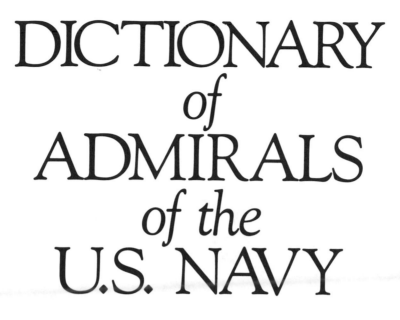

DICTIONARY
of
ADMIRALS
of the
U.S. NAVY

DICTIONARY
of
ADMIRALS
of the
U.S. NAVY
VOLUME 1
1862–1900

E PLURIBUS UNUM

William B. Cogar

NAVAL INSTITUTE PRESS • ANNAPOLIS, MARYLAND

Library of Congress Cataloging-in-Publication Data

Cogar, William B., 1949–
    Dictionary of admirals of the U.S. Navy / by William B.
Cogar.
        p. cm.
    Bibliography: p.
    Contents: v. 1. 1862–1900.
    ISBN 0-87021-431-4 (v. 1) :
    1. Admirals—United States—Registers. 2. United States. Navy—
Registers.   I. Title.
V11.U7C69   1989
359.3'31'092273—dc20   89-3339
                                                                   CIP

Book design by Bea Jackson
Printed in the United States of America

9 8 7 6 5 4 3 2

First printing

Photo Credits:

Appleton's Cyclopedia of American Biography [James Grant Wilson and John Fiske, eds. (New York: D. Appleton & Co., 1888)]: p. 175.

Naval Historical Center: p. 6, p. 7, p. 8, p. 9, p. 10, p. 11 bottom, p. 12, p. 15 top and bottom, p. 16, p. 17, p. 18, p. 19, p. 20, p. 21, p. 22, p. 23, p. 24, p. 25, p. 26, p. 27 top and bottom, p. 30, p. 31 top, p. 32, p. 33, p. 34, p. 37, p. 39, p. 40, p. 43, p. 45, p. 48, p. 52, p. 54, p. 55, p. 62 top and bottom, p. 65, p. 67, p. 68 top, p. 69, p. 70, p. 72 bottom, p. 73, p. 74, p. 76, p. 77, p. 80 top and bottom, p. 81, p. 82, p. 83, p. 84, p. 86, p. 90 top and bottom, p. 92, p. 93, p. 94, p. 95, p. 96, p. 97, p. 98, p. 99, p. 102 top and bottom, p. 103, p. 104, p. 105, p. 106 top and bottom, p. 107, p. 109, p. 110, p. 111, p. 112, p. 115, p. 116, p. 117, p. 118, p. 119, p. 121, p. 123, p. 125, p. 126, p. 127, p. 129, p. 130, p. 135, p. 136, p. 137, p. 138, p. 139, p. 140, p. 141, p. 142, p. 143, p. 144, p. 147 top, p. 149, p. 150, p. 152, p. 154, p. 157, p. 158, p. 163, p. 166, p. 167, p. 168, p. 170, p. 171, p. 172, p. 173, p. 174, p. 176, p. 177, p. 178, p. 179, p. 180, p. 181, p. 182, p. 183, p. 187, p. 188, p. 189 top and bottom, p. 190, p. 191, p. 192, p. 195, p. 197, p. 198 top and bottom, p. 201, p. 203 top, p. 204, p. 207, p. 208.

National Cyclopedia of American Biography (New York: James T. White & Co., 1906): p. 199.
Nimitz Library, U.S. Naval Academy: p. 28, p. 53 top.
U.S. Naval Academy Museum: p. 11 top, p. 31 bottom, p. 38, p. 44, p. 49, p. 53 bottom, p. 113, p. 133, p. 213.

U.S. Naval Institute: p. 3, p. 4, p. 5, p. 13, p. 36, p. 41, p. 46, p. 50, p. 56, p. 57, p. 58, p. 60, p. 63, p. 66, p. 68 bottom, p. 72 top, p. 75, p. 78, p. 79, p. 85, p. 87, p. 88, p. 91, p. 100, p. 114, p. 120, p. 122, p. 124, p. 128, p. 131, p. 134, p. 146, p. 147 bottom, p. 153, p. 155, p. 159, p. 162, p. 164, p. 184, p. 185, p. 200, p. 203 bottom, p. 209, p. 211, p. 212.

Contents

Preface

For the historian, there is nothing more frustrating than researching important facets of history only to find a dearth of reliable information. This is certainly the case with the lives and professional careers of those men who have occupied the flag ranks of the American navy. While more thorough and accurate career records have been kept during the past few decades, this was not the case for the nineteenth and early twentieth centuries. So little research has been done in this area that both the scholar and the nonscholar continually face numerous obstacles to obtaining small bits of information, much less complete career records. It is my hope that this volume alleviates at least some of this frustration and that the volume will assist many in discovering material heretofore difficult to find.

There are many who deserve my warmest expressions of gratitude for the inspiration, help, constructive criticism, and general encouragement shown in the course of my research on this work. I have been particularly pleased and heartened by the considerable number of people who have enthusiastically stated that the navy needs just such a work and that the final product will benefit many.

Several people who have assisted me in this work deserve special mention. The librarians and staff of the Nimitz Library of the U.S. Naval Academy have been extremely cooperative and professional, frequently steering me towards new information. In particular, Alice S. Creighton, head of Special Collections, and Pamela Sherbert and Mary Rose Catalfamo of that same department were extremely helpful. Each showed remarkable patience, tenacity, and consistently even-tempered dispositions when bombarded by my many requests. Katherine M. Dickson, Barbara Manvel, and William R. McQuade of the Nimitz Library Reference Department frequently lent their expertise. Professor William W. Jeffries, archivist and director of the Naval Academy's Museum, James W. Cheevers, curator of the museum, and Jane H. Price of the Naval Academy Archives were also cooperative.

The Naval Institute and its staff have been most encouraging and helpful with this project. I am particularly indebted to Paul W. Wilderson, the acquisitions editor, and Anthony F. Chiffolo, manuscript editor. No one could be as fortunate as I in having such friendly and patient editors. Likewise, thanks and appreciation are extended to Deborah Estes of the Acquisitions Department and to Patty M. Maddocks, director of the Institute's Library and Photographic Services, for their worthy suggestions and recommendations. Mr. Richard Hobbs, formerly of the Naval Institute, is deserving of my thanks and appreciation since he had a very integral part in getting the entire project off the ground.

Thanks must also be extended to Dr. Dean C. Allard, senior historian of the Naval Historical Center at the Washington Navy Yard, and to Kathleen L. Rohr and Bernard F. Calvalcante, who were very helpful and patient with my many requests to see particular files and manuscripts housed at the Naval Historical Center. Agnes Hooper and Charles S. Haberlein of the center's photographic department were also extremely helpful and knowledgeable.

Many of my colleagues in the History Department of the Naval Academy have been invariably helpful by offering their suggestions and criticisms. I am particularly indebted to my colleague and friend William R. Roberts, who read much of the manuscript and gave me invaluable assistance. Others in the History Department who provided assistance included Frederick C. Harrod, Craig L. Symonds, Robert W. Love, and particularly Jack Sweetman, who first suggested the entire idea to me. To all my colleagues, I extend my thanks for their help and their patience.

Lastly, and by far most importantly, the greatest debt is to my wife, Jackie, and our children, who have lived with this project for what must surely seem an eternity. They have patiently and unselfishly given up many evenings and weekends of normal family activities so that I could use those times to produce this volume.

Introduction

During the late nineteenth and early twentieth centuries, the United States grew and assumed a position of international power and prestige. For many and different reasons, the nation began to look overseas beyond its natural geographical borders. Quite naturally, the sea services played a very significant role in this process. Not only were they expanded greatly, but also the extent to which they were used and the manner in which they were employed changed dramatically and permanently.

Those men who occupied the ranks of admiral in the U.S. Navy were individuals who deserve recognition for their efforts and whose lives, actions, attitudes, and values reflect in great part those of the nation at large. Some of these men, like Admirals David G. Farragut, John A. Dahlgren, William T. Sampson, Stephen B. Luce, and George A. Dewey, are quite well known. They have attracted the attention of scholars and serve as the subjects of numerous biographies, published articles, and theses. Other admirals are not nearly so famous, nor are their deeds as well known. Nevertheless, their contributions to this nation's history are also important.

Unfortunately, there is no published work that provides reliable and detailed information on every man who reached the rank of admiral in the United States Navy after 1862, when the rank of admiral was finally adopted. The official military records for many—indeed most—of the men in this volume are far from complete. For the scholar as well as for the nonscholar, the quest for reliable personal information and career summaries is extremely laborious and tedious. It entails the examination of several if not many different sources. While a considerable amount of work was done around the turn of the century on the careers of officers in the sea services, these works are not only incomplete but also frequently inaccurate, and usually conclude around 1902 at the latest.

This volume intends to provide as reliable and as complete information as possible on every admiral of the United States Navy between the Civil War and the end of the century. Subsequent volumes will do the same from 1901 to the present. This volume contains 211 admirals. It includes those officers who reached the rank of admiral after retirement as well as those who did so while still on active duty.

Each entry begins with personal information together with a list of the ranks the officer achieved and the dates of each of his promotions. There then follows a chronological summary of the man's career, beginning when he first entered the service and concluding with either his retirement or his death. Dates of tours of duty are recorded as accurately as possible. In some of the records of the earlier careers, however, it is unclear whether a date meant the issuance of the order for an officer to report to a particular ship or station or the time the officer actually reported to his new billet. For the most part, the dates that are included in this volume are those of the particular officer's actually reporting to his new duty station. For some officers, the dates are unknown or approximate and are indicated as such with question marks. Following the career summary for some of the entries is a section on "career highlights." This section is not intended to provide detailed accounts of actions, but rather simply to note an officer's more famous actions or deeds. The last section deals with bibliographical matters. Descriptions and locations of personal papers as well as any monographs, articles, or essays written by or about the officer have been included.

Ranks in the United States Navy

The history of ranks within the United States Navy is a complicated one. The following account does not attempt to trace all of the many changes that took place in the nineteenth century in the officer ranks of the United States Navy, although such a study is needed. What follows is rather a brief guide to explain the ranks held by the men in this volume in order to understand more clearly their careers.

Not surprisingly, many of our naval usages and titles are directly inherited from the Royal Navy. On 15 November 1776 the Continental Congress created the ranks of admiral, vice admiral, rear admiral, and commodore. While never filled, these were designed to be the naval equivalents of the highest ranks in the land forces: general, lieutenant general, major general, and brigadier general. Lesser ranks for both sea and land forces also followed their respective British models. Captains of ships of forty guns or more corresponded to colonels on land. Captains of ships of twenty to forty guns corresponded to lieutenant colonels. Captains of ships of ten to twenty guns were equivalent to majors; and navy lieutenants were equivalent to captains in the land forces.

While American military ranks closely followed British precedents, there was much that was distinctly American about the system of ranks adopted by the Continental Congress in 1776. Most notable was the resistance of the American government and public at large to the rank and title of admiral. There were attempts between the Revolution and the Civil War to fill the ranks of admiral, vice admiral, and rear admiral. These ranks were considered too reminiscent of aristocratic titles to be used by a young nation imbued with republican virtues, however. One exception was the appointment by the Continental Congress in November 1775 of Esek Hopkins as "Commander in Chief of the Fleet." This title was no longer used after Hopkins was suspended in March 1777.

By the time of the 27 March 1794 Act, which created the U.S. Navy, officers were divided between "line," or combatant officers, and "staff," or noncombatant officers. The former fought the enemy and held naval command. The latter supported the line officers. There were three different appointment sources. Commissioned officers received their appointments from the president by and with the consent of the Senate.

According to the 1794 Navy Act, commissioned officers included captains, lieutenants, chaplains, surgeons, and surgeon's mates. Of these, only captains and lieutenants were naval line officers. Warrant officers received their authority from either the president or the secretary of the navy. Warrant officers included sailing masters, pursers, boatswains, gunners, carpenters, sailmakers, and midshipmen. Finally, petty officers were appointed by the captain of each ship and included master's mates, captain's mates, boatswain's mates, coxswains, sailmaker's mates, and gunner's mates.

Although the rank of rear admiral did not exist again until the Civil War, there was from the beginning a need in the navy for a rank above that of captain. Any officer commanding a vessel was nominally termed a "captain." It was customary to call anyone who commanded a fleet or squadron of ships a "flag officer," a generic term indicating overall command and not rank. The flag officer identified himself and his vessel to others in the squadron by flying a flag or broad pennant from his "flagship." The title "commodore" was normally given to this senior officer as a courtesy, and it was usually retained by the officer after his cruise, although it conferred no official rank, pay, or other duty.

It was not until 16 January 1857 that the rank of "flag officer" was formally assigned to captains who commanded a fleet or squadron. It is unclear why the title of commodore was not officially adopted instead, since it meant the same as flag officer. Perhaps it was still too reminiscent of aristocratic privileges. In any case, the honorary title of commodore temporarily disappeared from use in the navy. It was replaced by the official title of "flag officer," which was used from 1857 to 1862. Flag officers flew the flag of a vice admiral if they had held the rank of captain for at least twenty years or the flag of a rear admiral if they had fewer than twenty years of sea service as a captain.

On 16 July 1862 Congress established nine grades of line officers. The rank of flag officer was officially abolished and the rank of commodore recognized in its place. The rank of commodore remained in use until it was again temporarily abolished for those on active duty by the 3 March 1899 Personnel Act. All commodores were advanced to rear admiral by this act, with the exception of those officers who held the rank of commodore on the Retired List.

There were also numerous changes within the lower ranks. Until the end of the eighteenth century, the only commissioned line officers were captains and lieutenants. An intermediate line officer rank was needed, and in 1799 the new rank of "master in command," or "master commandant," was placed between captain and lieutenant. The act of 3 March 1801, passed shortly after the Quasi-War with France, however, reduced the naval establishment and abolished the rank of master commandant. But the need to have an intermediate rank proved too great, and it was restored by Congress on 21 April 1806. The rank of master commandant was permanently changed on 3 March 1837 to "commander." This rank paralleled that of lieutenant colonel in the army and the Marine Corps.

The military rank of lieutenant is a very old one. In the Continental Navy lieutenants stood directly below captains. Lieutenants normally were former midshipmen or in some cases sailing masters. The "first lieutenant" was the officer next in line behind the ship's captain who took command of the ship should anything happen to the captain. First lieutenants were frequently termed "lieutenants commanding" because they were qualified to command smaller vessels and prize ships. This practice was officially recognized by the 16 July 1862 act, which created the rank of "lieutenant commander." This rank corresponded to that of major in the army and Marine Corps. Lieutenants in the navy had the equivalent rank of captain in the army and Marine Corps.

After the lieutenants came the "sailing masters," line or combatant officers who were appointed by means of a warrant rather than a commission. The legislation of 3 March 1837 changed "sailing master" to "master." The rank of master continued in use until 3 March 1883, when it was changed to "lieutenant (junior grade)." This rank corresponded to the rank of first lieutenant in the army and Marine Corps.

The rank of midshipman was the lowest warrant held by combatant officers. Midshipmen—normally boys or young men who received their training at sea—first appeared in the U.S. Navy in 1794. After the advent of steam, changes were made in the training and education of midshipmen. Naval schools were established at several of the navy yards; the most notable of these early schools was Philadelphia's. In 1845 the schools were replaced by the Naval School (renamed the Naval Academy in 1850) at Annapolis, Maryland. Midshipmen studied and were examined for promotion at these schools. Beginning with the act of 3 March 1837, the midshipmen who passed their examinations were known as "passed midshipmen." Sent to the fleet, they then waited for an opening in the rank of lieutenant or master, depending on the period. "Acting midshipmen" were young boys who received a year of shore education before being sent to the fleet as midshipmen. They then returned to shore and commenced studying for their examinations. The rank of "acting midshipman" was abolished by the act of 16 July 1862. This same act also stipulated that the appointment of midshipmen to the Naval Academy should reflect the distribution by state of the national population.

The same act also created the rank of "ensign," the lowest commissioned rank in the navy and the equivalent of a second lieutenant in the army and the Marine Corps. On 3 March 1883 Congress created the rank of "ensign (junior grade)." This rank did not parallel any rank in the army, however, and it was abolished on 26 June 1884.

On 15 July 1870 the rank of "midshipman" at the Naval Academy was changed to "cadet midshipman." Three years later, the course of study at the Naval Academy was extended from four to six years. The first four years were spent at Annapolis and the next two at sea. The cadet midshipman then returned to Annapolis, where he took his examination. After passing the examination, the cadet midshipman became a "midshipman" and waited to be promoted when a vacancy occurred among the navy's ensigns. The six year curriculum endured until 1912, when it was shortened to four years. Midshipmen at the Naval Academy continued to hold the rank of "cadet midshipman" or "cadet engineer" until 1882, when the rank of "naval cadet" was introduced in their stead. This rank remained in use until 1 July 1902, when the older and more traditional title of "midshipman" was restored.

The Civil War brought about a number of very important changes in the system of naval ranks. The act of 16 July 1862, for example, introduced the modern hierarchy of line commissions: midshipman, ensign, master, lieutenant, lieutenant commander, commander, captain, commodore, and rear admiral. The positions of ensign, lieutenant commander, commodore, and rear admiral were all new. The last rank in particular was created as a result of the wartime expansion of the navy and its division into several blockading squadrons stationed along the southern coastline, with a large command that encompassed the Mississippi River and its tributaries. David Glasgow Farragut was the first of nine officers initially appointed to the post of rear admiral in the United States Navy.

It was not long before additional flag officer ranks were superimposed on that of rear admiral. On 21 December 1864 Congress created the rank of vice admiral. This rank was held by one officer appointed from the list of active rear admirals. David G. Farragut, the senior rear admiral in the navy, became its first vice admiral. He was the senior officer in the navy and the equivalent of a lieutenant general in the army. To complete the flag officer ranks and to parallel the hierarchy of general officers in the army, Congress eventually created the rank of admiral on 25 July 1866. This law gave the navy one admiral, one vice admiral, and ten rear admirals on the active list. Not surprisingly, Farragut became the navy's first admiral, and his foster brother, Rear Admiral David Dixon Porter, succeeded him as vice admiral.

When Admiral Farragut died on 14 August 1870, Porter took his place at the head of the active list. Porter remained the only four-star admiral until his death in 1891. As part of the deep cutbacks that took place in the military after the Civil War, Congress on 24 January 1873 decreed that any vacancies in the positions of admiral and vice admiral would no longer be filled by promotion. Once these positions became vacant, they would cease to exist.

It was not until 3 March 1899 that Congress, in the jubilant aftermath of the Spanish-American War, restored the rank of admiral. The act of 3 March 1899 exempted the officer who held this position from mandatory retirement but stipulated that when the office became vacant, it would cease to exist. By this act, Rear Admiral George Dewey, the hero of the Battle of Manila Bay, became this country's third four-star flag officer or, as he was known officially, the Admiral of the Navy, a title Dewey held until his death in early 1917. In addition to its other provisions, the 3 March 1899 act divided the rank of rear admiral into lower and upper numbers or halves, corresponding respectively in pay and rank to brigadier generals and major generals in the army.

On 3 March 1915, the commanders of the Atlantic, Pacific, and Asiatic Fleets were given the temporary rank of admiral, while the officers next in line of command in each of these fleets received the temporary rank of vice admiral. The navy used these ranks until the following year, 1916, when Congress bestowed the temporary rank of admiral on the newly created Chief of Naval Operations. All flag officers reverted to the rank of rear admiral when they entered the Retired List.

From time to time during the nineteenth century, the need arose to augment the small standing navy. Owing to the temporary expansion of the navy and the pressing and immediate demand for more officers during the Civil War, for example, Congress on 24 July 1861 authorized the appointment of volunteer officers in an "acting" capacity. These men were released at the conclusion of the war with the exception of a limited number who received permission to transfer to the regular navy. According to the act of 25 July 1866, five lieutenant commanders, twenty lieutenants, fifty masters, and seventy-five ensigns could be appointed to the regular navy from the ranks of the volunteers.

Promotion and Retirement

Several notable attempts were made to reform the system of promotion by seniority as well as the system of voluntary retirement held by the navy throughout the nineteenth century. As early as June 1855, the navy sought to implement a controversial plan to regularize its promotion and retirement procedures. A five-man board of officers found 201 officers unfit for service. The board recommended the dismissal of 49 officers, the retirement on furlough pay of 81 officers, and the retirement of the remaining 71 officers on leave-of-absence. The navy immediately implemented the board's findings, although each officer had the right to request a hearing. These actions created such an outcry that in March 1859 Congress passed a law authorizing the president and the Senate to restore to active duty those officers retired by decisions of the board.

The coming of the Civil War in April 1861 led Secretary of the Navy Gideon Welles to propose further personnel reforms that would increase the efficiency of the service. On 3 August 1861 Congress voted to retire all officers unfit for service because of age or infirmity. On 21 December 1861 another, more far-reaching law provided for the mandatory retirement of all officers at age sixty-two or after forty-five years of service. Although Congress occasionally granted exceptions to this rule for one reason or another, it remained in effect for the rest of the century. In July of the following year, the legislators sought to improve the navy's system of advancement by seniority by creating a board to evaluate each officer for promotion. More than thirty years later, the Personnel Act of 3 March 1899 strengthened the system of promotion based on merit and seniority. While this act still left much to be desired, it also provided the mechanism to remove those officers deemed unsatisfactory.

Relative Rank

The possession of rank in any military society entitle the holder to certain social as well as official benefits and privileges. An officer's relative position when entering or leaving a ship, his place at the wardroom table, the cabin in which he slept, even the uniform he wore all depended on his rank. From the navy's earliest days, the line or combat officers insisted that they, the military backbone of the service, were the only officers entitled to hold rank. The sole function of the staff or noncombatant portion of the navy, the line officer argued, was to support the line. As a result, staff officers held functional titles such as fleet surgeon and assistant surgeon instead of ranks. By the late 1830s, however, the quasi-civilian staff officers began to demand that they be given ranks comparable to those of the line officers. The resulting conflict over the relative standing of these two groups of officers affected day-to-day matters of discipline and morale for the remainder of the century. Despite repeated attempts to redress this conflict, it was not until 1899 that the navy settled the issue of relative or assimilated rank, as it was also known. Even that settlement did not satisfy everyone.

The list of civil officers in the navy had grown by 1840 to include fleet surgeons, passed assistant surgeons, chaplains, pursers, engineers, and professors of mathematics. The General Regulations of 1841 offered the first official recognition of the comparability between line and staff officers. Article four of those regulations made surgeons,

pursers, chaplains, and secretaries the equivalent of lieutenants; passed assistant surgeons the equivalent of masters; other assistant surgeons and professors of mathematics
the equivalent of passed midshipmen; and clerks the equivalent of midshipmen. This
first attempt to establish a relative or equivalent ranking of line and staff officers
proved unsatisfactory, however, since the 1841 regulations ranked commissioned staff
officers with warrant officers in the line and vice-versa.

The demand that the staff be given assimilated rank increased in 1842 with the
creation of the bureau system. Surgeons and pursers now had representatives—bureau
chiefs—in Washington, D.C., and the bureau chiefs had direct access to the secretary
of the navy. The drive to win assimilated rank for the staff soon proved too strong for
the line officers. Medical officers spearheaded this drive and were the first staff officers
to receive relative rank on 31 August 1846. The pursers followed suit on 27 May 1847,
and the engineers on 13 January 1859. The secretary of the navy first announced these
changes in general orders. Congress later confirmed the secretary's actions in the naval
appropriations acts of 1854 and 1859.

During the Civil War a rapid increase in the size of the officer corps brought about
a readjustment of the relative ranking of line and staff officers. On 13 March 1863
Secretary of the Navy Gideon Welles issued a general order raising the relative ranks
of some staff officers and giving relative rank for the first time to others. Welles's 1863
order also included the first official list of all of the different groups of officers who
made up the staff: surgeons, paymasters, engineers, naval constructors, chaplains,
professors of mathematics, secretaries, clerks, carpenters, and sailmakers. All other
officers, the secretary added, belonged to the line.

Welles's 1863 order angered many line officers and made them all the more determined to strike back at the staff at the earliest opportunity. During the first few years
of Reconstruction, the controversy between line and staff consequently grew more
acrimonious than ever before. The line officers savored the first of several important
triumphs when on 25 July 1866 Congress increased their numbers while holding the
number of staff officers to prewar levels. On 1 April 1869 Secretary of the Navy Adolf
E. Borie, relying on the attorney general's opinion that only Congress had the authority to determine relative ranks, declared Welles's order of 1863 null and void. Overnight
staff officers saw their relative ranks either diminish or disappear entirely. They quickly
mounted a bitter campaign to restore the relative ranks given them in 1863. On 3
March 1871 Congress responded to the staff officers' demands by permanently granting
relative rank to all the staff officers named in the 1863 order at levels close to those
originally established by Welles. The one group of staff officers not covered by the 1871
act—professors of mathematics—finally received relative rank on 31 May 1872.

The question of relative rank was finally resolved by the Personnel Act of 3 March
1899, which abolished relative rank and made engineering officers a part of the line.
Another section of the 1899 act, however, stated that it shall not "be construed as
changing the titles of officers in the staff corps of the Navy." Thus, staff officers
continued to be addressed by functional title and line officers by rank. A change in
naval regulations in 1918 directed that ". . . every officer in the Navy shall be designated
and addressed by the title of his rank without any discrimination whatever. In written
communication the name of the corps to which a staff officer belongs shall be stated
immediately after his name." This remains current navy practice.

STAFF OFFICERS

The following categories of staff, or noncombatant, officers are discussed in order of their official recognition by the United States Navy and thus in their order of precedence. The staff officers ranked both with and after, i.e., with the line officers in rank but behind them in line or precedence.

Medical Corps

Surgeons and their assistants were present on board ships of the American navy since the earliest days, performing a most needed function. It was not until 24 May 1828 that Congress established a system of ranks and requirements for navy medical personnel similar to those used by contemporary civilian physicians. A board of senior medical officers examined all candidates for entry in the Medical Corps. Those admitted into the corps became assistant surgeons. Assistant surgeons had to pass an examination in order to become surgeons. The absence of any mandatory retirement system in the navy before 1862, however, meant that qualified assistant surgeons often had to wait a very long time for promotion. Assistant surgeons who had passed their examinations and were awaiting promotion thus became known as "passed assistant surgeons."

Surgeons assigned to squadrons with a hospital ship oversaw the medical activities of the squadron. If no hospital ship was present, the senior medical officer supervised surgeons throughout the squadron. The 24 May 1828 act designated any surgeon performing these duties a "fleet surgeon," whose rank and pay were to be determined by the secretary of the navy. The hierarchy of staff officers in the Medical Corps after 1828 hence included fleet surgeons, surgeons, passed assistant surgeons, and assistant surgeons.

The surgeons were the first staff officers to demand equivalent rank with line officers and the first to receive assimilated rank in 1846. In the 1846 General Regulations, surgeons ranked with lieutenants, passed assistant surgeons with masters, and assistant surgeons with passed midshipmen. Fleet surgeons and surgeons with more than twelve years of service ranked with commanders; all other surgeons ranked with lieutenants. Passed assistant surgeons came next after lieutenants, and assistant surgeons came next after masters. While staff officers could not exercise military command, the Navy Appropriations Act of 5 August 1854 authorized them to command subordinates in their own departments.

The 13 March 1863 General Order by Navy Secretary Gideon Welles increased the relative ranks of many staff officers. In the Medical Corps, for instance, fleet surgeons ranked with captains; surgeons who had more than fifteen years of service as surgeons ranked with captains; surgeons who had more than five years of service as surgeons ranked with commanders; surgeons who had fewer than five years of service as surgeons ranked with lieutenant commanders; passed assistant surgeons ranked with lieutenants; and assistant surgeons ranked with masters.

When Secretary Borie rescinded Welles's order in 1869, these relative ranks were temporarily reduced. Surgeons of the fleet and surgeons who had served more than twelve years in that capacity ranked with commanders; surgeons who had served fewer than twelve years as surgeons ranked with lieutenants; passed assistant surgeons ranked next after lieutenants; and assistant surgeons ranked next after masters. On 3 March

1871 Congress restored the relative ranks for medical personnel first announced in the 1863 order. The 1871 act also created the new positions of medical director and medical inspector.

A navy circular of 1 December 1871 further increased the relative ranks of medical officers: medical directors had the equivalent rank of captains; medical inspectors had the equivalent rank of commanders; surgeons had the equivalent rank of lieutenant commanders; passed assistant surgeons had the equivalent rank of lieutenants or masters; and assistant surgeons had the equivalent rank of masters or ensigns. The Personnel Act of 1899 eventually abolished the system of relative ranks, although it authorized no change in the titles of staff officers. A medical director thus held the rank of captain after 1899 but continued to be addressed as "medical director."

Pay Corps

Forerunners of today's supply officers, pursers were included by the 27 March 1794 act with the first noncombatant officers. Their status did not change significantly until 31 August 1842, when they became agents of the newly created Bureau of Provisions and Clothing. Navy agents and storekeepers represented the bureau on shore, while pursers represented it at sea.

Pursers became known as paymasters on 22 June 1860. The increased size of the navy during the Civil War necessitated an increase in the number of paymasters and the creation of the new rank of assistant paymaster on 17 July 1861. Congress established the Pay Corps as well as the ranks of pay director and pay inspector on 3 March 1871.

When staff officers first received relative ranks with line officers in 1841, pursers ranked with the rank of lieutenant. By order of the secretary of the navy on 27 May 1847, confirmed by Congress on 5 August 1854, pursers with twelve or more years of service ranked with commanders, while those with fewer than twelve years ranked with lieutenants.

The Civil War readjustments resulted in the creation of the Pay Department on 13 March 1863 and in new assimilated ranks. Fleet paymasters ranked with captains; paymasters after fifteen years ranked with captains; paymasters after five years ranked with commanders; paymasters in the first five years ranked with lieutenant commanders; and assistant paymasters ranked with masters. This correlation was revoked on 1 April 1869 but restored by Congress on 3 March 1871. New relative ranks were subsequently created on 1 December 1871. Pay directors now ranked with captains; pay inspectors ranked with commanders; paymasters ranked with lieutenant commanders; passed assistant paymasters ranked with lieutenants or masters; and assistant paymasters ranked with masters or ensigns. As with all staff corps, the entire issue of relative ranks was ended by the 1899 Personnel Act.

The name of the Bureau of Provisions and Clothing was changed by Congress in July 1892 to the Bureau of Supplies and Account. It was not until 11 July 1919 that Congress changed the name and officers were actually called "supply officers" and their corps, the "Supply Corps."

Engineer Corps

Although there was initial resistance by many line officers to steam power and thus to engineers in the naval service during the early days of steam propulsion, a chief engineer was appointed by the secretary of the navy on 12 July 1836. In October of the following year, Matthew C. Perry was authorized to appoint assistant engineers. Congress, however, did not officially create the Engineer Corps until 31 August 1842. The secretary of the navy was authorized to appoint a chief engineer, two first assistant engineers, two second assistant engineers, and three third assistant engineers for each steamship in the navy.

The number of engineers naturally grew as the navy increasingly used steam power. Relative ranks were granted to the engineers on 13 January 1859, but the new assimilated ranks for engineers still showed a decidedly inferior status. Chief engineers with more than twelve years of service ranked with commanders; chief engineers with twelve or fewer years of service ranked with lieutenants; first assistant engineers ranked next after lieutenants; second assistant engineers ranked with masters; and third assistant engineers ranked after masters.

The number of engineers grew dramatically during the Civil War, and with the 13 March 1863 order by Navy Secretary Gideon Welles, relative ranks for engineers changed. Fleet engineers ranked with captains; chief engineers with more than fifteen years of service ranked with captains; chief engineers with at least five years of service ranked with commanders; chief engineers in their first five years ranked with lieutenant commanders; first assistant engineers ranked with masters; second assistant engineers ranked with ensigns; and third assistant engineers ranked with midshipmen.

The order by Secretary Borie of 1 April 1869 nullifying the relative ranks set in 1863 created a new rank correlation. Fleet engineers and chief engineers with more than twelve years of service ranked with commanders; chief engineers with fewer than twelve years of service ranked with lieutenants; first assistant engineers ranked next after lieutenants; second assistant engineers ranked next after masters; and third assistant engineers ranked with midshipmen. The engineers, however, received some satisfaction when new relative ranks were imposed on 1 December 1871. The first ten chief engineers ranked with captains; the next fifteen chief engineers ranked with commanders; the next forty-five chief engineers ranked with lieutenant commanders; first assistant engineers ranked with lieutenants or masters; and second assistant engineers ranked with masters or ensigns. The rank of third assistant engineer was abolished on 15 July 1870, and those then in that rank were promoted to second assistant engineers.

Cadet engineers first appeared at the Naval Academy in 1867, although a class of acting third assistant engineers was ordered to the Academy in the preceding year. The first group of engineers graduated in 1868. Four years followed before the next class of cadet engineers was admitted. Beginning in 1872 cadet engineers underwent a two-year program. This was raised to four years with the class of 1874. Furthermore, on 24 February 1874, the title of "first assistant engineer" was changed to "passed assistant engineer," while that of "second assistant engineer" became simply "assistant engineer." On 5 August 1882, the titles "cadet engineer" and "cadet midshipman" were dropped, and every student at Annapolis was called a "naval cadet." By that same legislation, the engineering program was increased to six years.

By the Personnel Act of 1899, the Engineer Corps was amalgamated with the line and thus effectively abolished. Henceforward, naval officers were required to study line and engineering skills. All officers on engineering duty would enjoy the same rank and privileges as their peers on the bridge. However, the older and more senior engineering officers remained on restricted duties in their particular fields, and thus there remained special categories of engineering officers serving only on shore duty. While there was no attempt to restore an engineer corps, there was passed an act on 29 August 1916 making provisions for "Officers for Engineering Duty Only" (EDO). Officers at or above the rank of lieutenant could apply and receive this assignment with the approval of the secretary of the navy. These officers could serve at sea but only until they reached the rank of commander. Thereafter their duties would be restricted to shore, the only exception being the EDOs serving as fleet or squadron engineers.

Chaplains

Chaplains at sea saw first and foremost to the spiritual welfare of the officers and crew. But early on, as evidenced in the Navy Regulations of 25 January 1802, the responsibility for educating midshipmen and crew members fell principally to chaplains, and many were appointed for their abilities as educators as well as for their clerical training. This was never a very effective system, and Congress on 2 June 1813 provided for the employment at sea of schoolmasters, who afforded some measure of help to the navy chaplains. After professors of mathematics were appointed and naval schools were created at some major yards, chaplains were relieved of most of their schoolmaster duties.

The 1841 General Regulations gave chaplains the relative rank of lieutenants. The next changes came on 13 March 1863 when chaplains with twelve or more years of service ranked with commanders, while those with fewer than twelve years of service ranked with lieutenant commanders. The act of 3 March 1871, granting relative ranks to nearly all classes of staff officers, did so for only eighteen chaplains. Since the total number of chaplains allowed was twenty-four, six chaplains were without rank. On 1 December 1871, the first four chaplains received the relative rank of captain; the next seven ranked with lieutenant commanders. Relative ranks ended on 3 March 1899, but the title of "chaplain" has remained to the present day.

Professors of Mathematics

Up to the middle of the nineteenth century, midshipmen received a haphazard education, both at sea and on land. Chaplains and schoolmasters shouldered the early responsibility of shipboard education. From time to time, efforts were made to modernize and strengthen the educational methods and procedures. One such effort came on 3 March 1835. Congress created a new class of staff officers, the professor of mathematics, a title assumed by schoolmasters since 1831, who relieved the chaplains of most of the educational duties. Furthermore, schools were established at the major navy yards by 1840.

Professors of mathematics served both at sea and in the shore schools. In 1841, six served at the naval schools at Boston, New York, and Philadelphia, eight served on board ships, and three awaited orders. The 1841 General Regulations establishing assimilated ranks placed professors of mathematics with passed midshipmen. In the following year, however, professors of mathematics who served at sea were allowed to live, mess, and receive the same rations as lieutenants.

With the establishment of the Naval School at Annapolis in 1845, Secretary of the Navy George Bancroft placed many of the language teachers and professors of mathematics in a "waiting orders" status in order to save money, since they were paid less in this status than when on active assignment. Three years later, Congress clarified the status of professors of mathematics by limiting their numbers to twelve and assigning them to duty at the Annapolis Naval School, at the Naval Observatory in Washington, D.C., and on ships of war for the purpose of instructing midshipmen.

With the 13 March 1863 General Order, professors of mathematics were officially designated staff officers and given relative rank with line officers. Professors with service of twelve or more years were ranked with commanders, while those with fewer than twelve years of service ranked with lieutenant commanders. The relative rank status for professors of mathematics was removed on 1 April 1869, but unlike other classes of staff officers, professors were not included in the legislation of 3 March 1871 that restored relative ranks. This was remedied by legislation passed on 31 May 1872. Three professors were ranked with captains, four ranked with commanders, and five ranked with either lieutenant commanders or lieutenants.

By the early twentieth century, the role of the professors of mathematics had outlived its usefulness. Congress provided on 29 August 1916 that no further appointments be made to the Corps of Professors of Mathematics. The corps would then cease to exist when the last professor of mathematics, either on the active or retired lists, died, resigned, or retired. The Corps of Professors of Mathematics became extinct when the last professor retired from the active list on 1 July 1936.

Naval Constructors

When Congress authorized the president on 27 March 1794 to build six frigates, naval constructors were appointed to oversee the work at the six sites: Portsmouth, New Hampshire; Boston; New York; Philadelphia; Baltimore; and Gosport (Norfolk), Virginia. These men were and remained civilians. Designated "Principal Naval Constructor of the Navy," Joshua Humphreys advised the secretary of the navy and recommended six sites for permanent navy yards to replace those rented for the first shipbuilding program. Sites were eventually purchased at the six sites above, although Washington, D.C., was substituted for Baltimore. The individual naval constructors reported directly to the Board of Navy Commissioners when it was appointed in early 1815. When Samuel Humphreys was appointed "Chief Constructor" in 1826, resident naval constructors reported to the board through Humphreys.

With the substitution of the bureaus system for the Board of Navy Commissioners in 1842, the Bureau of Construction, Equipment, and Repair oversaw the design, building, supplying, and repair of vessels for sea. This administrative change was not accompanied by any changes in the status of the civilian naval constructors, although beginning in 1844 they began to receive the same travel and ration allowances that officers did. The act creating the bureaus stipulated that the chief of the Bureau of Construction, Equipment, and Repair was to be a "skilful" naval constructor. In spite of this, the first five bureau chiefs were naval officers and not civilian naval constructors.

It was not until the Civil War that naval constructors finally became officers. The 3 March 1863 General Order by Secretary Welles stated that naval constructors were henceforth considered staff officers with corresponding assimilated ranks. Naval constructors with more than twenty years of service ranked with captains; naval constructors after twelve years with commanders; naval constructors in their first twelve years of service ranked with lieutenant commanders; and assistant naval constructors ranked with masters.

Naval constructors became commissioned officers by an act of 25 July 1866, and their appointments were made by the president and confirmed by the Senate. Like other staff officers, naval constructors had their relative rank removed in 1869 but restored two years later. Subsequently, the first two naval constructors ranked with captains; the next three naval constructors ranked with commanders; and all remaining naval constructors ranked with lieutenant commanders. Assistant naval constructors ranked with lieutenants or masters. As with all ranks in the navy, naval constructors saw the end of relative ranks with the 1899 Personnel Act.

Civil Engineers

Civil engineers were first employed for naval work in 1802 when President Thomas Jefferson requested Benjamin Henry Latrobe to submit plans for a drydock. Subsequent civil engineers were appointed by the secretary of the navy and acted in a civilian capacity. William S. P. Sanger, resident engineer at Norfolk, was appointed in 1836 civil engineer for the navy and is regarded as the "Father" of the Civil Engineering Corps. He continued to serve under the Bureau of Yards and Docks after August 1842.

By the act of 2 March 1867, civil engineers were given commissioned officer status. This small group of officers, whose function was to build, maintain, and to an extent operate the shore establishment of the navy, had a status somewhat different from other staff officers since they performed functions almost exclusively on shore. Seven civil engineers, including Sanger, were commissioned on 28 March 1867.

Although Congress authorized the president on 3 March 1871 to determine relative rank for civil engineers, no action was taken until 24 February 1881 when the secretary of the navy assigned relative rank to the ten civil engineers who then made up that corps. The first civil engineer received the relative rank of captain; the next two ranked with commanders; the next three ranked with lieutenant commanders; and the final four ranked with lieutenants. It is uncertain why the Navy Department delayed for a decade implementing the 1871 legislation on relative rank for civil engineers. Perhaps it was because this small group did not serve at sea and because the bureau chief was a line officer. It was not until 1898 that a civil engineer, Mordecai T. Endicott, was appointed chief of the Bureau of Yards and Docks. In the following year, relative ranks were ended.

Administration and Management

The United States Navy was officially created on 27 March 1794 when Congress authorized the president to construct six frigates to counter the threat of corsairs from the Barbary States then attacking American commerce in the Mediterranean. Although the threat subsided, construction continued on three of the frigates, and to oversee management of the new sea service, the Navy Department was created on 30 April 1798. Its chief officer was the secretary of the navy, who was responsible for executing presidential orders concerning the construction of vessels, the procurement of armaments and naval stores, and the enlistment of sailors. The secretary was assisted by a principal clerk and a few lesser clerks.

This system remained in effect until the conclusion of the War of 1812. That conflict clearly demonstrated the inadequacies of the navy's administrative structure. Congress consequently created the Board of Navy Commissioners on 7 February 1815. Composed of three "post captains," who were appointed by the president and confirmed by the Senate, as well as a secretary and a staff of clerks, the Board performed day-to-day ministerial functions such as overseeing the construction, equipping, and arming of war vessels as well as procuring all naval materials for the smooth running of the navy. The board was accountable to the secretary of the navy, and the secretary of the navy still retained control and direction of naval forces. This system worked relatively well until 1842.

As the navy expanded and became technologically different and more complicated, there was confusion between the secretary of the navy and the Board of Navy Commissioners over authority and responsibility. On 31 August 1842, the Board of Commissioners was abolished, and the navy's administration was reorganized into five bureaus. Each bureau was headed by a bureau chief, appointed by the president with the approval of the Senate. These chiefs were individually accountable to the secretary of the navy. Except for adding more bureaus early in the Civil War and redefining some bureaus' functions, this system remained essentially the same for over a century. The 1842 bureaus worked as follows:

The Bureau of Navy Yards and Docks was responsible for the operation of the navy yards and for the construction and maintenance of docks, wharves, and buildings. This bureau was originally the largest, most powerful, and subsequently most important bureau of the entire administrative machinery. The Bureau of Construction, Equipment, and Repair oversaw the design, construction, repair, and supply of naval vessels. It was also charged with the development of steam propulsion and naval architecture. The Bureau of Ordnance and Hydrography managed the naval magazines, manufactured and provisioned guns and munitions, and collected and distributed hydrographic information. The Bureau of Provisions and Clothing paid officers and men and provided clothing, consumable supplies, food, and "small stores" for sale to crews. The bureau's representatives ashore were the navy agents and storekeepers, while afloat they were the pursers. The Bureau of Medicine and Surgery provided medical supplies and was responsible for the navy's hospitals, dispensaries, and laboratories.

The law establishing the bureau system specified that the chiefs of the bureaus of Navy Yards and Docks and of Ordnance and Hydrography be captains of the navy; that the chief of the Bureau of Construction, Equipment and Repairs be a "skilful" naval constructor; and that the chief of the Bureau of Medicine and Surgery be a naval surgeon. No stipulation was attached to the chief of the Bureau of Provisions and Clothing, and this post was filled by either an officer or a civilian.

During the Civil War, numerous changes were made in the management of the navy owing to the need for more specialization than the original five bureaus could provide. On 5 July 1862, Congress restructured the navy's administration, expanding and modifying the existing bureaus. The results were: the Bureau of Equipment and Recruiting; the Bureau of Construction and Repair; the Bureau of Steam Engineering; the Bureau of Navigation; the Bureau of Ordnance; the Bureau of Provisions and Clothing; the Bureau of Yards and Docks; and the Bureau of Medicine and Surgery. The chiefs of the Bureaus of Navigation, Ordnance, Yards and Docks, and Equipment and Recruiting were to be line officers; the chief of the Bureau of Construction and Repair, a naval constructor; the Bureau of Steam Engineering, a chief engineer; and the Bureau of Medicine and Surgery, a naval surgeon.

The Bureau of Navigation was designed to be the scientific bureau and took over the hydrographic work formerly under the Bureau of Ordnance and Hydrography. This new bureau was responsible now for the Naval Observatory, the Hydrographic Office, the Naval Almanac Office, and the Naval Academy. It did not oversee personnel until 28 April 1865, when Secretary of the Navy Gideon Welles transferred the Office of Detail, which he established within the secretary's office to handle officer personnel, to the Bureau of Navigation. This resulted in split responsibility for personnel matters: the enlisted ranks in the Bureau of Equipment and Recruiting, and the officers in the Bureau of Navigation.

On 25 June 1889, an order moved recruiting to the Bureau of Navigation, and equipment functions such as the procurement of chronometers, compasses, and similar items was moved from Navigation to the Bureau of Equipment and Recruiting. Not surprisingly, then, the latter bureau was renamed on 1 July 1889 simply the Bureau of Equipment. The Hydrographic Office was officially put under the Bureau of Equipment on 9 May 1898, where it remained until 30 June 1914, when an act formally abolished the Bureau of Equipment. The only other change in administrative format to the bureaus during the nineteenth century was on 19 July 1892, when Congress changed the name of the Bureau of Provisions and Clothing to the Bureau of Supplies and Accounts.

The idea of creating a panel to assist the secretary of the navy in coordinating the work of the eight bureaus surfaced during the Civil War with Secretary Gideon Welles and again in March 1877 with Secretary of the Navy Richard W. Thompson. However, nothing came of these ideas. With the major building program in the 1880s, the division of shipbuilding responsibilities among three bureaus proved to be a major problem. Proposals to centralize and improve the system were again made, but nothing came of any attempt to centralize responsibility until the twentieth century. In 1889, however, Secretary Benjamin F. Tracy organized a "Construction Board" composed of the chiefs of the Bureaus of Construction and Repairs, Steam Engineering, Equipment and Recruiting, Ordnance, and Yards and Docks. Furthermore, to improve the administration, Tracy made some modifications by transferring functions from one bureau to another.

In the 1880s, a move to create a naval militia began. Several states added naval branches to their existing militia forces, and by 1894 twenty-five such branches had been created. Congress first took action to support this nonregular auxiliary on 2 March 1891 by providing money for arms and munitions as authorized by the secretary of the navy. This was followed on 3 August 1894 by an act that allowed the navy to loan vessels to state naval militia. Finally, the United States Auxiliary Naval Force was created during the Spanish-American War on 26 May 1898 and was asked to assist the regular forces in various ways.

Owing to the Spanish-American War, a Naval War Board was established in 1898 to plan and implement strategy. Navy Secretary John D. Long drew from its members to establish the General Board on 13 March 1900 to improve management of the Navy Department and to help coordinate the growing size and complexity of the navy. Headed by Admiral George Dewey and consisting of the chief of the Bureau of Navigation, the president of the Naval War College, the head of the navy's intelligence service, and eight other senior officers, the General Board acted in a purely advisory capacity, although in 1904 there was an unsuccessful attempt to give the General Board legal status and administrative responsibility. It was not until 1915 that the Office of Naval Operations was created. Under the authority and direction of the secretary of the navy, the chief of naval operations was responsible for the fleet's operations and its readiness for war.

Bureau Chiefs (1842–1901)

Bureau of Navy Yards and Docks
(renamed Bureau of Yards and Docks, 1862)

Commo Lewis Warrington	1 Sep 1842–24 May 1846
RAdm Joseph Smith	25 May 1846–30 Apr 1869
RAdm Daniel Ammen	1 May 1869–30 Sep 1871
RAdm C. R. P. Rodgers	1 Oct 1871–21 Sep 1874
RAdm John C. Howell	22 Sep 1874–30 Jun 1878
Capt Richard L. Law	1 Jul 1878–4 Jun 1881
RAdm Edward T. Nichols	4 Jun 1881–1 Mar 1885
RAdm David B. Harmony	27 Mar 1885–2 Apr 1889
Commo George B. White	2 Apr 1889–27 Feb 1890
Commo Norman H. Farquhar	6 Mar 1890–6 Mar 1894

Commo Edmund O. Matthews	16 Mar 1894–16 Mar 1898
RAdm Mordecai T. Endicott	4 Apr 1898–8 Jan 1907

Bureau of Equipment and Recruiting
(renamed Bureau of Equipment, 1889; abolished, 1914)

RAdm Andrew H. Foote	17 Jul 1862–3 Jun 1863
Cdr Albert N. Smith	4 Jun 1863–8 Sep 1866
RAdm Melancton Smith	17 Sep 1866–17 Jul 1870
RAdm William Reynolds	18 Jul 1870–31 Jan 1875
Commo Robert W. Shufeldt	1 Feb 1875–19 Nov 1878
Commo Earl English	20 Nov 1878—5 Sep 1884
Commo Winfield S. Schley	6 Sep 1884–31 Jul 1889
Commo George Dewey	1 Aug 1889–30 Jun 1893
Commo French E. Chadwick	1 Jul 1893–6 Sept 1897
RAdm Royal B. Bradford	7 Sep 1897–27 Oct 1903

Bureau of Navigation

RAdm Charles H. Davis	17 Jul 1862–27 Apr 1865
Capt Percival Drayton	28 Apr 1865–4 Aug 1865
Adm David D. Porter	Ad interim
RAdm Thornton A. Jenkins	24 Aug 1865–11 Apr 1869
RAdm James Alden	12 Apr 1869–30 Sep 1871
RAdm Daniel Ammen	1 Oct 1871–4 Jun 1878
Capt William D. Whiting	11 Jun 1878–13 Oct 1881
Commo James G. Walker	22 Oct 1881–31 Oct 1889
RAdm Francis M. Ramsay	1 Nov 1889–5 Apr 1897
RAdm Arent S. Crowinshield	8 Apr 1897–30 Apr 1902

Bureau of Ordnance and Hydrography
(renamed Bureau of Ordnance, 1862)

Commo William M. Crane	1 Sep 1842–18 Mar 1846
Commo Lewis Warrington	25 May 1846–12 Oct 1851
Commo Charles Morris	13 Oct 1851–21 Jan 1856
Capt Duncan N. Ingraham	10 Mar 1856–23 Sep 1860
Capt G. A. Magruder	24 Sep 1860–23 Apr 1861
Capt A. A. Harwood	24 Apr 1861–22 Jul 1862
RAdm John A. Dahlgren	22 Jul 1862–24 Jun 1863
Cdr Henry A. Wise	25 Jun 1863–1 Jun 1868
RAdm John A. Dahlgren	22 Jul 1868–23 Jul 1869
RAdm A. Ludlow Case	10 Aug 1869–9 Apr 1873
Commo William N. Jeffers	10 Apr 1873–7 Jun 1881
Commo Montgomery Sicard	1 Jul 1881–13 Jan 1890
Commo William M. Folger	12 Feb 1890–2 Jan 1893
Commo William T. Sampson	28 Jan 1893–27 May 1897
RAdm Charles O'Neil	1 Jun 1897–15 Mar 1904

Bureau of Construction, Equipment, and Repair
(renamed Bureau of Construction and Repair, 1862)

Commo David Conner	1 Sep 1842–1 Mar 1843
Capt Beverley Kennon	2 Mar 1843–9 Apr 1844
Commo Charles Morris	10 Apr 1844–31 May 1847
Commo Charles W. Skinner	1 Jun 1847–28 Feb 1852
Commo William B. Shubrick	1 Mar 1852–30 Jun 1853
Chief Naval Constructor Samuel Hartt	1 Jul 1853–16 Nov 1853
Chief Naval Constructor John Lenthall	17 Nov 1853–22 Jan 1871
Chief Naval Constructor Isaiah Hanscom	23 Jan 1871–27 Apr 1877
Chief Naval Constructor James W. Easby	28 Apr 1877–13 Dec 1881
Chief Naval Constructor Theodore D. Wilson	3 Mar 1882–7 Jul 1893
RAdm Philip Hichborn	23 Jul 1893–4 Mar 1901

Bureau of Steam Engineering

Engineer in Chief Benjamin F. Isherwood	5 Jul 1862–16 Mar 1869
Engineer in Chief James W. King	23 Mar 1869–14 Mar 1873
Engineer in Chief W. W. W. Wood	31 Mar 1873–3 Mar 1877
Engineer in Chief William H. Shock	4 Mar 1877–15 Jun 1883
Engineer in Chief Charles H. Loring	18 Jan 1884–8 Aug 1887
RAdm George W. Melville	9 Aug 1887–8 Aug 1903

Bureau of Provisions and Clothing
(renamed Bureau of Supplies and Accounts, 1892)

Charles W. Goldsborough	1 Sep 1842–30 Jan 1844
Commo William B. Shubrick	31 Jan 1844–14 Apr 1846
Gideon Welles	15 Apr 1846–8 Jul 1849
Purser William Sinclair	9 Jul 1849–30 Sep 1854
Pay Director Horatio Bridge	1 Oct 1854–11 Jul 1869
Paymaster General Edward T. Dunn	12 Jul 1869–17 Feb 1873
Paymaster General John O. Bradford	18 Feb 1873–22 Feb 1877
Paymaster General James H. Watmough	23 Feb 1877–17 Nov 1877
Paymaster General George F. Cutter	18 Nov 1877–30 Aug 1881
Paymaster General Joseph A. Smith	27 Jun 1882–29 Jan 1886
Paymaster General James Fulton	17 Nov 1886–15 Mar 1890
RAdm Edwin Stewart	16 May 1890–5 May 1899
RAdm Albert S. Kenny	5 May 1899–1 Jul 1903

Bureau of Medicine and Surgery

Surgeon William P. C. Barton	1 Sep 1842–31 Mar 1844
Surgeon Thomas Harris	1 Apr 1844–30 Sep 1853
Surgeon William Whelan	1 Oct 1853–11 Jun 1865
Surgeon Phineas J. Horwitz	12 Jun 1865–30 Jun 1869
Surgeon-General William M. Wood	1 Jul 1869–24 Oct 1871
Surgeon-General Jonathan M. Foltz	25 Oct 1871–9 Jun 1872
Surgeon-General James C. Palmer	10 Jun 1872–4 Jul 1873
Surgeon-General Joseph Beale	5 Jul 1873–30 Dec 1876
Surgeon-General William Grier	2 Feb 1877–5 Oct 1878
Surgeon-General J. Winthrop Taylor	21 Oct 1878–19 Aug 1879

Surgeon-General Philip S. Wales	26 Jan 1880–26 Jan 1884
Surgeon-General Francis M. Gunnell	27 Mar 1884–26 Mar 1888
Surgeon-General John M. Browne	2 Apr 1888–9 May 1893
Surgeon-General James R. Tryon	7 Sep 1893–7 Sept 1897
RAdm William K. Van Reypen	22 Oct 1897–25 Jan 1902

Abbreviations

act.	acting	Dec	December
Adm, adm	admiral	dept.	department
Afr.	African	dir.	director
AK	Alaska	dist.	district
AL	Alabama	div.	division
Am.	American	E.	East
Apr	April	engr.	engineer
AR	Arkansas	Ens	ensign
Asia.	Asiatic	Ensjg	ensign (junior grade)
asst.	assistant	equip.	equipment
Atl.	Atlantic	Eur.	European
Aug	August	evol.	evolution
AZ	Arizona	exam.	examining/examination
bd.	board	exec.	executive
BGen	brigadier general	expd.	expedition
Blk.	Blockading	expl.	exploring
Braz.	Brazil	Feb	February
bur.	bureau	FL	Florida
bvt.	brevet	flgs.	flagship
c.	circa	flot.	flotilla
CA	California	flt.	fleet
Capt, capt	captain	ft.	feet/fort
capt.yd.	captain of yard	GA	Georgia
Cdr, cdr	commander	Gen, gen	general
CO	Colorado	gov.	governor
Col	colonel	HI	Hawaii
Commo	commodore	hosp.	hospital
comdt.	commandant	HQ	headquarters
const.	constructor	IA	Iowa
cst.	coast	ID	Idaho
CT	Connecticut	IL	Illinois
DC	District of Columbia	IN	Indiana
DE	Delaware	Ind.	India

insp.	inspector	OR	Oregon
inst.	instructor	ord.	ordnance
Jan	January	PA	Pennsylvania
Jul	July	Pac.	Pacific
Jun	June	PAsst.	passed assistant
KS	Kansas	Paymstr.	paymaster
KY	Kentucky	P.I.	Philippine Islands
LA	Louisiana	PMidn	passed midshipman
LCdr	lieutenant commander	prac.	practice
LtCol	lieutenant colonel	pres.	president
LtGen	lieutenant general	prof.	professor
L.h.	lighthouse	q.v.	*quod vide* [which see]: see also
lib.	library		
Lt, lt	lieutenant	RAdm	rear admiral
Ltjg	lieutenant (junior grade)	rec.	receiving
lv.	leave	rel.	relative
l.o.a.	leave of absence	ret.	retirement
MA	Massachusetts	Ret.Lst.	Retired List
Mar	March	RI	Rhode Island
Maj	major	Rndv.	Rendezvous
math.	mathematics	S.	South
MB	Marine Barracks	s.a.	settle accounts
MD	Maryland	SC	South Carolina
ME	Maine	SD	South Dakota
Med.	Mediterranean	sec.	secretary
medl.	medical	Sep	September
MGen	major general	serv.	service
MI	Michigan	spec.	special
Midn, midn	midshipman/midshipmen	sqdn.	squadron
MN	Minnesota	sta.	station
MO	Missouri	supt.	superintendent
MS	Mississippi	surg.	surgeon
Mstr, mstr	master	surv.	surveying
MT	Montana	temp.	temporary
N.	North	TN	Tennessee
nav.	navigation	torp.	torpedo
NB	Nebraska	TX	Texas
NC	North Carolina	univ.	university
ND	North Dakota	U.S.	United States
NH	New Hampshire	USA	United States Army
NJ	New Jersey	USMA	United States Military Academy
NM	New Mexico		
n.d.	no date	USMC	United States Marine Corps
Nov	November		
NV	Nevada	USN	United States Navy
NWC	Naval War College	USNA	United States Naval Academy
NY	New York		
Oct	October	UT	Utah
off.	officer	VA	Virginia
OH	Ohio	VAdm	vice admiral
OK	Oklahoma	VT	Vermont

W.	West	w.o.	waiting orders
WA	Washington	WV	West Virginia
WI	Wisconsin	WY	Wyoming

Collections and Libraries

ALP	Abraham Lincoln Papers, IL State Historical Society
ASHF	American Swedish Historical Foundation, Philadelphia, PA
ASAL	Archibald Stevens Alexander Lib., Rutgers Univ.
BAKL	Baker Lib., Harvard Univ.
BL	Bancroft Lib., Univ. of CA, Berkeley
BLYU	Beinecke Lib., Yale Univ.
EFMC	Eric F. Menke Collection, Georgetown Univ.
EMHL	Eleutherian Mills Historical Lib., Greenville, DE
FDRL	Franklin D. Roosevelt Library, Hyde Park, NY
GARL	George Arents Research Lib., Syracuse Univ.
HHL	Henry Huntington Lib., San Marino, CA
LC	Lib. of Congress, Washington, DC
LSUL	Louisiana State Univ. Lib.
ISHS	Illinois State Historical Society, Springfield, IL
MCHC	Marine Corps Historical Center, Washington Navy Yard
NHF,LC	Naval Historical Foundation, Lib. of Congress
NHF,WNY	Naval Historical Foundation, Washington Navy Yard
NL	Nimitz Lib., U.S. Naval Academy, Annapolis, MD
NYHS	New York Historical Society
NYPL	New York Public Lib.
RHTRL	Robert Hudson Tannahill Research Lib., Dearborn, MI
SCL	South Caroliniana Lib., Columbia, SC
SHC	Southern Historical Collection, Univ. of NC
SML	Sterling Memorial Lib., Yale Univ.
USMA	U.S. Military Academy, West Point, NY
USNAM	U.S. Naval Academy Museum, Annapolis, MD
WLCL	William L. Clements Lib., Ann Arbor, MI
WPL	William Perkins Lib., Duke Univ.

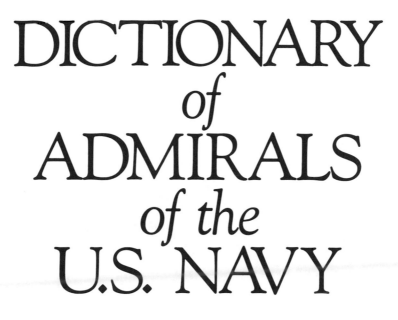

DICTIONARY
of
ADMIRALS
of the
U.S. NAVY

JAMES ALDEN Born in Portland, ME, on 31 Mar 1810, son of James and Elizabeth (Tate) Alden. Married Sarah Ann Thompson in 1838 but left no issue. Died in San Francisco on 6 Feb 1877. Buried in Portland, ME.

Ranks Midn (1 Apr 1828); PMidn (14 Jun 1834); Lt (25 Feb 1841); Cdr (14 Sep 1855); Capt (2 Jan 1863); Commo (25 Jul 1866); RAdm (19 Jun 1871); placed on Ret.Lst. (31 Mar 1872).

Career Summary Received appointment from ME (1 Apr 1828); Naval Station, Boston (Sep 1828–Apr 1830); *Concord*, Med.Sqdn. (May 1830–Jul 1833); l.o.a. (Jul–Oct 1833); Navy Yard, Norfolk, VA (Oct 1833–May 1834); l.o.a. (May–Aug 1834); Navy Yard, Boston (Aug 1834–Jun 1835); l.o.a. (Jun 1835–Jun 1836); Navy Yard, Boston (Jun–Jul 1836); l.o.a. (Jul 1836–Feb 1837); on furlough (Feb 1837–Jul 1838); *Porpoise*, U.S.Expl.Expd. (Jul 1838–Jul 1842); l.o.a. (Jul–Oct 1842); Navy Yard, Boston (Dec 1842–Feb 1844); *Constitution*, spec. cruise (Feb 1844–Oct 1846); l.o.a. (Oct–Dec 1846); Naval Observatory, Washington, DC (Dec 1846–Jul 1847); Home Sqdn. (Jul–Aug 1847); l.o.a. (Aug–Sep 1847); insp. of provisions and clothing, Navy Yard, Boston (Sep 1847–May 1849); cst.surv. duty (May 1849–Sep 1860); w.o. (Sep 1860–Apr 1861); temp. duty, Navy Yard, Norfolk, VA (Apr 1861); cdr, *South Carolina*, Gulf Blk.Sqdn. (May 1861–Jan 1862); cdr, *Richmond*, W.Gulf Blk.Sqdn. (Jan 1862–Aug 1863); cdr, *Ft. Jackson*, NY (Aug–Sep 1863); l.o.a. (Sep–Oct 1863); cdr, *Brooklyn*, W.Gulf Blk.Sqdn. (Nov 1863–Jan 1865); w.o. (Jan–Aug 1865); l.o.a. (Aug–Nov 1865); member, court-martial bd. (Nov 1865); cdr, flgs. *Susquehanna*, N.Atl.Sqdn. (Oct 1866–Jan 1867); w.o. (Jan–Mar 1867); cdr, *Minnesota*, spec.serv. (May 1867–Jan 1868); w.o. (Jan–Mar 1868); member, Naval Exam.Bd., Boston (Mar 1868); comdt., Navy Yard, Mare Island, CA (Aug 1868–Apr 1869); chief, Bur. of Nav., Washington, DC (Apr

JAMES ALDEN
1810–1877

1869–Sep 1871); cdr, Eur.Flt., *Wabash* (Oct 1871–Jul 1872); placed on Ret.Lst. (31 Mar 1872).

Career Highlights Member of famed Wilkes Expedition of 1838–42; was present at capture of Vera Cruz, Tuspan, and Tabasco during Mexican War. During the war with the Indians in Puget Sound, he volunteered with survey steamer *Active* to aid army: their arrival in the spring of 1856 at San Juan Island prevented violence between the Royal Navy and the U.S. Army. In Civil War, commanded steam sloop *Brooklyn* in Battle of Mobile Bay in Aug 1864.

JOHN JAY ALMY
1815–1895

JOHN JAY ALMY Born in Newport, RI, on 24 Apr 1815, son of Samuel and Phoebe (Irish) Almy. Married, with three children, including a son, Lt A. C. Almy, USN. Died at his home in Washington, DC, on 16 May 1895. Buried in the Congressional Cemetery, Washington, DC.

Ranks Midn (2 Feb 1829); PMidn (3 Jul 1835); Lt (8 Mar 1841); Cdr (24 Apr 1861); Capt (3 Mar 1865); Commo (31 Dec 1869); RAdm (24 Aug 1873); placed on Ret.Lst. (24 Apr 1877).

Career Summary Received appointment from RI (2 Feb 1829); w.o. (Feb 1829–Apr 1830); *Concord*, Med.Sqdn. (Apr 1830–Dec 1832); l.o.a. (Dec 1832–Mar 1833); *Vincennes*, Pac.Sqdn. (Mar 1833–Oct 1835); l.o.a. (Oct 1835–Jan 1836); *Natchez*, Norfolk, VA (Jan–Apr 1836); w.o. and l.o.a. (Apr–Sep 1836); rec. ship, Navy Yard, NY (Sep 1836–Mar 1837); cst.surv. duty (Mar–Nov 1837); l.o.a. (Nov 1837–Mar 1838); cst.surv. duty (Mar–Jun 1838); *Cyane*, W.Ind. and Med. Sqdns. (Jun 1838–Jun 1841); l.o.a. (Jun–Sep 1841); Depot of Charts, Washington, DC (Dec 1841–Dec 1842); *Bainbridge*, Home Sqdn. (Dec 1842–May 1843); *Macedonian*, W.Ind.Sqdn. (May 1844–May 1845); l.o.a. (May–Sep 1845); Hydrographic Office and Naval Observatory, Washington, DC (Sep 1845–Nov 1846); *Ohio*, Gulf of Mexico and Pac.Sqdn. (Nov 1846–Apr 1850); l.o.a. (Apr–May 1850); Navy Yard, Boston (May–Nov 1850); l.o.a. (Nov 1850–Mar 1851); cst.surv. duty (May 1851–Sep 1857); cdr, *Fulton*, Home and Braz. Sqdns. (Sep 1857–May 1859); Navy Yard, NY (May 1859–May 1862); cdr, *South Carolina*, S.Atl.Blk.Sqdn. (Jun 1862–Jul 1863); cdr, *Connecticut*, N.Atl.Blk.Sqdn. (Jul 1863–Oct 1864); w.o. (Oct–Nov 1864); spec. duty, NY (Nov 1864–Jan 1865); cdr, *Juniata*, S.Atl. and Braz. Sqdns. (Jan 1865–Jun 1867); w.o. (Jun 1867–Jan 1868); member, bd. to appraise ironclads (Jan–Feb 1868); ord. duty, Navy Yard, NY (May 1868–Feb 1870); w.o. (Feb–Jun 1870); chief signal off., Washington, DC (Jun 1870–May 1871); member, Bd. of Visitors, USNA (May 1871–Jun 1873); chief signal off., Washington, DC (Jun–Jul 1873); w.o. (Jul–Sep 1873); cdr, N.Pac.Sqdn., *Pensacola* (Sep 1873–Jul 1876); home and w.o. (Jul 1876–Mar 1877); pres., Bd. of Inspection (Mar–Apr 1877); placed on Ret.Lst. (24 Apr 1877).

Career Highlights Conducted successful operations

against Confederate blockade runners while commanding *Connecticut*, capturing or destroying over $1,000,000 worth of prizes in 1864 alone. At retirement, had the largest amount of sea service (27 years and 10 months) credited to any naval officer.

References
Personal Papers: a) FDRL. b) 3 volumes (1873–76) in NYHS. c) 2 volumes (1857–66) in NYPL.

DANIEL AMMEN
1820–1898

DANIEL AMMEN Born in Brown County, OH, on 15 May 1820. A boyhood friend of future Gen and Pres. Ulysses S. Grant. Spent a few months at West Point where his brother and later army Gen Jacob Ammen taught. Married to Mary Jackson, then to Zoe Atocha. Had five children. Resided in Beltsville, then Ammendale, MD. Died at the Naval Hosp., Washington, DC, on 11 Jul 1898. Buried in Arlington National Cemetery.

Ranks Midn (7 Jul 1836); PMidn (1 Jul 1842); Mstr (10 May 1849); Lt (4 Nov 1849); Cdr (16 Jul 1862); Capt (25 Jul 1866); Chief, Bur. of Yards and Docks with rank of Commo (1 May 1869); Commo (1 Apr 1872); RAdm (11 Dec 1877); retired (4 Jun 1878).

Career Summary Appointed from OH (7 Jul 1836); w.o. (Jul–Sep 1836); *Relief*, S.Seas Surv. and Expl.Expd. (Sep 1836–Jul 1837); *Macedonian*, S.Seas Surv. and Expl.Expd. (Jul 1837–Mar 1838); *Levant* and *Vandalia*, W.Ind.Sqdn. (Mar 1838–Nov 1839); w.o. (Nov 1839–Mar 1840); *Preble*, Med.Sqdn. (Mar 1840–May 1841); rec. ship *Ohio*, Boston (May–Jul 1841); Naval School, Philadelphia (Aug 1841–Jul 1842); w.o. (Jul–Oct 1842); surv. duty, DE Bay and rec. ship *Experiment*, Philadelphia (Oct 1842–Oct 1843); *Lexington*, Med.Sqdn. (Oct 1843–Oct 1844); l.o.a. (Oct 1844–Apr 1845); *Vincennes*, E.Ind.Sqdn. (Apr 1845–Apr 1847); cst.surv. duty (May 1847–Oct 1849); *St. Lawrence*, Med.Sqdn. (Jan–Nov 1850); l.o.a. (Nov–Dec 1850); cst.surv. duty (Dec 1850–Jul 1852); spec. duty, San Francisco Bay (Jul–Nov 1852); *Water Witch*, expl. and surv. duty (Feb 1853–May 1854); *Bainbridge*, Braz.Sqdn. (May 1854–Jan 1855); l.o.a. (Jan–Apr 1855); Naval Observatory, Washington, DC (Apr 1855–Aug 1857); *Saranac*, Pac.Sqdn. (Sep 1857–Jun 1858); *Merrimack*, Pac.Sqdn. (Jun 1858–Feb 1860); Naval Rndv., Baltimore (Mar 1860–May 1861); exec.off., *Roanoke*, Atl.Blk.Sqdn. (May–Sep 1861); cdr, *Seneca*, S.Atl.Blk.Sqdn. (Sep 1861–Aug 1862); cdr, *Sebago*, S.Atl.Blk.Sqdn. (Aug–Sep 1862); cdr, *Patapsco*, N.Atl.Blk.Sqdn. (Oct 1862–Jun 1863); sick lv. (Jun–Sep 1863); spec. duty, S.Atl.Blk.Sqdn., *Philadelphia* (Sep 1863–Jan 1864); sick lv. (Jan–Mar 1864); temp. cdr, *Shenandoah*, N.Atl.Blk.Sqdn. (Mar–Apr 1864); cdr, *Mohican*, S.Atl.Blk.Sqdn. (Oct 1864–Apr 1865); spec. duty recovering naval machinery in NC (Jul–Aug 1865); cdr, *Miantonomah*, N.Atl.Sqdn. (Sep 1865–Mar 1866); w.o. (Mar–Nov 1866); spec. duty, Hartford, CT (Nov 1866–Aug 1867); cdr, flgs. *Piscataqua*, Asia.Sqdn. (Aug 1867–Feb 1869); chief, Bur. of Yards and Docks, Washington, DC (May 1869–Sep 1871); chief, Bur. of Nav., Washington, DC (Oct 1871–Jun 1878); retired (4 Jun 1878).

Career Highlights In May 1864 while in charge of some 220 conscripted seamen sailing from NY to Aspinwall on the CA passenger steamer *Ocean Queen*, suppressed an open mutiny. During career and after retirement, involved with designing a variety of crafts and weapons for the navy, including the ram *Katahdin* for harbor defense and a cask life raft that became standard design for life boats in the naval service.

References
Personal Papers (1836–98): a) Univ. Research Lib., Univ. CA, Los Angeles. b) Correspondence between Ammen and Pres. Rutherford B. Hayes in Rutherford B. Hayes Lib., Fremont, OH.

Writings: a) *U.S. Commission on Site for Naval Observatory* (Washington, DC: 1879). b) "The Purpose of a Navy, and the Best Methods of Rendering It Efficient," *U.S. Naval Institute Proceedings* 17 (1879): 119–30. c) *The American Inter-Oceanic Ship Canal Question* (Philadelphia: 1880). d) *The Atlantic Coast*, part II of *The Navy in the Civil War* (NY: 1883). e) *The Old Navy and the New* (Philadelphia: 1891, 1898).

THEODORUS BAILEY Born on 12 Apr 1805, at Chateaugay (Plattsburg), NY, son of William and Phoebe (Platt) Bailey. Married Sarah Ann Platt on 23 Jun 1830. Died in Washington, DC, on 10 Feb 1877. Buried in Oak Hill Cemetery, Washington, DC.

Ranks Midn (1 Jan 1818); Lt (3 Mar 1827); Cdr (6 Mar 1849); Capt (15 Dec 1855); Commo (16 Jul 1862); Act. RAdm (22 Nov 1862); RAdm (25 Jul 1866); placed on Ret.Lst. (10 Oct 1866).

Career Summary Received appointment from NY (1 Jan 1818); w.o. (Jan 1818–1819); *Cyane*, Afr.Cst. and W.Indies (1819–Dec 1820); flgs. *Franklin*, Pac.Sqdn. (May 1821–Sep 1824); l.o.a. and w.o. (Sep 1824–May 1825); Navy Yard, NY (May–Jul 1825); *Shark*, Home Sqdn. (Jul 1825–Sep 1826); l.o.a. (Sep–Nov 1826); rec. ship *Fulton*, NY (Nov 1827–May 1829); l.o.a. (May 1829–Jan 1831); *Natchez*, W.Ind.Sqdn. (Jan–Sep 1831); l.o.a. and w.o. (Sep 1831–Apr 1833); *Vincennes*, Pac.Sqdn. (Apr 1833–Jun 1836); l.o.a. (Jun–Nov 1836); spec. recruiting duty for Expl.Expd. (Nov 1836–Jun 1837); w.o. (Jun–Sep 1837); temp. duty, *Ohio*, NY (Sep 1837–Jan 1838); Navy Yard, NY (Jan 1838–Apr 1840); l.o.a. (Apr–Sep 1840); *Constitution*, E.Ind.Sqdn. (Sep 1840–May 1844); l.o.a. and w.o. (May 1844–May 1845); Naval Rndv., NY (Jun 1845–May 1846); cdr, *Lexington*, Pac.Sqdn. (May 1846–Oct 1848); home, l.o.a., and w.o. (Oct 1848–Sep 1853); cdr, *St. Mary's*, Pac.Sqdn. (Sep 1853–Dec 1856); home and l.o.a. (Dec 1856–

THEODORUS BAILEY
1805–1877

May 1861); cdr, *Colorado*, W.Gulf Blk.Sqdn. (May 1861–May 1862); cdr, Naval Sta., Sacket's Harbor, NY (May–Nov 1862); cdr, E.Gulf Blk.Sqdn., *Cayuga* (Nov 1862–Sep 1864); cdr, Navy Yard, Portsmouth, NH (Sep 1864–Oct 1867); placed on Ret.Lst. (10 Oct 1866); spec. bd. duties, Washington, DC (Mar 1869–Apr 1873).

Career Highlights During the Mexican War, commanded storeship *Lexington* in blockade and capture of San Blas in Baja California in Jan 1848: cited for his efficient and valuable aid to the Pac.Sqdn. by fitting out and leading several expeditions against the enemy. During the Civil War, served as RAdm Farragut's [*q.v.*] second-in-command during the passage up the MS River and the capture of New Orleans.

References
Personal Papers: a) 1 volume (1846–48) at BL. b) 220 items (1828–85) at GARL.

GEORGE BEALE BALCH Born in Shelbyville, TN, on 3 Jan 1821. Married twice: two sons and four daughters. Died on 16 Apr 1908 at Raleigh, NC. Buried at USNA Cemetery.

Ranks Midn (30 Dec 1837); PMidn (29 Jun 1843); Lt (16 Aug 1850); Cdr (16 Jul 1862); Capt (25 Jul 1866); Commo (13 Aug 1872); RAdm (5 Jun 1878); placed on Ret.Lst. (3 Jan 1883).

Career Summary Appointed from AL (30 Dec 1837); w.o. (Dec 1837–Apr 1838); *Cyane* and *Grampus*, Med.Sqdn. (Apr 1838–Aug 1841); l.o.a. (Aug–Dec 1841); rec. ship *Pennsylvania*, Norfolk, VA (Dec 1841–Apr 1842); *Falmouth*, Pac.Sqdn. (Apr–Aug 1842); Naval School, Philadelphia (Sep 1842–Jul 1843); Depot of Charts, Washington, DC (Jul 1843–May 1845); *Southampton* and prize schooner *Merchant and Worden*, Afr.Sqdn. (May 1845–Feb 1846); *Princeton*, Home and Med. Sqdns. (Apr 1846–Jul 1849); l.o.a. (Jul–Sep 1849); Naval Observatory, Washington, DC (Sep 1849–Jun 1850); l.o.a. (Jun–Sep 1850); on furlough (Oct 1850–Mar 1851); w.o. (Mar–Jun 1851); Naval Observatory, Washington, DC (May–Jul 1851); *Plymouth*, Asia.Sqdn. (Jul 1851–Jan 1855); l.o.a. (Jan–Apr 1855); *Michigan*, on Great Lakes (Apr–May 1855); l.o.a. (May–Sep 1855); Navy Yard, Washington, DC (Sep 1855–Jun 1857); *Plymouth*, Home Sqdn. (Jun–Nov 1857); *Jamestown*, Home Sqdn. (Dec 1857–Sep 1858); w.o. (Sep–Nov 1858); *St. Mary's*, Pac.Sqdn. (Dec 1858–Oct 1860); USNA (Nov 1860–Jan 1861); w.o. (Jan–Mar 1861); Naval Observatory, Washington, DC (Mar–Aug 1861); *Sabine*, then cdr, *Pocahontas*, S.Atl.Blk.Sqdn. (Aug 1861–Sep 1862); w.o. (Sep–Oct 1862); *Pawnee*, S.Atl.Blk.Sqdn. (Oct 1862–Feb 1865); temp. duty, Navy Yard, Washington, DC (Mar 1865–Jan 1868); w.o. (Jan–Mar 1868); cdr, flgs. *Contoocook* [renamed *Albany*], N.Atl.Sqdn. (Mar 1868–Jan 1870); w.o. (Jan–Apr 1870); Navy Yard, Washington, DC (Apr 1870–Sep 1872); spec. duty, Washington, DC (Oct 1872–Jan 1873); w.o. (Jan–

GEORGE BEALE BALCH
1821–1908

Mar 1873); gov., Naval Asylum, Philadelphia (Apr 1873–Mar 1876); w.o. (Mar–May 1876); member, L.h. Bd. (Jun 1876–Aug 1877); member, Naval Exam. and Ret. Bds. (Sep 1877–Aug 1879); supt., USNA (Aug 1879–Jun 1881); cdr, Pac.Sta., *Pensacola* (Jul 1881–Jan 1883); placed on Ret.Lst. (3 Jan 1883).

Career Highlights During the Mexican War, participated in the attack on Alvarado in Aug 1846 and with the Mosquito Fleet at the bombardment and landing at Vera Cruz in Mar 1847. In Apr 1854, wounded at Shanghai, China, commanding an advance post during action between Chinese Imperial forces and Taiping rebels.

References
Personal Papers: 420 items (1830–1924) at SHC.

CHARLES HENRY BALDWIN
1822–1888

CHARLES HENRY BALDWIN Born in New York City on 3 Sep 1822, son of Edwin and Miss (Carey) Baldwin. Married twice, to Caroline Pamelia Tohree and to Mrs. Mary Reade. A son and a daughter. Died at his home in New York City on 17 Nov 1888. Buried in St. Mark's Churchyard, New York City.

Ranks Midn (24 Apr 1839); PMidn (2 Jul 1845); Mstr. (17 Jan 1853); Lt (2 Dec 1853); resigned (28 Feb 1854); received commission as Act.Lt (27 Dec 1861); Cdr (18 Nov 1862); Capt (12 Jun 1869); Commo (8 Aug 1876); RAdm (31 Jan 1883); placed on Ret.Lst. (3 Sep 1884).

Career Summary Received appointment from NY (24 Apr 1839); w.o. (Apr–Jun 1839); *Brandywine* and *Fairfield*, Med.Sqdn. (Jun 1839–Jan 1843); sick lv. (Jan–Mar 1843); *Vandalia*, Home Sqdn. (Mar 1843–May 1844); rec. ship *New Hampshire*, NY (May–Jun 1844); *Michigan*, on Great Lakes (Jun–Aug 1844); Naval School, Philadelphia (Sep 1844–Jun 1845); l.o.a. (Jun–Aug 1845); *Congress*, Pac.Sqdn. (Aug 1845–Jan 1849); l.o.a. and w.o. (Jan–Jun 1849); on furlough, commanding mail steamers *Baltic* and *Pacific* (Jun 1849–Apr 1851); w.o. (Apr–May 1851); cst.surv. duty (May–Jun 1851); on furlough (Jun 1851–Dec 1853); ordered to Braz.Sqdn. (Feb 1854); resigned commission and entered Pacific Mail Service (28 Feb 1854); commissioned (27 Dec 1861); cdr, *Clifton*, W.Gulf Blk.Sqdn. (Jan–Jul 1862); cdr, *Vanderbilt*, spec.serv. (Sep 1862–Oct 1864); spec. duty, Navy Yard, NY (Oct–Nov 1864); ord. duty, Navy Yard, Mare Island, CA (Dec 1864–Jul 1867); l.o.a. (Jul 1867–Oct 1868); flt.capt., N.Pac.Sqdn., *Pensacola* (Jan–Jun 1869); insp. of ord., Navy Yard, Mare Island, CA (Jun 1869–Sep 1871); cdr, *Colorado*, Asia.Sqdn. (Sep 1871–Mar 1873); cdr, Naval Rndv., San Francisco (Apr–Oct 1873); exec.off., Navy Yard, Mare Island, CA (Oct 1873); cdr, Naval Rndv., San Francisco (Oct 1873–Jun 1874); w.o. and l.o.a. (Jun 1874–Oct 1876); member, Naval Ret.Bd. (Oct 1876–Dec 1877); w.o. and l.o.a. (Dec 1877–Mar 1880); member, L.h. Bd. (Apr 1880–Feb 1883); cdr, Eur. Sta., *Lancaster* (Mar 1883–Sep 1884); placed on Ret.Lst. (3 Sep 1884).

Career Highlights During the Mexican War, saw action at Mazatlan from Nov 1847 to Jun 1848. Participated in actions on lower Mississippi during Civil War. As commander of Eur.Sta., was U.S. representative at the court of Czar Alexander III and Empress Maria Feodorovna at Moscow in May and Jun 1883.

ALBERT SMITH BARKER Born in Hanson, MA, on 31 Mar 1843, son of Josiah and Eliza (Cushing) Barker. Educated at the Pierce Academy. Married Ellen Blackman Maxwell in 1894. Died on 30 Jan 1916, in Washington, DC. Buried in Arlington National Cemetery.

Ranks Act.Midn (25 Oct 1859); title changed to Midn (16 Jul 1862); Ens (22 Nov 1862); Lt (22 Feb 1864); LCdr (25 Jul 1866); Cdr (28 Mar 1877); Capt (5 May 1892); RAdm (10 Oct 1899); placed on Ret.Lst. (31 Mar 1905).

Career Summary Received appointment from MA (25 Oct 1859); USNA (Oct 1859–May 1861); *Mississippi*, W.Gulf Blk.Sqdn. (May 1861–Mar 1863); *Monongahela*, W.Gulf Blk.Sqdn. (Mar–Aug 1863); *Niagara*, spec.serv. (Sep 1863–Feb 1864); flt. lt, flgs. *Lancaster*, Pac. Sqdn. (May 1864–Mar 1867); w.o. (Mar–May 1867); flt. lt, flgs. *Guerriere*, S.Atl.Sta. (May 1867–Jul 1869); w.o. and l.o.a. (Jul–Nov 1869); *Terror*, Boston and N.Atl.Sqdn. (Dec 1869–Nov 1870); *Dictator*, N.Atl.Sqdn. (Nov 1870): w.o. (Nov 1870–May 1871); *Wachusett*, Eur.Sta. (Jun 1871–May 1873); w.o. (Jun–Aug 1873); torp. duty, Newport, RI (Sep 1873–Jul 1874); temp. duty, exec.off., *Intrepid*, spec.serv. (Jul–Aug 1874); USNA (Sep 1874–Feb 1876); cdr, *Palos*, Asia.Sqdn. (Mar 1876–Aug 1877); w.o. (Sep 1877–May 1878); Torp.Sta., Newport, RI (Jun–Sep 1878); w.o. (Sep–Oct 1878); insp., 8th L.h. Dist., New Orleans (Nov 1878–Jan 1882); s.a. and w.o. (Jan–Jul 1882); cdr, *Montauk*, Philadelphia (Jul–Dec 1882); cdr, *Enterprise*, hydrographic surv. duty (Dec 1882–Mar 1886); w.o. (Mar–Aug 1886); asst., then insp., 2nd L.h. Dist., Boston (Sep 1886–Nov 1889); s.a. and w.o. (Nov–Dec 1889); Bur. of Nav., Washington, DC (Dec 1889–Dec 1891); ord. instructions, Navy Yard, Washington, DC (Jun 1891–Mar 1892); cdr, flgs. *Philadelphia*, N.Atl.Sqdn. and Naval Review Flt. (Jul 1892–Aug 1894); l.o.a. and w.o. (Aug 1894–Jan 1895); capt.yd., Navy Yard, Mare Island, CA (Feb 1895–Mar 1897); cdr, *Oregon*, Pac.Sta. (Mar 1897–Jan 1898); home and l.o.a. (Jan–Feb 1898); spec. duty, member of Army and Navy Bd. of Strategy and member of War Bd., Washington, DC (Mar–May 1898); cdr, flgs. *Newark*, E.Sqdn., N.Atl.Flt. (May–Aug 1898); cdr, *Oregon*, and chief of staff, E.Sqdn., N.Atl.Flt. (Aug 1898–May 1899); temp. cdr, Asia.Flt., *Baltimore* (May–Jun 1899); home and w.o. (Jun–Oct 1899); comdt., Navy Yard and Sta., Norfolk, VA (Oct 1899–Jul 1900); comdt., Navy Yard and Sta., NY (Jul 1900–Apr 1903); cdr, N.Atl.Flt., *Kearsarge* (Apr 1903–Mar 1905); placed on Ret.Lst. (31 Mar 1905).

ALBERT SMITH BARKER
1843–1916

Career Highlights Saw action on lower Mississippi River in 1862. Witnessed Spanish bombardment of Callao, Peru, in May 1866. Was at Min River in China when French fleet sank Chinese men-of-war at Pagoda Anchorage in 1885. While at the Torp.Sta. at Newport, RI, in 1873–74, was apparently the first person in the U.S. to fire high explosive shells. During Spanish-American War, was present at bombardment of Santiago, Cuba, in Jul 1898.

References

Personal Papers: covering 1883–1905, in NHF, WNY.

Writings: a) "The Firing of High Explosives from Great Guns," U.S. Naval Institute *Proceedings* 39 (1886): 547–61. b) *Deep–Sea Soundings; A Brief Account of the Work done by the USS* ENTERPRISE *in Deep–Sea Soundings during 1883–1886* (NY: 1892). c) *Everyday Life in the Navy: The Autobiography of Rear Admiral Albert S. Barker* (Boston: c.1928).

GEORGE WILLIAM BEAMAN Born on 7 May 1837, in Rutland, VT, son of George Hudson and Eleanor Kettle (Gookin) Beaman. Educated at Rutland High School and the Troy Conference Academy. War correspondent with *The Missouri Democrat* from Aug 1861 to Mar 1862. Married Rebecca Swift Goldsmith on 2 May 1866: one son, William Major Beaman. Died on 3 May 1917 at his home in Cambridge, MA.

Ranks Act.Asst.Paymstr. (5 Mar 1862); Asst.Paymstr. (11 Jun 1862); Paymstr. (28 Mar 1866); Pay Insp. (12 Sep 1891); Pay Dir. (9 Apr 1899); placed on Ret.Lst. with rank of RAdm (7 May 1899).

Career Summary Private, 3rd Regiment, MO Reserve Corps (May–Aug 1861); received appointment from MO as Act.Asst.Paymstr. (5 Mar 1862); capt's clerk (Mar–May 1862); w.o. (May–Jul 1862); *Seneca*, S.Atl.Blk.Sqdn. (Aug 1862–May 1863); *Union*, E. and W. Gulf Blk.Sqdns. (May 1863–Aug 1864); w.o. (Aug–Dec 1864); asst. purchasing paymstr., Cairo, IL (Dec 1864–Feb 1865); spec. duty, MS Flot. (Feb–Aug 1865); s.a. and w.o. (Aug–Dec 1865); *Algonquin*, NY [never commissioned] (Dec 1865–Mar 1866); s.a. and w.o. (Mar–May 1866); prac. ship *Marion*, USNA (May 1866–Sep 1868); s.a. and w.o. (Sep–Dec 1868); *Cyane*, N. and S. Pac.Stas. (Jan–Jul 1869); *Ossipee*, N. and S. Pac.Stas. (Jul 1869–Mar 1872); s.a. and w.o. (Mar–Oct 1872); Navy Yard, Norfolk, VA (Oct 1872–Jan 1876); s.a. and w.o. (Jan–Dec 1876); *Franklin*, Norfolk, VA (Dec 1876–Feb 1877); s.a. and w.o. (Feb–Mar 1877); *Monongahela*, Asia.Sta. (May 1877–Nov 1879); s.a. and w.o. (Nov 1879–Jun 1880); Naval Asylum, Philadelphia (Jun 1880–Sep 1883); s.a. and w.o. (Sep 1883–Mar 1885); *Shenandoah*, Pac.Sta. (Apr 1885–Oct 1886); s.a. and w.o. (Oct–Dec 1886); gen. storekeeper, Navy Yard, Boston (Jan 1887–Jun 1889); s.a. and w.o. (Jun–Dec 1889); *Baltimore*, on trials and flgs., N.Atl.Sqdn. (Dec 1889–Jul 1890); gen. storekeeper, Navy

GEORGE WILLIAM BEAMAN
1837–1917

Yard, Mare Island, CA (Sep 1890–Dec 1892); s.a. and w.o. (Dec 1892–Jul 1893); *New York*, N.Atl.Sta. (Aug 1893–Dec 1894); flt.paymstr., N.Atl.Sta., *New York* (Dec 1894–Mar 1896); s.a. and w.o. (Mar–May 1896); paymstr., Navy Yard, Boston (May 1896–Apr 1899); s.a. and w.o. (Apr–May 1899); placed on Ret.Lst. (7 May 1899).

GROVE SPOONER BEARDSLEE Born in Verona, Oneida County, NY, on 22 Jan 1838. Likely related to RAdm Lester Anthony Beardslee [*q.v.*]. Died in Atlantic City, NJ, on 7 Mar 1906. Buried in Syracuse, NY.

Ranks Asst.Surg. (1 Jul 1861); PAsst.Surg. (22 Jun 1864); Surg. (25 Jul 1866); Medl.Insp. (24 Apr 1884); Medl.Dir. (22 Jan 1891); placed on Ret.Lst. as Medl.Dir. with rank of RAdm (22 Jan 1900).

Career Summary Received appointment from NY (1 Jul 1861); *Lancaster*, Pac., then W.Gulf Blk.Sqdns. (Oct 1861– Apr 1863); *St. Mary's*, Pac.Sqdn. (Apr 1863–Mar 1864); return and w.o. (Mar–May 1864); Naval Hosp., NY (May–Oct 1864); *Lackawanna*, W.Gulf Blk.Sqdn. (Nov. 1864–Jul 1865); w.o. (Jul–Aug. 1865); Naval Hosp., NY (Aug–Oct 1865); *Brooklyn*, flgs., and *Juniata*, S.Atl.Sqdn. (Oct 1865–Jun 1867); w.o. (Jun 1867–Mar 1868); rec. ship *Independence*, Mare Island, CA (Apr 1868–Jan 1870); *St. Mary's*, Pac.Sta. (Jan 1870–Jun 1873); Naval Hosp., Norfolk, VA (Jul 1873–Apr 1874); rec. ship *Vermont*, NY (Apr 1874); Navy Yard, Boston (Apr 1874–Sep 1876); *Dictator*, N.Atl.Sta. (Sep 1876–May 1877); l.o.a. (May 1877–May 1878); w.o. (May–Jun 1878); Navy Yard, NY (Jun 1878–Jan 1880); w.o. (Jan–Aug 1880); *Galena*, Eur.Sta. (Aug 1880–Oct 1883); l.o.a. (Oct 1883–Oct 1884); w.o. (Oct 1884–Mar 1885); Navy Yard, Norfolk, VA (Mar 1885–Jun 1886); flgs. *Brooklyn*, Asia.Sqdn. (Jun 1886–May 1889); w.o. (May–Jun 1889); l.o.a. (Jul 1889–May 1890); Navy Yard, Washington, DC (May 1890–Jul 1893); member, then pres., Naval Exam. and Ret. Bds., Washington, DC (Jan 1893–Jan 1900); placed on Ret.Lst. (22 Jan 1900).

LESTER ANTHONY BEARDSLEE Born in Little Falls, NY, on 1 Feb 1836, son of John and Mary (Anthony) Beardslee. Likely related to Grove Spooner Beardslee, USN [*q.v.*]. Educated at local schools. Married Evelyn Small in Jan 1863. Retired to Beaufort, SC. Died in Augusta, GA, on 10 Nov 1903.

Ranks Act.Midn (5 Mar 1850); PMidn (20 Jun 1856); Mstr (22 Jan 1858); Lt (23 Jul 1859); LCdr (16 Jul 1862); Cdr (12 Jun 1869); Capt (26 Nov 1880); Commo (23 Jan 1894); RAdm (21 May 1895); placed on Ret.Lst. (1 Feb 1898).

Career Summary Received appointment from NY (5 Mar 1850); USNA (Mar 1850–May 1851); *Plymouth*, E.Ind.Sqdn. (May 1851–Jan 1855); l.o.a. (Jan–Oct 1855); USNA (Oct 1855–Jun 1856); *Merrimack*, spec.serv. (Aug

GROVE SPOONER BEARDSLEE
1838–1906

LESTER ANTHONY BEARDSLEE
1836–1903

1856–Apr 1857); w.o. (Apr–Jun 1857); *Germantown*, E.Ind.Sqdn. (Jul 1857–Apr 1860); w.o. (Apr–Nov 1860); *Saratoga*, Afr.Sqdn. (Nov 1860–Jan 1863); exec.off., *Nantucket*, N.Atl.Sqdn. (Jan–Apr 1863); sick lv. and w.o. (Apr–Aug 1863); spec. duty, NY (Aug–Oct 1863); exec.off., *Wachusett*, spec.serv. off Braz. (Oct 1863–Jan 1865); *Connecticut*, spec.serv., W.Indies (Jan–Jun 1865); sick lv. (Jun 1865–Mar 1866); cdr, *Ashuelot*, Asia.Sqdn. (Dec 1866–Jul 1868); home and w.o. (Jul–Oct 1868); exec.off., *Lackawanna*, Pac.Sqdn. (Oct 1868–Feb 1869); w.o. (Mar–Jun 1869); Hydrographic Office, Washington, DC (Oct 1869–Apr 1870); cdr, *Palos*, Pac.Sqdn. (Apr–Oct 1870); w.o. (Dec 1870–Jan 1871); Hydrographic Office, Washington, DC (Jan 1871–Aug 1872); equip.off., Navy Yard, Washington, DC (Oct 1872–Sep 1875); spec. duty, Bur. of Equip., Washington, DC (Oct 1875–Aug 1876); member, bd. to test metals (Apr 1875–Apr 1879); temp. cdr, *Speedwell*, Washington, DC (Jun–Oct 1878); cdr, *Jamestown*, AK coast (May 1879–Sep 1880); spec. duty (Nov 1880–Nov 1881); l.o.a. (Nov 1881–Mar 1883); cdr, rec. ship *Franklin*, Norfolk, VA (Apr 1883–May 1884); cdr, *Powhatan*, N.Atl.Sqdn. (May 1884–May 1886); w.o. (May 1886–May 1887); Torp.Sta., Newport, RI (Jun–Sep 1887); w.o. (Sep 1887–Aug 1888); NWC (Aug–Nov 1888); w.o. (Nov 1888–May 1889); cdr, rec. ship *Vermont*, NY (Jul 1889–Oct 1891); cdr, Naval Sta., Port Royal, SC (Nov 1891–Jul 1894); cdr, Pac. Sta., *Philadelphia* (Aug 1894–Aug 1897); pres., Exam. and Ret. Bd. (Oct 1897–Jan 1898); placed on Ret.Lst. (1 Feb 1898).

Career Highlights While on *Plymouth*, was a member of Commodore Perry's party at the memorable landing at Kurihama, Japan, Jul 1853. During Civil War, was on monitor *Nantucket* during the ironclad attack on Charleston Harbor in Apr 1863. Served on board the *Wachusett* off Brazil, participating in the capture of the Confederate cruiser *Florida*, commanding the latter as prize to Hampton Roads, VA. While commanding tug *Palos* to meet Pac.Sqdn. in 1870, took first U.S. flag through the recently completed Suez Canal.

Reference
Personal Papers: 128 items (1850–1900) in NHF,LC.

JOHN COLT BEAUMONT Born in Wilkes-Barre, PA, on 27 Aug 1821, son of Andrew and Julia (Colt) Beaumont. Married Fanny Dorrance on 27 Oct 1852. Married again to Fannie King in 1874. Had three children. Died in Durham, NH, on 2 Aug 1882. Buried in Oak Hill Cemetery, Washington, DC.

Ranks Midn (1 Mar 1838); PMidn (20 May 1844); Mstr (30 Aug 1851); Lt (29 Aug 1852); Cdr (16 Jul 1862); placed on Ret.Lst. (27 Apr 1868); restored to Active List as Capt (10 Jun 1872); Commo (14 Jun 1874); RAdm (25 Nov 1881); placed on Ret.Lst. (3 Feb 1882).

JOHN COLT BEAUMONT
1821–1882

Career Summary Received commission from PA (1 Mar 1838); w.o. (Mar–May 1838); *Erie*, Atl.Coast (May 1838–Sep 1840); l.o.a. (Sep–Oct 1840); *Constellation*, spec. cruise (Oct 1840–May 1844); l.o.a. (May–Nov 1844); *Jamestown*, Afr.Cst. (Nov 1844–Aug 1846); l.o.a. (Aug–Nov 1846); *Ohio*, W.Ind.Sqdn. (Nov 1846–Oct 1847); l.o.a. (Oct 1847–Feb 1848); Naval Observatory, Washington, DC (Feb–Aug 1848); cst.surv. duty (Aug 1848–May 1849); *Independence*, Med.Sqdn. (Jun 1849–Jun 1852); l.o.a. (Jun–Sep 1852); Naval Observatory, Washington, DC (Sep 1852–May 1854); w.o. (May–Jul 1854); *San Jacinto*, Eur. and W.Ind. Sqdns. (Jul 1854–May 1855); l.o.a. and w.o. (May–Oct 1855); *Potomac*, Home Sqdn. (Oct 1855–Aug 1856); *Wabash*, Home Sqdn. (Aug 1856–Feb 1858); l.o.a. (Feb–May 1858); rec. ship *North Carolina*, NY (May 1858–Apr 1859); *Hartford*, E.Ind.Sqdn. (May 1859–Jan 1862); cdr, *Aroostook*, N.Atl.Sqdn. (Feb–Jul 1862); sick lv. and w.o. (Jul–Oct 1862); cdr, *Sebago*, S.Atl.Blk.Sqdn. (Oct 1862–Apr 1863); cdr, *Nantucket*, S.Atl.Blk.Sqdn. (Apr–Oct 1863); spec. duty, S.Atl.Blk.Sqdn. (Oct–Dec 1863); cdr, *Mackinaw*, N. and S. Atl.Sqdns. (Feb 1864–May 1865); w.o. (May–Jul 1865); sick lv. (Jul 1865–Mar 1866); cdr, *Miantonomah*, Eur.Sta. (Mar 1866–Jul 1867); w.o. (Jul 1867–Apr 1868); placed on Ret.Lst. (27 Apr 1868); restored to Active List (10 Jun 1872); w.o. (Jun–Dec 1872); exec.off., Navy Yard, Washington, DC (Dec 1872–Jun 1873); cdr, *Powhatan*, spec.serv. (Jul 1873–Jul 1874); member, Bd. of Inspection and Surv. (Jul 1874–Mar 1875); w.o. (Mar 1875–Aug 1876); chief signal off., Navy Dept., Washington, DC (Sep 1876–Apr 1879); comdt., Navy Yard, Portsmouth, NH (May 1879–Dec 1881); w.o. (Dec 1881–Feb 1882); placed on Ret.Lst. (3 Feb 1882).

GEORGE EUGENE BELKNAP Born on 22 Jan 1832, at Newport, NH, son of Sawyer and Martha (Aiken) Belknap. First wife was Ellen D. Reed, whom he married on 8 Dec 1861. Second wife was Frances G. Prescott, whom he married in Calcutta, India, on 23 Dec 1866. Received honorary Doctorate of Laws from Dartmouth College in 1894. Died at Key West, FL, on 7 Apr 1903. Buried in Arlington National Cemetery.

Ranks Act.Midn (7 Oct 1847); PMidn (10 Jun 1853); Mstr (15 Sep 1855); Lt (16 Sep 1855); LCdr (16 Jul 1862); Cdr (25 Jul 1866); Capt (25 Jan 1875); Commo (2 Jun 1885); RAdm (12 Feb 1889); placed on Ret.Lst. (22 Jan 1894).

Career Summary Received appointment from NH (7 Oct 1847); USNA (Oct–Dec 1847); *Porpoise*, Afr.Cst. (Dec 1847–Apr 1850); l.o.a. (Apr–Jul 1850); *Raritan*, Pac.Sqdn. (Jul 1850–Jun 1853); l.o.a. (Jun–Oct 1853); USNA (Oct 1853–Jan 1854); cst.surv. duty (Jan–Oct 1854); *Falmouth*, spec. duty, W.Indies (Nov 1854–Aug 1855); *Saratoga*, Boston (Aug–Oct

GEORGE EUGENE BELKNAP
1832–1903

1855); rec. ship *Ohio*, Boston (Nov 1855–Mar 1856); *Portsmouth*, Asia.Sta. (Apr 1856–Jun 1858); l.o.a. (Jun–Jul 1858); rec. ship *Ohio*, Boston (Jul–Oct 1858); *America* (Nov–Dec 1858); w.o. (Dec 1858–Jan 1859); *St. Louis*, Home Sqdn. (Jan 1859–Oct 1861); l.o.a. (Oct–Nov 1861); exec.off., *Huron*, S.Atl.Blk.Sqdn. (Nov 1861–Jun 1862); w.o. (Jun–Sep 1862); exec.off., *New Ironsides*, Norfolk, VA, S.Atl.Blk.Sqdn., and Philadelphia (Sep 1862–Aug 1864); cdr, *Seneca*, NY and N.Atl.Blk.Sqdn. (Sep–Nov 1864); cdr, *Canonicus*, N. and S. Atl.Blk.Sqdns. (Nov 1864–Jun 1865); w.o. (Jun–Jul 1865); USNA and prac. sqdn. (Jul–Aug 1865); w.o. (Aug–Nov 1865); exec.off., *Shenandoah*, Asia.Sqdn. (Nov 1865–Feb 1867); cdr, flgs. *Hartford*, Asia.Sqdn. (Feb 1867–Aug 1868); w.o. (Aug–Sep 1868); USNA (Oct 1868); w.o. (Oct–Nov 1868); Naval Rndv., NY (Nov 1868–Jan 1869); w.o. (Jan–Apr 1869); nav. duty, Navy Yard, Boston (Apr 1869–May 1872); cdr, *Tuscarora*, S.Pac.Sta. (May 1872–Oct 1874); w.o. (Oct–Nov 1874); spec. duty, Washington, DC, and Boston (Nov–Dec 1874); cdr, rec. ship *Ohio*, Boston (Jan–Mar 1875); capt.yd., Navy Yard, Pensacola, FL (Mar 1875–Apr 1876); spec. duty, deep sea soundings (May–Dec 1876); comdt., Navy Yard, Pensacola, FL (Dec 1876–Jan 1881); w.o. (Jan–Mar 1881); cdr, *Alaska*, Pac.Sqdn. (Apr 1881–Jan 1883); w.o. (Jan–May 1883); capt.yd., Navy Yard, Norfolk, VA (Jun 1883–May 1885); supt., Naval Observatory, Washington, DC (Jun 1885–Jun 1886); comdt., Navy Yard, Mare Island, CA (Jun 1886–Mar 1889); cdr, Asia.Sta., flgs. *Omaha* and *Marion* (Apr 1889–Feb 1892); home and w.o. (Feb–Apr 1892); pres., Bd. of Inspection and Survey (Apr 1892–Jan 1894); placed on Ret.Lst. (22 Jan 1894).

Career Highlights Guarded the American consulate against the barrier forts at Canton, China, in Oct and Nov 1856. During the Civil War, commanded boats from *St. Louis* during the two reinforcement ventures to Ft. Pickens in Apr 1861. While commanding *New Ironsides*, involved in bombardments of Charleston and harbor in Apr 1863, receiving commendation from RAdm Du Pont [*q.v.*]. Led expedition against natives on Formosa in Jun 1867.

Achieved greatest recognition with scientific research and experimentation. From 1872 to 1874, participated in survey across Isthmus of Panama for inter-ocean canal route. Made deep sea soundings between the western U.S. and Japan for possible submarine cables. Invented different types of cylinders for taking seabed samples. For scientific efforts, received acclaim from the international scientific world.

References

Personal Papers: 1400 items (1857–1903) in NHF, LC.

Writings: a) *The Depth of the Pacific of the East Coast of Japan* (1890). b) "Some Aspects of Naval Administration, in War, with its Attendant Belongs of Peace," U.S. Naval Institute *Proceedings* 86 (1898): 263–300. c) *Oration Delivered by*

Rear-Admiral George E. Belknap, U.S. Navy (Boston: 1902). d) *Letters of Captain George Hamilton Perkins, USN*, ed. and arr. by George E. Belknap (Concord, NH: 1908).

CHARLES HEYER BELL Born in New York City on 15 Aug 1798. Died on 19 Feb 1875 at New Brunswick, NJ, where he was buried.

Ranks Midn (18 Jun 1812); Lt (28 Mar 1820); Cdr (10 Sep 1840); Capt (12 Aug 1854); Act.RAdm (16 Jul 1862); transferred to Ret.Lst. with rank of Commo (16 Jul 1862); RAdm on Ret.Lst. (25 Jul 1866)

Career Summary Received appointment from NY (18 Jun 1812); w.o. (Jun 1812–Feb 1813); *Macedonian*, New London, CT (Feb 1813–1814); duty on Lake Ontario (1814–Apr 1815); *Macedonian*, Med.Sqdn. (Apr–Dec 1815); on furlough (Dec 1815–May 1817); rec. ship *Asp*, Baltimore (May–Nov 1817); *Congress*, Portsmouth, NH (Nov–Dec 1817); *Hornet* (Dec 1817–Feb 1818); prize *Cyane* (Feb–Apr 1818); *Guerriere*, Med.Sqdn. (Apr 1818–Jun 1819); Navy Yards, NY and Washington, DC (Jun–Nov 1819); *Ontario*, Med.Sqdn. (Nov 1819–May 1824); l.o.a. (May–Aug 1824); cdr, *Ferret*, W.Ind.Sqdn. (Aug 1824–Feb 1825); return to U.S. then member, court of inquiry (Feb–May 1825); w.o. (May 1825–Jun 1828); *Erie*, W.Ind.Sqdn. (Jul 1828–Aug 1829); l.o.a. (Aug 1829–Mar 1830); spec. duty, Washington, DC (Mar–Apr 1830); on furlough, commanding revenue cutter on NY Sta. (Apr 1830–Jun 1832); Navy Yard, NY (Jun 1832–Apr 1833); exec.off., flgs. *Vincennes*, Pac.Sqdn. (Apr 1833–Jan 1835); cdr, *Dolphin*, Pac.Sqdn. (Jan–May 1835); l.o.a. and w.o. (May 1835–Jul 1839); cdr, *Dolphin*, spec. duty to Afr.Cst. (Jul 1839–Jul 1840); l.o.a. (Jul–Sep 1840); cdr, *Dolphin*, Afr.Sqdn. (Sep 1840–May 1841); l.o.a. and w.o. (May 1841–Jul 1844); cdr, *Yorktown*, Afr.Sqdn. (Jul 1844–Jun 1846); l.o.a. and w.o. (Jun 1846–May 1848); Navy Yard, NY (Jun 1848–Jun 1850); w.o. (Jun–Aug 1850); spec. inspection duty of mail steamers at NY (Aug 1850–Jul 1855); cdr, *Constellation*, Med.Sqdn. and spec. duty to W.Indies (Jul 1855–Aug 1858); l.o.a. and w.o. (Aug 1858–Apr 1859); pres., Naval Exam.Bd. (Apr–Jun 1859); comdt., Navy Yard and Sta., Norfolk, VA (Jun 1859–Aug 1860); w.o. (Aug–Sep 1860); cdr, Med.Sqdn., *Richmond* (Sep 1860–Jul 1861); w.o. (Jul–Sep 1861); member, Bd. to Better Organize Navy, NY (Sep–Dec 1861); cdr, Pac.Sqdn., *Lancaster* (Jan 1862–Oct 1864); transferred to Ret.Lst. (16 Jul 1862); return to U.S. and w.o. (Oct 1864–Mar 1865); comdt., Navy Yard, NY (May 1865–May 1868); pres., Bd. of Visitors, USNA (May–Jun 1868, Nov 1868–Jan 1869).

References
Personal Papers: 1 volume (1813–22), SHC.

HENRY HAYWOOD BELL Born in Orange County, NC, on 13 Apr 1808. Married. Died by drowning in Osaka,

CHARLES HEYER BELL
1798–1875

HENRY HAYWOOD BELL
1808–1868

Japan on 11 Jan 1868. Temporarily interred at Hiogo, Japan; body was later moved to the U.S.

Ranks Midn (4 Aug 1823); Lt (3 Mar 1831); Cdr (12 Aug 1854); Commo (16 Jul 1862); RAdm (25 Jul 1866); placed on Ret.Lst. (12 Apr 1867); died (11 Jan 1868).

Career Summary Received appointment from NC (4 Aug 1823); *Erie*, Med.Sqdn. (Aug 1823–Dec 1827); *Grampus*, W.Ind.Sqdn. (Jan 1828–Dec 1830); *Vincennes*, W.Ind.Sqdn. (Dec 1830–Sep 1835); *Constitution*, W.Ind.Sqdn. (Sep 1830– Sep 1839); *United States*, Home Sqdn., then *Marion*, Med.Sqdn. (Sep 1839–Jun 1842); *Hunter*, spec.serv. (Aug 1842– Jun 1843); cdr, *Hunter*, spec.serv. (Jun 1843–Jan 1846); l.o.a. (Jan–Apr 1846); *United States*, Afr.Sqdn., and cdr, *Boxer*, Med.Sqdn. (Apr 1846–May 1848); Navy Yard, Philadelphia (Jan 1849–Feb 1850); w.o. (Feb–Jun 1850); Navy Yard, Norfolk, VA (Jun 1850–Aug 1851); w.o. (Aug 1851–May 1852); ord. duty, Navy Yard, NY (May 1852–Jun 1855); w.o. (Jun– Sep 1855); cdr, flgs. *San Jacinto*, E.Ind.Sqdn. (Sep 1855–Aug 1858); l.o.a. and w.o. (Aug 1858–May 1859); member, Bd. of Examiners, USNA (May–Jul 1859); ord. duty, Cold Spring, NY (Jul 1859–Feb 1861); w.o. (Feb–Jun 1861); asst.insp. of ord., Navy Yard, Washington, DC (Jun 1861–Jan 1862); flt.capt, W.Gulf Blk.Sqdn., *Pensacola* (Jan 1862–Jan 1864); l.o.a. (Jan–Apr 1864); insp. of ord., Navy Yard, NY (Apr– Sep 1864); w.o. (Sep 1864–Jul 1865); cdr, E.Ind.Sqdn., *Hartford* (Jul 1865–Jan 1868); died (11 Jan 1868).

Career Highlights A participant in capture and destruction of the four barrier forts near Canton, China, in Nov 1856. Although a North Carolinian, remained loyal to Union, serving as RAdm Farragut's [*q.v.*] chief of staff and flt.capt on lower MS River, at capture of New Orleans, and at siege of Vicksburg in 1862.

ANDREW ELLICOTT KENNEDY BENHAM Born in Richmond County, NY, on 10 Apr 1832. Married Emma H. Seaman in 1863. Died at Lake Mahopac, NY, on 11 Aug 1905. Buried in Arlington National Cemetery.

Ranks Act.Midn (24 Nov 1847); PMidn (10 Jun 1853); Mstr (15 Sep 1855); Lt (16 Sep 1855); LCdr (16 Jul 1862); Cdr (25 Jul 1866); Capt (12 Mar 1875); Commo (30 Oct 1885); RAdm (28 Feb 1890); placed on Ret.Lst. (10 Apr 1894).

Career Summary Received appointment from NY (24 Nov 1847); USNA (Dec 1847–Jan 1848); *Plymouth* and *Dolphin*, E.Ind.Sqdn. (Jan 1848–Feb 1851); l.o.a. (Feb–Jul 1851); *Saranac*, Home Sqdn. (Jul 1851–Jun 1852); USNA (Oct 1852– Jun 1853); flgs. *Princeton*, E.Ind.Sqdn. (Jul–Sep 1853); *St. Mary's*, Pac.Sqdn. (Sep 1853–Dec 1856); cst.surv. duty (Feb 1857–Sep 1858); *Westernport*, Braz.Sqdn. and Paraguay Expd. (Sep 1858–May 1859); w.o. (May–Jun 1859); *Crusader*, Home Sqdn. (Jun 1859–Sep 1861); l.o.a. (Sep–Oct 1861); *Bienville*, S.Atl.Blk.Sqdn. (Oct 1861–Dec 1862); *Sacramento*, N.Atl.

ANDREW ELLICOTT KENNEDY
BENHAM
1832–1905

Blk.Sqdn. (Dec 1862–Sep 1863); cdr, *Penobscot*, W.Gulf. Blk.Sqdn. (Sep 1863–Jul 1865); w.o. (Jul–Sep 1865); Navy Yard, NY (Sep 1865–Aug 1866); rec. ship *Vermont*, NY (Aug–Nov 1866); *Susquehanna*, spec.serv. (Nov 1866–Jan 1867); rec. ship *Vermont*, NY (Jan–Jun 1867); w.o. (Jun 1867–Mar 1868); Navy Yard, NY (Apr 1868–May 1870); w.o. (May–Oct 1870); insp., 1st L.h. Dist., Portland, ME (Oct 1870–Dec 1871); cdr, *Canonicus* then *Saugus*, N.Atl.Sta. (Jan 1872–Apr 1874); w.o. (Apr–Sep 1874); Naval Rndv., NY (Sep–Dec 1874); insp., 6th L.h. Dist., Charleston, SC (Jan 1875–Feb 1878); s.a. and w.o. (Feb–Sep 1878); cdr, *Richmond*, Asia.Sta. (Sep 1878–Sep 1881); home and w.o. (Aug–Nov 1881); Navy Yard, Portsmouth, NH (Dec 1881–Sep 1884); asst., then insp., 3rd L.h. Dist., Tompkinsville, NY (Sep 1884–Nov 1887); s.a. and w.o. (Nov 1887–May 1888); pres., Bd. of Improvement, Navy Yard, League Island, PA (Nov 1888–Jan 1889); cdr, Navy Yard, Mare Island, CA (Mar 1889–Jun 1891); w.o. (Jun 1891–Jun 1892); cdr, S.Atl.Sta., *Newark* (Jun 1892–May 1893); cdr, N.Atl.Sta., *San Francisco* (Jun 1893–Apr 1894); placed on Ret.Lst. (10 Apr 1894).

CHARLES STUART BOGGS Born in New Brunswick, NJ, on 28 Jan 1811, son of Robert Morris and Mary (Lawrence) Boggs. Married Sophia Dore on 4 Dec 1832. Married Henrietta (Molt) Bull on 8 Apr 1875. Died at his home in New Brunswick, NJ, on 22 Apr 1877.

Ranks Midn (1 Nov 1826); PMidn (28 Apr 1832); Lt (6 Sep 1837); Cdr (14 Sep 1855); Capt (16 Jul 1862); Commo (25 Jul 1866); RAdm (1 Jul 1870); retired (29 Jan 1872).

Career Summary Appointed from NJ (1 Nov 1826); w.o. (Nov 1826–Feb 1827); Navy Yard, Boston (Feb 1827–Aug 1830); *Porpoise*, W.Ind.Sqdn. (Aug 1830–Jan 1832); w.o. (Jan–Aug 1832); rec. ship *Hudson*, NY (Aug 1832–Feb 1834); on furlough (Feb 1834–Jan 1835); Navy Yard, NY (Jan–Aug 1835); Naval Rndv., NY (Aug–Nov 1835); *North Carolina*, Norfolk, VA and Pac.Sqdn. (Nov 1835–Aug 1842); *Marion*, Braz.Sqdn. (Aug–Sep 1842); w.o. (Sep–Dec 1842); *Saratoga*, Afr.Cst. (Dec 1842–Jun 1845); l.o.a. (Jun 1845–Jan 1846); *Potomac*, Home Sqdn. (Jan–Apr 1846); *Princeton*, Home Sqdn. (Apr 1846–May 1848); return home and w.o. (May 1848–Sep 1849); rec. ship *North Carolina*, NY (Sep 1849–Jan 1851); exec.off., *St. Lawrence*, spec. duty, World's Fair, London, England (Jan–Aug 1851); Navy Yard, NY (Sep 1851–Sep 1854); temp. duty, insp. of provisions, Navy Yard, NY (Sep 1854–Nov 1855); cdr, mail steamers *Illinois* and *St. Louis* (Nov 1855–Dec 1859); insp., 12th L.h. Dist., San Francisco (Jan 1860–Dec 1861); cdr, *Varuna*, Navy Yard, NY (Dec 1861–Jan 1862); cdr, *Juniata*, Philadelphia and N.Atl.Blk.Sqdn. (May 1862–Jan 1863); cdr, *Sacramento*, N.Atl.Blk.Sqdn. (Jan–Sep 1863); spec. duty, NY (Oct 1863–Jan 1865); cdr, *Connecticut*, W.Indies and Navy Yard, Philadelphia (Jan 1865–Mar 1866); cdr, *De*

CHARLES STUART BOGGS
1811–1877

Soto, N.Atl.Sqdn. (Mar 1866–Aug 1868); w.o. (Aug–Nov 1868); spec. duty (Nov 1868–Jul 1869); insp., 3rd L.h. Dist., Tompkinsville, NY (Jul 1869–Dec 1870); cdr, Eur.Flt., *Franklin* (Jan–Oct 1871); home and w.o. (Oct 1871–Jan 1872); retired (29 Jan 1872); sec., L.h. Bd. (Feb 1872–May 1873).

Career Highlights During Mexican War, was at siege of Vera Cruz: commanded boat sent from *Princeton* that destroyed the captured brig *Truxton*. Commanded the *Varuna* during capture of Fts. St. Philip and Jackson and of New Orleans in 1862.

References
Personal Papers: 1 vol., c.1845, ASAL.

GEORGE MILTON BOOK
1845–1921

GEORGE MILTON BOOK Born in New Castle, PA, on 25 May 1845, son of William and Ann (Emery) Book. Married Mary Sippy on 7 May 1867. Had at least one son. Died on 22 Jan 1921 in New Castle, PA.

Ranks Act.Midn (23 Nov 1861); title changed to Midn (16 Jul 1862); Ens (1 Dec 1866); Mstr (12 Mar 1868); Lt (26 Mar 1869); placed on Ret.Lst. (8 Feb 1871); restored to Active List (20 Dec 1875); LCdr (28 May 1881); Cdr (16 Dec 1891); Capt (29 Mar 1899); transferred to Ret.Lst. as RAdm (8 Mar 1900).

Career Summary Received appointment from PA (23 Nov 1861); USNA (Nov 1861–Oct 1865); *Dakotah*, W.Ind.Sqdn. (Oct–Nov 1865); sick lv. (Nov 1865–Jun 1866); *Rhode Island*, W.Ind.Sqdn. (Jun–Nov 1866); *Mackinaw*, W.Ind.Sqdn. (Nov 1866–Apr 1867); w.o. (Apr–Jul 1867); apprentice ship *Portsmouth* (Jul 1867–Oct 1868); rec. ship *New Hampshire*, Norfolk, VA (Oct 1868–Mar 1869); *Seminole*, Navy Yard, Boston (Apr–May 1869); rec. ship *Potomac*, Philadelphia (May–Sep 1869); w.o. (Sep–Oct 1869); *Benicia*, on trials (Nov 1869–Jan 1870); sick lv. (Jan–Oct 1870); *Swatara*, N.Atl.Sqdn. (Oct–Nov 1870); sick lv. (Nov 1870–Feb 1871); placed on Ret.Lst. (8 Feb 1871); restored to Active List (20 Dec 1875); *Ossipee*, N.Atl.Sqdn. (Jul 1874–Oct 1875); Navy Yard, Norfolk, VA (Oct 1875–May 1876); *Adams*, S.Atl.Sta. (Jun 1876–Jul 1879); w.o. (Jul–Oct 1879); cdr, *Montauk*, N.Atl.Sta. (Nov 1879–Dec 1881); *Enterprise*, N.Atl.Sta. (Jan 1882); exec.off., *Palos*, Asia.Sta. (Jan 1882–Oct 1884); cdr, *Palos*, Asia.Sta. (Oct 1884–Mar 1885); rec. ship *Vermont*, NY (Dec 1885–Nov 1888); cdr, *Pint*, Pac.Sqdn. (Jan–May 1889); suspended (May–Dec 1889); Navy Yard, NY (Jan 1890–Aug 1891); w.o. (Aug 1891–Apr 1892); Navy Yard, NY (May 1892–Feb 1893); cdr, *Alert*, Asia.Sta. (Apr–Oct 1893); home and w.o. (Oct 1893–May 1894); Navy Yard, Pensacola, FL (Jun–Sep 1894); w.o. (Sep 1894–Apr 1895); various bd. duties (Apr–Aug 1895); Navy Yard, Norfolk, VA (Aug 1895–Jul 1896); w.o. (Jul 1896–Apr 1897); cdr, *Marion*, Pac.Sta. (May–Dec 1897); Navy Yard, Mare Island, CA (Dec 1897–Jan 1898); cdr, *Mohican*, Pac.Sta.

(Jan–Oct 1898); cdr, *Adams*, Pac.Sta. (Oct 1898–Sep 1899); w.o. (Sep 1899–Mar 1900); transferred to Ret.Lst. (8 Mar 1900).

DANIEL LAWRENCE BRAINE Born in New York City on 18 May 1829. Educated at seminary in Newburg, NY. Married, with four children. Died on 30 Jan 1898 in Brooklyn, NY, where he was buried.

Ranks Midn (30 May 1846); PMidn (8 Jun 1852); Mstr (15 Sep 1855); Lt (16 Sep 1855); LCdr (16 Jul 1862); Cdr (25 Jul 1866); Capt (11 Dec 1874); Commo (2 Mar 1885); Act.RAdm (6 Oct 1886); RAdm (4 Sep 1887); placed on Ret.Lst. (18 May 1891).

Career Summary Received appointment from TX (30 May 1846); *Austin*, Galveston, TX, and Pensacola, FL (May–Aug 1846); *Mississippi*, Home Sqdn. (Sep 1846–Jan 1847); *John Adams*, Home Sqdn. (Jan 1847–Apr 1848); l.o.a. (Apr–Jun 1848); *Michigan*, on Great Lakes (Jun–Nov 1848); *Savannah*, S.Atl. and Pac. Stas. (Nov 1848–Dec 1849); *St. Mary's*, E.Ind.Sqdn. (Dec 1849–Jun 1850); l.o.a. (Jun–Nov 1850); *Saranac*, Home and W.Ind. Sqdns. (Nov 1850–Jul 1851); l.o.a. (Jul–Oct 1851); USNA (Oct 1851–Jun 1852); *St. Louis*, Med.Sqdn. (Jul 1853–May 1855); l.o.a. (May–Oct 1855); cst.surv. duty (Oct 1855–Oct 1857); *Vincennes*, Afr.Sqdn. (Oct 1857–Feb 1859); w.o. (Feb–Apr 1859); rec. ship *North Carolina*, NY (Apr–Sep 1859); flgs. *Roanoke*, Home Sqdn. (Oct 1859–May 1860); l.o.a. (May–Jun 1860); rec. ship *North Carolina*, NY (Jun 1860–May 1861); cdr, *Monticello*, N.Atl.Blk.Sqdn. (May 1861–Jul 1863); temp. ord. duty, Navy Yard, NY (Jul–Aug 1863); cdr, *Vicksburg*, spec.serv. and N.Atl.Blk.Sqdn. (Aug 1863–Oct 1864); cdr, *Pequot*, N.Atl.Blk.Sqdn. (Oct 1864–May 1865); ord. duty, Navy Yard, NY (May 1865–Feb 1868); cdr, *Shamokin*, Braz.Sqdn. (Feb–Dec 1868); w.o. (Dec 1868–Mar 1869); ord. duty, Navy Yard, NY (Mar–Jun 1869); equip.off., Navy Yard, NY (Jun 1869–Jun 1872); w.o. (Jun–Sep 1872); member, Bd. of Inspection (Sep–Dec 1872); cdr, *Juniata*, Eur. and Med. Sqdns. (Feb 1873–Jan 1875); return home and w.o. (Mar–Apr 1875); cdr, rec. ship *Vermont*, NY (Apr–Jun 1875); cdr, rec. ship *Colorado*, NY (Jun 1875–May 1878); l.o.a. (May–Dec 1878); cdr, *Powhatan*, N.Atl.Sta. (Dec 1878–Mar 1881); sick lv. (Mar 1881–Jun 1883); member, Bd. of Inspection and Surv. (Jun 1883–Mar 1885); spec. duty, NY (Mar–Jul 1885); pres., bd. to visit naval and mercantile vessels, NY (Jul 1885–Jul 1886); cdr, S.Atl.Sta., *Lancaster* (Aug 1886–Aug 1888); return home and w.o. (Aug 1888–Nov 1889); comdt., Navy Yard, NY (Nov 1889–May 1891); placed on Ret.Lst. (18 May 1891).

Career Highlights During Mexican War, participated in the capture of Tabasco, Tuscan, Tampico, and Vera Cruz. Commanded *Juniata* in 1873 and 1874 to search for the *Polaris* Expedition in Greenland.

DANIEL LAWRENCE BRAINE
1829–1898

SAMUEL LIVINGSTON BREESE
1794–1870

SAMUEL LIVINGSTON BREESE Born in Utica, NY, in 1794. Married, with at least one son, Capt S. L. Breese, USN. Died at Mount Aury, PA, on 17 Dec 1870.

Ranks Midn (17 Dec 1810); Act.Lt (21 Mar 1815); Lt (27 Apr 1816); Mstr.Comdt. (22 Dec 1835); Capt (8 Sep 1841); placed on Ret.Lst. as RAdm (16 Jul 1862).

Career Summary Received appointment from NY (17 Dec 1810); under tuition (Aug–Sep 1811); *Congress*, spec.serv. (Sep 1811–Feb 1814); on furlough (Feb–May 1814); duty, Lake Champlain, NY (May 1814–Mar 1815); duty, Flying Sqdn. (Mar 1815–Aug 1817); duty, Sacket's Harbor, NY (Aug 1817–Jan 1819); *Hornet*, Med. and W.Ind. Sqdns. (Jan 1819–Mar 1821); flgs. *Constitution*, Med.Sqdn. (Mar 1821–Aug 1824); l.o.a. (Aug 1824–May 1827); *Lexington*, Med.Sqdn. (May 1827–Apr 1832); l.o.a. (May 1830–May 1831); Navy Yard, Philadelphia (Apr 1832–Apr 1835); l.o.a. (Apr–Jun 1837); *Ontario*, W.Ind.Sqdn. (Jun 1837–Sep 1838); l.o.a. (Sep 1838–Apr 1839); cdr, Naval Rndv., Baltimore (Apr 1839–Mar 1840); cdr, *Preble*, spec.serv. (Mar–Nov 1840); l.o.a. (Nov 1840–Feb 1841); cdr, *Cumberland*, Med.Sqdn. (Aug 1843–Nov 1845); l.o.a. (Nov 1845–Feb 1846); Navy Dept., Washington, DC (Jul 1846); cdr, *Albany*, Home Sqdn. (Oct 1846–Aug 1847); w.o. (Aug–Oct 1847); temp. spec. duty, Great Lakes (Oct 1847–Sep 1848); member, Bd. on Rank, Washington, DC (Oct 1850–Sep 1851); member, Bd. of Examiners (Oct–Nov 1851); temp. duty, Navy Dept., Washington, DC (Nov 1851–Mar 1852); cdr, Navy Yard and Sta., Norfolk, VA (Apr 1852–May 1855); cdr, Med.Sqdn., *Congress* (Jun 1855–Jan 1858); l.o.a. (Jan–Apr 1858); cdr, Navy Yard, NY (Oct 1858–Oct 1861); w.o. (Oct 1861–Jul 1862); placed on Ret.Lst. (16 Jul 1862); insp., 2nd L.h. Dist., Boston (Jul–Oct 1862); w.o. (Oct 1862–Apr 1864); pres., court-martial bd. (Apr 1864–Jul 1865); port adm, Philadelphia (Apr 1869–Sep 1870).

References
Personal Papers: a) 4 vols, WPL. b) correspondence between Breese and RAdm Thomas Tingey Craven [*q.v.*] (1855–66), EFMC.

GEORGE ADAMS BRIGHT Born on 9 Apr 1837 in Bangor, ME. Married, with a son and a daughter. Died in Washington, DC, on 12 Mar 1905. Buried in Arlington National Cemetery.

Ranks Act.Asst.Surg. (15 May 1861); Asst.Surg. (8 Aug 1864); PAsst. Surg. (31 Dec 1867); Surg. (12 Sep 1874); Medl.Insp. (11 May 1893); Medl.Dir. (19 Oct 1897); transferred to Ret.Lst. with rank of RAdm (9 Apr 1899).

Career Summary Received appointment from ME (15 May 1861); Navy Yard, Boston (May 1861); *South Carolina*, Gulf Blk. and N.Atl.Blk. Sqdns. (May 1861–Mar 1864); return home and w.o. (Mar–Jul 1864); Navy Yard, Philadelphia (Jul–Aug 1864); *New Ironsides*, N.Atl.Blk.Sqdn. (Aug 1864–

Apr 1865); w.o. (Apr–May 1865); prac. ship *Marion* (Jun 1865–Oct 1866); *Susquehanna*, spec. duty (Nov 1866–Sep 1867); w.o. (Sep 1867–Jan 1868); Naval Hosp., Washington, DC (Jan 1868–Jan 1869); *Kenosha* [renamed *Plymouth*], Eur.Sqdn. (Jan 1869–Jun 1873); w.o. (Jun–Jul 1873); l.o.a. (Jul–Oct 1873); USNA (Oct 1873–Aug 1876); *Tuscarora*, Mexican cst.surv. (Oct 1876–May 1880); Naval Hosp., Mare Island, CA (May 1880–May 1883); w.o. (May–Aug 1883); Naval Rndv., Philadelphia (Aug–Sep 1883); *Galena*, N.Atl.Sta. (Oct 1883–Nov 1884); w.o. (Nov 1884–May 1885); bd. duty (May 1885); training ship *Constellation* (May–Sep 1885); w.o. (Sep–Oct 1885); *Brooklyn*, N.Atl.Sta. (Oct 1885–Jun 1886); Navy Yard, Norfolk, VA (Jul 1886–Jun 1889); w.o. (Jun–Aug 1889); member, Naval Exam.Bd., USNA (Sep–Oct 1889); w.o. (Oct 1889–Aug 1890); prac. ship *Constellation* (Aug–Sep 1890); senior member, Exam.Bd., USNA (Sep–Oct 1890); w.o. (Oct–Dec 1890); spec. duty (Dec 1890–May 1891); spec. duty, *Newark* (Jun 1891–Jul 1894); flt.surg., S.Atl.Sta., *Newark* (Oct 1893–Jul 1894); l.o.a. (Jul–Oct 1894); w.o. (Oct–Dec 1894); Navy Yard, NY (Dec 1894–Sep 1895); Naval Hosp., Washington, DC (Sep 1895–Apr 1899); transferred Ret.Lst. (9 Apr 1899).

GEORGE BROWN Born in Rushville, IN, on 19 Jun 1835, son of William J. and Susan (Tompkins) Brown. Married Kate Morris on 4 Oct 1871. Had two sons, Paymstr. George Brown, Jr., USN, and Lt Hugh Brown, USN. Died at his home in Indianapolis, IN, on 29 Jun 1913. Buried at Crown Hill Cemetery in Indianapolis.

GEORGE BROWN
1835–1913

Ranks Act.Midn (5 Feb 1849); PMidn (12 Jun 1855); Mstr (16 Sep 1855); Lt (2 Jun 1856); LCdr (16 Jul 1862); Cdr (25 Jul 1866); Capt (25 Apr 1877); Commo (4 Sep 1887); Act.RAdm (28 Dec 1889); RAdm (27 Sep 1893); placed on Ret.Lst. (19 Jun 1897).

Career Summary Received appointment from IN (5 Feb 1849); USNA (Feb–Jul 1849); *Cumberland*, Med.Sqdn. (Jul 1849–Jul 1851); l.o.a. (Jul–Oct 1851); *St. Lawrence*, Pac.Sqdn. (Oct 1851–Sep 1854); USNA (Oct–Nov 1855); sick lv. (Nov 1854–Oct 1856); USNA (Oct 1855–Jun 1856); w.o. (Jun–Dec 1856); *Falmouth*, Braz.Sqdn. (Jan–Jun 1857); *Supply*, NY (Aug 1857); *Falmouth*, Braz.Sqdn. (Sep 1857–May 1859); l.o.a. (May–Aug 1859); *Supply*, Afr.Sqdn. (Aug–Dec 1859); *Portsmouth*, Afr.Sqdn. (Dec 1859–Feb 1860); cdr, prize slaver *Virginia* (Feb–Apr 1860); Navy Yard, Norfolk, VA (Apr–May 1860); *Pawnee*, Navy Yard, Philadelphia (Jun–Aug 1860); *Powhatan*, spec.serv. (Aug 1860–Mar 1861); w.o. (Mar–Apr 1861); *Powhatan*, Home Sqdn. (Apr–Nov 1861); l.o.a. and court of inquiry (Nov 1861); *Octarora*, Mortar Flot. (Dec 1861–Sep 1862); w.o. (Sep–Oct 1862); cdr, *Indianola*, MS Sqdn. (Oct 1862–Feb 1863); prisoner of war (24 Feb–25 May 1863); spec. duty, Cincinnati (Jun 1863); w.o. (Jun–Sep 1863); cdr,

Itasca then *Pocahontas*, W.Gulf Blk.Sqdn. (Sep 1863–Jul 1865); Navy Yard, Washington, DC (Aug–Oct 1865); cdr, *Hornet*, spec.serv. (Oct–Nov 1865); Navy Yard, Washington, DC (Nov 1865–Feb 1866); l.o.a. (Feb–May 1866); ord. duty, Navy Yard, Washington, DC (May 1866–Jul 1867); l.o.a. to command *Stonewall* to Japan (Aug 1867–May 1869); w.o. (May 1869–Jan 1870); spec. duty, Washington, DC (Jan–Jun 1870); w.o. (Jun–Sep 1870); cdr, *Michigan*, on Great Lakes (Sep 1870–Oct 1873); w.o. (Oct–Nov 1873); ord. duty, Navy Yard, Boston (Nov 1873–Dec 1876); spec. duty, Bur. of Yards and Docks, Boston (Dec 1876–Mar 1877); w.o. (Mar–Apr 1877); insp., 10th L.h. Dist., Buffalo, NY (Jun 1877–Jan 1878); s.a. and w.o. (Jan–Apr 1878); cdr, *Alaska*, Pac.Sta. (Apr 1878–Apr 1881); insp., 3rd L.h. Dist., Tompkinsville, NY (May 1881–Nov 1884); s.a. and w.o. (Nov 1884–Apr 1885); temp. duty, Washington, DC (Apr–Jun 1885); capt.yd., Navy Yard, Norfolk, VA (Jun 1885–Mar 1886); comdt., Navy Yard, Norfolk, VA (Mar 1886–Dec 1889); cdr, Pac.Sta., *San Francisco* (Jan 1890–Jan 1893); temp. duty, Washington, DC (Feb–Jun 1893); comdt., Navy Yard, Norfolk, VA (Jul 1893–Jun 1897); placed on Ret.Lst. (19 Jun 1897); spec. duty, inspecting west coast navy yards and stas. (Aug 1898).

Career Highlights While commanding the ironclad *Indianola* on MS River, engaged several Confederate vessels on 24 Feb 1863, resulting in the surrender of his ship and his and his crew's capture. Eventually exchanged at Richmond later in the year.

References

Writings: *Pacific Squadron, U.S. Navy Regulation*, 2nd. ed. (1891).

ANDREW BRYSON
1822–1892

ANDREW BRYSON Born in New York City on 22 Jul 1822. Married, with two daughters and a son: the eldest daughter married Medl. Dir. John Y. Taylor, USN. Died in Washington, DC, on 7 Feb 1892.

Ranks Midn (1 Dec 1837); PMidn (29 Jun 1843); Mstr (30 Jan 1851); Lt (30 Aug 1851); Cdr (16 Jul 1862); Capt (25 Jul 1866); Commo (14 Feb 1873); RAdm (25 Mar 1880); placed on Ret.Lst. (30 Jan 1883).

Career Summary Received appointment from NY (1 Dec 1837); w.o. (Dec 1873–Feb 1838); *Levant*, W.Ind.Sqdn. (Feb 1838–Jun 1842); l.o.a. (Jun–Sep 1842); Naval School, Philadelphia (Sep 1842–Jun 1843); *Macedonian* then *Decatur*, Afr.Sqdn. (Jul 1843–Jan 1845); l.o.a. (Jan–Apr 1845); *Michigan*, on Great Lakes (Apr 1845–May 1849); *John Adams*, Navy Yard, Boston (May–Jun 1849); on furlough (Jun 1849–Jan 1850); exec.off., *Erie*, Med.Sqdn. (Feb–Oct 1850); w.o. (Oct 1850–Mar 1851); exec.off., *Relief*, Braz.Sqdn. (Mar–Sep 1851); *Bainbridge*, Braz.Sqdn. (Sep 1851–Aug 1853); l.o.a. and w.o. (Aug–Dec 1853); rec. ship *Ohio*, Boston (Dec 1853–Nov 1856); w.o. (Nov–Dec 1856); *Saratoga*, Home Sqdn. (Dec 1856–Jan

1858); l.o.a. (Jan–May 1858); rec. ship *Ohio*, Boston (May–Oct 1858); exec.off., *Preble*, Braz.Sqdn. and Paraguay Expd. (Oct 1858–Sep 1860); l.o.a. and w.o. (Sep 1860–Jan 1861); Navy Yard, NY (Jan–Oct 1861); cdr, *Chippewa*, spec.serv. (Oct 1861–Jun 1863); cdr, *Lehigh*, S.Atl.Blk.Sqdn. (Aug 1863–Apr 1864); w.o. (Apr–May 1864); Navy Yard, NY (May–Oct 1864); cdr, *Essex*, and 7th Div., MS Sqdn. (Oct 1864–Aug 1865); cdr, 7th Div., MS Sqdn. (Oct 1864–Aug 1865); cdr, 8th Div., MS Sqdn. (Apr–May 1865); flt.capt, MS Sqdn. (May–Aug 1865); w.o. (Aug 1865–Apr 1866); cdr, *Michigan*, on Great Lakes (Apr 1866–Apr 1868); w.o. (Apr–Jun 1868); member, Naval Exam.Bd., Philadelphia (Jun–Aug 1868); cdr, rec. ship *Ohio*, Boston (Oct 1868–Oct 1870); Navy Yard, Boston (Oct 1870–Sep 1871); cdr, *Brooklyn*, Eur.Sta. (Oct 1871–Jul 1873); w.o. (Jul–Nov 1873); member, Naval Exam. and Ret. Bds. (Nov 1873–May 1874); w.o. (May–Sep 1874); comdt., Navy Yard, Portsmouth, NH (Sep 1874–Jul 1876); w.o. (Jul 1876–Mar 1879); pres., Bd. of Examiners, USNA (Mar–Apr 1879); w.o. (Apr–Sep 1879); cdr, S.Atl.Sta., *Shenandoah* (Sep 1879–Jul 1881); return home and w.o. (Jul 1881–Feb 1882); member, Naval Exam.Bd. (Feb–Sep 1882); w.o. (Sep 1882–Jan 1883); placed on Ret.Lst. (30 Jan 1883).

WILLIAM GEORGE BUEHLER Born in Philadelphia, PA, on 25 Mar 1837, son of William Olds and Henrietta Ruhamah Buehler. Educated in private schools in Harrisburg, PA. Married to Caroline Rogers. Died in Haverford, PA, on 10 Aug 1919.

Ranks 3rd Asst.Engr. (21 Nov 1857); 2nd Asst.Engr. (8 Oct 1861); 1st Asst.Engr. (6 Oct 1862); Chief Engr. (10 Nov 1863); Chief Engr. with rel. rank of Cdr (25 May 1894); Capt (3 Mar 1899); retired with rank of RAdm (29 Mar 1899).

Career Summary Received appointment from PA (21 Nov 1857); spec. duty, NY (Jan–Feb 1858); *Niagara*, spec.serv. (Feb–Aug 1858); w.o. (Aug–Sep 1858); *Niagara*, spec.serv. (Sep–Oct 1858); w.o. (Dec 1858–Mar 1859); *Michigan*, on Great Lakes (Mar–Jun 1859); w.o. (Jun–Dec 1859); *Narragansett*, on trials and Pac.Sqdn. (Dec 1859–Sep 1861); *Aroostook*, N.Atl. and W.Gulf Blk.Sqdns. (Nov 1861–Aug 1863); report and w.o. (Aug–Oct 1863); *Galena*, W.Gulf Blk.Sqdn. (Oct 1863–Jan 1865); *Suwanee*, Pac.Sqdn. (Jan 1865–Mar 1867); *Chattanooga*, Navy Yard, Philadelphia (May–Jun 1867); w.o. (Jun–Sep 1867); *Wampanoag*, spec.serv. (Sep 1867); Naval Rndv., Philadelphia (Sep 1867–Jun 1868); w.o. (Jun–Dec 1868); Navy Yard, League Island, PA (Dec 1868–Nov 1870); *Terror*, N.Atl.Sta. (Nov 1870–Jan 1872); report and w.o. (Jan–Feb 1872); spec. duty, Philadelphia (Feb 1872–May 1873); w.o. (May–Jun 1873); spec. duty, Wilmington, DE (Jun–Dec 1873); *Franklin*, N.Atl.Sta. (Dec 1873–Mar 1874); *Ticonderoga*, N.Atl.Sta. (Apr–Oct 1874); w.o. (Oct–Nov 1874); flgs. *Brooklyn*, S.Atl.Sta. (Nov 1874–Dec 1875); spec. duty, Quintaid

WILLIAM GEORGE BUEHLER
1837–1919

Iron Works, NY (Dec 1875–Aug 1876); w.o. (Aug–Sep 1876); spec. duty, Quintaid and Continental Iron Works, NY (Sep 1876–May 1877); member, Bd. of Exam., League Island, PA (Jun–Sep 1877); *Plymouth*, N.Atl.Sta. (Oct 1877–May 1879); *Kearsarge*, N.Atl.Sta. (May–Dec 1879); *Powhatan*, N.Atl.Sta. (Dec 1879–Oct 1880); spec. duty, Philadelphia (Oct 1880–May 1885); *Pensacola*, Eur.Sta. (May 1885–Feb 1888); w.o. (Feb–Sep 1888); member, Bd. of Inspection and Surv. (Oct 1888–Oct 1893); temp. duty, Naval Exam.Bd., Philadelphia, PA (Oct 1893–Dec 1894); chief engr., Navy Yard, Portsmouth, NH (Dec 1894–Mar 1899); retired (29 Mar 1899).

CHARLES CARROLL CARPENTER Born in Greenfield, MA, on 27 Feb 1834, son of David N. and Phebe Maria (Newcomb) Carpenter. Attended Norwich Univ. in CT from 1848 to 1850. Married Anna Brown on 15 Dec 1862, having seven children. Died on 1 Apr 1899 at the Adams Nervine Sanitarium in Jamaica Plains, MA. Buried in South Cemetery in Portsmouth, NH.

Ranks Act.Midn (1 Oct 1850); PMidn (20 Jun 1856); Mstr (22 Jan 1858); Lt (23 Jan 1858); LCdr (16 Jul 1862); Cdr (10 Feb 1869); Capt (25 Mar 1880); Commo (15 May 1893); Act.RAdm (12 Jul 1894); RAdm (11 Nov 1894); placed on Ret.Lst. (27 Feb 1896).

Career Summary Received appointment from MA (1 Oct 1850); USNA (Oct 1850–Nov 1851); *Portsmouth*, Pac.Sqdn. (Nov 1851–Apr 1855); l.o.a. (Apr–Oct 1855); USNA (Oct 1855–Jun 1856); w.o. (Jun–Jul 1856); *Merrimack*, on trials (Aug 1856–Apr 1857); flgs. *Roanoke*, Home Sqdn. (Apr–Sep 1857); rec. ship *Ohio*, Boston (Sep 1857–Jan 1858); *Colorado*, Norfolk, VA (Jan–Apr 1858); w.o. (Apr–Jun 1858); *Dolphin*, spec.serv., W.Indies (Jun–Sep 1858); rec. ship *Ohio*, Boston (Nov 1858–Jun 1859); *Mohawk*, coast of Cuba, W. and E. Gulf Blk.Sqdns. (Jun 1859–Apr 1862); w.o. (Apr–May 1862); *Flag*, S.Atl.Blk.Sqdn. (May–Nov 1862); w.o. (Nov–Dec 1862); *Sacramento*, Navy Yard, Portsmouth, NH (Dec 1862); *Catskill*, S.Atl.Blk.Sqdn. (Dec 1862–Sep 1863); USNA (Oct 1863–Jun 1865); flgs. *Hartford*, then cdr, *Wyoming*, Asia.Sqdn. (Jun 1865–Feb 1868); w.o. (Feb–Aug 1868); Navy Yard, Portsmouth, NH (Sep 1868–Apr 1869); w.o. (Apr–Jul 1869); insp. of supplies, Navy Yard, Portsmouth, NH (Jul 1869–Mar 1871); cdr, *Nantasket*, N.Atl.Sta. (Mar 1871–Jul 1872); w.o. (Sep–Nov 1872); Navy Yard, Portsmouth, NH (Sep 1872–Oct 1875); w.o. (Sep–Nov 1875); cdr, *Huron*, N.Atl.Sqdn. (Nov 1875–Sep 1876); w.o. (Sep 1876–May 1878); torp. instruction, Newport, RI (May–Sep 1878); w.o. (Sep 1878–Mar 1880); equip. duty, Navy Yard, Boston (Apr 1880–Jun 1882); cdr, flgs. *Hartford*, N.Atl.Sta. (Jun 1882–Jul 1884); w.o. (Jul–Sep 1884); Navy Yard, Portsmouth, NH (Sep–Dec 1884); w.o. (Dec 1884–Oct 1887); senior member, gen. court-martial (Oct–Dec 1887); w.o. (Jan–Apr 1888); cdr, rec. ship *Wabash*, Boston (Apr 1888–

CHARLES CARROLL CARPENTER
1834–1899

May 1890); capt.yd., then comdt., Navy Yard, Portsmouth, NH (Jun 1890–Jan 1894); w.o. (Jan–Mar 1894); pres., gen. court-martial (Mar–Jul 1894); cdr, Asia.Sqdn., *Monocacy* (Aug–Sep 1894), then on *Baltimore* (Sep 1894–Nov 1895); home and l.o.a. (Nov 1895–Feb 1896); placed on Ret.Lst. (27 Feb 1896); comdt., Navy Yard, Portsmouth, NH (Apr–Aug 1898).

SAMUEL POWHATAN CARTER Born in Elizabethton, TN, on 6 Aug 1819, son of Alfred Moore and Evaline (Parry) Carter. Attended Washington College in TN and Princeton Univ. Married Carrie Potts. Died in Washington, DC, on 26 May 1891. Buried at Oak Hill Cemetery in Washington, DC.

Ranks U.S. Navy: Midn (14 Feb 1840); PMidn (11 Jul 1846); Mstr (12 Sep 1854); Lt (18 Apr 1855); LCdr (16 Jul 1862); Cdr (25 Jun 1865); Capt (28 Oct 1870); Commo (13 Nov 1878); placed on Ret.Lst. (6 Aug 1881); RAdm on Ret.Lst. (16 May 1882). U.S. Army: Col (Jul 1861); Act.BGen (Sep 1861); BGen (1 May 1862); Bvt.MGen (13 Mar 1865); mustered out of Army (Jan 1866).

Career Summary Received appointment from TN (14 Feb 1840); w.o. (Feb–Apr 1840); rec. ship *Delaware*, Hampton Roads, VA (Apr–Oct 1840); *Dale*, Pac.Sqdn. (Oct 1840–Oct 1843); w.o. (Oct 1843–Jun 1844); rec. ship *North Carolina*, NY (Jun–Sep 1844); *Michigan*, on Great Lakes (Sep 1844–Jan 1845); *Potomac*, Home Sqdn. (Jan–Dec 1845); Naval School, Annapolis, MD (Dec 1845–Jul 1846); w.o. (Jul–Nov 1846); *Ohio*, Home Sqdn. (Dec 1846–Jun 1847); Naval Observatory, Washington, DC (Jun 1847–Aug 1848); *St. Lawrence*, Med.Sqdn. (Aug 1848–Sep 1850); l.o.a. (Sep–Oct 1850); asst.prof. of math., USNA (Oct 1850–Jun 1853); act.mstr, USNA (Nov 1851–Jun 1853); *Relief*, Braz.Sqdn. (Jun 1853–Sep 1855); *San Jacinto*, E.Ind.Sqdn. (Sep 1855–Oct 1857); asst. to exec.off. and asst.inst. of seamanship, USNA (Oct 1857–Mar 1860); *Seminole*, Braz.Sqdn. (Mar 1860–Jul 1861); spec. duty, Washington, DC (Jul 1861); organizing TN Brigade, eastern TN (Jul–Sep 1861); cdr, TN Brigade and various cavalry units (Sep 1861–Feb 1863); cdr, troops in southeastern KY (Feb–May 1863); cdr, Southeastern KY Dist. (May–Jul 1863); cdr, cavalry div., 23rd Army Corps (Jul–Sep 1863); provost marshal gen, E. TN (Sep 1863–Jan 1865); div. cdr, Dist. of Newbern, NC (Jan–Apr 1865); cdr, 3rd Div., 23rd Army Corps (Apr–Jul 1865); cdr, Western NC (May–Aug 1865); cdr, 23rd Army Corps (Jul–Aug 1865); l.o.a. and w.o. (Aug 1865–Jan 1866); mustered out of army (Jan 1866); cdr, *Monocacy*, Asia.Sqdn. (Mar 1866–May 1869); Navy Yard, Philadelphia (Oct 1869–Jan 1870); comdt. of midn, USNA (Feb 1870–Jul 1873); cdr, *Alaska*, Eur.Sta. (Jul 1873–Jul 1876); member, Naval Exam.Bd. (Aug 1876–Jan 1877); member, L.h. Bd. (Jan 1877–Aug 1881); placed on Ret.Lst. (6 Aug 1881).

Career Highlights The only American officer to be

SAMUEL POWHATAN CARTER
1819–1891

both an admiral in the navy and a general in the army. Declaring loyalty to the Union before his native TN seceded, was chosen by TN Governor Andrew Johnson to recruit, train, and lead militia volunteers in the eastern part of state. Conducted many cavalry operations in eastern TN, eastern and central KY, and NC.

AUGUSTUS LUDLOW CASE
1813–1893

AUGUSTUS LUDLOW CASE Born in Newburg, NY, on 3 Feb 1813. Married and had two sons, one of whom, Augustus L. Case, Jr., graduated from USNA in 1871. Died on 17 Feb 1893 in Washington, DC. Buried in Newport, RI.

Ranks Midn (1 Apr 1828); PMidn (14 Jun 1834); Lt (25 Feb 1841); Cdr (14 Sep 1855); Capt (2 Jan 1863); Commo (8 Dec 1867); RAdm (24 May 1872); placed on Ret.Lst. (3 Feb 1875).

Career Summary Received appointment from NY (1 Apr 1828); w.o. (Apr–Jul 1828); rec. ship *Robert Fulton*, NY (Jul–Aug 1828); *Hudson*, Braz.Sqdn. (Aug 1828–Aug 1831); l.o.a. (Aug–Nov 1831); Navy Yard and Naval School, NY (Nov 1831–Jul 1832); l.o.a. (Jul–Aug 1832); *St. Louis*, W.Ind.Sqdn. (Aug 1832–Aug 1833); l.o.a. (Aug–Oct 1833); Navy Yard and Naval School, NY (Oct 1833–Jun 1834); l.o.a. and w.o. (Jun 1834–Jul 1835); Navy Yard, NY (Jul–Oct 1835); l.o.a. and w.o. (Oct 1835–Apr 1836); *Experiment*, cst.surv. duty (Apr–Nov 1836); *Pioneer*, *Relief*, and *Vincennes*, U.S. Expl.Expd. (Nov 1836–Jun 1842); w.o. (Jun–Sep 1842); l.o.a. and w.o. (Sep 1842–Mar 1843); *Brandywine*, E.Indies (Mar 1843–Sep 1845); l.o.a. (Sep 1845–Dec 1846); *Fredonia*, *Mahonese*, *Porpoise*, *Raritan*, *John Adams*, and *Germantown*, Home Sqdn. (Dec 1846–Feb 1848); l.o.a. and w.o. (Feb 1848–Oct 1849); *Vincennes*, spec.serv., Pac. Ocean (Oct 1849–Oct 1851); cdr, *Warren*, Pac.Sqdn. (Oct 1851–Mar 1853); return to U.S. and l.o.a. (Mar–May 1853); insp., 3rd L.h. Dist., Tompkinsville, NY (May 1853–Jul 1857); w.o. (Jul 1857–Sep 1858); cdr, *Caledonia*, Braz.Sqdn. and Paraguay Expd. (Oct 1858–Jun 1859); w.o. (Jun 1859–Mar 1861); spec. duty, asst. to cdr, Office of Detail, Navy Dept., Washington, DC (Mar–Apr 1861); flt.capt, N.Atl.Blk.Sqdn., *Minnesota* (Apr 1861–Jan 1863); cdr, *Iroquois*, N.Atl.Blk.Sqdn. (Jan–Oct 1863); spec. duty, Washington, DC (Oct 1863–Mar 1864); spec. duty, Navy Yard, NY (Mar 1864–Apr 1865); flt.capt, Eur.Sqdn., *Colorado* (Apr 1865–Sep 1866); insp., 3rd L.h. Dist., Tompkinsville, NY (Nov 1866–Jul 1869); chief, Bur. of Ord., Washington, DC (Aug 1869–Apr 1873); cdr, Eur.Sqdn., *Wabash* then *Franklin* (Jun 1873–Feb 1875); placed on Ret.Lst. (3 Feb 1875).

Career Highlights During Mexican War, participated in capture of Vera Cruz, Alvarado, and Tobasco, overseeing landing of troops, ordnance, and material for siege of Vera Cruz. In 1874, commanded Eur.Sqdn. that combined with the N and S Atl.Sqdns at Key West, FL, to conduct maneuvers as show of force to Spain over *Virginius* affair.

Silas Casey Born in East Greenwich, RI, on 11 Sep 1841, son of army General Silas and Abbie (Pearce) Casey. Married Sophie Gray Heberton in Oct 1865. Died on 14 Aug 1913 in Warm Springs, VA. Buried in Arlington National Cemetery.

Ranks Act.Midn (25 Sep 1856); Midn (15 Jun 1860); Mstr (31 Aug 1861); Lt (16 Jul 1862); LCdr (25 Jul 1866); Cdr (14 Jun 1874); Capt (12 Feb 1889); Commo (11 May 1898); RAdm (3 Mar 1899); placed on Ret.Lst. (11 Sep 1903).

Career Summary Received appointment from NY (25 Sep 1856); USNA (Sep 1856–Jun 1860); *Niagara*, spec. cruise, and Atl. and Gulf Blk.Sqdns. (Jun 1860–Jun 1862); l.o.a. and w.o. (Jun–Aug 1862); *Unadilla*, S.Atl.Blk.Sqdn. (Aug–Sep 1862); exec.off., *Wissahickon*, S.Atl.Blk.Sqdn. (Sep 1862–May 1863); w.o. (May–Jun 1863); exec.off., *Quaker City*, N.Atl.Blk.Sqdn. (Jun 1863–May 1865); w.o. (May–Jun 1865); nav.off., *Winooski*, Atl.Sqdn. (Jun 1865–Jul 1867); w.o. (Jul–Sep 1867); USNA (Oct 1867–Jan 1870); exec.off., flgs. *Colorado*, Asia.Sqdn. (Jan 1870–Mar 1873); ord. duty and equip.off., Navy Yard, Philadelphia (Apr 1873–Aug 1874); senior aide to comdt., Navy Yard, Philadelphia (Aug 1874–Mar 1875); w.o. (Mar–Jul 1875); cdr, *Portsmouth*, Pac.Sqdn. (Jul 1875–Aug 1876); w.o. (Jul–Sep 1876); insp., 12th L.h. Dist., San Francisco (Sep 1876–Sep 1879); s.a. and w.o. (Sep 1879–Jan 1880); cdr, *Wyoming*, Eur.Sta. (Feb 1880–Jan 1882); home and w.o. (Jan–Apr 1882); equip.off., Navy Yard, Washington, DC (May 1882–Jul 1884); insp., 5th L.h. Dist., Baltimore (Jul 1884–Mar 1885); s.a. and w.o. (Mar–May 1885); torp. instruction, Newport, RI (Jun–Sep 1885); cdr, rec. ship *Dale*, Washington, DC (Sep 1885–Jan 1887); insp., 5th L.h. Dist., Baltimore (Jan 1887–Nov 1889); s.a. and l.o.a. (Nov 1889–Jul 1890); *Newark*, Philadelphia (Jul 1890–Feb 1891); cdr, *Newark*, N.Atl.Sqdn. (Feb 1891–May 1893); l.o.a. (May 1893–Feb 1894); member, Naval Exam.Bd. (Feb–Apr 1894); cdr, rec. ship *Vermont*, NY (Apr 1894–Mar 1897); cdr, *New York*, N.Atl.Sqdn. (Mar–Dec 1897); home and l.o.a. (Dec 1897–Jan 1898); comdt., Navy Yard and Sta., League Island, PA (Jan 1898–Jan 1901); cdr, Pac.Sta., *Iowa* (Jan–Aug 1901), then *Wisconsin* (Aug 1901–Dec 1902), then *New York* (Dec 1902–Feb 1903); w.o. (Mar–Sep 1903); placed on Ret.Lst. (11 Sep 1903).

References
Personal Papers: 300 items (1771–1941), NHF,LC.
Additional Sources: U.S. Library of Congress, Manuscript Division, *Silas Casey, Stanford Caldwell Hooper; A Register of their Papers in the Library of Congress* (Washington, DC: Lib. of Congress, 1968).

Thomas Thompson Caswell Born in Providence, RI, on 4 Jan 1840, son of Alexis and Esther Lois (Thompson) Caswell. Attended Brown Univ., where his father was president, from 1858–61, receiving the A.M. degree. Married Ger-

Silas Casey
1841–1913

Thomas Thompson Caswell
1840–1913

trude E. Ford on 26 Sep 1867. After she died in 1894, married Elizabeth Blanchard Randall on 11 Oct 1897. Survived by one daughter. Died on 9 Jul 1913 in Weekapaug, RI. Buried in USNA Cemetery.

Ranks Asst.Paymstr. (9 Sep 1861); Paymstr. (17 Sep 1863); resigned (10 Jun 1871); resignation acceptance withdrawn (13 Dec 1871); Pay Insp. (31 Aug 1881); Pay Dir. (25 Dec 1892); retired with rank of RAdm (5 Jun 1899).

Career Summary Received appointment from RI (9 Sep 1861); w.o. (Sep–Nov 1861); *Huron*, S.Atl.Blk.Sqdn. (Nov 1861–Oct 1862); w.o. (Oct–Nov 1862); *Sangamon*, S.Atl.Blk.Sqdn. (Nov 1862–Jul 1863); w.o. (Jul–Aug 1863); *Seminole*, W.Gulf Blk.Sqdn. (Aug 1863–Feb 1864); s.a. and w.o. (Feb–Mar 1864); *Pawtuxet*, N.Atl.Sqdn. (Mar–Dec 1864); s.a. and w.o. (Dec 1864–May 1865); *National Guard*, Eur.Sqdn. (May 1865–Jun 1867); s.a. and w. o. (Jun–Aug 1867); paymstr., Navy Yard, Norfolk, VA (Sep 1867–Nov 1870); additional duty, insp. of provisions and clothing, Navy Yard, Norfolk, VA (Jan–Mar 1868, Oct–Nov 1869); s.a. and w.o. (Nov–Dec 1870); *Tennessee*, spec.serv. (Jan–Apr 1871); s.a. and w.o. (Apr–Jun 1871); resigned (10 Jun 1871); restored to duty (13 Dec 1871); w.o. (Dec 1871–Jan 1872); *Pensacola*, Pac.Sqdn. (Jan–Sep 1872); flt.paymstr., Pac.Sqdn., *Pensacola* (Oct 1872–Jun 1875); s.a. and w.o. (Aug–Oct 1875); insp. of provisions and clothing, Navy Yard, Norfolk, VA (Jan 1876–Jan 1879); s.a. and w.o. (Jan–Aug 1879); Navy Yard, Washington, DC (Aug 1879–Sep 1880); insp. of provisions and clothing, Navy Yard, Washington, DC (Oct 1880–May 1881); Navy Pay Office, NY (May 1881–Aug 1884); flt.paymstr., Pac.Sta., *Hartford* (Jul 1884–Jan 1887); s.a. and w.o. (Jan–Aug 1887); USNA (Aug 1887–Aug 1890); sick lv. (Aug 1890–Sep 1891); in charge, Navy Pay Office, Washington, DC (Sep 1891–Oct 1894); s.a. and w.o. (Oct 1894–Apr 1895); USNA (Apr 1895–Apr 1899); s.a. and w.o. (Apr–Jun 1899); retired (5 Jun 1899).

RALPH CHANDLER Born in New York City on 3 Aug 1829. Died in Hong Kong, China, on 11 Feb 1889. Buried at Happy Valley, Hong Kong, China.

Ranks Midn (27 Sep 1845); PMidn (6 Oct 1851); Mstr (15 Sep 1855); Lt (16 Sep 1855); LCdr (16 Jul 1862); Cdr (25 Jul 1866); Capt (4 Jun 1874); Commo (1 Mar 1884); RAdm (7 Oct 1886); died (11 Feb 1889).

Career Summary Received appointment from NY (27 Sep 1845); Naval School, Annapolis, MD (Sep 1845–Jul 1846); flgs. *Independence*, Pac.Sqdn. (Aug 1846–May 1849); l.o.a. (May–Sep 1849); *Vincennes*, Pac.Sqdn. (Sep 1849–Oct 1851); l.o.a. (Oct–Nov 1851); USNA (Nov 1851–Jun 1852); *St. Louis*, Med.Sqdn. (Jul 1852–May 1855); l.o.a. (May–Jul 1855); cst.surv. duty (Jul 1855–Aug 1860); l.o.a. (Aug–Nov 1860); *Vandalia*, E.Ind. and S.Atl.Blk. Sqdns. (Nov 1860–Dec 1861); *San Jacinto*, N.Atl. and E.Gulf Blk. Sqdns. (Jan 1862–Mar

RALPH CHANDLER
1829–1889

1863); *Roanoke*, Navy Yard, NY (Mar–May 1863); cdr, *Hunts-ville*, E.Gulf Blk.Sqdn. (May 1863–Jul 1864); cdr, Naval Rndv., NY (Aug–Nov 1864); cdr, *Maumee*, N.Atl.Blk.Sqdn. (Nov 1864–Jan 1865); cdr, *Sangamon*, N.Atl.Blk.Sqdn. (Jan–Aug 1865); w.o. (Aug–Dec 1865); cdr, *Don*, spec.serv. (Jan 1866–May 1868); w.o. (May–Aug 1868); member, court-martial, NY (Aug–Sep 1868); ord. duty, Navy Yard, NY (Nov 1868–Mar 1869); cdr, *Tallapoosa*, spec.serv. (Mar 1869–Feb 1870); Navy Yard, NY (May 1870–Apr 1874); cdr, *Swatara*, transit of planet Venus expd. (May 1874–Jun 1875); cdr, rec. ship *Ohio*, Boston (Jul–Oct 1875); cdr, rec. ship *Wabash*, Boston (Oct 1875–Aug 1878); cdr, *Lackawanna*, N.Atl.Sta. (Sep 1878–Apr 1880); w.o. (Mar–May 1880); member, Advisory Bd. for Harbor Improvement, Philadelphia (May 1880–Feb 1881); Navy Yard, Boston (Oct 1881–Jun 1884); comdt., Navy Yard, NY (Dec 1884–Oct 1886); cdr, Asia.Sta., *Marion* (Nov 1886–Feb 1889); died (11 Feb 1889).

References
Personal Papers: a) 4 vols (1849–64), BAKL. b) 1 box (1847–87) with Port R. Chandler Papers, NYHS.

Writings: a) "Rigging and Equipment of Vessels of War," U.S. Naval Institute *Proceedings* 21 (1883): 483–88. b) "Auto-biography," unpublished (1887). c) "Private Journal," 2 vols. [n.d.]; Vol. I: 1874–75; Vol. II: 1860–61.

JOHN HOWE CLARK Born in Greenland, NH, on 16 Apr 1837, son of Samuel Wallace and Rebecca E. (Howe) Clark. Received the A.B. degree from Dartmouth College in 1857, and the M.D. degree from Harvard in 1862. Remained a bachelor. Died in Amherst, MA, on 30 Nov 1913. Buried in Amherst's Meadowview Cemetery.

Ranks Asst.Surg. (19 Oct 1861); PAsst.Surg. (24 Apr 1865); Surg. (14 May 1867); Medl.Insp. (8 Jan 1885); Medl.Dir. (4 Mar 1893); placed on Ret.Lst. as Medl.Dir. with rank of RAdm (16 Apr 1899).

Career Summary Received appointment from NH (19 Oct 1861); w.o. (Oct 1861–Apr 1862); Naval Hosp., W.Gulf Blk.Sqdn. (Jun 1862–Jun 1864); Navy Yard, Portsmouth, NH (Jul 1864–Apr 1865); *Mohongo*, Pac.Sqdn. (Apr 1865–Aug 1867); home and w.o. (Aug–Dec 1867); rec. ship *Vandalia*, Portsmouth, NH (Dec 1867–Nov 1869); *Alaska*, Asia.Sta. (Dec 1869–Feb 1873); home and w.o. (Feb–Mar 1873); Naval Rndv., NY (Apr–Jun 1873); Naval Hosp., Chelsea, MA (Jun 1873–Nov 1875); *Hartford* and *Worcester*, N.Atl.Sta. (Nov 1875–Jan 1876); *New Hampshire*, N.Atl.Sta. (Mar 1876–Oct 1878); rec. ship *Wabash*, Boston (Oct 1878–Feb 1881); member, Naval Exam.Bd. (Mar–Jul 1881); rec. ship *Wabash*, Boston (Jul 1881–Apr 1882); member, Naval Medl. Exam.Bd., Philadelphia (Apr–Sep 1882); w.o. (Sep–Nov 1882); rec. ship *Wabash*, Boston (Nov 1882–Feb 1883); member, Naval Medl. Exam.Bd. (Feb–Mar 1883); w.o. (Mar–Apr 1883); flt.surg., Pac.Sta.,

Lackawanna (May 1883–Jan 1885); flt.surg., Pac.Sta., *Hartford* (May 1885–Apr 1886); return to U.S. and w.o. (Apr–Aug 1886); spec. duty, Portsmouth, NH, and in charge, Naval Hosp., Widow's Island, ME (Sep 1886–Jan 1890); member, Naval Exam.Bd. (Jan 1888–Jan 1890); flt.surg., Pac.Sta., *Baltimore* (Jan 1890–Mar 1891), then *San Francisco* (Mar 1891–May 1892); l.o.a. (May–Aug 1892); spec. duty, USNA (Aug–Sep 1892); w. o. (Sep 1892–Apr 1893); pres., Bd. of Medl. Examiners, and Naval Ret.Bd., NY (May 1893–May 1895); in charge, Naval Hosp., Chelsea, MA (May 1895–May 1898); home and w.o. (May–Jun 1898); member, Ret.Bd., Washington, DC (Jun 1898–Apr 1899); placed on Ret.Lst. (16 Apr 1899).

CHRISTOPHER JAMES CLEBORNE
1838–1909

CHRISTOPHER JAMES CLEBORNE Born in Edinburgh, Scotland, on 16 Dec 1838. Educated at the Collegiate School of St. James and the Bristol Academy in Bristol, England. Began medical schooling at the Univ. of Edinburgh, transferring and completing the degree in Mar 1860 at Univ. of PA. Married, with two sons. Was a resident physician at the PA Hosp. in 1860 before entering USN. Died on 2 Oct 1909 at his home in Washington, DC. Buried in Arlington National Cemetery.

Ranks Asst.Surg. (9 May 1861); PAsst.Surg. (26 Oct 1863); Surg. (24 Nov 1863); Medl.Insp. with rank of Cdr (7 Jan 1878); Medl.Dir. with rank of Capt (18 Sep 1887); retired as Medl.Dir. with rank of RAdm (10 Nov 1899).

Career Summary Received appointment from PA (9 May 1861); *Jamestown*, N.Atl.Sqdn. (May 1861–Jan 1862); *Dale*, S.Atl.Blk.Sqdn.(Jan–Jul 1862); sick lv. (Jul–Aug 1862); w.o. (Aug–Sep 1862); *Aroostook*, W.Gulf Blk.Sqdn. (Sep 1862–Aug 1863); return and w.o. (Aug–Sep 1863); Naval Rndv., Philadelphia (Sep 1863–Mar 1864); *Ticonderoga*, S.Atl. Blk.Sqdn. (Mar 1864–May 1865); w.o. (May–Jun 1865); recorder, Naval Medl. Bd., Philadelphia (Jun–Dec 1865); flgs. *Rhode Island*, W.Ind.Sqdn. (Dec 1865–Dec 1866); *Iroquois*, NY (Jan–Sep 1867); training ship *Saratoga* (Oct 1867–Apr 1869); w.o. (Apr–May 1869); prac. ship *Macedonian*, USNA (May 1869); w.o. (May–Sep 1869); flgs. *Powhatan*, S.Pac.Sqdn. (Sep–Dec 1869); w.o. (Dec 1869–Jan 1870); member, Naval Medl. Exam.Bd., Philadelphia (Jan–Aug 1870); w.o. (Aug–Sep 1870); Naval Sta., League Island, PA (Oct 1870–Nov 1871); *Juniata*, Eur.Sqdn. (Dec 1871–Jul 1872); *Plymouth*, Eur.Sqdn. (Jul 1872–Jul 1874); *Brooklyn* and *Congress*, Eur.Sqdn. (Jul 1874–Oct 1874); w.o. (Oct 1874–Apr 1875); Navy Yard, Portsmouth, NH (Apr 1875–Apr 1879); flt.surg., N.Atl.Flt., *Powhatan* (Apr–Dec 1879), then *Tennessee* (Dec 1879–Apr 1881); Navy Yard, Portsmouth, NH (Apr 1881–Oct 1884); w.o. (Oct–Dec 1884); member, Medl. Exam.Bd., Philadelphia (Dec 1884–Dec 1887); dir., Naval Hosp., Norfolk, VA (Jan 1888–Apr 1891);

dir., Naval Hosp., Chelsea, MA (Apr 1891–Aug 1894); dir., Naval Hosp., Norfolk, VA (Aug 1894–Feb 1899); Naval Hosp., Philadelphia (Feb–Nov 1899); retired (10 Nov 1899).

JOHN MELLON BRADY CLITZ Born in Sacket's Harbor, NY, on 1 Dec 1821, the son of Capt John Clitz, USN. His brother was Col Henry Boynton Clitz, USA. Died on 9 Oct 1897 at St. Elizabeth's Asylum in Washington, DC.

Ranks Act.Midn (12 Apr 1837); PMidn (29 Jun 1843); Mstr (16 Aug 1850); Lt (6 Apr 1851); Cdr (16 Jul 1862); Capt (25 Jul 1866); Commo (28 Dec 1872); RAdm (13 Mar 1880); retired (16 Oct 1883).

Career Summary Received appointment from MI (12 Apr 1837); w.o. (Apr–Jun 1837); *Ontario*, W.Ind.Sqdn. (Jun 1837–Aug 1841); rec. ship *Columbus*, Boston (Aug–Dec 1841); l.o.a. (Oct 1841–Feb 1842); *Missouri*, on trials (Feb–Aug 1842); Naval School, Philadelphia (Sep 1842–Jun 1843); Depot of Charts, Washington, DC (Jun 1843–Nov 1844); *St. Mary's*, Med.Sqdn. (Nov 1844–Jul 1845); *Falmouth*, Home Sqdn. (Jul 1845–Nov 1846); l.o.a. (Nov–Dec 1846); Naval Observatory, Washington, DC (Dec 1846–Feb 1847); *Hecla, Petrita, Mississippi*, Home Sqdn. (Feb 1847–Apr 1848); l.o.a. (Apr–Jun 1848); Naval Observatory, Washington, DC (Jun 1848–Jun 1849); *Cumberland*, Med.Sqdn. (Jun 1849–Jul 1851); l.o.a. and w.o. (Jul–Dec 1851); cst.surv. duty (Dec 1851–Jul 1852); Naval Observatory, Washington, DC (Jul–Sep 1852); *Mississippi*, E.Ind.Sqdn. (Sep 1852–Apr 1855); l.o.a. (Apr–Aug 1855); spec. duty, Washington, DC (Aug 1855–Jun 1856); w.o. (Jun–Oct 1856); rec. ship *Allegheny*, Baltimore (Oct 1856); w.o. (Oct 1856–Mar 1857); *Decatur*, Pac.Sqdn. (Mar 1857–Aug 1859); l.o.a. (Aug–Oct 1859); Navy Yard, NY (Oct 1859–Jan 1861); *Iroquois* (Feb 1861–Jan 1862); cdr, *Penobscot*, N.Atl.Blk.Sqdn. (Feb–Dec 1862); return home and w.o. (Dec 1862–Jan 1863); cdr, *Juniata*, E.Gulf Blk.Sqdn. (Feb–Dec 1863); cdr, *Osceola*, N.Atl.Blk.Sqdn. (Dec 1863–May 1865); Navy Yard, Boston (May 1865–May 1868); member, Naval Exam.Bd., Boston (May–Oct 1868); cdr, *Pawnee*, Norfolk, VA, and S.Atl.Sqdn. (Dec 1868–Jul 1869); ord. duty, Navy Yard, NY (Jul 1869–Nov 1870); cdr, *California*, Pac.Flt. (Dec 1870–Nov 1872); home and w.o. (Nov 1872–Jan 1876); cdr, Naval Station, Port Royal, SC (Jan 1876–Apr 1877); w.o. (Apr 1877–Mar 1878); insp., 3rd L.h. Dist., Tompkinsville, NY (Apr 1878–Jun 1880); s.a. and w.o. (Jun–Aug 1880); cdr, Asia.Sta., *Richmond* (Sep 1880–Apr 1883); return home and w.o. (Apr–Oct 1883); retired (16 Oct 1883).

EDMUND ROSS COLHOUN Born at Chambersburg, PA, on 6 May 1821, son of Alexander and Margaretta A. (Ross) Colhoun. Married Mary Ann Reed on 31 Jul 1845 in Philadelphia. Three sons and three daughters; the eldest son was Paymstr. Samuel Reed Colhoun, USN. Died in Washing-

JOHN MELLON BRADY CLITZ
1821–1897

EDMUND ROSS COLHOUN
1821–1897

ton, DC, on 17 Feb 1897. Buried in Arlington National Cemetery.

Ranks Midn (1 Apr 1839); PMidn (2 Jul 1845); Mstr (26 Jan 1853); resigned (27 Jun 1853); reappointed as Act.Lt (24 Sep 1861); Cdr (17 Nov 1862); Capt (2 Mar 1869); Commo (26 Apr 1876); RAdm (3 Dec 1882); placed on Ret.Lst. (6 May 1883).

Career Summary Received appointment from MO (1 Apr 1839); *Marion*, Braz.Sqdn. (Sep 1839–Nov 1841); Naval School, Philadelphia (Nov 1841–Apr 1842); *Congress*, Med. and Braz. Sqdns. (Apr 1842–Aug 1844); Naval School, Philadelphia (Sep. 1844–Jun 1845); l.o.a. (Jun–Aug 1845); Hydrographic Office, Washington, DC (Aug 1845); l.o.a. (Aug–Dec 1845); *Cumberland*, Home Sqdn. (Dec 1846–Feb 1847); l.o.a. (Feb–Mar 1847); *Raritan*, Home Sqdn. (Mar–Jul 1847); rec. ship *Experiment*, Philadelphia (Jan 1848–Jul 1849); *Albany*, Home Sqdn. (Jul 1849–Sep 1850); l.o.a. (Sep–Nov 1850); rec. ship *Union*, Philadelphia (Nov 1850–Oct 1851); *St. Lawrence*, Pac.Sqdn. (Oct 1851–Jun 1853); resigned (27 Jun 1853); received appointment (24 Sep 1861); *Hunchback*, N.Atl.Blk.Sqdn. (Sep 1861–Oct 1862); cdr, *Ladona*, N.Atl.Blk.Sqdn. (Oct 1862–Jun 1863); cdr, *Weehawken*, S.Atl.Blk.Sqdn. (Jun–Dec 1863); sick lv. (Dec 1863–Feb 1864); cdr, *Saugus*, Navy Yard, Philadelphia, and N.Atl.Blk.Sqdn. (Feb–Dec 1864); w.o. (Dec 1864–Mar 1865); spec. duty, NY (Mar 1865–Feb 1866); l.o.a. (Feb–Aug 1866); w.o. (Aug–Oct 1866); flt.capt and chief of staff, S.Pac.Sqdn., *Powhatan* (Dec 1866–Aug 1867); return home and w.o. (Jun 1867–Apr 1869); cdr, *Dictator*, N.Atl.Sta. (Jun 1869–Jul 1870); insp. of ord., Navy Yard, Philadelphia (Aug 1870–Dec 1871); exec.off., Navy Yard, Boston (Dec 1871–May 1873); cdr, flgs. *Hartford*, Asia.Sqdn. (Jul 1873–Apr 1874); cdr, Asia.Sta., *Hartford* (Apr–Aug 1874); cdr, flgs. *Richmond*, S.Pac.Sta. (Aug 1874–Apr 1875); w.o. (Jul–Aug 1875); l.o.a. (Aug 1875–Jul 1876); spec. Centennial duty, Philadelphia (Jul–Oct 1876); member, Exam. and Ret. Bds. (Oct 1876–Mar 1877); cdr, Navy Yard, Mare Island, CA (Apr 1877–Jan 1881); w.o. (Jan–May 1881); spec. duty, insp. of vessels in CA (May 1881–Apr 1882); w.o. (Apr 1882–May 1883); placed on Ret.Lst. (6 May 1883).

References
Personal Papers: 1200 items (1839–88), NHF,LC.

NAPOLEON COLLINS Born in Fayette County, PA, on 4 May 1814. Died at Callao, Peru, on 9 Aug 1875. Buried in Protestant Cemetery at Callao, then reinterred in the U.S. in 1876.

Ranks Midn (2 Jan 1834); PMidn (16 Jul 1840); Lt (6 Nov 1846); Cdr (16 Jul 1862); Capt (25 Jul 1866); Commo (19 Jan 1871); RAdm (9 Aug 1874); died (9 Aug 1875).

Career Summary Received appointment from PA (2 Jan 1834); W.Ind.Sqdn. (Sep 1834–Jun 1836); *Natchez*,

NAPOLEON COLLINS
1814–1875

W.Ind.Sqdn. (Jun 1836–Sep 1839); Naval School, NY (Sep–Nov 1839); Naval School, Philadelphia (Nov 1839–Sep 1840); *Boston* then flgs. *Constellation*, E.Ind.Sqdn. (Sep 1840–May 1844); Naval Observatory, Washington, DC (May–Aug 1846); w.o. (Aug 1846–Feb 1847); *Decatur*, Home Sqdn. (Feb 1847–Nov 1849); l.o.a. (Nov 1849–Jun 1850); *Michigan*, on Great Lakes (Jun 1850–Apr 1853); cdr, *John P. Kennedy* then *Susquehanna*, N.Pac.Expd. and E.Ind.Sqdn. (Apr 1853–Mar 1855); l.o.a. (Mar–May 1855); on furlough (Jun 1855–Jun 1856); Navy Yard, Mare Island, CA (Jun–Aug 1856); *John Adams*, Pac.Sta. (Aug 1856–Apr 1858); l.o.a. (Apr–Aug 1858); *Michigan*, on Great Lakes (Aug 1858–Dec 1859); w.o. (Dec 1859–Oct 1860); *Vandalia*, E.Ind.Sqdn. (Nov 1860–May 1861); cdr, *Anacostia*, Potomac Flot. (May–Aug 1861); cdr, *Unadilla*, S.Atl.Blk.Sqdn. (Sep 1861–Sep 1862); cdr, *Octorora*, "Flying Sqdn." (Sep 1862–Sep 1863); cdr, *Wachusett*, spec.serv. (Nov 1863–Dec 1864); w.o. (Dec 1864–Sep 1866); cdr, *Sacramento*, spec.serv. (Sep 1866–Nov 1867); w.o. (Nov 1867–Feb 1868); suspended from duty (Feb 1868–Mar 1869); w.o. (Mar 1869–Jan 1870); Navy Yard, Norfolk, VA (Feb 1870–Jan 1871); w.o. (Jan–Sep 1871); insp., 10th L.h. Dist., Buffalo, NY (Sep 1871–Jul 1874); cdr, S.Pac.Sqdn., *Richmond* (Aug 1874–Aug 1875); died (9 Aug 1875).

Career Highlights Captured Confederate steamer *Florida* in harbor of Bahia, Braz., on 7 Oct 1864. Braz. complained, demanded *Florida*'s return or rendition. Collins was court-martialled in Apr 1865, found guilty of neutrality violation, and sentenced to dismissal. Sentence overturned by Secretary of the Navy Gideon Welles.

GEORGE HENRY COOPER Born at Fort Diamond, NY Harbor, on 27 Jul 1822. Married, with three sons and a daughter. Died in Brooklyn, NY, on 17 Nov 1891.

Ranks Midn (4 Aug 1837); PMidn (29 Jun 1843); Mstr (11 Oct 1850); Lt (8 May 1851); Cdr (16 Jul 1862); Capt (2 Dec 1867); Commo (5 Jun 1874); RAdm (15 Nov 1881); placed on Ret.Lst. (27 Jul 1884).

Career Summary Received appointment from NY (4 Aug 1837); *Concord*, W.Ind.Sqdn. (Aug 1837–Nov 1838); l.o.a. (Nov 1838–Jan 1839); *Constitution*, flgs., and *St. Louis*, S.Pac.Sqdn. (Jan 1839–Sep 1842); l.o.a. (Sep–Nov 1842); Naval School, Philadelphia (Nov 1842–Jun 1843); *Macedonian* and *Saratoga*, W.Ind. and Afr.Sqdns. (Jun 1843–Nov 1844); l.o.a. (Nov 1844–Feb 1845); in ordinary, Navy Yard, Norfolk, VA (Feb–Jun 1845); despatch vessel, *Flirt*, spec.serv. (Jun 1845–Feb 1846); w.o. (Feb–Mar 1846); despatch vessel *Flirt*, spec.serv. (Mar 1846–Jan 1847); Naval Rndv., Norfolk, VA (Jan–Mar 1847); *Decatur* and *Raritan*, Home Sqdn. (Mar–Jul 1847); rec. ship *Pennsylvania*, Norfolk, VA (Jul 1847–Dec 1848); storeship *Supply* (Dec 1848–Sep 1849); l.o.a. (Sep 1849); Navy Yard, Norfolk, VA (Sep 1849–Mar 1850); Navy Yard,

GEORGE HENRY COOPER
1822–1891

Norfolk, VA (Mar–Dec 1850); flgs. *Susquehanna*, E.Ind.Sqdn. (Dec 1850–Mar 1855); l.o.a. (Mar 1855); temp. duty, Naval Rndv., Navy Yard, Norfolk, VA (Mar 1855–Nov 1856); ord. duty, Navy Yard, Norfolk, VA (Nov 1856–May 1857); prac. ship *Preble* (May 1857–Feb 1858); *Colorado*, W.Ind.Sqdn. (Mar–Aug 1858); flgs. *Roanoke*, Home Sqdn. (Aug 1858–May 1860); l.o.a. (May–Jul 1860); Navy Yard, Portsmouth, NH (Aug 1860–Sep 1861); insp., *Curlew*, Pittsburgh, PA (Sep–Dec 1861); Navy Yard, NY (Dec 1861–Mar 1862); cdr, supply ship *Massachusetts* (Mar–Dec 1862); temp. cdr, *Connecticut*, spec. duty and Aspinwall, Panama (Dec 1862–Jul 1863); cdr, *Sonoma*, S.Atl.Blk.Sqdn. (Jul 1863–Jul 1864); spec. duty, fitting out ships outside navy yards (Jul–Sep 1864); cdr, *Glaucus*, N.Atl.Blk.Sqdn. (Sep 1864–May 1865); w.o. (May–Jun 1865); spec. duty, NY (Jun 1865); cdr, *Winooski*, spec.serv. (Jun 1865–Jul 1867); w.o. (Jul–Aug 1867); ord. duty, Navy Yard, Norfolk, VA (Sep 1867–Dec 1869); cdr, *Colorado*, Navy Yard, NY, and Asia.Sqdn. (Jan 1869–Jul 1871); w.o. (Jul–Sep 1871); Navy Yard, Norfolk, VA (Sep 1871–Nov 1873); cdr, *Terror*, League Island, PA (Dec 1873); exec.off., Navy Yard, Norfolk, VA (Dec 1873); cdr, *Roanoke*, Navy Yard, NY (Dec 1873–Dec 1874); cdr, Navy Yard, Pensacola, FL (Jan 1874–Apr 1876); w.o. (Apr–Oct 1876); pres., Bd. of Exam., USNA (Oct–Nov 1876); w.o. (Nov–Dec 1876); insp., 13th L.h. Dist., Portland, OR (Jan–Mar 1877); pres., Bd. of Inspection (Apr 1877–Apr 1880); cdr, Navy Yard, NY (May 1880–Apr 1882); cdr, N.Atl.Sqdn., *Tennessee* (May 1882–Jul 1884); placed on Ret.Lst. (27 Jul 1884).

CHARLES STANHOPE COTTON
1843–1909

CHARLES STANHOPE COTTON Born in Milwaukee, WI, on 15 Feb 1843, son of Lester Holt and Mary Ann Cotton. Married Rebecca Cecilia Robertson on 30 Aug 1865. Died on 19 Feb 1909 in Nice, France.

Ranks Act.Midn (23 Sep 1858); title changed to Midn (16 Jul 1865); Ens (11 Nov 1862); Lt (22 Feb 1864); LCdr (25 Jul 1866); Cdr (25 Apr 1877); Capt (28 May 1892); RAdm (27 Mar 1900); retired (16 Feb 1904).

Career Summary Received appointment from WI (23 Sep 1858); USNA (Sep 1858–May 1861); *St. Lawrence*, Philadelphia (May–Sep 1861); spec. duty, Philadelphia (Sep–Nov 1861); flgs. *Minnesota*, N.Atl.Blk.Sqdn. (Nov 1861–Oct 1862); *Iroquois*, N.Atl.Blk.Sqdn. (Nov 1862–Jul 1863); *Oneida*, W.Gulf Blk.Sqdn. (Mar 1864–Aug 1865); w.o. (Aug–Nov 1865); *Shenandoah*, Asia.Sta. (Nov 1865–May 1869); l.o.a. (May–Sep 1869); USNA (Sep 1869–Jul 1870); *California*, Navy Yard, Portsmouth, NH (Sep 1870); Navy Yard, Portsmouth, NH (Oct–Dec 1870); *Tennessee*, Santo Domingo Expd. (Jan–Apr 1871); exec.off., *Ticonderoga*, S.Atl.Sta. (Apr 1871–Feb 1874); w.o. (Feb–Apr 1874); Navy Yard, Portsmouth, NH (Apr 1874–May 1876); torp. instruction, Newport, RI (Jun–Sep 1876); exec.off., rec. ship *Worcester*, Norfolk, VA (Sep–

Oct 1876); Navy Yard, NY (Oct 1876–Jul 1880); w.o. (Jul–
Aug 1880); cdr, *Monocacy*, Asia.Sta. (Sep 1880–Sep 1883);
temp. cdr, *Alert*, Asia.Sta. (Jun–Jul 1881); home and w.o.
(Sep–Dec 1883); insp. of ord., Navy Yard, Norfolk, VA (Jan
1884–Sep 1887); asst., then insp., 15th L.h. Dist., St. Louis,
MO (Oct 1887–Nov 1890); s.a. and w.o. (Nov 1890–Mar
1891); cdr, *Mohican*, Pac.Sqdn. (Apr 1891–Apr 1892); cdr,
Bering Sea Patrol Sqdn., *Mohican* (Jun–Oct 1891); cdr, rec.
ship *Independence*, Mare Island, CA (May 1892–Aug 1894);
cdr, flgs. *Philadelphia*, Pac.Sta. (Aug 1894–Sep 1897); home
and w.o. (Sep 1897–Jan 1898); ord. instruction, Navy Yard,
Washington, DC (Jan–Apr 1898); cdr, *Harvard*, N.Atl.Flt.
(Apr–Sep 1898); capt.yd., Navy Yard, Mare Island, CA (Oct
1898–Apr 1899); cdr, rec. ship *Independence*, Mare Island, CA
(Apr 1899–Mar 1900); pres., Ret.Bd., Washington, DC (Mar–
Jul 1900); comdt., Navy Yard and Naval Sta., Norfolk, VA
(Jul 1900–Apr 1903); cdr, Eur.Sqdn., *Brooklyn* (Apr 1903–Feb
1904); retired (16 Feb 1904).

Career Highlights During the Civil War, observed the
action from on board the *Minnesota* between the *Monitor*
and the *Merrimack* in Hampton Roads. Participated in the
Battle of Mobile Bay and the eventual surrender of Ft. Morgan in Aug 1864. Sent first cable on 11 May 1898 reporting
arrival of Spanish Adm Cervera's fleet at Martinique. Later,
at the Battle of Santiago Bay, he and the *Harvard* took
numerous Spanish prisoners from the *Infanta Maria Teresa*
and the *Almirante Oquendo*.

References
Personal Papers: 600 items (1860–1921), log of *Minnesota*
(1861) in NHF,WNY.

THOMAS CRABBE Born in MD in 1788, moving to Lancaster, PA, before entering the navy. Surname was originally
spelled "Crabb" until changed officially in Jul 1845. Died in
Princeton, NJ, on 29 Jun 1872.

Ranks Midn (15 Nov 1809); Lt (4 Feb 1815); Mstr.Comdt.
(3 Mar 1835); Cdr (3 Mar 1835); Capt (8 Sep 1841); placed
on Ret.Lst. with rank of Commo (16 Jul 1862); RAdm on
Ret.Lst. (25 Jul 1866).

Career Summary Received appointment from PA (15
Nov 1809); *President*, Atl.Coast (Nov 1810–Apr 1811); on fur-
lough (Apr–Oct 1811); Navy Yard, Philadelphia (Oct 1811–
Feb 1812); Navy Yard, Gosport, VA (Feb–Jul 1812); under
instruction, Washington, DC (Jul–Aug 1812); *Constellation*,
Navy Yard, Washington, DC, and Hampton Roads, VA (Aug
1812–Jul 1815); *John Adams*, Med.Sqdn. (Jul–Aug 1815); *Con-
stellation*, Med.Sqdn. (Aug 1815–Nov 1816); home and w.o.
(Nov 1816–Jan 1817); Navy Yard, NY (Jan–Apr 1817); Navy
Yard, Norfolk, VA (Apr 1817–Jul 1819); *Constellation*,
Braz.Sqdn. (Jul 1819–Nov 1820); w.o. (Nov 1820–Mar 1821);
schoolship *Guerriere*, Norfolk, VA (Mar 1821–Nov 1822);

Peacock, W.Ind.Sqdn. (Dec 1822–Jul 1823); attached to W.Ind.Sqdn. (Sep 1823–Feb 1824); Navy Yard, Norfolk, VA (Feb–Sep 1824); l.o.a. (Sep–Nov 1824); Navy Yard, Washington, DC (Nov 1824–Apr 1827); *Java*, Med.Sqdn. (Apr 1827–Apr 1828); *Delaware*, Med.Sqdn. (Apr 1828–Apr 1829); home and l.o.a. (Jul 1829–Aug 1830); Navy Yard, Portsmouth, NH (Aug 1830–Nov 1833); l.o.a. (Nov 1833–May 1834); w.o. (May 1834–Aug 1836); *Vandalia*, W.Ind.Sta. (Aug–Sep 1836); cdr, *Vandalia*, W.Ind.Sqdn. (Sep 1836–Oct 1837); l.o.a. (Oct 1837–Jan 1838); w.o. (Jan 1838–Mar 1841); cdr, Naval Rndv., Baltimore (Mar–Apr 1841); w.o. (Apr 1841–Jul 1847); cdr, flgs. *Brandywine*, Braz.Sqdn. (Jul 1847–Jun 1848); w.o. (Jun 1848–Oct 1851); cdr, *San Jacinto*, Med.Sqdn. (Nov 1851–Jul 1853); l.o.a. (Jul–Nov 1853); w.o. (Nov 1853–Jun 1854); member, court-martial bd., Philadelphia (Jun 1854); cdr, Afr.Sqdn., *Jamestown* (Jan 1855–Jun 1857); l.o.a. (Jun–Sep 1857); w.o. (Sep 1857–Mar 1861); member, court-martial bd., Washington, DC (Mar–Jun 1861); w.o. (Jun–Aug 1861); member, court of inquiry, Navy Yard, Philadelphia (Aug 1861–Nov 1862); placed on Ret.Lst. (16 Jul 1862); pres., gen. court-martial, Navy Yard, Philadelphia (Nov 1862–Jan 1863); pres., gen. court-martial, Navy Yard, Philadelphia (Feb 1863); member, gen. court-martial, Navy Yard, NY (Mar 1863); president, gen. court-martial, Navy Yard, Philadelphia (Jun–Sep 1863); prize commissioner, Eastern Dist., Philadelphia (Sep 1864–Oct 1865).

References
Personal Papers: 1 journal (1815), USMA.

THOMAS TINGEY CRAVEN
1808–1887

THOMAS TINGEY CRAVEN Born in Washington, DC, on 20 Dec 1808, the son of Tunis and Hannah (Tingey) Craven. His father was a Navy purser and storekeeper while his maternal grandfather, Commo Thomas Tingey (1750–1829) was for long comdt. of the Washington Navy Yard. Married Virginia Wingate, then married Emily Truxton. Eight children: three sons graduated from USNA; one daughter, Ida, married future Asst. Secretary of the Navy Frank W. Hackett. Brother was Cdr Tunis Augustus Macdonough Craven, killed commanding *Tecumseh* at Battle of Mobile Bay on 5 Aug 1864. Died at the Boston Navy Yard on 23 Aug 1887. Buried in Geneva, NY. In 1929, bodies of Craven and his wife were reinterred at Arlington National Cemetery.

Ranks Midn (1 May 1822); PMidn (24 May 1828); Lt (27 May 1830); Cdr (16 Dec 1852); Capt (7 Jun 1861); Commo (10 Jul 1862); RAdm (10 Oct 1866); transferred to Ret.Lst. (30 Dec 1869).

Career Summary Received appointment from NH (1 May 1822); *United States*, Pac.Sqdn. (Oct 1823–May 1826); *Peacock*, Pac.Sqdn. (May 1826–Oct 1827); l.o.a. (Oct 1827–Apr 1828); examination and w.o. (Apr–Aug 1828); *Erie*,

W.Ind.Sqdn. (Aug 1828–Aug 1829); l.o.a. and w.o. (Aug 1829–Nov 1831); rec. ship at NY (Nov–Dec 1831); *Boxer*, Braz.Sqdn. (Jan 1831–Jun 1833); *Peacock*, spec. duty to Arabia (Jun 1833–Mar 1834); *Boxer*, Braz.Sqdn. (Mar–Jul 1834); l.o.a. (Jul 1834–Feb 1835); rec. ship at NY (Feb 1835–Mar 1836); l.o.a. (Mar 1836–Sep 1837); *John Adams*, Hampton Roads, VA (Sep 1837–Apr 1838); 1st lt, *Vincennes*, U.S.Expl.Expd. (Apr 1838–Jul 1839); *Boxer*, Pac.Sqdn. (Oct 1839–Feb 1840); l.o.a. (Feb–Apr 1840); spec. duty studying steam propulsion, Navy Yard, NY (Apr 1840–Jun 1841); l.o.a. (Jun 1841–Mar 1842); cdr, rec. ship at Buffalo, NY (Mar–Aug 1842); w.o. (Aug 1842–Mar 1843); *Macedonian*, Afr.Cst. (Mar–Nov 1843); cdr, *Porpoise*, Afr.Sqdn. (Nov 1843–Nov 1844); l.o.a. (Nov 1844–May 1846); Naval Rndv., NY (May 1846–Jun 1847); *Ohio*, Pac.Sqdn. (Jun–Nov 1847); home and l.o.a. (Nov 1847–May 1849); exec.off., flgs. *Independence*, Med.Sqdn. (May–Nov 1849); home and w.o. (Nov 1849–Jun 1850); comdt. of midn, USNA (Jun 1850–Jun 1855); cdr, flgs. *Congress*, Med.Sqdn. (Jun 1855–Jan 1858); l.o.a. (Jan–Feb 1858); comdt. of midn, USNA (Feb 1858–Oct 1860); w.o. (Oct 1860–Apr 1861); cdr, Naval Rndv., Portland, ME (Apr–Jun 1861); cdr, Potomac Flot., *Yankee* (Jun–Dec 1861); cdr, *Brooklyn*, W.Gulf Blk.Sqdn. (Dec 1861–Aug 1862); cdr, *Niagara*, spec.serv., Eur. waters (Aug 1862–Sep 1865); suspended from duty (Sep 1865–Jul 1866); comdt., Navy Yard, Mare Island, CA (Jul 1866–Aug 1868); cdr, N.Pac.Sqdn., *Ossipee* (Aug 1868–Apr 1869); comdt., Navy Yard, Mare Island, CA (Apr–Dec 1869); transferred to Ret.Lst. (30 Dec 1869); port adm, San Francisco (Jan–Oct 1870).

Career Highlights Twice comdt. of midn at USNA. Captured Confederate raider *Georgia* off Portugal in Aug 1864. In Mar 1865, tried unsuccessfully to blockade CSS *Stonewall* at El Ferrol, Spain. Subsequently court-martialled in Dec 1865, receiving two year suspension of duty. Verdict overruled a year later by Secretary of the Navy Gideon Welles.

References
Personal Papers: a) c.19 items (1865, 1868–69) in John Bigelow Papers and in Thomas Turner Letterbooks, NYPL. b) 170 items (1841–69) in GARL. c) 1 vol. (1863–65) in WPL. d) ¼ ft. (1855–61) in EFMC.

JOHNSTON BLAKELEY CREIGHTON Born in RI on 12 Nov 1822. Married, with two daughters and a son. Died at his home in Morristown, NJ, on 13 Nov 1883.

Ranks Midn (10 Feb 1838); PMidn (20 May 1844); Mstr (16 Dec 1852); Lt (9 Oct 1853); LCdr (16 Jul 1862); Cdr (23 Sep 1862); Capt (26 Nov 1868); Commo (9 Nov 1874); RAdm (11 May 1882); placed on Ret.Lst. (21 Nov 1882).

Career Summary Received appointment from RI (10 Feb 1838); w.o. (Feb–Mar 1883); *Levant*, W.Ind.Sqdn. (Mar–Sep 1838); l.o.a. (Sep–Oct 1838); *Constellation*, *Natchez*, and

JOHNSTON BLAKELEY
CREIGHTON
1822–1883

Macedonian, W.Ind.Sqdn. (Oct 1838–Oct 1841); l.o.a. (Oct–Dec 1841); *Columbia*, Braz.Sqdn. (Jan 1842–Sep 1843); l.o.a. (Sep–Oct 1843); Naval School, Philadelphia (Sep 1843–May 1844); *Truxtun*, Afr.Cst. (May 1844–Nov 1845); l.o.a. (Nov 1845–May 1846); *Dale* then *Lexington*, Pac.Sqdn. (May 1846–Jun 1849); l.o.a. and w.o. (Jun 1849–Mar 1850); rec. ship *North Carolina*, NY (Mar–May 1850); *Michigan*, on Great Lakes (May 1850–Mar 1852); *Cumberland*, Med.Sqdn. (Apr 1852–Apr 1855); l.o.a. and w.o. (May–Oct 1855); Navy Yard, Boston (Oct 1855–Jul 1858); *Sabine*, Navy Yard, NY (Aug 1858); *Roanoke*, Home Sqdn. (Aug 1858–May 1860); l.o.a. and w.o. (May 1860–Jan 1861); Naval Rndv., NY (Feb–Aug 1861); flgs. *Lancaster*, Pac.Sqdn. (Oct 1861–Feb 1862); return to U.S. and w.o. (Feb–Mar 1862); cdr, *Ottawa*, S.Atl.Blk.Sqdn. (Apr–Sep 1862); spec. duty to Pac.Sqdn. and back (Oct–Nov 1862); spec. duty, NY (Dec 1862–Jan 1863); cdr, *Mahaska*, S.Atl.Blk.Sqdn. (Feb 1863–Feb 1864); w.o. (Feb–Mar 1864); temp. ord. duty, Navy Yard, Boston (Apr–Jul 1864); cdr, *Mingo*, S.Atl.Blk.Sqdn. (Jul 1864–Apr 1865); temp. ord. duty, Navy Yard, Boston (Mar 1865–Dec 1866); ord. duty, Navy Yard, NY (Dec 1866–Apr 1867); cdr, *Oneida*, Asia.Sqdn. (May 1867–Apr 1869); return and w.o. (Apr–Jun 1869); spec. duty, NY (Jun 1869–Sep 1871); cdr, *Guerriere*, Eur.Sqdn. (Sep 1871–Mar 1872); spec. duty (Mar–Jun 1872); w.o. (Jun–Aug 1872); cdr, *Worcester* and chief of staff, N.Atl.Sta. (Aug 1872–May 1873); w.o. (May–Jul 1873); member, Naval Exam.Bd. (Jul 1873–Oct 1874); w.o. (Oct 1874–Jun 1876); comdt., Navy Yard, Norfolk, VA (Jul 1876–Jul 1879); w.o. (Jul 1879–Nov 1882); placed on Ret.Lst. (21 Nov 1882).

BARTLETT JEFFERSON
CROMWELL
1840–1917

BARTLETT JEFFERSON CROMWELL Born near Springplace, GA, on 9 Feb 1840, the son of Andrew Forgison and Sarah (Ragon) Cromwell. Married Lizzie H. Huber on 31 Dec 1866; three daughters, each marrying naval officers. Died in Montrose, PA, on 24 Jun 1917. Buried in Arlington National Cemetery.

Ranks Act.Midn (21 Sep 1857); Midn (1 Jun 1861); Lt (16 Jul 1862); LCdr (25 Jul 1866); Cdr (24 Oct 1874); Capt (26 Mar 1889); Commo (10 Aug 1898); RAdm (3 Mar 1899); placed on Ret.Lst. (9 Feb 1902).

Career Summary Received appointment from NE (21 Sep 1857); USNA (Sep 1857–Jun 1861); *Iroquois*, *St. Lawrence*, and *Quaker City*, spec.serv. and S.Atl.Blk.Sqdn. (Sep 1861–Oct 1862); *Conemaugh*, S.Atl.Blk.Sqdn. (Oct 1862–Jun 1863); prize, *Atlanta* (Jun–Oct 1863); *Proteus*, E.Gulf Blk.Sqdn. (Oct 1863–May 1865); exec.off., *Shawmut*, Braz.Sqdn. (Jun 1865–Dec 1866); w.o. (Dec 1866–Jan 1867); USNA (Jan 1867–Sep 1869); *Miantonomah*, spec.serv. and N.Atl.Sta. (Oct 1869–Jul 1870); *Plymouth*, Eur.Sqdn. (Jul 1870–Mar 1872); *Juniata*, Eur.Sqdn. (Mar–May 1872); l.o.a. (May–Aug 1872); torp.

duty, Newport, RI (Sep 1872–Jun 1873); w.o. (Jun–Sep 1873); exec.off., *Powhatan*, spec.serv. (Sep 1873–Sep 1874); insp. of ord., Navy Yard, League Island, PA (Sep 1874–Feb 1878); cdr, *Rio Bravo*, spec.serv. (Feb–Oct 1878); cdr, *Ticonderoga*, spec.serv. (Nov 1878–Sep 1881); l.o.a. (Sep 1881–Jan 1882); insp. of ord., Navy Yard, Portsmouth, NH (Feb 1882–Sep 1884); cdr, Naval Rndv., Philadelphia (Oct 1884–May 1885); w.o. (May 1885–Jun 1886); court-martial duty, Boston (Jun–Aug 1886); w.o. (Aug–Dec 1886); Navy Yard, League Island, PA (Dec 1886–Dec 1889); ord. duty, Philadelphia and Chester, PA (Dec 1889–Jan 1890); cdr, flgs. *Omaha*, Asia.Sta. (Feb 1890–Jun 1891); l.o.a. (Jun–Aug 1891); capt.yd., Navy Yard, League Island, PA (Sep–Oct 1891); capt.yd., Navy Yard, Norfolk, VA (Oct 1891–Oct 1894); home and w.o. (Oct–Dec 1894); cdr, *Atlanta*, N.Atl.Sta. (Dec 1894–Sep 1895); court-martial and bd. duties (Sep 1895–Dec 1898); comdt., Naval Sta., and cdr, *Resolute*, Havana, Cuba (Dec 1898–Nov 1899); pres., Naval Ret.Bd. (Nov 1899–Mar 1900); comdt., Naval Sta., Portsmouth, NH (Mar 1900–Apr 1901); cdr, S.Atl.Sta., *Chicago* (Apr–Jul 1901); cdr, Eur.Sta., *Chicago* (Jul 1901–Feb 1902); placed on Ret. Lst. (9 Feb 1902).

References
Personal Papers: 4 items (1878) in LSUL.

PEIRCE CROSBY Born in Delaware County, PA, on 16 Jan 1824, son of John P. and Catharine (Beale) Crosby. Married four times: to Matilda Boyer on 16 Oct 1850, to Julia Wells in Mar 1861, to Miriam Gratz on 15 Feb 1870, and to Louise Audenried on 24 Jun 1880. Died on 15 Jun 1899 in Washington, DC.

Ranks Midn (5 Jun 1838); PMidn (20 May 1844); Mstr (4 Nov 1852); Lt (3 Sep 1853); LCdr (16 Jul 1862); Cdr (22 Sep 1862); Capt (27 May 1868); Commo (3 Oct 1874); RAdm (10 Mar 1882); placed on Ret.Lst. (29 Oct 1883).

Career Summary Received appointment from PA (5 Jun 1838); w.o. (Jun–Sep 1838); flgs. *Ohio*, Med.Sqdn. (Sep 1838–Jul 1841); l.o.a. (Jul–Oct 1841); rec. ship *Experiment*, Philadelphia (Oct 1841–Feb 1842); *Mississippi*, Home Sqdn. (Feb–May 1842); *Congress* and *Preble*, Med.Sqdn. (Jun 1842–Sep 1843); l.o.a. (Sep–Nov 1843); Naval School, Philadelphia (Nov 1843–Jul 1844); cst.surv. duty (Jul 1844–Feb 1847); *Decatur* and *Petrel*, Home Sqdn. (Feb 1847–Aug 1848); l.o.a. (Nov 1848–Feb 1849); *Relief*, spec.serv. (Feb 1849–Aug 1850); l.o.a. (Aug–Oct 1850); Navy Yard, Philadelphia (Oct 1850–Aug 1852); *Saranac*, Navy Yard, Philadelphia (Aug–Sep 1852); rec. ship *Union*, Philadelphia (Sep 1852–Mar 1853); *Savannah*, Navy Yard, Norfolk, VA (Mar–Jun 1853); w.o. (Jun–Nov 1853); *Germantown*, Braz.Sqdn. (Nov 1853–Feb 1857); l.o.a. (Feb–Mar 1857); rec. ship *Princeton*, Philadelphia (Mar 1857–Jun 1858); *Saratoga*, Home Sqdn. (Jun 1858–Jul 1860); l.o.a. (Jul–Sep 1860); rec. ship *Princeton*, Philadelphia (Sep 1860–Apr

PEIRCE CROSBY
1824–1899

1861); *Cumberland*, N.Atl.Blk.Sqdn. (Apr–Sep 1861); cdr, *Pembina*, Navy Yard, NY and S.Atl.Blk.Sqdn. (Sep–Oct 1861); sick lv. (Oct–Dec 1861); cdr, *Pinola*, W.Gulf Blk.Sqdn. (Jan–Oct 1862); cdr, *Sangamon*, N.Atl.Blk.Sqdn. (Nov 1862–Jan 1863); flt.capt, N.Atl.Blk.Sqdn., *Minnesota* (Jan–Oct 1863); cdr, *Florida*, then cdr, *Keystone State*, N.Atl.Blk.Sqdn. (Nov 1863–Nov 1864); cdr, *Muscoota*, N.Atl.Blk.Sqdn. (Nov–Dec 1864); *Metacomet*, W.Gulf Blk.Sqdn. (Dec 1864–Aug 1865); w.o. (Aug–Sep 1865); cdr, *Shamokin*, Braz. coast (Sep 1865–Jun 1868); return home and w.o. (Jun–Sep 1868); member, Naval Exam. and Ret. Bds., Philadelphia (Oct 1868–Mar 1869); w.o. (Mar–Dec 1869); insp. of ord., Navy Yard, Norfolk, VA (Jan–Sep 1870); Navy Yard, Philadelphia (Sep 1870–Feb 1872); cdr, *Powhatan*, N.Atl.Sqdn. (Feb 1872–Jul 1873); w.o. (Jul–Aug 1873); exec.off., Navy Yard, Washington, DC (Sep 1873–Oct 1874); w.o. (Oct 1874–Oct 1877); cdr, Naval Sta., League Island, PA (Nov 1877–Jan 1881); w.o. (Jan 1881–Apr 1882); cdr, S.Atl.Sta., *Brooklyn* (Jun 1882–Feb 1883); cdr, Asia.Sta., *Richmond* (Apr–Oct 1883); placed on Ret.Lst. (29 Oct 1883).

Career Highlights Saw action in the attacks on Tuscan and Tabasco in 1847 during the war with Mexico. Participated in attack upon the Confederate forts at Hatteras Inlet, on the lower Mississippi, and in capture of New Orleans. In the attack on Mobile Bay, helped plan and execute clearing of torpedoes from the channels in the Bay.

JOHN ADOLPHUS BERNARD
DAHLGREN
1809–1870

JOHN ADOLPHUS BERNARD DAHLGREN Born in Philadelphia on 13 Nov 1809, son of Bernard Ulrich and Martha (Rowan) Dahlgren. Married Mary Clement Bunker on 8 Jan 1839: seven children. Married again to Sarah Madeleine Vinton Goddard on 2 Aug 1865: three children. Died at the Washington Navy Yard on 12 Jul 1870. Buried in Philadelphia's Laurel Hill Cemetery.

Ranks Act.Midn (1 Feb 1826); PMidn (28 Apr 1832); Lt (8 Mar 1837); Cdr (14 Sep 1855); Capt (16 Jul 1862); RAdm (7 Feb 1863); died (12 Jul 1870).

Career Summary Received appointment from PA (1 Feb 1826); *Macedonian*, Braz.Sqdn. (Apr 1826–Nov 1828); l.o.a. (Nov 1828–Jun 1829); *Ontario*, Med.Sqdn. (Jun 1829–Nov 1831); l.o.a. (Nov 1831–Jan 1832); w.o. (Jan–Apr 1832); l.o.a. and w.o. (Apr 1832–Apr 1833); rec. ship *Sea Gull*, Philadelphia (Apr–Jun 1833); l.o.a. (Jun 1833–Feb 1834); rec. ship *Sea Gull*, Philadelphia (Feb 1834); cst.surv. duty (Feb 1834–Jun 1838); l.o.a. and w.o. (Jun 1838–May 1842); rec. ship *Experiment*, Philadelphia (May 1842–Aug 1843); flag lt, Med.Sqdn., *Cumberland* (Aug 1843–Nov 1845); l.o.a. and w.o. (Nov 1845–Jan 1847); spec.ord. duty, Navy Dept., Washington, DC (Jan–Mar 1847); ord. duty, Navy Yard, Washington, DC (Mar 1847–Feb 1857); temp. duty, Naval School, Annapolis, MD (Oct 1847); cdr, ord. prac. ship *Plymouth* (Feb–Nov 1857); in charge of ord., Navy Yard, Washington, DC, and to continue on prac. ship *Plymouth* (Nov 1857–Apr 1861); cdr, Navy Yard, Washington, DC (Apr 1861–Jul 1862); chief, Bur. of Ord., Washington, DC (Jul 1862–Jun 1863); cdr, S.Atl.Blk.Sqdn., *Wabash* (Jul 1863–Jun 1865); w.o. (Jun 1865–Jan 1866); bd. duties, Washington, DC (Jan 1866); w.o. (Jan–May 1866); pres., Bd. of Visitors, USNA (May–Sep 1866); cdr, S.Pac.Sqdn., *Powhatan* (Dec 1866–Jul 1868); chief, Bur. of Ord., Washington, DC (Jul 1868–Jul 1869); comdt., Navy Yard, Washington, DC (Aug 1869–Jul 1870); died (12 Jul 1870).

Career Highlights Famed inventor of much naval ord., including gun named for him and used extensively during Civil War. In charge of ord. activities at Washington Navy Yard from 1845 until the outbreak of Civil War when, owing to resignation and subsequent dismissal of all superior ranking officers, found himself in command of the Yard along with additional duties as chief of the Bur. of Ord. Rewarded by Congress with additional ten years of active duty and rank of rear admiral for his ord. developments. From Jul 1863 commanded S.Atl.Blk.Sqdn., helping to close port of Charleston, SC.

References

Personal Papers: a) 66 items (1847–70) in EMHL. b) 10,000 items (1824–89) in LC. c) 75 items (1843–70) in NHF,LC. d) c.1861–65 in ALP. e) 1 vol. (1855) in NL. f) 1848–1849 in NYHS. g) 2 vols. (1829–85) in NYPL. h) 2 ft. (1823–1945) in GARL. i) 8 items (1850–70) in ASHF. j) 2 items (1864–65) in SCL. k) 1 item, Joshua D. Warren's Journals in NHF,WNY.

Writings: a) *The System of Boat Armament in the United States Navy* (1852). b) *Shells and Shell Guns* (1857). c) *Memoir of Ulrich Dahlgren, by his father, Rear Admiral Dahlgren* (Phil.: 1872). d) *Maritime International Law* (1877).

Selected Additional Sources: a) Sarah Madeleine Vinton Dahlgren, "Biographical Sketch" in her husband's work *Maritime International Law* (1877). b) ———, *Memoir of John A. Dahlgren, Rear Admiral, United States Navy, by his Widow* (New York: 1882). c) Ralph Earle, "John Adolphus Dahlgren (1809–1870)," U.S. Naval Institute *Proceedings* 265 (Mar 1925): 424–36. d) Clarence S. Peterson, *Admiral John A. Dahlgren, Father of U.S. Naval Ordnance* (New York: 1945).

CHARLES HENRY DAVIS Born in Boston, MA, on 16 Jan 1807, son of Daniel and Lois (Freeman) Davis. Attended Harvard University for two years before entering service. In 1842, completed studies at Harvard, taking a degree in math. In 1842, married Harriet Mills, sister of eminent Harvard astronomer Benjamin Pierce. Had six children including Anna, who married Henry Cabot Lodge; Evelyn, who married Brooks Adams; and RAdm Charles

CHARLES HENRY DAVIS
1807–1877

Henry Davis, USN (1845–1921). Died on duty as supt. of Naval Observatory in Washington, DC, on 18 Feb 1877. Buried in Cambridge, MA.

Ranks Act.Midn (12 Aug 1823); PMidn (23 Mar 1829); Lt (3 Mar 1831); Cdr (12 Jun 1854); Capt (15 Nov 1861); Commo (16 Jul 1862); RAdm (7 Feb 1863); died (18 Feb 1877).

Career Summary Received appointment from MA (12 Aug 1823); *United States* then *Dolphin*, S.Pac.Sta. (Oct 1823–Apr 1827); l.o.a. (Apr–Jul 1827); *Erie*, W.Ind.Sta. (Jul 1827–Jun 1828); l.o.a. (Jun 1828–Jun 1829); *Ontario*, Med.Sqdn. (Jun 1829–May 1832); l.o.a. (May 1832–Apr 1833); rec. ship *Columbus*, Boston (Apr–Oct 1833); flag lt, Pac.Sta., *Vincennes* (Oct 1833–Feb 1835); l.o.a. and w.o. (Feb–Dec 1835); Naval Rndv., Boston (Dec 1835–Oct 1836); spec. duty (Oct 1836–Jan 1837); *Independence*, Braz.Sqdn. (Jan 1837–Apr 1840); l.o.a. (Apr–Jul 1840); in ordinary, Boston (Aug–Oct 1840); l.o.a. and w.o. (Oct 1840–Oct 1841); Naval Rndv., Boston (Oct 1841–Apr 1842); cst.surv. duty (Apr 1842–Aug 1843); l.o.a. and w.o. (Aug 1843–Feb 1844); spec. duty, Navy Yard, Boston (Feb–Apr 1844); cst.surv. duty (Apr 1844–Jul 1849); supt., Nautical Almanac Office, Harvard Univ., Cambridge, MA (Jul 1849–Nov 1856); cdr, *St. Mary's*, Pac.Sta. (Dec 1856–Feb 1859); l.o.a. and w.o. (Feb–Aug 1859); supt., Nautical Almanac Office, Harvard Univ., Cambridge, MA (Aug 1859–May 1861); spec. duty, exec.off., Bur. of Detail, Navy Dept., Washington, DC (May–Sep 1861); chief of staff and flt.capt., S.Atl.Blk.Sqdn. (Sep 1861–Jan 1862); Navy Dept., Washington, DC (Feb–Apr 1862); asst.cdr, then cdr, Upper MS Flot. (May–Oct 1862); chief, Bur. of Nav., Washington, DC (Jul 1862–Apr 1865); supt., Naval Observatory, Washington, DC (Apr 1865–May 1867); cdr, S.Atl.Sqdn., *Guerriere* (May 1867–Jul 1869); w.o. (Jul–Aug 1869); spec. duty relating to Isthmian canal (Aug 1869–Sep 1870); cdr, Navy Yard, Norfolk, VA (Oct 1870–Jul 1873); member, L.h. Bd., Washington, DC (Jul 1873–Jan 1874); supt., Naval Observatory, Washington, DC (Feb 1874–Feb 1877); died (18 Feb 1877).

Career Highlights One of the navy's greatest scientists in hydrographic studies and surveys from about 1842 to 1856, publishing numerous works on tides and other related subjects, including helping to establish *American Ephemeris and Nautical Almanac*. Became first supt. of Nautical Almanac Office; eventually helped found National Academy of Sciences in 1863.

In 1857, arranged for surrender of filibuster William Walker and followers, escorting them safely to Panama. A planner and organizer of naval strategy during early months of Civil War, especially with blockade and the expeditions against Hatteras and Port Royal. Served as second in command, and after incapacity of RAdm Andrew Foote [*q.v.*], commander of the Upper MS Gunboat Flot., participating in battle and surrender of Memphis, remaining off Vicksburg until Sep 1862 although appointed chief of Bur. of Nav. in preceding Jul.

References
Personal Papers: RHTRL.
Writings: a) *The Laws of Deposits of the Flood Tides: Its Dynamic Action and Office* (Washington, DC: 1852). b) *Report on Interoceanic Canals and Railroads between the Atlantic and Pacific Oceans* (Washington, DC: 1867). c) ed., *Narrative of the North Polar Expeditions* (Washington, DC: 1876).
Additional Sources: Charles Henry Davis, *Life of Charles Henry Davis, Rear Admiral, 1807–1877* (Boston: 1899).

JOHN LEE DAVIS Born in Carlisle, IN, on 3 Sep 1825, son of John Wesley and Ann (Hoover) Davis. Married Frances Robinson on 2 Dec 1855: one daughter. Died in Washington, DC, on 12 Mar 1889. Buried in Rock Creek Cemetery in Washington, DC.

Ranks Act.Midn (9 Jan 1841); Midn (25 Jan 1842); PMidn (10 Aug 1847); Mstr (14 Sep 1855); Lt (15 Sep 1855); LCdr (16 Jul 1862); Cdr (25 Jul 1866); Capt (14 Feb 1873); Commo (4 Feb 1882); Act.RAdm (19 Dec 1883); RAdm (30 Oct 1885); placed on Ret.Lst. (3 Sep 1887).

JOHN LEE DAVIS
1825–1889

Career Summary Received appointment from IN (9 Jan 1841); w.o. (Jan–Feb 1841); rec. ship *North Carolina*, NY (Feb–Apr 1841); *Fairfield*, Med.Sqdn. (Apr 1841–Jan 1845); l.o.a. (Jan–Feb 1845); *Lexington*, Home Sqdn. (Feb–Jul 1845); *Potomac* and *Porpoise*, Home Sqdn. (Jul 1845–Aug 1846); Naval School, Annapolis, MD (Oct 1846–Aug 1847); *Cumberland*, Home Sqdn. (Sep 1847–Feb 1848); *Plymouth*, *Preble*, then *Dolphin*, E.Ind.Sqdn. (Feb 1848–Feb 1851); l.o.a. (Feb–May 1851); cst.surv. duty (May–Nov 1851); w.o. (Nov 1851–Mar 1852); *Perry*, Afr.Sqdn (Apr 1852–Jul 1854); l.o.a. and w.o. (Jul–Nov 1854); cst.surv. duty (Nov 1854–Oct 1857); *Vandalia*, Pac.Sqdn. (Nov 1857–Jan 1860); l.o.a. (Jan–Apr 1860); w.o. (Apr 1860–Feb 1861); exec.off., *Water Witch*, Gulf Sqdn. (Mar–Nov 1861); exec.off., *Potomac*, W.Gulf Blk.Sqdn. (Nov 1861); exec.off., *Colorado*, W.Gulf Blk.Sqdn. (Nov 1861–Jun 1862); cdr, *Vixen*, S.Atl.Blk.Sqdn. (Jul 1862); cdr, *Wissahickon*, S.Atl.Blk.Sqdn. (Jul 1862–Aug 1863); cdr, *Montauk* (Aug 1863–May 1864); w.o. (May–Jul 1864); cdr, *Sassacus*, N.Atl.Blk.Sqdn. (Jul 1864–May 1865); Navy Yard, Philadelphia (May 1865–Aug 1866); spec.bd. duties (Aug 1866–Jul 1868); Navy Yard, Washington, DC (Sep 1868–Sep 1871); cdr, *Wyoming*, N.Atl.Sta. (Oct 1871–Oct 1872); member, Naval Exam.Bd., USNA (Nov–Dec 1872); w.o. (Dec 1872–Mar 1873); member, L.h. Bd., Washington, DC (Apr 1873–Jan 1877); cdr, *Trenton*, flgs., and *Constellation*, Eur.Sqdn. (Jan 1877–Jan 1880); w.o. (Jan–Dec 1880); member, Bd. of Inspection and Surv. (Dec 1880–Feb 1882); member, Naval Exam.Bd. (Feb 1882–Apr 1883); member, L.h. Bd., Washington, DC (Apr–Nov 1883); cdr, Asia.Sqdn., *Trenton* (Dec 1883–Nov 1886); return home and w.o. (Nov–Dec 1886); pres., Naval Ret.Bd. (Dec 1886–Sep 1887); placed on Ret.Lst. (3 Sep 1887).

BENJAMIN FRANKLIN DAY Born in Plymouth, OH, on 16 Jan 1841, son of Benjamin Franklin and Prussia Brunnel (King) Day. Married Flora Inez Baldwin on 22 Sep 1869: two sons. Died in Rockbridge, VA, on 3 Jul 1933.

Ranks Act.Midn (20 Sep 1858); resigned (24 Nov 1860); reinstated (29 Jun 1861); title changed to Midn (16 Jul 1862); Lt (1 Aug 1862); LCdr (25 Jul 1866); Cdr (8 Aug 1876); Capt (5 Nov 1891); RAdm (29 Mar 1899); retired (28 Mar 1900).

Career Summary Received appointment from OH (20 Sep 1858); USNA (Sep 1858–Nov 1860); resigned (24 Nov 1860); reinstated (29 Jun 1861); USNA (Jun–Oct 1861); *New London*, then *Colorado*, W.Gulf Blk.Sqdn. (Oct 1862–Feb 1864); w.o. (Feb–Mar 1864); *Saugus*, N.Atl.Blk.Sqdn. (Mar 1864–May 1865); w.o. (May–Aug 1865); *Tuscarora*, Pac.Sqdn. (Aug 1865–Dec 1867); w.o. (Jan–Apr 1868); *Contoocook*, flgs., and *Albany*, N.Atl.Sqdn. (Apr 1868–Jan 1870); w.o. (Jan–Mar 1870); *Alaska*, Navy Yard, Boston (Mar 1870); w.o. (Mar–Jun 1870); Hydrographic Office, Washington, DC (Jun 1870–Jan 1871); *Ticonderoga*, Navy Yard, Boston (Jan–Apr 1871); w.o. (Apr–Jun 1871); *Congress*, spec.serv. and Eur.Sta. (Jun 1871–Mar 1874); *Shenandoah*, Key West, FL (Mar 1874); *Wabash*, Navy Yard, Boston (Apr–Jun 1874); exec.off., rec. ship *New Hampshire*, Norfolk, VA (Jul 1874–Aug 1875); l.o.a. (Aug–Dec 1875); cdr, *Manhattan*, N.Atl.Sta. (Dec 1875–Jul 1876); w.o. (Jul 1876–Apr 1877); cdr, naval force, Rio Grande River, *Rio Bravo* (Apr 1877–Feb 1878); w.o. (Feb 1878–May 1879); Navy Yard, Norfolk, VA (May 1879–Mar 1880); w.o. (Mar 1880–May 1881); torp. instruction, Newport, RI (Jun–Sep 1881); w.o. (Sep–Nov 1881); insp., 8th L.h. Dist., New Orleans (Jan 1882–Jan 1884); w.o. (Jan 1884–May 1885); cdr, *Mohican*, Pac.Sta. (May 1885–Aug 1888); w.o. (Aug 1888–May 1889); equip.off., Navy Yard, Boston (May 1889–Feb 1892); capt.yd., Navy Yard, NY (Feb–Jun 1892); w.o. (Jun–Dec 1892); cdr, *Boston*, spec. cruise, Hawaiian Islands (Feb–Dec 1893); w.o. and l.o.a. (Dec 1893–May 1894); cdr, *Baltimore*, Asia.Sta. (Jul 1894–Feb 1896); l.o.a. (Feb–Apr 1896); pres., Steel Bd. (Apr 1896–Jan 1897); member, Naval Exam. and Ret. Bd. and other bd. duties (Jan 1897–Mar 1900); retired (28 Mar 1900).

JOHN DECAMP Born in NJ on 5 Oct 1812. Died on 24 Jun 1875 in Burlington, NJ.

Ranks Midn (1 Oct 1827); PMidn (10 Jun 1833); Lt (28 Feb 1838); Cdr (14 Sep 1855); Capt (16 Jul 1862); transferred to Ret.Lst. (13 Mar 1869); Commo on Ret.Lst. to date from 8 Dec 1867; RAdm on Ret.Lst. (13 Jul 1870).

Career Summary Received appointment from FL (1 Oct 1827); Naval School, NY (Jul–Oct 1828); *Vandalia*, Braz.Sqdn. (Oct 1828–Nov 1829); *Hudson*, Braz.Sqdn. (Nov 1829–Aug 1831); l.o.a. (Aug–Dec 1831); *Peacock*, Braz.Sta. (Dec 1831–Mar 1834); *Enterprise*, Braz.Sqdn. (Mar–Apr 1834); l.o.a.

JOHN DeCAMP
1812–1875

(Apr–Aug 1834); *Potomac*, Med.Sqdn. (Aug–Nov 1834); home and sick lv. (Nov 1834–Jul 1835); Navy Yard, NY (Jul 1835–Jun 1836); *Constellation*, W.Ind.Sqdn. (Sep 1836–Jul 1837); *Concord*, W.Ind.Sqdn. (Oct 1837–Jun 1838); rec. ship *Columbus*, Boston (Oct 1838–Sep 1839); *United States*, Home Sqdn. (Oct 1839–Mar 1840); *Potomac*, Braz.Sqdn. (Mar 1840–Aug 1842); l.o.a. (Aug 1842–Sep 1843); rec. ship *North Carolina*, NY (Sep–Oct 1843); *Boston*, Braz.Sqdn. (Oct 1843–Jan 1846); l.o.a. (Jan–Jul 1846); *Mississippi*, flgs., and *Supply*, W.Ind.Sqdn. (Jul 1846–Sep 1847); l.o.a. and w.o. (Sep 1847–Apr 1849); *Falmouth*, Pac.Sqdn. (Apr 1849–Nov 1850); l.o.a. (Feb 1850–Feb. 1853); flgs. *Constitution*, Afr.Sqdn. (Feb–Nov 1853); cdr, prize schooner *H. N. Campbell* (Nov 1853–Jan 1854); w.o. (Jan–Sep 1854); Navy Yard, NY (Sep 1854–May 1856); w.o. (May 1856–Oct 1857); Insp., 12th L.h. Dist., San Francisco (Oct 1857–Jan 1860); w.o. (Jan 1860–Jan 1861); cdr, *Relief*, Gulf Blk.Sqdn. (Jan–Oct 1861); cdr, *Iroquois*, W.Gulf Blk.Sqdn. (Dec 1861–Mar 1862); cdr, *Wissahickon*, W.Gulf Blk.Sqdn. (Mar–Aug 1862); w.o. (Aug 1862–Aug 1863); cdr, *Wabash*, S.Atl.Blk.Sqdn. (Aug 1863–Oct 1864); w.o. (Oct 1864–Feb 1865); cdr, rec. ship *Constellation*, Norfolk, VA (Feb–Oct 1865); sick lv. (Oct 1865–Jan 1866); cdr, *Potomac*, Pensacola, FL (Jan 1866–Jul 1867); cdr, rec. ship *Potomac*, League Island, PA (Jul 1867–Oct 1870); transferred to Ret.Lst. (13 Mar 1869).

References
Personal Papers: 100 items (1805–77) in NYHS.

JOHN CHARLES PHILIP DE KRAFFT Born in Washington, DC, on 12 Jan 1826, son of Frederick Cornelius de Krafft, who served as a midn until 1810. Married, with one son. Died at his home in Washington, DC, on 29 Oct 1885. Buried in Arlington National Cemetery.

Ranks Midn (19 Oct 1841); PMidn (10 Aug 1847); Mstr (14 Sep 1855); Lt (15 Sep 1855); LCdr (16 Jul 1862); Cdr (25 Jul 1866); Capt (20 Nov 1872); Commo (1 Oct 1881); RAdm (2 Jun 1885); died (29 Oct 1885).

Career Summary Received appointment from IL (19 Oct 1841); *Independence*, Navy Yard, NY, and flgs., Home Sqdn. (Dec 1841–Jun 1842); *Congress*, then *Preble*, Med.Sqdn. (Jun 1842–Sep 1843); l.o.a. (Sep–Nov 1843); *Raritan*, Norfolk, VA, and *Cumberland*, Home Sqdn. (Nov 1843–Jan 1847); l.o.a. (Jan–Feb 1847); *Union*, Navy Yard, Norfolk, VA (Feb–May 1847); w.o. (May–Jun 1847); *Ohio*, Pac.Sqdn. (Jun 1847–Jan 1848); Naval School, Annapolis, MD (Jan–Jul 1848); l.o.a. (Jul–Nov 1848); *Vixen*, Home Sqdn. (Nov 1848); *Raritan*, Home Sqdn. (Nov 1848–Apr 1850); l.o.a. (Apr–Jul 1850); Naval Observatory, Washington, DC (Jul 1850–Feb 1851); l.o.a. (Feb–May 1851); *Plymouth*, Home Sqdn. (May 1851); *Vixen*, Home Sqdn. (May 1851–Apr 1852); l.o.a. (Apr–Dec 1852); cst.surv. duty (Dec 1852–Nov 1853); w.o. (Nov 1853–

JOHN CHARLES PHILIP
DE KRAFFT
1826–1885

May 1854); *Michigan*, on Great Lakes (May 1854–Oct. 1855); w.o. (Oct 1855–Mar 1856); *John Adams*, Pac.Sqdn. (Apr 1856–Apr 1858); l.o.a. (Apr–Jul 1858); *Michigan*, on Great Lakes (Aug 1858–Sep 1859); w.o. (Sep 1859–Apr 1860); *Niagara*, spec.serv. (May 1860–Jun 1862); Navy Yard, Washington, DC (Jun 1862–Sep 1863); w.o. (Sep–Oct 1863); cdr, *Conemaugh*, W.Gulf Blk.Sqdn. (Oct 1863–Feb 1866); w.o. (Feb–Mar 1866); ord. duty, Navy Yards, Philadelphia and Washington, DC (Mar–Dec 1866); w.o. (Dec 1866–Mar 1867); spec. duty, Philadelphia (Mar 1867–Feb 1868); flt.capt and chief of staff, N.Atl.Sqdn., *Contoocook* (Feb 1868–Aug 1869); w.o. (Aug–Oct 1869); spec. duty, Philadelphia (Oct 1869–Oct 1870); Navy Yard, Portsmouth, NH (Oct 1870–Sep 1872); cdr, *California*, and chief of staff, N.Pac.Sta. (Oct 1872–Sep 1873); cdr, flgs. *Richmond*, N.Pac.Sta. (Sep 1873–Mar 1874); cdr, flgs. *Hartford*, Asia.Sqdn. (May 1874–Mar 1875); l.o.a. (Mar–Oct 1875); capt.yd., Navy Yard, Washington, DC (Oct 1875–Jan 1876); w.o. (Jan 1876–Sep 1877); Navy Yard, Washington, DC (Nov 1877–Jul 1880); temp. comdt., Navy Yard, Washington, DC (Jan–Jul 1880); hydrographer, Bur. of Nav., Washington, DC (Jul 1880–Jun 1883); w.o. (Jun–Aug 1883); pres., Bd. of Inspection and Survey (Aug 1883–Oct 1885); w.o. (Oct 1885); died (29 Oct 1885).

GEORGE DEWEY
1837–1917

GEORGE DEWEY Born on 26 Dec 1837 in Montpelier, VT, the son of Dr. Julius Yemans and Sophia Dewey. Attended Norwich Univ. before his appointment to the USNA. Married Susan Boardman Goodwin, daughter of the Governor of NH, on 24 Oct 1867. Had one son. Remarried on 9 Nov 1899 to Mildred MacLean Hazen, widow of BGen William B. Hazen, USA. Died at his home in Washington, DC, on 16 Jan 1917. Body first interred at Arlington National Cemetery, then reinterred at Episcopal Cathedral in Washington, DC.

Ranks Act.Midn (23 Sep 1854); Midn (11 Jun 1858); PMidn (19 Jan 1861); Mstr (23 Feb 1861); Lt (19 Apr 1861); LCdr (3 Mar 1865); Cdr (13 Apr 1872); Capt (27 Sep 1884); Chief of Bur. of Equip. and Recruiting with rank of Commo (1 Aug 1889–30 Jun 1893); Commo (28 Feb 1896); RAdm (11 May 1898); Adm of the Navy (2 Mar 1899); died (16 Jan 1917).

Career Summary Received appointment from VT (23 Sep 1854); USNA (Sep 1854–Jun 1858); *Wabash*, Med.Sqdn. (Jun 1858–Dec 1859); l.o.a. (Dec 1859–May 1860); *Pawnee* then *Powhatan*, W.Ind.Sqdn. (Jun–Dec 1860); w.o. (Dec 1860–Apr 1861); exec.off., *Mississippi*, W.Gulf Blk.Sqdn. (May 1861–Mar 1863); exec.off., *Monongahela*, flgs., and *Brooklyn*, W.Gulf Blk.Sqdn. (Mar–Sep 1863); w.o. (Sep–Nov 1863); *Agawam*, N.Atl.Blk.Sqdn., then exec.off., *Colorado*, Navy Yard, Portsmouth, NH (Nov 1863–Feb 1865); exec.off., *Kearsarge*, Eur.Sta. (Mar 1865–Feb 1866); *Canandaigua*, Eur.Sta. (Feb–

Aug 1866); exec.off., flgs. *Colorado*, Eur.Sqdn. (Aug 1866–
Aug 1867); w.o. (Aug–Sep 1867); USNA (Oct 1867–Sep 1870);
cdr, *Narragansett*, spec.serv. (Oct 1870–Feb 1871); cdr, store-
ship *Supply* (Feb–Jul 1871); Navy Yard, Boston (Jul–Dec 1871);
Torp.Sta., Newport, RI (Dec 1871–Jan 1873); spec. duty (Feb–
Mar 1873); cdr, *Narragansett*, Pac.Surv. (Mar 1873–Jul 1875);
w.o. (Jul–Aug 1875); insp., 2nd L.h. Dist., Tompkinsville, NY
(Oct 1875–Aug 1877); member, then secretary, L.h. Bd.,
Washington, DC (Sep 1877–Oct 1882); cdr, *Juniata*, Asia.Sta.
(Oct 1882–May 1883); sick lv. (May 1883–Jul 1884); Navy
Dept., Washington, DC (Aug 1884); w.o. (Aug–Sep 1884);
cdr, *Dolphin*, Chester, PA (Oct 1884–Mar 1885); cdr, flgs.
Pensacola, Eur.Sta. (Mar 1885–Feb 1888); w.o. (Feb 1888–Jul
1889); chief, Bur. of Equipment and Recruiting, Washington,
DC (1 Aug 1889–30 Jun 1893); member, L.h. Bd., Washing-
ton, DC (May 1893–Oct 1895); various bd. duties (Jul 1893–
Jan 1898); pres., Bd. of Inspection and Survey (Jul 1893–Nov
1897); cdr, Asia.Sta., *Olympia* (Jan 1898–Oct 1899); Navy
Dept., Washington, DC (Oct 1899–Mar 1900); pres., Gen.Bd.,
Washington, DC (Mar 1900–Jan 1917); chairman, Joint Army
and Navy Bd., Washington, DC (1903–Jan 1917); died (16
Jan 1917).

Career Highlights Navigated the *Mississippi* on 24 Apr
1862 past Fts. Jackson and St. Philip. In following year during
run past Port Hudson, *Mississippi* ran aground and had to
be burned to avoid capture: received praise for evacuating
crew while under fire.

Victory at Manila Bay on 1 May 1898 assured hero's
place. Made admiral of the navy, created for him and highest
rank ever held at that time. From 1900 to death, served as
first and only pres. of navy's new Gen.Bd. established to
advise the secretary of the navy on matters such as war
strategies against Germany and Japan (Plan Black and Plan
Orange, respectively), and programs to build large battleship
fleets, gain overseas naval bases, and construct an isthmian
canal.

References

Personal Papers: a) 25,000 items (1820–1919) in LC. b) 4
ft. of papers (1893–1917) in NHF,WNY. c) 14 items (1890–
1943) in NHF,LC. d) 1 item in Dr. George V. W. Voorhees
Papers, ASAL. e) 2 items (1864–1865, 1898) in NYPL. f) $1/4$
ft. (1844–1912) in GARL. g) some letters to Dewey in Elwell
Stephen Otis Papers, Univ. of Rochester Lib., Rochester, NY.
h) Dewey's Despatches from Manila Bay, 1898: Chicago Historical Society.

Writings: *Autobiography of George Dewey, Admiral of the
Navy* (NY: 1913).

Selected Additional Sources: a) Dewey, Adelbert M.,
*The Life of George Dewey, Rear Admiral, U.S.N. and Dewey
Family History* (NY: 1898). b) ———, *The Life and Letters of
Admiral Dewey* (NY: 1899). c) Ellis, Edward S., *Dewey and*

Other Commanders (NY: 1899). d) Clemes, Will M., *Life of Admiral George Dewey* (NY: 1899). f) Halstead, Murat, *Life and Achievements of Admiral Dewey from Montpelier to Manila* (Chicago: 1899). g) Hamm, Margherita A., *Dewey, the Defender: A Life Sketch of America's Great Admiral* (NY: 1899). h) Handford, Thomas W., *Admiral Dewey, the Hero of Manila* (Chicago: 1899). i) Stickney, Joseph L., *Life and Glorious Deeds of Admiral Dewey* (Chicago: 1899). j) Williams, Henry L., *Taking Manila; or, In the Philippines with Dewey* (NY: 1899). k) Young, Louis S., *Life and Heroic Deeds of Admiral Dewey* (NY: 1899). l) Fiske, Bradley A., "Admiral Dewey: An Appreciation," U.S. Naval Institute *Proceedings* 169 (Mar 1917): 434–36. m) Sargent, Nathan. *Admiral Dewey and the Manila Campaign* (Washington, DC: 1947). n) West, Richard S., *Admirals of Empire: The Combined Story of George Dewey, Alfred Thayer Mahan, Winfield Scott Schley, and William Thomas Sampson* (Indianapolis: 1948). o) Spector, Ronald, *Admiral of the New Navy: The Life and Career of George Dewey* (Baton Rouge: 1974).

EDWARD DONALDSON
1816–1889

EDWARD DONALDSON Born in Baltimore, MD, on 17 Nov 1816. Died at his home in Baltimore on 15 May 1889.

Ranks Cadet Midn (21 Jul 1835); PMidn (22 Jun 1841); Mstr (20 May 1847); Lt (23 Oct 1847); Cdr (16 Jul 1862); Capt (25 Jul 1866); Commo (28 Sep 1871); RAdm (21 Sep 1876); retired (29 Sep. 1876).

Career Summary Received appointment from MD (21 Jul 1835); *Falmouth*, W.Ind.Sqdn. (Jul–Aug 1835); l.o.a. (Aug–Nov 1835); *Warren*, then *Vandalia*, W.Ind.Sqdn. (Nov 1835–Feb 1837); l.o.a. (Feb–May 1837); rec. ship *Fox*, Baltimore (May–Sep 1837); *Columbia*, E.Ind.Sqdn. (Oct 1837–Jun 1840); l.o.a. (Jun–Sep 1840); Naval School, Philadelphia (Sep 1840–Jun 1841); *Phoenix* and *Wave*, Mosquito Flt. (Aug 1841–Oct 1842); l.o.a. (Oct–Dec 1842); rec. ship *Pennsylvania*, Norfolk, VA (Dec 1842–Jan 1843); *Truxtun*, spec.serv. (Feb 1843–Jan 1844); l.o.a. (Jan–Mar 1844); Depot of Charts, Washington, DC (Mar 1844); l.o.a. (Mar–May 1844); rec. ship *Ontario*, Baltimore (May–Oct 1844); *Erie*, Afr.Sqdn. (Oct 1844–Apr 1845); l.o.a. (Apr–Sep 1845); cst.surv. duty (Oct 1845–Mar 1847); *Vanderbilt*, cst.surv. duty (Mar 1847–Jan 1848); *Plymouth*, E.Ind.Sqdn. (Feb 1848–Feb 1851); l.o.a. (Feb–Aug 1851); Naval Rndv., Baltimore (Aug 1851–Nov 1852); *Water Witch*, survey and expl. duty (Nov 1852–Apr 1854); w.o. (Apr–Oct 1854); rec. ship *Ontario*, Baltimore (Nov 1854–Dec 1855); *Merrimack*, spec.serv. (Jan 1856–Apr 1857); *Roanoke*, Norfolk, VA (Apr–May 1857); l.o.a. (May–Oct 1857); rec. ship *Allegheny*, Baltimore (Oct–Dec 1857); sick lv. and w.o. (Dec 1857–May 1858); rec. ship *Allegheny*, Baltimore (May 1858–May 1859); *San Jacinto*, Afr.Sqdn. (Jun–Nov 1859); l.o.a. (Nov 1859–Sep 1860); rec. ship, *Pennsylvania*, Norfolk, VA (Sep 1860–Apr 1861); Naval Rndv., Philadelphia (Apr–Jul

1861); temp. duty, *Keystone State*, S.Atl.Sqdn. (Jul–Oct 1861);
cdr, *Keystone State*, S.Atl.Sqdn. (Oct–Nov 1861); cdr, *Scioto*,
W.Gulf Blk.Sqdn. (Nov 1861–Jul 1862); sick lv. and w.o. (Jul–
Aug 1862); cdr, rec. ship *Princeton*, Philadelphia (Aug 1862–
Jun 1863); cdr, *Keystone State*, N.Atl.Blk.Sqdn. (Jun 1863–Feb
1864); cdr, *Seminole*, W.Gulf Blk.Sqdn. (Feb–Sep 1864); ord.
duty, Baltimore, (Sep 1864–Apr 1865); cdr, *Susquehanna*, NY
(Apr 1865); sick lv. (Apr–Oct 1865); cdr, rec. ship, *Allegheny*,
Baltimore (Oct 1865–Mar 1868); w.o. (Mar–Aug 1868); mem-
ber, court-martial bd., NY (Aug–Sep 1868); w.o. (Sep 1868–
Mar 1869); Navy Yard, Norfolk, VA (Mar 1869–Feb 1870);
w.o. (Feb 1870–Feb 1871); Navy Yard, Norfolk, VA (Feb–Sep
1871); w.o. (Oct 1871–May 1872); cdr, Naval Sta., Mound
City, IL (Jun 1872–May 1873); w.o. (May 1873–Sep 1876);
retired (29 Sep 1876).

References
Personal Papers: 10 items (1834–77) in MD Historical
Society.

MICHAEL COYLE DRENNAN Born in Easton, PA, on
10 Oct 1838, son of Cornelius and Bridget (Cooke) Drennan.
Early education at Minerva Academy in Easton. Received
the M.D. from the Univ. of PA Medical School. Married
Ellen Johnson in Jun 1864: one daughter. Died on 23 Mar
1915 in Easton, PA, where he was buried.

Ranks Act.Asst.Surg. (15 Apr 1863); resigned (18 Mar
1865); Act.Asst.Surg. (9 Feb 1867); Asst.Surg. (30 Jun 1868);
PAsst.Surg. (13 Jun 1870); Surg. (20 Apr 1879); Medl.Insp.
(28 May 1895); Medl.Dir. (16 Apr 1899); placed on Ret.Lst.
as Medl.Dir. with rank of RAdm (24 Oct 1899).

Career Summary Received appointment from PA as
Act.Asst.Surg. (15 Apr 1863); *Commodore Jones*, NY (Apr–
Dec 1863); w.o. (Dec 1863–Jul 1864); *St. Lawrence*, Hampton
Roads, VA (Jul–Dec 1864); w.o. (Dec 1864–Feb 1865); *Emma*,
Hampton Roads, VA (Feb–Mar 1865); resigned (18 Mar 1865);
reappointed (9 Feb 1867); Naval Rndv., Philadelphia (Feb
1867–Jun 1868); storeship *Purveyor*, NY (Jun 1868–Apr 1869);
w.o. (Apr–May 1869); *Macedonian*, USNA (May–Sep 1869);
Naval Hosp., Norfolk, VA (Oct 1869–Oct 1870); *Nantasket*,
then *Congress*, N.Atl.Sta. (Oct 1870–May 1871); sick lv. (May–
Aug 1871); USNA (Aug 1871–Apr 1872); *Portsmouth*, then
Lancaster, S.Atl.Sta. (Apr 1872–Sep 1873); return home and
w.o. (Sep–Nov 1873); recruiting duty, Chicago (Nov–Dec
1873); w.o. (Dec 1873–Mar 1874); rec. ship *Potomac*, League
Island, PA (Mar–Apr 1874); *Pawnee*, N.Atl.Sta. (Apr–Sep
1874); l.o.a. and w.o. (Sep–Dec 1874); Navy Yard, NY (Dec
1874–May 1875); *Ashuelot*, Asia.Sta. (May 1875–Jan 1877);
Naval Hosp., Yokohama, Japan (Jan 1877–Sep 1878); return
home and w.o. (Sep 1878–Jul 1879); Naval Sta., New London,
CT (Jul 1879–Dec 1881); *Enterprise*, spec.serv. (Jan–Nov 1882);
Kearsarge, Eur.Sta. (Nov 1882–Jun 1885); return home and

MICHAEL COYLE DRENNAN
1838–1915

w.o. (Jun–Aug 1885); USNA (Sep–Oct 1885); w.o. (Oct–Nov 1885); prac. ship *New Hampshire*, Newport, RI (Nov 1885–Nov 1886); l.o.a. (Nov 1886–Sep 1887); USNA (Sep–Oct 1887); w.o. (Oct 1887–Feb 1888); rec. ship *Vermont*, NY (Feb–Nov 1888); *Atlanta*, spec.serv. (Nov 1888–Oct 1891); l.o.a. and w.o. (Oct 1891–May 1892); spec. duty, USNA (May–Jun 1892); Navy Yard, Norfolk, VA (Jul 1892–Mar 1893); rec. ship *Vermont*, NY (Apr 1893–Aug 1895); flt.surg., N.Atl.Sqdn., *New York* (Aug 1895–Apr 1898); home and w.o. (Apr–May 1898); bd. duty, USNA (May–Jun 1898); rec. duty, Navy Yard, NY (Jun–Jul 1898); home and w.o. (Jul–Aug 1898); bd. duty, USNA (Sep–Oct 1898); recruiting duty, Chicago (Nov–Dec 1898); Marine Recruiting Rndv., Philadelphia (Jan–Oct 1899); placed on Ret.Lst. (24 Oct 1899).

SAMUEL FRANCIS DU PONT
1803–1865

SAMUEL FRANCIS DU PONT Born at Goodstay in Bergen Point [present day Bayonne], NJ, on 27 Sep 1803, son of Victor Marie and Gabrielle Josephine de la Fite (de Pelleport) Du Pont. Attended boarding school at Mount Airy College near Germantown, PA, from 1812 to 1817, when he entered the navy at the age of twelve. Again attended Mount Airy College briefly in 1820. Married Sophie Madeleine Du Pont, first cousin and daughter of the founder of the Du Pont powder firm, on 27 Jun 1833. Died in Philadelphia on 23 Jun 1865. Buried at his residence near Wilmington, DE.

Ranks Midn (19 Dec 1815); Lt (28 Apr 1826); Cdr (28 Oct 1842); Capt (14 Sep 1855); RAdm (16 Jul 1862); died (23 Jun 1865).

Career Summary Received appointment from DE (19 Dec 1815); remained in school in PA (Dec 1815–Feb 1817); *Franklin*, Med.Sqdn. (May 1817–Nov 1818); *Erie*, Med.Sqdn. (Nov 1818–Jan 1820); Navy Yard, Philadelphia, and l.o.a. to study (Mar 1820–Feb 1821); Navy Dept., Washington, DC (Feb–Apr 1821); flgs. *Constitution*, Med.Sqdn. (Apr 1821–Jul 1822); home and examination (Jul–Sep 1822); *Congress*, W.Ind. and S.Atl Sqdns. (Sep 1822–Dec 1823); l.o.a. and w.o. (Dec 1823–Jul 1824); flgs. *North Carolina*, Med.Sqdn. (Jul 1824–Dec 1826); *Porpoise*, Med.Sqdn. (Dec 1826–May 1827); home and l.o.a. (May 1827–Jun 1829); *Ontario*, Med.Sqdn. (Jun 1829–Apr 1832); home, l.o.a., and w.o. (Apr 1832–Dec 1835); exec.off., *Warren*, Gulf of Mexico (Dec 1835–Apr 1836); exec.off., *Constellation*, Gulf of Mexico (Apr–Jun 1836); cdr, *Grampus*, spec.serv., Caribbean (Jun–Nov 1836); home, l.o.a., and w.o. (Nov 1836–Sep 1838); *Ohio*, flgs., Med. and Afr. Sqdns., then as rec. ship, Boston (Sep 1838–Apr 1840); home and w.o. (Apr–Oct 1840); l.o.a. (Oct–Nov 1840); *North Carolina*, Med.Sqdn. (Nov 1840–Jul 1841); home and w.o. (Jul 1841–Jun 1842); court-martial duty, NY (Jun–Oct 1842); member, Bd. to Review Navy Regulations, Washington, DC (Nov 1842–Jan 1843); home and w.o. (Feb–Jul 1843); cdr, *Perry*, Braz.Sqdn. (Aug 1843–

Jan 1844); home and sick lv. (Jan 1844–Aug 1845); member, bd. to consider establishing a naval school at Annapolis, MD (Aug–Sep 1845); cdr, flgs. *Congress*, Pac.Sqdn. (Oct 1845–Jul 1846); cdr, *Cyane*, Pac.Sqdn. (Jul 1846–Oct 1848); l.o.a. (Oct 1848–Jun 1849); member, spec.bd. on examinations and curriculum at Naval School, Annapolis, MD (Jun–Sep 1849); appointed, then rejected, as supt., Naval School, Annapolis, MD (Sep–Oct 1849); l.o.a. (Oct 1849–Jan 1850); bd. duties (Jan–May 1850); cdr, rec. ship *Union*, Philadelphia (May 1850–May 1852); member, L.h. Bd., Washington, DC (Apr 1851–Apr 1857); member, Naval Efficiency Bd., Washington, DC (Jun–Sep 1855); cdr, *Minnesota*, Asia.Sta. (Apr 1857–May 1859); l.o.a. and w.o. (May 1859–Dec 1860); pres., Bd. of Examiners, USNA (Dec 1860); cdr, Navy Yard, Philadelphia (Dec 1860–Sep 1861); senior member, Strategy Bd., Washington, DC (Jun 1861); cdr, S.Atl.Blk.Sqdn., *Wabash* (Sep 1861–Jul 1863); inactive duty (Jul 1863–Mar 1865); member, Naval Promotion Bd. (Mar 1865); died (23 Jun 1865).

Career Highlights Sat on the board which supported Navy Secretary George Bancroft's idea of establishing a single naval school at Annapolis, MD. In the Mexican War, landed troops at San Diego; cleared Gulf of CA of Mexican naval forces; and participated in actions at Guaymas, Mazatlan, La Paz, and San Jose, efforts for which he received official commendation. Worked for improvement of Naval Academy and for development of steam power in the service. Headed Naval Efficiency Board in 1855 and recommended retirement of many naval officers, thereby assisting in developing a retirement policy. As one of the highest ranking officers at outset of Civil War, was very influential in planning navy's strategy and operations. As commander of S.Atl.Blk.Sqdn., successfully directed attacks and capture of Port Royal, SC, in Nov 1861, thus making the Union blockade more efficient and tighter. Under severe government and public pressure to take Charleston Harbor, led unsuccessful ironclad attacks in Apr 1863.

References

Personal Papers: a) c.49,000 items (1806–88) in EMHL. b) 3 items (1862–63) in SCL. c) 2 items (1845–46) in BLYU. d) logbook (1846–47) *Cyane* kept by Du Pont and William Merrine in SC Historical Society, Charleston, SC.

Writings: a) *Report on the National Defenses* (Washington, DC: 1852). b) *Official Despatches and Letters of Rear Admiral Du Pont, U.S. Navy, 1846–1848* (Wilmington, DE: 1883). c) *Samuel Francis Du Pont: A Selection from his Civil War Letters* 3 vols. ed. John D. Hayes (Ithaca, NY: 1969).

Additional Sources: a) Du Pont, Henry A., *Rear-Admiral Samuel Francis Du Pont, United States Navy: A Biography* (NY: 1926). b) Merrill, James M., *Du Pont, the Making of an Admiral: A Biography of Samuel Francis Du Pont* (NY: 1986).

GEORGE FOSTER EMMONS
1811–1884

GEORGE FOSTER EMMONS Born in Clarendon, VT, on 23 Aug 1811, son of Horatio and Abigail (Foster) Emmons. Married Frances Thornton on 10 Jan 1843: three sons and one daughter. Died in Princeton, NJ, on 23 Jul 1884. Buried in Baltimore.

Ranks Midn (1 Apr 1828); PMidn (14 Jun 1834); Act.Lt (11 Jul 1838); Lt (25 Feb 1841); Cdr (28 Jan 1856); Capt (7 Feb 1863); Commo (20 Sep 1868); RAdm (25 Nov 1872); placed on Ret.Lst. (23 Aug 1873).

Career Summary Appointed from VT (1 Apr 1828); w.o. (Apr–Jul 1828); Naval School, NY (Jul 1828–May 1829); Naval Sta., NY (May 1829–Jan 1830); *Brandywine*, spec.serv., W.Ind. and Med. Sqdns. (Jan 1830–Jul 1833); l.o.a. (Jul–Oct 1833); Naval School, NY (Oct 1833–Jun 1834); l.o.a. and w.o. (Jun 1834–Nov 1836); *Consort, Pioneer*, then *Macedonian*, W.Ind.Sqdn. (Nov 1836–1838); *Peacock*, U.S.Expl.Expd. (1838–Jul 1841); *Flying Fish*, U.S.Expl.Expd. (Jul–Nov 1841); flgs. *Vincennes*, U.S.Expl.Expd. (Nov 1841–Jun 1842); w.o. (Jun–Sep 1842); rec. ship *Ontario*, Baltimore (Sep 1842–Sep 1843); *Boston*, Braz.Sqdn. (Sep 1843–Jan 1846); l.o.a. and w.o. (Jan–Oct 1846); Naval Rndv., Baltimore (Oct 1846–Jun 1847); *Ohio, Warren*, then *Southampton*, Pac.Sqdn. (Jun 1847–Jan 1850); w.o. (Jan–Sep 1850); Bur. of Construction and Repair, Washington, DC (Sep 1850–Jun 1853); duty on, then cdr, *Savannah*, Braz.Sqdn. (Jun 1853–Nov 1856); l.o.a. and w.o. (Nov 1856–Apr 1861); spec. duty, Washington, DC (Apr–May 1861); member, L.h. Bd., Washington, DC (May–Oct 1861); cdr, *St. Mary's, Hatteras, R. R. Cuyler, Monongahela*, then *Brooklyn*, Pac. and W.Gulf Blk. Sqdns. (Oct 1861–Dec 1863); spec. duty, Washington, DC (Dec 1863–Oct 1864); cdr, *Lackawanna*, W.Gulf Blk.Sqdn. (Oct 1864–Jul 1865); w.o. (Jul 1865–Feb 1866); cdr, *Pensacola*, Navy Yard, NY (Mar 1866); w.o. (Mar–Oct 1866); cdr, *Ossipee*, Pac.Sqdn. (Nov 1866–Sep 1868); return to U.S. and w.o. (Sep 1868–Mar 1869); pres., Naval Exam. and Ret. Bd., Philadelphia (Mar 1869); w.o. (Mar–May 1869); senior member, Ord.Bd., Washington, DC (May–Jul 1869); w.o. (Jul–Oct 1869); in charge, Hydrographic Office, Washington, DC (Oct 1869–Sep 1870); cdr, Navy Yard, Philadelphia (Oct 1870–Oct 1872); w.o. (Oct 1872–Aug 1873); placed on Ret.Lst. (23 Aug 1873).

Career Highlights In 1837, escorted General Santa Anna back to Mexico after his defeat in TX. Served on the famed U.S.Expl.Expd. under the command of Lt Charles Wilkes [*q.v.*]. During the Civil War, served as flt.capt under RAdm John A. Dahlgren [*q.v.*] off Charleston Harbor in 1863.

References

Personal Papers: a) excerpts from journal on *Ossipee* (1867) in BL. b) 11 vols., 4,000 items (1836–50) in SML.

Writings: *The Navy of the United States, from the Commencement, 1775–1853, with a Brief History of Each Vessel's Service and Fate* (1853).

MORDECAI THOMAS ENDICOTT Born in May's Landing, NJ, on 26 Nov 1844, son of Thomas Doughty and Ann (Pennington) Endicott. Educated in Presbyterian parochial schools. Received the Civil Engineering degree in 1868 from Rensselaer Polytechnical Institute in Troy, NY. Married Elizabeth Adams on 29 May 1872. Had seven daughters. In practice as a civil engineer and in mining from Jul 1868 to his entry into the service. Died at his home in Washington, DC, on 5 Mar 1926. Buried in Arlington National Cemetery.

Ranks Civil Engr. (13 Jul 1874); Civil Engr. with rel. rank of Cdr (16 Feb 1882); Civil Engr. with rel. rank of Capt (21 Mar 1898); Chief, Bur. of Yards and Docks with rank of Commo (4 Apr 1898); Chief, Bureau of Yards and Docks with rank of RAdm (3 Mar 1899); transferred to Ret.Lst. as Civil Engr. with rank of RAdm (26 Nov 1906); recalled to active duty (12 Oct 1917); permanently retired (30 Jun 1920).

Career Summary Received appointment from NJ (13 Jul 1874); Navy Yard, League Island, PA (Jul 1874–Apr 1886); Navy Yard, Norfolk, VA (May 1886–Oct 1889); Member, Bd. of Improvement, Navy Yard, NY (Oct 1889–Apr 1890); Bur. of Yards and Docks, Washington, DC (Apr 1890–Apr 1898); chief, Bur. of Yards and Docks, Washington, DC (Apr 1898–Jan 1907); transferred to Ret.Lst. (26 Nov 1906); spec. temp. duty, Navy Dept., Washington, DC (Jan 1907–Jun 1909); temp. duty, Dept. of Justice, Washington, DC (Nov 1914–Apr 1917); Bur. of Yards and Docks, Washington, DC (Oct 1917–Oct 1919); member, Bd. of Awards and Medals, Navy Dept., Washington, DC (Mar–Oct 1919, Jan–Jun 1920).

References
Additional Sources: "Memoirs of Deceased Members," *Transactions of the American Society of Civil Engineers* 91 (1927): 1051–56.

MORDECAI THOMAS ENDICOTT
1844–1926

FREDERICK ENGLE Born on 23 Oct 1799 in Delaware County, PA. Married, with children. Died in Philadelphia on 12 Feb 1868.

Ranks Midn (6 Dec 1814); Lt (13 Jan 1825); Cdr (8 Sep 1841); Capt (14 Sep 1855); transferred to Ret.Lst. with rank of Commo (16 Jul 1862); RAdm on Ret.Lst. (25 Jul 1866).

Career Summary Received appointment from PA (6 Dec 1814); *Firefly*, Med.Sqdn. (Jan–Nov 1815); on furlough (Dec 1815–Feb 1817); *Boxer*, W.Ind.Sqdn. (Feb–Oct 1817); w.o. (Jan–May 1818); *Guerriere*, Med.Sqdn. (May 1818–Oct 1820); l.o.a. (Oct 1820–Jan 1821); Navy Yard, Philadelphia (Jan 1821–Dec 1822); *Ferret* and *Sea Gull*, W.Ind.Sqdn. (Dec 1822–Aug 1825); l.o.a. (Aug 1825–Mar 1826); flgs. *Brandywine*, Pac.Sqdn. (Jul 1826–Oct 1829); l.o.a. (Oct 1829–Dec 1830); *Vincennes*, W.Ind.Sqdn. (Dec 1830–Jul 1832); l.o.a. (Sep–Dec 1832); w.o. (Dec 1832–Oct 1833); Naval Rndv., Philadelphia (Oct 1833–Oct 1836); flgs. *Constellation*, then cdr, *Grampus*, W.Ind.Sqdn. (Oct 1836–Nov 1837); l.o.a. (Aug 1837–May 1838); w.o. (May

FREDERICK ENGLE
1799–1868

1838–Apr 1840); cdr, rec. ship *Experiment*, Philadelphia (Apr 1840–Oct 1841); w.o. (Oct 1841–Feb 1842); Navy Yard, Philadelphia (Feb 1842–Jan 1845); w.o. (Jan–Jul 1845); cdr, *Princeton*, Home Sqdn. (Jul 1845–Jul 1849); l.o.a. (Jul–Oct 1849); w.o. (Oct 1849–Mar 1850); Naval Rndv., NY (Mar 1850–May 1852); w.o. (May–Nov 1852); cdr, rec. ship *Union*, Philadelphia (Nov 1852–Oct 1855); w.o. (Oct 1855–Jul 1856); cdr, *Minnesota*, Navy Yard, Washington, DC (Jul–Aug 1856); cdr, flgs. *Wabash*, Home Sqdn. (Aug 1856–Feb 1858); l.o.a. (Feb–May 1858); member, Bd. of Examiners (May–Dec 1858); temp. cdr, Navy Yard, Philadelphia (Dec 1858–Sep 1859); w.o. (Sep 1859–Jul 1860); *Brooklyn*, spec.surv. duty (Jul 1860–Jan 1861); w.o. (Jan–May 1861); spec. duty, Navy Dept., Washington, DC (May 1861); cdr, E.Ind.Sqdn., *Hartford* (Jul–Dec 1861); member, Bd. of Examiners (Dec 1861–Aug 1862); transferred to Ret.Lst. (16 Jul 1862); gov., Naval Asylum, Philadelphia (Aug 1862–May 1866); pres., Bd. of Examiners (Jun 1864–Nov 1866).

EARL ENGLISH
1824–1893

EARL ENGLISH Born in Crosswicks, NJ, on 18 Feb 1824. Received early education in Trenton, NJ. Married, with two daughters. Died on 16 Jul 1893 in Washington, DC. Buried in Oak Hill Cemetery in Washington, DC.

Ranks Midn (25 Feb 1840); PMidn (11 Jul 1846); Mstr (1 Mar 1855); Lt (14 Sep 1855); LCdr (16 Jul 1862); Cdr (25 Jul 1866); Capt (28 Sep 1871); Commo (25 Mar 1880); RAdm (4 Sep 1884); placed on Ret.Lst. (18 Feb 1886).

Career Summary Received appointment from NJ (25 Feb 1840); w.o. (Feb–May 1840); rec. ship *Columbus*, Boston (May–Sep 1840); *Constellation*, E.Ind.Sqdn. (Sep 1840–May 1844); l.o.a. (May–Jul 1844); *Princeton*, spec.serv. (Jul 1844–Jul 1845); l.o.a. and w.o. (Jul–Oct 1845); Naval School, Annapolis, MD (Oct 1845–Jul 1846); flgs. *Independence*, Pac.Sqdn. (Aug 1846–May 1849); l.o.a. (May–Sep 1849); *Vixen*, Home Sqdn. (Sep 1849–Aug 1850); w.o. (Aug 1850); Naval Rndv., Philadelphia (Aug–Nov 1850); *Southampton*, Pac.Sqdn. (Nov 1850–Sep 1852); rec. ship *Union*, Philadelphia (Sep 1852–Apr 1853); *Dolphin*, spec.serv. (Apr–Nov 1853); l.o.a. (Nov–Dec 1853); cst.surv. duty (Dec 1853–Aug 1855); w.o. (Aug–Oct 1855); *Levant*, E.Ind.Sqdn. (Oct 1855–Apr 1858); Navy Yard, Philadelphia (Apr 1858–Aug 1859); *Wyoming*, Pac.Sqdn. (Aug 1859–Nov 1861); spec. duty, NY (Dec 1861–Jan 1862); cdr, *Westfield*, NY (Jan–Feb 1862); spec. duty, NY (Feb–Mar 1862); cdr, *Somerset*, E.Gulf Blk.Sqdn. (Mar–Sep 1862); cdr, *Sagamore*, E.Gulf Blk.Sqdn. (Oct 1862–Oct 1863); return home and w.o. (Oct–Dec 1863); cdr, *Pontiac*, under construction, Philadelphia (Dec 1863–May 1864); cdr, *Wyalusing*, N.Atl.Blk.Sqdn. (May 1864–Jun 1865); l.o.a. and w.o. (Jun–Dec 1865); temp. ord. duty, Navy Yard, NY (Dec 1865–Dec 1866); cdr, *Iroquois*, then cdr, flgs. *Delaware*, Asia.Sqdn. (Jan 1867–Nov 1870); w.o. (Nov 1870–Feb 1871); member, Bd. of

Inspection and Survey (Feb 1871–Aug 1872); Navy Yard, Portsmouth, NH (Sep 1872–Mar 1874); cdr, *Congress*, Eur.Sta. (Apr 1874–Jul 1876); comdt., Navy Yard, Portsmouth, NH (Aug 1876–Nov 1878); chief, Bur. of Equip. and Recru:ting, Washington, DC (Nov 1878–Sep 1884); cdr, Eur.Sta., *Lancaster* (Sep 1884–Feb 1885); cdr, S.Atl.Sta., *Lancaster* (Jul–Nov 1885); return home and w.o. (Nov 1885–Feb 1886); placed on Ret.Lst. (18 Feb 1886).

JAMES ENTWISTLE Born in Paterson, NJ, on 8 Jan 1837. Educated in public schools there. Retired to Paterson where he died on 23 Mar 1910. Buried in that city's Fairlawn Cemetery.

Ranks 3rd Asst.Engr. (29 Oct 1861); 2nd Asst.Engr. (3 Aug 1863); 1st Asst.Engr. with rel. rank of Lt (11 Oct 1866); Chief Engr. (1 Jul 1887); Chief Engr. with rel. rank of Cdr (14 Oct 1896); Chief Engr. with rel. rank of Capt (10 Feb 1899); Capt (3 Mar 1899); placed on Ret.Lst. with rank of RAdm (8 Jul 1899).

Career Summary Received appointment from PA (29 Oct 1861); *Aroostook*, N.Atl. and W.Gulf Blk. Sqdns. (Nov 1861–Feb 1865); w.o. (Feb–Apr 1865); *Mahongo*, Pac.Sqdn. (Apr 1865–Sep 1867); w.o. (Sep 1867); temp. duty, *Wampanoag*, on trials (Sep 1867–Feb 1868); w.o. (Feb–Mar 1868); *Ammonoosuc*, Boston (Mar–Jun 1868); w.o. (Jun–Sep 1868); *Nipsic*, S.Atl.Sqdn. (Oct 1868–Dec 1869); w.o. (Dec 1869–Jan 1870); *Michigan*, on Great Lakes (Jan–Mar 1870); w.o (Mar–Sep 1870); Navy Yard, League Island, PA (Oct 1870–Jan 1872); *Canonicus* and *Saugus*, N.Atl.Sta. (Jan 1872–Jun 1873); sick lv. (Jun–Nov 1873); *Franklin*, N.Atl.Sta. (Nov 1873); *Florida* [renamed *Wampanoag*], in ordinary, NY (Nov 1873–Jan 1874); *Powhatan*, N.Atl.Sta. (Jan–Mar 1874); *Franklin*, Eur.Sta. (Mar 1874–Dec 1876); w.o. (Dec 1876–Mar 1877); Bur. of Steam Engineering, Washington, DC (Mar–Jun 1877); w.o. (Jun–Jul 1877); spec. duty, NY (Jul 1877–Dec 1878); Navy Yard, Mare Island, CA (Jan 1879–Feb 1881); *Palos*, Asia.Sta. (Apr–Aug 1881); *Ashuelot*, Asia.Sta. (Aug 1881–May 1883); suspended from duty (May 1883–May 1884); w.o. (May–Jun 1884); *Alarm*, spec.serv. (Jun–Sep 1884); w.o. (Sep–Dec 1884); various bd. duty (Dec 1884–Aug 1886); rec. ship *Minnesota*, NY (Aug 1886–Jul 1887); w.o. (Jul–Sep 1887); *Enterprise*, Eur.Sqdn. (Oct 1887–May 1890); w.o. (May–Jun 1890); insp. of machinery, Bath Ironworks, Bath, ME (Jun 1890–Nov 1895); *Boston*, Asia.Sta. (Dec 1895–Oct 1896); Navy Yard, Mare Island, CA (Oct 1896–Mar 1897); flt.engr., Asia.Flt., *Olympia* (Mar 1897–Dec 1898); *Raleigh*, Asia.Sta. (Dec 1898–Apr 1899); home and w.o. (Apr–Jul 1899); placed on Ret.Lst. (8 Jul 1899).

Career Highlights Participated in Battle of Manila Bay while flt.engr. of Asia.Flt. Advanced on 11 Feb 1901 two numbers on Ret.Lst. for eminent and conspicuous conduct in battle at Manila Bay.

JAMES ENTWISTLE
1837–1910

HENRY ERBEN
1832–1909

HENRY ERBEN Born in New York City on 6 Sep 1832, son of Henry Erben. Married Caroline Augusta Vulte. One son and one daughter. Died in New York City on 23 Oct 1909; buried there.

Ranks Act.Midn (17 Jun 1848); PMidn (12 Jun 1855); Mstr (16 Sep 1855); Lt (27 Dec 1856); LCdr (16 Jul 1862); Cdr (6 May 1868); Capt (1 Nov 1879); Commo (3 Apr 1892); RAdm (31 Jul 1894); placed on Ret.Lst. (6 Sep 1894).

Career Summary Received appointment from NY (17 Jun 1848); *St. Lawrence*, spec.serv. (Aug 1848–Nov 1850); l.o.a. (Nov 1850–Jan 1851); *St. Lawrence*, spec.serv. (Jan–Aug 1851); l.o.a. (Aug–Oct 1851); *St. Lawrence*, Pac.Sqdn. (Oct 1851–Jul 1853); l.o.a. (Jul–Oct 1853); USNA (Oct–Dec 1853); dismissed from USNA for misconduct for one year and turned back (20 Dec 1853); cst.surv. duty (Dec 1853–Jul 1854); l.o.a. (Jul–Oct 1854); USNA (Oct 1854–Jun 1855); *Potomac*, Home Sqdn. (Jul–Oct 1855); w.o. (Oct–Nov 1855); spec. duty, Port-Au-Prince, Haiti (Nov 1855–Mar 1856); l.o.a. and w.o. (Mar–Jun 1856); *Supply*, spec.serv. (Jun 1856–Feb 1857); l.o.a. (Feb–Jun 1857); *Mississippi*, E.Ind.Sqdn. (Jul 1857–Nov 1859); *Supply*, Gulf Sta. (Feb 1860–Mar 1861); *Release*, Gulf and Atl.Blk Sqdns. (Mar–Sep 1861); spec. duty, St. Louis (Sep 1861); *Huntsville*, Gulf Blk.Sqdn. (Oct 1861–Apr 1862); cdr, *St. Louis*, MS Sqdn. (Apr–Jun 1862); cdr, *Sumter*, MS Sqdn. (Jun–Sep 1862); naval howitzer battery, Indian River, MD (Oct 1862); exec.off., *Patapsco*, N.Atl.Blk.Sqdn. (Oct 1862–Jul 1863); w.o. (Jul–Oct 1863); spec. duty, NY (Oct–Nov 1863); *Niagara*, spec. duty, Atl. Coast (Nov 1863–May 1864); cdr, *Chino*, Boston (May–Jul 1864); cdr, *Tunxis*, Navy Yard, Philadelphia (Jul–Sep 1864); cdr, *Ponola*, W.Gulf Blk.Sqdn. (Oct 1864–Jul 1865); w.o. (Jul–Sep 1865); temp. duty, Navy Yard, NY (Sep 1865–Dec 1866); cdr, *Huron*, then *Kansas*, S.Atl.Sta. (Jan 1867–Sep 1869); w.o. (Sep–Dec 1869); ord. duty, Navy Yard, NY (Jan 1870–Sep 1871); w.o. (Sep 1871–Jun 1872); nav. duty, Navy Yard, NY (Jul 1872–Aug 1873); Navy Yard, NY (Aug–Sep 1873); Naval Rndv., NY (Sep 1873–Sep 1874); cdr, *Tuscarora*, N.Pac.Sta. (Oct 1874–Aug 1875); w.o. (Aug–Sep 1875); aide, Navy Yard, Portsmouth, NH (Sep 1875–Oct 1878); w.o. (Oct–Nov 1878); cdr, nautical schoolship *St. Mary's* (Nov 1878–Dec 1882); w.o. (Dec 1882–Jun 1883); cdr, *Pensacola*, spec.serv. (Jul 1883–Jun 1884); w.o. (Jun–Nov 1884); capt.yd., Navy Yard, Portsmouth, NH (Nov 1884–Sep 1886); spec. duty, pres., Bd. to Inspect Vessels, NY (Oct 1886–Oct 1889); w.o. (Oct 1889–Jan 1890); member, spec. bd. (Jan–Mar 1890); pres., gen. court-martial (Mar–May 1890); member, Bd. of Inspection and Survey (May 1890–Mar 1891); gov., Naval Home, Philadelphia (Mar–May 1891); comdt., Navy Yard, NY (May 1891–May 1893); cdr, Eur.Sta., *Chicago* (Jun 1893–Aug 1894); home and w.o. (Aug–Sep 1894); placed on Ret.Lst. (6 Sep 1894); in charge, Patrol Flt., US Coast (Apr–Jul 1898).

Career Highlights While on storeship *Supply*, participated in experiment bringing camels from Egypt to TX for War Department. At Pensacola when Navy Yard surrendered in early 1861. Aided transfer of Union troops from Fort Barrancas to Fort Pickens on 9 Jan 1861. Saw action on Mississippi River at bombardment of Fort Pillow, in capture of Memphis, at siege of Vicksburg, against the batteries, at Baton Rouge, and in destruction of Confederate ram *Arkansas* in 1862. With naval howitzer battery with Gen George McClellan during the Antietam campaign in Oct 1862. Commanded several monitors off Charleston Harbor during 1863 and 1864. In war with Spain, commanded Patrol Flt. designed to protect entire coast of U.S., from Galveston, TX, to Bar Harbor, ME.

References

Personal Papers: 2 ft. (1848–1903) in NYHS.

Other Sources: J. M. Ellicott, "With Erben and Mahan on the *Chicago*," U.S. Naval Institute *Proceedings* 463 (Sep 1941): 1234–50; 548 (Oct 1948): 1247–49.

DONALD McNEILL FAIRFAX Born at Mt. Eagle, Fairfax County, VA, on 10 Mar 1821, son of George William and Isabella (McNeill) Fairfax. Married Josephine Foote, daughter of RAdm Andrew Hull Foote, USN [*q.v.*]. Died at his home in Hagerstown, MD on 10 Jan 1894. Buried in Rose Hill Cemetery in Hagerstown.

Ranks Midn (12 Aug 1837); PMidn (29 Jun 1843); Mstr (4 Aug 1850); Lt (26 Feb 1851); Cdr (16 Jul 1862); Capt (25 Jul 1866); Commo (24 Aug 1873); RAdm (11 Jul 1880); placed on Ret.Lst. (30 Sep 1881).

Career Summary Received appointment from NC (12 Aug 1837); w.o. (Aug–Sep 1837); rec. ship *Hudson*, NY (Sep–Dec 1837); *John Adams*, E.Ind.Sqdn and spec.serv. (Dec 1837–Sep 1840); l.o.a. (Sep–Nov 1840); rec. ship *North Carolina*, NY (Nov 1840–Apr 1841); *Fairfield* then *Brandywine*, Med.Sqdn. (May 1841–Jul 1842); l.o.a. (Jul–Sep 1842); Naval School, Philadelphia (Sep 1842–Jul 1843); *Missouri*, E.Ind.Sqdn. (Aug–Oct 1843); Depot of Charts, Naval Observatory, Washington, DC (Nov 1843–Mar 1844); cst.surv. duty (Jun 1844–Mar 1845); *Porpoise*, Home Sqdn. (Mar–Apr 1845); *Columbus, Vincennes, Erie,* then *Cyane*, spec.serv. to Far E., then Pac.Sqdn. (Apr 1845–Oct 1848); l.o.a. (Oct 1848–Apr 1849); Naval Rndv., NY (Apr–Dec 1849); w.o. (Dec 1849–Apr 1850); *Congress*, Braz.Sqdn. (Apr 1850–Jul 1853); l.o.a. and w.o. (Jul 1853–Feb 1854); Navy Yard, Washington, DC (Mar–May 1854); l.o.a. and w.o. (May 1854–Jan 1855); spec. duty, astronomical observations, Navy Department, Washington, DC (Jan–Apr 1855); w.o. (Apr–Jun 1855); flgs. *Potomac*, Home Sqdn. (Jun 1855–Aug 1856); flgs. *Wabash*, Home Sqdn. (Aug 1856–Feb 1858); l.o.a. (Feb–May 1858); ord. duty, Navy Yard, NY (May 1858–Jun 1859); *Mystic*, then exec.off., *Constella-*

DONALD McNEILL FAIRFAX
1821–1894

tion, then *San Jacinto,* Afr.Sqdn. (Jul 1859–Nov 1861); ord. duty, Philadelphia (Dec 1861–May 1862); cdr, *Cayuga,* W.Gulf Blk.Sqdn. (May–Dec 1862); return home and w.o. (Dec 1862–Jan 1863); cdr, *Nantucket,* S.Atl.Blk.Sqdn. (Jan–Apr 1863); cdr, *Montauk,* S.Atl.Blk.Sqdn. (Apr–Aug 1863); comdt. of midn, USNA (Sep 1863–Oct 1865); l.o.a. (Oct 1865); spec. duty, Philadelphia (Oct–Dec 1865); cdr, flgs. *Rhode Island,* Home Sqdn. (Dec 1865–Jan 1867); cdr, flgs. *Susquehanna,* Home Sqdn. (Jan 1867–Jan 1868); w.o. (Jan–Apr 1868); ord. duty, Navy Yard, Boston (Jun 1868–Sep 1869); Navy Yard, Portsmouth, NH (Sep 1869–Sep 1872); w.o. (Sep 1872–Sep 1874); special duty, Rio de Janeiro, Braz. (Sep–Nov 1874); comdt., Naval Sta., New London, CT (Dec 1874–Jul 1876); w.o. (Jul 1876–Apr 1877); comdt., Naval Sta., New London, CT (May 1877–Oct 1878); w.o. (Oct 1878–Apr 1879); member, Naval Exam. and Ret. Bds. (May–Oct 1879); gov., Naval Asylum, Philadelphia (Oct 1879–Sep 1881); placed on Ret.Lst. (30 Sep 1881).

Career Highlights While on *John Adams* during its circumnavigation of the world, participated in destruction of several pirate villages on Sumatra in 1839 in reprisal for attacks upon merchant vessels in the area. On board the *Princeton* in Feb 1844 when Robert Stockton's "Peacemaker" exploded and killed several people. During the Mexican War, took part in the capture of Mazatlan and Lower California. In 1858, participated in surrender of the filibuster Walker and his command. On board the *San Jacinto* in 1861 when that vessel stopped the British mail packet *Trent* and removed the Confederate agents Mason and Slidell. Saw action off New Orleans in 1862, and commanded two monitors during attacks against Charleston in 1863.

References

Writings: "Captain Wilkes's Seizure of Mason and Slidell," *Battles and Leaders of the Civil War,* II (1887): 135–42.

NORMAN VAN HELDREICH FARQUHAR

NORMAN VAN HELDREICH FARQUHAR Born in Pottsville, PA, on 11 Apr 1840, son of George W. and Amilie (von Schrader) Farquhar. Married Addie W. Pope on 26 Apr 1862. Died in Jamestown, RI, on 3 Jul 1907. Buried in Arlington National Cemetery.

Ranks Act.Midn (27 Sep 1854); dismissed (11 Mar 1857); restored (23 Mar 1857); Midn (9 Jun 1859); Lt (31 Aug 1861); LCdr (5 Aug 1865); Cdr (12 Dec 1872); Capt (4 Mar 1886); Commo (21 Jul 1897); RAdm (3 Mar 1899); placed on Ret.Lst. (11 Apr 1902).

Career Summary Received appointment from PA (27 Sep 1854); USNA (Sep 1854–Jun 1859); found deficient and turned back (Jun 1857); *San Jacinto* and prize brig *Delicia,* Afr.Sqdn. (Jun 1859–Feb 1860); w.o. (Feb–Mar 1860); *Saratoga,* Afr.Sqdn (Mar 1860); *San Jacinto* and *Constellation,*

NORMAN VAN HELDREICH
FARQUHAR
1840–1907

Afr.Sqdn. (Apr–Jul 1860); *Mystic* and prize brig *Friction*, Afr.Sqdn. (Jul 1860–Aug 1860); w.o. (Aug–Nov 1860); *Saratoga* then *Sumter*, Afr.Sqdn. (Nov 1860–Sep 1861); l.o.a. and w.o. (Sep–Nov 1861); *Mystic*, N.Atl.Blk.Sqdn. (Nov 1861–Mar 1862); *Sonoma*, N.Atl.Blk.Sqdn. (Mar–Apr 1862); *Mahaska*, N.Atl.Blk.Sqdn. (Apr 1862–Jan 1863); *Rhode Island*, W.Ind.Sqdn. (Jan 1863–Apr 1864); w.o. (Apr–May 1864); *Santiago de Cuba*, N.Atl.Blk.Sqdn. (May 1864–Jun 1865); w.o. (Jun–Jul 1865); USNA (Jul 1865–Sep 1868); *Swatara*, Eur.Sqdn. (Oct 1868–Jun 1869); Navy Yard, Boston (Jun–Aug 1869); exec.off., flgs. *Severn*, N.Atl.Sta. (Aug 1869–Sep 1870); cdr, *Kansas*, Tehauntepec and Nicaragua Surveying Expd. (Sep 1870–Aug 1871); w.o. (Aug–Sep 1871); ord. duty, Navy Yard, Boston (Sep 1871–Apr 1872); exec.off., Navy Yard, Boston (Apr–Oct 1872); exec.off., *Powhatan*, N.Atl.Sta. (Oct–Dec 1872); cdr, *Santee*, and in charge, buildings and grounds, USNA (Dec 1872–Sep 1877); cdr, *Portsmouth*, spec.serv. (Sep 1877–Mar 1878); w.o. (Mar–Aug 1878); cdr, *Quinnebaug*, then cdr, *Wyoming*, Eur.Sqdn. (Sep 1878–May 1881); comdt. of cadets, USNA (Jun 1881–May 1886); torp. instruction, Newport, RI (Jun–Sep 1886); w.o. (Sep 1886–Jan 1887); bd. duties (Jan–May 1887); cdr, *Trenton*, Pac.Sta. (May 1887–Jul 1889); member, Bd. of Visitors, Torp. Sta., Newport, RI (Jul 1889); bd. duties (Aug–Oct 1889); member, L.h. Bd., Washington, DC (Nov 1889–Mar 1890); chief, Bur. of Yards and Docks, Washington, DC (Mar 1890–Mar 1894); comdt., Navy Yard, League Island, PA (Mar 1894–Jun 1896); cdr, *Newark*, N.Atl.Sta. (Jun–Dec 1896); pres., Naval Exam.Bd., Washington, DC (Dec 1896–May 1897); comdt., Navy Yard, Norfolk, VA (Jun 1897–Oct 1899); cdr, N.Atl.Sta., *Kearsarge* (Oct 1899–May 1901); chairman, L.h. Bd., Washington, DC (May 1901–Apr 1902); placed on Ret.Lst. (11 Apr 1902).

Career Highlights While a midn with the Afr.Sqdn., brought a slaver to U.S. with a crew of only ten and no other officers. Participated in both actions at Fort Fisher in 1864–65. While commanding *Trenton*, was at Samoa when the infamous hurricane of 16 Mar 1889 hit, saving 450 officers and men of his crew although losing the *Trenton* plus 150 men of the *Vandalia*.

References
Writings: a) "The Barometer in High Southern Latitudes," U.S. Naval Institute *Proceedings* 5 (1878): 113–26. b) "How May the Sphere of Usefulness of Naval Officers be Extended in Time of Peace with Advantage to the Country and the Naval Service?" U.S. Naval Institute *Proceedings* 24 (1883): 195–202. c) "Inducements for Retaining Trained Seamen in the Navy, and Best System of Rewards for Long and Faithful Service," U.S. Naval Institute *Proceedings* 33 (1885): 175–206.

DAVID GLASGOW FARRAGUT
1801–1870

DAVID GLASGOW FARRAGUT Born at Campbell's Station, near Knoxville, TN, on 5 Jul 1801, son of George and Elizabeth (Shine) Farragut. Adopted by Commo David Porter, USN, in 1808, after his mother died. Married twice: to Susan C. Marchant on 24 Sep 1823, who died in 1840, and to Virginia Loyall on 26 Dec 1843. One son, Loyall Farragut. Died in Portsmouth, NH, on 14 Aug 1870. Buried in Woodlawn Cemetery, Westchester County, NY.

Ranks Midn (17 Dec 1810); Lt (13 Jan 1825); Cdr (8 Sep 1841); Capt (14 Sep 1855); RAdm (16 Jul 1862); VAdm (21 Dec 1864); Adm (25 Jul 1866); died (14 Aug 1870).

Career Summary Received appointment from TN (17 Dec 1810); *Essex*, N. and S.Atl. waters (Aug 1811–Mar 1814); prize mstr, *Alexander Barclay* (1813); prisoner of war (Mar–Nov 1814); *Spark*, NY (Nov 1814–Apr 1815); flgs. *Independence*, Med.Sqdn. (Apr–Dec 1815); *Macedonian*, Med.Sqdn. (Dec 1815–Jan 1816); flgs. *Washington*, l.o.a. for study, then *Franklin*, Med.Sqdn. (Jan 1816–Oct 1820); Navy Yard, NY (Nov 1820–Jan 1821); Navy Yard, Norfolk, VA (Jan 1821–May 1822); *John Adams*, *Greyhound*, *Sea Gull*, and cdr, *Ferret*, Mosquito Flt. (May 1822–Apr 1825); court of inquiry, Washington, DC (Apr–Jun 1825); Navy Yard, Norfolk, VA (Jul–Aug 1825); *Brandywine*, Med.Sqdn. (Aug 1825–Jun 1826); l.o.a. (Jun–Nov 1826); rec. ship *Alert*, Norfolk, VA (Nov 1826–Oct 1828); exec.off., *Vandalia*, Braz.Sqdn. (Oct 1828–Feb 1830); l.o.a. (Feb–Dec 1830); rec. ships *Congress* and *Java*, Norfolk, VA (Dec 1830–Dec 1832); exec.off., *Natchez*, spec.serv. (Dec 1832–Jul 1834); l.o.a. and w.o. (Jul 1834–Jul 1837); Naval Rndv., Norfolk, VA (Jul 1837–Mar 1838); cdr, *Erie*, W.Ind.Sqdn. (Mar 1838–Nov 1840); in ordinary, Norfolk, VA (Nov 1840–Feb 1841); flgs. *Delaware*, Braz.Sqdn. (Feb–Sep 1841); exec.off., flgs. *Delaware*, then cdr, *Decatur*, Braz.Sqdn. (Sep 1841–Feb 1843); l.o.a. (Feb–Apr 1843); exec.off., then cdr, rec. ship *Pennsylvania*, Norfolk, VA (Apr 1844–Oct 1845); Navy Yard, Norfolk, VA (Oct 1845–Mar 1847); cdr, *Saratoga*, Home Sqdn. (Mar 1847–Apr 1848); Navy Yard, Norfolk, VA (Apr 1848–Apr 1850); w.o. (Apr 1850–Mar 1851); ord. duty, Navy Yard, Washington, DC (Mar 1851–Apr 1852); ord. duty, Navy Yard, Norfolk, VA (Apr 1852–Aug 1854); spec. duty, establish and command Navy Yard, Mare Island, CA (Aug 1854–May 1858); w.o. (May–Dec 1858); cdr, *Brooklyn*, spec. duty, Gulf of Mexico (Jan 1859–Oct 1860); l.o.a. and w.o. (Oct 1860–Apr 1861); member, Naval Ret. Bd. and for Better Organization of Navy, NY (Sep–Dec 1861); cdr, W.Gulf Blk.Sqdn., *Hartford* (Jan 1862–Jan 1865); cdr, naval forces, James River, VA (Jan–Feb 1865); spec. duty, Washington, DC (Feb–Mar 1865); home and w.o. (Mar–May 1865); pres., Bd. of Visitors, USNA (May 1865–Jan 1866); w.o. (Jan 1866–Jun 1867); cdr, Eur.Sqdn., *Franklin* (Apr 1867–Nov 1868); w.o. (Nov 1868–Aug 1870); died (14 Aug 1870).

Career Highlights America's first officer to reach admiral rank. By special acts, Congress created for him the ranks of VAdm and Adm. Given first command, a captured prize in 1813, at the age of twelve. Wounded while on the *Essex* at Valparaiso when that vessel was destroyed by the British in Mar 1814. Led a landing party against pirates in Cuba in Jul 1823 while attached to the Mosquito Flt. A Southerner by birth and marriage, resisted family and peer pressure and remained loyal to the Union. Commanded W.Gulf Blk.Sqdn. from early 1862 through most of the Civil War, taking New Orleans, Vicksburg, and thus closing the southern half of the river. Hero of the Battle of Mobile Bay on 5 Aug 1864.

References

Personal Papers: a) 102 items (1863–80) in HHL. b) 1 vol. (1864): diary kept by Alexander McKinley, private secretary to Farragut, in EMHL. c) 12 items (1810–69) in LC. d) 400 items (1816–69) in NHF,WNY. e) 3 items in Christopher C. Auger Papers in IL State Historical Society, Springfield, IL. f) 100 items, 4 vols. (1817–70) in USNAM. g) 7 items (1862–64) in Concord Free Lib., Concord, MA. h) 8 items (1862–64) in NYHS. i) 5 items (1863–70) in NYPL. j) 10 items (1864–70) in GARL.

Writings: a) *Experiments to Ascertain the Strength and Endurance of Navy Guns* (Washington, DC: 1854). b) *Reports of the Naval Engagements on the Mississippi River . . .* (Washington, DC 1862).

Selected Additional Sources: a) Phineas C. Headley, *The Life and Naval Career of Vice-Admiral David Glascoe [sic.] Farragut* (1865). b) Loyall Farragut, *The Life and Letters of David Glasgow Farragut, First Admiral of the United States Navy* (NY: 1879). c) James Barnes, *Midshipman Farragut* (NY: 1896). d) ———, *David G. Farragut* (Boston: 1899). e) John Randolph Spears, *David G. Farragut* (Philadelphia: c.1905). f) Alfred Thayer Mahan, *Admiral Farragut* (NY: 1905). g) Caspar F. Goodrich, "Farragut," U.S. Naval Institute *Proceedings* 250 (Dec 1923): 1961–86. h) John C. Watson, "Farragut and Mobile Bay—Personal Reminiscences," U.S. Naval Institute *Proceedings* 291 (May 1927): 551–57. i) Albert Mordell, "Farragut at the Crossroads," U.S. Naval Institute *Proceedings* 336 (Feb 1931): 151–61. j) Richard S. West, "The Relations between Farragut and Porter," U.S. Naval Institute *Proceedings* 389 (Jul 1935): 985–97. k) Rose Nelson Chavanne, *David Farragut, Midshipman* (NY: 1941). l) Charles Lee Lewis, *David Glasgow Farragut: Admiral in the Making* 2 vol., (Annapolis: 1941). m) ———, *David Glasgow Farragut: Our First Admiral* (Annapolis: 1943). n) Richard S. West, Jr., "Admiral Farragut and General Butler," U.S. Naval Institute *Proceedings* 640 (Jun 1956): 635–43; 648 (Feb 1957): 214–15. o) Edwin P. Hoyt, *Damn the Torpedoes! The Story of America's First Admiral: David Glasgow Farragut* (NY: 1970).

JOHN CARSON FEBIGER
1821–1898

JOHN CARSON FEBIGER Born on 14 Feb 1821 in Pittsburgh, PA. Died on 9 Oct 1898 at his home of Londonderry (near Easton), MD. Buried in Arlington National Cemetery.

Ranks Midn (4 Sep 1838); PMidn (20 May 1844); Mstr (13 Jul 1852); Lt (30 Apr 1853); LCdr (16 Jul 1862); Cdr (27 Aug 1862); Capt (6 May 1868); Commo (9 Aug 1874); RAdm (4 Feb 1882); placed on Ret.Lst. (1 Jul 1882).

Career Summary Received appointment from OH (4 Sep 1838); w.o. (Sep–Oct 1838); *Macedonian*, W.Ind.Sqdn. (Oct 1838–Oct 1840); *Concord*, Braz.Sqdn. (Oct 1840–May 1844); l.o.a. (May–Aug 1849); *Potomac*, Home Sqdn. (Aug 1844–Dec 1845); l.o.a. (Dec 1845–May 1846); *Dale*, then *Columbus*, Pac.Sqdn. (May 1846–Mar 1848); l.o.a. (Mar–Jun 1848); on furlough (Jun 1848–Sep 1849); w.o. (Sep 1849–May 1850); *Dale*, then *Portsmouth*, Afr.Sqdn. (May 1850–Jun 1851); l.o.a. and w.o. (Jun–Dec 1851); cst.surv. duty (Dec 1851–Jun 1857); *Germantown*, E.Ind.Sqdn. (Jul 1857–Apr 1860); l.o.a. and w.o. (Apr–Oct 1860); cst.surv. duty (Oct 1860–May 1861); *Savannah*, Atl.Blk.Sqdn. (May–Nov 1861); l.o.a. (Nov–Dec 1861); cdr, *Kanawha*, W.Gulf Blk.Sqdn. (Dec 1862–Feb 1863); return home and w.o. (Feb–May 1863); cdr, *Osage*, MS Sqdn. (May–Jul 1863); w.o. (Jul–Oct 1863); cdr, *Mattabesset*, N.Atl.Blk.Sqdn. (Oct 1863–May 1865); w.o. (May–Oct 1865); cdr, *Stonewall*, Havana, Cuba (Oct–Nov 1865); w.o. (Nov 1865–Mar 1866); cdr, *Ashuelot*, then *Shenandoah*, Asia.Sqdn. (Mar 1866–Apr 1869); w.o. (Apr–Jul 1869); ord. duty, Navy Yard, Washington, DC (Jul 1869); l.o.a. (Jul–Sep 1869); insp., Naval Reserve Lands (Sep 1869–Jul 1872); cdr, *Omaha*, S.Pac.Sqdn. (Aug 1872–Jan 1874); home and w.o. (Jan–Apr 1874); member, Naval Exam. and Ret. Bds. (May 1874–Oct 1876); comdt., Navy Yard, Washington, DC (Oct 1876–Jun 1880); w.o. (Jun–Dec 1880); spec. bd. duty, Washington, DC (Dec 1880–Mar 1881); w.o. (Mar–Nov 1881); member, Naval Ret. Bd., Washington, DC (Nov 1881–Jul 1882); placed on Ret.Lst. (1 Jul 1882).

References
Personal Papers: Journal from *Chipola*, *Concord*, and *Macedonian* (1838–43) in NYHS.

JAMES MILTON FLINT Born in Hillsborough, NH, on 7 Feb 1838, son of Amos and Mary (Stickney) Flint. Educated in common schools and at Pembroke Academy. Received M.D. degree from Harvard University in Mar 1860. Married Carolina H. Conant on 27 Jun 1871. Died in Washington, DC, on 21 Nov 1919.

Ranks Act.Asst.Surg. (14 Apr 1862); Asst.Surg. (26 Oct 1863); PAsst.Surg. (13 Dec 1867); Surg. (24 Jun 1874); Medl. Insp. (4 Mar 1893); Medl.Dir. (6 Jun 1897); placed on Ret.Lst. as Medl.Dir. with rank of RAdm (7 Feb 1900).

Career Summary Received appointment from NH (14 Apr 1862); Navy Yard, NY (Apr 1862–Apr 1863); *Ethan Al-*

JAMES MILTON FLINT
1838–1919

len, E.Gulf Blk.Sqdn. (May 1862–Sep 1863); w.o. (Sep–Oct 1863); *Chocura*, Philadelphia (Oct 1863); w.o. (Oct–Nov 1863); *Hastings*, MS Sqdn. (Dec 1863–Jul 1865); w.o. (Jul–Oct 1865); rec. ship *Allegheny*, Baltimore (Oct 1865–Jul 1866); *Pensacola*, Pac.Sqdn. (Aug 1866–Sep 1867); return to U.S. and l.o.a. (Sep–Dec 1867); Naval Hosp., NY (Dec 1867–Jan 1868); Naval Hosp., Chelsea, MA (Jan–Jul 1868); *Franklin*, Eur.Sqdn. (Aug 1868–Apr 1870); return home and l.o.a. (Apr–May 1870); w.o. (May–Jul 1870); Naval Sta., Mound City, IL (Jul–Aug 1870); USNA (Sep 1870–Jan 1871); Navy Yard, Boston (Jan–Oct 1871); *Pensacola*, then *Saranac*, Pac.Sta. (Oct 1871–May 1874); return to U.S. and w.o. (Jun–Jul 1874); Torp.Sta., Newport, RI (Jul 1874–May 1876); Naval Hosp., Chelsea, MA (May 1876–Aug 1877); w.o. (Aug 1877–Oct 1878); *Enterprise*, Eur.Sta. (Oct 1878–May 1880); w.o. (May–Jun 1880); spec. duty, Bur. of Medicine and Surgery, Washington, DC (Jun 1880–Jun 1884); additional duty, Smithsonian Institution, Washington, DC (Jun 1881–Jun 1884); Fish Commission steamer, *Albatross* (Jun 1884–Jun 1887); spec. duty, U.S. Fish Commission (Jun 1887–Mar 1888); spec. duty, Smithsonian Institution, Washington, DC (Apr 1887–Oct 1891); *Miantonomah*, N.Atl.Sta. (Oct 1891–Mar 1893); l.o.a. and w.o. (Mar–May 1893); *Baltimore*, Asia.Sta. (May 1893–Jan 1895); home and l.o.a. (Jan–May 1895); Smithsonian Institution, Washington, DC, and various bd. duties (May 1895–Feb 1900); placed on Ret.Lst. (7 Feb 1900).

Career Highlights Three tours of duty with the Smithsonian Institution in Washington, DC, serving as curator of the division of medicine for the U.S. Natural History Museum.

References

Writings: a) *Recent Foraminifera: A Descriptive Catalogue of Specimens dredged by the U.S. Fish Commission steamer* Albatross (Washington, DC: U.S. National Museum, Annual Report, 1897). b) "Chinese Medicine," *Smithsonian Institution* XLV (1903): 180–82. c) *A Contribution to the Oceanography of the Pacific* (Washington, DC: 1905). d) *Directions for Collecting Information and Objects Illustrating the History of Medicine* (Washington, DC: 1905).

ANDREW HULL FOOTE Born in New Haven, CT, on 12 Sep 1806, son of Senator, and later Gov. of CT, Samuel A. and Eudocia (Hull) Foote. Cadet at USMA from Jun to Dec 1822 before accepting a commission in the navy. Twice married: to Caroline Flagg on 22 Jun 1828, and to Caroline Street on 27 Jan 1842. Three children. One daughter married RAdm Donald McNeill Fairfax, USN [*q.v.*] Died in New York City on 26 Jun 1863. Buried in New Haven, CT.

Ranks Act.Midn (4 Dec 1822); PMidn (24 May 1828); Lt (27 May 1830); Cdr (19 Dec 1852); Capt (29 Jun 1861); Flag Off. (13 Nov 1861); RAdm (16 Jul 1862); died (26 Jun 1863).

ANDREW HULL FOOTE
1806–1863

Career Summary Received appointment from CT (4 Dec 1822); *Grampus*, Mosquito Flt. (Dec 1822–Dec 1823); flgs. *Peacock*, Mosquito Flt. (Dec 1823–Jan 1824); flgs. *United States*, Pac.Sqdn. (Jan 1824–Apr 1827); l.o.a. (Apr–Aug 1827); *Natchez*, W.Ind.Sqdn. (Aug 1827–Feb 1828); l.o.a. (Feb–Apr 1828); w.o. (Apr–Oct 1828); *St. Louis*, Pac.Sqdn. (Oct 1828–Dec 1831); l.o.a. and w.o. (Dec 1831–May 1833); flgs. *Delaware*, Med.Sqdn. (May 1833–Feb 1836); l.o.a. and w.o. (Feb 1836–Oct 1837); *Fulton*, Atl.Sqdn (Oct–Nov 1837); *John Adams*, circumnavigation of globe (Nov 1837–Jun 1840); l.o.a. and w.o. (Jun 1840–Jun 1841); Navy Yard, NY (Jun–Aug 1841); l.o.a. (Aug–Nov 1841); comdt., Naval Asylum, Philadelphia (Nov 1841–Aug 1843); flgs. *Cumberland*, Med. Sqdn. (Aug 1843–Nov 1845); l.o.a. (Nov 1845–Apr 1846); Navy Yard, Boston (Jun 1846–Jun 1848); l.o.a. and w.o. (Jun 1848–Sep 1849); cdr, *Perry*, W.Afr.Sqdn. (Oct 1849–Dec 1851); l.o.a. and w.o. (Dec 1851–Mar 1854); Naval Asylum, Philadelphia (Mar 1854–Jun 1855); member, Naval Efficiency Bd., Washington, DC (Jun–Sep 1855); w.o. (Sep 1855–Mar 1856); cdr, *Portsmouth*, E.Ind.Sqdn. (Apr 1856–Jun 1858); l.o.a. (Jun–Oct 1858); cdr, Navy Yard, NY (Oct 1858–Aug 1861); cdr, naval operations, upper MS River and tributaries, St. Louis (Aug 1861–May 1862); sick lv. (May–Jul 1862); chief, Bur. of Equipment and Recruitment, Washington, DC (Jul 1862–Jun 1863); appointed cdr, S.Atl.Blk.Sqdn. (Jun 1863); died (26 Jun 1863).

Career Highlights As 1st lt of *Cumberland*, made vessel the first "temperance ship" in the navy. Worked to eliminate whiskey rations and to prohibit flogging. Personally led an assault force against the barrier forts at Canton, China, in Nov 1856, driving the Chinese away and making the forts and their guns inoperable. Commanded naval operations in the Western theater, headquartered at St. Louis, providing important naval support for operations on the upper Mississippi, Cumberland, and Tennessee Rivers, including actions at Forts Henry and Donelson, and at Island No. 10. Died en route to taking command of the S.Atl.Blk.Sqdn.

References

Personal Papers: a) 150 items (1837–63) in New Haven Colony Historical Society, New Haven, CT. b) 800 items (1838–63) in LC. c) c.1861–62 in Wallace-Dickey Papers and Abraham Lincoln Papers, ISHS. d) 7 items (1862) in Civil War Federal Collection, TN State Archives and Library, Nashville, TN. e) 1 letter to Foote by M. F. Maury (1856) in the Lib., Univ. of VA. f) letters of Foote and Gideon Welles on MS River campaigns in Western Reserve Historical Society, Cleveland, OH.

Writings: a) *Africa and the American Flag* (NY, 1854). b) *The African Squadron: Ashburton Treaty: Consular Sea Letters: reviewed in an Address by Commander A. H. Foote* (Philadelphia: 1855).

Additional Sources: a) James Mason Hoppin, *Life of An-*

drew Hull Foote, Rear-Admiral United States Navy (NY: 1874).
b) H. J. Maihater, "The Partnership," *U.S. Naval Institute Proceedings* 771 (May 1967): 49–57.

SAMUEL RHODES FRANKLIN Born in York, PA, on 24 Aug 1825. Two brothers in the Army: one was Gen William B. Franklin. Married daughter of RAdm Benjamin F. Sands [*q.v.*] on 10 Jan 1883. Died in Washington, DC, on 24 Feb 1909. Buried in Arlington National Cemetery.

Ranks Midn (18 Feb 1841); PMidn (10 Aug 1847); Mstr (18 Apr 1855); Lt (14 Sep 1855); LCdr (16 Jul 1862); Cdr (25 Jul 1866); Capt (13 Aug 1872); Commo (28 May 1881); RAdm (24 Jan 1885); placed on Ret.Lst. (24 Aug 1887).

Career Summary Received appointment from PA (18 Feb 1841); w.o. (Feb–Apr 1841); rec. ship *Hudson*, NY (Apr–Oct 1841); *United States, Relief*, and *Levant*, Pac.Sqdn. (Oct 1841–Apr 1847); l.o.a. (Apr–Oct 1847); Naval School, Annapolis, MD (Oct 1847–Jul 1848); cst.surv. duty (Aug 1848–May 1849); *Independence*, Med.Sqdn. (Jun 1849–Jun 1852); l.o.a. (Jun–Aug 1852); *Saranac*, Navy Yard, Philadelphia (Aug 1852); *Dolphin*, spec.serv. (Aug 1852–Mar 1853); w.o. (Mar–Apr 1853); cst.surv. duty (Apr 1853–Oct 1854); USNA (Oct 1854–Dec 1856); *Falmouth*, Braz.Sqdn. (Jan 1857–May 1859); s.a. and w.o. (May–Aug 1859); ord. duty, Navy Yard, Washington, DC (Aug–Nov 1859); Naval Observatory, Washington, DC (Nov 1859–Jun 1860); w.o. (Jun–Nov 1860); *Macedonian*, Home Sqdn. (Dec 1860–Jan 1862); temp. ord. duty, Navy Yard, Washington, DC (Jan–Mar 1862); *Dakotah*, N.Atl.Blk.Sqdn. (Mar–Jul 1862); cdr, *Victoria*, N.Atl. Blk.Sqdn. (Jul 1862–Oct. 1863); flt.capt., W.Gulf Blk.Sqdn., *Portsmouth* (Oct 1863–Jul 1865); return home and w.o. (Jul 1865–Jan 1866); cdr, *Saginaw*, N.Pac.Sqdn. (Feb 1866–Jul 1867); ord. duty, Navy Yard, Mare Island, CA (Jul 1867–Apr 1869); cdr, *Mohican*, N.Pac.Sqdn. (Apr 1869–Jan 1870); w.o. (Jan–May 1870); equipment duty, Navy Yard, Mare Island, CA (May 1870–Mar 1872); w.o. (Mar–Jun 1872); exec.off., Naval Sta., New London, CT (Jul–Sep 1872); exec.off., Navy Yard, Washington, DC (Sep–Dec 1872); w.o. (Dec 1872–Feb 1873); exec.off., Naval Sta., New London, CT (Mar–Apr 1873); cdr, *Wabash*, and chief of staff, Eur.Sqdn. (Jun 1873–Mar 1874); cdr, *Franklin*, and chief of staff, Eur.Sqdn. (Mar 1874–Dec 1876); w.o. (Dec 1876–Jan 1877); capt.yd., Navy Yard, Norfolk, VA (Jan–Oct 1877); Hydrographic Office, Washington, DC (Oct 1877–May 1878); in charge, Hydrographic Office, Bur. of Nav., Washington, DC (May 1878–Jun 1880); l.o.a. (Jun–Dec 1880); spec. duty, Bur. of Equipment and Recruiting, Washington, DC (Dec 1880–Feb 1882); member, Naval Exam.Bd. (Feb–Sep 1882); member, then pres., Naval Exam. and Ret. Bds. (Sep 1882–Feb 1884); supt., Naval Observatory, Washington, DC (Feb 1884–Mar 1885); cdr, Eur.Sta., *Franklin* then *Pensacola* (May 1885–Aug 1887);

SAMUEL RHODES FRANKLIN
1825–1909

placed on Ret.Lst. (24 Aug 1887); senior member, Naval Exam.Bd., Washington, DC (Jul–Aug 1898).

References

Personal Papers: a) journal from *Pensacola* (1885–87) in NYHS. b) 1 vol. in NYPL.

Writings: *Memoirs of a Rear Admiral Who has Served for More than Half a Century in the Navy of the United States* (NY: 1898).

JOSEPH P. FYFFE
1832–1896

JOSEPH P. FYFFE Born in Urbana, OH, on 26 Jul 1832. Married Eliza Moody. One son, who served as an Asst. Paymstr. Died in Pierce, NE, on 25 Feb 1896. Buried in Pierce.

Ranks Act.Midn (9 Sep 1847); PMidn (15 Jun 1854); Mstr (15 Jun 1855); Lt (16 Jun 1855); LCdr (16 Jul 1862); Cdr (2 Dec 1867); Capt (13 Jan 1879); Commo (28 Feb 1890); RAdm (10 Jul 1894); retired (20 Jul 1894).

Career Summary Received appointment from OH (9 Sep 1847); Naval School, Annapolis, MD (Oct 1847); *Cumberland* and *Stromboli*, Home Sqdn. (Oct 1847–Sep 1848); l.o.a. (Sep–Oct 1848); *Yorktown*, Afr.Sqdn. (Oct 1848–Sep 1850); home and l.o.a. (Sep 1850–Jan 1851); *St. Lawrence*, spec.serv. (Jan–Aug 1851); *Saranac*, Home Sqdn. (Nov 1851–Jun 1852); l.o.a. (Jun–Oct 1852); USNA (Oct 1852–Jun 1854); w.o. (Jun–Jul 1854); *San Jacinto*, spec.serv. in Eur. and W.Indies (Jul 1854–Mar 1855); *Release*, Arctic Expd. (Apr–Oct 1855); l.o.a. (Oct 1855–Feb 1856); *Relief*, Braz.Sqdn. (Feb 1856–Jul 1857); *Germantown*, E.Ind.Sqdn. (Jul 1857–Apr 1860); *Saranac*, Pac. Sqdn. (Dec 1860–Jul 1862); return and l.o.a. (Jul–Nov 1862); w.o. (Nov 1862–Apr 1863); MS Sqdn. (Oct 1862–Apr 1863); exec.off., flgs. *Minnesota*, N.Atl.Blk.Sqdn. (Apr 1863–Oct 1864); cdr, *Commodore Morris*, then *Hunchback*, N.Atl.Blk.Sqdn. (Oct 1864–Jun 1865); w.o. (Jun 1865–Mar 1866); Navy Yard, Boston (Mar 1866–Apr 1867); *Oneida*, Asia.Sqdn. (Apr 1867–Jun 1868); home, l.o.a., and w.o. (Jun 1868–Apr 1869); cdr, *Saugus*, spec.serv. (Apr 1869–Jan 1870); w.o. (Jan–Oct 1870); in charge, Nitre Depot, Malden, MA (Oct 1870–Oct 1873); recruiting duty, Detroit, MI (Nov 1873–May 1874); cdr, *Ajax*, N.Atl.Sta. (May–Jul 1874); insp., 14th L.h. Dist., Cincinnati (Aug 1874–Jun 1875); cdr, *Monocacy*, Asia.Sta. (Jul 1875–Oct 1877); return to U.S. and w.o. (Oct 1877–Sep 1879); cdr, rec. ship *St. Louis*, Philadelphia (Sep 1879–Jul 1880); cdr, rec. ship *Franklin*, Norfolk, VA (Jul 1880–Oct 1881); cdr, flgs. *Tennessee*, N.Atl.Sta. (Oct 1881–May 1882); cdr, flgs. *Pensacola*, Pac.Sta. (Aug 1882–May 1883); home and sick lv. (May 1883–Jun 1884); Navy Yard, Boston (Jun 1884–Nov 1887); w. o. (Nov 1887–May 1888); member, gen. court-martial (Jun–Jul 1888); w.o. (Jul 1888–Oct 1890); pres., bd. to examine naval and merchant vessels, Boston (Oct 1890–Jun 1891); cdr, Naval Sta., New London, CT (Jun 1891–Jun 1893); comdt., Navy Yard, Boston (Jul 1893–Jul 1894); retired (20 Jul 1894).

References
Personal Papers: 1 item (1892) in NHF,LC.
Other Sources: R. W. Daly, "Joe Fyffe—Officer and Gentleman," U.S. Naval Institute *Proceedings* 638 (Apr 1956): 417–25; 641 (Jul 1956): 763.

BANCROFT GHERARDI Born in Jackson, LA, on 10 Nov 1832, son of Donato and Jane (Bancroft) Gherardi, his mother being sister to future Secretary of the Navy George Bancroft. Married to Anna Talbot Rockwell. Two sons, including Capt Walter R. Gherardi, USN. Died in Stratford, CT, on 10 Dec 1903. Buried in Annapolis, MD.

BANCROFT GHERARDI
1832–1903

Ranks Act.Midn (29 Jun 1846); PMidn (8 Jun 1852); Mstr (15 Sep 1855); Lt (16 Sep 1855); LCdr (16 Jul 1862); Cdr (25 Jul 1866); Capt (9 Nov 1874); Commo (3 Nov 1884); RAdm (25 Aug 1887); placed on Ret.Lst. (10 Nov 1894).

Career Summary Received appointment from MA (29 Jun 1846); Naval School, Annapolis, MD (Jun–Dec 1846); *Ohio* then *Dale*, Pac.Sqdn. (Dec 1846–Aug 1849); home and w.o. (Aug 1849–Feb 1850); flgs. *Saranac*, Home Sqdn. (Feb 1850–Jul 1851); USNA (Aug 1851–Jun 1852); *St. Louis*, Med.Sqdn. (Jul 1852–May 1855); l.o.a. (May–Aug 1855); *Saratoga*, Home Sqdn. (Aug 1855–Aug 1857); Naval Rndv., Boston (Aug 1857–Jan 1858); l.o.a. (Jan–Mar 1858); *Niagara*, spec.serv. (Mar–Aug 1858); l.o.a. (Aug–Sep 1858); Naval Rndv., Boston (Sep 1858–Apr 1859); flgs. *Lancaster*, Pac.Sqdn. (May 1859–Oct 1861); l.o.a. (Oct–Nov 1861); *Chippewa*, N.Atl.Blk.Sqdn. (Nov 1861–May 1863); *Mohican*, spec.serv. (May–Aug 1863); cdr, *Chocura*, W.Gulf Blk.Sqdn. (Aug 1863–May 1864); cdr, *Port Royal*, W.Gulf Blk.Sqdn. (May–Dec 1864); cdr, *John P. Jackson*, W.Gulf Blk.Sqdn. (Dec 1864–Jan 1865); cdr, *Port Royal*, W.Gulf Blk.Sqdn (Jan 1865–Feb 1866); l.o.a. and w.o. (Feb–May 1866); Naval Observatory, Washington, DC (May–Jul 1866); Hydrographic Office, Washington, DC (Jul–Aug 1866); Naval Rndv., Philadelphia (Sep 1866–Jan 1867); cdr, *Tahoma*, spec. duty, Vera Cruz, Mexico (Jan–Jun 1867); nav. and equipment duty, Navy Yard, Philadelphia (Jun 1867–Jun 1870); w.o. (Jun–Oct 1870); cdr, *Jamestown*, Pac.Flt. (Nov 1870–Sep 1871); cdr, rec. ship *Independence*, Mare Island, CA (Sep 1871–Apr 1874); temp. cdr, flgs. *Richmond*, S.Pac.Sta. (Apr–Aug 1874); w.o. (Aug 1874–Jan 1875); cdr, flgs. *Pensacola*, N.Pac.Sta. (Jan 1875–Mar 1876); w.o. (Mar–Aug 1876); suspended (12 Aug 1876); restored to service (23 Feb 1877); w.o. (Feb 1877–Feb 1878); cdr, rec. ship *Colorado*, NY (May 1878–Jun 1881); w.o. (Jun–Jul 1881); cdr, flgs. *Lancaster*, Eur.Sta. (Aug 1881–Nov 1883); l.o.a. (Nov 1883–Sep 1884); member, Naval Exam. and Ret. Bds. (Sep 1884–Apr 1885); pres., Naval Exam.Bd. (Apr–Oct 1885); gov., Naval Asylum, Philadelphia (Oct 1885–Sep 1886); comdt., Navy Yard, NY (Oct 1886–Feb 1889); cdr, N.Atl.Sta., *Galena* (Feb 1889–Sep 1892); cdr, Spec.Sqdn., International Review, *Baltimore* (Sep 1892–Feb 1893); cdr, Naval Review Flt., Hampton Roads, VA, *Philadelphia* (Mar–May 1893); comdt., Navy Yard, NY (Jun 1893–Nov 1894); placed on Ret.Lst. (10 Nov 1894).

WILLIAM CAMPBELL GIBSON
1838–1911

WILLIAM CAMPBELL GIBSON Born in Albany, NY, on 23 Jul 1838, son of Joseph and Marion (Campbell) Gibson. Educated in Albany to 1847, then at Sand Lake Academy in Albany from 1847 to 1855. Served as clerk in the hardware business in Albany before joining merchant service. Married Aurelia A. Holbrook on 5 Aug 1875. Six children. Died at his home in Brooklyn, NY, on 10 May 1911. Buried in Greenwood Cemetery in Brooklyn.

Ranks Enlisted in Volunteer Navy (Aug 1861); Act. Master's Mate (15 Dec 1862); Act.Ens (22 Aug 1863); transferred to Regular Navy as Ens (12 Mar 1868); Mstr (18 Dec 1868); Lt (21 Mar 1870); LCdr (13 Jul 1884); Cdr (4 Jul 1893); Capt (18 Feb 1900); placed on Ret.Lst. with rank of RAdm (23 Jul 1900).

Career Summary Enlisted into Volunteer Navy (Aug 1861); *Fernandina*, N. and S. Atl.Blk.Sqdns. (Dec 1862–Aug 1863); Navy Yard, NY (Aug–Oct 1863); *Governor Buckingham*, N.Atl.Blk.Sqdn. (Oct 1863–Oct 1864); *Banshee*, N.Atl.Blk.Sqdn. (Oct 1864); cdr, *Resolute*, Potomac Flot. (Oct 1864–Jun 1865); *Ino*, Med.Sqdn. (Jul 1865–Jan 1867); *Guard*, Eur.Sta. (May 1867–Oct 1868); rec. ship, *Potomac*, Philadelphia (Oct–Dec 1868); *Narragansett*, W.Ind.Sta. (Jan–Jul 1869); w.o. (Jul–Sep 1869); Navy Yard, NY (Sep 1869–Jun 1870); *Mohican*, and storeship *Callao*, Pac.Sta. (Jul 1870–Oct 1873); w.o. (Nov–Dec 1873); recruiting duty, Burlington, VT (Dec 1873–Jan 1874); *Roanoke*, NY (Jan–Jun 1874); *Minnesota*, NY (Jun 1874–Jul 1875); *Frolic*, S.Atl.Sta. (Aug 1875–Oct 1877); w.o. (Oct 1877–Mar 1878); Navy Yard, NY (Mar 1878–Jan 1881); exec.off., *Yantic*, N.Atl.Sta. (Jan 1881–Jan 1884); w.o. (Jan–Mar 1884); Navy Yard, Pensacola, FL (Apr 1884–Jun 1888); w.o. (Jun–Sep 1888); exec.off., *Monongahela*, Pac.Sta. (Sep 1888–Feb 1890); cdr, *Monongahela*, Pac.Sta. (Feb–Sep 1890); l.o.a. (Sep–Nov 1890); spec. duty, then equip. duty, Navy Yard, NY (Nov 1890–Mar 1892); cdr, *Fern*, spec.serv. (Mar 1892–Nov 1893); equip.off., Navy Yard, Portsmouth, NH (Nov 1893–Nov 1896); home and w.o. (Nov–Dec 1896); cdr, training ship *Adams*, Pac.Flt. (Jan 1897–Apr 1898); Navy Yard, League Island, PA (Apr–May 1898); cdr, *City of Peking*, spec.serv. (May–Sep 1898); *Adams*, Navy Yard, Mare Island, CA (Sep 1898); w.o. (Sep–Oct 1898); senior member, Bd. of Insp., Navy Yard, NY (Oct 1898–Jan 1900); cdr, *Texas*, N.Atl.Sta. (Jan–Jul 1900); placed on Ret.Lst. (23 Jul 1900).

OLIVER S. GLISSON Born in Brookville, OH, on 18 Jan 1809, son of Thomas Glisson. Married, with at least two sons. Died on 20 Nov 1890 at his home in Philadelphia.

OLIVER S. GLISSON
1809–1890

Ranks Midn (1 Nov 1826); PMidn (28 Apr 1832); Lt (8 Mar 1837); Cdr (14 Sep 1855); Capt (16 Jul 1862); Commo (25 Jul 1866); RAdm (10 Jun 1870); placed on Ret.Lst. (18 Jan 1871).

Career Summary Received appointment from IN (1 Nov 1826); Naval Sta., Pensacola, FL (Dec 1826–Feb 1828); *Erie*, Pensacola, FL (Feb 1828–Sep 1830); Naval School, NY (Sep 1830–Jun 1831); *Spark*, spec. duty (Jun–Nov 1831); w.o. and l.o.a. (Nov 1831–Dec 1832); Navy Yard, Norfolk, VA (Dec 1832–May 1833); *Delaware*, Med.Sqdn. (May 1833–Dec 1834); l.o.a. (Dec 1834–May 1835); Navy Yard, Norfolk, VA (May 1835–Mar 1836); act.mstr, *Grampus*, Washington, DC (Mar–Oct 1836); Naval Rndv., Norfolk, VA (Oct 1836–Mar 1837); *Fairfield*, Braz.Sqdn. (Mar 1837–Apr 1840); l.o.a. (Apr–Sep 1840); Navy Yard, Norfolk, VA (Sep 1840–Jun 1842); *Warren*, then *Marion*, W.Ind.Sqdn. (Jun 1842–Jul 1843); l.o.a. (Jul–Aug 1843); Navy Yard, Norfolk, VA (Aug 1843–Dec 1844); *Saratoga*, Braz.Sqdn. (Dec 1844–Jan 1847); l.o.a. (Jan–Mar 1847); *Saratoga*, Home Sqdn. (Mar 1847–May 1848); cdr, *Reefer*, Home Sqdn. (May 1847); Navy Yard, Norfolk, VA (Jun 1848–Jun 1850); w.o. (Jun–Aug 1850); spec. duty, war steamers under construction (Aug 1850–May 1852); *Powhatan*, E.Ind.Sqdn. (May 1852–Feb 1856); l.o.a. and w.o. (Feb 1856–Mar 1857); Naval Asylum, Philadelphia (Mar 1857–May 1860); w.o. (May 1860–Apr 1861); cdr, *Ice Boat*, Philadelphia (Apr–May 1861); cdr, *Mount Vernon*, N.Atl.Blk.Sqdn. (May 1861–Aug 1862); l.o.a. (Aug–Oct 1862); cdr, *Mohican*, spec.serv. (Oct 1862–Apr 1864); cdr, *Santiago de Cuba*, spec.serv. (May 1864–Jun 1865); w.o. (Jun 1865–Jan 1867); cdr, Naval Sta., League Island, PA (Jan 1867–Apr 1870); w.o. (Apr–Jul 1870); cdr, Eur.Flt., *Franklin* (Aug 1870–Jan 1871); placed on Ret.Lst. (18 Jan 1871).

Career Highlights On board *Powhatan* during Commo Matthew C. Perry's expedition to Japan. In the Civil War, commanded *Mount Vernon* and helped save the transport *Mississippi* that had run aground off North Carolina and that had on board 1500 troops heading for New Orleans and the action there. Participated in both actions against Fort Fisher, NC.

References
Sources: *To the Loving Memory of Rear Admiral Oliver S. Glisson, U.S.N., by his two Sons* (Baltimore: 1891).

SYLVANUS WILLIAM GODON
Born in Philadelphia, PA, on 18 Jun 1809. Widower with no children. Died in Blois, France, on 17 May 1879.

Ranks Midn (4 Mar 1819); PMidn (4 Jun 1831); Lt (17 Dec 1836); Cdr (14 Sep 1855); Capt (16 Jul 1862); Commo (2 Jan 1863); Act.RAdm (16 May 1865); RAdm (25 Jul 1866); placed on Ret.Lst. (18 Jun 1871).

Career Summary Received appointment from PA (4

SYLVANUS WILLIAM GODON
1809–1879

Mar 1819); w.o. (Mar 1819–Jan 1820); on furlough (Jan 1820–Jun 1823); Navy Yard, Philadelphia (Jun 1823–Apr 1826); *Macedonian*, Braz.Sqdn. (Apr 1826–Nov 1828); Naval School, Norfolk, VA (Nov 1828–Jun 1829); *Natchez*, Med.Sqdn. (Jun 1829–Feb 1830); l.o.a. (Feb–Mar 1830); Naval School, Norfolk, VA (Mar–Jul 1830); rec. ship *Congress*, Norfolk, VA (Jul–Sep 1830); Naval School, NY (Sep 1830–Mar 1831); w.o. (Mar–May 1831); l.o.a. (May–Jun 1831); *Potomac, Shark*, and *Peacock*, Pac.Sqdn. (Jul 1831–Oct 1837); l.o.a. (Oct 1837–Mar 1839); *Cyane*, Med.Sqdn. (Mar 1839–Jun 1840); *Ohio*, Navy Yard, Boston (Jun 1840–Jun 1841); l.o.a. and w.o. (Jun 1841–Feb 1842); Naval Rndv., Philadelphia (Feb 1842–Sep 1843); *Boston*, Braz.Sqdn. (Sep 1843–Jan 1846); l.o.a. and w.o. (Jan–Oct 1846); Naval Rndv., Philadelphia (Oct 1846–Feb 1847); *Vesuvius*, NY (Feb 1847–Feb 1848); Navy Dept., Washington, DC (Apr–Oct 1848); ord. duty, Navy Yard, Washington, DC (Oct–Nov 1848); w.o. (Nov 1848–Apr 1849); spec. duty, war steamers under construction (Apr 1849–Dec 1850); exec.off., *Susquehanna*, E.Ind.Sqdn. (Dec 1850–Jun 1853); w.o. (Jun 1853–Apr 1854); Navy Yard, Philadelphia (Apr 1854–Jun 1855); member, Naval Efficiency Bd., Washington, DC (Jun–Sep 1855); Navy Yard, Philadelphia (Sep–Oct 1855); w.o. (Oct 1855–Mar 1858); l.o.a. and w.o. (Mar 1858–Oct 1859); cdr, *Mohican*, Pac.Sqdn. (Oct 1859–Jul 1862); cdr, *Powhatan*, S.Atl.Blk.Sqdn. (Aug 1862–Mar 1863); sick lv. (Mar–Nov 1863); member, Naval Examining Bd. (Nov–Dec 1863); spec. duty, Navy Yard, Philadelphia (Dec 1863–Jul 1864); cdr, *Susquehanna*, then cdr, *Brooklyn*, S.Atl.Blk.Sqdn. (Jul 1864–Sep 1867); w.o. (Sep 1867–Jan 1868); comdt., Navy Yard, NY (May 1868–Oct 1870); w.o. (Oct 1870–Jul 1872); placed on Ret.Lst. (18 Jun 1871).

References

Personal Papers: 91 items (1831–49) in Cincinnati Historical Society, Cincinnati, OH.

LOUIS MALESHERBES
GOLDSBOROUGH
1805–1877

LOUIS MALESHERBES GOLDSBOROUGH Born in Washington, DC, on 18 Feb 1805, son of Charles Washington and Catherine (Roberts) Goldsborough. His father served as chief clerk of the Navy Dept. from 1798 to 1813, and secretary of the Bd. of Navy Commissioners from 1815 to 1842. Married Elizabeth Wirt on 11 Nov 1833. Three children. A brother was Commo John Rodgers Goldsborough, USN. Died in Washington, DC, on 20 Feb 1877.

Ranks Midn (18 Jun 1812); Lt (13 Jan 1825); Cdr (8 Sep 1841); Capt (14 Sep 1855); RAdm (16 Jul 1862); placed on Ret.Lst. (6 Oct 1873).

Career Summary Received appointment from Washington, DC (18 Jun 1812); never in actual service (Jun 1812–Jul 1816); Navy Yard, Boston (Jul 1816–Sep 1817); flgs. *Franklin*, Med.Sqdn. (Sep 1817–Apr 1820); *Guerriere*, Navy Yard, Norfolk, VA (Apr 1820–Oct 1821); flgs. *Franklin*, Pac.Sqdn. (Oct

1821–Oct 1824); survey duty (Oct 1824–Jun 1825); court-martial duty (Jul–Aug 1825); l.o.a. to study in Europe, then w.o. (Aug 1825–Dec 1830); in charge, Depot of Charts and Instruments, Washington, DC (Dec 1830–Feb 1833); l.o.a. and w.o. (Feb 1833–Sep 1839); *United States*, Pac.Sqdn. (Sep 1839–Sep 1841); *Marion*, Braz.Sqdn. (Sep 1841–Jun 1842); l.o.a. (Jun–Nov 1842); Navy Dept., Washington, DC (Nov 1842–Jan 1843); Navy Yard, Portsmouth, NH (Jan 1843–Apr 1845); w.o. (Apr 1845–Nov 1846); exec.off., *Ohio*, Home Sqdn. (Nov 1846–Jun 1847); w.o. (Jun–Oct 1847); cdr, Naval Rndv., Baltimore (Oct 1847–Jan 1849); detached duty, senior naval member, commission exploring recently acquired lands of CA and OR (Jan 1849–Dec 1850); Navy Dept., Washington, DC (Dec 1850–Apr 1851); w.o. (Apr 1851–Mar 1852); cdr, flgs. *Cumberland*, Med.Sqdn. (Apr–Nov 1852); cdr, flgs. *Levant*, Med.Sqdn. (Nov 1852–Apr 1853); return and w.o. (Apr–Oct 1853); supt., USNA (Nov 1853–Sep 1857); w.o. (Sep 1857–Jan 1859); spec. duty, Washington, DC (Jan–Jun 1859); cdr, flgs. *Congress*, Braz.Sta. (Jun 1859–Sep 1861); cdr, Atl., then N.Atl.Blk.Sqdn., *Minnesota* and *Philadelphia* (Sep 1861–Sep 1862); w.o. (Sep–Oct 1862); spec. administrative duties, Washington, DC (Oct 1862–Apr 1865); cdr, Eur.Sqdn., *Colorado* (Apr 1865–Aug 1867); w.o. (Aug 1867–Mar 1869); senior member, bd. to examine steam engines (Mar–Oct 1869); port adm, Washington, DC (Oct 1869–Sep 1870); insp. of hulls in ordinary (Oct 1869–Oct 1870); cdr, Navy Yard, Washington, DC (Oct 1870–Oct 1873); placed on Ret.Lst. (6 Oct 1873).

Career Highlights With Med.Sqdn., commanded volunteer boat expedition in Sep 1827 against pirates, recapturing brig HMS *Comet*. Recommended creation of a Depot of Charts and Instruments: became the superintendent in Dec 1830. In 1833, while on leave, conducted a group of German immigrants into FL to estate of his father-in-law, William Wirt, then commanded steamboat expedition and company of volunteers during the Seminole War. During the Mexican War, was present at bombardment of Vera Cruz in Mar 1847 and in following month led a landing party at Tuxpan. Served as supt. of USNA from 1853 to 1857. Although at retirement age when Civil War began, was appointed flag officer of the Atl.Blk.Sqdn., assisting the army in the capture of Roanoke Island, NC, in Feb 1862. Participated in the Peninsular Campaign during the spring of 1862, eventually asking to be relieved of command owing to public criticism of this campaign's failure.

References

Personal Papers: a) 8,000 items (1817–74) in LC. b) 2 vols., 3 boxes (1821–73) in NYPL. c) 523 items, 1 vol. (1827–77) WPL. d) in Wirt Family Papers in SHC. e) in Gardiner Collection in Historical Society of PA, Philadelphia.

Additional Sources: a) Thorton A. Jenkins, *Rear Admiral Goldsborough and the Retiring Laws of the Navy* (Washington, DC: 1868). b) Melancton Smith, *Naval Retiring Laws and Rear Admiral Goldsborough* (Washington, DC: 1868). c) Caspar F. Goodrich, "Memorabilia of the Old Navy," U.S. Naval Institute *Proceedings* 112 (1904): 823–30. d) Edward C. Gardiner, "Narrative of Rear Admiral Goldsborough, U.S. Navy," U.S. Naval Institute *Proceedings* 365 (Jul 1933): 1023–31, 1091; 369 (Nov 1933): 1669–70.

JOSEPH FOSTER GREEN
1811–1897

JOSEPH FOSTER GREEN Born in Bath, ME, on 24 Nov 1811, son of Peter N. Green. Died in Brookline, MA, on 9 Dec 1897. Buried in Bath, ME.

Ranks Midn (1 Nov 1827); PMidn (10 Jun 1833); Lt (28 Feb 1838); Cdr (14 Sep 1855); Capt (16 Jul 1862); Commo (2 Dec 1867); RAdm (13 Jul 1870); transferred to Ret.Lst. (25 Nov 1872).

Career Summary Received appointment from ME (1 Nov 1827); w.o. (Nov 1827–Jul 1828); Navy Yard, Boston (Jul–Nov 1828); *Dolphin*, Pac.Sqdn. (Nov 1828–Mar 1829); *Vandalia*, Braz.Sqdn. (Mar 1829–Aug 1831); l.o.a. (Aug–Nov 1831); *Grampus*, Afr. Sqdn. (Nov 1831–Aug 1832); l.o.a. (Aug–Dec 1832); Naval School, Norfolk, VA (Oct 1832–Jun 1833); l.o.a. and w.o. (Jun 1833–Feb 1834); rec. ship *Columbus*, Boston (Feb–Aug 1834); *Potomac*, Med.Sqdn. (Aug 1834–Mar 1837); l.o.a. and w.o. (Mar–Sep 1837); Navy Yard, Boston (Sep 1837–May 1838); *Erie*, W.Ind.Sqdn. (May 1838–Jun 1840); l.o.a. (Jun–Sep 1840); in ordinary, Boston (Sep 1840–Jan 1842); *Columbia*, Braz.Sqdn. (Jan 1842–Jan 1845); l.o.a. and w.o. (Jan–Sep 1845); Naval Rndv., Boston (Sep 1845–Nov 1846); *Ohio*, Pac.Sqdn. (Nov 1846–Apr 1850); l.o.a. (Apr–Jun 1850); Navy Yard, Boston (Jun 1850–Apr 1852); *Princeton*, spec.serv. (Apr–Jun 1852); ord. duty, Navy Yard, Boston (Sep 1852–Dec 1854); asst.exec.off., USNA (Jan–May 1855); comdt. of midn, USNA (May 1855–Mar 1858); w.o. (Mar–Oct 1858); cdr, *America*, spec.serv. (Nov–Dec 1858); w.o. (Dec 1858–Feb 1860); ord. duty, Navy Yard, Boston (Feb 1860–Jun 1862); cdr, *Canandaigua*, S.Atl.Blk.Sqdn. (Jun 1862–Dec 1864); return home and w.o. (Dec 1864–Mar 1865); spec. duty (Mar–Jun 1865); ord. duty, Navy Yard, Boston (Jun 1865–Jun 1868); pres., Bd. to Select Powder Magazine (Jun–Jul 1868); w.o. (Jul 1868–Mar 1869); member, Bd. to Survey Ord. (Mar 1869–Jan 1870); cdr, Southern Sqdn., Atl.Flt., *Congress* (Jan 1870–Jun 1871); w.o. (Jun 1871–Mar 1872); pres., Bd. of Naval Examiners, Washington, DC (Mar–Jul 1872); cdr, N.Atl.Sta., *Worcester* (Aug 1872–May 1873); transferred to Ret.Lst. (25 Nov 1872).

References
Personal Papers: 60 items (1828–1960) in NHF,LC.

THEODORE PHINNEY GREENE
1809–1887

THEODORE PHINNEY GREENE Born in Montreal, Canada, on 1 Nov 1809, moving to VT at early age. Died in Jaffrey, NH, on 30 Aug 1887. Survived by wife and son.

Ranks Midn (1 Nov 1826); PMidn (28 Apr 1832); Lt (20 Dec 1837); Cdr (14 Sep 1855); Capt (16 Jul 1862); Commo (24 Jul 1867); placed on Ret.Lst. (1 Nov 1871); RAdm on Ret.Lst. (24 May 1872).

Career Summary Received appointment from VT (1 Nov 1826); *Warren*, Med.Sqdn. (Nov 1826–Jul 1830); *Java*, Med.Sqdn. (Jul–Sep 1830); *Ontario*, Med.Sqdn. (Sep 1830–Aug 1831); *Brandywine*, Med.Sqdn. (Aug–Sep 1831); *Constellation*, Med.Sqdn. (Sep–Nov 1831); l.o.a. (Nov 1831–Jul 1833); *Vincennes*, Pac. and E.Ind. Sqdns. (Aug 1833–Jun 1836); l.o.a. (Jun–Dec 1836); Navy Yard, NY (Dec 1836–Jan 1837); *Independence*, Braz.Sqdn. (Jan 1837–Apr 1840); l.o.a. (Apr–Oct 1840); rec. ship *Columbia*, Boston (Oct 1840–Jan 1842); *Grampus*, Home Sqdn. (Jan–Sep 1842); l.o.a. (Sep 1842–Jan 1843); *St. Louis*, Norfolk, VA (Jan–Mar 1843); *Lexington*, Med.Sqdn. (Mar 1843–May 1844); w.o. (May 1844–Aug 1845); *Congress*, Pac.Sqdn. (Aug 1845–Jan 1849); l.o.a. (Jan–Mar 1849); w.o. (Mar 1849–Sep 1851); *Cyane*, Home Sqdn. (Sep 1851–Oct 1853); l.o.a. (Oct–Nov 1853); Navy Yard, Boston (Nov 1853–Oct 1857); insp., 1st L.h. Dist., Portland, ME (Oct 1857–Dec 1860); s.a. and w.o. (Dec 1860–Apr 1861); Navy Yard, Mare Island, CA (May 1861–Mar 1863); cdr, *Shenandoah*, Philadelphia (May 1863); cdr, *Santiago de Cuba*, "Flying Sqdn." (May–Dec 1863); w.o. (Dec 1863–Apr 1864); cdr, *San Jacinto*, E.Gulf Blk.Sqdn. (Apr–Dec 1864); temp. cdr, E.Gulf Blk.Sqdn., *San Jacinto* (Jul–Oct 1864); cdr, *Richmond*, W.Gulf Blk.Sqdn. (Dec 1864–Jul 1865); w.o. (Jul–Oct 1865); ord. duty, Navy Yard, Portsmouth, NH (Oct 1865–Oct 1866); cdr, flgs. *Powhatan*, Pac.Sqdn. (Dec 1866–Jan 1868); home and w.o. (Jan–May 1868); member, Bd. of Visitors, USNA (May–Jun 1868); cdr, Navy Yard, Pensacola, FL (Oct 1868–Jun 1870); w.o. (Jun 1870–Nov 1871); transferred to Ret.Lst. (1 Nov 1871).

References
Personal Papers: 1 vol. (1863–64) in NYHS.

JAMES AUGUSTIN GREER Born in Cincinnati, OH, on 28 Feb 1833, son of James and Caroline (King) Greer. Married to Mary Randolph Webb: a daughter and two sons. Died in Washington, DC, on 17 Jun 1904. Buried in Arlington National Cemetery.

Ranks Act.Midn (10 Jan 1848); PMidn (15 Jun 1854); Mstr (15 Sep 1855); Lt (16 Sep 1855); LCdr (16 Jul 1862); Cdr (25 Jul 1866); Capt (26 Apr 1876); Commo (19 May 1886); Act.RAdm (24 Aug 1887); RAdm (3 Apr 1892); placed on Ret.Lst. (28 Feb 1895).

Career Summary Received appointment from OH (10 Jan 1848); Naval School, Annapolis, MD (Jan–Mar 1848); *Saratoga*, Home Sqdn. (Mar 1848–Nov 1849); l.o.a. (Nov 1849–Feb 1850); *Saranac*, Home Sqdn. (Feb–Aug 1850); *St. Mary's*, Pac.Sqdn. (Aug 1850–Dec 1852); l.o.a. (Dec 1852–Jan 1853); *Columbia*, Home Sqdn. (Jan–Oct 1853); USNA (Oct

JAMES AUGUSTIN GREER
1833–1904

1853–Jun 1854); w.o. (Jun–Aug 1854); *Independence*, Pac.Sqdn. (Sep 1854–Oct 1857); l.o.a. (Oct–Dec 1857); Navy Yard, Norfolk, VA (Dec 1857–Oct 1858); *Southern Star*, Paraguay Expd. (Oct 1858—Jun 1859); w.o. (Jun–Aug 1859); *Sumter*, then *San Jacinto*, Afr.Sqdn. (Aug 1859–Nov 1861); *St. Louis*, spec.serv. (Jan–Oct 1862); Navy Dept., Washington, DC (Oct–Dec 1862); cdr, *Carondelet*, then *Benton*, MS Sqdn. (Jan 1863–Aug 1864); spec. duty, Cincinnati (Aug–Sep 1864); cdr, Naval Sta., Mound City, IL (Oct–Nov 1864); cdr, flgs. *Black Hawk*, MS Sqdn. (Nov–Dec 1864); w.o. (Dec 1864–Jan 1865); USNA (Jan 1865–Sep 1866); cdr, *Mohongo*, N.Pac.Sta. (Oct 1866–Sep 1867); cdr, *Tuscarora*, N.Pac.Sta. (Nov–Dec 1867); w.o. (Jan–Jun 1868); ord. duty, Navy Yard, Philadelphia (Jul 1868–Mar 1869); USNA (Mar 1869–Jul 1873); cdr, *Tigress*, spec.serv., *Polaris* Relief Expd. (Jul–Nov 1873); w.o. (Nov–Dec 1873); member, Bd. of Inspection (Dec 1873–Nov 1875); cdr, *Lackawanna*, Pac. Sta. (Nov 1875–Mar 1877); w.o. (Mar–Aug 1877); cdr, *Constitution*, spec.serv. (Aug 1877); w.o. (Aug 1877–Jan 1878); member, Bd. of Examiners (Jan–Mar 1878); temp. cdr, *Constellation*, spec.serv., Paris Exposition (Mar–Jul 1878); w.o. (Jul 1878–Mar 1879); cdr, *Hartford*, S.Atl.Sta. (Apr–Dec 1879); w.o. (Dec 1879–Mar 1880); member, Bd. of Inspection (Apr 1880–Apr 1882); capt.yd., Navy Yard, Washington, DC (Apr 1882–Aug 1884); w.o. (Aug 1884–Apr 1885); member, Ret.Bd. (Apr–Dec 1885); member, then pres., Naval Exam.Bd. (Apr 1885–Jul 1887); member, then pres., Naval Ret.Bd. (Jun 1886–Jul 1887); cdr, Eur.Sta., *Lancaster* (Aug 1887–Jun 1889); member, various bds. and spec. duties (Jun 1889–Feb 1895); placed on Ret.Lst. (28 Feb 1895).

Career Highlights On *San Jacinto* when that vessel stopped British mail steamer *Trent* and removed the Confederate emissaries Mason and Slidell in 1861. Participated in numerous Civil War actions, including siege at Vicksburg and the Red River Campaign.

FRANCIS HOYT GREGORY
1789–1866

FRANCIS HOYT GREGORY Born in Norwalk, CT, on 9 Oct 1789. From Mar 1802 to his entry into the service, served in merchant service. Died in Brooklyn, NY, on 4 Oct 1866. Buried in New Haven, CT.

Ranks Midn (16 Jan 1809); resigned (30 Aug 1813); resignation revoked (3 Sep 1813); Lt (28 Jun 1814); Mstr.Comdt. (24 Apr 1828); Capt (18 Jan 1838); placed on Ret.Lst. with rank of RAdm (16 Jul 1866).

Career Summary Received appointment from CT (16 Jan 1809); *Revenge*, NY Flot. (Jan–Mar 1809); *Vesuvius*, W.Ind.Sqdn. (Mar 1809–Jun 1810); on furlough for merchant serv. (Jun 1810–Feb 1811); Gunboat No. 182, New Orleans (Feb–Apr 1811); cdr, Gunboat No. 182, New Orleans, then NY Stas. (Apr 1811–Mar 1812); Gunboat duty, NY (Apr–Sep 1812); duty, Lake Ontario (Sep 1812–Aug 1814); resigned (30 Aug 1813); resignation revoked (3 Sep 1813); prisoner of war

(Aug 1814–Jun 1815); *Congress*, then *United States*, Med.Sqdn. (Jun 1815–Oct 1817); *Constellation*, en route home (Oct–Nov 1817); *Washington*, NY (Oct 1818–Aug 1821); cdr, *Grampus*, W.Ind.Sqdn. (Aug 1821–Oct 1822); w.o. (Oct 1822–Jan 1824); supernumerary, *Washington*, NY (Jan 1824); Navy Yard, NY (Jan 1824–Jun 1825); *Brandywine*, spec.serv., then Med.Sqdn. (Jun 1825–Jul 1826); Navy Yard, NY (Jul–Sep 1826); on furlough (Sep 1826–Apr 1827); Navy Yard, NY (Apr 1827–Mar 1831); cdr, *Falmouth*, Pac.Sqdn. (Mar 1831–Feb 1834); w.o. (Feb 1834–Jun 1841); cdr, rec. ship *North Carolina*, NY (Jun 1841–Oct 1843); cdr, *Raritan*, Braz. and W.Ind. Sqdns. (Oct 1843–Dec 1846); cdr, *Cumberland* (Dec 1846–Jan 1847); l.o.a. and w.o. (Jan 1847–Aug 1849); cdr, Afr.Sqdn., *Portsmouth* (Oct 1849–Jun 1851); l.o.a. and w.o. (Jun 1851–Feb 1852); comdt., Navy Yard and Sta., Boston (May 1852–Nov 1855); *Merrimack*, Boston (Nov 1855–Feb 1856); w.o. (Feb 1856–Jan 1859); spec. duty, NY (Jan–Dec 1859); w.o. (Dec 1859–Jul 1861); spec.serv. supervising construction of gunboats (Jul 1861–Oct 1866); placed on Ret.Lst. (16 Jul 1862).

Career Highlights Served under Commo Isaac Chauncey on Lake Ontario during War of 1812, participating in attack on Little York, Canada, on 27 Apr 1813 and against Fort George on 27 May of that year. With Chauncey in actions and skirmishes on Lake Ontario until captured by British in Aug 1814. Sent to England as prisoner until Jun 1815. Saw much service in the Med. against Algerine pirates and in the W.Indies.

WILLIAM HARKNESS Born in Ecclefechan, Scotland, on 17 Dec 1837, son of James and Jane Weild Harkness. Emigrated in 1840 to Jersey City, NJ, where his father became Presbyterian minister. Studied at Lafayette College in PA from 1854 to 1856, then at Rochester Univ. from 1856 to 1858. Took the A.B. degree in 1858, the A.M. in 1861, and the LL.D. in 1874. Received the A.M. from Lafayette College in 1865. Studied medicine at the Homeopathic College, NY, receiving the M.D. in 1862. Remained unmarried. Died on 28 Feb 1903 at his home in Jersey City, NJ.

Ranks Prof. of Math. with rel.rank of LCdr (24 Aug 1863); Prof. of Math. with rel.rank of Cdr (31 May 1872); Prof. of Math. with rel.rank of Capt (30 Jun 1897); placed on the Ret.Lst. as Prof. of Math. with rel.rank of RAdm (17 Dec 1899).

WILLIAM HARKNESS
1837–1903

Career Summary Aide, U.S. Naval Observatory, Washington, DC (1 Aug 1862); received appointment from NY as prof. of math. (24 Aug 1863); Naval Observatory, Washington, DC (Aug 1862–Oct 1865); *Monadnock*, spec.serv. (Oct 1865–Jun 1866); report and w.o. (Jun–Oct 1866); Hydrographic Office, Washington, DC (Oct 1866–Oct 1867); Naval Observatory, Washington, DC (Oct 1867–Jun 1874); *Swatara*, spec. scientific serv. (Jun 1874–Jun 1875); spec. duty, Naval

Observatory, Washington, DC (Jun 1875–May 1897); asst.supt., Naval Observatory, Washington, DC (Oct 1892–Sep 1894); dir., Nautical Almanac Office, Washington, DC (Jun 1897–Dec 1899); dir. of astronomy, Naval Observatory, Washington, DC (Sep 1894–Dec 1899); placed on Ret.Lst. (17 Dec 1899).

Career Highlights First served as a surgeon with the Army at the First Battle of Bull Run and again during the attack on Washington in 1864. Became one of the U.S.'s foremost astronomers. Discovered the coronal line K1474 during the total eclipse of the sun in Aug 1869. Member from 1871 of the U.S. Transit of Venus Commission. Headed the Venus parties at Hobart, Tasmania, in 1874 and again in Washington, DC, in 1882. Discovered in 1879 theory of the focal curve of achromatic telescopes. Designed most of the large instruments at the U.S. Naval Observatory used during the latter part of the nineteenth and early part of the twentieth centuries.

References

Personal Papers: a) 4 vols. in U.S. Naval Observatory Lib., Washington, DC. b) 1.5 ft. (1849–1900) in Univ. of Rochester (NY) Lib.

Writings: *Observations on Terrestrial Magnetism and on the Deviation of the Compass of the United States Ironclad* Monadnock . . . *in 1865 and 1866* (Washington, DC: 1873).

Other Sources: S. DeCristofaro, "William Harkness, Successor to Maury," U.S. Naval Institute *Proceedings* 606 (Aug 1953): 877–79.

DAVID BUTTZ HARMONY Born in Easton, PA, on 3 Sep 1832, son of William J. and Ebba (Herster) Harmony. Died in Washington, DC, on 2 Nov 1917. Buried in Arlington National Cemetery.

Ranks Act.Midn (7 Apr 1847); PMidn (10 Jun 1852); Mstr (15 Sep 1855); Lt (16 Sep 1855); LCdr (16 Jul 1862); Cdr (25 Jul 1866); Capt (4 Feb 1875); Commo (23 Sep 1885); RAdm (26 Mar 1889); retired (26 Jun 1893).

Career Summary Received appointment from PA (7 Apr 1847); Naval School, Annapolis, MD (Jun–Aug 1847); *Brandywine*, Braz.Sqdn. (Aug–Nov 1847); *Ohio, Warren*, and *Falmouth*, Pac.Sqdn. (Nov 1847–Feb 1852); l.o.a. (Feb–Sep 1852); USNA (Sep 1852–Jun 1853); w.o. (Jun–Jul 1853); *Relief*, Braz.Sqdn. (Jul 1853–Jan 1854); w.o. (Jan–Feb 1854); *Relief*, Braz.Sqdn. (Feb 1854–Nov 1855); l.o.a. (Nov–Dec 1855); rec. ship *Ontario*, Baltimore (Jan 1856–Jan 1857); w.o. (Jan–Mar 1857); *Decatur*, Pac.Sqdn. (Mar 1857–Aug 1859); l.o.a. (Aug–Dec 1859); rec. ship *North Carolina*, NY (Dec 1859–Sep 1860); exec.off., *Iroquois*, Med.Sqdn. (Dec 1860–Jun 1861); exec.off., *Iroquois*, E.Gulf Blk.Sqdn. (Aug 1861–Oct 1862); *Nahant*, N.Atl.Blk.Sqdn. (Oct 1862–Aug 1863); sick lv. and w.o. (Aug–

DAVID BUTTZ HARMONY
1832–1917

Oct 1863); spec. duty, NY (Oct–Dec 1863); cdr, *Tahoma*, E.Gulf Blk.Sqdn. (Jan–Jul 1864); w.o. (Jul–Aug 1864); temp. cdr, Naval Rndv., NY (Aug–Dec 1864); cdr, *Sebago*, W.Gulf Blk.Sqdn. (Dec 1864–Jul 1865); w.o. (Jul–Nov 1865); temp. duty, Navy Yard, NY (Nov 1865–May 1867); cdr, *Frolic*, Eur.Sqdn (Jul 1867–May 1869); w.o. (May–Jun 1869); insp. of supplies, Navy Yard, NY (Jun 1869–Jan 1872); w.o. (Jan 1872–Nov 1873); cdr, *Kearsarge*, Asia.Sta. (Nov 1873–Feb 1875); cdr, flgs. *Hartford*, Asia.Sta. (Feb–Oct 1875); w.o. (Oct 1875–Mar 1876); cdr, Naval Rndv., NY (Mar–Jun 1876); w.o. (Jun 1876–Jan 1878); cdr, *Plymouth*, N.Atl.Sta. (Feb 1878–May 1879); w.o. (May–Sep 1879); cdr, flgs. *Powhatan*, N.Atl.Sta. (Oct–Dec 1879); cdr, flgs. *Tennessee*, N.Atl.Sta. (Dec 1879–Jun 1881); cdr, rec. ship *Colorado*, NY (Jun 1881–Apr 1883); spec. duty, Navy Dept., Washington, DC (Apr 1883); member, Exam. and Ret. Bds. (Apr 1883–Mar 1885); chief, Bur. of Yards and Docks, Washington, DC (Mar 1885–Apr 1889); chairman, L.h. Bd., Washington, DC (Mar 1889–May 1891); cdr, Asia.Sta., *Lancaster* (Feb 1892–Jun 1893); retired (26 Jun 1893).

Career Highlights During Civil War, participated in attacks on Ft. Jackson and Ft. St. Philip, on Chalmette Batteries, at New Orleans, against Vicksburg, against the Confederate ram *Arkansas*, against defenses of Charleston, and in the capture of Mobile.

ANDREW ALLEN HARWOOD Born in Settle, Bucks County, PA, on 9 Oct 1802, son of John Edmund Harwood. Died in Marion, MA, on 28 Aug 1884.

Ranks Act.Midn (1 Jan 1818); Lt (3 Mar 1827); Cdr (2 Oct 1848); Capt (14 Sep 1855); Commo (16 Jul 1862); placed on Ret.Lst. (9 Oct 1864); RAdm on Ret.Lst. (16 Feb 1869).

Career Summary Received appointment from PA (1 Jan 1818); *Saranac*, W.Ind.Sta. (Apr–Dec 1818); *Hornet*, W.Ind.Sta. (Mar 1819–Feb 1822); Navy Yard, Philadelphia (Feb–May 1822); rec. ship, Navy Yard, Philadelphia (May–Aug 1822); *Sea Gull*, W.Ind.Sta. (Dec 1822–Sep 1823); Navy Yard, Philadelphia (Dec 1823–Mar 1824); l.o.a. (Mar–Jul 1824); *Constitution*, Med.Sqdn. (Jul 1824–Jul 1827); return to U.S. and l.o.a. (Jul 1827–Oct 1828); rec. ship *Sea Gull*, Philadelphia (Oct. 1828–Mar 1830); l.o.a. and w.o. (Mar 1830–Mar 1831); Navy Yard, NY (Aug 1831–May 1832); *United States*, Med.Sqdn. (May 1832–Aug 1833); spec.serv. and l.o.a. (Aug 1833–Jun 1834); on furlough (Jun 1834–Jul 1835); *Shark*, Med.Sqdn. (Aug 1835–Jan 1838); l.o.a. and w.o. (Jan 1838–Apr 1840); spec.serv., Navy Yard, NY (Apr 1840–May 1843); asst.insp. of ord., Bur. of Ord. and Hydrography, Washington, DC (May 1843–Oct 1852); cdr, *Cumberland*, Med.Sqdn. (Nov 1852–Jul 1855); l.o.a. and w.o. (Jul 1855–Mar 1858); member, Bd. of Examination (Mar–Sep 1858); insp. of ord.,

ANDREW ALLEN HARWOOD
1802–1884

and temp. chief, Bur. of Ord. and Hydrography, Washington, DC (Sep 1858–Apr 1861); member, Bd. of Examiners (May–Aug 1861); chief, Bur. of Ord. and Hydrography, Washington, DC (Apr 1861–Jul 1862); comdt., Navy Yard, Washington, DC, and Potomac Flot. (Jul 1862–Dec 1863); l.o.a. (Dec 1863–Jun 1864); member, Bd. of Examiners, Washington, DC (Jun–Jul 1864); secretary, L.h. Bd., Washington, DC (Jul 1864–Mar 1869); placed on Ret.Lst. (9 Oct 1864); member, Permanent Court, Washington, DC (Mar–Sep 1869); judge advocate, Ret.Bd., Washington, DC (Sep 1869–Oct 1870); judge advocate, USN (Oct 1870–Oct 1871).

References
Personal Papers: Harwood Family Papers, 555 items (1767–1969) in Stanford Univ. Lib., Stanford, CA.

Writings: a) *The Practice of Naval Summary Courts-Martial* (Washington, DC: 1863). b) *The Law and Practice of United States Navy Courts Martial* (New York: 1867).

PHILIP HICHBORN
1839–1910

PHILIP HICHBORN Born in Charlestown, MA, on 4 Mar 1839, son of Philip and Martha (Gould) Hichborn. Graduated from Boston High School, then indentured to government as shipwright apprentice at Boston Navy Yard from 1855 to 1860. By direction of Navy Dept., took course of special instruction in ship construction, calculation, and design. Moved to CA in 1860 and advanced through the civilian positions in the Mare Island Navy Yard's Construction Dept. to become Mstr. Shipwright there in 1862. Married with two children. Died on 1 May 1910 in Washington, DC. Buried in Boston's Mount Auburn Cemetery.

Ranks Asst.Naval Const. (26 Jul 1869); Naval Const. (12 Mar 1875); Naval Const. with rel. rank of Capt (22 Jan 1889); Chief Const. (12 Jul 1893); Chief Const. with rank of RAdm (3 Mar 1899); placed on Ret.Lst. (4 Mar 1901).

Career Summary Received appointment from CA (26 Jul 1869); Navy Yard, Mare Island, CA (Jun 1869–May 1870); Navy Yard, Philadelphia (Jun 1870–Dec 1875); Navy Yard, League Island, PA (Dec 1875–Oct 1884); member, Bd. of Inspection and Survey (Sep 1883–Oct 1884); asst. to chief, Bur. of Construction and Repair, and naval const., Navy Yard, Washington, DC (Nov 1884–Jul 1893); chief const., and chief, Bur. of Construction and Repair, Washington, DC (Jul 1893–Mar 1901): placed on Ret.Lst. (4 Mar 1901).

Career Highlights Invented such things as the Franklin Life Buoy and the Hichborn Balanced Turrets.

References
Writings: a) *Report on European Dockyards* (Washington, DC: 1886, 1889). b) "Sheathed or Unsheathed Ships?" U.S. Naval Institute *Proceedings* 48 (1889): 21–56. c) "Designs for the *Denver* Class, Sheathed Protected Cruisers," U.S. Naval Institute *Proceedings* 92 (1899): 892–96. d) *Standard Design for Boats of the United States Navy* (Washington, DC: 1900).

FRANCIS JOHN HIGGINSON Born in Boston, MA, on 19 Jul 1843, son of Stephen and Agnes Gordon (Cochrane) Higginson. Married Grace Glenwood Haldane on 5 Jan 1878. Died at his residence in Kingston, NY, on 12 Sep 1931.

Ranks Act.Midn (21 Sep 1857); Lt (1 Aug 1862); LCdr (25 Jul 1866); Cdr (10 Jun 1876); Capt (27 Sep 1891); Commo (10 Aug 1898); RAdm (3 Mar 1899); placed on Ret.Lst. (19 Jul 1905).

Career Summary Received appointment from MA (21 Sep 1857); USNA (Sep 1857–May 1861); turned back (21 Jun 1859); *Colorado*, W.Gulf Blk.Sqdn. (Jul 1861–Jun 1862); *Vixen*, *Powhatan*, then *Housatonic*, S.Atl.Sqdn. (Jul 1862–May 1864); USNA (Jun 1864–Jun 1865); flgs. *Hartford*, Asia.Sqdn. (Jun 1865–Aug 1868); w.o. (Aug–Sep 1868); exec.off., rec. ship *New Hampshire*, Norfolk, VA (Sep–Dec 1868); flgs. *Franklin*, Med.Sqdn. (Dec 1868–Nov 1869); *Richmond*, Eur.Sta. (Nov 1869–Sep 1871); exec.off., *Shenandoah*, Eur.Sta. (Sep 1871–Jul 1873); w.o. (Aug–Sep 1873); USNA (Sep–Nov 1873); exec.off., *Franklin*, N.Atl.Sta. (Dec 1873–Mar 1874); exec.off., *Dictator*, N.Atl.Sta. (Mar–May 1874); l.o.a. (May–Jul 1874); cdr, Naval Rndv., Boston (Jul 1874–Jan 1875); exec.off., rec. ship *Ohio*, Boston (Jan–May 1875); torp. instruction, Newport, RI (Jun–Oct 1875); spec. duty, Bur. of Ord., Washington, DC (Oct 1875–Jan 1878); cdr, *Despatch*, Med.Sqdn. (Feb 1878–Jul 1879); w.o. (Jul 1879–Jun 1880); insp., 5th L.h. Dist., Baltimore (Jun 1880–Jun 1882); s.a. and w.o. (Jun–Sep 1882); cdr, *Miantonomah*, spec.serv. (Oct 1882–Mar 1883); w.o. (Mar–Jun 1883); cdr, *Monocacy*, Asia.Sta. (Aug 1883–Apr 1886); w.o. (Apr–Aug 1886); torp. instruction, Newport, RI (Sep 1886–Sep 1887); NWC (Sep–Oct 1887); comdt., Naval Training Sta., and cdr, *New Hampshire*, Newport, RI (Oct 1887–Jul 1890); w.o. and l.o.a. (Jul 1890–Dec 1891); cdr, *Atlanta*, S.Atl.Sqdn. (Dec 1891–May 1893); w.o. (May 1893–Jun 1894); capt.yd., Navy Yard, Mare Island, CA (Jul 1894–Feb 1895); cdr, *Monterey*, Pac.Sqdn. (Feb–Sep 1895); l.o.a. (Sep–Dec 1895); spec.bd. duties, NY (Dec 1895–Jun 1896); capt.yd., Navy Yard, NY (Jun 1896–Jul 1897); cdr, *Massachusetts*, N.Atl.Sqdn. and Flt. (Jul 1897–Sep 1898); member, L.h. Bd. and other bd. duties, Washington, DC (Sep 1898–Apr 1901); cdr, N.Atl.Flt., *Kearsarge* (May 1901–Jul 1903); comdt., Navy Yard, Washington, DC (Jul 1903–Jul 1905); placed on Ret.Lst. (19 Jul 1905).

Career Highlights During the Civil War, participated in actions on lower Mississippi River and in capture of New Orleans. In attacks against Fort Sumter, was exec.off. of *Housatonic* when it was blown up in Feb 1865 by a torpedo boat in Charleston Harbor. Commanded *Massachusetts* during Spanish-American War: advanced three numbers for eminent and conspicuous conduct in battle at Santiago.

References
Writings: a) *Manufacture of Wrought Iron Tubes for Conversion of Dahlgren XI Inch Shell Guns to VIII Inch M.L. Rifle*

FRANCIS JOHN HIGGINSON
1843–1931

. . . (Washington, DC: 1876). b) *Naval Battles in the Century* (Toronto: 1906).

HENRY KUHN HOFF
1809–1878

HENRY KUHN HOFF Born in PA in 1809. Married to Louisa Alexina Wadsworth Bainbridge, the daughter of Commo William Bainbridge. Had at least one son. Died in Washington, DC, on 25 Dec 1878. Buried in St. James the Less Cemetery in Philadelphia.

Ranks Act.Midn (28 Oct 1823); PMidn (23 Mar 1829); Lt (3 Mar 1831); Cdr (6 Feb 1854); Capt (30 Jun 1861); Commo (16 Jul 1862); RAdm (13 Apr 1867); transferred to Ret.Lst. (19 Sep 1868).

Career Summary Received appointment from SC (28 Oct 1823); *Porpoise*, Afr.Sqdn. (May 1824–Apr 1825); sick lv. (Apr–Jul 1825); *Brandywine*, spec.serv. and Med.Sqdn. (Jul 1825–Feb 1826); *Constitution*, Med.Sqdn. (Feb 1826–Aug 1828); w.o. (Jul 1829–Mar 1830); Navy Yard, NY (Jun 1830–Jun 1831); *Potomac*, Pac.Sqdn. (Jun 1831–Jun 1834); spec. recruiting duty, Norfolk, VA (Nov 1836–Jan 1837); flgs. *Independence*, spec.serv. Braz.Sqdn. (Jan 1837–Sep 1838); l.o.a. (Oct 1838–Jan 1839); rec. ship *Experiment*, Philadelphia (Sep 1840–Sep 1841); *Savannah*, S.Pac.Sqdn. (Aug 1843–Apr 1844); *Relief*, S.Pac. Sta. (Apr 1844–Oct 1845); Navy Yard, Philadelphia (Nov 1845–Dec 1847); w.o. (Dec 1847–Jul 1848); *St. Lawrence*, Eur.Sqdn. (Jul 1848–Nov 1850); Naval Rndv., Philadelphia (Mar 1852–Dec 1853); w.o. (Dec 1853–Sep 1855); cdr, flgs. *San Jacinto*, E.Ind.Sqdn. (Sep 1855–Sep 1856); cdr, *Independence*, Pac.Sqdn. (Sep 1856–Sep 1857); cdr, *John Adams*, Pac.Sqdn. (Sep 1857–Apr 1858); member, Bd. of Visitors, USNA (May–Jun 1857); cdr, rec. ship *Princeton*, Philadelphia (Jun 1858–Aug 1861); cdr, *Lancaster*, Pac.Sqdn. (Sep 1861–Aug 1862); w.o. (Sep–Dec 1862); member, Gen. Court-Martial Bd., Philadelphia (Dec 1862); member, Naval Ret.Bd. (Dec 1862–Mar 1863); member, Bd. of Visitors, USNA (May–Jul 1863); member, Exam.Bd., Newport, RI (Jul 1863); member, court of inquiry, Boston (Jan–Feb 1867); member, gen. court-martial, Washington, DC (Feb–May 1864); in charge of ord., Philadelphia (May 1864–Apr 1867); cdr, N.Atl.Sta., *Contoocook* (Feb 1868–Aug 1869); transferred to Ret.Lst. (19 Sep 1868); member, Bd. of Examiners, Washington, DC (Oct 1869–Sep 1870); pres., Bd. of Visitors, USNA (May–Jun 1870).

JOHN ADAMS HOWELL Born in Bath, NY, on 16 Mar 1840, son of William and Frances A. (Adams) Howell. Married Arabella E. Krause of St. Croix, West Indies, in May 1867. Died at Warrenton, VA, on 10 Jan 1918. Buried in Warrenton. Survived by one daughter.

Ranks Act.Midn (27 Sep 1854); Midn (11 Jun 1858); PMidn (19 Jan 1861); Mstr (23 Feb 1861); Lt (18 Apr 1861); LCdr (3 Mar 1865); Cdr (6 Mar 1872); Capt (1 Mar 1884);

JOHN ADAMS HOWELL
1840–1918

Commo (21 May 1895); RAdm (10 Aug 1898); placed on Ret.Lst. (16 Mar 1902).

Career Summary Received appointment from NY (27 Sep 1854); USNA (Sep 1854–Jun 1858); *Macedonian* and *Wabash*, Med.Sqdn. (Jun 1858–Dec 1859); l.o.a. (Dec 1859–Mar 1860); *Pocahontas* and *Pawnee*, Home Sqdn. (Mar–Dec 1860); *Supply* and *Montgomery*, Atl. and E.Gulf Blk.Sqdns. (Feb 1861–Jul 1862); w.o. (Jul–Oct 1862); *Ossipee*, N.Atl. and W.Gulf Blk.Sqdns. (Oct 1862–Jun 1865); *De Soto*, spec.serv. and N.Atl.Sqdn. (Jul 1865–May 1867); l.o.a. (May–Aug 1867); instructor of astronomy and nav., USNA (Aug 1867–Jun 1871); cst.surv. duty (Jun 1871–Dec 1874); USNA (Dec 1874–Jul 1879); cdr, *Adams*, Pac. Sta. (Aug 1879–Apr 1881); asst., Bur. of Ord., Washington, DC (May–Sep 1881); insp. of ord., Navy Yard, Washington, DC (Sep 1881–Jul 1884); member, USNA Advisory Bd., Washington, DC (Oct 1882–Nov 1888); cdr, *Atlanta*, spec.serv. and Sqdn. of Evol. (Dec 1888–Dec 1890); w.o. (Dec 1890–Jan 1891); steel insp. duty (Jan–Jun 1891); member, then pres., Steel Bd. (Jul 1891–Sep 1894); comdt., Navy Yard, Washington, DC (Feb 1893–Jun 1896); comdt., Navy Yard, League Island, PA (Jun 1896–Jan 1898); cdr, Eur.Sta., *San Francisco* (Jan–Apr 1898); cdr, 1st Sqdn., N.Atl.Flt., *San Francisco* (Apr–Oct 1898); temp. cdr, N.Atl.Flt., *New York* (Aug 1898); pres., Naval Exam.Bd. (Nov 1898–Oct 1900); pres., Naval Ret.Bd. (Nov 1898–Mar 1902); placed on Ret.Lst. (16 Mar 1902).

Career Highlights Saw action at Battle of Mobile Bay in Aug 1864. As cdr of Northern Patrol Sqdn., cruised and protected American coast from ME to DE Capes during war with Spain. Inventor of torpedoes, gyroscopes for their guidance, torpedo launchers, explosive shells, a superior form of disappearing gun carriage, and an amphibious lifeboat.

References
Writings: *A Textbook on Surveying, Projection and Portable Instruments for Use at the Naval Academy* (1876).

JOHN CUMMING HOWELL Born in Philadelphia, PA, on 24 Nov 1819, son of Richard Lewis Howell and Rebecca A. (Stockton) Howell. Grandson of Richard Howell, governor of NJ from 1794 to 1801. Educated at Washington College in PA. Married Mary Stockton, daughter of Commo Robert F. Stockton, USN: one daughter. Died on 12 Sep 1892 in Folkestone, England.

Ranks Midn (9 Jun 1836); PMidn (1 Jul 1842); Mstr (21 Feb 1849); Lt (2 Aug 1849); Cdr (16 Jul 1862); Capt (25 Jul 1866); Commo (29 Jan 1872); RAdm (25 Apr 1877); placed on Ret.Lst. (24 Nov 1881).

Career Summary Received appointment from PA (9 Jun 1836); *Boston*, W.Ind.Sqdn. (Jun 1836–May 1839); l.o.a. (May–Oct 1839); *Levant* and *Macedonian*, W.Ind.Sqdn. (Oct 1839–Oct 1840); *Poinsett*, spec.serv. (Oct–Dec 1840); rec. ship *Dela-*

JOHN CUMMING HOWELL
1819–1892

ware, Norfolk, VA (Dec 1840–Jan 1841); l.o.a. and w.o. (Jan–Jun 1841); Naval School, Philadelphia (Jun 1841–Jun 1842); *Congress*, *Columbia*, and *Perry*, Med., Braz., and E.Ind. Sqdns. (Jun 1842–Sep 1845); l.o.a. (Sep–Dec 1845); naval storekeeper, Macao, China (Dec 1845–Mar 1848); return and w.o. (Mar–Sep 1848); rec. ship *Union*, Philadelphia (Sep 1848–Sep 1849); *Raritan*, Home Sqdn. (Sep 1849–Apr 1850); l.o.a. and w.o. (Apr–Aug 1850); *St. Mary's*, Pac.Sta. (Aug–Sep 1850); *Saratoga*, E.Ind.Sqdn. (Sep 1850–Nov 1853); sick lv. (Nov 1853–Jan 1854); rec. ship *Union*, Philadelphia (Jan 1854–Apr 1856); *Susquehanna*, Med. and Home Sqdns. (Apr 1856–May 1858); l.o.a. (May–Jun 1858); rec. ship *Princeton* and Naval Rndv., Philadelphia (Jun 1858–Mar 1860); *Seminole*, Braz.Sqdn. (Mar 1860–Jul 1861); *Minnesota*, N.Atl.Blk.Sqdn. (Jul–Oct 1861); cdr, *Tahoma*, E.Gulf Blk.Sqdn. (Oct 1861–Dec 1862); return home and w.o. (Dec 1862–Feb 1863); cdr, *Lehigh*, N.Atl.Blk.Sqdn. (Feb–Jul 1863); spec. duty, Navy Yard, NY (Jul–Aug 1863); cdr, *Metacomet* (Aug–Sep 1863); *Nereus*, N.Atl.Blk.Sqdn. (Sep 1863–May 1865); flt.capt, N.Atl.Sqdn., *Minnesota* (May–Oct 1865); cdr, Naval Rndv., Philadelphia (Oct 1865–Jun 1868); w.o. (Jun–Aug 1868); court-martial duty, NY (Aug 1868); bd. duties, Philadelphia (Aug–Dec 1868); flt.capt and chief of staff, Eur.Sqdn., *Franklin* (Dec 1868–Nov 1871); w.o. (Nov–Dec 1871); cdr, Navy Yard, League Island, PA (Dec 1871–Oct 1872); cdr, Navy Yard, Portsmouth, NH (Oct 1872–Sep 1874); chief, Bur. of Yards and Docks, Washington, DC (Sep 1874–Jun 1878); spec. duty, Navy Dept., Washington, DC (Jul–Aug 1878); cdr, N.Atl.Sta., *Powhatan* (Sep 1878–Jan 1879); cdr, Eur.Sqdn., *Trenton* (Jan 1879–Oct 1881); w.o. (Oct–Nov 1881); member, Naval Ret.Bd. (Nov 1881); placed on Ret.Lst. (24 Nov 1881).

Career Highlights During the Civil War, participated in action at Hatteras Inlet in 1861 and in both attacks on Fort Fisher, NC, in late 1864 and early 1865. While chief of the Bur. of Yards and Docks, he occasionally served as act. assistant secretary of the navy.

HENRY LYCURGUS HOWISON Born in Washington, IN, on 10 Oct 1837, son of Henry and Juliet Virginia (Jackson) Howison. Married Hannah J. Middleton on 3 Oct 1865. Made his home in Yonkers, NY, where he died on 31 Dec 1914. Buried in Oak Hill Cemetery, Washington, DC.

Ranks Act.Midn (26 Sep 1854); Midn (11 Jun 1858); PMidn (19 Jan 1861); Mstr (23 Feb 1861); Lt (19 Apr 1861); LCdr (3 Mar 1865); Cdr (19 Aug 1872); Capt (2 Mar 1885); Commo (21 Mar 1897); RAdm (30 Sep 1898); placed on Ret.Lst. (10 Oct 1899).

Career Summary Received appointment from IN (26 Sep 1854); USNA (Sep 1854–Jun 1858); *Wabash*, Med.Sqdn. (Jun 1858–Dec 1859); l.o.a. (Dec 1859–Mar 1860); *Pocahontas*, Home Sqdn. (Mar–Nov 1860); *Pawnee*, Home Sqdn. (Nov–

HENRY LYCURGUS HOWISON
1837–1914

Dec 1860); USNA (Jan 1861); *Pawnee*, Navy Yard, Washington, DC (Feb–Mar 1861); *Pocahontas*, spec.serv. (Mar–Sep 1861); temp. duty with army (Jun–Jul 1861); exec.off., *Augusta*, S.Atl.Blk.Sqdn. (Sep 1861–Jun 1863); exec.off., *Nantucket*, S.Atl.Blk.Sqdn. (Jun 1863–Feb 1864); exec.off., *Catskill*, S.Atl.Blk.Sqdn. (Feb–May 1864); *Bienville*, W.Gulf Blk.Sqdn. (May 1864–Apr 1865); asst.insp. of ord., Navy Yard, Washington, DC (May 1865–Aug 1866); nav., then exec.off., flgs. *Pensacola*, Pac.Sta. (Aug 1866–Nov 1868); asst.insp. of ord., Navy Yard, Washington, DC (Dec 1868–Jan 1870); aide to supt., exec.asst., and cdr, *Constitution*, USNA (Feb 1870–Dec 1872); cdr, *Shawmut*, Gulf of Mexico (Jan–Oct 1873); Navy Yard, Washington, DC (Oct 1873–Jan 1874); cdr, *Shawmut*, Gulf of Mexico (Jan 1874–Feb 1875); head, Dept. of Seamanship, USNA (Feb 1875–Oct 1878); cdr, practice ship *Mayflower* (May–Sep 1876); cdr, practice ship *Constellation* (Jun–Sep 1878); insp. of ord., Navy Yard, Washington, DC (Oct 1878–Sep 1881); member, Naval Advisory Bd. (Jul–Nov 1881); cdr, gunnery training ship *Minnesota* (Nov 1881–Feb 1882); Bur. of Equipment and Recruiting, Washington, DC (Feb–Apr 1882); member, Naval Inspection Bd. (Apr 1882–Apr 1885); member, Bd. of Appraisals, Investigations, Examinations, and Retirements (Apr 1885–Feb 1886); cdr, *Vandalia*, Pac.Sqdn. (Feb 1886–Apr 1888); w.o. (Apr–Jun 1888); pres., Steel Inspecting Bd. (Jun 1888–Mar 1890); member, L.h. Bd., Washington, DC (Mar 1890–Jul 1892); capt.yd., Navy Yard, Mare Island, CA (Aug 1892–Jul 1893); comdt., Navy Yard and Naval Sta., Mare Island, CA (Jul 1893–Jun 1896); cdr, *Oregon*, Pac.Sta. (Jun 1896–Mar 1897); comdt., Navy Yard and Naval Sta., Boston (May 1897–Mar 1899); cdr, S.Atl.Sta., *Chicago* (Mar–Oct 1899); placed on Ret.Lst. (10 Oct 1899).

AARON KONKLE HUGHES Born in Elmira, NY, on 31 Mar 1822. Died at his home in Washington, DC, on 4 May 1906. Buried in Arlington National Cemetery.

Ranks Act.Midn (20 Oct 1838); PMidn (28 May 1844); Mstr (19 Dec 1852); Lt (18 Oct 1853); LCdr (16 Jul 1862); Cdr (16 Nov 1862); placed on Ret.Lst. (24 Oct 1864); recommissioned on Active List (1 Aug 1868); Capt (10 Feb 1869); Commo (4 Feb 1875); RAdm (2 Jul 1882); placed on Ret.Lst. (31 Mar 1884).

Career Summary Received appointment from NY (20 Oct 1838); w.o. (Oct 1838–Jan 1839); flgs. *Constitution*, Pac.Sqdn. (Jan 1839–Nov 1841); l.o.a. (Nov 1841–Feb 1842); *Boxer*, Gulf of Mexico and W.Indies (Feb–Nov 1842); l.o.a. (Nov 1842–Jan 1843); rec. ship *Pennsylvania*, Norfolk, VA (Jan–Jun 1843); *Macedonian*, Afr.Sqdn. (Jun 1843–Jan 1844); home and l.o.a. (Jan–Sep 1844); Naval School, Philadelphia (Sep 1844–Jun 1845); l.o.a. (Jun–Oct 1845); *Columbia*, Braz.Sqdn. (Oct 1845–Jul 1846); cst.surv. duty (Aug–Oct

AARON KONKLE HUGHES
1822–1906

1846); *Michigan*, on Great Lakes (Oct 1846–Jul 1848); l.o.a. and w.o. (Jul–Nov 1848); rec. ship *North Carolina*, NY (Nov 1848–Aug 1850); *St. Mary's*, Pac.Sqdn. (Aug–Sep 1850); *Albany*, W.Indies and Gulf of Mexico (Sep 1850–Nov 1852); w.o. (Nov 1852–Jan 1853); rec. ship *Ontario*, Baltimore (Jan–Jun 1853); l.o.a. and w.o. (Jun–Dec 1853); *Decatur*, Pac.Sqdn. (Jan 1854–Aug 1856); return, l.o.a., and w.o. (Aug 1856–Jan 1857); exec.off., rec. ship *Allegheny*, Baltimore (Jan–Oct 1857); exec.off., storeship *Supply*, Afr. and Braz. Sqdns. (Nov 1857–Aug 1858); w.o. (Aug–Sep 1858); rec. ship *Allegheny*, Baltimore (Sep 1858–Jun 1859); exec.off., *San Jacinto*, Afr.Sqdn. (Jun 1859–Jan 1860); exec.off., *Portsmouth*, Afr.Sqdn. (Jan–Jun 1860); *San Jacinto*, and prize master, *Storm King*, Afr.Sqdn. (Jun–Oct 1860); w.o. (Oct–Dec 1860); rec. ship *Princeton*, Philadelphia (Dec 1860–Apr 1861); exec.off., *Ice Boat*, Philadelphia (Apr–May 1861); exec.off., *Mississippi*, Gulf Sqdn. (May–Oct 1861); cdr, *Water Witch*, Gulf Blk.Sqdn.(Oct 1861–Apr 1862); w.o. (Apr–May 1862); cdr, *Mohawk*, S.Atl.Blk.Sqdn. (May 1862–Jun 1863); w.o. (Jun–Jul 1863); cdr, *Cimmaron*, S.Atl.Blk.Sqdn. (Jul 1863–May 1864); w.o. (May–Oct 1864); placed on Ret.Lst. (24 Oct 1864); temp. ord. duty, MS River Sqdn. (Oct 1864–Feb 1865); exec.off., Naval Sta., Mound City, IL (Feb 1865–Feb 1866); w.o. (Feb–Apr 1866); member, general court-martial, Philadelphia (Apr–Aug 1866); insp., 6th L.h. Dist., Charleston, SC (Aug 1866–Jul 1868); l.o.a. and w.o. (Jul 1868–May 1870); recommissioned on Active List (1 Aug 1868); in charge of ironclads, New Orleans (Jun–Oct 1870); cdr, rec. ship *Ohio*, Boston (Oct 1870–Jan 1872); additional duty, exec.off., Navy Yard, Boston (Sep 1871–Jan 1872); w.o. (Jan 1872–Aug 1873); cdr, *Pensacola*, and chief of staff, Pac.Sqdn. (Sep 1873–Jan 1875); w.o. (Jan 1875–Apr 1877); cdr, Naval Sta., Port Royal, SC (Apr 1877–Jun 1878); w.o. (Jun 1878–Jun 1879); comdt., Navy Yard, Norfolk, VA (Jul 1879–Jul 1882); w.o. (Jul–Dec 1882); cdr, Pac.Sta., *Hartford* (Jan 1883–Mar 1884); placed on Ret.Lst. (31 Mar 1884).

References
Personal Papers: 6 vols. (1839–94) in NYPL.

JOHN IRWIN Born in Pittsburgh, PA, on 15 Apr 1832. Married, with a daughter and a son who later served as a navy paymaster. Died at his home in Washington, DC, on 29 Jul 1901.

Ranks Act.Midn (9 Sep 1847); PMidn (10 Jun 1853); Mstr (15 Sep 1855); Lt (16 Sep 1855); LCdr (16 Jul 1862); Cdr (25 Jul 1866); Capt (15 May 1875); Commo (4 Mar 1886); RAdm (19 May 1891); placed on Ret.Lst. (15 Apr 1894).

Career Summary Received appointment from PA (9 Sep 1847); *Cumberland*, Home Sqdn. (Oct 1847–Mar 1848); l.o.a. (Mar–Jun 1848); rec. ship *Pennsylvania*, Norfolk, VA (Jun–Jul 1848); *St. Lawrence*, Med.Sqdn. (Jul 1848–Nov 1850); l.o.a.

JOHN IRWIN
1832–1901

(Nov 1850–Feb 1851); *John Adams* and *Porpoise*, Afr.Sqdn.
(Mar 1851–Jul 1852); USNA (Oct 1852–Jun 1853); *Fulton*,
Home Sqdn. (Jun 1853–Jul 1856); l.o.a. (Jul–Oct 1856);
cst.surv. duty (Oct 1856–Jun 1858); *Savannah*, Home Sqdn.
(Jul 1858–Nov 1860); l.o.a. (Nov 1860–Apr 1861); rec. ship
Pennsylvania, Norfolk, VA (Apr 1861); Navy Yard,
Washington, DC (Apr–May 1861); flgs. *Wabash*,
S.Atl.Blk.Sqdn. (May 1861–May 1863); w.o. (May–Aug 1863);
ord. duty, Navy Yard, Boston (Aug–Nov 1863); ord. duty,
Navy Yard, Philadelphia (Nov 1863–Jan 1864); cdr, *Katahdin*
and then *Genesee*, W.Gulf Blk.Sqdn. (Jan 1864–Jul 1865); w.o.
(Jul–Aug 1865); spec. duty, Philadelphia (Aug 1865–Jan 1867);
w.o. (Jan–Mar 1867); cdr, *Lenapee*, spec.serv., Wilmington,
NC (Mar–Oct 1867); w.o. (Oct–Nov 1867); cdr, *Newbern* and
then *Gettysburg*, N.Atl.Sqdn. (Nov 1867–Oct 1869); w.o. (Oct
1869–Jan 1870); cdr, *Yantic*, N.Atl.Flt. (Feb 1870–Mar 1871);
w.o. (Apr–Oct 1871); Naval Sta., League Island, PA (Oct
1871–Mar 1873); cdr, rec. ship *Sabine*, Portsmouth, NH (Mar
1873–Oct 1875); w.o. (Oct 1875–Mar 1876); cdr, flgs.
Pensacola, Pac.Sta. (Mar 1876–Jan 1879); cdr, rec. ship *Independence*, Mare Island, CA (Feb–May 1879); in charge, Nav.
Dept., Navy Yard, Mare Island, CA (May 1879–Feb 1882);
capt.yd., Navy Yard, Mare Island, CA (Apr 1881–Nov 1883);
comdt., Navy Yard, Mare Island, CA (Mar–Nov 1883); senior member, Bd. of Inspection, Mare Island, CA (Nov 1883–
Jan 1888); w.o. (Jan 1888–Mar 1889); member, Bd. of Examination (Mar 1889–May 1891); comdt., Navy Yard, Mare
Island, CA (Jun 1891–May 1893); cdr, Pac.Sta., *Philadelphia*
(Jun 1893–Apr 1894); placed on Ret.Lst. (15 Apr 1894).

References
Personal Papers: (1863–98) in NYHS.

THORNTON ALEXANDER JENKINS Born in Orange
County, VA, on 11 Dec 1811, son of William Jenkins. Married
twice, his second wife being the daughter of a navy paymaster. Five children. Died in Washington, DC, on 9 Aug 1893.
Buried in Arlington National Cemetery.

Ranks Midn (1 Nov 1828); PMidn (14 Jun 1834); Lt (9
Dec 1839); Cdr (14 Sep 1855); Capt (16 Jul 1862); Commo
(25 Jul 1866); RAdm (15 Aug 1870); placed on Ret.Lst.
(11 Dec 1873).

Career Summary Received appointment from VA
(1 Nov 1828); *Natchez*, W.Ind.Sqdn. (Dec 1828–Sep 1831);
Naval School, Norfolk, VA (Sep 1831–Aug 1832); *Vandalia*,
W.Ind.Sqdn. (Aug 1832–Jul 1833); Naval School, Norfolk,
VA (Jul 1833–May 1834); cst.surv. duty (Sep 1834–Mar 1842);
Congress, Braz. and Med. Sqdns. (Apr 1842–Mar 1845);
spec.serv. with lighthouses in Europe and U.S. (May 1845–
Mar 1847); *Germantown*, Home Sqdn. (Mar–Sep 1847); cdr,
Relief, Home Sqdn. (Sep 1847–May 1848); rec. ship *Ontario*,
Baltimore (Oct 1848–Mar 1849); cst.surv. duty (Mar 1849–

THORNTON ALEXANDER
JENKINS
1811–1893

Apr 1851); secretary, L.h. Bd., Washington, DC (Apr–May 1851); cst.surv. duty (May 1851–Sep 1852); secretary, L.h. Bd., Washington, DC (Sep 1852–Sep 1858); cdr, *Preble*, Braz.Sta. and Gulf of Mexico (Sep 1858–Oct 1860); member, Bd. of Examiners, USNA (Dec 1860–Feb 1861); secretary, L.h. Bd. and on spec.serv., Washington, DC (Feb 1861–Jun 1862); cdr, *Wachusett*, James and Potomac Rivers (Jun–Sep 1862); cdr, *Oneida*, W.Gulf Blk.Sqdn. (Sep 1862–Feb 1863); flt.capt., chief of staff, and cdr, *Hartford*, W.Gulf Blk.Sqdn. (Feb–May 1863); *Monogahela*, W.Gulf Blk.Sqdn. (May–Jul 1863); cdr, *Richmond* and cdr, second division, W.Gulf Blk.Sqdn. (Jul 1863–Jan 1865); court-martial duty, James River (Mar–Apr 1865); spec.serv., Mississippi and Ohio Rivers (May–Aug 1865); chief, Bur. of Nav. and Detail, Washington, DC (Aug 1865–Apr 1869); secretary, L.h. Bd., Washington, DC (Apr 1869–Feb 1872); cdr, Asia.Sta., *Hartford* (Apr 1872–Dec 1873); placed on Ret.Lst. (11 Dec 1873).

Career Highlights During Civil War, was Farragut's [*q.v.*] flt.capt and chief of staff. Wounded in fight below Port Hudson on lower Mississippi. Present at Battle of Mobile Bay.

References

Personal Papers: a) 59 items (1846–92) in HHL. b) 7 items in NL.

Writings: a) "Papers relating to Exploration of the Isthmus of Darien, 1859, USS *Preble*, T.A. Jenkins, Commander." b) *Code of Flotilla and Boat Squadron Signals for the United States Navy* (Washington, DC: 1861). c) *Instructions for Hydrographic Surveyors* (Washington, DC: 1868). d) *The Rule of the Road at Sea and Inland Waters* (Washington, DC: 1869). e) *The Barometer, Thermometer, Hygrometer, and Atmospheric Appearances at Sea and on Land as Aids in Foretelling Weather* (Washington, DC: 1869). f) *Ships' Compasses* (Washington, DC: 1869).

JAMES EDWARD JOUETT Born near Lexington, KY, on 27 Feb 1828, son of the artist Matthew Harris and Margaret H. (Mamer) Jouett. Married Galana Stockett in 1852. One son, James Stockett Jouett. Died at his home near Sandy Springs, MD, on 30 Sep 1902. Buried in Arlington National Cemetery.

Ranks Act.Midn (10 Sep 1841); PMidn (10 Aug 1847); Mstr (14 Sep 1855); Lt (15 Sep 1855); LCdr (16 Jul 1862); Cdr (25 Jul 1866); Capt (7 Jan 1874); Commo (11 Jan 1883); Act.RAdm (20 Sep 1884); RAdm (19 Feb 1886); placed on Ret.Lst. (27 Feb 1890).

Career Summary Received appointment from KY (10 Sep 1841); *Independence*, Home Sqdn. (Dec 1841–May 1843); *Decatur*, Afr.Sqdn. (May 1843–Jan 1845); l.o.a. (Jan–Jun 1845); *John Adams*, Home Sqdn. (Jun 1845–Nov 1846); USNA (Nov 1846–Jul 1848); *St. Lawrence*, Eur.Sqdn. (Aug 1848–Nov 1850); l.o.a. (Nov 1850–Mar 1851); cst.surv. duty (Mar–Nov 1851);

JAMES EDWARD JOUETT
1828–1902

Lexington, Pac.Sqdn. (Nov 1851–Mar 1852); l.o.a. (Mar–Sep 1853); *St. Mary's*, Pac.Sqdn. (Sep 1853–Dec 1856); l.o.a. (Jan–Mar 1857); *Michigan*, on Great Lakes (Mar–May 1857); *Plymouth*, spec.serv. (May–Jun 1857); *Michigan*, on Great Lakes (Jun 1857–Oct 1858); chartered steamer *W. W. Chapin*, S.Atl.Sta. (Oct 1858–May 1859); w.o. (May–Aug 1859); *Crusader*, Home Sqdn. (Sep 1859–Mar 1861); *Michigan*, on Great Lakes (Mar–Jun 1861); Navy Yard, Pensacola, FL (Jun 1861); *Santee*, W.Gulf Blk.Sqdn. (Jun–Dec 1861); home and w.o. (Dec 1861–Apr 1862); cdr, *Montgomery*, W.Gulf Blk.Sqdn. (Apr 1862–Mar 1863); cdr, *R. R. Cuyler*, W.Gulf Blk.Sqdn. (Mar–Dec 1863); cdr, *Metacomet*, W.Gulf Blk.Sqdn. (Dec 1863–Dec 1864); Navy Yard, NY (Mar–Aug 1865); l.o.a. (Aug–Dec 1865); Naval Rndv., Philadelphia (Dec 1865–Aug 1866); capt.yd., Navy Yard, NY (Sep 1866–Mar 1868); cdr, *Michigan*, on Great Lakes (Apr 1868–Sep 1870); insp., 5th L.h. Dist., Baltimore (Sep–Dec 1870); ord. duty, Navy Yard, Norfolk, VA (Dec 1870–May 1873); member, Bd. of Inspection (May–Dec 1873); cdr, *Dictator*, Navy Yard, NY (Dec 1873–Jan 1874); member, Bd. of Inspection (Jan–Jul 1874); cdr, *Powhatan*, N.Atl.Sqdn. (Jul 1874–Mar 1876); member, Bd. of Inspection (Mar–Aug 1876); w.o. (Aug 1876–Mar 1877); member, Bd. of Inspection (Mar 1877–Mar 1880); w.o. (Mar–Jun 1880); cdr, Naval Sta., Port Royal, SC (Jul 1880–Jan 1883); cdr, sta. ship *Wyoming*, Port Royal, SC (Jul 1880–Oct 1882); member, various bds., NY (Jan 1883–Sep 1884); cdr, N.Atl.Sqdn., *Tennessee* (Sep 1884–Jun 1886); pres., Bd. of Inspection and Survey (Jun 1886–Feb 1890); placed on Ret.Lst. (27 Feb 1890).

Career Highlights During Mexican War, among detachment of sailors and marines at Port Isabel, TX, protecting Gen Zachary Taylor's base camp during the Battle of Palo Alto. Was with Commodore M. C. Perry's cruise to Far East in 1853–1855. In early 1861, was captured at Pensacola, FL. Refusing a parole, managed an escape. In Nov 1861, led boats from *Santee* into harbor of Galveston, TX, and was seriously wounded in hand-to-hand combat, though succeeding in capturing and burning Confederate armed cruiser *Royal Yacht*. Took part as cdr of *Metacomet* in Battle of Mobile Bay in Aug 1864, beating off two Confederate gunboats and capturing the *Selma*. Commanded force sent to Isthmus of Panama in 1885 that quashed rioting there and restored the transit across the isthmus.

References

Additional Sources: Alexander Pirtle, *Life of James Edward Jouett, Rear Admiral, U.S.N.* (Louisville: 1896).

ALBERT KAUTZ Born in Georgetown, OH, on 29 Jan 1839, son of George and Dorthea (Lewing) Kautz. Brother was Gen August V. Kautz, USA. Married, with one son, Austin Kautz, who served in the navy. Died in Florence, Italy, on 5 Feb 1907. Buried in Arlington National Cemetery.

ALBERT KAUTZ
1839–1907

Ranks Act.Midn (28 Sep 1854); Midn (11 Jun 1858); PMidn (19 Jan 1861); Mstr (23 Feb 1861); Lt (21 Apr 1861); LCdr (31 May 1865); Cdr (3 Sep 1872); Capt (2 Jun 1885); Commo (6 Apr 1897); RAdm (25 Dec 1898); placed on Ret.Lst. (29 Jan 1901).

Career Summary Received appointment from OH (28 Sep 1854); USNA (Sep 1854–Jun 1858); *Colorado, Roanoke, Savannah,* and *Saratoga,* Home Sqdn. (Jun 1858–Jul 1860); l.o.a. (Jun–Sep 1860); w.o. (Sep 1860–Apr 1861); *Perry,* spec.serv. (Apr–May 1861); *Flag,* N.Atl.Blk.Sqdn. (May–Jun 1861); cdr, prize brig *Hannah Balch* (Jun 1861); prisoner of war (Jun–Nov 1861); l.o.a. (Nov–Dec 1861); *Hartford,* W.Gulf Blk.Sqdn. (Jan 1861–Feb 1863); *Juniata,* W.Ind.Sqdn. (Feb–Dec 1863); w.o. (Dec 1863–Jan 1864); *Nereus,* Navy Yard, NY (Jan–Feb 1864); 1st lt, *Cyane,* Pac.Sqdn. (Feb 1864–Jul 1865); home and w.o. (Jul–Nov 1865); *Tonawanda,* Navy Yard, Washington, DC (Nov–Dec 1865); w.o. (Dec 1865–Jan 1866); *Winooski,* Home Sqdn. (Jan–Aug 1866); flgs. *Pensacola,* Pac.Sqdn. (Aug 1866–Jul 1868); w.o. (Jul–Dec 1868); rec. ship *New Hampshire,* Norfolk, VA (Dec 1868–May 1869); Navy Yard, Boston (May 1869–Aug 1871); l.o.a. (Aug–Nov 1871); w.o. (Nov 1871–Feb 1872); *Powhatan,* Home Sqdn. (Feb 1872); w.o. (Feb–Mar 1872); insp., 7th L.h. Dist., Key West, FL (Mar 1872–Aug 1873); w.o. (Aug–Oct 1873); cdr, *Monocacy,* Asia.Sta. (Oct 1873–Sep 1875); w.o. (Sep–Dec 1875); insp., 14th L.h. Dist., Cincinnati, Ohio (Jan 1876–Jun 1880); s.a. and w.o. (Jun–Jul 1880); cdr, *Michigan,* on Great Lakes (Aug 1880–Aug 1883); w.o. (Aug 1883–Mar 1884); Bur. of Equip. and Recruiting, Washington, DC (Mar–Jun 1884); equip.off., Navy Yard, Boston (Jul 1884–Oct 1887); l.o.a. (Nov 1887–Dec 1888); w.o. (Jan–Aug 1889); member, gen court-martial (Aug 1889); w.o. (Aug–Oct 1889); capt.yd., Navy Yard, Portsmouth, NH (Oct 1889–May 1890); cdr, *Pensacola,* Pac.Sqdn. (Jun 1890–Mar 1892); senior member of bd., Navy Yard, Mare Island, CA (Mar–Jun 1892); capt.yd., Navy Yard, Boston (Jun 1892–Aug 1894); cdr, rec. ship *Wabash,* Boston (Aug 1894–Apr 1897); pres., Exam. and Ret. Bd. (Apr–Oct 1897); comdt., Naval Sta., Newport, RI (Oct 1897–Oct 1898); cdr, Pac.Sta., *Philadelphia,* then *Iowa* (Oct 1898–Jan 1901); placed on Ret.Lst. (29 Jan 1901).

Career Highlights Taken prisoner off Cape Hatteras on 25 Jun 1861. Paroled by Pres. Jefferson Davis along with Lt John L. Worden [*q.v.*] and another officer; subsequently became first officers exchanged in the war. He then served on the staff of RAdm Farragut [*q.v.*] on lower Mississippi River, commanding first division of guns against Confederate Forts Jackson and St. Philip, the Chalmette batteries, and the capture of New Orleans.

LOUIS KEMPFF
1841–1920

LOUIS KEMPFF Born near Belleville, IL, on 11 Oct 1841,

son of Frederick and Henrietta Kempff. Married Cornelia R. Selby on 16 Jul 1873. Two sons and a daughter. One son was Capt Clarence S. Kempff, USN. Died in Santa Barbara, CA, on 29 Jul 1920. Buried in Santa Barbara.

Ranks Act.Midn (25 Sep 1857); title changed to Midn (16 Jul 1862); Lt (1 Aug 1862); LCdr (26 Jul 1866); Cdr (9 Mar 1876); Capt (19 May 1891); RAdm (3 Mar 1899); placed on Ret.Lst. (11 Oct 1903).

Career Summary Received appointment from IL (25 Sep 1857); USNA (Sep 1857–May 1861); turned back (22 Jun 1858); *Vandalia*, Atl.Blk.Sqdn. (May–Nov 1861); flgs. *Wabash*, Atl.Blk.Sqdn. (Nov 1861–Mar 1862); *Susquehanna*, W.Gulf Blk.Sqdn. (Mar 1862–May 1863); *Sonoma*, W.Ind.Sqdn. (Jun–Jul 1863); *Connecticut*, N.Atl.Blk.Sqdn. (Jul 1863–Oct 1864); w.o. (Oct–Nov 1864); *Suwanee*, Pac.Sqdn. (Nov 1864–Mar 1867); return home (Mar–May 1867); exec.off., apprentice ship *Portsmouth* (Jun 1867–Oct 1868); exec.off., rec. ship *Independence*, Mare Island, CA (Oct 1868–Jun 1869); exec.off., *Mohican*, Pac.Sta. (Jun–Sep 1869); exec.off., rec. ship *Independence*, Mare Island, CA (Sep 1869–Nov 1870); Pac.Sqdn. (Nov 1870–May 1871); exec.off., *Mohican*, Pac.Sqdn. (May 1871–Jun 1872); exec.off., *Saranac*, Pac.Sta. (Jul–Nov 1872); exec.off., flgs. *California*, N.Pac.Sta. (Nov 1872–Apr 1873); w.o. (Apr–Aug 1873); Naval Rndv., San Francisco (Aug 1873–Nov 1874); insp., 13th L.h. Dist., Portland, OR (Nov 1874–Oct 1876); w.o. (Oct 1876–Mar 1877); senior aide to comdt., Navy Yard, Mare Island, CA (Apr 1877–Mar 1878); equip.off., Navy Yard, Mare Island, CA (Mar 1878–Mar 1880); w.o. (Mar–Sep 1880); cdr, Naval Rndv., San Francisco (Sep 1880–Apr 1881); w.o. (Apr–Jun 1881); cdr, *Alert*, Asia.Sta. (Jul 1881–Jul 1882); w.o. (Jul 1882–Jan 1883); ord.off., Navy Yard, Mare Island, CA (Jan 1883–Oct 1885); cdr, *Adams*, Pac.Sta. (Oct 1885–May 1888); w.o. (May–Jun 1888); act. capt.yd., Navy Yard, Mare Island, CA (Jun 1888–Jul 1890); member, Bd. of Inspection, San Francisco (Jul 1890–Feb 1893); cdr, *Monterey*, Pac.Sqdn. (Feb 1893–Feb 1895); home and l.o.a. (Feb–Apr 1895); NWC (Jun–Oct 1895); member, Naval Exam. and Ret. Bd., Washington, DC (Oct 1895–Sep 1896); cdr, rec. ship *Independence*, Mare Island, CA (Oct 1896–Apr 1899); comdt., Navy Yard, Mare Island, CA (May 1899–Mar 1900); junior sqdn. cdr, Asia.Sta., *Oregon* (Apr–May 1900); senior sqdn. cdr, Asia.Flt., *Newark*, then *Kentucky* (May 1900–Mar 1902); home and w.o. (Mar–Jun 1902); comdt., Pac. Naval Dist., San Francisco (Jun 1902–Oct 1903); placed on Ret.Lst. (11 Oct 1903); spec. duty (Oct 1904–Aug 1905).

Career Highlights During Civil War, saw action at Port Royal in Nov 1861, and at Fernandina, Jacksonville, and St. Augustine, FL. Participated in the retaking of Norfolk in May 1862. While senior sqdn. cdr of Pac.Sqdn., was participant in allied actions against Boxers in China.

References
Personal Papers: a) 7 items (1860–62) at ISHS. b) "Letter from the Senior Squadron Commander U.S. Naval Force on Asiatic Station," U.S. Naval Institute *Proceedings* 98 (1901): 373–74.

ALBERT SEWALL KENNY
1841–1930

ALBERT SEWALL KENNY Born in Keosanqua, IA, on 19 Jan 1841, son of Sewall and Mary (Strong) Kenny. Received A.B. from Univ. of VT in 1861. Married Ellen Barnes on 27 Oct 1874. Died on 17 May 1930 at his home in Washington, DC. Buried in Moravian Cemetery, Staten Island, NY.

Ranks Asst.Paymstr. (19 Mar 1862); Paymstr. (9 Mar 1865); Pay Insp. with rel. rank of Cdr (31 Jul 1884); Pay Dir. with rel. rank of Capt (26 Sep 1897); Paymstr. Gen. with rel. rank of RAdm (13 Dec 1899); to Ret.Lst. (19 Jan 1903).

Career Summary Received appointment from VT (19 Mar 1862); w.o. (Mar–Apr 1862); *South Carolina*, S.Atl.Blk.Sqdn. (Apr 1862–May 1864); s.a. and w.o. (May 1864); *Santiago de Cuba*, N.Atl.Blk.Sqdn. (May 1864–Jun 1865); s.a. and w.o. (Jun 1865–Mar 1866); storeship *J. C. Kuhn* [renamed *Purveyor*], Eur.Sqdn. (Mar 1866–Nov 1867); s.a. and w.o. (Nov 1867–Apr 1868); Navy Pay Office, San Francisco (Jun 1868–Jul 1871); s.a. and w.o. (Jul 1871–Mar 1872); flgs. *Plymouth*, Eur.Sta. (May 1872–Jun 1873); s.a. and w.o. (Jun 1873–Jan 1874); *Roanoke*, N.Atl.Sta. (Jan–Dec 1874); judge advocate, court of inquiry, Rio de Janeiro, Brazil (Jun–Sep 1874); USNA (Jan 1875–Jul 1880); s.a. and w.o. (Jul 1880–Jan 1881); spec. duty, Navy Dept., Washington, DC (Jan–Mar 1881); spec. duty, Washington, DC (Mar–Jul 1881); flt.paymstr., N.Atl.Sta., *Tennessee* (Jul 1881–May 1884); s.a. and w.o. (May–Jun 1884); spec. duty, court of inquiry (Jun–Dec 1884); w.o. (Dec 1884–Sep 1885); Navy Yard, Boston (Sep 1885–Nov 1887); Bur. of Provisions and Clothing, Washington, DC (Nov 1887–Jul 1890); duty connected with *Philadelphia*, Navy Yard, NY (Jul–Aug 1890); s.a. and w.o. (Aug–Sep 1890); gen. storekeeper, Navy Yard, NY (Oct 1890–Jun 1893); *Chicago*, Eur.Sta. (Jun 1893–May 1895); l.o.a. (May 1895–Jan 1896); in charge, Navy Pay Office, NY (Jan–May 1896); gen. storekeeper, Navy Yard, NY (Jun 1896–May 1899); paymstr. gen. and chief, Bur. of Supplies and Accounts, Washington, DC (May 1899–Jul 1903); transferred to Ret.Lst. (19 Jan 1903).

AUGUSTUS HENRY KILTY Born in Annapolis, MD, on 25 Nov 1807. Died on 10 Nov 1879 at Baltimore, MD.

Ranks Midn (4 Jul 1821); dismissed (8 Jun 1831); reinstated (6 Aug 1831); PMidn (28 Apr 1832); Lt (6 Sep 1837); placed on Reserve List (13 Sep 1855); Cdr (14 Sep 1855); Capt (16 Jul 1862); Commo (25 Jul 1866); placed on Ret.Lst. (25 Nov 1868); RAdm on Ret.Lst. (13 Jul 1870).

Career Summary Received appointment from MD (4 Jul 1821); accepted commission (2 Dec 1824); w.o. (Dec 1824–

AUGUSTUS HENRY KILTY
1807–1879

Jun 1825); *Decoy, John Adams,* and *Constellation,* W.Ind.Sqdn. (Jun 1825–Jul 1827); l.o.a. (Jul–Oct 1827); w.o. (Oct 1827–Jun 1828); *Hudson,* Braz.Sqdn. (Jun 1828–Jul 1829); l.o.a. (Jul–Nov 1829); w.o. (Nov 1829–Jun 1830); *Florida,* LA cst.surv. (Jun 1830–Mar 1831); examination and w.o. (Mar–Jun 1831); dismissed (8 Jun 1831); reinstated (6 Aug 1831); Naval School, Norfolk, VA (Aug 1831–Apr 1832); l.o.a. (Aug 1832–Feb 1833); *Grampus,* W.Ind.Sqdn. (Feb 1833–Feb 1834); l.o.a. (Feb–Aug 1834); rec. ship *Sea Gull,* Philadelphia (Aug 1834–Jul 1836); w.o. (Jul 1835–Mar 1837); *Fairfield,* Braz.Sqdn. (Mar–Apr 1837); l.o.a. (Apr 1837–Apr 1838); *John Adams,* E.Ind.Sqdn. (May 1838–Jun 1840); l.o.a. and w.o. (Jun 1840–Jan 1842); rec. ship *Columbus,* Boston (Jan–Apr 1842); *Columbus,* Med. and Braz. Sqdns. (Apr 1842–May 1844); l.o.a. (May 1844–Apr 1846); *United States,* Afr. and Med. Sqdns. (May 1846–Feb 1849); l.o.a. and w.o. (Feb–Sep 1849); Naval Rndv., Baltimore (Oct 1849–Oct 1851); w.o. (Oct 1851–Jul 1854); rec. ship *North Carolina,* NY (Jul 1854–Sep 1855); placed on Reserved List (13 Sep 1855); on furlough (Sep 1855–Jun 1859); cdr, Naval Rndv., Baltimore (Jun 1859–Apr 1861); w.o. (Apr–Sep 1861); insp., 10th L.h. Dist., Buffalo, NY (Sep 1861); spec. duty, St. Louis, MO, then cdr, *Mound City* (Sep 1861–Aug 1862); cdr, Expd. into Arkansas (Jun–Aug 1862); sick lv. (Aug 1862–Apr 1863); ord. duty, Naval Sta., Baltimore (Apr 1863–Sep 1864); cdr, *Roanoke,* N.Atl.Sqdn. (Sep 1864–Jun 1865); cdr, rec. ship *Vermont,* NY (Jun–Dec 1865); spec. duty, Baltimore (Dec 1865–Oct 1866); w.o. (Oct 1866–Jul 1867); cdr, Navy Yard, Norfolk, VA (Aug 1867–Oct 1870); placed on Ret.Lst. (25 Nov 1868).

LEWIS ASHFIELD KIMBERLEY Born in Troy, NY, on 2 Apr 1830. Married Annie M. Cushman, daughter of Capt Charles H. Cushman, USN, in 1874. Had a son and a daughter. Died at his home in West Newton, MA, on 28 Jan 1902. Buried at Mount Auburn Cemetery in Boston, MA.

Ranks Act.Midn (8 Dec 1846); PMidn (8 Jun 1852); Mstr (15 Sep 1855); Lt (16 Sep 1855); LCdr (16 Jul 1862); Cdr (25 Jul 1866); Capt (3 Oct 1874); Commo (27 Sep 1884); RAdm (26 Jan 1887); placed on Ret.Lst. (2 Apr 1892).

Career Summary Received appointment from IL (8 Dec 1846); Naval School, Annapolis, MD (Dec 1846–Jun 1847); *Jamestown,* Afr. and Med. Sqdns. (Jun 1847–May 1850); l.o.a. (May–Jun 1850); *Raritan,* Pac.Sqdn. (Jun 1850–Oct 1852); USNA (Oct 1852–Jun 1853); *Decatur,* Afr.Sqdn. (Jul–Sep 1853); *Dale,* Afr.Sqdn. (Sep 1853–Jan 1856); l.o.a. (Jan–Mar 1856); rec. ship *Ohio,* Boston (Mar 1856–Jul 1857); *Germantown,* E.Ind.Sqdn. (Aug 1857–Apr 1860); l.o.a. (Apr–Oct 1860); *Richmond,* Med.Sqdn. (Oct 1860–Jul 1861); *Potomac* and flgs. *Hartford,* W.Gulf Blk.Sqdn. (Jul 1861–Dec 1864); l.o.a. (Dec 1864–Feb 1865); flgs. *Colorado,* Eur.Sqdn. (Feb 1865–Sep 1866); w.o. (Sep 1866–May 1867); cdr, rec. ship *Vermont,* NY (May 1867–May 1870); w.o. (May–Aug 1870);

LEWIS ASHFIELD KIMBERLEY
1830–1902

cdr, *Benicia*, Asia.Sqdn. (Aug 1870–Sep 1872); w.o. (Sep–Oct 1872); Bur. of Equip. and Recruiting, Washington, DC (Oct 1872–Nov 1873); cdr, *Canonicus*, N.Atl.Sqdn. (Dec 1873–May 1874); l.o.a. (May 1874–Mar 1875); cdr, *Monongahela*, S.Atl.Sta. (Mar 1875–Jul 1876); w.o. (Jul 1876–Feb 1877); cdr, flgs. *Omaha*, S.Pac.Sta. (Feb 1877–Apr 1878); w.o. (Apr 1878–Apr 1880); capt.yd., Navy Yard, NY (May 1880–Jun 1883); member, then pres., Exam. and Ret.Bd. (Jun 1883–Apr 1885); comdt., Navy Yard, Boston (Apr 1885–Mar 1887); cdr, Pac.Sta. (Apr 1887–Jan 1889); home and w.o. (Jan 1889–Feb 1890); pres., Naval Exam.Bd. (Feb 1890–Apr 1892); pres., Bd. of Inspection and Survey (Mar 1890–Apr 1892); placed on Ret.Lst. (2 Apr 1892).

Career Highlights Participated in actions against Port Hudson batteries, Grand Gulf, and at Battle of Mobile Bay during Civil War. Was with expedition to Korea, commanding force which landed and captured the Korean forts. Received commendation from the secretary of the navy for conduct of affairs during and after the hurricane which struck Samoa on 15 and 16 Mar 1889.

References

Personal Papers: a) 50 items (1889–96) in NHF,LC. b) c.50 items (1847–91) in Chicago Historical Society, Chicago.

WILLIAM ALEXANDER KIRKLAND
1836–1898

WILLIAM ALEXANDER* KIRKLAND Born in Hillsboro, NC, on 3 Jul 1836, son of Alexander McKenzie and Anna McKenzie (Cameron) Kirkland. Married Dona Concolacion Victoria Gowlandon 15 May 1861 in Montevideo, Uruguay. One daughter. Died on 12 Aug 1898 at the Navy Yard on Mare Island, CA. Buried in Brooklyn, NY.

Ranks Act.Midn (2 Jul 1850); PMidn (20 Jun 1856); Mstr (22 Jan 1858); Lt (18 Mar 1858); LCdr (16 Jul 1862); Cdr (2 Mar 1869); Capt (1 Apr 1880); Commo (27 Jun 1893); RAdm (1 Mar 1895); placed on Ret.Lst. (3 Jul 1898).

Career Summary Received appointment from NC (2 Jul 1850); USNA (Jul 1850–Nov 1851); *Portsmouth* and *St. Lawrence*, Pac.Sqdn. (Nov 1851–Apr 1855); l.o.a. (Apr–Oct 1855); USNA (Oct 1855–Jun 1856); w.o. (Jun–Aug 1856); *St. Lawrence*, Braz.Sqdn. (Sep 1856–Jun 1857); *Falmouth*, Braz.Sqdn. (Jun 1857–Aug 1859); l.o.a. (Jun–Aug 1859); *Release*, *Congress*, *Pulaski*, and *Jamestown*, Home, Braz., and Pac. Sqdns. (Aug 1859–Aug 1863); *Wyoming*, E.Ind.Sqdn. (Jan 1863–Jul 1864); cdr, *Owasco*, W.Gulf Blk.Sqdn. (Jul 1864–Jun 1865); return and w.o. (Jun–Aug 1865); cdr, *Wasp*, S.Atl.Sqdn. (Aug 1865–May 1869); return and w.o. (May–

---

*Bur. of Nav. records show his middle name to be "Ashe," but his marriage certificate and his widow's petition for a pension stated his middle name to be "Alexander." It is unknown when he changed it. Later documents show that his daughter claimed it was "Alexander."

Nov 1869); cdr, *Wasp*, S.Atl.Sqdn. (Dec 1869–Mar 1870); w.o. and l.o.a. (Mar 1870–Dec 1872); cdr, *Supply*, spec.serv. (Dec 1872–Feb 1873); cdr, *Guard*, spec.serv. (Feb 1873–Apr 1874); w.o. (Apr–May 1874); temp. duty, Bur. of Ord., Washington, DC (May–Oct 1874); cdr, *Wasp*, S.Atl.Sta. (Nov 1874–May 1877); w.o. (May–Sep 1877); cdr, rec. ship *Passaic*, Washington, DC (Sep 1877–Jan 1878); cdr, *Supply*, spec.serv. (Jan–Oct 1878); l.o.a. (Oct 1878–Dec 1880); temp. court-martial duty, *Hartford*, Asia.Sta. (Dec 1878–Jan 1879); cdr, *Shenandoah*, S.Atl.Sta. (Apr 1881–May 1882); l.o.a. (May–Jul 1882); Navy Yard, Norfolk, VA (Jul 1882–Apr 1883); cdr, rec. ship *Colorado*, NY (Apr 1883–Mar 1884); capt.yd., Navy Yard, NY (Mar 1884–Apr 1887); cdr, rec. ship *Vermont*, NY (Apr 1887–Jul 1889); w.o. (Jul–Aug 1889); pres., court of inquiry (Aug–Sep 1889); supervisor of harbor, NY (Oct 1889–Jul 1891); comdt., Navy Yard, League Island, PA (Jul 1891–Feb 1894); cdr, Eur.Sta., *Chicago* (Apr 1894–Feb 1895), then *San Francisco* (Feb–Nov 1895); w.o. and l.o.a. (Nov 1895–May 1896); cdr, Navy Yard, Mare Island, CA (Jun 1896–Jul 1898); placed on Ret.Lst. (3 Jul 1898).

References
Personal Papers: 46 items (1894–1901) at East Carolina Univ. Naval Collections, Greenville, NC.

JOSEPH LANMAN Born in Norwich, CT, on 11 Jul 1811, son of Peter and Abigail (Trumbull) Lanman. Uncle was CT Senator James Lanman. Married Ann Cornelia Williams, daughter of Capt Job G. Williams, USMC, on 20 Sep 1842. Four children. Died on 13 Mar 1874 at his home in Norwich, CT.

Ranks Midn (1 Jan 1825); PMidn (4 Jun 1831); Lt (3 Mar 1835); Cdr (14 Sep 1855); Capt (16 Jul 1861); Commo (29 Aug 1862); RAdm (8 Dec 1867); placed on Ret.Lst. (18 Jul 1872).

Career Summary Received appointment from CT (1 Jan 1825); w.o. (Jan 1825–Apr 1826); *Macedonian*, Braz.Sqdn. (Jan 1826–Nov 1828); l.o.a. (Nov 1828–Aug 1829); *Peacock*, W.Ind.Sqdn. (Aug 1829–Aug 1830); l.o.a. and w.o. (Aug 1830–Jul 1831); rec. ship, NY (Jul 1831–Mar 1832); w.o. (Mar 1832–Mar 1833); *Dolphin* and *Vincennes*, Pac.Sqdn. (Apr 1833–Jun 1836); l.o.a. and w.o. (Jun–Dec 1836); Navy Yard, NY (Dec 1836–May 1837); l.o.a. (May–Aug 1837); Med.Sqdn. (Sep 1837–Nov 1838); l.o.a. (Nov 1838–Feb 1839); *Warren*, W.Ind.Sqdn. (Feb 1839–Apr 1841); l.o.a. (Apr–Oct 1841); *Macedonian*, W.Ind.Sqdn. (Oct 1841–Aug 1842); l.o.a. and w.o. (Aug 1842–Mar 1843); ord. duty (Mar 1843–Jun 1846); w.o. (Jun–Jul 1846); *Preble*, Pac.Sqdn. (Jul 1846–Feb 1849); l.o.a. (Feb–Apr 1849); spec. duty on war steamers (Apr 1849–Oct 1851); *San Jacinto*, Med.Sqdn. (Nov 1851–Jul 1853); Navy Yard, Washington, DC (Aug 1853–Oct 1856); w.o. (Oct 1856–Mar 1857); cdr, *Michigan*, on Great Lakes (Apr 1858–Dec

JOSEPH LANMAN
1811–1874

1859); spec. bd. duty (Jan 1860–Mar 1861); w.o. (Mar 1861); ord. duty, Navy Yard, Mare Island, CA (Apr 1861–Feb 1862); cdr, *Saranac*, Pac.Sqdn. (Feb–Sep 1862); cdr, *Lancaster*, Pac.Sqdn. (Sep 1862–Aug 1864); cdr, *Minnesota*, N.Atl.Blk.Sqdn. (Sep 1864–Feb 1865); w.o. (Feb–Jun 1865); spec. duty, NY (Jun–Jul 1865); cdr, *Powhatan*, Navy Yard, Boston (Jul–Sep 1865); cdr, Atl.Sqdn., *New Hampshire* (Oct 1865–Nov 1866); w.o. (Nov 1866–Jul 1867); comdt., Navy Yard, Portsmouth, NH (Oct 1867–May 1869); cdr, S.Atl.Sqdn., *Lancaster* (Jun 1869–May 1872); w.o. (Jun–Jul 1872); placed on Ret.Lst. (18 Jul 1872).

References
Personal Papers: a) 1 vol. (1869–70) at USNAM. b) Journal (1834–35) in CT Historical Society, Hartford, CT.

JAMES LAWRENCE LARDNER
1802–1881

JAMES LAWRENCE LARDNER Born in Philadelphia on 20 Nov 1802, son of John and Margaret (Salter) Lardner. Served a short time in merchant service before entering navy. Married Margaret Wilmer on 2 Feb 1832. Married Ellen Wilmer on 23 Jun 1853. Had seven children. Died in Philadelphia on 12 Apr 1881. Buried in Frankford, PA.

Ranks Midn (10 May 1820); Lt (17 May 1828); Cdr (21 Nov 1851); Capt (19 May 1861); Commo (16 Jul 1862); Act.RAdm (15 Sep 1862); placed on Ret.Lst. (20 Nov 1864); RAdm on the Ret.Lst. (25 Jul 1866).

Career Summary Received appointment from PA (10 May 1820); *Dolphin* and flgs. *Franklin*, Pac.Sqdn. (Jul 1821–Sep 1824); l.o.a. (Sep 1824–Aug 1825); *Brandywine*, Med.Sqdn. (Aug 1825–Oct 1826); *Brandywine*, flgs., and *Dolphin*, Pac.Sqdn. (Oct 1826–Jun 1830); l.o.a. and w.o. (Jun 1830–May 1832); *Experiment*, Atl.Cst. (May–Sep 1832); on furlough (Sep 1832–Mar 1833); w.o. (Mar–May 1833); flgs. *Delaware*, Med.Sqdn. (May 1833–Jun 1834); l.o.a. and w.o. (Jun 1834–Oct 1836); flgs. *Independence*, Braz.Sqdn. (Mar 1837–May 1838); return, l.o.a., and w.o. (May 1838–Dec 1839); Navy Yard, Philadelphia (Dec 1839–Aug 1841); *Warren*, W.Ind.Sqdn. (Aug–Sep 1841); *Cyane* and *United States*, Pac.Sqdn. (Sep 1841–Oct 1844); l.o.a. and w.o. (Oct 1844–Nov 1845); cdr, rec.ship *Experiment*, Philadelphia (Nov 1845–Jul 1848); w.o. (Jul 1848–May 1850); cdr, *Porpoise*, and *Dale*, Afr.Sqdn. (May 1850–Apr 1853); l.o.a. and w.o. (Apr–Dec 1853); Naval Asylum, Philadelphia (Jan–Mar 1854); w.o. (Mar 1854–Jun 1855); flt.capt, Home Sqdn., *Columbia* (Jun–Oct 1855); w.o. (Oct 1855–Aug 1857); member, Bd. to Prepare Naval Regulations, Washington, DC (Aug 1857–Feb 1858); w.o. (Feb 1858–Nov 1860); Navy Yard, Philadelphia (Nov 1860–Sep 1861); cdr, *Susquehanna*, N.Atl.Blk.Sqdn. (Sep 1861–May 1862); cdr, E.Gulf Blk.Sqdn., *St. Lawrence* (May–Dec 1862); sick lv. (Dec 1862–Jan 1863); member, gen. court-martial bd., Navy Yard, Boston (Jan–May 1863); cdr, W.Ind.Sqdn., *Powhatan* (Jun 1863–Oct 1864); w.o. (Oct–Nov

1864); placed on Ret.Lst. (20 Nov 1864); spec. duty, Washington, DC (Nov 1864–Apr 1865); member, Naval Exam.Bd., Philadelphia (Apr 1865–Aug 1866); member, Naval Exam.Bd., NY (Mar–May 1869); gov., Naval Asylum, Philadelphia (Jun 1869–Jun 1872).

ELIE AUGUSTUS FREDERICK LAVALLETTE Born in Alexandria, VA, on 3 May 1790, son of Elie Lavallette, a chaplain in the navy. Served from 1800 on board the *Philadelphia* with his father and rated as a captain's clerk. Married, with a son, Stephen Decatur Lavallette, and a daughter. Died in Philadelphia on 18 Nov 1862. Buried in Philadelphia's Laurel Hill Cemetery.

Ranks Sailing Mstr (25 Jun 1812); Act.Lt (4 Jun 1814); Lt (9 Dec 1814); Mstr.Comdt. (3 Mar 1831); Capt (23 Feb 1840); placed on Ret.Lst. with rank of RAdm (16 Jul 1862).

Career Summary Received appointment from PA (25 Jun 1812); Delaware River Flot., Philadelphia (Jun–Oct 1812); *John Adams*, NY Sta. (Oct 1812–May 1813); *Alert*, NY (May–Aug 1813); Lake Champlain Sta. (Sep 1813–Jan 1815); *Spitfire*, NY (Jan–Mar 1815); on furlough and w.o. (Mar 1815–Apr 1817); member, gen. court-martial, Erie, PA (Apr–Jun 1817); *Despatch*, survey duty (Jun–Dec 1817); *Guerriere*, spec.serv. and Med.Sqdn. (Jun–Dec 1818); *United States*, Med.Sqdn. (Dec 1818–Jun 1819); *North Carolina*, Philadelphia (Jun 1819–Nov 1822); *Peacock*, W.Ind.Sqdn. (Dec 1822–Feb 1823); Navy Yard, Norfolk, VA (Feb 1823); cdr, Gunboat #158, W.Ind.Sqdn. (Feb–Aug 1823); Navy Yard, Philadelphia (Aug 1823–Jun 1824); *Constitution*, Med.Sqdn. (Jul 1824–Jul 1828); w.o. (Aug–Nov 1828); rec. duty, Naval Rndv., Philadelphia (Nov 1828–Mar 1831); Navy Yard, Norfolk, VA (Mar–Jul 1831); l.o.a. (Jul–Sep 1831); Navy Yard, Norfolk, VA (Sep 1831–Jun 1832); l.o.a. (Jun–Aug 1832); Navy Yard, Norfolk, VA (Aug–Dec 1832); l.o.a. (Dec 1832–Feb 1833); cdr, *Fairfield*, Pac.Sqdn. (May 1833–Dec 1835); l.o.a. (Dec 1835–Feb 1836); w.o. (Feb 1836–Feb 1837); member, gen. court-martial, Philadelphia (Mar 1837); cdr, Naval Rndv., Philadelphia (Mar 1837–Mar 1840); w.o. (Mar–Apr 1840); cdr, *Ohio*, Med.Sqdn. (May 1840–Jul 1841); l.o.a. (Jul–Oct 1841); w.o. (Oct 1841–Mar 1842); member, gen. court-martial, Baltimore (Mar 1842); w.o. (Mar–May 1842); cdr, Navy Yard and Sta., Pensacola, FL (May 1842–May 1845); cdr, Navy Sta., Memphis, TN (Jan–Jul 1846); cdr, *Independence*, flgs., and *Congress*, Pac.Sqdn (Jul 1846–Jan 1849); additional duty, gov., Mazatlan, Mexico (1847–Jun 1848); l.o.a. (Jan–Apr 1849); member, gen. court-martial, Navy Yard, Portsmouth, NH (May–Jun 1849); w.o. (Jun 1849–Jun 1850); l.o.a. (Jun–Sep 1850); w.o. (Sep–Nov 1850); member, gen. court-martial, Navy Yard, Washington, DC (Dec 1850); cdr, Afr.Sqdn., *Germantown* (Jan–Apr 1851); l.o.a. (Apr–Jul 1851); w.o. (Jul 1851–Jun 1854); member, gen. court-martial, Navy Yard,

ELIE AUGUSTUS FREDERICK
LAVALLETTE
1790–1862

Philadelphia (Jul 1854); w.o. (Jul 1854–Aug 1856); cdr, Navy Yard, Washington, DC (Aug 1856–May 1858); cdr, Med.Sqdn., *Wabash* (May 1858–Dec 1859); l.o.a. (Dec 1859–Mar 1860); pres., Bd. of Examiners (Jun 1860); cdr, Naval Sta., Sacket's Harbor, NY (Feb 1861–May 1862); pres., court of inquiry, Navy Yard, Washington, DC (Sep–Oct 1861); w.o. (May–Jul 1862); member, Advisory Bd. on Promotions, Washington, DC (Jul–Aug 1862); retired (16 Jul 1862).

Career Highlights Served as only lt on *Saratoga*, Commo Thomas Macdonough's flgs., at Battle of Lake Champlain, Sep 1814. Promoted for his gallantry in the action, and received the thanks of Congress and a silver medal.

References
Personal Papers: 558 items, 10 vols. (1826–1928) in WPL.

SAMUEL PHILLIPS LEE
1812–1897

SAMUEL PHILLIPS LEE Born in Sully, Fairfax County, VA, on 13 Feb 1812, son of Francis Lightfoot and Jane (Fitzgerald) Lee. Educated by private tutors in Sully, belonged to the illustrious and old Virginia Lees, his paternal grandfather being Richard Henry Lee, signer of the Declaration of Independence. His third cousins were the Confederate Gen Robert E. Lee and Capt Sydney Smith Lee, who commanded all Confederate naval forces in VA during the Peninsular campaign. Married Elizabeth Blair on 27 Apr 1843. One son, Francis Preston Blair Lee who sat in the Senate from MD from 1913 to 1917. Died in Silver Spring, MD, on 5 Jun 1897. Buried in Arlington National Cemetery.

Ranks Midn (22 Nov 1825); PMidn (4 Jun 1831); Lt (9 Feb 1837); Cdr (14 Sep 1855); Capt (16 Jul 1862); Act.RAdm (2 Sep 1862); Commo (25 Jul 1866); RAdm (22 Apr 1870); placed on Ret.Lst. (13 Feb 1873).

Career Summary Received appointment from VA (22 Nov 1825); *Hornet*, W.Ind.Sta. (Feb–Aug 1827); l.o.a. (Aug–Sep 1827); Navy Yard, NY (Sep–Oct 1827); *Delaware* and flgs. *Java*, Med.Sqdn. (Oct 1827–Aug 1830); Naval School, Norfolk, VA (Oct 1830–Jul 1831); Navy Yard, Boston (Jul 1831–Sep 1832); l.o.a. and w.o. (Sep 1832–Apr 1834); *Brandywine* and *Vincennes*, Pac. Sqdn. (Apr 1834–Jun 1836); l.o.a. and w.o. (Jun 1836–Jul 1837); *Pioneer*, Navy Yard, NY, and U.S.Expl.Expd. (Jul 1837–Jul 1839); l.o.a. (Jul–Dec 1839); *Hornet*, W.Ind.Sqdn. (Dec 1839–Aug 1840); l.o.a. (Aug 1840–Nov 1841); Naval Rndv., Alexandria, VA (Dec 1841–Apr 1842); cst.surv. duty (Apr 1842–Sep 1844); w.o. (Sep–Nov 1844); Navy Yard, Pensacola, FL (Nov 1844–Sep 1845); w.o. (Sep 1845–Mar 1846); cdr, cst.surv. duty (Mar 1846–Jun 1851); w.o. (Jun–Jul 1851); cdr, *Dolphin*, spec.serv. (Jul 1851–Jul 1852); spec. duty, Naval Observatory, Washington, DC (Jul 1852–Apr 1854); w.o. (Apr–Jul 1854); Naval Observatory, Washington, DC (Jul 1854–Oct 1855); w.o. (Oct 1855–Mar 1858); member, Naval Exam.Bd. and w.o. (Mar 1858–Oct 1860); cdr,

Vandalia, E.Ind. and S.Atl.Blk. Sqdns. (Nov 1860–Oct 1861); Navy Dept., Washington, DC (Oct 1861–Jan 1862); cdr, *Oneida*, W.Gulf Blk.Sqdn. (Jan–Aug 1862); cdr, N.Atl.Blk.Sqdn., *Philadelphia* (Sep 1862–Jan 1863), then *Minnesota* (Jan 1863–May 1864), then *Agawan* (May–Jun 1864), then *Malvern* (Jun–Oct 1864); cdr, MS Sqdn., *Black Hawk* (Oct 1864–Apr 1865), then *Tempest* (Apr–Aug 1865); w.o. (Aug 1865–Aug 1866); pres., Naval Exam.Bd., Hartford, CT (Aug 1866–Dec 1867); w.o. (Dec 1867–Apr 1868); member, Naval Exam.Bd., Philadelphia (Apr–May 1868); pres., court-martial bd., NY (Aug–Sep 1868); w.o. (Sep 1868–Feb 1869); pres., Bd. of Examiners and other bd. duties (Feb–Oct 1869); in charge, Signal Service, Washington, DC (Oct 1869-Jun 1870); spec. duty, Navy Dept., Washington, DC (Jun–Aug 1870); cdr, N.Atl.Sqdn., *Worcester* (Aug 1870–Aug 1872); placed on Ret.Lst. (13 Feb 1873).

Career Highlights During Mexican War, participated in second Tabasco Expd. During the Civil War, saw action on lower reaches of the Mississippi River in 1862. Commanded advance division below Vicksburg in 1862 before called back to command the N.Atl.Blk.Sqdn.

References

Personal Papers: a) 19,000 items (1860–69) at NHF,LC. b) 50 boxes (1733–1916) in Blair-Lee Papers, Princeton Univ. Lib. c) 1 item (1861) in NC Dept. of Cultural Resources, Raleigh, NC.

Writings: *Report and Charts of the Cruise of the U.S. brig DOLPHIN, by Lt S. P. Lee* (1854).

Additional Sources: Dudley T. Cornish and Virginia J. Laas, *Lincoln's Lee: The Life of Samuel Phillips Lee, United States Navy, 1812–1897* (Lawrence, KS: 1986).

WILLIAM EDGAR LeROY Born in New York City on 24 Mar 1818. Married first to Mary Elizabeth Nicoll, then in Nov 1881 to Mrs. Mary Bertram Stump. Had one son. Died on 10 Dec 1888 in New York City. Buried in Tarrytown, NY.

Ranks Midn (11 Jan 1832); PMidn (23 Jun 1838); Lt (13 Jul 1843); Cdr (1 Jul 1861); Capt (25 Jul 1866); Commo (3 Jul 1870); RAdm (5 Apr 1874); placed on Ret.Lst. (24 Mar 1880).

Career Summary Received appointment from NY (11 Jan 1832); w.o. (Jan 1832–May 1833); *Delaware*, Med.Sqdn. (May 1833–Feb 1836); l.o.a. and w.o. (Feb–Jul 1836); rec. ship *Hudson*, and Naval School, NY (Jul–Sep 1836); *Dolphin*, Braz.Sqdn. (Sep 1836–Sep 1837); l.o.a. and w.o. (Sep 1837–Aug 1838); rec. ship *Hudson*, NY (Aug–Sep 1838); *Ohio* and *Constitution*, Med. and Pac.Sqdns. (Sep 1838–Jul 1841); l.o.a. (Jul–Dec 1841); rec. ship *Hudson*, NY (Oct 1841–May 1842); Depot of Charts, Naval Observatory, Washington, DC (May–Sep 1842); rec. ship *Hudson*, NY (Sep–Dec 1842); *Erie* and *Cyane*, Pac.Sqdn. (Dec 1842–Oct 1844); l.o.a. (Oct 1844–Jan 1845); *Mississippi*, Home Sqdn. (Jan 1845–Aug 1846); *Poto-*

WILLIAM EDGAR LeROY
1818–1888

mac, Home Sqdn. (Aug–Oct 1846); l.o.a. (Oct 1846–Jan 1847); *Polk*, Home Sqdn. (Feb–May 1847); l.o.a. (May–Jun 1847); *Allegheny*, Pittsburgh, PA (Jun–Oct 1847); l.o.a. (Oct–Dec 1847); *Savannah*, Pac.Sqdn. (Dec 1847–Oct 1851); l.o.a. and w.o. (Oct 1851–Mar 1853); *Savannah*, Braz.Sqdn (Mar 1853–Nov 1856); l.o.a. and w.o. (Nov 1856–Jun 1857); Naval Sta., Sacket's Harbor, NY (Jun 1857–Jun 1858); Navy Yard, NY (Jun 1858–Jun 1859); cdr, *Mystic*, Afr.Sqdn. (Jun 1859–Oct 1861); l.o.a. (Oct–Nov 1861); cdr, *Keystone State*, S.Atl.Blk.Sqdn. (Nov 1861–Jun 1863); l.o.a. and w.o. (Jun–Sep 1863); cdr, *Oneida*, then *Ossipee*, W.Gulf Blk.Sqdn. (Sep 1863–Jun 1865); w.o. (Jun–Oct 1865); Naval Rndv., NY (Oct 1865–Apr 1867); flt.capt, Eur.Sqdn., and cdr, *Franklin* (Jun 1867–Dec 1868); return and w.o. (Dec 1868–Apr 1870); Navy Yard, NY (Apr–Jul 1870); w.o. (Jul–Sep 1870); spec. duty, New London, CT (Oct 1870–Feb 1871); w.o. (Feb–Dec 1871); senior member, Naval Inspection and Exam. Bds. (Jan 1872–May 1874); spec. duty, Washington, DC (May 1874); cdr, S.Atl.Sta., *Lancaster* (Jun 1874–Feb 1876); cdr, N.Atl.Sta., *Hartford* (Feb–Aug 1876); w.o. and l.o.a. (Aug 1876–Aug 1877); cdr, Eur.Sta., *Trenton* (Oct 1877–Jan 1879); return and w.o. (Jan–Apr 1879); bd. duties (Apr–Jun 1879); l.o.a. and w.o. (Jun 1879–Mar 1880); placed on Ret.Lst. (24 Mar 1880).

JOHN WILLIAM LIVINGSTON
1804–1885

JOHN WILLIAM LIVINGSTON Born in New York City on 22 May 1804, son of Dr. William and Eliza (Livingston) Turk. His father was a navy surgeon who died in 1854. In 1843, changed his name from Turk to his mother's maiden name of Livingston. Married. Died at his home in New York City on 10 Sep 1885. Buried in Greenwood Cemetery in New York City.

Ranks Midn (4 Mar 1823); PMidn (23 Mar 1829); Lt (21 Jun 1832); Cdr (24 May 1855); Commo (16 Jul 1862); transferred to Ret.Lst. (12 May 1866); RAdm on Ret.Lst. (26 May 1868).

Career Summary Received appointment from NY (4 Mar 1823); Navy Yard, NY (Jun 1824–Jan 1825); *Constitution*, Med.Sqdn. (Jan 1825–Nov 1826); l.o.a. (Nov 1826–Jul 1827); Navy Yard, Boston (Jul–Aug 1827); *Delaware*, Med.Sqdn. (Aug 1827–Feb 1829); w.o. (Feb 1829–Mar 1831); Navy Yard, NY (Mar 1831–Jul 1832); l.o.a. and w.o. (Jul 1832–Mar 1833); watch off., *Dolphin*, Pac.Sqdn. (May 1833–Dec 1835); l.o.a. (Dec 1835–Mar 1836); rec. ship at NY (Mar–Jun 1836); l.o.a. and w.o. (Jun–Dec 1836); Navy Yard, NY (Dec 1836–Sep 1837); flgs. *Columbia*, E.Ind.Sqdn. (Oct 1837–Jun 1840); l.o.a. (Jun–Nov 1840); Naval Rndv., NY (Nov 1840–Dec 1842); l.o.a. and w.o. (Dec 1842–Jul 1843); temp. duty, rec. ship *Franklin*, Boston (Jul–Oct 1843); *Raritan*, Philadelphia (Oct–Nov 1843); w.o. (Nov 1843–Aug 1845); flgs. *Congress*, Pac.Sqdn. (Aug 1845–Jan 1849); l.o.a. and w.o. (Jan–Sep 1849); Navy Yard, NY (Sep 1849–Sep 1851); cdr, *John Han-*

cock, spec.serv. (Sep–Oct 1851); w.o. (Oct 1851–Oct 1855); cdr, *St. Louis*, Afr.Sqdn. (Oct 1855–Feb 1858); l.o.a. and w.o. (Feb 1858–Jun 1859); cdr, rec. ship *Ohio*, Boston (Jun–Aug 1859); w.o. (Aug 1859–Apr 1861); Navy Yard, Norfolk, VA (Apr–May 1861); cdr, *Penguin*, Atl.Blk.Sqdn. (May–Aug 1861); cdr, *Bienville*, Atl.Blk.Sqdn. (Sep 1861); cdr, *Cumberland*, James River Flot. (Sep 1861–Feb 1862); sick lv. and w.o. (Feb–May 1862); cdr, Naval Sta., Norfolk, VA (May 1862–Nov 1864); cdr, Naval Sta., Mound City, IL (Dec 1864–Dec 1865); w.o. (Dec 1865–May 1866); transferred to Ret.Lst. (12 May 1866); court-martial duty (Oct 1866–Mar 1867); court-martial duty, Philadelphia (Apr–Jul 1867).

Career Highlights Assisted in destroying pirate towns along Sumatran coasts while with *Columbia* during her circumnavigation. Served off coast of CA and Mexico during Mexican War, participating in capture of Guaymas and San Blas. Commanded Navy Yard in Norfolk, VA, after Confederates abandoned it, repairing damages in order to use it as a refitting base for ships on blockade duty.

JOHN LOWE Born in Liverpool, England, on 11 Dec 1838, son of John and Mary (Blinston) Lowe. Educated in Liverpool and, after emigrating to the U.S. and settling in OH in Columbus, where he studied engineering. Married Josephine L. Dyer on 5 Nov 1867, having one daughter. Served as a private in the Union army at the outbreak of the Civil War. Retired to Washington, DC, where he died on 29 Aug 1930.

JOHN LOWE
1838–1930

Ranks Private, 2nd OH Regiment, U.S. Volunteers (17 Apr 1861); medical discharge (Jul 1861); 3rd Asst.Engr. (14 Aug 1861); 2nd Asst.Engr. (21 Apr 1863); 1st Asst.Engr. (11 Oct 1866); title changed to PAsst.Engr. (24 Feb 1874); Chief Engr. (16 Jun 1883); Chief Engr. with rel. rank of Cdr (15 Jan 1895); Chief Engr. with rel. rank of Capt (1 Mar 1899); Capt (3 Mar 1899); placed on Ret.Lst. with rank of RAdm (11 Dec 1900).

Career Summary Enlisted as Private, 2nd Ohio Regiment, U.S. Volunteers (17 Apr 1861); 2nd Ohio Regiment, (Apr–Jul 1861); discharged (Jul 1861); received appointment from OH as 3rd Asst.Engr. (14 Aug 1861); w.o. (Aug–Oct 1861); *Huron*, S.Atl.Blk.Sqdn. (Oct 1861–Jun 1864); w.o. (Jun–Jul 1864); *Shawmut*, N.Atl.Blk.Sqdn. (Jul 1864–Dec 1866); *Madawaska*, on trials (Dec 1866–Feb 1867); spec. duty, *Richmond*, Navy Yard, Boston (Feb–May 1867); spec. duty, *Maumee*, Philadelphia (May–Dec 1867); Navy Yard, Washington, DC (Dec 1867–Nov 1868); *Tallapoosa*, Navy Yard, Washington, DC, and spec.serv. (Nov 1868–Feb 1870); *Palos*, Navy Yard, Boston (Feb–Jun 1870); *Alaska*, Pac.Sqdn. (Jun 1870–Feb 1873); w.o. (Feb–Mar 1873); Navy Yard, Washington, DC (Mar–Nov 1873); *Manhattan*, spec.serv. (Nov 1873–Feb 1874); spec. duty, Navy Yard, Boston (Feb–Jul 1874); *Intrepid*, spec.serv. (Jul 1874–Jul 1876); w.o. (Jul–Nov 1876); *Despatch*, spec.serv., Eur. (Nov 1876–Jul 1879); w.o. (Jul–Dec 1879); rec. ship *Passaic*, Washington, DC (Dec. 1879–Oct 1880); Navy Yard, Washington, DC (Oct 1880–Oct 1883); *Yantic* and *Bear*, Greely Relief Expd. (Oct 1883–Nov 1884); w.o. (Nov–Dec 1884); member, Bd. of Examiners, Chester, PA (Dec 1884–Jan 1885); Navy Yard, Washington, DC (Jan–Dec 1885); *Dolphin*, N.Atl.Sta. (Dec 1885–Jan 1887); *Thetis*, spec.serv. and Alaskan waters (Jan 1887–Feb 1889); w.o. (Feb–May 1889); Vulcan Iron Works, Chicago, IL (May–Oct 1889); w.o. (Oct–Dec 1889); Navy Yard, Washington, DC (Jan 1890–Jan 1892); insp. of machinery, *New York*, under construction, Philadelphia (Jan 1892–Aug 1893); *New York*, S.Atl.Sta. (Aug 1893–Jan 1895); w.o. (Jan–Jun 1895); spec. duty, monitor flt., Richmond, VA (Jan 1895–Jan 1896); flt.engr., Pac.Sta., *Philadelphia* (Jan 1896–Dec 1897); l.o.a. (Dec 1897–Feb 1898); naval insp., Continental Iron Works, Brooklyn, NY (Feb–Nov 1898); member, Engr. Exam.Bd., Philadelphia (Nov 1898–Sep 1899); chief engr., Navy Yard, League Island, PA (Jan–Sep 1899); insp. of engineering material, Hartford, CT and elsewhere (Sep 1899–Dec 1900); placed on Ret.Lst. (11 Dec 1900).

Career Highlights One of the first to enlist at outbreak of Civil War. Saw action and was wounded at the First Battle of Bull Run. Participated in the Greely Relief Expd. in 1884. In 1898 became the world's first naval officer to serve on a submarine torpedo boat. Continued work with submarines after retirement, participating in Oct 1901 in important experiment at Peconic Bay, NY, where he was submerged for fifteen hours in a submarine torpedo boat. Received a medal from Congress for this "meritorious service."

References
Personal Papers: a) 600 items (1860–1945) in NHF,LC. b) 1 item (1838) in NHF,WNY.

STEPHEN BLEECKER LUCE
1827–1917

STEPHEN BLEECKER LUCE Born in Albany, NY, on 25 Mar 1827, son of Vinal and Charlotte (Bleecker) Luce. Married on 7 Dec 1854 to Elisa Henley, daughter of Commo John C. Henley. Three children. Retired to Newport, RI, where he died on 28 Jul 1917. Buried in St. Mary's Church, Portsmouth, RI.

Ranks Midn (19 Oct 1841); PMidn (10 Aug 1848); Mstr (14 Sep 1855); Lt (15 Sep 1855); LCdr (16 Jul 1862); Cdr (25 Jul 1866); Capt (28 Dec 1872); Commo (25 Nov 1881); Act.RAdm (20 Sep 1884); RAdm (5 Oct 1885); placed on Ret.Lst. (25 Mar 1889).

Career Summary Received appointment from NY (19 Oct 1841); *North Carolina*, NY (Oct 1841–Mar 1842); *Congress*, Med. and Braz. Sqdns. (Apr 1842–Mar 1845); *Columbus*, E.Ind.Sqdn. (May 1845–Mar 1848); Naval School, Annapolis, MD (Apr 1848–Jul 1849); *Vandalia*, Pac.Sta. (Aug 1849–Oct 1852); spec. duty in astronomy, Washington, DC (Dec 1852–May 1853); *Vixen*, Home Sqdn. (May 1853–Feb

1854); cst.surv. duty (May 1854–Nov 1857); *Jamestown*, W.Ind.Sqdn. (Nov 1857–Feb 1860); asst. instructor of seamanship and gunnery, USNA (May 1860–May 1861); *Wabash*, Atl.Blk.Sqdn. (May 1861–Jan 1862); USNA, Newport, RI (Jan 1862–Oct 1863); cdr, *Macedonian*, special duty, Eur. (Jun–Oct 1863); cdr, *Nantucket*, N.Atl.Blk.Sqdn. (Oct 1863–Aug 1864); cdr, *Sonoma*, N.Atl.Blk.Sqdn. (Aug 1864); *Canandaigua*, N.Atl.Blk.Sqdn. (Aug 1864); cdr, *Pontiac*, N.Atl.Blk.Sqdn. (Sep 1864–Jun 1865); USNA (Sep–Oct 1865); comdt. of midn, USNA (Oct 1865–Jun 1868); cdr, *Mohongo*, Pac.Sqdn. (Sep 1868–May 1869); cdr, *Juniata*, Med.Sqdn. (Jul 1869–Jul 1872); equip.off., then capt.yd., Navy Yard, Boston (Sep 1872–Oct 1875); cdr, *Minnesota*, spec. duty (Dec 1873); cdr, flgs. *Hartford*, N.Atl.Sta. (Nov 1875–Aug 1877); insp. of training ships (Aug–Dec 1877); cdr, training ship *Minnesota* (Jan 1878–Feb 1881); cdr, U.S. Naval Training Sqdn., *New Hampshire* (Apr 1881–Jun 1884); cdr, N.Atl.Sqdn., *Tennessee* (Jul–Sep 1884); pres., NWC (Sep 1884–Jun 1886); cdr, naval forces, N.Atl.Sta., *Richmond* (Jun 1886–Feb 1889); placed on Ret.Lst. (25 Mar 1889); spec. duty, NWC (1901–Nov 1910).

Career Highlights Career centered around the education and training system of the service. Campaigned hard and finally successfully in 1884 to found the NWC at Newport, RI. Served as pres. of U.S. Naval Institute from 1887 to 1898. Represented U.S. in 1892 at Columbian Historical Exposition in Madrid, Spain, commemorating 400th anniversary of the founding of America. Served as member of Bd. of Awards in 1901. Pres. of Bd. of Visitors for USNA in 1901.

References

Personal Papers: a) 8,000 items (1799–1938) in NHF,LC. b) ½ box (1876–1919) at NWC, Newport, RI. c) See: *David Foote Sellers, Stephen B. Luce: A Register of their Papers in the Library of Congress* (Washington, DC: 1978).

Writings: a) *Seamanship . . . compiled from Various Authorities for use at the Naval Academy* (editions, 1862–77). b) *Manning and Improvement of the Navy: Address Delivered at the United States Naval Academy* (Washington, DC: 1873). c) *Textbook of Seamanship. The Equipping and Handling of Vessels Under Sail or Steam* (editions, 1884–98). c) *The Story of the Monitor* (1902). d) *Naval Songs: A Collection of Originals . . . by S. B. Luce* (2nd ed., 1902).

Selected Additional Sources: a) Albert Gleaves, *Life and Letters of Stephen B. Luce: Rear Admiral, U.S.N., Founder of the Naval War College* (New York: 1925). b) John Kobler, *Luce: His Time, Life and Fortune* (Garden City: 1968). c) W. A. Swanberg, *Luce and His Empire* (New York: 1972). d) John D. Hayes and John B. Hattendorf, eds., *The Writings of Stephen B. Luce* (Newport: 1975). e) Ronald H. Spector, *Professors of War: The Naval War College and the Development of the Naval Profession* (Newport: 1977).

GEORGE ARMSTRONG LYON
1837–1914

GEORGE ARMSTRONG LYON Born in Erie, PA, on 23 Dec 1837, son of Reverend George A. and Mary (Sterrett) Lyon. Educated at Dartmouth College, graduating in 1858. Admitted to PA bar in 1861. Married Rose Vincent on 21 Jun 1877. One son. Died in Philadelphia on 6 Mar 1914. Buried in Erie, PA.

Ranks Asst.Paymstr. (11 Jun 1862); Paymstr. (23 Jan 1866); Pay Insp. (15 Sep 1888); Pay Dir. (15 Mar 1898); placed on Ret.Lst. as Pay Dir. with rank of RAdm (23 Dec 1898).

Career Summary Received appointment from PA (11 Jun 1862); w.o. (Jun–Jul 1862); duty with MS Flot., Cairo, IL (Jul 1862–Dec 1863); s.a. and w.o. (Dec 1863–Mar 1864); *Pontoosuc*, N.Atl.Blk.Sqdn. (Mar 1864–Jul 1865); s.a. and w.o. (Jul–Dec 1865); rec. ship *Potomac*, Pensacola, FL (Dec 1865–Jul 1867); s.a. and w.o. (Jul–Sep 1867); storeship *Idaho*, Asia.Sqdn. (Oct 1867–Apr 1870); s.a. and w.o. (Apr 1870–Feb 1871); *Worcester* (Feb–Jul 1871); s.a. and w.o. (Jul–Sep 1871); *Michigan*, on Great Lakes (Sep 1871–Oct 1874); s.a. and w.o. (Oct 1874–Aug 1875); insp. of provisions and clothing, Navy Yard, Washington, DC (Sep 1875–Oct 1878); s.a. and w.o. (Oct 1878–Jul 1879); Naval Rndv., St. Louis, MO (Jul–Sep 1879); Naval Rndv., Cincinnati, OH (Sep–Oct 1879); w.o. (Oct 1879–May 1881); Navy Yard, Washington, DC (May 1881–Jun 1883); additional duty, insp. of provisions and clothing, Navy Yard, Washington, DC (Sep–Oct 1882); *Trenton*, Asia.Sta. (Sep 1883–Jun 1884); flt.paymstr., Asia.Sta., *Trenton* (Jun 1883–Feb 1886); s.a. and w.o. (Feb–Jul 1886); l.o.a. and w.o. (Jul 1886–Aug 1887); Navy Pay Office, Navy Yard, Portsmouth, NH (Sep 1887–Jul 1890); s.a. (Jul–Sep 1890); in charge, Navy Pay Office, San Francisco (Sep 1890–Sep 1893); s.a. and w.o. (Sep 1893–Mar 1894); spec. bd. duty, Washington, DC (Mar–Sep 1894); in charge, Navy Pay Office, Boston (Oct 1894–Mar 1896); flt.paymstr., N.Atl.Sta., *New York* (Mar 1896–Jul 1897); s.a. and w.o. (Jul–Dec 1897); member, Naval Exam.Bd., Washington, DC (Dec 1897–Mar 1898); in charge, Navy Pay Office, Philadelphia (Apr 1898–Dec 1899); placed on Ret.Lst. (23 Dec 1899).

JOHN MARSTON Born in Boston, MA, on 26 Feb 1796. Died in Philadelphia on 8 Apr 1885.

Ranks Act.Midn (15 Apr 1813); Lt (13 Jan 1825); Cdr (8 Sep 1841); Capt (14 Sep 1855); transferred to Ret.Lst. (21 Dec 1861); Commo on Ret.Lst. (16 Jul 1862); RAdm on Ret.Lst. (28 Mar 1881).

Career Summary Received appointment from MA (15 Apr 1813); *President*, spec. cruise (Apr–Dec 1813); Navy Yard, Portsmouth, NH (Jan 1814–Mar 1815); *Washington* then *Java*, spec.serv. and Med.Sqdn. (Mar 1815–Feb 1817); l.o.a. (Feb–May 1817); *Prometheus*, spec.serv. (May 1817–Jul 1819); flgs. *Constellation*, Braz.Sqdn. (Jul 1819–May 1820); Navy Yard, Philadelphia (May 1820–Mar 1821); flgs. *Constitution*,

JOHN MARSTON
1796–1885

Med.Sqdn. (Mar 1821–Oct 1822); Navy Yard, Philadelphia (Oct 1822–May 1823); *Congress*, spec.serv., and Navy Yard, Norfolk, VA (May 1823–Jul 1825); *Brandywine*, spec.serv. and Med.Sqdn. (Jul 1825–Jun 1826); l.o.a. (Jun 1826–Nov 1831); on furlough (Nov 1831–Aug 1832); *Vandalia*, W.Ind.Sqdn. (Aug 1832–Mar 1833); l.o.a. and w.o. (Mar 1833–Sep 1837); ord. duty, Philadelphia (Sep–Oct 1837); temp. duty, *Pennsyl-vania*, Navy Yard, Norfolk, VA (Oct 1837–Sep 1839); *United States* and *Potomac*, Braz.Sqdn. (Oct 1839–Feb 1842); l.o.a. and w.o. (Feb 1842–Oct 1848); cdr, *Yorktown*, Afr.Sqdn. (Oct 1848–Dec 1850); w.o. (Dec 1850–Feb 1851); l.o.a. and w.o. (Feb 1851–May 1852); Navy Yard, Philadelphia (Jul 1852–Jul 1855); w.o. (Jul 1855–Sep 1860); cdr, flgs. *Cumberland*, Home and N.Atl.Sqdns. (Oct 1860–Sep 1861); cdr, *Roanoke*, N.Atl.Blk.Sqdn. (Sep 1861–Mar 1862); transferred to Ret.Lst. (21 Dec 1861); bd. duties, New London, CT (Aug–Oct 1862); insp., 2nd L.h. Dist., Boston (Oct 1862–Nov 1865).

References
Personal Papers: a) 250 items (1850–1862) in NHF,LC. b) 1 vol. (1850) in USNAM.

EDMUND ORVILLE MATTHEWS Born in Baltimore, MD, on 24 Oct 1836, son of John and Mary Righter (Lever-ing) Matthews. Married twice: to Hattie R. Hammond on 20 May 1878, and, after her death, to her sister, Alzaida R. Hammond. Retired to Cambridge, MA, where he died on 29 Jan 1911. Buried in Newport, RI.

Ranks Act.Midn (2 Oct 1851); Midn (9 Jun 1855); PMidn (15 Apr 1858); Mstr (4 Nov 1858); Lt (27 Jun 1860); LCdr (16 Jul 1862); Cdr (22 Apr 1870); Capt (14 Sep 1881); Commo (21 Jul 1894); RAdm (19 Jun 1897); placed on Ret.Lst. (24 Oct 1898).

Career Summary Received appointment from MO (2 Oct 1851); USNA (Oct 1851–Jun 1855); l.o.a. (Jun–Oct 1855); *Potomac*, Home Sqdn. (Oct 1855–Aug 1856); *Wabash*, Home Sqdn. (Aug 1856); *Saratoga*, Home Sqdn. (Aug 1856–Jan 1858); l.o.a. (Jan–Apr 1858); *Macedonian*, Med.Sqdn. (May 1858–Jul 1860); l.o.a. (Jul–Oct 1860); instructor of math., USNA (Oct 1860–May 1861); *Wabash*, N.Atl.Sqdn (May–Oct 1861); sick lv. (Oct 1861); instructor of seamanship, USNA, Newport, RI (Nov 1861–Jun 1864); cdr, *Sonoma*, S.Atl.Blk.Sqdn. (Jun 1864–Jun 1865); w.o. (Jun–Aug 1865); apprentice ship *Savannah* (Aug–Nov 1865); USNA (Nov 1865–Jun 1869); head, Torp. Corps, Newport, RI (Jun 1869–Jun 1873); l.o.a. and w.o. (Jun–Dec 1873); cdr, *Ashuelot*, Asia.Sta. (Jan 1874–Apr 1877); w.o. (Apr 1877–Mar 1878); inspector of ord., Navy Yard, NY (Apr 1878–Mar 1881); w.o. (Mar–Aug 1881); cdr, *Powhatan*, spec.serv. (Aug 1881–Feb 1883); w.o. (Feb–Apr 1883); cdr, training ship *New Hampshire* (Apr–Jun 1883); member, Gun Foundry Bd. with duty in Europe (May 1883–Dec 1884); w.o. (Dec 1884–Sep 1885); senior member,

EDMUND ORVILLE MATTHEWS
1836–1911

Bd. of Appraisement (Sep–Oct 1885); cdr, *Brooklyn*, Asia.Sta. (Oct 1885–Sep 1887); home and w.o. (Sep–Nov 1887); capt.yd., Navy Yard, Boston (Dec 1887–May 1890); cdr, rec. ship *Wabash*, Boston (May 1890–Nov 1892); bd. duties (Nov 1892–Mar 1894); chief, Bur. of Yards and Docks, Washington, DC (Mar 1894–Mar 1898); pres., Exam. and Ret. Bd. (Mar 1898–Apr 1899); placed on Ret.Lst. (24 Oct 1898).

References

Personal Papers: "A Long Life in Review; Service Record of Rear Admiral Edmund Orville Matthews in the United States Navy" ed. W. N. Matthews (Naval Historical Center, Washington Navy Yard, c.1933).

EDWARD MAY
1838–1917

EDWARD MAY Born in Leicester, MA, on 20 Jan 1838, son of Samuel and Sarah (Russell) May. Educated in private schools and at the Leicester Academy. Married Mary Mignot Blodgett on 4 Oct 1871. One daughter. Made his home in Jamaica Plain, MA. Died in Boston on 5 Feb 1917. Buried at Forest Hills, MA.

Ranks Asst.Paymstr. (6 Sep 1861); Paymstr. (14 Apr 1862); Pay Insp. (25 Sep 1875); Pay Dir. (24 Dec 1883); placed on Ret.Lst. as Pay Dir. with rank of RAdm (20 Jan 1900).

Career Summary Received appointment from MA (6 Sep 1861); *Unadilla*, S.Atl.Blk.Sqdn. (Sep 1861–Jul 1862); w.o. (Jul–Sep 1862); *Clara Dobson*, MS Flot. (Sep 1862–May 1864); w.o. (May–Aug 1864); spec. duty, Washington, DC (Aug 1864–Apr 1866); *Lackawanna*, N.Pac.Sqdn. (May 1866–Feb 1869); s.a. and w.o. (Feb–Apr 1869); Navy Yard, Boston (Jun 1869–Nov 1871); in charge of stores, Honolulu, Hawaiian Islands (Nov 1871–Sep 1874); s.a. and w.o. (Sep 1874–May 1875); *Constitution*, Navy Yard, Philadelphia (May–Sep 1875); s.a. and w.o. (Sep–Nov 1875); flt.paymstr., N.Atl.Sta., *Hartford* (Nov 1875–Jul 1877); s.a. and w.o. (Jul–Oct 1877); insp. of provisions and clothing, Navy Yard, Portsmouth, NH (Nov 1877–Aug 1881); s.a. and w.o. (Aug 1881–Jun 1882); l.o.a. (Jul 1882–Jan 1883); w.o. (Jan–Apr 1883); insp. of provisions and clothing, Navy Yard, Norfolk, VA (Apr 1883–Sep 1884); s.a. and w.o. (Sep 1884–Jan 1885); spec. duty, examining accounts of disbursing officers (Jan–Dec 1885); w.o. (Dec 1885–Mar 1886); Navy Pay Office, Norfolk, VA (Mar–May 1886); s.a. and w.o. (May–Jun 1886); spec. duty, Norfolk, VA (Jun–Dec 1886); Pay Office, Boston (Dec 1886–Dec 1889); s.a. (Dec 1889–Apr 1890); gen. storekeeper, Navy Yard, Norfolk, VA (Apr–Jul 1890); Navy Pay Office, Washington, DC (May 1890–Sep 1891); in charge, Navy Pay Office, Boston (Oct 1891–Oct 1894); temp. duty, pres., Naval Examining Bd., Washington, DC (Dec 1891–Jan 1892); s.a. and w.o. (Oct 1894–Jan 1895); gen. storekeeper, Navy Yard, Portsmouth, NH (Feb–Mar 1895); gen. storekeeper, Navy Yard, Boston (Apr 1895–Mar 1896); in charge, Navy Pay Office, Boston (Mar 1896–Jan 1900); placed on Ret.Lst. (20 Jan 1900).

EDWARD YORKE McCAULEY Born in Philadelphia, PA, on 2 Nov 1827, son of Daniel Smith and Sarah (Yorke) McCauley. Married Josephine Berkeley on 28 Jan 1858. One son. Practiced business in St. Paul, MN, between 1859 and 1861. Received honorary LL.D. from Hobart College in 1892. Died on Canonicut Island in Narragansett Bay, RI, on 14 Sep 1894. Buried in Philadelphia.

EDWARD YORKE McCAULEY
1827–1894

Ranks Midn (9 Sep 1841); PMidn (10 Aug 1847); Mstr (1 Jul 1855); Lt (14 Sep 1855); resigned (19 Aug 1859); re-entered service as Act.Lt (11 May 1861); LCdr (16 Jul 1862); Cdr (25 Jul 1866); Capt (3 Sep 1872); Commo (7 Aug 1881); RAdm (2 Mar 1885); placed on Ret.Lst. (25 Jan 1887).

Career Summary Received appointment from PA (9 Sep 1841); w.o. (Sep 1841–Feb 1842); *Fairfield* and *Delaware*, Med.Sqdn. (Mar 1842–Dec 1843); flgs. *Cumberland*, Med.Sqdn. (Dec 1843–Nov 1845); Naval School, Annapolis, MD (Jan–Apr 1846); *United States*, Afr.Sqdn. (May 1846–Feb 1848); Naval School, Annapolis, MD (Feb–Jul 1848); w.o. (Jul–Aug 1848); rec. ship *Experiment*, Philadelphia (Aug–Sep 1848); *Constitution*, Med.Sqdn. (Oct 1848–Oct 1850); sick lv. (Oct 1850–Oct 1851); flgs. *Independence*, Med.Sqdn. (Oct 1851–Jun 1852); l.o.a. (Jun–Aug 1852); *Saranac*, Navy Yard, Philadelphia (Aug 1852); *Powhatan*, E.Ind.Sqdn. (Aug 1852–Feb 1856); l.o.a. (Feb–May 1856); rec. ship *Princeton*, Philadelphia (Jun 1856–Mar 1857); *Niagara*, Cable Expd. (Apr–Nov 1857); w.o. (Nov 1857–Feb 1858); *Niagara* (Mar–Aug 1858); l.o.a. (Aug–Sep 1858); Naval Observatory, Washington, DC (Sep 1858–Feb 1859); w.o. (Feb–Aug 1859); *Supply*, spec. duty (Aug 1859); resigned (19 Aug 1859); act.lt, volunteer serv. (11 May 1861); spec. duty, Secretary of Navy's Office, Washington, DC, then *Flag*, *Fort Henry*, and *Tioga*, S.Atl. and E.Gulf Blk.Sqdns. (May 1861–Jul 1864); temp. duty, Navy Yard, Portsmouth, NH (Jul–Aug 1864); w.o. (Aug–Sep 1864); *Black Hawk*, MS Sqdn. (Oct–Nov 1864); cdr, *Benton*, and 5th Division, MS Sqdn. (Nov 1864–Jul 1865); w.o. (Jul–Aug 1865); spec.duty, Philadelphia (Aug 1865–Jan 1867); w.o. (Jan–Feb 1867); flt.capt, and chief of staff, N.Atl.Sqdn., *Susquehanna* (Feb 1867–Jan 1868); w.o. (Jan–Aug 1868); Navy Yard, Portsmouth, NH (Sep 1868–Nov 1870); head, French Dept., USNA (Nov 1870–Aug 1872); ord. duty, Navy Yard, Philadelphia (Aug–Oct 1872); cdr, *Hartford*, Asia.Sta. (Oct 1872–Jun 1873); cdr, *Lackawanna*, Asia.Sta. (Jun 1873–May 1875); w.o. (May–Nov 1875); capt.yd., Navy Yard, Boston (Nov 1875–Jul 1878); supt., Naval Asylum, Philadelphia (Jul 1878–Jun 1880); w.o. (Jun 1880–Sep 1881); spec. duty, Bur. of Nav., Washington, DC (Sep 1881–Oct 1883); flgs. *Hartford*, N.Atl.Sta. (Oct–Nov 1883); w.o. (Nov 1883–Nov 1884); comdt., Navy Yard, League Island, PA (Nov 1884–May 1885); cdr, Pac.Sta., *Hartford* (May 1885–Nov 1886); return home and w.o. (Nov 1886–Jan 1887); placed on Ret.Lst. (25 Jan 1887).

References
Personal Papers: 224 items, 3 vols., (1845–76) in NYHS.

Writings: a) "Seamanship and Gunnery; Private Scribbling" (1845–1847) in NYHS. b) *A Manual for the Use of Students in Egyptology* (Philadelphia: 1881). c) *A Dictionary of the Egyptian Language* (Philadelphia: 1883).

Additional Sources: Allan B. Cole, ed. *With Perry in Japan; the Diary of Edward Yorke McCauley* (1942).

ALEXANDER HUGH McCORMICK
1842–1915

ALEXANDER HUGH McCORMICK Born in Washington, DC, on 9 May 1842, son of Alexander and Eliza (Van Horn) McCormick. Married Isabella Howard on 9 Feb 1864. Four children. Retired to Annapolis, MD, where he died on 21 Aug 1915. Buried in Congressional Cemetery, Washington, DC.

Ranks Act.Midn (21 Sep 1859); resigned (22 May 1861); reinstated as Act.Midn (3 Jun 1861); title changed to Midn (16 Jul 1862); Ens (22 Dec 1862); Lt (22 Feb 1864); LCdr (25 Jul 1866); Cdr (30 Sep 1876); Capt (3 Apr 1892); RAdm (9 Sep 1899); placed on Ret.Lst. (26 Mar 1900).

Career Summary Received appointment from TX (21 Sep 1859); USNA (Sep 1859–May 1861); *Quaker City*, Chesapeake Bay Blockade (Jun–Oct 1861); rec. ship *North Carolina*, NY (Oct–Dec 1861); *Norwich*, S.Atl.Blk.Sqdn. (Jan 1862–Apr 1863); *Housatonic*, S.Atl.Blk.Sqdn. (Apr–Jul 1863); *Wabash*, S.Atl.Blk.Sqdn. (Jul–Sep 1863); w.o. (Sep 1863–Feb 1864); *Iroquois*, spec.serv. (Feb 1864–Oct 1865); w.o. (Oct 1865–Feb 1866); *Chattanooga*, Philadelphia (Feb–Sep 1866); instructor, Dept. of Math., USNA (Sep 1866–Jun 1869); flgs. *Lancaster*, S.Atl.Sta. (Jun 1869–Jul 1872); *Portsmouth*, spec.serv. (Jul–Aug 1872); instructor, Dept. of Astronomy and Nav., USNA (Sep 1872–Jun 1875); cdr, prac. ship *Fortune* (Jul–Sep 1873); exec.off., flgs. *Pensacola*, Pac.Sta. (Jul 1875–Nov 1876); w.o. (Nov 1876–Feb 1877); Bur. of Ord., Washington, DC (Feb 1877–Nov 1881); cdr, *Essex*, Pac. and Asia. Sqdns. (Nov 1881–Jan 1885); inspector of ord., Navy Yard, Washington, DC (Feb 1885–Oct 1888); Bur. of Ord., Washington, DC (Oct–Nov 1889); inspector of ord., Navy Yard, NY (Dec 1889–May 1892); cdr, *Lancaster*, Asia. Sta. (Jun 1892–Jun 1894); home, l.o.a. and bd. duties (Jun–Oct 1894); capt.yd., Navy Yard, Norfolk, VA (Oct 1894–Oct 1897); member, Armor and Personnel Bds. (Aug 1897–Jan 1898); cdr, *Oregon*, Pac.Sta. and spec.serv. (Jan–Mar 1898); home and sick lv. (Mar–Oct 1898); comdt., Navy Yard, Washington, DC (Oct 1898–Mar 1900); placed on Ret.Lst. (26 Mar 1900).

References
Writings: *Manual Exercises for Great Guns and Small Arms* (1881).

DAVID STOCKTON McDOUGAL
1809–1882

DAVID STOCKTON McDOUGAL Born in Chillicothe, OH, on 27 Sep 1809, son of Dr. John and Margaret (Stockton) McDougal. Dropped his middle name of "Stockton" in later life. Married Caroline Sterrett in 1833. Children included a son, Cdr Charles J. McDougal, USN, who died in 1881 while in service. Two grandsons in sea service, Adm David McDougal LeBreton, USN (1884–1973), and Gen Douglas C. McDougal, USMC (1876–1964). Died in San Francisco on 7 Aug 1882. Buried in the Mare Island Cemetery.

Ranks Midn (1 Apr 1828); PMidn (14 Jun 1834); Lt (25 Feb 1841); Cdr (24 Jan 1857); Capt (2 Mar 1864); Commo (12 Jun 1869); placed on Ret.Lst. (27 Sep 1871); RAdm on Ret.Lst. (24 Aug 1873).

Career Summary Received appointment from OH (1 Apr 1828); Naval School, NY (Aug 1828–May 1829); Naval Sta., NY (May 1829–Apr 1830); *Boston*, Med.Sqdn. (May 1830–Sep 1831); *Brandywine*, Med.Sqdn. (Sep 1831–Jul 1833); l.o.a. (Jul–Oct 1833); Naval School, NY (Oct 1833–May 1834); l.o.a. (May–Sep 1834); Navy Yard, NY (Sep 1834–Jul 1835); l.o.a. (Jul 1835–Mar 1836); rec. ship *Hudson*, NY (Mar–Jun 1836); *Natchez*, W.Ind.Sqdn. (Jul 1836–Nov 1838); *Grampus*, W.Ind.Sta. (Nov 1838–Feb 1839); l.o.a. (Feb–Mar 1839); rec. ship *North Carolina*, NY (Mar–Sep 1839); l.o.a. (Sep–Dec 1839); cst.surv. duty (Dec 1839–Feb 1841); l.o.a. (Feb–May 1841); *Fulton*, spec.serv. (May–Dec 1841); *Falmouth*, Home Sqdn. (Dec 1841–Mar 1843); l.o.a. (Mar–Jul 1843); *Falmouth*, Home Sqdn. (Jul 1843–Jan 1844); l.o.a. (Jan–Jun 1844); *Michigan*, on Great Lakes (Jun 1844–Jan 1847); *Mississippi*, Home Sqdn. (Jan–Jun 1847); l.o.a. (Jun 1847–Feb 1848); *St. Mary's*, Navy Yard, Norfolk, VA (Feb–Mar 1848); *Bainbridge*, Afr.Cst. (Mar 1848–Jul 1850); l.o.a. (Jul–Oct 1850); w.o. (Oct 1850–Jun 1851); *Michigan*, on Great Lakes (Jun 1851–Mar 1854); cdr, *Warren*, San Francisco, then Navy Yard, Mare Island, CA (Apr 1855–Feb 1856); cdr, *John Hancock*, OR coast (Feb–Aug 1856); cdr, *Warren*, Navy Yard, Mare Island, CA (Aug 1856–Oct 1857); home and w.o. (Nov 1857–Feb 1858); Navy Yard, Mare Island, CA (Feb 1858–May 1861); cdr, *Wyoming*, Pac., then Asia.Sqdns. (May 1861–Jul 1864); temp. cdr, then cdr, Navy Yard, Mare Island, CA (Aug 1864–Aug 1865); l.o.a. and w.o. (Aug 1865–Apr 1867); cdr, *Pensacola*, N.Pac.Sqdn. (Apr–Jul 1867); w.o. (Jul–Dec 1867); cdr, flgs. *Powhatan*, S.Pac.Sqdn. (Jan 1868–Dec 1869); cdr, S.Sqdn., Pac.Flt., *Ossipee* (Jan 1870–Feb 1872); placed on Ret.Lst. (27 Sep 1871).

RICHARD WORSAM MEADE Born in New York City on 9 Oct 1837, son of Capt Richard Worsam Meade, USN (1807–1870), and Clara (Meigs) Meade, daughter of NY Congressman Henry Meigs. Was nephew of Gen George G. Meade, USA. Two brothers were Paymstr. Henry Meigs Meade, USN, and BGen Robert Leamy Meade, USMC. Received education at Worcester Academy and Fordham School before service. Married Rebecca Paulding, daughter of RAdm Hiram Paulding [*q.v.*], on 6 Jun 1865. One son and

RICHARD WORSAM MEADE
1837–1897

four daughters. Resided in Germantown, PA. Died in Washington, DC, on 4 May 1897. Buried in Arlington National Cemetery.

Ranks Act.Midn (2 Oct 1850); PMidn (20 Jun 1856); Mstr (22 Jan 1858); Lt (23 Jan 1858); LCdr (16 Jul 1862); Cdr (20 Sep 1868); Capt (13 Mar 1880); Commo (5 May 1892); RAdm (7 Sep 1894); ret. (20 May 1895).

Career Summary Received appointment from CA (2 Oct 1850); USNA (Oct 1850–Nov 1851); *San Jacinto*, Med.Sqdn. (Nov 1851–Apr 1853); *St. Louis*, Med.Sqdn. (Apr 1853–Feb 1854); return and w.o. (Feb–May 1854); *Columbia*, W.Ind.Sqdn. (May 1854–Apr 1855); l.o.a. (Apr–Oct 1855); USNA (Oct 1855–Jun 1856); w.o. (Jun–Jul 1856); *Merrimack*, spec.serv. (Aug 1856–Apr 1857); *Cumberland*, Afr.Sqdn. (May 1857–Jan 1859); *Dale*, Afr.Sqdn. (Jan–May 1859); l.o.a. (May–Sep 1859); *Saranac*, Pac.Sqdn. (Nov 1859–Mar 1860); *Cyane*, Pac.Sqdn. (Mar 1860–Jul 1861); sick lv., Naval Hosp., NY (Aug–Oct 1861); instructor of gunnery, rec. ship *Ohio*, Boston (Oct 1861–Jan 1862); exec.off., *Dakotah*, N.Atl.Blk.Sqdn. (Jan–Mar 1862); sick lv., Naval Hosp, Chelsea, MA (Mar–Jun 1862); exec.off., *Conemaugh*, S.Atl.Blk.Sqdn. (Jun–Sep 1862); cdr, *Louisville*, Western Flot. (Sep–Dec 1862); sick lv. (Dec 1862–Jan 1863); ord. duty, Navy Yard, NY (Jan–Sep 1863); cdr, *Marblehead*, S.Atl.Blk.Sqdn. (Sep 1863–May 1864); cdr, *Chocura*, W.Gulf Blk.Sqdn. (May 1864–Jul 1865); head, Seamanship Dept., USNA (Jul 1865–Aug 1868); cdr, *Saginaw*, Pac.Sqdn. (Nov 1868–May 1869); spec. duty, USNA (May–Nov 1869); spec. ord. duty, Cold Spring, NY (Nov 1869–Jul 1870); cdr, schooner *America*, USNA (Jul–Dec 1870); w.o. (Dec 1870–Feb 1871); cdr, *Narragansett*, Pac.Sta. (Feb 1871–Apr 1873); spec. duty, Washington, DC (May–Jun 1873); inspector of ord. and nav.off., Navy Yard, NY (Jun 1873–May 1876); w.o. (May 1876–Nov 1878); spec. duty as senior off., Bd. to Revise Ord. Instructions, Washington, DC (Nov 1878–Jan 1879); cdr, *Vandalia*, N.Atl. and W.Ind. Stas. (Jan 1879–May 1882); l.o.a. and w.o. (May–Jul 1882); member, Bd. of Insp., Surv. and Appraisement (Jul 1882–Jun 1883); capt.yd., Navy Yard, NY (Jul 1883–Mar 1884); l.o.a. (Mar 1884–Nov 1885); member, Exam. and Ret. Bd., Washington, DC (Nov–Dec 1885); spec. duty, cdr, *Dolphin*, N.Atl.Sta. (Dec 1885–Jul 1886); pres., Bd. of Inventory (Jul 1886–Sep 1887); comdt., Navy Yard, Washington, DC (Sep 1887–Sep 1890); l.o.a. and w.o. (Sep 1890–Sep 1893); pres., Naval Exam. and Ret. Bd. (Sep 1893–Aug 1894); cdr, N.Atl.Sqdn., *New York* (Aug 1894–May 1895); resigned (20 May 1895).

Career Highlights During Civil War, was at Battle of Stono River in SC in Dec 1863. In Jul 1863, in command of naval battalion helping to quell riots in New York City. Captured or destroyed seven blockade runners while on blockade off TX and LA coasts in 1864 and 1865.

References

Personal Papers: 18 vols., 3 boxes in NYHS.

Writings: a) *Manual of the Boat Exercises at the U.S. Naval Academy* (Washington, DC: 1868). b) *A Treatise on Naval Architecture and Ship-Building* (Washington, DC: 1869). c) *Ordnance Instruction for the United States Navy* 5th ed. (Washington, DC: 1880). d) translator: 1) Crisenoy, Jules Etienne Gigault de, *Our Naval School and Naval Officers. A Glance at . . . the French Navy Prior to the late Franco-Prussian War* (1873). 2) Dislere, Paul, *The Iron-clad Ships of the World* (1875).

Additional Sources: W. F. Brown, "A Tribute of Respect . . . in Memory of Commander Richard Worsam Meade; rear admiral (retired), United States Navy." Grand Army of the Republic, Department of New York, Lafayette Post 40.

GEORGE WALLACE MELVILLE Born in New York City on 10 Jan 1841, son of Alexander and Sarah Douther (Wallace) Melville. Educated in public schools, the Christian Brothers School, and at Brooklyn Collegiate and Polytechnic Institute. Worked in Brooklyn for engineering firm of James Binns until he entered the navy. Received an honorary D.Engr. from the Stevens Institute of Technology in 1898, Georgetown Univ. in 1899, as well as an M.S. from Columbia Univ. in 1899, a Doctorate of Science from the Univ. of PA, and the LL.D. from Georgetown Univ. in 1899. Married twice, having two daughters by his first wife. Second wife was Estella Smith Polis, whom he married in Oct 1907. Retired to Philadelphia, where he died on 17 Mar 1912. Buried in South Laurel Hill Cemetery, Philadelphia.

Ranks 3rd Asst.Engr. (29 Jul 1861); 2nd Asst.Engr. (18 Dec 1862); 1st Asst.Engr. (30 Jan 1865); Chief Engr. (4 Mar 1881); Engr. in Chief and Chief, Bur. of Steam Engineering with rank of Commo (9 Aug 1887); Chief Engr. with rel. rank of Capt (6 Aug 1895); Capt (3 Mar 1899); Chief, Bur. of Steam Engineering with rank of RAdm (4 Mar 1899); placed on Ret.Lst. (10 Jan 1903).

GEORGE WALLACE MELVILLE
1841–1912

Career Summary Received appointment from NY (29 Jul 1861); w.o. (Jul–Aug 1861); *Michigan*, on Great Lakes (Aug 1861–Jul 1862); *Dakotah* and *Wachusett*, N.Atl.Blk. and W.Ind.Sqdns. (Jul 1862–Dec 1864); torp. boats and *Maumee*, Hampton Roads, VA and N.Atl.Blk.Sqdn. (Dec 1864–Jun 1865); w.o. (Jun–Sep 1865); *Chattanooga*, Philadelphia (Sep–Nov 1865); on furlough (Nov–Dec 1865); *Chattanooga*, Philadelphia (Dec 1865–Aug 1866); w.o. (Aug–Sep 1866); spec. duty, Boston (Sep 1866–Jan 1867); *Tacony*, spec.serv. (Jan–Sep 1867); w.o. (Sep–Dec 1867); *Penobscot*, Navy Yard, NY (Dec 1867–Jun 1869); w.o. (Jun–Jul 1869); Navy Yard, Norfolk, VA (Jul–Aug 1869); *Lancaster*, flgs., and *Portsmouth*, S.Atl.Sqdn. (Aug 1869–Aug 1872); w.o. (Aug 1872–Jun 1873); chief engr., *Tigress*, spec.serv. (Jun–Nov 1873); Navy Yard, Philadelphia (Nov 1873–Mar 1875); flgs. *Tennessee*, Asia.Sqdn. (Mar 1875–Oct 1878); Navy Yard, League Island, PA (Oct 1878–Apr 1879); chief engr., *Jeanette*, expl. duty (Apr 1879–Dec 1882);

spec. duty (Dec 1882–Jan 1883); w.o. (Jan 1883); in charge of stores, Navy Yard, League Island, PA (Jan 1883–Mar 1884); *Thetis*, spec. duty (Mar–Nov 1884); insp. of coal, Navy Yard, NY (Nov 1884–Dec 1886); additional duty, insp. of coal, Navy Yard, Philadelphia (Aug 1885–Dec 1886); *Atlanta*, Philadelphia, and on trials (Dec 1886–Jan 1887); spec. duty, Philadelphia (Jan–Aug 1887); chief, Bur. of Steam Engineering, Washington, DC (Aug 1887–Aug 1903); placed on Ret.Lst. (10 Jan 1903).

Career Highlights While on *Wachusett*, played integral role in destroying Confederate cruiser *Florida* in Brazil. Was on *Tigress* which in Apr 1873 rescued survivors from *Polaris* off Labrador. On *Jeanette* from 1879 until she sank on 11 Jun 1881 after nearly two years of being trapped or drifting in ice, commanding the only boat of the three that left the ship that survived. Congress commended his efforts to find remaining crew members. On board another Arctic rescue effort that did reach some survivors of the famous Greely Expd. in 1884. Was rewarded for all his efforts in Arctic exploration by being promoted over forty-four officers to become engr. in chief in Aug 1887, serving as such for seventeen years. An innovative administrator, was instrumental in the adoption of steam propulsion. Influential in the decision to incorporate engineering corps with the line in 1899.

References
Personal Papers: a) 125 items (1871–1911) in NHF,LC. b) Material relating to Arctic Exploration in Explorers Club, New York City.

Writings: a) *In the Lena Delta: A Narrative of the Search for Lieutenant–Commander DeLong* (Boston: 1885). b) "Causes for the Adoption of Water-Tube Boilers in the United States Navy," U.S. Naval Institute *Proceedings* 92 (1899): 896–903.

Additional Sources: a) R. H. Thurston, "Rear Admiral G. W. Melville, U.S.N., and Applied Science in Construction of the New Fleet," *Popular Science Monthly* (Dec 1903): 183–86. b) William L. Cathcart, "George Wallace Melville," *Journal of the American Society of Naval Engineers* 24 (May 1912): 477–511. c) Edward Ellsberg, *Hell on Ice: The Saga of the* Jeanette (New York: 1938). d) George W. Grupp, "Rear Admiral George Wallace Melville as a Man and Engineer-in-Chief of the Navy," U.S. Naval Institute *Proceedings* 543 (May 1948): 612–17.

WILLIAM MERVINE
1791–1868

WILLIAM MERVINE Born in Philadelphia, PA, on 14 Mar 1791, the son of John and Zibia (Wright) Mervine. Married Amanda Maria Crane on 12 Jan 1815. Six children. Died in Utica, NY, on 15 Sep 1868.

Ranks Midn (16 Jan 1809); Act.Lt (25 Aug 1813); Lt (4 Feb 1815); Mstr Comdt. (12 Jun 1834); Capt (8 Sep 1841); placed on Ret.Lst. with rank of Commo (16 Jul 1862); RAdm on Ret.Lst. (6 Aug 1866).

Career Summary Received appointment from PA (16 Jan 1809); gunboats, Naval Sta., Philadelphia (Mar–Jun 1809); on furlough (Jun 1809–May 1810); *Siren*, Naval Sta., New Orleans (May 1810–Dec 1811); on furlough (Dec 1811–May 1812); *John Adams*, Boston (Jun–Sep 1812); duty, Lake Ontario (Oct 1812–May 1813); *Hamilton*, Lake Ontario (May–Jun 1813); *Madison*, Lake Ontario (Jun–Jul 1813); *General Pike*, Lake Ontario (Jul–Aug 1813); *Oneida*, Lake Ontario (Aug 1813–Jun 1815); *Jones*, Lake Ontario (Jun 1815–Apr 1818); *Cyane*, Afr. and W.Ind. Sqdns. (May 1818–Jan 1823); sick lv. (Jan–May 1823); l.o.a. (May–Sep 1823); *Cyane*, Med.Sqdn. (Sep 1823–Oct 1824); *Nonesuch*, Med.Sqdn. (Oct–Dec 1824); flgs. *North Carolina*, Med.Sqdn. (Dec 1824–Jun 1825); *Cyane*, Med.Sqdn. (Jun–Oct 1825); l.o.a. (Nov 1825–Dec 1826); Navy Yard, Boston (Dec 1826–May 1827); *Natchez*, W.Ind. and Home Sqdns. (May 1827–Jan 1829); l.o.a. and w.o. (Jan 1829–Mar 1832); cdr, *Experiment*, Atl.Cst. (Mar 1832–Jul 1833); l.o.a. and w.o. (Jul 1833–Jul 1836); cdr, *Natchez*, W.Ind.Sqdn. (Jul 1836–Apr 1838); l.o.a. and w.o. (Apr 1838–Jun 1845); cdr, *Cyane*, Pac.Sqdn. (Jul 1845–Jul 1846); cdr, flgs. *Savannah*, Pac.Sqdn. (Jul 1846–Sep 1847); military comdt., Monterey, CA (Jul–Sep 1846); l.o.a. and w.o. (Sep 1847–Jul 1852); cdr, *Powhatan*, Home Sqdn. (Aug–Nov 1852); cdr, *Independence*, Navy Yard, NY (Nov 1852–Apr 1853); w.o. (Apr 1853–Jun 1854); Navy Dept., Washington, DC (Jun–Aug 1854); cdr, Pac.Sqdn., *Independence* (Sep 1854–Nov 1857); l.o.a. and w.o. (Nov 1857–May 1861); cdr, Gulf Blk.Sqdn., *Mississippi* (May–Sep 1861); w.o. (Sep 1861–Jul 1862); placed on Ret.Lst. (16 Jul 1862); spec. duty as presiding off., Naval Ret.Bd., Washington, DC (Oct 1862–Apr 1864); spec. duty, courts-martial and other bds., Navy Yards, NY, and Philadelphia (1864–1865).

Career Highlights Served in War of 1812 on Lake Ontario; wounded in 1813. With Pac.Sqdn. during Mexican War, landed with sailors and marines on 7 Jul 1846 and captured Monterey, CA. Failed in a similar attack against Los Angeles the following Oct. Initial commander of Gulf Blk.Sqdn., setting up and directing blockade from Key West, FL, to Galveston, TX.

References

Additional Sources: U.S. Navy Department, *Letters Sent and Received by William Mervine, Commanding the Pacific Squadron, 1855–1860* (Washington, DC: 1947).

EDWARD MIDDLETON Born in Charleston, SC, on 11 Dec 1810, son of Henry and Mary Helen (Hering) Middleton. His father was SC governor from 1810 to 1812, and his grandfather, Arthur Middleton, was colonial governor of SC and a signer of the Declaration of Independence. Died at his home in Washington, DC, on 27 Apr 1883. Buried in Greenwood Cemetery, New York City.

EDWARD MIDDLETON
1810–1883

Ranks Midn (1 Jul 1828); PMidn (14 Jun 1834); Lt (25 Feb 1841); Cdr (2 Apr 1856); Capt (24 Apr 1863); Commo (26 Nov 1868); placed on Ret.Lst. (11 Dec 1872); RAdm on Ret.Lst. (15 Aug 1876).

Career Summary Received appointment from SC (1 Jul 1828); *Java*, Med.Sqdn. (Oct 1828–May 1831); l.o.a. (May–Aug 1831); rec. ship *Franklin*, NY (Sep 1831–Sep 1832); *Vandalia*, W.Ind.Sqdn. (Sep 1832–Jul 1833); Naval School, NY (Jul 1833–Mar 1834); rec. ship *Hudson*, NY (Jun 1834–Jul 1835); *Constitution*, Med.Sqdn. (Jul 1835–Sep 1837); on furlough (Sep 1837–Aug 1838); l.o.a. (Aug 1838–Jun 1839); rec. ships *Hudson* then *North Carolina*, NY (Jun–Oct 1839); *Marion*, Braz.Sqdn. (Nov 1839–May 1842); l.o.a. (May 1842–May 1843); rec. ship *Pennsylvania*, Norfolk, VA (May–Jun 1843); *Decatur*, Navy Yard, Norfolk, VA (Jun 1843); exec.off., *Onkahya*, spec.serv. (Jun–Dec 1843); *Lexington*, Med.Sqdn. (Feb 1844–Mar 1845); l.o.a. (Mar–Dec 1845); *Cumberland*, Home Sqdn. (Dec 1845–Apr 1846); on furlough (Apr 1846–Mar 1847); w.o. (Mar–May 1847); *Princeton*, Med.Sqdn. (Jun 1847–Jul 1849); Navy Yard, Philadelphia (Sep 1849–Mar 1851); l.o.a. (Mar 1851–Jan 1852); *Independence*, Med.Sqdn. (Jan–Jun 1852); l.o.a. (Jun–Sep 1852); rec.ship *North Carolina*, NY (Sep 1852–Feb 1854); exec.off., then cdr, *Decatur*, Pac.Sqdn. (Feb 1854–Apr 1857); l.o.a. and w.o. (Apr 1857–Jun 1861); cdr, *St. Mary's*, Pac.Sqdn. (Aug 1861–Mar 1865); spec. duty, Navy Yard, NY (Mar 1865–Sep 1866); w.o. (Sep 1866–Oct 1867); Navy Yard, Mare Island, CA (Oct 1867–Aug 1868); cdr, *Pensacola*, Pac.Sqdn. (Aug 1868–Jan 1869); cdr, *Lackawanna*, Pac.Flt. (Feb 1869–May 1870); comdt., Navy Yard, Pensacola, FL (Jun 1870–Mar 1873); placed on Ret.Lst. (11 Dec 1872).

References
Personal Papers: a) 200 items (1810–93) in SHC. b) 1 item (1864) in SCL.

JOSEPH NELSON MILLER
1836–1909

JOSEPH NELSON MILLER Born in Springfield, OH, on 22 Nov 1836. Married twice; the first time on 22 Nov 1866, and the second to Helen Wills on 13 Nov 1877. One daughter. Died in East Orange, NJ, on 25 Apr 1909. Buried in Arlington National Cemetery.

Ranks Act.Midn (1 Oct 1851); Midn (10 Jun 1854); PMidn (22 Nov 1856); Mstr (22 Jan 1858); Lt (19 Feb 1860); LCdr (16 Jul 1862); Cdr (25 Jan 1870); Capt (28 May 1881); Commo (16 Apr 1894); RAdm (21 Mar 1897); placed on Ret.Lst. (22 Nov 1898).

Career Summary Received appointment from OH (1 Oct 1851); USNA (Oct 1851–Jun 1854); l.o.a. (Jun–Sep 1854); *Independence*, Pac.Sta. (Sep 1854–Oct 1856); w.o. (Nov 1854–Feb 1857); asst.prof. of ethics, USNA (Feb 1857–Oct 1858); *Preble*, Paraguay Expd. and Home Sqdn. (Oct 1858–Sep 1860); asst.prof. of ethics, USNA (Sep 1860–Apr 1861);

cdr, *Perry*, Atl.Blk.Sqdn. (May–Nov 1861); *Cambridge*, N.Atl.Blk.Sqdn. (Nov 1861–May 1862); exec.off., training ship *John Adams*, USNA, Newport, RI (May–Sep 1862); *Pocahontas*, Navy Yard, Philadelphia (Sep 1862); exec.off., *Passaic*, N.Atl.Blk.Sqdn. (Sep 1862–Jun 1863); spec. duty with ironclads, NY (Jun–Sep 1863); exec.off., *Sacramento*, N.Atl.Blk.Sqdn. (Sep–Nov 1863); exec.off., then cdr, *Sagamon* and *Nahant*, S.Atl.Blk.Sqdn. (Nov 1863–Jul 1864); exec.off., *Monadnock*, Navy Yard, Boston and N.Atl.Blk.Sqdn. (Sep 1864–Jan 1865); USNA (Feb 1865–Sep 1867); exec.off., *Powhatan*, Pac. and N.Atl. Sqdns. (Oct 1867–Dec 1869); w.o. (Dec 1869–Feb 1870); asst.equip.off., Navy Yard, NY (Feb–Apr 1870); chief of staff and cdr, *Ossipee*, Southern Sqdn., Pac.Flt. (Apr 1870–Nov 1872); w.o. (Nov 1872–Jan 1873); exec.off., Naval Sta., New London, CT (Jan–Feb 1873); asst. hydrographer, Washington, DC (Feb–Nov 1873); cdr, *Ajax*, N.Atl.Sqdn. (Dec 1873–May 1874); asst. hydrographer, Washington, DC (Jun 1874–Aug 1875); cdr, *Tuscarora*, Pac.Sta. (Sep 1875–Aug 1876); cdr, *Portsmouth*, spec.serv. (Aug 1876); w.o. (Aug–Dec 1876); asst., Bur. of Yards and Docks, Washington, DC (Dec 1876–Mar 1877); insp., 11th L.h. Dist., Detroit, MI (Mar 1877–Oct 1880); spec. duty, Washington, DC (Oct 1880–May 1881); cdr, rec. ship *Wabash*, Boston (May 1881–Apr 1882); chief of staff and cdr, *Tennessee*, N.Atl.Sqdn. (May–Jul 1882); w.o. (Jul–Oct 1882); member, Court of Inquiry for *Jeanette* (Oct 1882–Mar 1883); member, gen. court-martial (Mar–Jul 1883); w.o. (Jul–Sep 1883); chief of staff and cdr, *Tennessee*, N.Atl.Sqdn. (Sep 1883–Sep 1884); pres., Bd. of Inspection of Foreign Vessels, NY (Sep 1884–Apr 1885); cdr, rec. ship *Wabash*, Boston (Apr 1885–Apr 1888); capt.yd., Navy Yard, NY (Apr 1888–May 1891); cdr, flgs. *Chicago*, Sqdn. of Evol. (May 1891–Jul 1892); l.o.a., bd. duty, and w.o. (Jul–Oct 1892); cdr, rec. ship *Vermont*, NY (Nov 1892–Apr 1894); w.o. (Apr–Jul 1894); comdt., Navy Yard, Boston (Aug 1894–May 1897); spec.serv. to England, *Brooklyn* (May 1897); cdr, Pac.Sta., *Brooklyn* (May–Oct 1897), then *Baltimore* (Oct 1897–Mar 1898), then *Bennington* (Mar–Oct 1898); w.o. (Oct–Nov 1898); placed on Ret.Lst. (22 Nov 1898).

Career Highlights Saw action during Civil War at Ft. McAllister in Mar 1863, against Ft. Sumter in Apr 1863, and in both attacks against Ft. Fisher in late 1864 and early 1865. Represented service in London for Queen Victoria's Diamond Jubilee in 1897.

MERRILL MILLER Born in Bellafontaine, OH, on 13 Sep 1842, son of Henry and Mary Miller. Married Sarah Katherine Lynch on 11 Jul 1865. Retired to Berkeley, CA, where he died on 5 Aug 1914. Buried in USNA Cemetery.

Ranks Act.Midn (28 Nov 1859); title changed to Midn (16 Jul 1862); Ens (13 Oct 1862); Lt (22 Feb 1864); LCdr (25

MERRILL MILLER
1842–1914

Jul 1866); Cdr (25 Nov 1877); Capt (25 Feb 1893); RAdm (1 Jul 1900); placed on Ret.Lst. (13 Sep 1904).

Career Summary Received appointment from OH (28 Nov 1859); USNA (Nov 1859–May 1861); *Potomac* and *Santee*, Atl. and W.Gulf Blk.Sqdns. (May 1861–Aug 1862); l.o.a. (Aug–Oct 1862); *Black Hawk*, Mississippi Sqdn. (Oct 1862–Jul 1863); w.o. (Jul–Oct 1863); *Powhatan*, N.Atl.Blk.Sqdn. (Oct 1863–Jun 1865); w.o. (Jun–Sep 1865); *Monadnock*, spec.serv. (Sep 1865–Jun 1866); l.o.a. and w.o. (Jun–Oct 1866); USNA (Oct 1866–Jun 1869); flgs. *Lancaster*, S.Atl.Sqdn. (Jun 1869–Jan 1872); w.o. (Jan–Jun 1872); exec.off., rec. ship *Sabine*, Portsmouth, NH (Jun 1872–Mar 1873); exec.off., flgs. *Worcester*, N.Atl.Sta. (Mar 1873–Aug 1874); sick lv. (Aug–Dec 1874); USNA (Dec 1874–Sep 1879); w.o. (Sep 1879–May 1880); torp. instruction, Newport, RI (Jun–Sep 1880); cdr, *Yantic*, N.Atl.Sta. (Sep 1880–Jan 1881); sick lv. (Jan–Jun 1881); asst., then insp., 6th L.h. Dist., Charleston, SC (Jul 1881–Jan 1885); cdr, *Marion*, Asia.Sta. (Jan 1885–Nov 1887); home and w.o. (Nov 1887–Oct 1888); nav.off., Navy Yard, Portsmouth, NH (Nov 1888–Dec 1889); Naval Home, Philadelphia (Dec 1889–Jun 1892); w.o. (Jun–Aug 1892); insp., 1st L.h. Dist., Portland, ME (Sep 1892–Apr 1893); s.a. and w.o. (Apr–Jun 1893); cdr, rec. ship *Franklin*, Norfolk, VA (Jun 1893–Apr 1894); cdr, *Raleigh*, .N.Atl.Sqdn. (Apr 1894–Jan 1897); l.o.a. (Jan–Mar 1897); cdr, rec. ship *Vermont*, NY (Mar 1897–Mar 1900); comdt., Navy Yard, Mare Island, CA (Mar–Jul 1900); comdt., Navy Yard and Naval Sta., Mare Island, CA (Jul 1900–Jul 1903); cdr, Pac. Naval Dist., San Francisco (Oct 1903–Sep 1904); placed on Ret.Lst. (13 Sep 1904).

Career Highlights During the Civil War commanded the mortar boats during siege of Vicksburg in 1863. Saw subsequent action on James River and in both attacks at Ft. Fisher in Dec and Jan of 1864–65.

JOHN BERRIEN MONTGOMERY Born in Allentown, NJ, on 17 Nov 1794, son of Dr. Thomas West and Mary (Berrien) Montgomery. Married Mary Henry in Aug 1820. Nine children. Died in Carlisle, PA, on 25 Mar 1873. Buried in Oak Hill Cemetery in Washington, DC.

Ranks Midn (4 Jun 1812); Lt (1 Apr 1818); Cdr (9 Dec 1839); Capt (6 Jan 1853); transferred to Ret.Lst. (21 Dec 1861); Commo on Ret.Lst. (16 Jul 1862); RAdm on Ret.Lst. (25 Jul 1866).

Career Summary Received appointment from NJ (4 Jun 1812); *Hamilton*, *Madison*, and *General Pike*, Lake Ontario (Jun 1812–Aug 1813); *Niagara*, Lake Erie (Aug 1813–Jan 1815); on furlough (Jan–Mar 1815); *Ontario*, Med.Sqdn. (Mar 1815–Aug 1817); *Hornet*, Med.Sqdn. and NY (Aug 1817–Feb 1818); *Cyane*, Afr.Sqdn. (Feb 1818–May 1821); *Erie*, Med.Sqdn. (May 1821–Nov 1826); l.o.a. (Nov 1826–Apr 1828); Naval Rndv., Carlisle, PA (Apr 1828–Aug 1830); exec.off., *Peacock*,

JOHN BERRIEN MONTGOMERY
1794–1873

W.Ind.Sqdn. (Aug 1830–Aug 1831); l.o.a. (Aug 1831–Jan 1833); recruiting duty, Naval Rndv., Philadelphia (Jan–Aug 1833); recruiting duty, Naval Rndv., NY (Aug 1833–Feb 1835); exec.off., *Constitution*, spec.serv. (Feb–Jul 1835); cdr, rec. ship *Columbus*, Boston (Mar 1837–Jun 1839); l.o.a. and w.o. (Jun 1839–Jun 1841); cdr, Naval Rndv., Boston (Jun 1841–Jan 1844); w.o. (Jan–Oct 1844); cdr, *Portsmouth*, Pac.Sqdn. (Oct 1844–May 1848); l.o.a. and w.o. (May 1848–Mar 1849); exec.off., Navy Yard, Washington, DC (May 1849–Oct 1851); w.o. (Oct 1851–Mar 1853); ord. duty (Mar–Jun 1853); l.o.a. and w.o. (Jun 1853–May 1854); member, Bd. of Exam. (May 1854–Apr 1857); cdr, flgs. *Roanoke*, Home Sqdn. (May–Sep 1857); w.o. (Sep 1857–May 1859); cdr, Pac.Sqdn., *Lancaster* (May 1859–Jan 1862); transferred to Ret.Lst. (21 Dec 1861); w.o. (Jan–May 1862); comdt., Navy Yard, Boston (Jun 1862–Dec 1863); comdt., Navy Yard, Washington, DC (Dec 1863–Oct 1865); w.o. (Oct 1865–Jul 1866); comdt., Naval Sta., Sacket's Harbor, NY (Jul 1866–Sep 1869).

Career Highlights Commissioned three days after War of 1812 was declared, saw action on several schooners on Lake Ontario and with *Niagara* at the Battle of Lake Erie in Sep 1813. Early in Mexican War he occupied San Francisco with *Portsmouth*.

References
Additional Sources: a) J. M. Ellicott, "John Berrien Montgomery," U.S. Naval Institute *Proceedings* 374 (Apr 1934): 533–37. b) Fred Blackburn Rogers, *Montgomery and the Portsmouth* (San Francisco: John Howell Series on the U.S. Navy in California, 1958).

JAMES ROBERT MADISON MULLANY Born in New York City on 26 Oct 1818, son of Col James R. and Maria (Burger) Mullany. Married twice. Died in Bryn Mawr, PA, on 17 Sep 1887. Buried in Philadelphia.

Ranks Midn (7 Jan 1832); PMidn (23 Jun 1838); Lt (29 Feb 1844); Cdr (18 Oct 1861); Capt (25 Jul 1866); Commo (15 Aug 1870); RAdm (5 Jun 1874); placed on Ret.Lst. (26 Oct 1879).

Career Summary Received appointment from NY (7 Jan 1832); w.o. (Jan–Feb 1832); *Constellation*, Med.Sqdn. (Feb 1832–Nov 1834); l.o.a. and w.o. (Nov 1834–Jun 1835); rec. ship *Hudson*, NY (Jun 1835–Feb 1836); l.o.a. (Feb–Apr 1836); *United States*, Med.Sqdn. (May 1836–May 1838); l.o.a. (May–Nov 1838); Naval Rndv., NY (Nov 1838–Aug 1839); *Dolphin*, Braz. and Afr. Sqdns. (Aug 1839–Jul 1840); l.o.a. (Jul–Oct 1840); rec. ship *North Carolina*, NY (Oct 1840–Jul 1841); Naval Rndv., NY (Jul–Dec 1841); *Missouri*, spec.serv. (Dec 1841–Jun 1842); l.o.a. (Jun–Aug 1842); rec. ship *North Carolina*, NY (Aug 1842–Mar 1844); *Oregon*, spec.serv. (Mar–Apr 1844); l.o.a. and cst.surv. duty (Apr 1844–May 1848); *St. Louis* and *Brandywine*, Braz.Sqdn. (Jun 1848–Dec 1850); l.o.a.

JAMES ROBERT MADISON
MULLANY
1818–1887

and w.o. (Dec 1850–Jun 1851); rec. ship *North Carolina*, NY (Jun–Sep 1851); training ship *John Hancock*, USNA (Sep–Oct 1851); rec. ship *North Carolina*, NY (Oct 1851–Aug 1852); *Cyane*, Navy Yard, NY (Aug–Sep 1852); rec. ship *North Carolina*, NY (Sep–Nov 1852); *Columbia*, Home Sqdn. (Nov 1852–Mar 1855); l.o.a. (Mar–Jun 1855); ord. duty, NY (Jun 1855–May 1858); *Arctic*, spec. cruise, Cuban waters (May–Jul 1858); w.o. (Jul–Sep 1858); *Niagara*, spec.serv. (Sep–Dec 1858); w.o. (Dec 1858–Apr 1859); *Constellation*, Navy Yard, Norfolk, VA (Apr–May 1859); *Sabine*, Home Sqdn. (May 1859–Jun 1861); ord. duty, Navy Yard, NY (Jun 1861–Apr 1862); cdr, *Bienville*, W.Gulf Blk.Sqdn. (Apr 1862–Apr 1865); spec. duty (Apr–May 1865); ord. insp., Navy Yard, NY (May 1865–May 1868); member, Bd. of Visitors, USNA (May–Jun 1868); member, Bd. on Powder Magazines (Jun–Jul 1868); pres., court-martial bd. (Aug 1868); w.o. (Aug–Nov 1868); cdr, *Richmond*, Eur.Sqdn. (Dec 1868–Nov 1871); cdr, Med.Sqdn., then Eur.Flt., *Richmond* (Oct 1870–Nov 1871); w.o. (Nov 1871–Aug 1872); cdr, Navy Yard, Philadelphia (Oct 1872–Jun 1874); cdr, Naval Sta., League Island, PA (Apr 1873–Jun 1874); cdr, N.Atl.Sta., *Worcester* (Jun 1874–Feb 1876); gov., Naval Asylum, Philadelphia (Feb 1876–Oct 1879); placed on Ret.Lst. (26 Oct 1879).

References

Personal Papers: in Floyd T. Starr collection at Historical Society of PA, Philadelphia.

ALEXANDER MURRAY
1816–1884

ALEXANDER MURRAY Born in Pittsburgh, PA, on 2 Jan 1816. Grandfather was Capt Alexander Murray, USN, who served in the Revolutionary War and became the navy's ranking officer from 1811 to 1821. Died on 10 Nov 1884 in Washington, DC. Buried in Pittsburgh.

Ranks Midn (22 Aug 1835); PMidn (22 Jun 1841); Mstr (22 Mar 1847); Lt (12 Aug 1847); placed on Reserved List (13 Sep 1855); restored to Active List (29 Jan 1858); Cdr (16 Jul 1862); Capt (25 Jul 1866); Commo (19 Jun 1871); RAdm (26 Apr 1876); placed on Ret.Lst. (30 Apr 1878).

Career Summary Received appointment from PA (22 Aug 1835); w.o. (Aug–Nov 1835); *Warren, Grampus, Constellation, St. Louis,* and *Vandalia,* W.Ind.Sqdn. (Nov 1835–Nov 1838); l.o.a. (Nov 1838–Feb 1839); rec. ship *Hudson*, NY (Feb–May 1839); *Poinsett,* and *Van Buren*, spec.serv., FL coast (May 1839–Feb 1840); l.o.a. (Feb–May 1840); rec. ship *Hudson*, NY (May–Sep 1840); Naval School, Philadelphia (Sep 1840–Jul 1841); *Van Buren*, "Mosquito Flt." (Aug 1841–Jul 1842); l.o.a. and w.o. (Jul 1842–Feb 1843); *Shark, United States,* and *Levant*, Pac.Sqdn. (Feb 1843–Jul 1845); return to U.S., l.o.a., and w.o. (Aug 1845–May 1846); *Bonita*, NY (May–Jun 1846); *Vixen*, Home Sqdn. (Jun 1846–Jun 1847); l.o.a. (Jun–Sep 1847); cst.surv. duty (Sep 1847–Jun 1849); *Independence*, Med.Sqdn. (Jun 1849–Oct 1850); return to U.S., l.o.a., and w.o. (Oct

1850–Aug 1852); *Albany*, W.Indies (Aug–Sep 1852); w.o. (Sep–Oct 1852); rec. ship *Pennsylvania*, Norfolk, VA (Oct–Dec 1852); cdr, *Fulton*, W.Ind.Sqdn. (Dec 1852–May 1853); rec. ship *Pennsylvania*, Norfolk, VA (May–Aug 1853); l.o.a. (Aug–Nov 1853); w.o. (Nov 1853–Sep 1855); placed on Reserved List (13 Sep 1855); on furlough (Sep 1855–Jan 1858); restored to Active List (29 Jan 1858); w.o. (Jan–Apr 1858); cst.surv. duty (Apr 1858–Sep 1860); *Cumberland*, Home Sqdn. (Oct 1860–Jul 1861); cdr, *Louisiana*, N.Atl.Blk.Sqdn. (Jul 1861–May 1862); cdr, *Sebago*, N.Atl.Blk.Sqdn. (May–Jun 1862); sick lv. (Jun–Jul 1862); Navy Yard, Portsmouth, NH (Jul 1862–Aug 1865); temp. duty, Hampton Roads, VA (Dec 1862–Apr 1863); cdr, *Rhode Island*, spec.serv. (Aug–Dec 1865); w.o. (Dec 1865–Mar 1866); cdr, *Augusta*, spec. duty (Mar 1866–Jul 1867); w.o. (Jul 1867–Mar 1868); member, Naval Exam.Bd., Boston (Mar–May 1868); w.o. (May–Aug 1868); Navy Yard, Philadelphia (Oct 1868–Sep 1870); insp., 11th L.h. Dist., Detroit, MI (Oct 1870–Oct 1873); w.o. (Oct 1873–Feb 1874); member, L.h. Bd., Washington, DC (Feb 1874–Jun 1876); cdr, Pac.Sqdn., *Pensacola*, (Jul 1876–Apr 1878); placed on Ret.Lst. (30 Apr 1878).

References
Personal Papers: 54 items (1812–68) in MD Historical Society, Baltimore, MD.

EDWARD TATTNALL NICHOLS Born in Savannah, GA, on 1 Mar 1823. Died at Pomfret, CT, on 12 Oct 1886. Buried in Providence, RI.

Ranks Act.Midn (14 Dec 1836); Midn (26 Dec 1838); PMidn (1 Jul 1842); Mstr (2 Aug 1849); Lt (13 Mar 1850); Cdr (16 Jul 1862); Capt (25 Jul 1866); Commo (24 May 1872); RAdm (26 Feb 1878); placed on Ret.Lst. (1 Mar 1885).

Career Summary Received appointment from GA (14 Dec 1836); spec. duty, U.S.Expl.Expd. (Jan–Nov 1837); rec. ship *Hudson*, NY (May 1838); *Erie* and *Levant*, W.Ind.Sqdn. (May 1838–Oct 1841); Naval School, Philadelphia (Oct 1841–Jul 1842); *Columbus*, Med.Sqdn. (Jul 1842–Dec 1843); *John Adams*, Braz.Sqdn. (Dec 1843–May 1844); w.o. (May–Nov 1844); *Colonel Harney*, spec.serv., Atl. Coast (Nov 1844–Jun 1845); *Columbia* and *Saratoga*, Braz. Sqdn. (Oct 1845–Jan 1847); l.o.a. (Jan–Jul 1847); *Stromboli*, Home Sqdn. (Jul 1847–Sep 1848); *Savannah*, Pac.Sqdn. (Dec 1848–Oct 1851); l.o.a. (Oct 1851–Jan 1852); Navy Yard, Pensacola, FL (Jan 1852–Feb 1853); *Saranac*, Med.Sqdn. (Feb–Jul 1853); w.o. (Jul–Oct 1853); *Saranac*, Med.Sqdn. (Nov 1853–Jun 1856); Navy Yard, Portsmouth, NH (Aug 1856–Aug 1858); *Jamestown*, Home Sqdn. (Sep 1858–Feb 1860); Navy Yard, Boston (May 1860–Oct 1861); cdr, *Winona*, then *Iroquois*, W.Gulf Blk.Sqdn. (Oct 1861–Oct 1862); l.o.a. (Oct 1862); cdr, *Alabama*, S.Atl.Blk.Sqdn. (Oct 1862–Aug 1863); w.o. (Aug 1863); cdr, *Mendota*, N.Atl.Blk.Sqdn. (Aug 1863–May 1865); w.o. (May–Aug 1865); spec. duty, NY (Aug 1865–Aug 1868); w.o. (Aug

EDWARD TATTNALL NICHOLS
1823–1886

1868–Jan 1870); chief of staff, Asia.Sqdn., *Colorado* (Feb 1870–May 1872); w.o. (Jun–Oct 1872); member, Bd. of Examiners, USNA (Nov–Dec 1972); w.o. (Dec 1872–Mar 1873); member, Exam. and Ret. Bds., Washington, DC (Apr–Oct 1873); comdt., Navy Yard, Boston (Oct 1873–Oct 1876); w.o. (Oct 1876–Mar 1877); member, Exam. and Ret. Bds. (Apr–Jul 1877); cdr, S.Atl.Sqdn., *Hartford* (Aug 1877–Nov 1879); w.o. (Nov 1879–Jun 1880); insp., 3rd L.h. Dist., Tompkinsville, NY (Jun 1880–May 1881); chief, Bur. of Yards and Docks, Washington, DC (Jun 1881–Mar 1885); placed on Ret.Lst. (1 Mar 1885).

Career Highlights Received surrender of Ft. St. Philip on lower Mississippi River on 28 Apr 1862. Engaged Confederate ram *Arkansas*. Present at bombardment of Vicksburg batteries in Jul 1862.

References
Writings: *The Battle of New Orleans: Compiled from the Letters of the USS* Winona *under Command of Edward T. Nichols, 1861–1862,* comp. Donald B. Sayner (Tucson: 1976).

JAMES WILLIAM AUGUSTUS
NICHOLSON
1821–1887

JAMES WILLIAM AUGUSTUS NICHOLSON Born in Dedham, MA, on 10 Mar 1821, son of Nathaniel Dowse and Hannah (Gray) Nicholson. Married Mary Heap. Died in New York City on 28 Oct 1887. Buried in Woodlawn Cemetery, Westchester Co., NY.

Ranks Midn (10 Feb 1838); PMidn (20 May 1844); Mstr (11 Jun 1851); Lt (24 Apr 1852); Cdr (16 Jul 1862); Capt (25 Jul 1866); Commo (8 Nov 1873); RAdm (1 Oct 1881); placed on Ret.Lst. (10 Mar 1883).

Career Summary Received appointment from NY (10 Feb 1838); *Levant,* W.Ind.Sqdn. (Feb 1838–Sep 1839); l.o.a. (Sep–Oct 1839); *Natchez* and *Warren,* W.Ind.Sqdn. (Oct 1839–Jan 1841); l.o.a. (Jan–Apr 1841); *Fairfield* and *Brandywine,* Med.Sqdn. (May 1841–Jul 1842); l.o.a. (Jul–Nov 1842); Navy Yard, NY (Nov 1842–Apr 1843); *Somers,* Home Sqdn. (May–Oct 1843); Naval School, Philadelphia (Oct 1843–May 1844); *Princeton,* Home Sqdn. (May 1844–Mar 1846); w.o. (Mar–May 1846); *Lexington* and *Savannah,* Pac.Sqdn. (May 1846–Sep 1847); l.o.a. (Sep–Dec 1847); *Fredonia,* spec.serv. (Dec 1847–Jul 1848); l.o.a. and w.o. (Jul 1848–Apr 1849); flgs. *Raritan,* W.Ind.Sqdn. (Apr 1849–Apr 1850); l.o.a. (Apr–Jul 1850); cst.surv. duty (Jul–Oct 1850); w.o. (Oct–Dec 1850); *Southampton,* Pac.Sqdn. (Dec 1850–Aug 1852); l.o.a. and w.o. (Aug 1852–Feb 1853); *Macedonian,* spec.serv. (Feb 1853); *Vandalia,* spec. expd. to Japan (Feb 1853–Nov 1854); return to U.S., sick lv., and w.o. (Nov 1854–Oct 1855); Navy Yard, NY (Oct 1855–Feb 1857); *Release,* spec.serv. (May–Aug 1857); w.o. (Aug–Oct 1857); *Vincennes* and *Supply,* Afr.Sqdn. (Oct 1857–Mar 1860); l.o.a. and w.o. (Mar–Jul 1860); rec. ship *North Carolina,* NY (Jul 1860–Apr 1861); *Pocahontas,* Potomac River (Apr–Aug 1861); *Pensacola,* Navy Yard, Washington, DC

(Aug–Oct 1861); cdr, *Isaac Smith*, S.Atl.Blk.Sqdn. (Oct 1861–Sep 1862); ord. duty, Navy Yard, NY (Sep 1862–Jun 1863); cdr, *Shamrock*, Navy Yard, NY (Jun–Dec 1863); cdr, *Manhattan*, W.Gulf Blk.Sqdn. (Jan–Dec 1864); w.o. (Dec 1864–Feb 1865); cdr, *Mohongo*, Pac.Sqdn. (Mar 1865–Oct 1866); return and w.o. (Oct–Nov 1866); spec. duty, NY (Nov 1866–May 1867); w.o. (May–Sep 1867); cdr, *Wampanoag*, NY and spec.serv. (Sep 1867–Apr 1868); w.o. (Apr–Jun 1868); member, Naval Exam.Bd., Philadelphia (Jun–Aug 1868); Navy Yard, NY (Sep 1868–May 1871); cdr, *Lancaster*, then *Portsmouth*, S.Atl.Flt. (May 1871–Aug 1872); w.o. (Aug 1872–Mar 1873); member, Bd. of Examiners, USNA (Mar–Jun 1873); w.o. (Jun–Nov 1873); member, Naval Exam. and Ret. Bds. (Nov 1873–Aug 1876); comdt., Navy Yard, NY (Sep 1876–May 1880); w.o. (May 1880–Sep 1881); cdr, Eur.Sta., *Lancaster* (Sep 1881–Mar 1883); placed on Ret.Lst. (10 Mar 1883).

Career Highlights Was with Commo M. C. Perry to Japan in 1853, participating in all official meetings with the Japanese. During Civil War saw action at Port Royal, SC, in Nov 1861 and commanded a monitor at Mobile Bay. As cdr of Eur.Sta., assisted British in bombardment of Alexandria, Egypt, in 1881.

CHARLES STUART NORTON Born in Albany, NY, on 10 Aug 1836. Married Mary E. Pentz on 29 Mar 1872. Married again on 25 Jul 1906 to Elisabeth Killough. Died at his home in Westfield, NJ, on 24 Jun 1911. Buried in Arlington National Cemetery.

Ranks Act.Midn (3 Oct 1851); Midn (9 Jun 1855); PMidn (15 Apr 1858); Mstr (4 Nov 1858); Lt (24 Nov 1860); LCdr (16 Jul 1862); Cdr (1 Jul 1870); Capt (12 Oct 1881); Commo (31 Jul 1894); Act.RAdm (19 Dec 1894); RAdm (1 Feb 1898); placed on Ret.Lst. (10 Aug 1898).

Career Summary Received appointment from NY (3 Oct 1851); USNA (Oct 1851–Jun 1853); *Potomac*, Home Sqdn. (Jul 1855–Aug 1856); *Wabash*, Home Sqdn. (Aug 1856–Feb 1858); l.o.a. (Feb–May 1858); *Wabash*, Eur. Sqdn. (May 1858–Dec 1859); l.o.a. (Dec 1859–Mar 1860); *Seminole*, Braz. then S.Atl.Blk. Sqdns. (Mar 1860–Jul 1862); l.o.a. and w.o. (Jul–Oct 1862); *Maratanza*, N.Atl.Blk.Sqdn. (Oct 1862–Jul 1863); *Fort Jackson*, N.Atl.Blk.Sqdn. (Jul 1863–Mar 1864); sick lv. and w.o. (Mar–Apr 1864); *R. R. Cuyler* then *Maratanza*, W.Gulf and N.Atl. Blk.Sqdns. (Apr–Oct 1864); *Lackawanna*, W.Gulf Blk.Sqdn. (Nov–Dec 1864); *Richmond*, W.Gulf Blk.Sqdn. (Dec 1864–Jul 1865); w.o. (Jul–Nov 1865); *Monongahela*, W.Ind.Sqdn. (Nov–Dec 1865); w.o. (Dec 1865–Feb 1866); *Algonquin*, NY (Feb–Mar 1866); w.o. (Mar–Apr 1866); *Shamrock*, Eur.Sqdn. (Apr 1866–Jul 1868); Navy Yard, Portsmouth, NH (Jul–Aug 1868); rec. ship *Vermont*, NY (Aug 1868–Sep 1869); cdr, *Frolic*, Navy Yard, NY (Sep 1869); w.o. (Sep–Nov 1869); ironclad duty, New Orleans (Nov 1869–Jun

CHARLES STUART NORTON
1836–1911

1871); w.o. (Jun 1871–Jan 1872); insp., 6th L.h. Dist., Charleston, SC (Jan 1872–Jan 1874); w.o. (Jan 1874–Feb 1875); cdr, *Shawmut*, N.Atl.Sqdn. (Feb–Jul 1875); sick lv. (Jul–Dec 1875); cdr, *Passaic*, N.Atl.Sqdn. (Jan–Jul 1876); w.o. (Jul 1876–May 1877); Torp.Sta., Newport, RI (May–Sep 1877); w.o. (Sep 1877–Jan 1878); cdr, rec. ship *Passaic*, Washington, DC (Jan–Feb 1878); insp., 6th L.h. Dist., Charleston, SC (Mar 1878–Jul 1881); cdr, rec. ship *Independence*, Mare Island, CA (Jul 1881–Oct 1883); cdr, *Shenandoah*, S.Pac.Sta. (Nov 1883–Apr 1886); gen. court-martial duty (Jun–Aug 1886); member, Bd. of Inspection and Survey (Aug 1886–Jul 1889); capt.yd., Navy Yard, Norfolk, VA (Jul 1889–Oct 1891); cdr, rec. ship *Vermont*, NY (Oct 1891–Nov 1892); member, Naval Exam. and Ret. Bds. (Nov 1892–Nov 1894); cdr, S.Atl.Sta., *Newark* (Jan 1895–Apr 1896); comdt., Navy Yard, Washington, DC (May 1896–Oct 1898); placed on Ret.Lst. (10 Aug 1898).

JAMES SHEDDEN PALMER
1810–1867

JAMES SHEDDEN PALMER Born at Elizabethtown, NJ, on 13 Oct 1810. Remained unmarried. Died from yellow fever at St. Thomas, Virgin Islands, on 7 Dec 1867. Buried in New York City.

Ranks Ship's Boy (26 Aug 1824); Midn (1 Jan 1825); PMidn (4 Jun 1831); Lt (17 Dec 1836); placed on Reserved List (13 Sep 1855); Cdr (14 Sep 1855); Capt (16 Jul 1862); Commo (7 Feb 1863); RAdm (25 Jul 1866); died (7 Dec 1867).

Career Summary Served as ship's boy, flgs. *John Adams*, "Mosquito Flt." (Aug 1824–Mar 1825); received appointment from NJ as midn (1 Jan 1825); Navy Yard, NY (May 1825–Apr 1826); *Lexington*, Navy Yard, NY, then spec.serv., then Med.Sqdn. (May 1826–Nov 1829); *Delaware*, Med.Sqdn. (Nov 1829–Jan 1830); sick lv. (Jan–Sep 1830); l.o.a. to study math. in NY (Sep 1830–Apr 1831); rec. ship *Fox*, Baltimore (Jul 1831); on furlough due to ill health (Jul 1831–Oct 1832); Navy Yard, NY (Oct 1832–May 1833); flgs. *Delaware*, Med.Sqdn. (May 1833–Feb 1834); *Shark*, Med.Sqdn. (Feb–Dec 1834); flgs. *Delaware*, Med.Sqdn. (Dec 1834–Feb 1836); l.o.a. and w.o. (Feb 1836–Feb 1838); flgs. *Columbia*, E.Ind.Sqdn. (Mar 1838–Jun 1840); l.o.a. and w.o. (Jun 1840–Dec 1841); flgs. *Independence*, Home Sqdn. (Dec 1841–Dec 1843); *Potomac*, Navy Yard, Boston (Dec 1843–Sep 1844); l.o.a., on furlough, and w.o. (Sep 1844–Jun 1846); ord. duty, Navy Yard, Philadelphia (Jun 1846–Mar 1847); cdr, *Flirt*, Home Sqdn. (Mar–Aug 1847); sick lv. (Aug 1847–Nov 1848); spec. duty, Philadelphia (Nov 1848–Apr 1849); sick lv. (Apr 1849–Feb 1851); Naval Rndv., Philadelphia (Feb 1851–Mar 1853); l.o.a. and w.o. (Apr 1853–Sep 1859); placed on Reserved List (13 Sep 1855); cdr, *Iroquois*, Med.Sqdn. (Sep 1859–Jan 1862); l.o.a. and w.o. (Jan–Mar 1862); cdr, *Iroquois*, W.Gulf Blk.Sqdn. (Mar–Aug 1862); cdr, flgs. *Hartford*, W.Gulf Blk.Sqdn (Aug 1862–Jan 1864); cdr, naval forces, MS River, New Orleans, and *Pensacola* (Jan–Apr 1864); cdr, New Orleans and *Monongahela* (Apr–Aug 1864); cdr, 1st Division,

Ironclads, W.Gulf Blk.Sqdn., *Richmond* (Aug–Nov 1864); act.cdr, W.Gulf Blk.Sqdn., *Hartford* then *Richmond* (Nov 1864–Feb 1865); *Richmond*, W.Gulf Blk.Sqdn., (Feb–May 1865); gen. court-martial duty, Washington, DC (May–Dec 1865); cdr, N.Atl.Sqdn., *Rhode Island* (Dec 1865–Dec 1867); died (7 Dec 1867).

References
Other Sources: Charles Moran, "James Shedden Palmer: A Forgotten Protagonist of the Risorgimento," U.S. Naval Institute *Proceedings* 443 (Jan 1940): 31–43.

RUFUS PARKS Born in Bangor, ME, on 9 Apr 1837. Married with a son. Made his home in Norfolk, VA. Died at Jamestown, RI, on 9 Aug 1913. Buried in Richmond, VA.

Ranks Captain's Clerk (Nov 1860); Act.Paymstr. (3 Jun 1861); Asst.Paymstr. (12 Sep 1861); Paymstr. (14 Apr 1862); dismissed (2 Mar 1867); dismissal revoked (23 Jul 1872); Pay Insp. (23 Feb 1877); Pay Dir. (10 Aug 1886); placed on Ret.Lst. as Pay Dir. with rank of RAdm (9 Apr 1899).

Career Summary Received appointment as captain's clerk (Nov 1860); *Vandalia*, E.Ind. and S.Atl.Blk. Sqdns. (Nov 1860–Jan 1863); s.a. (Jan–Feb 1863); storeship *Falmouth*, Aspinwall, Panama (Mar–Oct 1863); home and w.o. (Oct 1863–Mar 1864); spec. duty, Navy Yard, NY (Mar–Apr 1864); *San Jacinto*, E.Gulf Blk.Sqdn. (Apr 1864–Mar 1865); w.o. (Mar–Sep 1865); *Monadnock*, spec.serv. (Sep 1865–Jul 1866); w.o. (Jul–Aug 1866); supply ship *Jamestown*, Aspinwall, Panama (Sep–Oct 1866); w.o. (Oct 1866–Mar 1867); dismissed (2 Mar. 1867); dismissal revoked and annulled (23 Jul 1872); w.o. (Jul 1872–Feb 1873); Navy Yard, Portsmouth, NH (Apr 1873–Nov 1874); flt.paymstr., S.Atl.Sta., *Brooklyn* (Dec 1874–Jul 1876); s.a. and w.o. (Jul–Sep 1876); Navy Pay Office, Norfolk, VA (Sep 1876–Oct 1880); flt.paymstr., Pac.Sqdn., *Pensacola* (Oct 1880–Jun 1884); s.a. and w.o. (Jun–Sep 1884); insp. of provisions and clothing, Navy Yard, Norfolk, VA (Sep 1884–Dec 1886); gen. storekeeper, Navy Yard, Norfolk, VA (Jan 1887–Dec 1888); s.a. and w.o. (Dec 1888–May 1889); gen. storekeeper, Navy Yard, Boston (Jun 1889–Jun 1892); s.a. and w.o. (Jun–Nov 1892); gen. storekeeper, Navy Yard, League Island, PA (Dec 1892–Apr 1893); in charge, Navy Pay Office, Baltimore (Apr–May 1893); gen. storekeeper, Navy Yard, NY (Jun 1893–Jun 1896); s.a. and w.o. (Jun–Jul 1896); in charge, Navy Pay Office, Philadelphia (Jul 1896–Apr 1898); gen. storekeeper, Navy Yard, Washington, DC (Apr 1898–Apr 1899); placed on Ret.Lst. (9 Apr 1899).

ENOCH GREENLEAFE PARROTT Born in Portsmouth, NH, on 27 Nov 1815, son of Enoch Greenleafe and Susan (Parker) Parrott. Remained a bachelor. Died in New York City on 10 May 1879. Buried at St. John's Church in Portsmouth, NH.

ENOCH GREENLEAFE PARROTT
1815–1879

Ranks Midn (10 Dec 1831); PMidn (15 Jun 1837); Lt (8 Sep 1841); Cdr (24 Apr 1861); Capt (25 Jul 1866); Commo (22 Apr 1870); RAdm (8 Nov 1873); retired (4 Apr 1874).

Career Summary Received appointment from NH (10 Dec 1831); *Boxer* and *Natchez*, Braz.Sqdn. (Dec 1831–Oct 1835); l.o.a. and w.o. (Oct 1835–Jun 1836); Navy Yard, Boston (Jun 1836–Feb 1837); Naval School, NY (Feb–Jun 1837); Naval Rndv., NY (Jun–Dec 1837); Navy Yard, Boston (Dec 1837–Apr 1839); *Fulton*, spec.serv. (Apr–Dec 1839); *Consort*, survey duty (Dec 1839–Oct 1840); cst.surv. duty (Oct 1840–Nov 1842); w.o. (Nov–Dec 1842); *Saratoga*, Afr.Sqdn. (Dec 1842–Aug 1845); flgs. *Congress*, Pac.Sqdn. (Aug 1845–Jan 1849); l.o.a. and w.o. (Jan–Sep 1849); rec. ship *Franklin*, Boston (Sep 1849–Dec 1850); w.o. (Dec 1850–Feb 1851); *St. Lawrence*, spec.serv. and Pac.Sqdn. (Feb–Aug 1851); l.o.a. and w.o. (Aug 1851–Jun 1852); *St. Louis* and *St. Mary's*, Med. and Pac. Sqdns. (Jul 1852–May 1853); l.o.a. and w.o. (May 1855–Feb 1856); Naval Observatory, Washington, DC (Feb 1856–Feb 1858); cdr, *Despatch*, spec.serv. (Mar 1858–Mar 1859); Naval Observatory, Washington, DC (Apr 1859–Apr 1861); Navy Yard, Norfolk, VA (Apr–May 1861); cdr, *Perry*, Atl.Blk.Sqdn. (May–Aug 1861); cdr, *Augusta*, Atl. then S.Atl.Blk. Sqdns. (Aug 1861–Sep 1863); cdr, *Canonicus*, N.Atl.Blk.Sqdn. (Sep 1863–Feb 1865); cdr, *Monadnock*, N.Atl.Blk.Sqdn. (Feb 1865); cdr, *Miantonomoh*, Navy Yard, NY (Feb–May 1865); cdr, *Agementicus*, spec.serv. (May–Oct 1865); cdr, rec. ship *Ohio*, Boston (Oct 1865–Sep 1868); w.o. (Sep 1868–Feb 1869); member, Bd. of Examiners (Feb–Mar 1869); member, Bd. of Visitors, USNA (Apr–May 1869); w.o. (May 1869–Mar 1870); comdt., Navy Yard, Mare Island, CA (Apr 1871–Sep 1872); comdt., Navy Yard, Boston (Aug 1872–Oct 1873); cdr, Asia.Sta., *Hartford* (Nov 1873–Mar 1874); sick lv. (Mar–Apr 1874); retired (4 Apr 1874).

Career Highlights Served during Mexican War with expedition under John C. Fremont from Monterey to Los Angeles, participating in the capture of Guaymas and Mazatlan. During Civil War, was with expedition which tried to destroy in Apr 1861 the Navy Yard at Norfolk, VA. Was on the *Perry* that captured first Confederate privateer of the war, the *Savannah*, receiving commendation from Navy Department.

References
Personal Papers: 433 items, 2 vols (1831–1929) in WPL.

THOMAS HARMAN PATTERSON
1820–1889

THOMAS HARMAN PATTERSON Born in New Orleans, LA, on 10 May 1820, son of Daniel Todd and George Ann (Pollock) Patterson. Married Maria Wainwright on 5 Jan 1847. Five children. Died in Washington, DC, on 9 Apr 1889. Buried in the Congressional Cemetery in Washington, DC.

Ranks Act.Midn (5 Apr 1836); Midn (3 Mar 1837);

PMidn (1 Jul 1842); Mstr (31 Oct 1848); Lt (23 Jun 1849); Cdr (16 Jul 1862); Capt (13 Apr 1867); Commo (2 Nov 1871); RAdm (28 Mar 1877); placed on Ret.Lst. (10 May 1882).

Career Summary Received appointment from LA (5 Apr 1836); w.o. (Apr–Jul 1836); *Porpoise*, spec.surv. duty (Jul 1836–Feb 1837); l.o.a. (Feb–Mar 1836); Navy Yard, Washington, DC (Mar–Apr 1837); duty with U.S.Expl.Expd. (Apr–Jun 1837); *Falmouth*, Pac.Sqdn. (Jun 1837–Jun 1840); l.o.a. (Jun–Oct 1840); Navy Yard, Washington, DC (Oct 1840–Aug 1841); Naval School, Philadelphia (Aug 1841–Jul 1842); Depot of Charts, Naval Observatory, Washington, DC (Aug 1842–Aug 1843); *Lawrence*, W.Ind.Sqdn. (Aug 1843–Apr 1844); cst.surv. duty (Apr 1844–Jul 1849); *Vandalia*, Pac.Sqdn. (Jul 1849–Oct 1852); l.o.a. (Oct–Dec 1852); spec. duty, Washington, DC (Dec 1852–Jan 1855); flgs. *Jamestown*, Afr.Sqdn. (Jan 1855–Jun 1857); Navy Yard, Washington, DC (Jul 1857–Aug 1859); w.o. (Aug–Oct 1859); *Mohican*, Afr.Sqdn. (Nov 1859–Oct 1861); cdr, *Chocura*, Hampton Roads and York River (Oct 1861–Oct 1862); senior officer, naval forces, York and Pamunkey Rivers, *Chocura* (Jun–Oct 1862); cdr, *James Adger*, S.Atl.Blk.Sqdn. (Nov 1862–Jun 1865); temp. duty, Washington, DC (Jan–May 1864); w.o. (Jun–Sep 1865); cdr, flgs. *Brooklyn*, S.Atl.Sqdn. (Oct 1865–Sep 1867); w.o. (Sep–Dec 1867); Navy Yard, Washington, DC (Dec 1867–May 1871); senior member, Bd. to Examine Inventions (May–Dec 1871); spec. duty, Washington, DC (Dec 1871–Sep 1872); act.chief, Bur. of Equipment and Recruiting, Washington, DC (Sep 1872–Sep 1873); comdt., Navy Yard, Washington, DC (Oct 1873–Oct 1876); pres., Naval Exam. and Ret. Bds. (Oct 1876–Aug 1877); cdr, Asia.Sta., *Richmond* (Oct 1878–Sep 1880); w.o. (Oct 1880–Jun 1881); spec. duty, preparations for new Navy Regulations (Jun 1881–May 1882); placed on Ret.Lst. (10 May 1882).

THOMAS PATTISON Born on 8 Feb 1822 in Troy, NY, son of Elias and Olivia (Gardiner) Pattison. Married Serafina Catalina Webster on 1 Jul 1850. One daughter, Maria Webster Pattison. Died on 17 Dec 1891 at New Brighton, Staten Island, NY.

Ranks Midn (2 Mar 1839); PMidn (2 Jul 1845); Mstr (17 Feb 1854); Lt (19 Sep 1854); LCdr (16 Jul 1862); Cdr (3 Mar 1865); Capt (3 Jul 1870); Commo (11 Dec 1877); RAdm (1 Nov 1883); placed on Ret.Lst. (8 Feb 1884).

Career Summary Received appointment from NY (2 Mar 1839); w.o. (Mar–Apr 1839); *St. Louis*, Pac.Sqdn. (Apr 1839–Sep 1842); l.o.a. (Sep–Dec 1842); rec. ship *Ohio*, Boston (Dec 1842–Jul 1843); l.o.a. and w.o. (Aug 1839–Apr 1844); rec. ship *North Carolina*, NY (Apr–Jun 1844); l.o.a. (Jun–Sep 1844); Naval School, Philadelphia (Sep 1844–Jul 1845); l.o.a. and w.o. (Jul 1845–Apr 1846); *Princeton*, *Raritan*, and *Cumberland*, Home Sqdn. (Apr 1846–Jan 1847); l.o.a. (Jan–Feb 1847);

THOMAS PATTISON
1822–1891

Active, Home Sqdn. (Feb 1847); *Electra, Scorpion*, and *Reefer*, Home Sqdn. (Feb 1847–Aug 1848); l.o.a. and w.o. (Aug 1848–May 1849); *Water Witch*, Home Sqdn (May 1849–May 1850); l.o.a. and w.o. (May–Oct 1850); cst.surv. duty (Oct 1850–Aug 1851); w.o. (Aug–Sep 1851); training ship *John Hancock*, USNA (Sep–Oct 1851); w.o. (Oct–Nov 1851); *Portsmouth*, Pac.Sqdn. (Nov 1851–Apr 1855); l.o.a. and w.o. (Apr–Sep 1855); rec. ship *Ohio*, Boston (Sep 1855–Mar 1856); Navy Yard, Boston (Mar 1856–Jun 1857); *Mississippi*, E.Ind.Sqdn. (Jun 1857–Jan 1860); l.o.a. and w.o. (Jan–Jun 1860); Naval Sta., Sacket's Harbor, NY (Jun 1860–Apr 1861); exec.off., *Perry*, Atl.Sqdn. (Apr–Jul 1861); Navy Yard, Washington, DC (Aug–Oct 1861); cdr, *Philadelphia*, Potomac Flot. (Oct–Dec 1861); cdr, *Sumter*, S.Atl.Blk.Sqdn. (Dec 1861–Nov 1862); w.o. (Nov–Dec 1862); cdr, *Clara Dolson*, Mississippi River Sqdn., then comdt., Naval Sta., Memphis, TN (Dec 1862–Aug 1865); l.o.a. (Aug–Nov 1865); cdr, *Muscoota*, Gulf Sqdn. (Nov 1865–Sep 1866); return home and w.o. (Sep–Dec 1866); Navy Yard, Norfolk, VA (Dec 1866–Apr 1870); l.o.a. and w.o. (Apr 1870–Jun 1872); cdr, rec. ship, *Ohio*, Boston (Jun–Oct 1872); cdr, *Richmond*, and *Saranac*, N.Atl. and Pac. Sqdns. (Nov 1872–Jun 1874); cdr, rec. ship *Independence*, Mare Island, CA (Jun 1874–Jun 1877); w.o. (Jun 1877–Dec 1878); cdr, Naval Sta., Port Royal, SC (Jan 1879–Jul 1880); comdt., Navy Yard, Washington, DC (Jul 1880–Jun 1883); l.o.a. and w.o. (Jul 1883–Feb 1884); placed on Ret.Lst. (8 Feb 1884).

HIRAM PAULDING
1797–1878

HIRAM PAULDING Born in Cortlandt, Westchester County, NY, on 11 Dec 1797, son of John and Esther (Ward) Paulding. Took leave in 1822 to attend Captain Alden Partridge's Military Academy in Norwich, VT. Married Ann Marie Kellogg in 1828. Six children. One daughter married future RAdm Richard W. Meade [*q.v.*] and another daughter married Gen Robert L. Meade, USMC. Died on 20 Oct 1878 at his home near Huntington, Long Island, NY. Buried in Huntington Cemetery.

Ranks Midn (1 Sep 1811); Lt (27 Apr 1816); Cdr (9 Feb 1837); Capt (29 Feb 1844); placed on Ret.Lst. with rank of Commo (21 Dec 1861); RAdm on Ret.Lst. (16 Jul 1862).

Career Summary Received appointment from NY (1 Sep 1811); flgs. *Constitution*, N.Atl. (Dec 1811–May 1813); Sacket's Harbor, Lake Ontario (May–Jun 1813); sick lv. (Jun–Jul 1813); Lake Champlain Flot. (Jul 1813–Sep 1814); *Ticonderoga* then *Eagle*, Lake Champlain (Sep 1814–Jan 1815); l.o.a. (Feb–Apr 1815); *Constellation*, Med.Sqdn. (May–Oct 1815); *Macedonian*, Med.Sqdn. (Oct 1815–Feb 1816); on furlough (Feb 1816–Jan 1817); flgs. *Independence*, Med.Sqdn. (Jan 1817–Jun 1818); *Macedonian*, Pac.Sqdn. (Jun 1818–Jun 1821); sick lv. at Valparaiso, Chile (Aug 1820–Mar 1821); l.o.a. (Jun 1821–Dec 1822); *Sea Gull*, W.Ind.Sqdn. (Jan—May 1823); *Peacock*, W.Ind.Sqdn. (May–Aug 1823); in ordinary (Aug–Nov

1823); *United States*, Pac.Sqdn. (Dec 1823–Aug 1825); *Dolphin*, Pac.Sqdn. (Aug 1825–Aug 1826); *United States*, Pac.Sqdn. (Aug 1826–Apr 1827); l.o.a. (Apr 1827–Jul 1828); Naval Rndv., Philadelphia (Jul–Sep 1828); l.o.a. (Sep 1828–Jun 1829); *Constellation*, Med.Sqdn. (Jun 1829–Nov 1830); Naval Rndv., NY (Nov 1830–Jul 1833); cdr, *Shark*, Med.Sqdn. (Sep 1833–Oct 1835); home, l.o.a., and w.o. (Oct 1835–Feb 1838); cdr, *Levant*, W.Ind.Sqdn. (Feb 1838–Jun 1839); home and l.o.a. (Jun 1839–Jul 1840); exec.off., Navy Yard, NY (Jul 1840–May 1841); l.o.a. (May 1841–Apr 1845); cdr, *Vincennes*, E.Ind.Sqdn. (May 1844–Apr 1847); l.o.a. and w.o. (Apr 1847–May 1848); member, spec.bd., Norfolk, VA, and Boston (May–Jul 1848); cdr, *St. Lawrence*, Eur. and Med. Sqdns. (Jul 1848–Nov 1850); l.o.a. and w.o. (Nov 1850–Jan 1853); comdt., Navy Yard, Washington, DC (Jan 1853–Jun 1855); cdr, Home Sqdn., *Wabash* (Jun 1855–Mar 1858); l.o.a. and w.o. (Mar 1858–Jul 1860); spec. duty, Navy Dept., and pres., Ret.Bd., Washington, DC (Jul 1860–Oct 1861); comdt., Navy Yard, NY (Oct 1861–May 1865); placed on Ret.Lst. (21 Dec 1861); gov., Naval Asylum, Philadelphia (May 1866–Jun 1869); port adm, Boston (Jun 1869–Oct 1870).

Career Highlights During War of 1812, saw action on Lakes Ontario and Champlain, commanding second division of guns at Battle of Lake Champlain. Served under Commo Stephen Decatur against Algerine pirates in 1815–16. In 1824, carried despatches from Callao, Peru, deep into the Andean Mountains to Simon Bolivar. In 1857, took into custody and sent home filibuster William Walker and 150 of his men from Nicaragua, an action approved by the American public but one which cost him his command. With Civil War, appointed by Pres. Lincoln to assist Navy Dept. with organizing the navy for war, including the unsuccessful destruction of the Navy Yard at Norfolk in 1861, for which Paulding received severe criticism. Retired for age, remained on duty in command of Navy Yard at NY. Sailors and marines under his command helped to quell the New York Draft Riots in 1863.

References

Personal Papers: among the Francis Barton Stockton papers in ASAL.

Writings: a) *Cruise of the* St. Lawrence, *1848–1850.* b) *Journal of a Cruise of the United States Schooner* Dolphin *Among the Islands in the Pacific Ocean* (NY:1831; new printing, Honolulu: 1970). c) *Bolivar in his Camp* (1834).

Additional Sources: a) Molly Elliot Seawell, *Midshipman Paulding* (c.1891). b) Rebecca (Paulding) Meade, *Life of Hiram Paulding, Rear Admiral, U.S.N.* (NY: 1910).

GEORGE FREDERICK PEARSON Born in NH on 6 Feb 1796. Died on 30 Jun 1867 at Portsmouth, NH, where he was also buried.

GEORGE FREDERICK PEARSON
1796–1867

Ranks Midn (11 Mar 1815); Lt (13 Jan 1825); Cdr (8 Sep 1841); Capt (14 Sep 1855); placed on Ret.Lst. with rank of Commo (16 Jul 1862); RAdm on Ret.Lst. (25 Jul 1866).

Career Summary Received appointment from NH (11 Mar 1815); *United States* and *Independence*, Med.Sqdn. (Jun 1815–Mar 1820); on furlough (Mar 1820–Oct 1821); *Franklin*, Pac.Sqdn. (Oct 1821–Aug 1822); Navy Yard, NY (Aug–Nov 1822); Navy Yard, Boston (Nov–Dec 1822); Navy Yard, Norfolk, VA (Dec 1822–Jul 1825); l.o.a. (Jul–Nov 1825); *Porpoise*, Med.Sqdn. (Nov 1825–Feb 1828); l.o.a. (Feb–Apr 1828); *Boston*, Med.Sqdn. (Apr 1828–Nov 1831); l.o.a. and w.o. (Nov 1831–May 1833); Navy Yard, Boston (May 1833–Jun 1834); l.o.a. and w.o. (Jun 1834–Feb 1835); *Constitution*, Med.Sqdn. (Feb 1835–Apr 1837); Navy Yard, Portsmouth, NH (Apr 1837–Sep 1841); w.o. (Sep–Dec 1841); rec. ship *Columbus*, Boston (Dec 1841–Dec 1842); w.o. (Dec 1842–Jul 1844); l.o.a. and w.o. (Jul 1844–Feb 1845); Navy Yard, Portsmouth, NH (Apr 1845–Oct 1846); cdr, *Boston*, Home Sqdn. (Oct 1846–Feb 1847); suspended (Feb 1847–Feb 1848); w.o. (Feb–Mar 1848); *Spitfire*, Home Sqdn. (Mar–Aug 1848); L.h. duty (Aug–Sep 1848); w.o. (Sep 1848–Mar 1849); L.h. duty (Sep 1848–Oct 1850); cdr, *Falmouth*, Pac.Sqdn., then *Congress*, Braz.Sqdn. (Nov 1850–Jul 1853); l.o.a. and w.o. (Jul 1853–Apr 1854); Navy Yard, Portsmouth, NH (May 1854–Oct 1855); w.o. (Oct 1855–Oct 1857); cdr, flgs. *Powhatan*, E.Ind.Sqdn. (Nov 1857–Aug 1860); l.o.a. (Aug 1860); comdt., Navy Yard, Portsmouth, NH (Aug 1860–Sep 1864); cdr, Pac.Sqdn., *Lancaster* (Oct 1864–Dec 1866); return and w.o. (Dec 1866–May 1867); member, Bd. of Visitors, USNA (May–Jun 1867); died (30 Jun 1867).

ALEXANDER MOSELY PENNOCK
1814–1876

ALEXANDER MOSELY PENNOCK Born in Norfolk, VA, on 1 Oct 1814, son of William Pennock. Married Margaret Loyall. Died in Portsmouth, NH, on 20 Sep 1876. Buried in Loyall family plot, Norfolk, VA.

Ranks Midn (1 Apr 1828); PMidn (14 Jun 1834); Lt (25 Feb 1841); Cdr (15 Dec 1855); Capt (2 Jan 1863); Commo (6 May 1868); RAdm (19 Jul 1872); died (20 Sep 1876).

Career Summary Received appointment from TN (1 Apr 1828); Naval School, Norfolk, VA (Apr–Oct 1828); *Guerriere*, Pac.Sqdn. (Oct 1828–Dec 1831); l.o.a. and w.o. (Dec 1831–Oct 1832); rec. ship *Congress*, Norfolk, VA (Oct 1832–Mar 1833); l.o.a. (Mar–Apr 1833); *Natchez*, Braz.Sqdn. (Apr 1833–Apr 1834); l.o.a. (Apr–Aug 1834); *Potomac*, Braz.Sqdn. (Aug 1834–Mar 1837); l.o.a. (Mar–Apr 1837); Naval Rndv., Norfolk, VA (Apr–Oct 1837); *Columbia* and *Decatur*, E.Ind. and Braz. Sqdns. (Oct 1837–Feb 1843); l.o.a. and w.o. (Feb–Aug 1843); Navy Yard, Norfolk, VA (Aug 1843–Apr 1844); *Lawrence*, Home Sqdn. (Apr–Nov 1844); l.o.a. (Nov–Dec 1844); Navy Yard, Norfolk, VA (Dec 1844–Jan 1847); Naval Rndv., Norfolk, VA (Jan–Sep 1847); *Supply*,

Home Sqdn. (Sep 1847–Dec 1848); Naval Rndv., Norfolk, VA (Dec 1848–Dec 1849); *Marion*, E.Ind.Sqdn. (Dec 1849–Jun 1852); l.o.a. and w.o. (Jun–Dec 1852); insp., 5th L.h. Dist., Norfolk, VA (Dec 1852–May 1856); w.o. (May–Dec 1856); spec. duty, *Niagara*, Navy Yard, NY and spec.serv. (Dec 1856–Nov 1857); w.o. (Nov 1857–Sep 1858); cdr, *Southern Star*, Braz.Sqdn. and Paraguay Expd. (Sep 1858–Jun 1859); w.o. (Jun–Oct 1859); insp., 3rd L.h. Dist., Tompkinsville, NY (Oct 1859–Sep 1861); flt.capt, MS Sqdn., *Benton*, and base cdr, Cairo, IL (Sep 1861–Apr 1865); Navy Yard, NY (Apr 1865–May 1867); cdr, flgs. *Franklin*, Eur.Sqdn. (May 1867–Mar 1869); return and w.o. (Mar–Oct 1869); member, Naval Exam.Bd., Washington, DC (Oct 1869–May 1870); member, Bd. of Visitors, USNA (May–Jun 1870); member, Naval Exam.Bd., Washington, DC (Jun 1870); comdt., Navy Yard, Portsmouth, NH (Jul 1870–Oct 1872); cdr, Pac.Sta., *California* (Oct 1872–May 1874); cdr, Asia.Sta., *Hartford* (May 1874–Jul 1875); w.o. (Jul–Nov 1875); spec. duty, revising Navy Regulations, Navy Dept., Washington, DC (Nov 1875–Aug 1876); w.o. (Aug–Sep 1876); died (20 Sep 1876).

THOMAS STOWELL PHELPS, SR. Born in Buckfield, ME, on 2 Nov 1822. Married Margaret Riche Levy. At least one son, RAdm Thomas Stowell Phelps, USN (1848–1915). Died in the Naval Hosp. in New York City on 10 Jan 1901.

Ranks Midn (17 Jan 1840); PMidn (11 Jul 1846); Mstr (1 Mar 1855); Lt (14 Sep 1855); LCdr (16 Jul 1862); Cdr (5 Aug 1865); Capt (19 Jan 1871); Commo (13 Jan 1879); RAdm (1 Mar 1884); placed on Ret.Lst. (2 Nov 1884).

Career Summary Received appointment from ME (17 Jan 1840); w.o. (Jan–Mar 1840); *Preble*, spec.serv., Labrador Cst., then Med.Sqdn. (Mar 1840–Sep 1843); l.o.a. (Sep–Oct 1843); *Boston*, Braz.Sqdn. (Oct 1843–Feb 1846); Naval School, Annapolis, MD (Feb–Jul 1846); w.o. (Jul–Oct 1846); *Boston*, Gulf Sqdn. (Oct 1846–Feb 1847); *Polk*, Home Sqdn. (Feb–May 1847); cst.surv. duty (May 1847–Jun 1849); *Independence*, Med.Sqdn. (Jun 1849–Dec 1850); *Constitution*, Med.Sqdn. (Dec 1850–Feb 1851); l.o.a. (Feb–May 1851); cst.surv. duty (May 1851–Aug 1852); rec. ship *Pennsylvania*, Norfolk, VA (Aug 1852–Jan 1853); *Fulton*, Home Sqdn. (Jan–Feb 1853); rec. ship *Pennsylvania*, Norfolk, VA (Feb–Dec 1853); survey duty on Elizabeth River, VA, then Navy Yard, Norfolk, VA (Dec 1853); *Decatur*, Pac.Sqdn. (Dec 1853–Mar 1857); l.o.a. (Mar–May 1857); ord. duty, Navy Yard, Norfolk, VA (May 1857–Sep 1858); *Western Port*, Braz.Sqdn. and Paraguay Expd. (Oct 1858–Jun 1859); *Crusader*, Home Sqdn. (Jun–Aug 1859); cdr, *Vixen*, cst.surv. and spec. duty (Aug 1859–Sep 1861); *Corwin*, spec. secret serv. (Sep 1861–Jan 1862); N.Atl.Blk.Sqdn. (Mar–Jun 1862); spec. duty, Potomac River (Jul 1862–Mar 1863); spec.surv. duties (Mar 1863–Dec 1864); cdr, *Saugus*, S.Atl.Blk.Sqdn. (Dec 1864–Jan 1865); cdr, *Jun-*

THOMAS STOWELL PHELPS, SR.
1822–1901

iata, S.Atl.Blk.Sqdn. (Jan–Feb 1865); cdr, *Lenapee*, Atl.Cst.Sqdn. (Mar 1865–Apr 1867); w.o. (Apr–Sep 1867); Navy Yard, Mare Island, CA (Oct 1867–Nov 1870); cdr, rec. ship *Independence*, Mare Island, CA (Nov 1870–Sep 1871); cdr, *Saranac*, N.Pac.Sta. (Sep 1871–Oct 1873); temp. duty, L.h. insp. (Oct–Nov 1873); w.o. (Nov 1873–Mar 1874); exec.off., Navy Yard, Mare Island, CA (Mar 1874–Apr 1877); w.o. (Apr–Sep 1877); cdr, rec. ship *Independence*, Mare Island, CA (Sep 1877–Feb 1879); w.o. (Feb–Dec 1879); cdr, Navy Yard, Mare Island, CA (Jan 1880–Mar 1883); cdr, S.Atl.Sta., *Brooklyn* (Jun 1883–Oct 1884); w.o. (Oct–Nov 1884); placed on Ret.Lst. (2 Nov 1884).

Career Highlights Served in the Indian War in Washington Territory and at the Battle of Seattle on 26 Jan 1856. Owing to cst.surv. experience, chosen at outset of Civil War to survey and chart Potomac River after many navigational aids had been destroyed or made inoperative by Confederate forces. Similarly engaged in secret survey work in VA waters, efforts noted by the secretary of the navy.

References
Writings: a) "Reminiscences of Seattle, Washington Territory, and U.S. Sloop of War, *Decatur*, During the Indian War of 1855–1856." *The United Service* 5 (1881): 669–706. b) "Cruise of the *Decatur*" in *The Papers of Francis Gregory Dallas, U.S. Navy; Correspondence and Journal, 1837–1859*, ed. Gardiner W. Allen (NY: 1917).

JOHN WOODWARD PHILIP
1840–1900

JOHN WOODWARD PHILIP Born in Kinderhook, NY, on 26 Aug 1840, son of Dr. John Henry Philip. Married, with two children. Died at Navy Yard in Brooklyn, NY, on 30 Jun 1900. Buried in the USNA Cemetery in Annapolis, MD.

Ranks Act.Midn (20 Sep 1856); Midn (1 Jun 1861); Lt (16 Jul 1862); LCdr (25 Jul 1866); Cdr (18 Dec 1874); Capt (31 Mar 1889); Commo (10 Aug 1898); RAdm (3 Mar 1899); died (30 Jun 1900).

Career Summary Received appointment from NY (20 Sep 1856); USNA (Sep 1856–Jun 1861); turned back (Jun 1857); *Marion*, Gulf Blk.Sqdn. (Jun 1861–Jun 1862); *Sonoma*, James River Flot. (Jul–Sep 1862); exec.off., *Chippewa, Pawnee*, then *Montauk*, S.Atl.Blk.Sqdn. (Sep 1862–Dec 1864); exec.off., *Wachusett*, Asia.Sqdn. (Jan 1865–Sep 1867); exec.off., *Hartford*, Asia.Sqdn. (Sep 1867–Aug 1868); USNA (Oct 1868); l.o.a. (Oct–Dec 1868); exec.off., *Richmond*, Eur.Sqdn. (Jan 1869–Nov 1871); w.o. (Nov 1871–Sep 1872); exec.off., flgs. *Hartford*, Asia.Sqdn. (Oct 1872–Jun 1873); cdr, *Monocacy*, Asia.Sqdn. (Jun 1873–Feb 1874); w.o. (Feb–Jun 1874); cdr, Naval Rndv., Boston (Jun–Jul 1874); l.o.a. to command steamer of Pacific Mail Steamship Company (Sep 1874–Jul 1876); cdr, *Adams*, N.Atl.Sta. (Jul 1876–Mar 1877); w.o. (Mar–Dec 1877); l.o.a. to command Woodruff Scientific Expd. (Dec 1877–Oct 1883) serving as cdr, *Tuscarora* (Dec 1877–Aug

1880) and *Ranger* (Aug 1880–Oct 1883); w.o. (Oct 1883–Jan 1884); spec. duty (Jan–Feb 1884); insp., 12th L.h. Dist., San Francisco (Apr 1884–Apr 1887); s.a. and w.o. (Apr 1887); cdr, rec. ship *Independence*, Mare Island, CA (Apr 1887–Apr 1890); member, Bd. of Inspection and Survey, San Francisco (May–Dec 1890); cdr, *Atlanta*, Sqdn. of Evol. (Dec 1890–Dec 1891); gen.insp., *New York*, Navy Yard, Philadelphia (Dec 1891–Sep 1892); spec. bd. duties (Sep 1892–Aug 1893); cdr, *New York*, S.Atl.Sqdn. (Aug 1893–Aug 1894); capt.yd., Navy Yard, Boston (Aug 1894–Oct 1897); cdr, *Texas*, N.Atl.Sqdn. (Oct 1897–Aug 1898); cdr, 2nd Sqdn., N.Atl.Sqdn., *Texas* (Sep 1898–Jan 1899); comdt., Navy Yard, NY (Jan 1899–Jun 1900); died (30 Jun 1900).

Career Highlights During Civil War, wounded at Stono River action. Commanded Woodruff Scientific Expedition (1877–83) which circumnavigated globe. During Spanish-American War commanded *Texas*, participating in Battle of Santiago on 3 Jul 1898, and being advanced five numbers for his service in the action.

References
Additional Sources: E. S. Maclay, *Life and Adventures of Jack Philip* (NY: 1903).

HENRY FERRY PICKING Born in Somerset County, PA, on 28 Jan 1840. Married Laura Sherwood on 2 May 1879. Died on 8 Sep 1899 at the Navy Yard in Boston. Buried in Forest Hills Cemetery, Boston.

Ranks Act.Midn (28 Sep 1857); Midn (1 Jun 1861); Lt (16 Jul 1862); LCdr (25 Jul 1866); Cdr (25 Jan 1875); Capt (4 Aug 1889); Commo (22 Nov 1898); RAdm (3 Mar 1899); died (8 Sep 1899).

Career Summary Received appointment from PA (28 Sep 1857); USNA (Sep 1857–Jun 1861); *St. Lawrence*, N.Atl.Blk.Sqdn. (Jun 1861–Sep 1862); w.o. (Oct–Dec 1862); USNA (Dec 1862–Jun 1864); serv. on, then cdr, *Nahant*, S.Atl.Blk.Sqdn. (Jun 1864–Aug 1865); w.o. (Aug–Oct 1865); *Swatara*, W.Ind. and Eur. Sqdns. (Oct 1865–Nov 1868); Navy Yard, League Island, PA (Dec 1868–Jan 1869); USNA (Jan 1869–Jan 1870); flgs. *Colorado*, Asia.Flt. (Feb 1870–Mar 1873); w.o. (Mar–May 1873); ord. duty, Navy Yard, Washington, DC (May–Jul 1873); l.o.a. (Jul–Aug 1874); Torp.Sta., Newport, RI (Aug 1873–Jun 1874); *Roanoke*, spec.serv., Navy Yard, NY (Jun–Nov 1874); Naval Rndv., NY (Dec 1874–Feb 1875); insp., 1st L.h. Dist., Portland, ME (Feb 1875–Nov 1878); s.a. and w.o. (Nov 1878–May 1879); cdr, *Kearsarge*, N.Atl.Sta. (May 1879–May 1881); w.o. (May–Jul 1881); insp., 1st L.h. Dist., Portland, ME (Aug 1881–Oct 1882); secretary, L.h. Bd., Washington, DC (Oct 1882–Sep 1887); cdr, naval forces, Northwestern Lakes, *Michigan* (Sep 1887–Nov 1889); in charge, Hydrographic Office, Washington, DC (Nov 1889–Sep 1890); insp., 3rd L.h. Dist., Tompkinsville, NY (Sep

HENRY FERRY PICKING
1840–1899

1890–Mar 1892); cdr, *Charleston*, Pac.Sqdn. and spec.serv. (Mar 1892–Feb 1894); l.o.a. (Mar–Jul 1894); bd. duties (Jul–Nov 1894); cdr, gunnery and training ship *Minnesota*, NY (Nov 1894–Sep 1895); member, Bd. of Inspection and Survey (Oct 1895–Apr 1897); cdr, rec. ship *Wabash*, Boston (Apr 1897–Nov 1898); bd. duties (Dec 1898–Mar 1899); comdt., Navy Yard, Boston (Mar–Sep 1899); died (8 Sep 1899).

References
Writings: *Report of Ice and Ice Movements in the North Atlantic Ocean* . . . (Washington, DC: 1890).

CHARLES HENRY POOR
1808–1882

CHARLES HENRY POOR Born in Cambridge, MA, on 11 Jun 1808, son of Moses and Charlotte (White) Poor. Married Mattie Stark on 13 May 1835. Eight children. Died in Washington, DC, on 5 Nov 1882. Buried in Oak Hill Cemetery in Washington, DC.

Ranks Act.Midn (1 Mar 1825); Midn (31 Dec 1825); PMidn (4 Jun 1831); Lt (22 Dec 1833); Cdr (14 Sep 1855); Capt (16 Jul 1862); Commo (2 Jan 1863); RAdm (20 Sep 1868); retired (9 Jun 1870).

Career Summary Received appointment from MA (1 Mar 1825); *John Adams*, W.Ind.Sqdn. (Mar 1825–Jun 1827); *Constellation*, Hampton Roads, VA (Jun–Jul 1827); l.o.a. (Jul–Sep 1827); *Delaware*, Med.Sqdn. (Sep 1827–Apr 1828); *Java*, Med.Sqdn. (Apr 1828–Jan 1830); l.o.a. and w.o. (Jan–Nov 1830); Naval School, Norfolk, VA (Nov 1830–Jun 1831); *Lexington*, Braz.Sqdn. (Jun 1831–Oct 1832); *Boxer*, Med.Sqdn. (Oct 1832–Jun 1834); l.o.a. (Jul 1834–Mar 1835); Naval Rndv., Norfolk, VA (Mar–May 1835); l.o.a. (May–Nov 1835); Naval Rndv., Norfolk, VA (Nov 1835–Apr 1836); w.o. (Apr 1836–Mar 1837); *Independence*, Braz.Sqdn. (Mar–Dec 1837); *Dolphin*, Braz.Sqdn. (Dec 1837–Jun 1838); *Independence*, Braz.Sqdn. (Jun 1838–Apr 1840); l.o.a. (Apr–Jul 1840); Navy Yard, Norfolk, VA (Jul 1840–Jan 1842); *Vandalia*, Home Sqdn. (Jan–Dec 1842); w.o. (Dec 1842–Jul 1843); flgs. *Macedonian*, Afr.Sqdn. (Jul 1843–May 1845); l.o.a. (May–Aug 1845); Navy Yard, Washington, DC (Sep 1845–Feb 1848); w.o. (Feb–Mar 1848); cdr, *Relief*, Gulf of Mexico (Mar 1848–Apr 1849); l.o.a. (Apr–Sep 1849); insp., Navy Yard, Norfolk, VA (Sep 1849–Nov 1851); w.o. (Nov 1851–Nov 1852); flgs. *St. Lawrence*, Pac. Sqdn. (Nov 1852–Apr 1855); l.o.a. (Apr–Jun 1855); Navy Yard, Norfolk, VA (Jun 1855–May 1858); member, Naval Exam.Bd. (May–Jul 1858); w.o. (Jul 1858–Apr 1859); member, Bd. to Examine Navy Yards (Apr–Jun 1859); cdr, *St. Louis*, Home Sqdn. (Jul 1859–Apr 1861); cdr, *Brooklyn*, Gulf Blk.Sqdn. (Apr–Oct 1861); court-martial duty (Oct–Nov 1861); l.o.a. (Nov–Dec 1861); ord. duty, Hampton Roads, VA (Dec 1861–Mar 1862); temp. cdr, then cdr, *Illinois*, Navy Yard, Portsmouth, NH (Mar–May 1862); cdr, *Roanoke*,

N.Atl.Blk.Sqdn. (May–Jun 1862); ord.off., N.Atl.Blk.Sqdn. (Jun–Oct 1862); cdr, *Saranac*, Pac.Sqdn (Oct 1862–Jun 1865); w.o. (Jun 1865–Nov 1866); cdr, Naval Sta., Mound City, IL (Nov 1866–May 1868); w.o. (May 1868–Jan 1869); comdt., Navy Yard, Washington, DC (Jan–Aug 1869); cdr, N.Atl.Sqdn., *Powhatan* (Sep 1869–Jun 1870); retired (9 Jun 1870).

Career Highlights In Civil War, commanded landing expedition which tried to reinforce Ft. Pickens in 1861. Commanded *Roanoke* during famous action off Newport News between *Monitor* and *Merrimack*.

References
Personal Papers: 4 items, including 2 vols (1855–70) in HHL.

DAVID DIXON PORTER Born in Chester, PA, on 8 Jun 1813, son of Commo David (1780–1843) and Evelina (Anderson) Porter. Adopted brother was RAdm David Glasgow Farragut, USN [*q.v.*]. Another brother was Commo William D. Porter, USN. Received some education at Columbia College, a preparatory school in Washington, DC. At age ten, accompanied his father on *John Adams* in 1824 to suppress piracy in West Indies. Married Georgia Ann Patterson, daughter of Commo Daniel T. Patterson, USN, on 10 Mar 1839. Eight children, one son being Commo Theodoric Porter, USN (1849–1920). Died in Washington, DC, on 13 Feb 1891. Buried in Arlington National Cemetery.

Ranks Midn, Mexican Navy (1826); Midn, USN (2 Feb 1829); PMidn (3 Jul 1835); Lt (27 Feb 1841); Cdr (22 Apr 1861); Act.RAdm (15 Oct 1862); RAdm (4 Jul 1863); VAdm (25 Jul 1866); Adm (15 Aug 1870); died (13 Feb 1891).

DAVID DIXON PORTER
1813–1891

Career Summary Appointed by his father as midn, Mexican Navy (1826); schooling, Mexico City (1826); schooner *Esmeralda*, (1826–1827?); brig *Guerrero*, W.Indies (Mar 1828); prisoner of war, Havana, Cuba (Mar–Dec 1828); received appointment as midn, USN (2 Feb 1829); *Constellation*, Med.Sqdn. (Jun 1829–Nov 1831); l.o.a. and w.o. (Nov 1831–May 1832); *United States*, Med.Sqdn. (May 1832–Dec 1834); l.o.a. (Dec 1834–Mar 1835); rec. ship *Sea Gull*, Philadelphia (Jul–Dec 1835); l.o.a. (Dec 1835–Apr 1836); cst.surv. duty (Apr 1836–Apr 1842); *Congress*, Med. and Braz. Sqdns. (Apr 1842–Mar 1845); l.o.a. (Mar–May 1845); Hydrographic Office, Naval Observatory, Washington, DC (May 1845–Mar 1846); spec. duty, commissioner to Santo Domingo (Mar–Jul 1846); Naval Observatory, Washington, DC (Jul–Nov 1846); Recruiting Office, New Orleans (Nov 1846–Jul 1847); 1st lt, *Spitfire*, Home Sqdn. (Jul–Aug 1847); Naval Observatory, Washington, DC (Oct 1847–Jan 1848); cst.surv. duty (Jan 1848–Oct 1849); l.o.a., on furlough commanding merchant mail steamers (Oct 1849–Apr 1855); cdr, *Supply*, spec.serv.,

Med. (Apr 1855–Feb 1857); s.a. (Feb–Apr 1857); spec. duty, Navy Yard, Portsmouth, NH (May 1857–Jun 1859); 1st lt, Navy Yard, Portsmouth, NH (Jun 1859–Aug 1860); cdr, training ship *Constitution*, USNA (Aug 1860); spec. duty, Pac. cst.surv. (Sep 1860–Apr 1861); cdr, *Powhatan*, spec. duty and blk. duty (Apr–Nov 1861); l.o.a. (Nov–Dec 1861); spec. duty, Washington, DC (Dec 1861–Feb 1862); cdr, Mortar Boat Flot., W.Gulf Blk.Sqdn., *Harriet Lane* (Feb–Oct 1862); cdr, MS River Sqdn., *Black Hawk* (Oct 1862–Oct 1864); cdr, N.Atl. Blk.Sqdn., *Malvern* (Oct 1864–Apr 1865); w.o. (Apr–May 1865); member, Bd. of Visitors, USNA (May–Aug 1865); ad interim chief, Bur. of Nav., Washington, DC (Aug 1865); supt., USNA (Aug 1865–Dec 1869); spec. duty, Navy Dept., Washington, DC (Dec 1869–Oct 1870); spec. duty, Washington, DC (Jan 1871–Aug 1876); w.o. (Aug–Oct 1876); duty examining Navy Yards (Oct–Dec 1876); head, Bd. of Insp. (Mar 1877–Feb 1891); died (13 Feb 1891).

Career Highlights First saw service under his father in the West Indies. Then entered Mexican navy, commanded by his father: saw considerable action and taken prisoner by Spanish in Havana, Cuba. During Mexican War, commanded seventy men against town of Tabasco and succeeded in capturing the main fort of the town. During Civil War, consulted by Pres. Lincoln on relief of Ft. Pickens: led relief expedition in spring 1861. Recommended and helped plan and execute attack upon lower Mississippi, receiving the surrender of Fts. Jackson and St. Philip. His mortar flot. was used against Vicksburg. As cdr of Mississippi River Sqdn., cooperated with army in taking various areas and campaigns, including Vicksburg in Jul 1863. Commanded N.Atl.Blk.Sqdn. when Fort Fisher and Wilmington, NC, were taken. For efforts and successes during war, received three different votes of thanks from Congress. Became supt. of USNA, instituting numerous changes and reforms in curriculum and instruction. Founding pres. of the Naval Institute in 1873. Wrote a great deal on naval subjects. Advanced to Adm in 1870, thus becoming highest ranking officer in navy.

References

Personal Papers: a) 750 items (1861–66) in HHL. b) 7000 items (1790–1899) in LC. c) Porter Family: 600 Items (1811–81) in NHF,LC. d) 1 item (1862) in ISHS. e) 6 vols. (1863–90) in USNAM. f) Porter Papers: 4 ft. (1805–1908) in WLCL. g) some in F. D. Roosevelt Library, Hyde Park, NY. h) log book of *Georgia* (1850–53) and Evelina Anderson Porter Papers in NYHS. i) 4 items (1866) in USMA. j) 14 items (1847–77) in WPL.

Writings: a) *Memoir of Commodore David Porter of the United States Navy* (Albany: 1875). b) *Allan Dare and Robert le Diable* (NY: c.1884). c) *Incidents and Anecdotes of the Civil War* (NY: 1885). d) *The Adventures of Harry Marline*

(NY: 1885). e) *The Naval History of the Civil War* (NY: 1886).

Selected Additional Sources: a) James Soley, *Admiral Porter* (NY: 1903). b) Malcolm W. Cagle, "Lieutenant David Dixon Porter and his Camels," U.S. Naval Institute *Proceedings* (Dec 1957: 1327–33). c) Richard S. West, Jr., *The Second Admiral: A Life of David Dixon Porter* (NY: 1937). d) Noel Bertram Gerson, *Yankee Admiral: A Biography of David Dixon Porter* (New York, 1968). e) Kenneth J. Hagan, "Admiral David Dixon Porter, Strategist for a Navy in Transition," U.S. Naval Institute *Proceedings* 94 (Jul 1968): 139–43.

LEVIN MINN POWELL Born in Winchester, VA, on 21 Apr 1803, son of Alfred Harrison Powell. Married but widowed. Died on 15 Jan 1885 at his residence in Washington, DC.

Ranks Midn (1 Mar 1817); Lt (28 Apr 1826); Cdr (24 Jun 1843); Capt (14 Sep 1855); placed on Ret.Lst. (21 Dec 1861); Commo on Ret.Lst. (16 Jul 1862); RAdm on Ret.Lst. (25 Jul 1866).

Career Summary Received appointment from VA (1 Mar 1817); w.o. (Mar 1817–Jul 1818); on furlough (Jul–Oct 1818); *Congress*, Navy Yard, Portsmouth, NH (Oct 1818–Jul 1821); l.o.a. (Jul–Aug 1821); on furlough (Aug 1821–Oct 1822); *Constitution*, Med.Sqdn. (Nov 1822–Jul 1823); l.o.a. (Jul–Aug 1823); *Ferret*, "Mosquito Flt." and W.Ind.Sqdn. (Aug 1823–Jun 1824); l.o.a. (Jun–Jul 1824); flgs. *North Carolina*, Med.Sqdn. (Jul 1824–Apr 1826); l.o.a. (Apr 1826–Aug 1827); *Delaware*, Navy Yard, Norfolk, VA, and flgs., Med.Sqdn. (Aug 1827–Jan 1830); l.o.a. (Jan 1830–May 1831); *Potomac*, Navy Yard, NY (May–Aug 1831); l.o.a. (Aug 1831–Dec 1832); *Natchez*, spec.serv., Charleston, SC (Dec 1832–Apr 1833); l.o.a. and w.o. (Apr 1833–Feb 1835); *Constitution*, spec.serv. (Feb–Aug 1835); l.o.a. (Aug–Sep 1835); 1st lt, *Vandalia*, W.Ind.Sqdn. (Oct 1835–Apr 1837); l.o.a. (Apr–Oct 1837); spec.serv., FL Everglades, l.o.a., and w.o. (Oct 1837–Sep 1840); cdr, *Consort*, surv.expds., Gulf of Mexico and Nantucket Island (Sep 1840–Nov 1841); l.o.a. (Nov–Dec 1841); cdr, rec. ship *Ontario*, NY (Dec 1841–Feb 1842); l.o.a. and w.o. (Feb–Sep 1842); *Flirt* and *Oregon*, surv.expd., Tampa Bay, FL (Sep 1842–Jul 1843); w.o. (Jul–Sep 1843); asst. insp. of ord. (Oct 1843–May 1849); cdr, *John Adams*, Braz. and Afr. Sqdns. (Jul 1849–Dec 1850); l.o.a. and w.o. (Dec 1850–Oct 1851); exec.off., Navy Yard, Washington, DC (Nov 1851–Nov 1854); w.o. (Nov 1854–Jun 1855); cdr, flgs. *Potomac*, N.Atl. and W.Ind. Sqdns. (Jun 1855–Aug 1856); l.o.a. and w.o. (Aug 1856–Jun 1858); supt. of mail steamers, NY (Jul 1858–May 1859); w.o. (May–Dec 1859); member, Bd. of Examiners (Jan 1860–Jan 1861); w.o. (Jan–Jul 1861); cdr, *Potomac*, Gulf Blk.Sqdn. (Jul 1861–Jun 1862); placed on Ret.Lst. (21 Dec 1861); bd. duties (Sep–Nov 1862); insp., 3rd L.h. Dist., Tompkinsville, NY

LEVIN MINN POWELL
1803–1885

(Nov 1862–Aug 1866); court-martial duty (Apr–Jul 1867); pres., Permanent Court, Navy Dept., Washington, DC (Mar 1869–Sep 1870; Oct 1870–Oct 1871).

GEORGE HENRY PREBLE
1816–1885

GEORGE HENRY PREBLE Born in Portland, ME, on 25 Feb 1816, son of Capt Enoch King and Sally (Cross) Preble. His paternal uncle was Commo Edward Preble, USN (1761–1807). Married Susan Cox on 18 Nov 1845. Four sons. Died at his home in Boston on 1 Mar 1885.

Ranks Midn (10 Oct 1835); PMidn (22 Jun 1841); Mstr (15 Jul 1847); Lt (5 Feb 1848); Cdr (16 Jul 1862); dismissed from service (20 Sep 1862); restored to rank (21 Feb 1863); Capt (29 Jan 1867); Commo (2 Nov 1871); RAdm (30 Sep 1876); placed on Ret.Lst. (25 Feb 1878).

Career Summary Received appointment from ME (10 Oct 1835); *United States*, Med.Sqdn. (May 1836–Nov 1838); *Warren, Macedonian, Levant*, and *Erie*, W.Ind.Sqdn. (Jan 1839–Sep 1840); Naval School, Philadelphia (Jan–Jun 1841); *Madison* and *Jefferson*, FL Expd. (Aug 1841–Aug 1842); sick lv. (Aug–Oct 1842); rec. ship *Ohio*, Boston (Oct 1842–May 1843); *St. Louis*, E.Ind.Sqdn. and spec. cruise (May 1843–Sep 1845); *Petrel*, Home Sqdn. (May 1846–May 1847); sick lv. (May 1847–Feb 1848); *Saratoga*, Gulf of Mexico (Feb 1848–Mar 1849); sick lv. (Mar–Apr 1849); exec.off., *Legree*, cst.surv. duty (Apr 1849–Jan 1851); *St. Lawrence*, spec. duty (Jan–Aug 1851); cdr, *Gallatin*, cst.surv. duty (Aug 1851–Dec 1852); *Vermont*, in ordinary, Boston (Dec 1852–Mar 1853); *Macedonian, Queen*, and *Confucius*, E.Ind.Sqdn. (Apr 1853–Aug 1856); insp., 1st L.h. Dist., Portland, ME (Sep 1856–Oct 1857); Navy Yard, Boston (Oct 1857–Sep 1859); exec.off., *Narragansett*, Pac.Sqdn. (Sep 1859–Nov 1861); cdr, *Katahdin*, W.Gulf Blk.Sqdn. (Jan–Aug 1862); cdr, *Oneida*, W.Gulf Blk.Sqdn. (Aug–Sep 1862); dismissed from service (20 Sep 1862); restored to rank (21 Feb 1863); w.o. (Feb–Apr 1863); en route to Portugal (Apr–Jun 1863); cdr, *St. Louis*, spec. duty, eastern Atl. (Jun 1863–Nov 1864); in charge, coal depot, Edisto River, SC (Nov 1864); cdr, Flt. Brigade, Port Royal, SC (Nov 1864–Apr 1865); cdr, *State of Georgia*, spec. duty, Aspinwall, Panama (Apr–Oct 1865); gen. insp. of supplies, and equip.off., Navy Yard, Boston (Oct 1865–Jul 1868); chief of staff, N.Pac.Sqdn., *Pensacola* (Aug–Dec 1868); cdr, flgs. *Pensacola*, Pac.Sqdn. (Aug 1868–Nov 1870); home and w.o. (Nov 1870–Jan 1871); cdr, Naval Rndv., Boston (Jan 1871–Nov 1873); spec. duty, Boston (Nov 1873–Jan 1874); w.o. (Jan–Apr 1874); spec. duty, Washington, DC (Apr–May 1874); cdr, Navy Yard, Philadelphia (Jun 1874–Jan 1876); w.o. (Jan–Mar 1876); spec. duty, Kittery, ME (Mar 1876–Feb 1877); cdr, S.Pac.Sqdn., *Omaha* (Mar 1877–Apr 1878); placed on Ret.Lst. (25 Feb 1878).

Career Highlights In 1844, commanded first armed American landing in China in order to protect residents and

American Consulate at Canton. During Mexican War, participated in siege and captures of Alvarado, Tampico, and Vera Cruz. Accompanied Commo M. C. Perry to Japan in 1853–56, making numerous surveys and sailing instructions of the East, many of which were published for American and British government use as well as for private use. During the Civil War, saw most of action on lower Mississippi River from Mar through Aug 1862. While commanding *Oneida* on blockade duty off Mobile, failed to stop Confederate cruiser *Oreto* [afterwards named the *Florida*] from breaking blockade; dismissed from service for his failure, but restored upon recommendation of pres. to Congress.

References

Personal Papers: a) 7 vols., 6 items (1861–82) in American Antiquarian Society, Worcester, MA. b) 44 vols., 6 boxes (1732–1887) in MA Historical Society, Boston, MA. c) c. 8 vols (c. 1839–70) in New England Historic Genealogical Society, Boston, MA. d) 1 vol. ["History of Portsmouth Navy Yard, 1603–1868"] in NH Historical Society, Concord, NH.

Writings: a) *The Chase of the Rebel Steamer of War, Oreto* . . . (Boston: 1862). b) *The Opening of Japan*, ed. by Boleslaw Szczesniak (Norman, OK: 1962). c) "Vessels of War Built at Portsmouth, New Hampshire, 1690–1860," *New England Register* XXII (1868): 393–403. d) *Genealogical Sketch of the First Three Generations of Prebles in America* (Boston: 1868). e) *The First Cruise of the United States Vessel*, Essex (Salem, MA, 1870). f) *Our Flag: Origin and Progress of the Flag of the United States of America* (Albany: 1872). g) *History of the Flag of the United States of America* . . . (Boston: 1872). h) *A Complete History of the Vessels of the United States Navy from 1797 to 1874* (Philadelphia: 1874). i) *Henry Knox Thatcher, Rear Admiral, U.S. Navy* (Boston: 1882). j) *A Chronological History of the Origin and Development of Steam Navigation* (Philadelphia: 1883). k) *History of the United States Navy Yard, Portsmouth, New Hampshire* (Washington: 1892). l) *History of the Boston Navy Yard, 1797–1875* (Washington, DC: microfilm, 1975).

HUGH YOUNG PURVIANCE Born on 22 Mar 1799 in Baltimore, MD, son of James and Eliza (Young) Purviance. Attended St. Mary's College in Maryland. Married Elizabeth R. Beatty on 23 Oct 1824. Two daughters. Died on 21 Oct 1882 in Baltimore. Buried in that city's Greenmount Cemetery.

Ranks Midn (3 Nov 1818); Lt (3 Mar 1827); Cdr (7 Mar 1849); Capt (28 Jan 1856); placed on Ret.Lst. (21 Dec 1861); Commo on Ret.Lst. (16 Jul 1862); RAdm on Ret.Lst. (25 Feb 1881).

Career Summary Received appointment from MD (3 Nov 1818); *Peacock*, Navy Yard, NY (Mar–Apr 1819); *Congress*, Pac.Sqdn. (Apr 1819–Aug 1821); *Franklin*, Pac.Sqdn.

HUGH YOUNG PURVIANCE
1799–1882

(Aug 1821–1824); *North Carolina*, Med.Sqdn. (Oct 1824–1827); *Falmouth*, W.Ind.Sqdn. (Mar 1828–Aug 1830); l.o.a. (Aug 1830–Dec 1831); *Peacock*, E.Ind.Sqdn. (Dec 1831–May 1834); l.o.a. and w.o. (May 1834–Jan 1835); Naval Rndv., Baltimore (Jan 1835–Jul 1836); spec. recruiting duty (Jul 1836–Feb 1837); cdr, *Fairfield*, Braz.Sqdn. (Mar 1835–May 1839); l.o.a. and w.o. (May–Dec 1839); Naval Rndv., Baltimore (Dec 1839–Jun 1841); *Brandywine*, Med.Sqdn. (Jun 1841–Jul 1842); l.o.a. (Jul–Aug 1842); Naval Rndv., Baltimore (Aug 1842–Oct 1843); cdr, *Consort*, Afr.Sqdn. (Oct 1843–May 1844); w.o. (May 1844–Apr 1846); Navy Dept., Washington, DC (May 1846); cdr, *Bonita*, Home Sqdn. (May–Jun 1846); flgs. *Cumberland*, Home Sqdn. (Jun–Sep 1846); l.o.a. and w.o. (Sep 1846–Sep 1849); cdr, rec. ship *Consort*, Baltimore (Sep 1849–Oct 1851); w.o. (Oct 1851–Dec 1852); cdr, *Marion*, Afr.Sqdn. (Dec 1852–Aug 1855); l.o.a. and w.o. (Aug 1855–Nov 1856); cdr, Naval Rndv., Baltimore (Nov 1856–Apr 1857); w.o. (Apr 1857–May 1859); member, Bd. of Examiners, USNA (May 1859–Jun 1861); cdr, *St. Lawrence*, S.Atl.Blk.Sqdn. (Jun 1861–May 1862); placed on Ret.Lst. (21 Dec 1861); insp., 5th L.h. Dist., Baltimore (Jul 1862–May 1865).

STEPHEN PLATT QUAKENBUSH Born in Albany, NY, on 23 Jan 1823, son of John N. and Nancy (Smith) Quakenbush. Married Cynthia Herrick Wright on 18 Jan 1849. Three children. Died in Washington, DC, on 4 Feb 1890. Buried at Oak Hill Cemetery in Washington, DC.

Ranks Midn (15 Feb 1840); PMidn (11 Jul 1846); Mstr (1 Mar 1855); Lt (14 Sep 1855); LCdr (16 Jul 1862); Cdr (25 Jul 1866); Capt (25 Jul 1871); Commo (13 Mar 1880); RAdm (28 Jul 1884); placed on Ret.Lst. (23 Jan 1885).

Career Summary Received appointment from NY (15 Feb 1840); w.o. (Feb–Apr 1840); rec. ship *Hudson*, NY (Apr–Sep 1840); *Boston*, E.Ind.Sqdn. (Sep 1840–Aug 1843); l.o.a. (Aug–Oct 1843); *Raritan*, and prize brig *Porpoise*, Braz.Sqdn. (Oct 1843–Jul 1845); l.o.a. (Jul–Oct 1845); Naval School, Annapolis, MD (Oct 1845–Jul 1846); *Albany*, and *Supply*, Home and Med. Sqdns. (Oct 1846–Dec 1848); l.o.a. (Dec 1848–Apr 1849); cst.surv. duty (Apr–Nov 1849); w.o. (Nov–Dec 1849); cst.surv. duty (Dec 1849–May 1850); mail steamer *Pacific* (May 1850–Apr 1851); w.o. (Apr–Jun 1851); mail steamer *Illinois* (Oct 1851–Apr 1852); *Perry*, Afr.Sqdn. (Apr 1852–Apr 1854); w.o. (Apr–Nov 1855); *Potomac*, Home Sqdn. (Nov 1855–Aug 1856); *Wabash*, Home Sqdn. (Aug 1856–Feb 1858); l.o.a. (Feb–Apr 1858); rec. ship *Princeton*, Philadelphia (Apr 1858–Jun 1859); *Congress*, Braz.Sqdn. (Jun 1859–Oct 1861); Navy Dept., Washington, DC (Oct–Nov 1861); cdr, *Delaware*, N.Atl.Blk.Sqdn. (Nov 1861–Sep 1862); cdr, *Unadilla*, S.Atl.Blk.Sqdn. (Sep 1862–Aug 1863); l.o.a. and w.o. (Aug–Oct 1863); cdr, *Pequot*, N.Atl.Blk.Sqdn. (Nov 1863–Oct 1864); w.o. (Oct–Dec 1864); cdr, *Patapsco*, S.Atl.Blk.Sqdn. (Dec

1864–Mar 1865); cdr, *Mingo*, S.Atl.Blk.Sqdn. (Mar–Jun 1865);
w.o. (Jun–Dec 1865); cdr, *Algonquin* [never commissioned],
Navy Yard, NY (Dec 1865–Jan 1866); w.o. (Jan–Feb 1866);
cdr, *Conemaugh*, N.Atl.Sqdn. (Feb 1866–Jul 1867); w.o. (Jul–
Aug 1867); Navy Yard, Norfolk, VA (Sep 1867–Nov 1870);
cdr, *Pawnee*, spec.serv. (Dec 1870–Feb 1871); w.o. (Feb–Apr
1871); Navy Yard, Norfolk, VA (Apr–Dec 1871); w.o. (Dec
1871–Jan 1872); cdr, *Terror*, N.Atl.Sta. (Jan 1872–Jan 1873);
w.o. (Jan–Aug 1873); cdr, rec. ship *New Hampshire*, Norfolk,
VA (Sep 1873–Aug 1875); w.o. (Aug 1875–Dec. 1880); cdr,
Naval Sta., Pensacola, FL (Jan 1881–May 1882); w.o. (May
1882–Jan 1885); placed on Ret.Lst. (23 Jan 1885).

References
Personal Papers: 2 items (1867–68) in WPL.

WALTER WELLS QUEEN Born in Washington, DC, on
6 Oct 1824, son of John William and Mary (Wells) Queen.
Married to Christiana Crosby, sister of RAdm Pierce Crosby,
USN [*q.v*]. Died in Washington, DC, on 24 Oct 1893. Buried
in Arlington National Cemetery.

Ranks Midn (7 Oct 1841); PMidn (10 Aug 1847); dismissed from service (12 Jun 1848); reinstated (27 Dec 1853);
Mstr (15 Sep 1855); Lt (16 Sep 1855); LCdr (16 Jul 1862); Cdr
(25 Jul 1866); Capt (4 Jun 1874); Commo (9 Feb 1884); RAdm
(28 Aug 1886); placed on Ret.Lst. (6 Oct 1886).

Career Summary Received appointment from NY (7
Oct 1841); *Macedonian* and *Marion*, W.Ind.Sqdn. (Oct 1841–
Jul 1843); *Warren*, Navy Yard, Philadelphia (Jul–Sep 1843);
Perry, E.Ind.Sqdn. (Sep 1843–Nov 1845); *Cumberland*, flgs.,
and *Ohio*, Home Sqdn. (Dec 1845–Jan 1848); Naval School,
Annapolis, MD (Jan–Jun 1848); dismissed from service for
duelling (12 Jun 1848); reinstated (27 Aug 1853); w.o. (Aug
1853–Feb 1854); *Relief*, Braz.Sqdn. (Feb 1854–Apr 1855);
Michigan, on Great Lakes (Apr 1855–Jan 1857); *San Jacinto*,
E.Ind.Sqdn. (Feb 1857–Aug 1858); l.o.a. (Aug–Sep 1858); rec.
ship *Allegheny*, Baltimore (Sep 1858–Apr 1859); *Lancaster*,
spec.serv. (May–Dec 1859); sick lv. and w.o. (Dec 1859–Aug
1860); *Powhatan*, W.Ind.Sqdn. (Aug 1860–Mar 1861); w.o.
(Mar–Apr 1861); *Powhatan*, spec.serv. (Apr–Nov 1861); l.o.a.
(Nov–Dec 1861); cdr, 2nd Division, Mortar Boat Flot., W.Gulf
Blk.Sqdn. (Dec 1861–Jul 1862); sick lv. and w.o. (Jul–Aug
1862); ord. duty, Navy Yard, Washington, DC (Aug 1862–
Mar 1863); ord.off., S.Atl.Blk.Sqdn., *Wabash* (Mar–Aug
1863); cdr, *Florida*, N.Atl.Blk.Sqdn. (Aug–Oct 1863); w.o.
(Oct–Nov 1863); cdr, *Wyalusing*, N.Atl.Blk.Sqdn. (Nov 1863–
May 1864); sick lv. and w.o. (May–Jul 1864); ord. duty, Navy
Yard, Philadelphia (Aug 1864); ord. duty, Scott Foundry,
Reading, PA (Aug 1864–Nov 1866); spec. duty, member of
Bd. to Examine Volunteer Officers for Entry to Regular
Navy, Hartford, CT, and Washington, DC (Nov 1866–Dec
1867); w.o. (Dec 1867–Feb 1868); cdr, *Tuscarora*, S.Pac. and

WALTER WELLS QUEEN
1824–1893

N.Atl. Sqdns. (Mar 1868–Jun 1870); cdr, Naval Rndv., Philadelphia (Aug–Sep 1870); cdr, rec. ship *Potomac*, League Island, PA (Oct 1870–Mar 1873); temp. duty, Naval Observatory, Washington, DC (Apr–Jun 1873); Navy Yard, Washington, DC (Jun 1873–Apr 1874); temp. cdr, rec. ship *Independence*, Mare Island, CA (May–Jun 1874); cdr, *Saranac*, N.Pac.Sta. (Jun 1874–Sep 1875); w.o. (Sep 1875–May 1876); cdr, rec. ships *Worcester* and *Franklin*, Norfolk, VA (Feb–Nov 1877); w.o. (Nov 1877–Mar 1878); capt.yd., Navy Yard, NY (May 1878–Mar 1880); cdr, flgs. *Trenton*, Eur. Sta. (Apr–Dec 1880); sick lv. and w.o. (Dec 1880–Sep 1881); spec. duty, Bur. of Yards and Docks, Washington, DC (Sep 1881–Jul 1883); l.o.a. and w.o. (Aug 1883–Apr 1885); member, Naval Ret.Bd., Washington, DC (Apr–Oct 1885); comdt., Navy Yard, Washington, DC (Oct 1885–Oct 1886); placed on Ret.Lst. (6 Oct 1886).

WILLIAM RADFORD
1809–1890

WILLIAM RADFORD Born in Fincastle, VA, on 9 Sep 1809, son of John and Harriet (Kennerly) Radford. Raised in VA, then near Maysville, KY, and finally in St. Louis, MO. His widowed mother married the MO governor, William Clark. Married Mary Elizabeth Lovell on 21 Nov 1848. Six children. Brother-in-law was Gen Stephen W. Kearney, USA. Died in Washington, DC, on 8 Jan 1890.

Ranks Midn (1 Mar 1825); PMidn (4 Jun 1831); Lt (9 Feb 1837); Cdr (14 Sep 1855); Capt (16 Jul 1862); Commo (24 Apr 1863); RAdm (25 Jul 1866); placed on Ret.Lst. (1 Mar 1870).

Career Summary Received appointment from MO (1 Mar 1825); *Brandywine*, spec. duty and Med.Sqdn. (Sep 1825–Jul 1828); l.o.a. (Jul 1828–May 1829); Navy Yard, NY (Jul–Sep 1828); *Erie*, W.Ind.Sqdn. (Sep 1828–May 1830); l.o.a. and w.o. (May 1830–Jun 1831); Navy Yard, Norfolk, VA (Jul–Sep 1831); l.o.a. (Sep 1831–Aug 1832); on furlough (Aug 1832–Aug 1833); w.o. (Aug 1833–Feb 1834); rec. ship *Sea Gull*, Philadelphia (Feb–Jun 1834); *John Adams*, Med.Sqdn. (Jun 1834–Jun 1835); l.o.a. and w.o. (Jun 1835–Sep 1837); *Boston*, W.Ind.Sqdn. (Sep 1837–Oct 1838); l.o.a. (Oct 1838–Dec 1840); *Preble* and *Brandywine*, Med.Sqdn. (Dec 1840–Jun 1841); Navy Yard, Norfolk, VA (Jun–Aug 1841); l.o.a. and w.o. (Aug–Dec 1841); rec. ship *Ontario*, New Orleans (Dec 1841–Feb 1842); cdr, *Ontario*, spec.serv., Gulf of Mexico (Feb–Dec 1842); Naval Rndv., New Orleans (Dec 1842–Aug 1843); *Savannah* and *Warren*, Pac.Sqdn. (Aug 1843–Sep 1847); l.o.a. and w.o. (Sep 1847–Mar 1848); temp. l.o.a. to serve with army (Mar–Jul 1848); l.o.a. and w.o. (Jul 1848–Jan 1849); Naval Rndv., NY (Jan 1849–Jan 1851); w.o. (Jan–Jun 1851); cdr, *Lexington*, Home Sqdn. (Jul 1851–Sep 1852); w.o. (Sep 1852–Sep 1858); insp., 3rd L.h. Dist., Tompkinsville, NY (Sep 1858–Oct 1859); w.o. (Oct 1859–Apr 1860); cdr, *Dakotah*, E.Ind.Sqdn. (May 1860–Jul 1861); return to U.S. and w.o. (Jul–Oct 1861); insp., 3rd L.h. Dist., Tompkinsville, NY (Oct 1861–Feb 1862); cdr,

Cumberland, N.Atl.Blk.Sqdn. (Feb–Mar 1862); member, Bd. of Examiners (May 1862); exec.off., Navy Yard, NY (May 1862–Jul 1864); w.o. (Jul–Aug 1864); cdr, *New Ironsides* and ironclad division, S.Atl.Blk.Sqdn. (Aug 1864–Feb 1865); cdr, James River Flot., *Dumbarton*, then *Phlox* (Feb–Apr 1865); cdr, Atl.Sqdn., *New Hampshire* (Apr–Oct 1865); comdt., Navy Yard, Washington, DC (Oct 1865–Jan 1869); cdr, Eur.Sqdn., *Franklin* (Feb 1869–Aug 1870); placed on Ret.Lst. (1 Mar 1870); member, Naval Exam.Bd., Washington, DC (Oct 1870–Jun 1872).

Career Highlights Saw action during Mexican War on Pac. coasts of Mexico and CA. In early 1862, commanded *Cumberland* but was away on spec. court-martial duty when that vessel was attacked and sunk by CSS *Virginia* [*Merrimack*]. Commanded an ironclad division at both attacks on Ft. Fisher, NC, in Dec and Jan 1864–65.

References

Personal Papers: 53 items (1847–90) in NHF,LC.

Additional Sources: Mme. Sophie (Radford) de Meissner, *Old Naval Days; Sketches from the Life of Rear Admiral William Radford, U.S.N., by his Daughter* (NY: 1920).

FRANCIS MUNROE RAMSAY Born in Washington, DC, on 5 Apr 1835, son of Bvt. MGen (USA) George Douglas and Frances Whetcroft (Munroe) Ramsay. Married Anna Josephine McMahon on 9 Jun 1869 in Buenos Aires, Argentina. Three children. Home was Washington, DC, where he died on 19 Jul 1914. Buried in Arlington National Cemetery.

Ranks Act.Midn (5 Oct 1850); PMidn (20 Jun 1856); Mstr (22 Jan 1858); Lt (23 Jan 1858); LCdr (16 Jul 1862); Cdr (25 Jul 1866); Capt (1 Dec 1877); Commo (26 Mar 1889); RAdm (11 Apr 1894); placed on Ret.Lst. (5 Apr 1897).

Career Summary Received appointment from PA (5 Oct 1850); USNA (Oct 1850–Nov 1851); *St. Lawrence*, Pac.Sqdn. (Nov 1851–Apr 1855); l.o.a. (Apr–Sep 1855); USNA (Oct 1855–Jun 1856); w.o. (Jun–Dec 1856); *Falmouth*, Braz.Sqdn. (Jan–Sep 1857); *Merrimack*, Pac.Sqdn. (Sep 1857–Feb 1860); l.o.a. (Feb–Apr 1860); ord. duty, Navy Yard, Washington, DC (Apr–Oct 1860); *Saratoga*, Afr.Sqdn. (Oct 1860–Jan 1862); l.o.a. (Jan–Mar 1863); cdr, *Choctaw*, MS Sqdn. (Mar 1863–Sep 1864); cdr, 3rd Division, MS Sqdn., *Choctaw* (Aug 1863–Sep 1864); cdr, 3rd and 4th Dists., MS Sqdn., *Choctaw* (May–Sep 1864); cdr, *Unadilla*, N.Atl.Blk.Sqdn. (Oct 1864–May 1865); head, Dept. of Gunnery, USNA (Jun 1865–Sep 1866); nav. duty, Navy Yard, Washington, DC (Sep 1866–May 1867); flt.capt and chief of staff, S.Atl.Sqdn., *Guerriere* (May 1867–Jul 1869); w.o. (Jul–Aug 1869); insp. of ord., Navy Yard, Washington, DC (Aug 1869–Aug 1872); temp. spec. duty, Bur. of Ord., Washington, DC (Aug–Sep 1872); naval attache, London, England, and Europe (Sep 1872–Sep 1873); Bur. of Ord., Washington, DC (Oct 1873–Jan 1874); cdr,

FRANCIS MUNROE RAMSAY
1835–1914

Ossipee, N.Atl.Sta. (Jan 1874–Jan 1875); w.o. (Jan–Apr 1875); Naval Asylum, Philadelphia (Apr 1875–Apr 1876); insp. of ord., Navy Yard, NY (May 1876–Apr 1878); Torp.Sta., Newport, RI (Apr–Sep 1878); insp. of ord. and in charge, Torp.Sta., Newport, RI (Sep 1878–Jan 1881); cdr, flgs. *Trenton*, Eur.Sta. (Feb–Nov 1881); supt., USNA (Nov 1881–Sep 1886); member, Bd. of Exam. (Oct 1886–Apr 1887); cdr, *Boston*, spec.serv. (May 1887–Feb 1889); comdt., Navy Yard, NY (Feb–Oct 1889); chief, Bur. of Nav., Washington, DC (Nov 1889–Apr 1897); placed on Ret.Lst. (5 Apr 1897).

Career Highlights Commanded numerous expds. on Mississippi and its tributaries during Civil War, including Yazoo River, siege and fall of Vicksburg, and Red River Expd. Saw action at both attacks on Ft. Fisher, NC, and in capture of Richmond.

GEORGE CAMPBELL READ
1787–1862

GEORGE CAMPBELL READ Born in Ireland in 1787, son of Benjamin Read. Emigrated with his family at an early age, settling in PA. Married. Died in Philadelphia on 22 Aug 1862. Buried in the Philadelphia Naval Asylum, although later disinterred and buried elsewhere.

Ranks Midn (2 Apr 1804); Lt (25 Apr 1810); Mstr Comdt. (27 Apr 1816); Capt (3 Mar 1825); placed on Reserve List (13 Sep 1855); RAdm on Ret.Lst. (16 Jul 1862).

Career Summary Received appointment from PA (2 Apr 1804); on furlough (Apr 1804–Aug 1806); *Vixen* (Aug 1806–Jul 1807); *Revenge*, Naval Sta., NY (Aug 1807–Nov 1809); *President*, Atl.Cst. (Nov 1809–Apr 1813); *John Adams*, NY (Apr–May 1813); cdr, *Scorpion*, Potomac Flot. (May–Sep 1813); cdr, *Vixen*, spec.serv. (Sep 1813–Apr 1814); Naval Sta., Sacket's Harbor, NY (Apr–Aug 1814); *Java*, under construction, Baltimore (Aug–Nov 1814); Navy Yard, NY (Nov 1814–Jun 1815); *Chippewa*, Med.Sqdn. (Jun 1815–Feb 1817); w.o. (Feb–Aug 1817); cdr, *Hornet*, W.Ind., N.Atl., and Med. Sqdns. (Aug 1817–Sep 1821); Navy Yard, NY (Sep 1821–Apr 1824); l.o.a. (Apr 1824–Jul 1825); *Brandywine*, spec.serv. and Med.Sqdn. (Jul 1825–May 1826); l.o.a. (May–Nov 1826); member, Bd. of Examiners, NY (Nov 1826–Jan 1827); l.o.a. and w.o. (Jan–Oct 1827); member, Bd. of Examiners (Oct 1827–Dec 1828); member, court of inquiry, NY (Dec 1828–Feb 1832); cdr, *Constellation*, Med.Sqdn. (Feb 1832–Nov 1834); l.o.a. (Nov 1834–Jul 1835); suspended (Jul 1835–Jul 1836); w.o. (Jul 1836–Sep 1837); cdr, flgs. *Columbia*, E.Ind.Sqdn. (Sep 1837–Jun 1840); l.o.a. and w.o. (Jun 1840–Nov 1841); cdr, Navy Yard, Philadelphia (Nov 1841–Dec 1844); w.o. (Dec 1844–Nov 1845); cdr, Afr.Sqdn., then Med.Sqdn., *United States* (Dec 1845–Feb 1849); l.o.a. (Feb–May 1849); w.o. (May 1849–Jun 1850); gov., Naval Asylum, Philadelphia (Jun–Aug 1850); cdr, Navy Yard and Sta., Philadelphia (Aug 1850–Aug 1853); w.o. (Aug 1853–Sep 1855); placed on Reserve List (13 Sep 1855); l.o.a. (Sep 1855–May 1861); gov., Naval Asylum, Philadelphia (May 1861–Aug 1862); died (22 Aug 1862).

Career Highlights On *Constitution* when she defeated HMS *Guerriere* in Jul 1812 and again on *United States* when she defeated HMS *Macedonian* in Aug 1812. Commanded two-ship sqdn. sailing on world cruise in 1838 that sought revenge for plundering of American *Eclipse* by Sumatrans, bombarding town of Quallah Battoo, and razing town of Mueke. Was instrumental at Philadelphia in founding of Naval Academy, serving as pres. of the Exam.Bd. which approved Academy's establishment.

References

Additional Sources: a) William Meacham Murrell, *Cruise of the frigate* Columbia *Around the World Under the Command of Commodore George C. Read, in 1838, 1839, and 1840* (Boston: 1840). b) F. W. Taylor, *The Flagship: or a Voyage Around the World in the United States Frigate* Columbia, *attended by her Consort the Sloop of War* John Adams *and Bearing the Broad Pennant of Commodore George C. Read* 2 vols. (NY: 1840). c) Charles O. Paullin, "Early Voyages of American Naval Vessels to the Orient; The Cruise of Commodore Read: 1838–1840," U.S. Naval Institute *Proceedings* 136 (1910): 1073–83.

JOHN JOSEPH READ Born in Mt. Holly, NJ, on 17 Jun 1842, son of Joseph S. and Mary (Black) Read. Retired to Mt. Holly, NJ. Died there on 24 Oct 1910. Buried in Mt. Holly.

Ranks Act.Midn (21 Sep 1858); title changed to Midn (16 Jul 1862); Ens (25 Nov 1862); Lt (22 Feb 1864); LCdr (25 Jul 1866); Cdr (11 Dec 1877); Capt (27 Apr 1893); RAdm (29 Nov 1900); placed on Ret.Lst. (17 Jun 1904).

Career Summary Received appointment from NJ (21 Sep 1858); USNA (Sep 1858–Mar 1861); Navy Yard, NY (Apr–May 1861); *Potomac*, W.Gulf Blk.Sqdn. (May 1861–Dec 1862); flgs. *Hartford*, W.Gulf Blk.Sqdn. (Dec 1862–Aug 1863); *Massachusetts* and *New Ironsides*, S.Atl.Blk.Sqdn. (Aug 1863–Aug 1864); w.o. (Aug–Sep 1864); exec.off., *R. R. Cuyler*, N.Atl.Blk.Sqdn. (Sep 1864–Jun 1865); w.o. (Jun–Aug 1865); *De Soto*, N.Atl.Blk.Sqdn. (Aug 1865–May 1866); *Rhode Island*, Atl.Sqdn. (May 1866–Jan 1867); exec.off., flgs. *Susquehanna*, N.Atl.Sqdn. (Jan 1867–Jan 1868); w.o. (Jan–Mar 1868); *Michigan*, on Great Lakes (Apr 1868–Jul 1870); *Guerriere*, Eur.Sta. (Aug 1870–Mar 1872); suspended (Sep 1871–Sep 1872); *Portsmouth*, Navy Yard, NY (Oct–Dec 1872); w.o. (Dec 1872–Jan 1873); exec.off., rec. ship *Vermont*, NY (Jan–Oct 1873); exec.off., *Kearsarge*, Asia.Sqdn. (Nov 1873–Jan 1874); exec.off., *Richmond*, N.Pac.Sta. (Jan 1874–May 1876); cdr, flgs. *Richmond*, S.Pac.Sta. (May 1876–Sep 1877); w.o. (Sep 1877–Jul 1878); Bur. of Yards and Docks, Washington, DC (Jul 1878–Jun 1879); insp., 15th L.h. Dist., St. Louis, MO (Jul 1879–Jul 1883); s.a. and w.o. (Jul–Aug 1883); cdr, *Michigan*, on Great Lakes (Aug 1883–Apr 1887); insp., 4th L.h. Dist.,

JOHN JOSEPH READ
1842–1910

Philadelphia (May 1887–May 1890); s.a. and w.o. (May 1890–Mar 1891); cdr, *Iroquois*, Pac.Sta. (Mar 1891–May 1892); l.o.a. (May–Jun 1892); insp., 11th L.h. Dist., Detroit, MI (Jul 1892–May 1893); s.a., w.o. and bd. duties (May–Jun 1894); temp. duty, Newport, RI (Jul–Aug 1894); cdr, rec. ship *Independence*, Mare Island, CA (Aug 1894–Feb 1895); cdr, flgs. *Olympia*, Asia.Sta. (Feb 1895–Jul 1897); home, l.o.a., and w.o. (Jul 1897–Apr 1898); cdr, rec. ship *Richmond*, Philadelphia (Apr 1898–Nov 1900); w.o. (Nov 1900–Mar 1901); comdt., Navy Yard, Portsmouth, NH (Apr 1901–Aug 1903); chairman, L.h. Bd., Washington, DC (Aug 1903–Jun 1904); placed on Ret.Lst. (17 Jun 1904).

Career Highlights Saw almost all major actions on the lower Mississippi, including siege and capture of Vicksburg. Participated in both actions at Ft. Fisher in Dec and Jan 1864–65.

GEORGE COLLIER REMEY
1841–1928

GEORGE COLLIER REMEY Born in Burlington, IA, on 10 Aug 1841, son of William Butler and Eliza Smith (Howland) Remey. Married Mary J. Mason on 8 Jul 1873. Three sons and two daughters. His home was in Washington, DC, where he died on 10 Feb 1928. Buried in Burlington, IA.

Ranks Act.Midn (20 Sep 1855); Midn (9 Jun 1859); Lt (31 Aug 1861); LCdr (25 Jun 1865); Cdr (25 Nov 1872); Capt (30 Oct 1885); Commo (19 Jun 1897); RAdm (22 Nov 1898); placed on Ret.Lst. (10 Aug 1903).

Career Summary Received appointment from IA (20 Sep 1855); USNA (Sep 1855–Jun 1859); *Hartford*, E.Ind.Sqdn. (Jun 1859–Dec 1861); l.o.a. (Dec 1861–Jan 1862); *Marblehead*, N. and S. Atl.Blk.Sqdns. (Jan 1862–Apr 1863); exec.off., *Canandaigua*, S.Atl.Blk.Sqdn. (Apr–Aug 1863); cdr, *Marblehead*, S.Atl.Blk.Sqdn. (Aug 1863); cdr, naval battery, Ft. Morris, SC (Aug–Sep 1863); prisoner of war (8 Sep 1863–15 Nov 1864); exec.off., *De Soto*, Baltimore (Feb–Apr 1865); *Mohongo*, Pac.Sqdn. (Apr 1865–Aug 1867); w.o. (Sep–Oct 1867); asst. instructor in naval gunnery, infantry tactics, and howitzer drill, USNA (Oct 1867–Apr 1869); *Sabine*, spec.serv. (May 1869–Jul 1870); w.o. (Jul–Aug 1870); spec. temp. ord. duty, Pittsburgh, PA (Sep 1870); second-in-command, Tehauntepec and Nicaraguan Surv.Expd. (Sep 1870–May 1871); w.o. (May–Sep 1871); Naval Observatory, Washington, DC (Sep 1871–Jan 1872); temp. cdr, *Frolic*, spec.serv. (Jan–Apr 1872); Naval Observatory, Washington, DC (Apr–Aug 1872); on staff, *Worcester*, flgs., and *Powhatan*, N.Atl.Sta. (Aug 1872–May 1873); w.o. and l.o.a. (May 1873–Jan 1874); Bur. of Yards and Docks, Washington, DC (Jan 1874–Nov 1875); cdr, naval forces, Rio Grande River, *Rio Bravo* (Nov 1875–Jan 1876); Bur. of Yards and Docks, Washington, DC (Jan–Dec 1876); w.o. (Dec 1876–Feb 1877); cdr, *Enterprise*, N.Atl.Sta. (Mar 1877–Apr 1878); w.o. (Apr–May 1878); torp. instruction,

Newport, RI (Jun–Sep 1878); w.o. (Sep 1878–Jun 1879); Bur. of Yards and Docks, Washington, DC (Jul 1879–Sep 1881); staff duty, *Lancaster*, Eur.Sta. (Sep 1881–Mar 1883); w.o. (Mar 1883–Jul 1884); equip.off., Navy Yard, Washington, DC (Jul 1884–Apr 1886); capt.yd., Navy Yard, Norfolk, VA (Apr 1886–Jul 1889); w.o. (Jul–Oct 1889); cdr, flgs. *Charleston*, Pac.Sqdn. (Nov 1889–Mar 1892); capt.yd., Navy Yard, Portsmouth, NH (May 1892–May 1895); w.o. and l.o.a. (May–Sep 1895); member, Naval Ret. and Exam.Bds. (Oct 1895–Jun 1896); comdt., Navy Yard, Portsmouth, NH (Jul 1896–Apr 1898); comdt., Naval Base, Key West, FL (May–Aug 1898); comdt., Navy Yard, Portsmouth, NH (Aug 1898–Mar 1900); cdr, Asia.Sta., *Brooklyn* (Apr 1900–May 1902); chairman, L.h. Bd., Washington, DC (May 1902–Aug 1903); placed on Ret.Lst. (10 Aug 1903).

Career Highlights During Civil War, commanded naval battery on Morris Island, SC, in late summer of 1863. Commanded second division of boats on the night attack against Ft. Sumter on 8 Sep 1863; taken prisoner and exchanged on 15 Nov 1864. As commander of naval base at Key West, FL, during the war with Spain, was responsible for supplies and maintenance of all vessels in the West Indies campaign. In 1900, commanded the Asia.Flt., overseeing naval operations during later phases of Philippine Insurrection. From Jul to Oct 1900, patrolled off China during the Boxer Rebellion and the Peking Relief Expd.

References
Personal Papers: a) Remey Family Papers, 1225 items (1855–1932) in LC. b) 1 item (1902–35) in NHF,LC. c) 6 vols. (1841–1928) typescript volumes prepared by his son, Charles Mason Remey, entitled "Life and Letters . . ." [see below] in State Historical Society, Iowa City, IA. d) 35 vols. (1939): Charles Mason Remey Family history in Minnesota Historical Society, St. Paul, MN. e) 9 ft. (1874–) papers of Charles M. Remey and included papers on his father, RAdm Remey in GARL. f) 1 vol. (1939) in WPL. g) 2 vols. (1841–1928) in Historical Society of PA, Philadelphia, PA.

Writings: "Reminiscences Written at the Request of and for the Interest of his Children," 1920.

Additional Sources: Charles Mason Remey, *Life and Letters of Rear Admiral George Collier Remey, United States Navy, 1841–1928* (Washington, DC: 1939).

WILLIAM REYNOLDS Born in Lancaster, PA, on 10 Dec 1815, son of John and Lydia (Moore) Reynolds. Educated at Lancaster Academy and in other private schools. Married Rebecca Krug. Died in Washington, DC, on 5 Nov 1879. Buried in Lancaster, PA.

Ranks Act.Midn (17 Nov 1831); PMidn (15 Jun 1837); Lt (8 Sep 1841); placed on Reserved List (24 Sep 1855); Cdr on Reserved List (9 Jun 1862); Capt (25 Jul 1866); Commo (10

WILLIAM REYNOLDS
1815–1879

Jun 1870); RAdm (12 Dec 1873); placed on Ret.Lst. (10 Dec 1877).

Career Summary Received appointment from PA (17 Nov 1831); *Boxer*, Braz. and W.Ind. Sqdns. (Dec 1831–May 1834); l.o.a. (May–Aug 1834); *Potomac*, Med.Sqdn. (Aug 1834–Feb 1836); l.o.a. and w.o. (Feb–Oct 1836); Naval School, Norfolk, VA (Oct–Nov 1836); Naval School, NY (Nov 1836–Jun 1837); temp. duty, *Pennsylvania*, Chester, PA, and Norfolk, VA (Oct 1837–Jan 1838); l.o.a. (Jan–Mar 1838); Depot of Charts, Washington, DC (Mar–Jul 1838); *Porpoise*, U.S.Expl.Expd. (Jul 1838–Jul 1842); l.o.a. (Jul 1842–Jun 1843); spec. duty, Navy Dept., Washington, DC (Jun–Aug 1843); *Cumberland* and *Plymouth*, Med.Sqdn. (Aug 1843–Dec 1845); l.o.a. and on furlough (Dec 1845–Dec 1846); *Allegheny*, spec.serv. (Feb 1847–Oct 1849); l.o.a. (Oct 1849–Mar 1850); Bur. of Construction and Repair, Washington, DC (Mar–Oct 1850); l.o.a. and on furlough (Oct 1850–May 1855); cdr, *Fredonia*, Valparaiso, Chile (May–Sep 1855); placed on Reserve List (24 Sep 1855); naval storekeeper, Honolulu, Territory of HI (Feb 1857–Jan 1862); sick lv. (Jan–Oct 1862); cdr, *Vermont*, then *New Hampshire*, Naval Depot, Port Royal, SC (Nov 1862–Jul 1865); l.o.a. and w.o. (Jul 1865–May 1866); cdr, *Lackawanna*, N.Pac.Sqdn. (May 1866–Jan 1869); w.o. (Feb–Mar 1869); pres., spec. bd. on weapons (Mar–May 1869); member, permanent Ord. Bd. (May 1869–Jul 1870); member, Bd. of Visitors, USNA (May–Jun 1870); chief, Bur. of Equip. and Recruiting, Washington, DC (Jul 1870–Jan 1875); spec. duty, Washington, DC (Feb–Apr 1875); cdr, Asia.Sta., *Tennessee* (Apr 1875–Aug 1877); w.o. (Sep–Dec 1877); placed on Ret.Lst. (10 Dec 1877).

Career Highlights Served with U.S.Expl.Expd. from 1838 to 1842.

References
Personal Papers: a) 2 items (1877–80) in NHF,LC. b) diaries made during U.S.Expl.Expd. (1830–65) in Franklin and Marshall College, Lancaster, PA.

Writings: *A List of the Reported Dangers to Navigation in the Pacific Oceans, Whose Positions are Doubtful.* (Washington, DC: 1866).

ALEXANDER COLDEN RHIND Born in New York City on 31 Oct 1821, son of Charles and Susan (Fell) Rhind. Father was U.S. diplomat to Turkish Empire from 1828 to 1831. Remained unmarried. Died at his home in New York City on 8 Nov 1897. Buried in Coldenham, NY.

Ranks Midn (3 Sep 1838); PMidn (2 Jul 1845); Mstr (30 Apr 1853); Lt (17 Feb 1854); dismissed from service (13 Sep 1855); recommissioned Lt (6 Jan 1859); LCdr (16 Jul 1862); Cdr (2 Jan 1863); Capt (2 Mar 1870); Commo (30 Sep 1876); RAdm (30 Oct 1883); placed on Ret.Lst. (31 Oct 1883).

ALEXANDER COLDEN RHIND
1821–1897

Career Summary Received appointment from AL (3 Sep 1838); *Ohio* and *Cyane*, Med.Sqdn. (Nov 1838–Jun 1841); l.o.a. (Jun–Oct 1841); *Warren*, W.Ind.Sqdn. (Oct 1841–Apr 1842); w.o. (Apr 1842–Jan 1843); rec. ship *Pennsylvania*, Norfolk, VA (Jan–Jun 1843); *Macedonian*, Afr.Sqdn. (Jun 1843–Apr 1844); *Falmouth*, NY (Apr–May 1844); *Phoenix*, spec.serv. (May–Aug 1844); Naval School, Philadelphia (Aug 1844–Jun 1845); *Washington*, cst.surv. duty (Jun 1845–Mar 1846); w.o. (Mar–Apr 1846); *Potomac*, Home Sqdn. (Apr–Aug 1846); *Albany*, NY (Sep–Dec 1846); w.o. (Dec 1846–Feb 1847); *Scorpion*, spec.serv. (Feb–Apr 1847); *Water Witch*, Home Sqdn. (May 1847–Jul 1848); l.o.a. (Aug–Nov 1848); cst.surv. duty, CA cst. (Nov 1848–c.1849); *St. Mary's*, E.Ind.Sqdn. (c.1849–Jun 1850); l.o.a. (Jun–Sep 1850); w.o. (Sep–Oct 1850); cst.surv. duty (Nov 1850–Apr 1853); l.o.a. (May 1854–Jun 1854); cst.surv. duty (Jun–Jul 1854); l.o.a. (Jul–Oct 1854); *John Adams*, Pac.Sqdn. (Oct 1854–Jul 1855); on furlough (Jul–Sep 1855); dismissed from service (13 Sep 1855); reinstated (6 Jan 1859); *Constellation*, Afr.Sqdn. (Apr 1859–Oct 1861); l.o.a. (Oct–Dec 1861); cdr, *Crusader*, S.Atl.Blk.Sqdn. (Dec 1861–Jul 1862); cdr, *Seneca*, S.Atl.Blk.Sqdn. (Jul–Oct 1862); cdr, *Keokuk*, S.Atl.Blk.Sqdn. (Oct 1862–Apr 1863); cdr, *Paul Jones*, S.Atl.Blk.Sqdn. (May–Jul 1863); cdr, flgs. *Wabash*, S.Atl.Blk.Sqdn. (Jul–Sep 1863); cdr, *Agawam*, N.Atl.Blk.Sqdn. (Oct 1863–Jun 1865); temp. cdr, *Louisiana*, N.Atl.Blk.Sqdn. (Dec 1864); l.o.a. (Jun 1865–May 1867); cdr, rec. ship *Vermont*, NY (May 1867–May 1868); cdr, Naval Rndv., NY (May–Dec 1868); w.o. (Dec 1868–Jan 1870); spec. duty, Navy Yard, NY (Jan–Apr 1870); w.o. (Apr 1870–Apr 1871); l.o.a. (May 1871–May 1872); w.o. (May–Aug 1872); cdr, *Congress*, Eur.Sta. (Aug 1872–Apr 1874); w.o. (Apr 1874–Sep 1875); insp., 3rd L.h. Dist., Tompkinsville, NY (Sep 1875–Jan 1877); w.o. (Jan–Mar 1877); insp., 3rd L.h. Dist. (Mar 1877–Apr 1878); l.o.a. and w.o. (May 1878–May 1880); pres., Bd. of Inspection and Survey (May 1880–Sep 1882); w.o. (Sep 1882–Mar 1883); gov., Naval Asylum, Philadelphia (Mar–Oct 1883); placed on Ret.Lst. (31 Oct 1883).

Career Highlights During the Mexican War, saw action at capture of Alvarado and Tobasco. During Civil War, commanded ironclad *Keokuk* in the 7 Apr 1863 attack on Charleston's defenses. Hit numerous times, *Keokuk* sank the next day without a loss of life, despite his gallant efforts to save her. Commanded powder boat *Louisiana*, which on 23 Dec 1864 was purposely blown up by him and his crew to try to destroy Ft. Fisher, NC, action for which Rhind received a commendation.

References
Additional Sources: *Reply to the Attacks of Mr. A. C. Rhind; dropped from the Rolls of the Navy by the Navy Board in 1855* (Baltimore: 1857) [viz., letters collected in defense of Cdr E. B. Boutwell, captain of USS *John Adams*].

CADWALADER RINGGOLD
1802–1867

CADWALADER RINGGOLD Born at Fountain Rock, Washington County, MD, on 20 Aug 1802, son of Gen (USA) Samuel and Maria (Cadwalader) Ringgold. His father served as congressman. Remained unmarried. Died in New York City on 29 Apr 1867. Buried in Greenmount Cemetery in Baltimore, MD.

Ranks Midn (4 Mar 1819); Lt (17 May 1828); Cdr (16 Jul 1849); placed on Reserve List (13 Sep 1855); reinstated to Active List (29 Jan 1858); Capt (2 Apr 1856); placed on Ret.Lst. with rank of Commo (16 Jul 1862); RAdm on Ret.Lst. (25 Jul 1866).

Career Summary Received appointment from MD (4 Mar 1819); flgs. *Columbus*, Med.Sqdn. (Dec 1819–Aug 1821); l.o.a. and w.o. (Aug 1821–Mar 1822); *Macedonian*, W.Ind.Sqdn. (Mar–Aug 1822); Naval Rndv., Baltimore (Nov–Dec 1822); *Grey Hound*, "Flying Sqdn.," W.Indies (Jan–May 1823); *Peacock*, "Flying Sqdn.," W.Indies (May–Jul 1823); *Weasel*, "Flying Sqdn.," W.Indies (Jul–Sep 1823); sick lv. (Sep 1823–Mar 1825); *North Carolina*, Med.Sqdn. (Mar–Dec 1825); l.o.a. and w.o. (Dec 1825–Oct 1828); *Vandalia*, Braz.Sqdn. (Nov 1828–Jan 1832); l.o.a. (Jan 1832–May 1833); *Delaware*, Navy Yard, Norfolk, VA (May–Jun 1833); sick lv. and w.o. (Jun 1833–Jun 1834); *Adams*, Med.Sqdn. (Jul 1834–May 1837); l.o.a. (May 1837–Apr 1838); cdr, *Porpoise*, U.S.Expl.Expd. (May 1838–Jul 1842); l.o.a. (Jul–Sep 1842); insp., Bur. of Provisions and Clothing, Washington, DC (Sep 1842–May 1846); w.o. (May 1846–Feb 1847); ord. duty (Feb 1847–Apr 1849); spec.surv. duty, CA cst. (Apr 1849–Dec 1850); w.o. (Dec 1850–Oct 1851); spec. duty, Navy Dept., Washington, DC (Oct 1851–May 1852); member, Bd. of Examiners (May–Aug 1852); l.o.a. (Aug–Sep 1852); cdr, N.Pac.Expl. and Surveying Expd., *Vincennes* (Sep 1852–Jul 1854); home and sick lv. (Jul 1854–Sep 1855); placed on Reserve List (13 Sep 1855); reinstated (29 Jan 1858); member, Bd. of Examiners (Mar 1858–Apr 1859); spec. duty in connection with N.Pac.Expd. (Apr–Oct 1859); member, Bd. of Examiners (Oct 1859–Aug 1861); cdr, *Sabine*, S.Atl.Blk.Sqdn. and spec. duties (Sep 1861–Oct 1863); transferred to Ret.Lst. (16 Jul 1862); w.o. (Oct 1863–Apr 1864); spec. duty, office of supt. of vessels being built, NY (Apr 1864–Apr 1867).

Career Highlights While with U.S.Expl.Expd., participated in skirmishes with Fiji Islanders in Aug 1840 that resulted from murder of two officers. Commanded N.Pac.Expl. and Surveying Expd., charting many islands until serious mental illness and subsequent relief by RAdm John Rodgers.

References
Writings: a) *A Series of Charts, with Sailing Directions . . . to the Bay of San Francisco, 1851* (1852). b) "Memorial of Commander Cadwalader Ringgold . . . to the Congress of the United States Navy, praying to be reinstated on the

Active List of the Service. . . ." (1856). c) *Correspondence to Accompany Maps and Charts of California.*

Additional Sources: Wilhelm Heine, *Die Expedition in die Seen von China, Japan und Ochotsk unter commande von Commodore Colin Ringgold und John Rodgers . . . 1853 bis 1856 . . .* (Leipzig: 1858–59).

HENRY BELLOWS ROBESON Born in New Haven, CT, on 5 Aug 1842, son of Dr. Abel Bellows and Susan (Taylor) Robeson. Married Katherine Nichols Bellows on 11 Jun 1872. Retired to Walpole, NH, where he died on 16 Jul 1914 and where he was buried.

Ranks Act.Midn (25 Sep 1856); Midn (15 Jun 1860); Mstr (31 Aug 1861); Lt (16 Jul 1862); LCdr (25 Jul 1866); Cdr (12 Feb 1874); Capt (25 Aug 1887); Commo (1 Feb 1898); retired with rank of RAdm (28 Mar 1899).

Career Summary Received appointment from CT (25 Sep 1856); USNA (Sep 1856–Jun 1860); *Niagara*, E.Ind.Sqdn., and Navy Yard, NY (Jun 1860–Jun 1862); *New Ironsides*, spec.serv. and S.Atl.Blk.Sqdn. (Jul 1862–Aug 1864); *Colorado*, N.Atl.Blk.Sqdn. and flgs., Eur.Sqdn. (Aug 1864–Aug 1867); w.o. (Aug–Sep 1867); *Piscataqua* [renamed *Delaware*], Asia. Sqdn. (Oct 1867–Nov 1870); w.o. (Nov 1870–Feb 1871); temp. duty, Springfield, MA (Feb–Oct 1871); spec. ord. duty, aid to RAdm Stephen C. Rowan [*q.v.*], Navy Yard, NY (Oct–Dec 1871); Torp.Sta., Newport, RI, and exec.off., *Minnesota* (Dec 1871–Dec 1873); exec.off., *Dictator*, N.Atl.Sta. (Dec 1873–Mar 1874); w.o. (Mar–Apr 1874); Navy Yard, NY (Apr 1874–Sep 1876); cdr, *Vandalia*, Eur.Sta. (Sep 1876–Feb 1877); w.o. (Mar–Apr 1877); cdr, *Despatch*, Navy Yard, Washington, DC (Apr–May 1877); cdr, *Vandalia*, Eur.Sta. (May 1877–Jan 1879); w.o. (Jan–May 1879); torp. instruction, Newport, RI (May–Sep 1879); USNA (Sep 1879–Aug 1883); cdr, *Miantonomah*, Navy Yard, NY (Sep 1883); w.o. (Sep–Dec 1883); Navy Yard, NY (Jan 1884–Feb 1888); member, Advisory Bd. (Feb 1888–Jan 1889); cdr, *Chicago*, Sqdn. of Evol. (Jan 1889–May 1891); l.o.a. (May–Jul 1891); supervisor, NY Harbor (Jul 1891–Jul 1892); w.o., l.o.a., and sick lv. (Jul 1892–Mar 1895); court-martial duty (Mar–May 1894); NWC (Jun–Sep 1895); capt.yd., Navy Yard, Portsmouth, NH (Oct 1895–Mar 1898); w.o. (Mar 1898–Mar 1899); retired (28 Mar 1899).

HENRY BELLOWS ROBESON
1842–1914

CHRISTOPHER RAYMOND PERRY RODGERS Born in Brooklyn, NY, on 14 Nov 1819, son of navy Commo George Washington (1787–1832) and Ann Maria (Perry) Rodgers. Maternal uncles included Oliver Hazard and Matthew C. Perry. Two brothers: Alexander Rodgers, who was killed during the attack on Chapultepec in 1847, and Cdr George W. Rodgers, who died commanding monitor *Catskill* during bombardment of Charleston in Aug 1863. Married Jane Slidell on 7 Jul 1845. Five children, two of whom rose

CHRISTOPHER RAYMOND PERRY
RODGERS
1819–1892

to flag rank in the navy, Raymond Perry Rodgers (1849–1925) and Thomas Slidell Rodgers (1858–1931). Died in Washington, DC, on 8 Jan 1892. Buried in USNA Cemetery.

Ranks Midn (5 Oct 1833); PMidn (8 Jul 1839); Lt (4 Sep 1844); Cdr (15 Nov 1861); Capt (25 Jul 1866); Commo (28 Aug 1870); RAdm (14 Jun 1874); placed on Ret.Lst. (14 Nov 1881).

Career Summary Received appointment from CT (5 Oct 1833); w.o. (Oct–Dec 1833); Naval School, NY (Dec 1833–Feb 1834); *Brandywine* and *Vincennes*, Pac.Sta. (Feb 1834–Jun 1836); l.o.a. and w.o. (Jun–Dec 1836); Navy Yard, NY (Dec 1836–Feb 1837); *Fairfield* and *Dolphin*, Braz.Sqdn. (Mar 1837–Apr 1839); Naval School, NY (Apr–Jul 1839); l.o.a. (Jul–Oct 1839); *Flirt, Wave*, and cdr, *Phoenix*, "Mosquito Flt." (Oct 1839–Oct 1842); l.o.a. (Oct–Dec 1842); *Saratoga*, Afr.Sqdn. (Dec 1842–May 1843); w.o. (May–Aug 1843); *Cumberland* and *Lexington*, Med.Sqdn. (Sep 1843–May 1845); l.o.a. (May–Nov 1845); cst.surv. duty (Nov 1845–Dec 1846); *Potomac* and *Albany*, Home Sqdn. (Jan–Aug 1847); cst.surv. duty (Aug 1847–Mar 1850); w.o. (Mar–Apr 1850); *Congress*, Braz.Sqdn. (Apr 1850–Aug 1851); return, l.o.a., and w.o. (Aug 1851–Nov 1852); flag lt, Afr.Sqdn., *Constitution* (Nov 1852–Jun 1855); l.o.a. (Jun–Jul 1855); cst.surv. duty (Jul 1855–Apr 1858); *Wabash*, Med.Sqdn. (May 1858–Dec 1859); l.o.a. (Dec 1859–Oct 1860); comdt. of midn, USNA (Oct 1860–Sep 1861); cdr, flgs. *Wabash*, S.Atl.Blk.Sqdn. (Oct 1861–Jul 1863); return and Navy Dept., Washington, DC (Jul–Oct 1863); bd. duty, Washington, DC (Oct–Nov 1863); flt.capt, S.Atl.Blk.Sqdn., *Wabash* (Aug 1862–Jul 1863); cdr, *New Ironsides*, S.Atl.Blk.Sqdn. (Apr–Jul 1863); cdr, *Iroquois*, spec.serv. (Nov 1863–Oct 1865); w.o. (Oct–Dec 1865); Navy Yard, Norfolk, VA (Oct 1865–Dec 1868); cdr, *Franklin*, Med.Sqdn. (Dec 1868–Nov 1870); spec. duty, Europe (Dec 1870–Aug 1871); Navy Dept., Washington, DC (Sep–Oct 1871); chief, Bur. of Yards and Docks, Washington, DC (Oct 1871–Sep 1874); act.chief, Bur. of Equipment and Recruiting, Washington, DC (Oct 1873–Sep 1874); supt., USNA (Sep 1874–Jun 1878); cdr, Pac.Sta., *Pensacola* (Jul 1878–Oct 1880); w.o. (Oct–Dec 1880); spec. duty, Washington, DC (Dec 1880–Apr 1881); spec. duty, Navy Dept., Washington, DC (Apr–Jun 1881); supt., USNA (Jun–Nov 1881); placed on Ret.Lst. (14 Nov 1881).

Career Highlights Saw action in Seminole War from 1839 to 1842. In Mexican War, participated in the taking of Vera Cruz, Tobasco, and Tuspan. Comdt. of midn at USNA in years up to Civil War, playing important role in moving the Academy to temporary home of Newport, RI. During the Civil War, served as flt.capt to RAdm Samuel F. Du Pont's [q.v.] S.Atl.Blk.Sqdn. Was twice supt. of Naval Academy, instituting numerous changes to both curriculum and to disciplinary system. Also served as pres. of Naval Institute from 1875–78 and again from 1882–83. Was pres. of International Meridian Conference of 1884, which established the prime meridian and the universal day.

References

Personal Papers: a) Rodgers Family: 15,500 items (1788–1944) in NHF,LC. b) Rodgers Family Papers: 11,150 items (1740–1957) in LC. c) 1840–42 and 1861–66 in NYHS.

Writings: "Du Pont's Attack on Charleston" for *Battles and Leaders of the Civil War* (1887–88).

Additional Sources: Stephen D. Brown, "Christopher Raymond Perry Rodgers: Mentor of the New Navy" in *Naval History: The Sixth Naval History Symposium*, 1983, ed. Daniel Masterson (Wilmington, DE: 1986).

FREDERICK RODGERS Born in Havre de Grace, MD, on 3 Oct 1842, son of Col Robert Smith and Sarah (Perry) Rodgers. Paternal grandfather was Commo John Rodgers, USN (1772–1838). Uncle was RAdm John Rodgers, USN (1812–1882) [*q.v.*]. His mother was daughter of Commo Matthew C. Perry. Younger brother was RAdm John Augustus Rodgers, USN (1848–1933). Married Sarah M. Fall on 2 Feb 1882. One son. He made his home at St. James, Long Island, NY, where he died on 3 Nov 1917. Buried in Rock Creek Cemetery in Washington, DC.

Ranks Act.Midn (25 Sep 1857); Midn (1 Jun 1861); Lt (16 Jul 1862); LCdr (25 Jul 1866); Cdr (4 Feb 1875); Capt (28 Feb 1890); Commo (25 Dec 1898); RAdm (3 Mar 1899); placed on Ret.Lst. (3 Oct 1904).

Career Summary Received appointment from MD (25 Sep 1857); USNA (Sep 1857–Jun 1861); *Wabash*, then cdr, C. P. Knapp, Atl.Blk.Sqdn. (Jun–Aug 1861); *Santee*, prize brig *Delta*, and *Kineo*, Gulf Blk.Sqdn. (Aug 1861–Aug 1863); *Mendota*, N.Atl.Blk.Sqdn. (Sep 1863); *Grand Gulf*, N.Atl. and W.Gulf Blk.Sqdns. (Sep 1863–Nov 1865); w.o. (Nov 1865–Feb 1866); *Chattanooga*, Philadelphia (Feb–Aug 1866); *Sacramento*, spec.serv. (Sep 1866–Jun 1867); return home and w.o. (Jun 1867–Mar 1868); *Michigan*, on Great Lakes (Apr 1868–Jun 1869); *Pensacola*, *St. Mary's*, and *Saranac*, N.Pac.Sta. (Sep 1869–Jul 1872); w.o. (Aug–Oct 1872); ord. duty, Navy Yard, Washington, DC (Nov 1872–Nov 1873); cdr, *Despatch*, spec.serv. (Nov 1873–Oct 1876); insp., 11th L.h. Dist., Detroit, MI (Oct 1876–Mar 1877); cdr, *Adams*, S.Atl. and Pac. Stas. (Mar 1877–Aug 1879); w.o. (Aug 1879–Feb 1881); insp., 4th L.h. Dist., Philadelphia (Feb 1881–Sep 1883); cdr, rec. ship *Independence*, Mare Island, CA (Nov 1883–Apr 1887); w.o. (Apr–Nov 1887); insp., 3rd L.h. Dist., Tompkinsville, NY (Dec 1887–Sep 1890); cdr, flgs. *Philadelphia*, N.Atl.Sqdn. (Sep 1890–Jul 1892); supervisor, NY Harbor (Jul 1892–Oct 1893); capt.yd., Navy Yard, NY (Oct 1893–Jun 1896); cdr,

FREDERICK RODGERS
1842–1917

Massachusetts, spec.serv. (Jun 1896–Jun 1897); member, Naval Ret.Bd., Washington, DC (Jun–Sep 1897); member, Bd. of Inspection and Survey, Washington, DC (Sep–Dec 1897); pres., Bd. of Inspection and Survey, Washington, DC (Dec 1897–Jun 1898); cdr, *Puritan*, N.Atl.Flt. (Jun–Oct 1898); pres., Bd. of Inspection and Survey (Oct 1898–Feb 1901); cdr, Senior Sqdn., Asia.Flt., *New York* (Feb–Mar 1901); cdr, Asia.Flt., *New York* (Mar–Dec 1902); home and l.o.a. (Dec 1902–Mar 1903); comdt., Navy Yard, NY (Mar 1903–Oct 1904); placed on Ret.Lst. (3 Oct 1904); spec. bd. duties (Oct 1904–Jan 1907).

Career Highlights Saw action during Civil War on Mississippi River at Donaldsonville, Port Hudson, and College Point. Was also on board ill-fated *Sacramento* when she sank in Bay of Bengal on 19 Jun 1867.

References

Personal Papers: a) Rodgers Family: 15,500 items (1788–1944) in NHF,LC. b) Rodgers Family: 11,150 items (1740–1957) in LC.

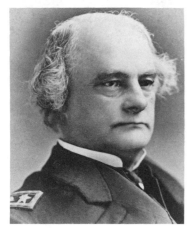

JOHN RODGERS
1812–1882

JOHN RODGERS Born in Sion Hall [Havre de Grace], MD, on 8 Aug 1812, son of navy Commo John (1772–1838) and Minerva (Denison) Rodgers. Early education in Washington, where his father was serving. Took l.o.a. in 1834 to attend University of VA. Married Ann Hodge on 27 Nov 1857. Two daughters and one son, VAdm William Ledyard Rodgers, USN (1860–1944). Brother was Col Robert Smith Rodgers, father of RAdm Frederick Rodgers, USN (1842–1917) [*q.v.*], and RAdm John Augustus Rodgers, USN (1848–1933). Died in Washington, DC, on 5 May 1882. Buried at Oak Hill Cemetery in Washington, DC.

Ranks Midn (18 Apr 1828); PMidn (14 Jun 1834); Lt (28 Jan 1840); Cdr (14 Sep 1855); Capt (16 Jul 1862); Commo (17 Jun 1863); RAdm (31 Dec 1869); died (5 May 1882).

Career Summary Received appointment from Washington, DC (18 Apr 1828); *Constellation* and *Concord*, Med.Sqdn. (Jun 1829–Dec 1832); l.o.a. (Dec 1832–Mar 1833); Navy School, Norfolk, VA (Mar–Dec 1833); l.o.a. (Dec 1833–Mar 1836); cst.surv. duty (Mar–Sep 1836); act.mstr, *Dolphin*, Braz.Sqdn. (Sep 1836–May 1839); l.o.a. (May–Nov 1839); cdr, *Wave*, and *Jefferson*, "Mosquito Flt." (Nov 1839–Jul 1842); l.o.a. (Jul–Nov 1842); cdr, *Boxer*, Home Sqdn. (Nov 1842–Jan 1844); l.o.a. (Jan–May 1844); spec.serv., Pittsburgh, PA (May 1844–Jan 1846); w.o. (Jan–Apr 1846); *United States* and *Marion*, Afr. and Med.Sqdns. (Apr 1846–Feb 1849); l.o.a. (Feb–Apr 1849); cst.surv. duty (Apr 1849–Oct 1852); cdr, *John Hancock*, Surveying and Expl.Expd., N.Pac. Ocean (Oct 1852–Jul 1854); cdr, Surveying and Exploring Expedition, N.Pac. Ocean, *Vincennes* (Jul 1854–Jul 1856); l.o.a. (Jul–Aug 1856); spec. duty, preparation of report on expd., Washington, DC (Aug 1856–May 1858); cdr, *Water Witch*, Navy Yard, Washington, DC (May–Jul 1858); spec. duty, Washington, DC (Jul 1858–Apr 1859); member, Bd. of Naval Examiners (Apr 1859–Apr 1861); spec. duty, NY and Washington, DC (Apr–May 1861); prisoner of war, then paroled (Apr 1861); spec. duty, supervisor of construction of ironclad gunboats, Cincinnati (May–Sep 1861); spec. duty, Navy Dept., Washington, DC (Sep–Oct 1861); cdr, *Flag*, S.Atl.Blk.Sqdn. (Oct 1861–Apr 1862); cdr, *Galena*, N.Atl.Blk.Sqdn. (Apr–Nov 1862); cdr, *Weehawken*, S.Atl.Blk.Sqdn. (Nov 1862–Jun 1863); cdr, *Canonicus*, Boston (Jul–Sep 1863); sick lv. and w.o. (Sep–Nov 1863); cdr, *Dictator*, spec.serv. (Nov 1863–May 1864); member, Bd. of Visitors, USNA (May–Sep 1864); cdr, *Vanderbilt*, spec.serv. (Sep 1864–Sep 1865); cdr, Spec.Sqdn., *Vanderbilt* (Sep 1865–Jun 1866); cdr, *Monadnock*, Navy Yard, Mare Island, CA (Jun 1866–Jun 1867); comdt., Navy Yard, Boston (Jul 1867–Dec 1869); cdr, Asia.Flt., *Colorado* (Feb 1870–May 1872); return and w.o. (May–Jul 1872); pres., Naval Exam. and Ret. Bds. (Jul 1872–Jun 1873); comdt., Navy Yard, Mare Island, CA (Jun 1873–Apr 1877); supt., Naval Observatory, Washington, DC (May 1877–May 1882); chairman, L.h. Bd., Washington, DC (May 1878–May 1882); pres., Naval Advisory Bd., Washington, DC (Jul–Nov 1881); died (5 May 1882).

Career Highlights Second-in-command of Expl.Expd. of N.Pac., assuming command when Cdr Cadwalader Ringgold [*q.v.*] became ill in 1854. Participated in unsuccessful attempt to destroy dry dock at Norfolk, VA, in Apr 1861, captured in process, although paroled shortly thereafter. Aide to RAdm Samuel F. Du Pont [*q.v.*] at taking of Port Royal, SC. Commanded an ironclad in May 1862 on unsuccessful gunboat expedition, stopped at Drewry's Bluff on way up James River to Richmond. In Jun 1863 while commanding ironclad *Weehawken*, forced larger Confederate ironclad *Atlanta* to surrender, for which he was given thanks of Congress and promoted to Commo. Served as pres. of Naval Institute, and as pres. of first Naval Advisory Bd. in 1881.

References

Personal Papers: a) Rodgers Family: 15,500 items (1788–1944) in NHF,LC. b) Rodgers Family: 11,150 items (1740–1957) in LC. c) 1 folder (1851–55) in NHF,WNY. d) 763 items; 168 vols in Historical Society of PA, Philadelphia, PA.

Additional Sources: a) Wilhelm Heine, *Die Expedition in die Seen von China, Japan und Ochotsk unter commande von Commodore Colin Ringgold und Commodore John Rodgers . . . 1853 bis 1856 . . .* (Leipzig: 1858–59). b) J. Russell Soley, "Rear-Admiral John Rodgers, President of the Naval Institute, 1879–82," U.S. Naval Institute *Proceedings* 20 (1882): 251–65. c) Asaph Hall, *Biographical Memoir of John Rodgers, 1812–1882* (Washington, DC: 1906). d) Allan B. Cole, ed. *Yankee Surveyors in the Shogun's Seas: Records of the U.S. Surveying Expedition* *to the North Pacific Ocean, 1853–56* (Princeton: 1947). e) Robert Erwin Johnson, *Rear Admiral John Rodgers, 1812–82* (Annapolis: 1967).

FRANCIS ASBURY ROE
1823–1901

FRANCIS ASBURY ROE Born on 4 Oct 1823 in Elmira, NY, son of Isaac and Hanna (Drake) Roe. Early education at Elmira Academy. Married Eliza J. Snyder in Sep 1849. Died on 28 Dec 1901 in Washington, DC.

Ranks Act.Midn (19 Oct 1841); Midn (3 Feb 1842); PMidn (10 Aug 1847); dismissed (23 Oct 1849); reappointed to previous rank (27 Sep 1850); Mstr (8 Aug 1855); Lt (14 Sep 1855); LCdr (6 Aug 1862); Cdr (25 Jul 1866); Capt (1 Apr 1872); RAdm (3 Nov 1884); placed on Ret.Lst. (4 Oct 1885).

Career Summary Received appointment from NY (19 Oct 1841); rec. ship *North Carolina*, NY (Oct 1841–Feb 1842); *John Adams*, Braz. and Afr. Sqdns. (Feb 1842–May 1844); *Yorktown*, Afr.Sqdn. (Sep 1844–Jun 1846); l.o.a. (Jun–Oct 1846); *Boston*, Home Sqdn. (Oct 1846–Feb 1847); *Allegheny*, Pittsburgh, PA (Feb–Oct 1847); USNA (Oct 1847–Jul 1848); l.o.a. (Jul–Sep 1848); *Albany*, W.Ind.Sqdn. (Sep 1848–Aug 1849); dismissed from service (23 Oct 1849); reappointed (27 Sep 1850); mail steamer *Georgia* (Oct 1850–Nov 1852); *Porpoise*, N.Pac.Expl.Expd. (Dec 1852–Aug 1854); exec.off., then cdr, *Vincennes*, N.Pac.Expl.Expd. (Aug 1854–Nov 1855); home and w.o. (Nov 1855–Feb 1856); cst.surv. duty (Feb 1856–Apr 1858); *Macedonian*, Med.Sqdn. (Apr 1858–Jul 1860); asst.insp. of ord., Navy Yard, NY (Sep 1860–Jul 1861); exec.off., *Pensacola*, W.Gulf Blk.Sqdn. (Aug 1861–Aug 1862); cdr, *Katahdin*, W.Gulf Blk.Sqdn. (Aug 1862–Feb 1863); home and l.o.a. (Feb–Aug 1863); cdr, *Neptune*, Navy Yard, NY (Sep 1863); cdr, *Sassacus*, N.Atl.Blk.Sqdn. (Sep 1863–Jul 1864); sick lv. (Jul–Nov 1864); cdr, *Michigan*, on Great Lakes (Nov 1864–Apr 1866); w.o. (Apr–Jun 1866); exec.off., then cdr, *Madawaska* (Jul 1866–Jan 1867); cdr, *Tacony*, and cdr, Mexican Gulf Division, N.Atl.Sta. (Jan–Aug 1867); flt.capt, Asia.Flt., *Delaware* (Aug 1867–Nov 1870); w.o. (Nov 1870–Mar 1872); w.o. (Mar–Aug 1872); cdr, Naval Rndv., San Francisco (Aug 1872–Mar 1873); w.o. (Mar–Jun 1873); exec.off., then capt.yd., Navy Yard, Boston (Jun 1873–Feb 1874); cdr, flgs. *Lancaster*, S.Atl.Sta. (Feb 1874–Jul 1875); Naval Sta., New London, CT (Aug 1875–Jul 1876); furlough (Jul 1876–Mar 1879); Bd. of Examiners, USNA (Mar–Apr 1879); pres., spec. Revisory Bd., Navy Dept., Washington, DC (Nov 1879–Jul 1882); w.o. (Jul 1882–Jul 1883); pres., Bd. of Examiners, Torp.Sta., Newport, RI (Jul–Aug 1883); gov., Naval Asylum, Philadelphia (Oct 1883–Oct 1885); placed on Ret.Lst. (4 Oct 1885).

Career Highlights Participated in 5 May 1864 action against Confederate ram *Albemarle*: commended by secretary of navy and advanced five numbers for his action. During Mexican revolution which ousted Prince Maximilian in 1867, witnessed last evacuation of French troops and escorted Generalissimo Santa Anna as a prisoner to Mexico. Acted as negotiator between various factions and the new revolutionary government at Vera Cruz and assisted in preserving order, efforts which warranted thanks and a congratulatory note from Pres. Andrew Johnson.

References

Personal Papers: a) 500 items (1842–1901) in NHF,LC. b) 1 item (n.d.) in Porter Collection in USMA.

Writings: a) *Naval Duties and Discipline, with the Policy and Principles of Naval Organization* (1865). b) "An American Sea Captain of Colonial Times, by Rear-Admiral Francis Asbury Roe" (Historical Papers of the Society of Colonial Wars of District of Columbia, no. 2, 1900).

Additional Sources: Marcus Benjamin, "Francis Asbury Roe" (Memorial Papers of the Society of Colonial Wars in District of Columbia, no. 4, 1903).

STEPHEN CLEGG ROWAN Born near Dublin, Ireland, on 25 Dec 1808, son of John Rowan. Emigrated to U.S. about 1818, settling in Piqua, OH. Married Mary Stark. At least one child. Died at his residence in Washington, DC, on 31 Mar 1890. Buried in Oak Hill Cemetery in Washington, DC.

Ranks Midn (1 Feb 1826); PMidn (28 Apr 1832); Lt (8 Mar 1837); Cdr (14 Sep 1855); Capt (16 Jul 1862); Commo (16 Jul 1862); RAdm (25 Jul 1866); VAdm (15 Aug 1870); transferred to Ret.Lst. (26 Feb 1889).

Career Summary Received appointment from OH (1 Feb 1826); *Delaware*, in ordinary, Norfolk, VA (Jun–Aug 1826); *Vincennes*, Pac.Sqdn. (Aug 1826–Jun 1830); on furlough (Aug 1830–Apr 1832); rec. ship *Hudson*, NY (Jul–Oct 1832); *St. Louis*, *Vandalia*, *Shark*, then *Vandalia*, W.Ind.Sqdn. (Oct 1832–May 1836); l.o.a. (May–Nov 1836); *Relief*, U.S.Expl.Expd. (Nov 1836–Dec 1837); l.o.a. (Dec 1837–Apr 1838); cst.surv. duty (Apr 1838–Mar 1841); *Delaware*, Braz. and Med. Sqdns. (Mar 1841–Mar 1844); l.o.a. (Mar–May 1844); rec. ship *Ontario*, Baltimore (May 1844–Jun 1845); *Cyane*, Pac.Sqdn. (Jun 1845–Oct 1848); l.o.a. (Oct 1848–Feb 1849); ord. duty, Navy Yard, NY (Feb 1849–Dec 1852); l.o.a. (Dec 1852–Feb 1853); cdr, *Relief*, Braz.Sqdn. (Feb 1853–Nov 1855); cdr, rec. ship *North Carolina*, NY (Dec 1855–May 1857); asst.insp. of ord., Navy Yard, NY (May 1857–Feb 1860); l.o.a. (Feb 1860–Jan 1861); cdr, *Pawnee*, spec.serv. (Jan–Oct 1861); cdr, *Brooklyn*, Philadelphia (Oct–Dec 1861); cdr, *Pawnee*, N.Atl.Blk.Sqdn. (Dec 1861–Jul 1862); cdr, *Powhatan*, W.Indies (Jul–Sep 1862); w.o. (Sep–Nov 1862); cdr, flgs. *New Ironsides*, S.Atl.Blk.Sqdn. (Nov 1862–Aug 1864); cdr, naval forces, NC Sounds, *Ironsides* (Sep 1864); w.o. (Sep 1864–Jun 1866); cdr, *Madawaska*, Navy Yard, NY (Jun–Aug 1866); cdr, Navy Yard, Norfolk, VA (Aug 1866–Aug 1867); cdr, Asia.Sqdn., *Piscata-*

STEPHEN CLEGG ROWAN
1808–1890

qua [renamed *Delaware*] (Aug 1867–Nov 1870); w.o. (Nov 1870–Feb 1871); spec. duty, Washington, DC (Feb–May 1871, Dec 1871–Jan 1872); pres., Bd. of Visitors, USNA (May–Oct 1871); cdr, spec. sqdn. to receive Russian sqdn. (Oct–Dec 1871); pres., spec. bd. to examine educational system at USNA (Jan–May 1872); comdt., Navy Yard and Naval Sta., NY (May 1872–Sep 1876); port adm, NY (May 1872–Oct 1876); member, spec. Bd. on Navy Yards (Oct–Dec 1876); port adm, NY (Dec 1876–Oct 1877); pres., Bd. of Examiners (Oct 1877–May 1880); temp. duty, member, Bd. of Visitors, USNA (May 1880–Sep 1881); spec. duty, Naval Guard of Honor (Sep 1881); gov., Naval Asylum, Philadelphia (Sep 1881–Jun 1882); supt., Naval Observatory, Washington, DC (Jun 1882–May 1883); chairman, L.h. Bd., Washington, DC (May 1883–Apr 1889); transferred to Ret.Lst. (26 Apr 1889).

Career Highlights During the Mexican War, participated in capture of Monterey. In Jul 1846, commanded landing party which took San Diego. Commanded naval battalion under Commo Robert F. Stockton and Gen Stephen W. Kearny in actions at Mesa and San Gabriel in upper CA in Jan 1847. Commanded landing party at successful attack near Mazatlan in Nov 1847 and in following Feb participated in bombardment of Guaymas. As commander of *Pawnee* in early 1861, he commanded only naval protection of the capital during Pres. Lincoln's inauguration and immediately after outbreak of war. Failing to relieve Ft. Sumter, attacked Confederate batteries at Aquia Creek on 25 May and thus fired first shots of war from a naval vessel. Was part of squadron attack on Fts. Hatteras and Clark, NC, in late Aug 1861. In Feb 1862, participated in joint army-navy operations at Roanoke Island, commanding navy gunboat and army squadrons that captured several key places in Albemarle and Pamlico Sounds. His efforts were rewarded by promotion to capt and to commo on the same day and, by nomination of the pres., the thanks of Congress. Then served under RAdm John Dahlgren [*q.v.*] and, during the latter's absence, as temp. cdr of S.Atl.Blk.Sqdn.

References

Personal Papers: a) 4 items (1826–90) in NHF,LC. b) Papers of Stephen C. Rowan: 1 microfilm reel (17 Aug 1826–26 Mar 1890) in National Archives, Washington, DC.

JOHN HENRY RUSSELL Born in Frederick, MD, on 4 Jul 1827, son of Robert Grier and Susan Hood (Worthington) Russell. Married Cornelia Pierpont Treadway in 1864. Three children. Lived in Washington, DC, where he died on 1 Apr 1897.

Ranks Midn (10 Sep 1841); PMidn (10 Aug 1847); Mstr (14 Sep 1855); Lt (15 Sep 1855); LCdr (16 Jul 1862); Cdr (25 Jul 1866); Capt (12 Feb 1874); Commo (30 Oct 1883); RAdm (4 Mar 1886); placed on Ret.Lst. (27 Aug 1886).

JOHN HENRY RUSSELL
1827–1897

Career Summary Received appointment from MD (10 Sep 1841); *Cyane* and *United States*, Pac.Sqdn. (Sep 1841–Oct 1844); l.o.a. (Oct 1844); *St. Mary's*, Gulf of Mexico (Oct 1844–Nov 1846); Naval School, Annapolis, MD (Nov 1846–Jan 1847); rec. ship *Pennsylvania*, Norfolk, VA (Jan–Feb 1847); *Allegheny*, spec.serv. (Feb–Oct 1847); Naval School, Annapolis, MD (Oct 1847–Jul 1848); l.o.a. (Jul–Sep 1848); *Relief* and *Perry*, Braz.Sqdn. (Sep 1848–Jul 1849); cst.surv. duty (Jul 1849–Jan 1850); mail steamer *Georgia*, NY and W.Ind. Line (Jan 1850–Dec 1852); *Vincennes*, N.Pac.Expl.Expd. (Dec 1852–Mar 1853); *Fenimore Cooper*, Navy Yard, NY (Mar–May 1853); *John P. Kennedy*, N.Pac.Expl.Expd. (May 1853–Jul 1856); l.o.a. (Jul–Aug 1856); ord. duty, Navy Yard, Washington, DC (Sep 1856–Apr 1858); *Wabash*, Med.Sqdn. (May 1858–Dec 1859); l.o.a. (Dec 1859–Jan 1860); ord.duty, Navy Yard, Washington, DC (Jan 1860–Apr 1861); spec. duty (Apr–May 1861); *Colorado*, Gulf Blk.Sqdn. (Jun–Oct 1861); report and w.o. (Oct–Dec 1861); cdr, *Kennebec*, W.Gulf Blk.Sqdn. (Jan 1862–Nov 1863); return and w.o. (Nov–Dec 1863); temp.ord.duty, Navy Yard, Washington, DC (Dec 1863–Apr 1864); l.o.a. and w.o. (Apr–Jun 1864); cdr, *Pontiac*, S.Atl.Blk.Sqdn. (Jun–Sep 1864); sick lv. (Sep–Nov 1864); cdr, *Cyane*, Pac.Sqdn. (Nov 1864–May 1865); return, sick lv., and w.o. (May–Dec 1865); ord.duty, Navy Yard, Norfolk, VA (Dec 1865–May 1866); Navy Yard, Mare Island, CA (Oct 1866–Jan 1870); cdr, *Ossipee*, Pac.Sqdn. (Jan 1870–Mar 1871); Navy Yard, Mare Island, CA (Apr 1871–Apr 1874); w.o. (Apr–Sep 1874); cdr, *Plymouth*, N.Atl.Sqdn. (Oct 1874–Oct 1875); w.o. (Oct–Dec 1875); spec. duty, Washington, DC (Dec 1875–Aug 1876); cdr, *Powhatan*, spec. duty (Aug 1876–Mar 1877); w.o. (Mar–Jun 1877); spec. duty (Jun 1877–Feb 1879); in charge, Nav. Dept., Navy Yard, Washington, DC (Feb 1879–Feb 1882); temp. capt.yd., Navy Yard, Washington, DC (Jul–Sep 1880); w.o. (Feb–Mar 1882); spec. duty, Washington, DC (Mar–Apr 1882); Hydrographic Office, Washington, DC (Apr 1882–Jul 1883); w.o. (Jul–Oct 1883); comdt., Navy Yard, Mare Island, CA (Nov 1883–May 1886); w.o. (May–Aug 1886); placed on Ret.Lst. (27 Aug 1886).

Career Highlights During the Mexican War, took part in securing Texas ports of Galveston, Corpus Christi, and Ft. Taylor on the Brazos River. Participated in blockade and capture of Vera Cruz. In the Civil War, tried to prevent vessels at the Norfolk Navy Yard from falling into Confederate hands: the last to leave the yard on 21 Apr 1861. On 14 Sep 1861, commanded successful boat operation at Pensacola, FL, to cut out and regain *Colorado*: wounded but received high praise from pres. and Navy Dept.

WILLIAM THOMAS SAMPSON Born in Palmyra, NY, on 9 Feb 1840, son of James and Hannah (Walker) Sampson. Married twice. His first wife was Margaret Sexton Aldrich,

WILLIAM THOMAS SAMPSON
1840–1902

whom he married in 1863. Second wife was Elizabeth Susan Burling, whom he married in 1882. Four daughters and two sons. Awarded LL.D. from Harvard University in 1899. Died on 6 May 1902 at his home in Washington, DC.

Ranks Act.Midn (24 Sep 1857); Midn (1 Jun 1861); Act.Mstr (13 May 1862); Lt (16 Jul 1862); LCdr (25 Jul 1866); Cdr (9 Aug 1874); Capt (26 Mar 1889); Act.RAdm (21 Apr 1898); Commo (3 Jul 1898); RAdm (3 Mar 1899); placed on Ret.Lst. (9 Feb 1902).

Career Summary Received appointment from NY (24 Sep 1857); USNA (Sep 1857–Apr 1861); Navy Yard, Washington, DC (Apr–May 1861); *Pocahontas*, Navy Yard, Washington, DC (May 1861); *Potomac* and *Water Witch*, Gulf Blk.Sqdn. (Jun 1861–Apr 1862); w.o. (Apr–May 1862); inst., USNA, and duties with training ship *John Adams* (May 1862–Jun 1864); exec.off., *Patapsco*, S.Atl.Blk.Sqdn. (Jun 1864–Feb 1865); return and report (Feb–Apr 1865); watch off., *Colorado*, Eur.Sqdn. (Apr 1865–Aug 1867); w.o. (Aug–Sep 1867); head, Dept. of Physics and Chemistry, USNA (Oct 1867–May 1871); exec.off., *Congress*, Eur.Sta. (Jun 1871–Mar 1874); *Wabash*, Navy Yard, Boston (Mar–Apr 1874); w.o. (Apr–May 1874); head, Physics Dept., USNA (May 1874–Dec 1878); temp. duty, cdr, *Alert*, Chester, PA (Mar–Aug 1875); temp. duty, cdr, training ship *Mayflower* (Jun–Sep 1877); w.o. (Jan–Sep 1879); Bur. of Nav., Washington, DC (Sep–Dec 1879); cdr, *Swatara*, Asia.Sqdn. (Dec 1879–Oct 1881); home and w.o. (Oct 1881–Jun 1882); asst.supt., and briefly act.supt., U.S. Observatory, Washington, DC (Jun 1882–Sep 1884); insp. of ord. and cdr, Naval Torp.Sta., Newport, RI (Oct 1884–Jul 1886); supt., USNA (Sep 1886–Jun 1890); cdr, *San Francisco*, San Francisco, and S.Pac.Sqdn. (Oct 1890–Jun 1892); supt., Gun Foundry, Washington, DC (Jul 1892–Jan 1893); chief, Bur. of Ord., Washington, DC (Jan 1893–May 1897); cdr, *Iowa*, N.Atl.Sqdn. (Jun 1897–Feb 1898); pres., Bd. of Inquiry, *Maine* (Feb–Mar 1898); cdr, N.Atl.Sta., *New York* (Mar–Aug 1898); cdr, N.Atl.Sta., *Resolute* (Sep 1898–Oct 1899); commissioner to Cuba (Sep–Dec 1898); comdt., Navy Yard and Naval Sta., Boston (Oct 1899–Oct 1901); w.o. (Oct 1901–Feb 1902); placed on Ret.Lst. (9 Feb 1902).

Career Highlights Graduated top of his class in 1861. Served several tours at USNA, including supt. Member of International Prime Meridian and Time Conference in 1884 and U.S. delegate to International Maritime Conference in 1887. While commander of Naval Torp.Sta. at Newport, RI, played important part in creation of NWC. Commander of N.Atl.Sta. during war with Spain, receiving much credit for Battle of Santiago. After war, served as one of three U.S. commissioners.

References

Writings: a) "The Navy and Its Prospects of Rehabilitation," U.S. Naval Institute *Proceedings* 36 (1886): 1–39. b)

"Outline of a Scheme for the Naval Defense of the Coast," U.S. Naval Institute *Proceedings* 49 (1889): 169–232. c) "Face Hardened Armor," U.S. Naval Institute *Proceedings* 72 (1894): 818–21. d) "Nauticus," pseudonym, *The Truth about the Schley Case* (Washington, DC: c.1900).

Selected Additional Sources: a) Sir William Athelstane Meredith, *With Sampson Through the War* (New York, 1899). b) James B. Parker, *Rear Admirals Schley, Sampson and Cervera* (NY, 1910). c) Louis J. Gulliver, "Sampson and Shafter at Santiago," U.S. Naval Institute *Proceedings* 436 (Jun 1939): 799–806. d) Richard Sedgewick Parker, *Admirals of the American Empire* (Indianapolis, 1948).

BENJAMIN FRANKLIN SANDS Born in Baltimore, MD, on 11 Feb 1812, son of Benjamin and Rebecca (Hooks) Sands. Raised in Louisville, KY. Married Henrietta Maria French. Eight children, one of whom was RAdm James Hoban Sands, USN (1845–1911). Died in Washington, DC, on 30 Jun 1883. Buried in Mt. Olive Cemetery in Washington, DC.

Ranks Midn (1 Apr 1828); PMidn (14 Jun 1834); Lt (16 Mar 1840); Cdr (14 Sep 1855); Capt (16 Jul 1862); Commo (25 Jul 1866); RAdm (27 Apr 1871); placed on Ret.Lst. (11 Feb 1874).

Career Summary Received appointment from KY (1 Apr 1828); Naval School, NY (May–Oct 1828); *Vandalia*, Braz.Sqdn. (Oct 1828–Dec 1831); l.o.a. (Dec 1831–Aug 1832); *St. Louis*, W.Ind.Sqdn. (Aug 1832–Jul 1833); l.o.a. (Jul–Oct 1833); Navy Yard, Norfolk, VA (Oct 1833–Jul 1834); l.o.a. (Jul 1834–Mar 1835); cst.surv. duty (Nov 1835–Aug 1842); *Columbus*, Med.Sqdn. (Aug 1842–May 1844); l.o.a. (May–Jun 1844); spec. duty, Depot of Charts and Instruments, Naval Observatory, Washington, DC (Jun 1844–Dec 1846); *Washington*, Home Sqdn. (Dec 1846–Sep 1847); l.o.a. (Sep–Dec 1847); cdr, *Porpoise*, Afr.Sqdn. (Dec 1847–Apr 1850); l.o.a. (Apr–May 1850); cst.surv. duty (May 1850–Sep 1858); Bur. of Construction, Equip., and Repair, Washington, DC (Sep 1858–Dec 1860); w.o. (Dec 1860–Mar 1861); spec. duty (Mar–Apr 1861); Bur. of Ord., Washington, DC (Apr–May 1861); cst.surv. duty (May 1861–Oct 1862); cdr, *Dakotah*, N.Atl.Blk.Sqdn. (Nov 1862–Jun 1863); temp. cdr, *Roanoke*, N.Atl.Blk.Sqdn. (Jun–Jul 1863); cdr, *Dakotah*, Baltimore (Jul–Oct 1863); cdr, *Fort Jackson*, N.Atl.Blk.Sqdn. (Oct 1863–Jul 1865); cdr, 2nd Division, W.Gulf Blk.Sqdn., *Fort Jackson* (Feb–Jun 1865); Navy Yard, Boston (Aug 1865–Dec 1866); w.o. (Dec 1866–May 1867); supt., Naval Observatory, Washington, DC (May 1867–Feb 1874); placed on Ret.Lst. (11 Feb 1874).

References
Personal Papers: those in NYHS.
Writings: *From Reefer to rear-Admiral; Reminiscences and*

BENJAMIN FRANKLIN SANDS
1812–1883

Journal Jottings of Nearly Half a Century of Naval Life, 1827–1874 (NY: 1899).

JOSHUA RATOON SANDS Born in Brooklyn, NY, on 13 May 1795, son of Joshua and Ann (Ayscough) Sands. Married three times: Mary Stevens, Henrietta Stevens, and Ellen Ann Crook. Four children. Died in Baltimore, MD, on 2 Oct 1883. Buried in Greenwood Cemetery in Brooklyn.

Ranks Act.Midn (18 Jun 1812); Lt (1 Apr 1818); Cdr (23 Feb 1840); Capt (25 Feb 1854); placed on Ret.Lst. (21 Dec 1861); Commo on Ret.Lst. (16 Jul 1862); RAdm on Ret.Lst. (26 Jul 1866).

Career Summary Received appointment from NY (18 Jun 1812); *Madison, Pike, Superior,* and shore battery duty, Lake Ontario (Sep 1812–Jun 1815); *Washington,* Med.Sqdn. (Jun 1815–1818); *Hornet,* Afr. and W.Ind. Sqdns. (1819–1821); *Franklin,* Pac.Sqdn. (Feb 1821–Jul 1825); court-martial duty, Washington, DC (Jul 1825–?); suspended (7 Jul 1827–Oct 1828); *Vandalia,* Braz.Sqdn. (Oct 1828–1830); w.o. (1830–Apr 1834); Naval Rndv., NY (Apr 1834–Nov 1839); w.o. (Nov 1839–May 1841); Navy Yard, NY (May 1841–Aug 1843); cdr, *Falmouth,* W.Ind.Sqdn. (Aug 1843–Jan 1846); l.o.a. (Jan–Jun 1846); cdr, *Vixen,* Home Sqdn. (Jun 1846–Jun 1847); report and w.o. (Jun 1847–Mar 1848); cdr, rec. ship *North Carolina,* NY (Mar 1848–Feb 1850); w.o. (Feb 1850–Jan 1851); cdr, *St. Lawrence,* spec. duty (Jan–Aug 1851); l.o.a. and w.o. (Aug 1851–Nov 1852); cdr, *Allegheny,* Navy Yard, Washington, DC (Nov 1852–Apr 1853); w.o. (Apr 1853–May 1855); member, Bd. of Naval Examiners (May 1855–Mar 1856); cdr, *Susquehanna,* Med.Sqdn. (Apr 1856–Apr 1858); w.o. (Apr 1858–Jun 1859); cdr, Braz.Sqdn., *Congress* (Jun 1859–Aug 1861); l.o.a. and w.o. (Aug 1861–Jul 1862); placed on Ret.Lst. (21 Dec 1861); insp., 10th L.h. Dist., Buffalo, NY (Jul 1862–Aug 1866); port adm, Norfolk, VA (Mar 1869–Oct 1872).

Career Summary Spent the entire War of 1812 on Lake Ontario, participating in the capture of York (Toronto) and acting as a despatcher from Commo Isaac Chauncey to the various vessels of the sqdn. Frequently in trouble over duelling. Participated in capture of Alvarado, Tobasco, Lagona, Vera Cruz, Tampico, and Tuspan during the Mexican War: despatched back to the U.S. with the flags, trophies, and cannon taken from the castles around Vera Cruz.

References
Personal Papers: various items (1830–79) in USNAM.
Additional Sources: Charles O. Paullin, "Duelling in the Old Navy," U.S. Naval Institute *Proceedings* 132 (1909): 1189–90.

JAMES FINDLAY SCHENCK Born in Franklin, OH, on 11 Jun 1807, son of Gen (USA) William Cortenus and Elizabeth (Rogers) Schenck. Attended U.S. Military Academy

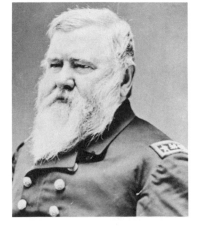

JAMES FINDLAY SCHENCK
1807–1882

from Jul 1822 to 1824 when he resigned. Married Dorothea Ann Smith on 27 Jul 1829. Four children. Died in Dayton, OH, on 21 Dec 1882.

Ranks Midn (1 Jul 1825); PMidn (4 Jun 1831); Lt (22 Dec 1835); Cdr (14 Sep 1855); Commo (2 Jan 1863); RAdm (21 Sep 1868); placed on Ret.Lst. (11 Jun 1869).

Career Summary Received appointment from OH (1 Jul 1825); *Hornet* and *Surprise*, W.Ind.Sqdn. (Aug 1825–Dec 1828); l.o.a. (Dec 1828–Dec 1829); *Brandywine*, Med.Sqdn. (Dec 1829–Jul 1830); l.o.a. (Jul 1830–Mar 1831); w.o. (Mar–Jun 1831); Navy Yard, Norfolk, VA (Jun–Sep 1831); l.o.a. and w.o. (Sep 1831–Apr 1832); *United States*, Navy Yard, NY and Med.Sqdn. (Apr 1832–Feb 1834); l.o.a. and w.o. (Feb 1834–May 1836); *Boston*, W.Ind.Sqdn. (Jun 1836–Apr 1838); l.o.a. and w.o. (Apr 1838–Aug 1839); *Dolphin*, Braz.Sqdn (Aug 1839–Jul 1840); l.o.a. and w.o. (Jul 1840–Nov 1841); rec. ship *Ontario*, NY (Nov 1841–Jan 1842); *Independence*, Home Sqdn. (Jan 1842–Dec 1843); *Preble*, Navy Yard, Portsmouth, NH (Dec 1843–Jul 1844); l.o.a. and w.o. (Jul 1844–Aug 1845); *Congress*, Pac. and E.Ind. Sqdns. (Aug 1845–Dec 1847); return and l.o.a. (Dec 1847–May 1849); cdr, mail steamer *Ohio* (May 1849–Dec 1852); l.o.a. (Dec 1852–Apr 1857); cdr, rec. ship *North Carolina*, NY (Apr 1857–Jun 1858); w.o. (Jun 1858–Jul 1859); cdr, *Saginaw*, E.Ind.Sqdn. (Aug 1859–Feb 1862); w.o. (Feb–Apr 1862); cdr, *St. Lawrence*, W.Gulf Blk.Sqdn. (May 1862–Apr 1863); return and w.o. (Apr 1863–Oct 1864); cdr, *Powhatan*, N.Atl.Blk.Sqdn. (Oct 1864–May 1865); cdr, 3rd Division, N.Atl.Blk.Sqdn., *Powhatan* (Oct 1864–May 1865); w.o. (May–Nov 1865); cdr, Naval Sta., Mound City, IL (Dec 1865–Nov 1866); placed on Ret.Lst. (11 Jun 1869).

Career Summary During the war with Mexico, served with Commo Robert F. Stockton's sqdn. on Pac. coast and in particular as chief military aide to Stockton. Commanded troops which landed and captured Santa Barbara and San Pedro, CA, marching on to make first capture of Los Angeles. During Civil War, commanded 3rd Division of RAdm David Dixon Porter's [*q.v.*] sqdn. during both attacks against Ft. Fisher, NC, in late 1864 and early 1865.

WINFIELD SCOTT SCHLEY Born at "Richlands" near Frederick, MD, on 9 Oct 1839, son of John Thomas and Georgiana Virginia (McClare) Schley. Married Annie R. Franklin on 10 Sep 1863. Two sons and a daughter. Resided in Washington, DC, dying in New York City on 2 Oct 1911. Buried in Arlington National Cemetery.

Ranks Act.Midn (20 Sep 1856); Midn (15 Jun 1860); Mstr (31 Aug 1861); Lt (16 Jul 1862); LCdr (25 Jul 1866); Cdr (10 Jun 1874); Capt (31 Mar 1888); Commo (6 Feb 1898); RAdm (3 Mar 1899); placed on Ret.Lst. (9 Oct 1901).

Career Summary Received appointment from MD (20 Sep 1856); USNA (Sep 1856–Jun 1860); *Niagara*, spec.serv.,

WINFIELD SCOTT SCHLEY
1839–1911

prize master *General Parkhill*, and Navy Yard, Philadelphia (Jun 1860–Jun 1861); *Keystone State*, Navy Yard, Philadelphia (Jun–Jul 1861); *Potomac*, and exec.off., *Winona*, W.Gulf Blk.Sqdn. (Jul 1861–Mar 1863); cdr, *Monongahela*, W.Gulf Blk.Sqdn. (Mar 1863); *Richmond*, W.Gulf Blk.Sqdn. (Apr–Aug 1863); l.o.a. (Aug–Sep 1863); ord. duty, Navy Yard, Washington, DC (Sep–Dec 1863); exec.off., *Wateree*, Pac.Sqdn. (Dec 1863–Feb 1866); w.o. (Mar–Aug 1866); act.asst.prof. of Spanish, USNA (Aug 1866–Oct 1869); exec.off., *Benicia*, Asia.Flt. (Nov 1869–Aug 1872); w.o. (Aug–Sep 1872); chairman, Dept. of Modern Languages, USNA (Sep 1872–Sep 1876); cdr, *Essex*, S.Atl.Sta. (Sep 1876–Oct 1879); w.o. (Oct–Nov 1879); spec.duty (Nov 1879–Aug 1880); asst., then insp., 2nd L.h. Dist., Boston (Aug 1880–Oct 1883); in charge of apprentice system, Bur. of Equipment and Recruiting, Washington, DC (Oct 1883–May 1884); cdr, *Thetis*, and in charge, Greely Relief Expd. (May–Sep 1884); chief, Bur. of Equipment and Recruiting, Washington, DC (Sep 1884–Jul 1889); cdr, *Baltimore*, Philadelphia, then flgs., N.Atl.Sqdn. (Jul 1889–Feb 1892); insp., 3rd L.h. Dist., Tompkinsville, NY (Mar 1892–Mar 1895); member, Bd. of Insp. and Survey (Mar–Oct 1895); cdr, flgs. *New York*, N.Atl.Sta. (Oct 1895–Mar 1897); chairman, L.h. Bd., Washington, DC (Mar 1897–Mar 1898); cdr, "Flying Squadron," *Brooklyn* (Apr–Jun 1898); cdr, 2nd Sqdn, N.Atl.Flt., *Brooklyn* (Jun–Jul 1898); member, Naval Exam.Bd. (Jul–Aug 1898); Puerto Rico Evacuation Commission, *New Orleans* and *Newark* (Aug–Nov 1898); home and w.o. (Nov 1898–Apr 1899); member, Naval Exam.Bd. (Apr–May 1899); l.o.a. and w.o. (May–Nov 1899); cdr, S.Atl.Sta., *Chicago* (Nov 1899–Apr 1901); w.o. (Apr–Oct 1901); placed on Ret.Lst. (9 Oct 1901).

Career Highlights During the Civil War, received distinction for dangerous volunteer duty in small boats against enemy fire while on blockade duty off Mobile Bay. Participated in nearly all engagements from Mar to Jul 1863 leading up to capture of Port Hudson. Participated in the attacks against forts on the Salee River in Korea in 1871. Commanded Greely Relief Expd., rescuing in 1884 Lt Adolphus W. Greely (USA) and six other survivors at Cape Sabine, Greenland. In Spanish-American War, commanded "Flying Squadron," then American forces during the Battle of Santiago on 3 Jul 1898, becoming deeply embroiled in controversy over credit for the victory between himself and RAdm William T. Sampson [*q.v.*].

References
Personal Papers: a) 4 vols. (1884–1935) in USNAM. b) 1 vol. (1885–91) in NL. c) some in FDRL. d) some in papers of Isidore Rayner in SHC.

Writings: a) (with Prof. J. R. Soley), *The Rescue of Greely* (NY: 1885). b) *Report of Winfield S. Schley, Commanding Greely Relief Expedition of 1884* (Washington, DC: 1887). c) "Official

Report on the Behavior of the U.S.S. *Baltimore*," U.S. Naval Institute *Proceedings* 62 (1892): 235-50. d) *Forty-Five Years under the Flag* (NY: 1904).

Selected Additional Sources: a) "Nauticus," pseudonym for RAdm William T. Sampson, *The Truth about the Schley Case* (Washington, DC: c.1900). b) James Parker, *Argument of Capt. James Parker on Behalf of Rear Admiral Winfield Scott Schley* (NY: 1902). c) George Edward Graham, *Schley and Santiago* (Chicago: 1902). d) James Parker, *Rear-Admirals Schley, Sampson and Cervera* (NY: 1910). e) Richard S. West, *Admirals of the American Empire* (Indianapolis: 1948).

GUSTAVUS HALL SCOTT Born in Fairfax County, VA, on 13 Jun 1812. Died at his residence in Washington, DC, on 23 Mar 1882. Buried in Oak Hill Cemetery, Washington, DC.

Ranks Midn (1 Aug 1828); PMidn (14 Jun 1834); Lt (25 Feb 1841); Cdr (27 Dec 1855); Capt (4 Nov 1863); Commo (10 Feb 1869); RAdm (14 Feb 1873); placed on Ret.Lst. (13 Jun 1874).

Career Summary Received appointment from VA (1 Aug 1828); w.o. (Aug–Oct 1828); *St. Louis*, Navy Yard, Washington, DC (Oct–Dec 1828); *Guerriere*, Pac.Sqdn. (Dec 1828–Dec 1831); l.o.a. (Dec 1831–May 1832); Naval School, Norfolk, VA (Jun–Aug 1832); l.o.a. (Aug–Sep 1832); Navy Yard, Norfolk, VA (Sep–Dec 1832); *Experiment*, Chesapeake Bay (Dec 1832–Jun 1833); Naval School, Norfolk, VA (Jun 1833–Jun 1834); l.o.a. (Jun–Sep 1834); *Vandalia*, W.Ind.Sqdn. (Sep 1834–Nov 1835); l.o.a. and w.o. (Nov 1835–May 1838); Navy Yard, Pensacola, FL (May–Aug 1838); *Levant*, W.Ind.Sqdn. (Aug 1838–Nov 1840); l.o.a. and w.o. (Nov 1840–Dec 1841); rec. ship *Pennsylvania*, Norfolk, VA (Dec 1841–Jan 1842); rec. ship *Hudson*, NY (Jan–Feb 1842); *Ontario*, W.Ind.Sqdn. (Feb–Apr 1842); *Columbus*, Med.Sqdn. (Apr 1842–Nov 1843); storeship *Pioneer* (Nov 1843–Mar 1844); *Colonel Harney*, Baltimore (Mar–May 1844); Depot of Charts and Instruments, Washington, DC (May 1844–May 1845); l.o.a. and w.o. (May 1845–Apr 1846); *United States*, Med.Sqdn. (May 1846–Feb 1849); l.o.a. (Feb–Jun 1849); ord. duty (Jun 1849–Sep 1851); w.o. (Sep–Nov 1851); *St. Lawrence*, Pac.Sqdn. (Nov 1851–Nov 1853); l.o.a. (Nov 1853–Feb 1854); *Michigan*, on Great Lakes (Mar 1854–Mar 1857); w.o. (Mar–Jun 1857); Insp., 11th L.h. Dist., Detroit, MI (Jun 1857–Dec 1860); w.o. (Jun 1860–Jun 1861); cdr, *Keystone State*, spec.serv. (Jun–Oct 1861); w.o. (Oct–Dec 1861); suspended (Dec 1861–Jun 1862); w.o. (Jun–Aug 1862); cdr, *Maratanza*, N.Atl.Blk.Sqdn. (Aug 1862–Jun 1863); cdr, *Wachusett*, Navy Yard, Philadelphia (Jun–Nov 1863); cdr, *De Soto*, E.Gulf Blk.Sqdn. (Nov 1863–Jun 1864); w.o. (Jun 1864); ord. duty (Jun–Aug 1864); cdr, rec. ship *Vermont*, NY (Aug–Nov 1864); cdr, *Canandaigua*, S.Atl.Blk.Sqdn. (Dec 1864–Apr 1865); cdr, *Saranac*, Pac.Sqdn. (Jun 1865–May

1867); return and w.o. (May 1867–Jun 1868); pres., Naval Exam.Bd., Philadelphia (Aug 1868); insp., 10th L.h. Dist., Buffalo, NY (Oct 1868–Feb 1871); w.o. (Feb 1871–Sep 1872); cdr, Naval Sta., League Island, PA (Oct 1872–Mar 1873); cdr, N.Atl.Sta., *Worcester* (May 1873–Jun 1874); placed on Ret.Lst. (13 Jun 1874).

THOMAS OLIVER SELFRIDGE, SR.
1804–1902

THOMAS OLIVER SELFRIDGE, SR. Born in Boston, MA, on 24 Apr 1804, son of Oliver Selfridge. Married Louisa Cary Soley in 1834. At least two sons, RAdm Thomas Oliver Selfridge, Jr., USN (1836–1924) [*q.v.*], and Cdr James R. Selfridge, USN. Resided in Washington, DC. Died in Waverly, MA, on 15 Oct 1902.

Ranks Midn (1 Jan 1818); Lt (3 Mar 1827); Cdr (11 Apr 1844); Capt (14 Sep 1855); Commo (16 Jul 1862); placed on Ret.Lst. (24 Apr 1866); RAdm on Ret.Lst. (25 Jul 1866).

Career Summary Received appointment from MA (1 Jan 1818); w.o. (Jan 1818–Apr 1819); flgs. *Independence*, Med.Sqdn. (Apr–Nov 1819); *Columbus*, Navy Yard, NY, and Med.Sqdn. (Nov 1819–Sep 1820); on furlough (Sep 1820–Jul 1824); *North Carolina*, flgs., then *Erie*, Med.Sqdn. (Jul 1824–Nov 1826); l.o.a. (Nov 1826–Jun 1829); *Natchez*, W.Ind.Sqdn. (Jun 1829–Aug 1832); l.o.a. and w.o. (Aug 1831–Aug 1832); Navy Yard, Portsmouth, NH (Aug–Dec 1832); l.o.a. and w.o. (Dec 1832–May 1833); *Delaware*, Med.Sqdn. (May 1833–Dec 1834); l.o.a. (Dec 1834–Sep 1835); rec. ship *Columbus*, Boston (Sep 1835–Sep 1836); *North Carolina*, Pac.Sqdn. (Oct 1836–Jul 1839); l.o.a. (Jul–Oct 1839); Naval Rndv., Boston (Oct 1839–Sep 1841); Navy Yard, Portsmouth, NH (Sep 1841–Apr 1845); *Columbus*, E.Ind.Sqdn., then cdr, *Dale*, Pac.Sqdn. (Apr 1845–Aug 1848); w.o. (Aug 1848–Jan 1850); cdr, Naval Rndv., Boston (Feb 1850–Feb 1852); w.o. (Feb–Oct 1852); Navy Yard, Boston (Oct 1852–Oct 1855); w.o. (Oct 1855–Apr 1861); cdr, *Mississippi*, W.Gulf Blk.Sqdn. (May 1861–Mar 1862); comdt., Navy Yard, Mare Island, CA (May 1862–Oct 1864); w.o. (Oct 1864–Dec 1865); comdt., Navy Yard, Philadelphia (Jan 1866–Aug 1868); placed on Ret.Lst. (24 Apr 1866); pres., Naval Ret. Bd., Philadelphia (Dec 1868–Mar 1869); senior member, Bd. on Vessels (Mar–Oct 1869); insp., 2nd L.h. Dist., Boston (Oct 1869–Sep 1870); member, Naval Ret.Bd., Philadelphia (Oct 1870–Jan 1872); comdt., Navy Yard, Mare Island, CA (Sep 1872–Jun 1873).

Career Highlights During Mexican War, participated in capture of Matanzas and Guaymas, receiving a severe wound during the latter which effectively incapacitated him for future sea duty. When he died in 1902, he was the senior officer on the Ret.Lst.

References

Personal Papers: a) 750 items (1809–1927) in NHF,LC. b) Journal (1861–62) kept on *Mississippi* in NHF,WNY. c)

Some papers in Smith Naval Collection and Aaron Cooke Collection, WLCL. d) See: U.S. Library of Congress, MSS Division, *Register of Thomas Oliver Selfridge, Sr. and Thomas Oliver Selfridge, Jr. . . . Papers in the Library of Congress* (Washington, DC: 1969).

Other Sources: "Extracts from the Letters of Lieutenant T. O. Selfridge, Written in 1833, During a Cruise of the 'U.S.S. Delaware,'" U.S. Naval Institute *Proceedings* 288 (Feb 1927): 184–87.

THOMAS OLIVER SELFRIDGE, JR. Born in Boston, MA, on 6 Feb 1836, son of Navy RAdm Thomas Oliver (1804–1902) [*q.v.*] and Louisa Cary (Soley) Selfridge. Married Ellen F. Shepley in Aug 1895. Four sons. Married Gertrude Wildes in 1907. Resided in Washington, DC, where he died on 4 Feb 1924. Buried in Forest Hills Cemetery in Boston.

Ranks Act.Midn (3 Oct 1851); Midn (10 Jun 1854); PMidn (22 Nov 1856); Mstr (22 Jan 1858); Lt (15 Feb 1860); LCdr (16 Jul 1862); Cdr (31 Dec 1869); Capt (24 Feb 1881); Commo (11 Apr 1894); Act.RAdm (12 Nov 1895); RAdm (28 Feb 1896); placed on Ret.Lst. (6 Feb 1898).

Career Highlights Received appointment from MA (3 Oct 1851); USNA (Oct 1851–Jun 1854); w.o. (Jun–Aug 1854); flgs. *Independence*, Pac.Sqdn. (Sep 1854–Sep 1856); w.o. (Sep–Dec 1856); cst.surv. duty, Pac. Ocean (Jan–Oct 1857); *Vincennes*, Afr.Sqdn. (Oct 1857–Apr 1860); l.o.a. (Apr–Sep 1860); flgs. *Cumberland*, Home Sqdn. (Oct 1860–Mar 1862); cdr, *Monitor*, Newport News, VA (Mar 1862); flag lt., N.Atl.Flt., *Minnesota* (Mar–Jul 1862); cdr, *Alligator*, MS Sqdn. (Jul–Aug 1862); cdr, *Cairo*, MS Sqdn. (Aug–Dec 1862); cdr, *Conestoga*, MS Sqdn. (Dec 1862–May 1863); cdr, *Manitou* (May–Jun 1863); cdr, naval battery, Vicksburg, MS (Jun–Jul 1863); cdr, *Conestoga*, MS Gunboat Flot. (Jul 1863–Mar 1864); cdr, *Osage*, Red River Expd. (Mar–May 1864); cdr, *Vindicator* and 5th Division, MS Sqdn. (May–Oct 1864); cdr, *Huron*, N.Atl.Blk.Sqdn. (Oct 1864–Jun 1865); w.o. (Jun–Aug 1865); USNA (Sep 1865–Sep 1868); cdr, *Nipsic*, W.Ind.Sqdn. (Oct 1868–Jun 1870); Navy Dept., Washington, DC (Jun–Nov 1870); in charge, Surveying Expd., Isthmus of Darien (Nov 1870–Jul 1871); spec. duty (Jul–Dec 1871); insp., 1st L.h. Dist., Portland, ME (Dec 1871–Aug 1872); asst.exec.off., Navy Yard, Boston (Aug–Dec 1872); survey duty, Isthmus of Darien (Dec 1872–May 1873); asst.exec.off., Navy Yard, Boston (May 1873–Feb 1874); survey duty, Isthmus of Darien (Mar–May 1874); Navy Yard, Boston (May 1874–Aug 1875); l.o.a. (Sep 1875–May 1877); torp. instruction, Newport, RI (May 1877–Apr 1878); spec. duty, survey of Amazon and Madeira Rivers, *Enterprise* (Apr–Oct 1878); cdr, *Enterprise*, Eur.Sta. (Oct 1878–May 1880); spec. duty, Bur. of Nav., Washington, DC (Jun 1880–Jan 1881); in charge, Torp.Sta., Newport, RI (Jan

THOMAS OLIVER SELFRIDGE, JR.
1836–1924

1881–Nov 1884); w.o. (Nov 1884–Feb 1885); cdr, *Omaha*, Asia.Sta. (Mar 1885–Mar 1887); spec. duty, Japan, then home (Mar 1887–Feb 1888); under arrest (May–Jun 1888); w.o. (Jun 1888–Apr 1889); member, gen. court-martial, and Bd. of Inspection (Apr 1889–May 1890); comdt., Navy Yard, Boston (May 1890–Jul 1893); w.o. and bd. duties (Jul 1893–Oct 1895); cdr, Eur.Sta., *New York*, then *Minneapolis*, then *San Francisco* (Nov 1895–Feb 1898); placed on Ret.Lst. (6 Feb 1898).

Career Highlights Graduated from USNA at head of class: first officer to receive a graduation diploma under the new and permanent system instituted at the Academy. During the Civil War, on *Cumberland* at Hampton Roads when Navy Yard at Norfolk was abandoned and partially destroyed. Distinguished himself during action between *Cumberland* and Confederate ironclad *Virginia* (formerly *Merrimack*) on 8 Mar 1862. Briefly commanded *Monitor* after that vessel's action against the *Virginia* on 9 Mar 1862. With MS Sqdn., commanded the unsuccessful experimental submarine torpedo boat *Alligator*. Commanded a land battery of naval guns during final siege and surrender of Vicksburg. Commanded a vessel on ill-fated Red River Expd. Commanded *Huron* at both attacks on Ft. Fisher, NC, leading one of four divisions of sailors and marines which made up the second attack landing force in Jan 1865. Received several foreign awards, including the Chevalier Legion of Honor from France and a gold medal from the Russian Czar Nicholas II in honor of the latter's coronation, to which Selfridge was the American naval delegate in 1896.

References
Personal Papers: a) 1900 items (1852–1927) in NHF,LC. b) See: U.S. Library of Congress, MSS Division, *Register of Thomas Oliver Selfridge, Sr. and Thomas Oliver Selfridge, Jr. . . . Papers in the Library of Congress* (Washington, DC: 1969).

Writings: a) "Origin of U.S. Ship *Portsmouth*," U.S. Naval Institute *Proceedings* 163 (1916): 913–14. b) "Plan of Selection," U.S. Naval Institute *Proceedings* 163 (1916): 915–16. c) *Memoirs of Thomas O. Selfridge, Jr., Rear Admiral, USN* (NY: 1924).

WILLIAM BRANFORD SHUBRICK
1790–1874

WILLIAM BRANFORD SHUBRICK Born at Belvedere, Bull's Island, SC, on 31 Oct 1790, son of Thomas and Mary (Branford) Shubrick. Father served as a colonel in Continental Army. Three brothers in the navy: Lt John Temple Shubrick, Capt Edward Shubrick, and Cdr Irvine Shubrick. Attended Harvard Univ. in 1805. Married Harriet Cordelia Wethered in Sep 1815. One child. Died on 27 May 1874 in Washington, DC.

Ranks Midn (20 Jun 1806); Lt (5 Jan 1813); MstrComdt. (28 Mar 1820); Capt (21 Feb 1831); placed on Ret.Lst. as RAdm (16 Jul 1862).

Career Summary Received appointment from SC (20 Jun 1806); *Chesapeake, Wasp,* and *Argus,* Med. and Home Sqdns. (Sep 1806–?); *Hornet,* spec.serv. (1811–1812); *Constellation,* Norfolk, VA (1812–Aug 1813); *Constitution,* spec.serv. (Aug 1813–Sep 1815); l.o.a. (Sep–Dec 1815); *Washington,* Med.Sqdn. (Dec 1815–Oct 1818); Naval Sta., Baltimore (Nov 1818–Mar 1820); cdr, Navy Yard, Charleston, MA (Mar 1820–Mar 1823); court of inquiry, NY (Mar 1823–Apr 1824); cdr, Navy Yard, Charleston, MA (Apr 1824–Jan 1826); l.o.a. (Jan–Apr 1826); cdr, *Lexington,* Braz.Sqdn. (Apr 1826–Apr 1827); Naval Rndv., Baltimore (Apr–Oct 1827); court-martial duty, Philadelphia (Oct 1827–Jul 1828); w.o. (Jul 1828–Mar 1829); cdr, *Natchez,* W.Ind. and Home Sqdns. (Mar–Jun 1829); l.o.a. (Jun 1829); Navy Yard, Washington, DC (Jun 1829–Jun 1833); l.o.a. and w.o. (Jun 1833–Apr 1834); insp. of ord. (Apr 1834–Dec 1838); cdr, W.Ind.Sqdn., *Macedonian* (Dec 1838–Oct 1840); comdt., Navy Yard, Norfolk, VA (Oct 1840–Oct 1843); w.o. (Oct 1843–Jan 1844); chief, Bur. of Provisions and Clothing, Washington, DC (Jan 1844–Apr 1846); cdr, Navy Yard, Washington, DC (Feb–Jul 1846); cdr, Pac.Sqdn., *Independence* (Aug 1846–Jul 1847); cdr, Pac.Cst. Naval Forces, *Independence* (Jul 1847–May 1849); l.o.a. (May–Jul 1849); pres., Bd. of Examiners (Jul–Sep 1849); pres., Bd. to Revise Navy Regulations at Naval School, Annapolis, MD (Sep–Oct 1849); w.o. (Oct 1849–Jun 1850); pres., Bd. of Naval Examiners (Jun 1850); cdr, Navy Yard, Philadelphia (Jun–Jul 1850); w.o. (Jul–Sep 1850); member, Bd. on Rel. Ranks (Sep 1850–Apr 1851); member, L.h. Bd., Washington, DC (Apr–Nov 1851); insp. of ordnance and ammunition, Washington, DC (Nov 1851–Feb 1852); chief, Bur. of Construction and Repair, Washington, DC (Mar 1852–Jun 1853); cdr, Eastern Sqdn., *Princeton* (Jul–Sep 1853); member, L.h. Bd., Washington, DC (Sep 1853–Jun 1855); pres., Naval Efficiency Bd., Washington, DC (Jun–Sep 1855); w.o. (Sep 1855–Aug 1857); pres., Bd. to Prepare Navy Regulations, Washington, DC (Aug 1857–Feb 1858); cdr, Braz.Sqdn. and Paraguay Expd., *Sabine* (Sep 1858–May 1859); chairman, L.h. Bd., Washington, DC (May 1859–Oct 1871); placed on Reserve List (16 Jul 1862).

Career Highlights Served on board *Wasp* in 1810 with James Fenimore Cooper, with whom he developed a long friendship: the novelist eventually dedicated two works to him. During War of 1812, served on *Constitution,* participating in the victories over the HMS *Cyane* and *Levant* in Feb 1815, receiving a medal from Congress for his actions. Temporarily in command of Pac.Sqdn. at outset of war with Mexico, instituting the seizure of Mazatlan and Guaymas. Commanded Eastern Sqdn. during summer of 1853, protecting American fishing interests and negotiating a treaty with the British over those fishing grounds off Labrador. Commanded the Paraguay Expd. in 1858–59 which sought redress for the attack on surveying steamer *Water Witch.*

References

Personal Papers: a) 15 items (1823–56) in NYHS. b) Other papers held by Mr. W. B. Shubrick Clymer, Mayfair Farm, Harrisville, NH.

Additional Sources: Susan Fenimore Cooper, *Rear Admiral William Branford Shubrick, A Sketch* (NY: 1877) [reprint from *Harper's Magazine,* Aug 1876].

ROBERT WILSON SHUFELDT
1822–1895

ROBERT WILSON SHUFELDT Born in Red Hook, NY, on 21 Feb 1822, son of George Adam and Mary (Wilson) Shufeldt. Educated at local schools then at Vermont's Middlebury College. Married Sarah H. Abercrombie on 16 Oct 1847. Six children, one son being the author, Robert Wilson Shufeldt. Died in Washington, DC, on 6 Nov 1895. Buried in Arlington National Cemetery.

Ranks Midn (11 May 1839); PMidn (2 Jul 1845); Mstr (21 Feb 1853); Lt (26 Oct 1853); resigned (20 Jun 1854); commissioned Cdr (19 Nov 1862); Capt (31 Dec 1869); Commo (21 Sep 1876); RAdm (7 May 1883); placed on Ret.Lst. (21 Feb 1884).

Career Summary Received appointment from NY (11 May 1839); *United States,* Home and W.Ind. Sqdns. (Oct 1839–Mar 1840); *Potomac,* Braz.Sqdn. (Mar 1840–Aug 1841); *Marion,* Braz.Sqdn. (Aug 1841–Jun 1842); l.o.a. (Jun–Aug 1842); rec. ship *Ohio,* Boston (Aug–Dec 1842); *Bainbridge,* Home Sqdn. (Dec 1842–Sep 1843); l.o.a. (Sep–Oct 1843); *Raritan,* Navy Yard, NY (Oct–Nov 1843); *Potomac,* Home Sqdn. (Nov 1843–Aug 1844); Naval School, Philadelphia (Aug 1844–Jun 1845); cst.surv. duty (Jun 1845–Feb 1846); w.o. (Feb–Apr 1846); *United States,* Afr.Sqdn. (May–Sep 1846); *Marion,* Afr. and Med. Sqdns. (Sep 1846–Sep 1848); l.o.a. (Sep 1848–Feb 1849); cst.surv. duty (Feb–Aug 1849); l.o.a. (Aug–Nov 1849); w.o. (Nov 1849–Apr 1850); mail steamers *Atlantic* (Apr 1850–Apr 1851) and *Georgia* (Apr–Sep 1851); on furlough (Sep 1851–Jun 1854); resigned (20 Jun 1854); consul gen. to Cuba (Apr 1861–Apr 1863); recommissioned (19 Nov 1862); cdr, *Fort Jackson,* S.Atl.Blk.Sqdn. (Apr–May 1863); cdr, *Conemaugh,* S.Atl.Blk.Sqdn. (May–Oct 1863); *Proteus,* E.Gulf Blk.Sqdn. (Oct 1863–Mar 1864); cdr, *Proteus,* E.Gulf Blk.Sqdn. (Mar 1864–May 1865); w.o. (May–Jun 1865); cdr, flgs. *Hartford,* Asia.Sqdn. (Jun 1865–Sep 1866); cdr, *Wachusett,* E.Ind.Sqdn. (Sep 1866–Feb 1868); w.o. (Feb–Apr 1868); l.o.a. (Apr–Nov 1868); cdr, Naval Rndv., NY (Dec 1868–Jan 1869); w.o. (Jan–Apr 1869); cdr, *Miantonomoh,* spec. duty, and N.Atl.Sta. (Oct 1869–May 1870); ord. duty, Navy Yard, Portsmouth, NH (May–Sep 1870); organized and commanded Tehauntepec and Nicaraguan Surveying Expd. (Sep 1870–Aug 1871); cdr, flgs. *Wabash,* Eur.Sta. (Aug 1871–Oct 1872); cdr, flgs. *Plymouth,* Eur.Sqdn. (Oct 1872–Jun 1873); w.o.

(Jun–Oct 1873); member, Bd. of Examiners, USNA (Oct–Nov 1873); exec.off., Navy Yard, NY (Dec 1873–Jan 1875); chief, Bur. of Equipment and Recruitment, Washington, DC (Feb 1875–Nov 1878); spec. duty, *Ticonderoga* (Nov 1878–Nov 1880); naval attaché, Peking, China (Mar 1881–Jun 1882); sick lv. (Aug–Oct 1882); pres., Naval Advisory Bd., Washington, DC (Oct 1882–Feb 1884); supt., Naval Observatory, Washington, DC (May 1883–Feb 1884); placed on Ret.Lst. (21 Feb 1884); pres., Bd. of Visitors, USNA (Mar 1884–Jun 1885).

Career Highlights After resigning in 1854, active in organizing and operating steamers between NY and Liverpool, between NY and New Orleans, and between NY and Havana. Also worked to open a route across the Tehauntepec region of Mexico. During the Civil War, appointed by Pres. Lincoln as consul gen. to Cuba, serving in a key role against Confederate raiders and privateers. Sent on a special diplomatic mission to Mexico in 1862. After the war, organized and initially commanded Nicaraguan Surveying Expd. in 1870–71. In 1878, served on a special commercial and diplomatic mission for State Dept. and as arbitrator of both U.S. and British governments in a boundary settlement with Liberia. As naval attaché to China, successfully negotiated the first treaty between Korea and a western nation in May 1882. Finally, as president of the Naval Advisory Bd., was instrumental in the new designs of steel cruisers and the foundation of the "New Navy."

References

Personal Papers: a) 15,000 (1836–1910); in NHF,LC. b) 160 items (1871–73) in NYPL. c) 195 items (1885–1924) in Academy of Natural Sciences Library, Philadelphia, PA.

Writings: *The Relation of the Navy to the Commerce of the United States* (Washington, DC: 1878).

Additional Sources: a) A. S. Hickey, "Rear Admiral Robert Wilson Shufeldt, United States Navy, Gentleman and Diplomat," U.S. Naval Institute *Proceedings* 479 (Jan 1943): 73–80. b) Russell W. Smith, "The Opening of Korea by Commodore Robert W. Shufeldt" (M.A. thesis, Univ. of Virginia, 1953). c) Frederick C. Drake, *The Empire of the Seas: A Biography of Rear Admiral Robert Wilson Shufeldt, USN* (Ithaca: 1970; Honolulu: 1984). d) William John Brinker, "Robert W. Shufeldt and the Changing Navy" (Ph.D. dissertation, Univ. of Indiana, 1973).

MONTGOMERY SICARD Born in New York City on 30 Sep 1836, son of Stephen and Lydia E. (Hunt) Sicard. Married Elizabeth Floyd on 20 May 1863. Three children. Resided in Westernville, NY, where he died on 14 Sep 1900.

Ranks Act.Midn (1 Oct 1851); Midn (9 Jun 1855); PMidn (15 Apr 1858); Mstr (4 Nov 1858); Lt (31 May 1860); LCdr

MONTGOMERY SICARD
1836–1900

(16 Jul 1862); Cdr (2 Mar 1870); Capt (7 Aug 1881); Commo (10 Jul 1894); RAdm (6 Apr 1897); placed on Ret.Lst. (30 Sep 1898).

Career Summary Received appointment from NY (1 Oct 1851); USNA (Oct 1851–Jun 1855); *Potomac*, Home Sqdn. (Jul 1855–Aug 1856); *Wabash*, Home Sqdn. (Aug 1856–Feb 1858); l.o.a. (Feb–Apr 1858); *Wabash*, Med.Sqdn. (Apr 1858–Dec 1859); l.o.a. (Dec 1859–Apr 1860); *Dakotah*, E.Ind.Sqdn. (Apr 1860–Dec 1861); exec.off., *Oneida*, and *Susquehanna*, W.Gulf Blk.Sqdn. (Jan 1862–May 1863); temp. ord. duty, Navy Yard, Portsmouth, NH (May–Nov 1863); exec.off., *Ticonderoga*, spec.serv. and N.Atl.Blk.Sqdn. (Nov 1863–Nov 1864); cdr, *Seneca*, N.Atl.Blk.Sqdn. (Nov 1864–Mar 1865); head, Dept. of Gunnery and Drawing, USNA (Mar 1865–Sep 1868); *Pensacola*, and cdr, *Saginaw*, N.Pac.Sqdn. (Oct 1868–Apr 1870); return and w.o. (Apr 1870–Apr 1871); cdr, rec. ship *Vandalia*, Portsmouth, NH (Apr 1871); w.o. (Apr–Aug 1871); ord. duty, Navy Yard, NY (Aug 1871–Jul 1872); insp. of ord., Navy Yard, Washington, DC (Jul 1872–Jun 1876); Bur. of Ord., Washington, DC (Jun 1876–Jun 1877); cdr, *Swatara*, N.Atl.Sta. (Aug 1877–Nov 1878); spec. ord. duty, Washington, DC (Nov 1878–Sep 1879); insp. of ord., Navy Yard, Boston (Oct 1879–Jun 1881); chief, Bur. of Ord., Washington, DC (Jul 1881–Jan 1890); pres., Steel Inspection Bd. (Mar 1890–Jul 1891); cdr, *Miantonomoh*, N.Atl.Sta., and Navy Yard, NY (Oct 1891–Nov 1893); l.o.a. (Nov 1893–Jan 1894); comdt., Naval Sta. and Navy Yard, Portsmouth, NH (Jan–Nov 1894); comdt., Naval Sta. and Navy Yard, NY (Nov 1894–May 1897); cdr, N.Atl.Sta., *New York* (May 1897–Mar 1898); sick lv. (Mar–Sep 1898); pres., Naval War Bd., Navy Dept., Washington, DC (Sep 1898); placed on Ret.Lst. (30 Sep 1898); senior member, Naval Exam.Bd., Washington, DC (Sep 1898–Apr 1899).

Career Highlights While with the W.Gulf Blk.Sqdn., participated in nearly all actions on the lower MS River, including bombardment of Vicksburg and action against the Confederate ram *Arkansas* in Jul 1862. Was at both attacks on Ft. Fisher, commanding part of second division in naval assault there on 15 Jan 1865. Remainder of career was mostly involved with naval ordnance. As chief of the Bur. of Ord., rewrote ord. instructions for navy. Established Naval Gun Factory at the Washington Navy Yard. During war with Spain, served as pres. of Naval War Bd.

References
Other Sources: Caspar F. Goodrich, "Two Episodes in Sicard's Life," U.S. Naval Institute *Proceedings* 258 (Aug 1924): 1278–80.

EDWARD SIMPSON
1824–1888

EDWARD SIMPSON Born in New York City on 3 Mar 1824, son of Edmund Shaw and Julia Elizabeth (Jones) Simpson. Married Mary Ann Ridgley in 1853. Five children, including a son, RAdm Edward Simpson, USN (1860–1930), and a daughter who married RAdm Charles Mitchell Thomas, USN (1846–1908). Died in Washington, DC on 1 Dec 1888. Buried in Cypress Hills Cemetery on Long Island, NY.

Ranks Midn (11 Feb 1840); PMidn (11 Jul 1846); Mstr (10 Jul 1854); Lt (18 Apr 1855); LCdr (16 Jul 1862); Cdr (3 Mar 1865); Capt (15 Aug 1870); Commo (26 Apr 1878); RAdm (9 Feb 1884); placed on Ret.Lst. (3 Mar 1886).

Career Summary Received appointment from NY (11 Feb 1840); *Decatur, Potomac,* and *Constitution,* Braz.Sqdn. (Feb 1840–Nov 1841); l.o.a. (Nov–Dec 1841); *Independence,* Home Sqdn. (Dec 1841–May 1842); *Congress,* Med. and Braz. Sqdns. (May 1842–Mar 1845); l.o.a. (Mar–Jun 1845); rec. ship *North Carolina,* NY (Jun–Sep 1845); Naval School, Annapolis, MD (Oct 1845–Jul 1846); *Vixen,* Home Sqdn. (Jul 1846–Dec 1847); l.o.a. (Dec 1847–Feb 1848); cst.surv. duty (Feb 1848–Jan 1849); *Washington,* spec.serv. (Jan–Nov 1849); w.o. (Nov 1849–Apr 1850); flgs. *Congress,* Braz.Sqdn. (Apr 1850–Jul 1853); l.o.a. (Jul–Aug 1853); asst.inst., naval gunnery and infantry tactics, USNA (Aug 1853–Dec 1854); w.o. (Dec 1854–Jan 1855); cst.surv. duty (Jan 1855–Feb 1856); w.o. (Feb–Mar 1856); *Portsmouth,* E.Ind.Sqdn. (Apr 1856–Jun 1858); l.o.a. (Jun–Jul 1858); head, Naval Gunnery, USNA, then rec. ship *North Carolina,* NY (Sep 1858–Sep 1861); duty at, then comdt. of midshipmen, USNA, Newport, RI (Sep 1861–Jun 1863); cdr, *Wabash,* S.Atl.Blk.Sqdn. (Jun 1863); cdr, *Passaic,* S.Atl.Blk.Sqdn. (Jun 1863–May 1864); spec. duty (May–Jun 1864); cdr, *Isonomia,* N.Atl.Blk.Sqdn. (Jul–Dec 1864); spec. duty (Jan–Feb 1865); flt.capt, W.Gulf Blk.Sqdn., *Stockdale* (Feb 1865–May 1866); spec. temp. duty, Navy Dept., Washington, DC (May–Jul 1866); cdr, *Mohican,* then cdr, *Mohongo,* N.Pac.Sqdn. (Jul 1866–Dec 1868); in charge, Hydrographic Office, Washington, DC (Dec 1868–Oct 1869); asst.chief, Bur. of Ord., Washington, DC (Oct 1869–Jul 1870); spec. ord. duty, Europe (Jul 1870–Sep 1872); spec. duty, Bur. of Ord., Washington, DC (Sep 1872–Jun 1873); insp. of ord., and in charge, Torp.Sta., Newport, RI (Jun–Dec 1873); cdr, *Franklin,* N.Atl.Sta. (Dec 1873–Mar 1874); cdr, *Wabash,* N.Atl.Sta. (Mar–Apr 1874); in charge, Torp.Sta., Newport, RI (Apr 1874–Jun 1875); cdr, *Omaha,* S.Pac.Sta. (Jul 1875–Mar 1877); return and w.o. (Mar–Oct 1877); capt.yd., Navy Yard, NY (Oct 1877–May 1878); w.o. (May–Sep 1878); cdr, Naval Sta., New London, CT (Oct 1878–Jan 1881); comdt., Navy Yard, League Island, PA (Jan 1881–Feb 1884); additional duty, pres., Gun Foundry Bd., Washington, DC (Apr 1883–Feb 1884); pres., Naval Advisory Bd. (Feb 1884–Oct 1885); pres., Bd. of Inspection and Survey (Oct 1885–Mar 1886); placed on Ret.Lst. (3 Mar 1886).

Career Highlights During Mexican War, participated in actions at Alvarado, Tobasco, Tampico, Tuspan, Coatzacoalcos, Laguna de Terminos, and Vera Cruz. During Civil War, saw much action in 1863–64 against forts in and around Charleston harbor, then served as flt.capt during operations against Mobile. Served as pres. of Naval Institute from 1886–88.

References

Personal Papers: a) 1 vol. (1877) on *Omaha* in Naval Training Center Historical Museum, San Diego, CA. b) 1 vol. (1840–43) and 2 items (1858–62) in MD Historical Society, Baltimore, MD. c) Private Collection with Simpson's grandson, Mr. E. R. Simpson, Ruxton, MD.

Writings: a) *A Treatise on Ordnance and Naval Gunnery* (Annapolis: 1859 and multiple editions). b) *Report on a Naval Mission to Europe*, 2 vols. (Washington, DC: 1873). c) "A Proposed Armament for the Navy," U.S. Naval Institute *Proceedings* VII (1881): 165–82. d) "The Navy and its Prospects of Rehabilitation," U.S. Naval Institute *Proceedings* XII (1886): 1–39. e) (with Sir Edward Reed), *Modern Ships of War* (NY: 1888).

JOSEPH S. SKERRETT
1833–1897

JOSEPH S. SKERRETT Born in Chillicothe, OH, on 18 Jan 1833. Died on 1 Jan 1897 in Washington, DC.

Ranks Act.Midn (12 Oct 1848); PMidn (15 Jun 1854); Mstr (15 Sep 1855); Lt (16 Sep 1855); LCdr (16 Jul 1862); Cdr (9 Jun 1867); Capt (5 Jun 1878); Commo (4 Aug 1889); RAdm (16 Apr 1894); retired (9 Jul 1894).

Career Summary Received appointment from OH (12 Oct 1848); Naval School, Annapolis, MD (Oct 1848–May 1849); flgs. *Mississippi*, Med.Sqdn. (May–Sep 1849); flgs. *Independence*, Med.Sqdn. (Sep 1849–Jun 1852); l.o.a. (Jun–Sep 1852); *Marion*, Afr.Sqdn. (Sep 1852–Jun 1854); l.o.a. (Jun–Sep 1854); USNA (Oct 1854–Jun 1855); flgs. *Potomac*, Home Sqdn (Jul 1855–Dec 1856); *Falmouth*, Braz.Sqdn. (Jan 1857–May 1859); l.o.a. (May–Jul 1859); Naval Rndv., Philadelphia (Jul 1859–Jun 1860); storeship *Release*, N.Atl.Sqdn. (Jun–Sep 1860); w.o. (Sep–Nov 1860); *Saratoga*, Afr.Sqdn. (Nov 1860–Jan 1863); ord. duty, Navy Yard, Washington, DC (Jan–May 1863); exec.off., *Shenandoah*, N.Atl.Blk.Sqdn. (May 1863–Jan 1864); spec. duty, Naval Committee, House of Representatives, Washington, DC (Feb 1864); cdr, *Aroostook*, W.Gulf Blk.Sqdn. (Mar 1864–Sep 1865); w.o. (Sep–Oct 1865); cdr, Naval Rndv., Washington, DC (Oct 1865–May 1867); cdr, apprentice ship *Portsmouth* (Jun 1867–Oct 1868); USNA (Oct 1868–May 1869); nav.off., Navy Yard, Norfolk, VA (May 1869–1870); asst. to comdt. of midshipmen, and senior instructor in seamanship, naval tactics, and naval construction, USNA (1870–Jul 1872); cdr, *Portsmouth*, Pac.Surv. duty (Aug 1872–Jul 1875); Navy Yard, Washington, DC (Aug 1875–Mar 1878); equip.off., Navy Yard, Washington, DC (Mar–Oct 1878); insp., 1st L.h. Dist., Portland, ME (Nov 1878–Aug 1881); cdr, flgs. *Richmond*, Asia.Sta. (Oct 1881–Aug 1884);

cdr, Asia.Sta. (Oct 1883–Jan 1884); Naval Asylum, Philadelphia (Sep 1884–Oct 1886); gov., Naval Asylum, Philadelphia (Oct 1886–May 1888); w.o. (May–Dec 1888); member, Naval Advisory Bd., Washington, DC (Dec 1888–Oct 1889); comdt., Navy Yard, Portsmouth, NH (Oct 1889–Sep 1890); comdt., Navy Yard, Washington, DC (Sep 1890–Dec 1892); cdr, Pac.Sta., *Boston* (Jan–Oct 1893); cdr, Asia.Sta., *Baltimore* (Dec 1893–Jul 1894); retired (9 Jul 1894).

JOHN DRAKE SLOAT Born in Goshen, NY, on 26 Jul 1781, son of Capt John and Ruth (Drake) Sloat. Father served in Continental Navy. Married Abby Gordon on 27 Nov 1814. Three children. Between 1801 and 1812, commanded a merchant ship. Died on Staten Island, NY, on 28 Nov 1867. Buried in Brooklyn's Greenwood Cemetery.

Ranks Midn (12 Feb 1800); discharged (21 May 1801); Sailing Mstr. (10 Jan 1812); Act.Lt (28 Apr 1813); Lt (24 Jul 1813); Mstr.Comdt. (21 Mar 1826); Capt (9 Feb 1837); placed on Reserve List (27 Sep 1855); Commo on Ret.Lst. (16 Jul 1862); RAdm on Ret.Lst. (6 Aug 1866).

Career Summary Received appointment from NY (12 Feb 1800); *President*, W.Indies (Mar 1800–May 1801); discharged (21 May 1801); reappointed (10 Jan 1812); *United States*, spec.serv., Navy Yard, NY, and New London, CT (Feb 1812–Mar 1815); on furlough (Mar 1815–Jun 1816); Navy Yard, NY (Jun 1816–Mar 1820); Navy Yard, Portsmouth, NH (Mar 1820–Jun 1821); in ordinary, *Washington*, NY (Jun–Aug 1821); *Franklin*, Pac.Sqdn. (Aug 1821–Sep 1822); *Congress*, W.Ind.Sqdn. (Sep 1822–Apr 1823); Navy Yard, NY (Apr–Dec 1823); cdr, *Grampus*, W.Ind.Sqdn. (Dec 1823–Aug 1825); l.o.a. and w.o. (Aug 1825–Jul 1828); Naval Rndv., NY (Jul–Sep 1828); l.o.a. (Sep–Oct 1828); cdr, *St. Louis*, Pac.Sqdn. (Oct 1828–Dec 1831); l.o.a. (Dec 1831–Dec 1832); cdr, Naval Rndv., NY (Dec 1832–Mar 1837); w.o. (Mar 1837–Oct 1840); comdt., Navy Yard, Portsmouth, NH (Oct 1840–Nov 1843); w.o. (Nov 1843–Aug 1844); cdr, Pac.Sqdn., *Savannah* (Aug 1844–Oct 1846); spec. duty, Philadelphia and NY (Nov 1846–Feb 1847); w.o. (Mar–Jun 1847); member, Bd. of Examiners (Jun–Aug 1847); w.o. (Aug 1847–Jan 1848); comdt., Navy Yard and Naval Sta., Norfolk, VA (Jan 1848–Feb 1851); w.o. (Feb 1851–Jan 1852); member, spec. bd. to locate navy yard on Pac. cst. (Jan–Dec 1852); spec. duty, Bur. of Construction and Repair, Hoboken, NJ (Dec 1852–Sep 1855); placed on Reserve List (27 Sep 1855).

Career Highlights Sailed in 1800 under Commo Thomas Truxton in W.Indies during Quasi-War against France. In War of 1812, served as sailing mstr. on *United States* under Commo Stephen Decatur, participating in that vessel's victory over HMS *Macedonian* in Oct 1812. Commanded Pac.Sqdn. when war with Mexico broke out, his forces occupying Monterey in Jul 1846. Claimed CA for U.S.

JOHN DRAKE SLOAT
1781–1867

References
Personal Papers: California Historical Society, San Francisco, CA.
Additional Sources: Edwin Allen Sherman, *The Life of the Late Rear Admiral John Drake Sloat* (1902).

DAVID SMITH Born in Scotland on 13 Dec 1834, emigrating at a young age to MA. Died in Washington, DC, on 27 May 1903.

Ranks 3rd Asst.Engr. (26 Aug 1859); 2nd Asst.Engr. (8 Jul 1861); 1st Asst.Engr. (25 Jul 1866); Chief Engr. (5 Mar 1871); Chief Engr. with rel. rank of Cdr (25 Aug 1889); Chief Engr. with rel. rank of Capt (6 Aug 1895); placed on Ret.Lst. (13 Dec 1896); Chief Engr. on Ret.Lst. with rank of RAdm (3 Mar 1899).

Career Summary Received appointment from MA (26 Aug 1859); w.o. (Aug–Sep 1859); *Narragansett*, spec.serv. (Sep–Dec 1859); spec. duty, Norfolk, VA (Dec 1859–Feb 1860); *Pocahontas*, Home Sqdn. (Mar 1860–Jun 1861); w.o. (Jun–Jul 1861); *Lancaster*, Pac.Sqdn. (Aug 1861–Aug 1864); w.o. (Aug–Sep 1864); *Tallapoosa*, N.Atl.Sqdn. (Sep 1864–May 1867); w.o. (May–Sep 1867); *Wampanoag*, Navy Yard, NY (Sep 1867–Feb 1868); spec.serv., NY (Feb 1868–Apr 1869); Bur. of Steam Engineering, Washington, DC (Apr 1869–Apr 1872); *Tuscarora*, S.Pac.Sta. (May 1872–Apr 1873); home and w.o. (Apr–Jun 1873); *Shenandoah*, Eur.Sqdn. (Aug 1873–Apr 1874); w.o. (Apr–May 1874); spec. duty, NY, and Washington, DC (May 1874–Sep 1879); *Nipsic*, spec.serv. and Eur.Sta. (Sep 1879–Mar 1883); w.o. (Mar–Oct 1883); Navy Yard, Washington, DC (Oct 1883–Nov 1885); duty under Advisory Bd., Chester, PA (Nov 1885–May 1887); *Boston*, Chester, PA, and spec. cruises, W.Indies (May 1887–Oct 1889); w.o. (Oct–Dec 1889); spec. duty, NY (Dec 1889–May 1890); duty, State, War, and Navy Building, Washington, DC (May–Nov 1890); member, Steel Inspection Bd. (Nov 1890–Nov 1893); *Philadelphia*, Pac.Sta. (Nov 1893–Jul 1895); flt.engr., Pac.Sta., *Philadelphia* (Apr 1894–Jul 1895); home and l.o.a. (Jul–Sep 1895); Bur. of Steam Engineering, Washington, DC (Sep 1895–Dec 1896); placed on Ret.Lst. (13 Dec 1896); spec. duty, Harrisburg, PA (May–Jul 1898); inspection duty, Bur. of Steam Engineering, Washington, DC (Jul 1898–Feb 1899).

JOSEPH SMITH Born in Hanover, MA, on 30 Mar 1790, son of Albert and Anne Lentham (Eels) Smith. Married Harriet Bryant on 1 Mar 1818. Four children, including Lt Joseph Bryant Smith, USN, commander of the *Congress* in 1862 who was killed in the attack against the CSS *Virginia* (formerly *Merrimack*). Died at his home in Washington, DC, on 17 Jan 1877.

Ranks Midn (16 Jan 1809); Lt (24 Jul 1813); Mstr.Comdt.

JOSEPH SMITH
1790–1877

(3 Mar 1827); Capt (9 Feb 1847); placed on Reserved List (17 Sep 1855); RAdm on Ret.Lst. (16 Jul 1862).

Career Summary Received appointment from MA (16 Jan 1809); Naval Sta., Portland, ME (Feb–Apr 1809); *Chesapeake*, spec.serv. (Apr–Nov 1809); on furlough (Nov 1809– Oct 1812); 1st lt, *Eagle*, Lake Champlain Sqdn. (Oct 1812– Jan 1815); *Constellation*, Med.Sqdn. (Jan 1815–Dec 1816); Navy Yard, Boston (Jan–Aug 1817); *John Adams*, spec.serv. (Aug– Sep 1817); Navy Yard, NY (Sep–Nov 1817); Navy Yard, Portsmouth, NH (Nov 1817–Apr 1818); *Guerriere*, spec.serv., and Med.Sqdn. (Apr 1818–Aug 1819); sick lv., and Navy Yard, Boston (Aug 1819–Jun 1824); on furlough (Jun 1824– Sep 1827); cdr, rec. ship, Boston (Sep 1827–Oct 1828); Navy Yard, Boston (Oct–Dec 1828); *Guerriere*, Med.Sqdn. (Dec 1828–Apr 1831); l.o.a. (Apr–Jun 1831); Navy Yard, Boston (Jun 1831–Aug 1834); l.o.a. and w.o. (Aug 1834–May 1836); Navy Yard, Boston (May 1836–Feb 1837); spec. duty, preparations for U.S.Expl.Expd. (Feb 1837–Feb 1838); spec. duty, Washington, DC (Feb–Sep 1838); cdr, *Ohio*, Med.Sqdn. (Sep 1838–Apr 1840); home and l.o.a. (Apr–Oct 1840); cdr, rec. ship *Columbus*, Boston (Oct 1840–Mar 1842); cdr, flgs. *Cumberland*, Med.Sqdn. (Aug 1843–Nov 1845); w.o. (Nov 1845– May 1846); chief, Bur. of Yards and Docks, Washington, DC (May 1846–Apr 1869); placed on Reserve List (17 Sep 1855); pres., Ret.Bd. (Oct 1870–Oct 1871).

Career Highlights During War of 1812, participated in Battle of Lake Champlain on 11 Sep 1814. Participated in Algerine War of 1815, helping to capture Algerine vessels. Served as chief of Bur. of Yards and Docks for nearly three decades: was the ranking naval officer for the construction of ironclad vessels in 1861. Was instrumental in building *Monitor*.

JOSEPH ADAMS SMITH Born in Machias, ME, on 1 Sep 1837, son of George S. and Delia T. (Adams) Smith. Educated at public schools in Machias before attending Bucsport Seminary in Maine and then to Plymouth, NH. Received the LL.D. from Harvard University. Married May Hamlin Bartlett on 26 Jan 1881. One daughter. Died in Philadelphia on 18 Aug 1907. Buried in Woodlawn Cemetery in Warren, PA.

Ranks Asst.Paymstr. (8 Oct 1861); Paymstr. (23 Aug 1862); Pay Insp. (15 May 1879); Pay Dir. (24 Nov 1891); placed on Ret.Lst. as Pay Dir. with rank of RAdm (1 Sep 1899).

Career Summary Received appointment from ME (8 Oct 1861); w.o. (Oct–Dec 1861); *Kearsarge*, spec.serv. (Dec 1861–Nov 1864); s.a. and w.o. (Nov 1864–Feb 1865); rec. ship *Constellation*, Norfolk, VA (Feb 1865–Jul 1866); rec. ship *New Hampshire*, Norfolk, VA (Jul–Oct 1866); flt.paymstr., Gulf Sqdn., *Estrella* (Oct 1866–May 1867); w.o. (May–Aug 1867); rec. ship *Ohio*, Boston (Sep 1867–Sep 1870); s.a. and w.o. (Sep–Nov 1870); *California*, spec.serv. (Dec 1870–Sep 1871);

JOSEPH ADAMS SMITH
1837–1907

s.a. and w.o. (Sep–Oct 1871); Navy Yard, Boston (Nov 1871–Dec 1873); *Minnesota*, Navy Yard, NY (Dec 1873); w.o. (Dec 1873–Apr 1874); practice ship *Constellation*, USNA (Apr–Oct 1874); s.a. and w.o. (Oct 1874–Apr 1875); flt.paymstr., Asia.Sta., *Tennessee* (Apr 1875–Jul 1878); s.a. and w.o. (Jul–Nov 1878); Navy Pay Office, Washington, DC (Nov 1878–Dec 1881); s.a. and w.o. (Dec 1881–Jun 1882); paymstr. gen., and chief, Bur. of Provisioning and Clothing, Washington, DC (Jun 1882–Jan 1886); suspended (Jun 1885–Jun 1889); gen. storekeeper, Navy Yard, Portsmouth, NH (Jun 1889–Apr 1892); gen. storekeeper, Navy Yard, Washington, DC (Apr 1892–Apr 1895); gen. storekeeper, League Island, PA (Apr 1895–Dec 1898): gen. storekeeper, purchasing paymstr., and paymstr. of sta., Havana, Cuba (Dec 1898–Apr 1899); gen. storekeeper, Navy Yard, League Island, PA (Apr–Aug 1899); s.a. and w.o. (Aug–Sep 1899); placed on Ret.Lst. (1 Sep 1899).

Career Highlights During most of Civil War, was on *Kearsarge*, commanding the powder division in the celebrated victory against Confederate cruiser *Alabama* on 19 Jul 1864.

References
Personal Papers: on *Kearsarge* and CSS *Alabama* in WPL.

MELANCTON SMITH
1810–1893

MELANCTON SMITH Born in New York City on 24 May 1810, the son of Col Melancton Smith, USA, who served in War of 1812. Married Mary Jackson in 1837. Died in Green Bay, WI, on 19 Jul 1893.

Ranks Midn (1 Mar 1826); PMidn (28 Apr 1832); Lt (8 Mar 1837); Cdr (14 Sep 1855); Capt (16 Jul 1862); Commo (25 Jul 1866); RAdm (1 Jul 1870); placed on Ret.Lst. (24 May 1871).

Career Summary Received appointment from NY (1 Mar 1826); Navy Yard, Portsmouth, NH, then *Brandywine* and *Vincennes*, Pac.Sqdn. (Jul 1826–Jun 1830); l.o.a. and w.o. (Jun 1830–Jan 1831); Naval School, NY (Jan–May 1831); *Potomac*, Navy Yard, NY (May–Jun 1831); Navy Yard, NY (Jun 1831–Jan 1832); l.o.a. and w.o. (Jan—Aug 1832); *St. Louis*, W.Ind.Sqdn. (Aug–Dec 1832); Navy Yard, Pensacola, FL (Dec 1832–Jul 1833); *Porpoise* and *Vandalia*, W.Ind.Sqdn. (Jul 1833–Aug 1834); l.o.a. and w.o. (Aug 1834–Jul 1835); Navy Yard, NY (Jul 1835–Jul 1836); *Natchez* and *Vandalia*, W.Ind.Sqdn. (Jul 1836–May 1838); l.o.a. and w.o. (May 1838–Jun 1839); *Poinsett*, spec.serv. (Jun 1839–Mar 1840); in ordinary, Navy Yard, NY (Mar 1840–Apr 1841); *Fairfield* and *Preble*, Med.Sqdn. (Apr 1841–Sep 1843); rec. ship *Ontario*, NY (Nov 1843–Oct 1844); storeship *Erie*, Pac.Sqdn. (Oct–Dec 1844); *Vandalia* and *Colonel Harney*, Home Sqdn. (Dec 1844–Jan 1846); exec.off., Navy Yard, Pensacola, FL (Jan 1846–Apr 1848); l.o.a. and w.o. (Apr–Sep 1848); *Constitution*, Med.Sqdn.

(Sep 1848–Jan 1851); w.o. (Jan 1851–Jun 1855); exec.off., flgs. *Potomac*, Home Sqdn. (Jun–Oct 1855); w.o. (Oct 1855–Oct 1857); insp., 2nd L.h. Dist., Boston (Oct 1857–Dec 1860); w.o. (Dec 1860–Apr 1861); Navy Dept., Washington, DC (Apr–May 1861); cdr, *Massachusetts*, Gulf Blk.Sqdn. (May 1861–Feb 1862); cdr, *Mississippi*, W.Gulf Blk.Sqdn. (Feb 1862–Mar 1863); cdr, *Monongahela*, W.Gulf Blk.Sqdn. (Mar–Jun 1863); return and w.o. (Jun–Jul 1863); cdr, *Onondaga*, under construction (Jul 1863–Apr 1864); cdr, *Mattabesett*, N.Atl.Blk.Sqdn. (Apr–May 1864); divisional off., James River, *Onondaga* (May–Oct 1864); *Wabash*, Navy Yard, Norfolk, VA (Oct 1864–Feb 1865); w.o. (Feb–Jun 1865); comdt., Navy Yard, Washington, DC (Jun 1865–Sep 1866); chief, Bur. of Equipment and Repair, Washington, DC (Sep 1866–Jul 1870); comdt., Navy Yard, Washington, DC (Jul–Oct 1870); comdt., Navy Yard, NY (Oct 1870–May 1872); placed on Ret.Lst. (24 May 1871); gov., Naval Asylum, Philadelphia (Jun 1872–Apr 1873).

Career Highlights Saw action in Florida's Seminole War from 1839 to 1840. At Civil War's outbreak, patrolled mouth of Mississippi River, fighting inconclusive battle with Confederate cruiser *Florida* on 19 Oct 1861. Participated in many actions on lower reaches of Mississippi River. Commanded small squadron in Albemarle Sound, NC, but failed to engage and capture Confederate ram *Albemarle*.

JAMES HANNA SPOTTS Born at Ft. Johnson, Wilmington Harbor, NC, on 11 Mar 1822, son of Maj Samuel Spotts, USA. Died on 9 Mar 1882 on board *Brooklyn* at anchor in Port Stanly, Falkland Islands, while commander of the S.Atl.Sqdn. Buried at Port Stanly.

Ranks Midn (2 Aug 1837); PMidn (29 Jun 1843); Mstr (8 Apr 1851); Lt (21 Nov 1851); Cdr (16 Jul 1862); Capt (25 Jul 1866); Commo (25 Sep 1873); RAdm (28 May 1881); died (9 Mar 1882).

Career Summary Received appointment from KY (2 Aug 1837); w.o. (Aug–Sep 1837); *John Adams*, E.Ind.Sqdn. (Sep 1837–Jun 1840); l.o.a. (Jun–Dec 1840); rec. ship *Delaware*, Norfolk, VA (Dec 1840–Mar 1841); *Delaware*, flgs., and *Potomac*, Braz.Sqdn. (Mar 1841–Aug 1842); Naval School, Philadelphia (Aug 1842–Jun 1843); l.o.a. (Jun–Sep 1843); *Lawrence*, Braz. and Home Sqdns. (Sep 1843–May 1844); *Falmouth*, Home Sqdn. (May–Sep 1844); l.o.a. and w.o. (Sep 1844–May 1845); *Southampton*, Afr.Sqdn. (May–Nov 1845); return to U.S., l.o.a., and w.o. (Nov 1845–May 1846); *Bonita*, spec.serv. (May–Jun 1846); *Lexington*, Pac.Sqdn. (Jun 1846–Jun 1849); l.o.a. and w.o. (Jun 1849–May 1850); cst.surv. duty (May–Aug 1850); w.o. (Aug 1850–Nov 1851); *Portsmouth*, Pac.Sqdn. (Nov 1851–Apr 1855); l.o.a. and w.o. (Apr–Oct 1855); Naval Rndv., Philadelphia (Oct 1855–Mar 1857); *Michigan*, on Great Lakes (Mar 1857–Aug 1858); *Cyane* and

JAMES HANNA SPOTTS
1822–1882

Saranac, Pac.Sqdn. (Sep 1858–Nov 1860); l.o.a. and w.o. (Nov 1860–May 1861); Navy Dept., Washington, DC (May–Jun 1861); cdr, *Magnolia*, E.Gulf Blk.Sqdn. (Jul 1861–Dec 1862); sick lv. (Dec 1862–Jan 1863); Naval Rndv., Burlington, VT (Jan–Mar 1863); w.o. (Mar–Jun 1863); cdr, *South Carolina*, S.Atl.Blk.Sqdn. (Jun 1863–Jan 1864); w.o. (Jan–Feb 1864); spec. duty, NY (Feb–Mar 1864); cdr, *Pawtuxet*, Navy Yards, Portsmouth, NH, and NY (Mar 1864–Jun 1865); Navy Yard, Mare Island, CA (Jun 1865–Oct 1867); w.o. (Oct 1867–Sep 1870); cdr, *Saranac*, then *Pensacola*, Pac.Sqdn. (Sep 1870–Oct 1872); w.o. (Oct–Nov 1872); insp., 12th L.h. Dist., San Francisco (Dec 1872–Dec 1874); w.o. (Dec 1874–Mar 1877); spec. duty, San Francisco (Mar 1877–May 1881); cdr, S.Atl.Sta., *Brooklyn* (Jul 1881–Mar 1882); died (9 Mar 1882).

FABIUS STANLY
1815–1882

FABIUS STANLY Born in New Bern, NC, on 15 Dec 1815, son of Honorable John Stanly, speaker of NC legislature and two-term NC congressman. His brother was Edward Stanly, five-term congressman and military gov. of NC in 1862. Died at his home in Washington, DC, on 5 Dec 1882. Buried in Oak Hill Cemetery, Washington, DC.

Ranks Midn (20 Dec 1831); PMidn (15 Jun 1837); Lt (8 Sep 1841); placed on Reserved List (13 Sep 1855); restored to Active List (29 Jan 1858); Cdr (19 May 1861); Capt (25 Jul 1866); Commo (1 Jul 1870); RAdm (12 Feb 1874); placed on Ret.Lst. (4 Jun 1874).

Career Summary Received appointment from NC (20 Dec 1831); w.o. (Dec 1831–Feb 1832); *Constellation*, Med.Sqdn. (Feb 1832–Nov 1834); l.o.a. and w.o. (Nov 1834–Jan 1836); *Concord*, W.Ind.Sqdn. (Jan–Dec 1836); Naval School, Norfolk, VA (Dec 1836–Apr 1837); Naval School, NY (Apr–Jun 1837); *Falmouth*, Pac.Sqdn. (Jun 1837–Jul 1839); l.o.a. (Jul–Oct 1839); *Consort*, surveying duty (Oct 1839–Nov 1840); *Fulton*, spec.serv. (Nov 1840–Apr 1841); *Delaware*, Braz.Sqdn. (Apr 1841–Jul 1843); sick lv. (Jul–Sep 1843); *Union*, spec.serv. (Sep 1843–Jan 1844); *Constitution*, spec.serv. (Jan–May 1844); *Princeton*, spec.serv. (May 1844–Jan 1846); l.o.a. (Jan–May 1846); *Dale*, *St. Mary's*, *Warren*, and *Congress*, Pac.Sqdn. (May 1846–Jan 1850); w.o. (Jan–Mar 1850); Navy Yard, Washington, DC (Mar–Nov 1850); w.o. (Nov 1850–Apr 1851); suspended (Apr 1851–Apr 1852); l.o.a. (Apr–Dec 1852); cdr, *Warren*, Pac.Sqdn. (Dec 1852–Apr 1854); on furlough (Apr–Nov 1854); exec.off., Navy Yard, Mare Island, CA (Nov 1854–Sep 1855); placed on Reserved List (13 Sep 1855); on furlough (Sep 1855–Jan 1858); restored to Active List (29 Jan 1858); w.o. (Jan–Aug 1858); cdr, *Supply*, Paraguay Expd. (Aug 1858–May 1859); l.o.a. (May–Jun 1859); cdr, *Wyandotte*, W.Ind.Sqdn. (Jun 1859–Dec 1860); w.o. (Dec 1860–Feb 1861); cdr, rec. ship *Independence*, Navy Yard, Mare Island, CA (Mar–Sep 1861); insp., 12th L.h. Dist., San Francisco (Sep 1861–Mar 1862); cdr, *Narragansett*, Pac.Sqdn. (Apr 1862–Oct 1863); ord.off., MS Sqdn., Cairo, IL (Nov 1863–Nov 1864);

cdr, *State of Georgia*, S.Atl.Blk.Sqdn. (Nov 1864–Apr 1865); spec. duty, Mound City, IL (Apr–Jun 1865); cdr, *Tuscarora*, Pac.Sqdn. (Jun 1865–Nov 1867); l.o.a. and w.o. (Nov 1867–May 1869); Naval Rndv., Baltimore (May 1869–Jun 1870); member, court-martial bd., Washington, DC (Oct–Dec 1870); insp., 5th L.h. Dist., Baltimore (Dec 1870–Jan 1874); w.o. (Jan–Jun 1874); placed on Ret.Lst. (4 Jun 1874).

OSCAR FITZALAN STANTON Born in Sag Harbor, Long Island, NY, on 18 Jul 1834, son of Joseph and Elizabeth (Cooper) Stanton. Married Caroline Eliza Gardner on 6 Jul 1859. Made his home in New London, CT, dying there on 5 Jul 1924. Buried at Cedar Grove Cemetery in New London.

Ranks Act.Midn (29 Dec 1849); PMidn (12 Jun 1855); Mstr (16 Sep 1855); Lt (2 Apr 1856); LCdr (16 Jul 1862); Cdr (12 Dec 1867); Capt (11 Jul 1879); Commo (19 May 1891); Act.RAdm (1 Aug 1893); RAdm (21 Jul 1894); retired (30 Jul 1894).

Career Summary Received appointment from NY (29 Dec 1849); USNA (Jan–Dec 1850); *Susquehanna*, E.Ind.Sqdn. (Dec 1850–Jun 1853); *Saratoga*, E.Ind.Sqdn. (Jun 1853–Sep 1854); USNA (Oct 1854–Jun 1855); *Constellation*, Med.Sqdn. (Jul 1855–Apr 1858); l.o.a. (Apr–Oct 1858); *Memphis*, Paraguay Expd. (Oct 1858–Jun 1859); l.o.a. (Jun–Aug 1859); storeship *Supply*, *Portsmouth*, and *Marion*, Afr.Sqdn. (Sep 1859–Oct 1860); l.o.a. (Oct–Dec 1860); *St. Mary's*, Pac.Sqdn. (Dec 1860–Mar 1862); w.o. (Apr–May 1862); *Saco*, Navy Yard, Boston, and exec.off., *Tioga*, James River, Potomac Flot. and "Flying Sqdn." (May 1862–Sep 1863); cdr, *Pinola*, W.Gulf Blk.Sqdn. (Sep 1863–Oct 1864); ord. duty, Navy Yard, NY (Dec 1864–Mar 1865); *Powhatan*, E.Gulf Blk.Sqdn. (Mar–Jul 1865); w.o. (Jul–Sep 1865); Navy Yard, NY (Sep–Nov 1865); USNA (Nov 1865–Apr 1867); cdr, *Tahoma*, Gulf Sqdn. (May–Aug 1867); w.o. (Aug 1867–Jun 1868); cdr, storeship *Purveyor*, Gulf of Mexico and W.Afr.Cst. (Jul 1868–Apr 1869); w.o. (Apr 1869–Jan 1870); rec. ship *Vandalia*, Portsmouth, NH (Feb 1870–Apr 1871); cdr, *Monocacy*, Asia.Sta. (Jan 1872–Jun 1873); *Yantic*, Asia.Sta. (Jun 1873–Aug 1874); Navy Yard, Norfolk, VA (Nov 1874–Mar 1877); w.o. (Mar 1877–May 1878); Torp.Sta., Newport, RI (Jun–Sep 1878); w.o. (Sep 1878–Sep 1879); cdr, training ship *Constitution* (Oct 1879–Jun 1881); w.o. (Jun–Nov 1881); Naval Asylum, Philadelphia (Nov 1881–Sep 1884); w.o. (Sep–Nov 1884); cdr, flgs. *Tennessee*, N.Atl.Sta. (Nov 1884–Oct 1885); w.o. (Sep–Oct 1885); cdr, Naval Sta., New London, CT (Oct 1885–Mar 1889); member, gen. court-martial (Apr–May 1889); senior member, Bd. of Examiners, Norfolk, VA (May–Jun 1890); cdr, rec. ship *New Hampshire*, and Training Sta., Norfolk, VA (Jun–Oct 1890); cdr, training ship *Richmond*, and Naval Sta., Newport, RI (Oct 1890–Jun 1891); gov., Naval Home, Philadelphia (Jul 1891–Jul 1893); pres., gen. court-martial, Norfolk, VA (Sep 1892); pres., court of inquiry, Philadelphia (Nov 1892); cdr, S.Atl.Sta., *Newark*

OSCAR FITZALAN STANTON
1834–1924

(Jul–Oct 1893); cdr, N.Atl.Sta., *Kearsarge* (Jan–Jul 1894), then *San Francisco* (Jul–Aug 1894); retired (30 Jul 1894); cdr, Naval Sta., New London, CT (Apr–Oct 1898).

Career Highlights Served on board *Susquehanna* as part of Commo Matthew C. Perry's expd. to Japan. During Civil War, commanded a gunboat at Battle of Mobile Bay in Aug 1864.

References

Personal Papers: 204 items (1850–1900) at Mystic Seaport, G. W. Blunt White Lib., Mystic, CT.

CHARLES STEEDMAN
1811–1890

CHARLES STEEDMAN Born in St. James's Parish, Santee, SC, on 20 Sep 1811, son of Charles John and Mary (Blake) Steedman. Married Sarah Bishop on 7 Feb 1843. Six children. Died in Washington, DC, on 13 Nov 1890. Buried in Mount Auburn, Cambridge, MA.

Ranks Midn (1 Apr 1828); PMidn (14 Jun 1834); Lt (25 Feb 1841); Cdr (14 Sep 1855); Capt (13 Dec 1862); Commo (25 Jul 1866); RAdm (25 May 1871); placed on Ret.Lst. (25 Sep 1873).

Career Summary Received appointment from SC (1 Apr 1828); w.o. (Apr–Aug 1828); Naval School, NY (Aug 1828–May 1829); Navy Yard, NY (May 1829–Mar 1830); *Natchez*, W.Ind.Sqdn. (Mar 1830–Sep 1831); l.o.a. (Sep–Oct 1831); *Fairfield*, W.Ind.Sqdn. (Oct 1831–Jul 1832); l.o.a. (Jul–Oct 1832); Navy Yard, Norfolk, VA (Oct 1832–Feb 1833); *Grampus*, W.Ind.Sqdn. (Feb 1833–Feb 1834); l.o.a. (Feb 1834–Feb 1835); *Constitution*, Med.Sqdn. (Feb 1835–Apr 1837); l.o.a. (Apr 1837–Dec 1838); flag lt, *Macedonian*, W.Ind.Sqdn. (Dec 1838–Oct 1840); l.o.a. and w.o. (Oct 1840–Aug 1841); *Dolphin* and *Mississippi*, Home and W.Ind.Sqdns. (Aug 1841–Sep 1842); home and sick lv. (Sep 1842–May 1843); cst.surv. duty (May 1843–Oct 1844); *St. Mary's*, W.Ind.Sqdn. (Oct 1844–May 1847); return and l.o.a. (Jun–Aug 1847); Naval Observatory, Washington, DC (Aug 1847–Jun 1849); *Cumberland*, Med.Sqdn. (Jul 1849–Jul 1851); l.o.a. and w.o. (Jul 1851–Jan. 1852); Naval Observatory, Washington, DC (Jan 1852–Jan 1855); *Jamestown*, Navy Yard, Philadelphia (Jan–Feb 1855); sick lv. (Feb 1855–May 1856); spec. duty, Washington, DC (May 1856–Apr 1858); w.o. (Apr–Sep 1858); cdr, *Dolphin*, Paraguay Expd. (Sep 1858–Dec 1860); s.a. and w.o. (Dec 1860–Apr 1861); insp., 4th L.h. Dist., Philadelphia, and cdr, *Maryland*, spec. duty, Chesapeake Bay (Apr–Sep 1861); spec. duty, St. Louis (Sep 1861); cdr, *Bienville*, S.Atl.Blk.Sqdn. (Oct 1861–Apr 1862); cdr, *Paul Jones*, S.Atl.Blk.Sqdn. (Apr 1862–Apr 1863); cdr, *Powhatan*, S.Atl.Blk.Sqdn. (Apr–Oct 1863); cdr, *Ticonderoga*, spec.serv. and N.Atl.Blk.Sqdn. (Oct 1863–May 1865); member, Naval Exam.Bd., Boston (May–Aug 1865); cdr, *Ticonderoga* and *Colorado*, Eur.Sqdn. (Sep 1865–Sep 1867); w.o. (Sep 1867–Feb 1868); spec. duty, Philadelphia (Feb 1868–Dec 1869); comdt., Navy Yard, Boston (Dec 1869–Sep 1872); cdr, S.Pac.Sqdn., *Pensacola* (Oct 1872–Sep 1873); placed on Ret.Lst. (24 Sep 1873).

Career Highlights At outbreak of Civil War, commanded Baltimore Railroad's *Maryland*, keeping communications open between Havre-de-Grace and Annapolis, MD, until damaged or destroyed railbridges could be repaired and communication restored between Washington and Philadelphia. Participated in the taking of Port Royal, SC.

References

Personal Papers: 170 items; 2 vols. (1835–1905) in WPL.

Additional Sources: a) Amos L. Mason, ed., *Memoirs and Correspondence of Charles Steedman, rear-Admiral, United States Navy, with his Autobiography and personal Journals, 1811–1890* (1912). b) Albert Gleaves, "An Officer of the Old Navy: Rear-Admiral Charles Steedman, U.S.N. (1811–1890)," U.S. Naval Institute *Proceedings* 145 (1913): 197–210.

ROGER NELSON STEMBEL Born in Middleton, MD, on 27 Dec 1810. Made his home in Washington, DC. Died on 20 Nov 1900 in New York City. Buried in Woodlawn Cemetery, New York City.

Ranks Midn (27 Mar 1832); PMidn (23 Jun 1838); Lt (26 Oct 1843); Cdr (1 Jul 1861); Capt (25 Jul 1866); Commo (13 Jul 1870); placed on Ret.Lst. (27 Dec 1872); RAdm on Ret.Lst. (5 Jun 1874).

Career Summary Received appointment from OH (27 Mar 1832); w.o. (Mar–Sep 1832); *Porpoise* and *Vandalia*, W.Ind.Sqdn. (Sep 1832–Dec 1837); Naval School, NY (Dec 1837–Jun 1838); Depot of Charts and Instruments, Washington, DC (Jul 1838–May 1839); *Brandywine*, Med.Sqdn. (May 1839–Jul 1842); l.o.a. and w.o. (Jul 1842–May 1843); cst.surv. duty (May 1843–Jan 1848); *Plymouth*, Navy Yard, NY (Jan–Feb 1848); w.o. (Feb 1848–Nov 1849); *Germantown*, Home Sqdn. (Nov 1849–Sep 1850); l.o.a. and w.o. (Sep 1850–Feb 1851); *Jamestown*, Braz.Sqdn. (Feb 1851–May 1854); l.o.a. and w.o. (May–Nov 1854); spec. duty, Washington, DC (Nov 1854–Apr 1857); w.o. (Apr–Jun 1857); *Mississippi*, E.Ind.Sqdn. (Jul 1857–Jan 1860); l.o.a. (Jan–Apr 1860); Naval Asylum, Philadelphia (May 1860–Jun 1861); spec. duty, Western Gunboat Flot., Cincinnati (Jun 1861–Aug 1862); sick lv. (Aug 1862–Jan 1863); cdr, Naval Rndv., Philadelphia (Feb 1863–Aug 1864); spec. duty, Pittsburgh, PA (Aug 1864–Jun 1865); w.o. (Jun–Jul 1865); Navy Yard, Philadelphia (Jul–Oct 1865); cdr, *Shenandoah*, Navy Yard, Philadelphia (Oct 1865); cdr, *Canandaigua*, Eur.Sqdn. (Oct 1865–Dec 1866); return and w.o. (Dec 1866–Aug 1869); cdr, Naval Rndv., Boston (Aug 1869–Jan 1871); cdr, Northern Sqdn., Pac.Sta., *Saranac* (Feb 1871–Oct 1872); return and w.o. (Oct–Dec 1872); placed on Ret.Lst. (27 Dec 1872).

ROGER NELSON STEMBEL
1810–1900

THOMAS HOLDUP STEVENS
1819–1896

THOMAS HOLDUP STEVENS Born in Middletown, CT, on 27 May 1819, son of navy Capt Thomas Holdup (1795–1841) and Elizabeth Sage Stevens. Father commanded sloop *Trippe* during Battle of Lake Erie in War of 1812 and eventually rose to command Washington Navy Yard. Married Anna Maria Christie on 2 Nov 1844. Nine children, including future RAdm Thomas Holdup Stevens, USN (1848–1914). Died in Rockville, MD, on 15 May 1896. Buried in Arlington National Cemetery.

Ranks Act.Midn (14 Dec 1836); PMidn (1 Jul 1842); Mstr (25 Jul 1848); Lt (10 May 1849); dropped from service (13 Sep 1855); recommissioned Lt (10 May 1857); Cdr (16 Jul 1862); Capt (25 Jul 1866); suspended (1 Sep 1871); suspension remitted (26 Nov 1872); Commo (20 Nov 1872); RAdm (27 Oct 1879); placed on Ret.Lst. (27 May 1881).

Career Summary Received appointment from CT (14 Dec 1836); *Independence*, Braz.Sqdn. (Feb 1837–Apr 1840); l.o.a. (Apr–Jun 1840); Depot of Charts and Instruments, Washington, DC (Jun–Sep 1840); Navy Yard, Washington, DC (Oct 1840–Apr 1841); cst.surv. duty (Apr–Sep 1841); Naval School, Philadelphia (Sep 1841–Jul 1842); rec. ship *Pennsylvania*, Norfolk, VA (Aug–Sep 1842); cst.surv. duty (Sep 1842–Aug 1843); l.o.a. (Aug–Sep 1843); *Michigan*, on Great Lakes (Sep 1843–Sep 1844); naval storekeeper, Honolulu, Sandwich Islands (Oct 1844–Dec 1847); on Chilean ship *Maria Helena*, and shipwrecked, Christmas Island (Dec 1848–Apr 1849); Navy Yard, Sacket's Harbor, NY (Jun–Sep 1849); *Michigan*, on Great Lakes (Sep 1849–Aug 1850); w.o. (Aug 1850–Jan 1851); *Germantown*, Navy Yard, NY (Jan–Feb 1851); cdr, *Ewing*, surv. duty, Pac.Cst. (Mar 1851–Jan 1855); w.o. (Jan–Sep 1855); released from service (13 Sep 1855); recommissioned (10 May 1857); cdr, *Colorado*, Home Sqdn. (Mar–Aug 1858); *Roanoke*, Home Sqdn. (Aug 1858–May 1860); l.o.a. and w.o. (May 1860–Jan 1861); *Michigan*, on Great Lakes (Mar–Jul 1861); *Pensacola*, Navy Yard, Washington, DC (Jul 1861); cdr, *James Adger*, Navy Yard, NY (Jul–Aug 1861); cdr, *Penguin*, Potomac Flot. (Aug–Sep 1861); cdr, *Ottawa*, Atl.Blk.Sqdn. (Sep 1861–Apr 1862); cdr, *Maratanza*, N.Atl.Blk.Sqdn. (Apr–Aug 1862); cdr, *Sonoma*, "Flying Sqdn." (Sep 1862–Jun 1863); w.o. (Jun–Aug 1863); cdr, *Patapsco*, S.Atl.Blk.Sqdn. (Aug 1863–Apr 1864); cdr, *Oneida*, W.Gulf Blk.Sqdn. (May–Aug 1864); cdr, *Winnebago*, W.Gulf Blk.Sqdn. (Aug 1864); cdr, *Oneida*, W.Gulf Blk.Sqdn. (Aug 1864–Aug 1865); w.o. (Aug–Nov 1865); spec. duty, Naval Rndv., NY (Nov 1865–Mar 1866); w.o. (Mar–Aug 1866); insp., 11th L.h. Dist., Detroit, MI (Aug 1866–Sep 1869); w.o. (Sep 1869–Jul 1870); cdr, *Guerriere*, Eur.Sqdn. (Aug 1870–Sep 1871); suspended under court-martial (Sep 1871–Mar 1872); w.o. (Mar–May 1872); suspended from rank and duty for three years (1 Sep 1871); remainder of suspension remitted (26 Nov 1872); w.o. (Nov 1872–Jun 1873); comdt., Navy Yard, Norfolk, VA (Jul 1873–Jun 1876); spec. duty, chairman, Harbor Bd., Norfolk, VA (Jun 1876–Aug 1880); cdr, Pac.Sqdn., *Pensacola* (Oct 1880–Jul 1881); placed on Ret.Lst. (27 May 1881).

Career Highlights After duty at Honolulu, returned home on board Chilean *Maria Helena*, which wrecked on Christmas Island in 1848. Surviving the wreck, spent three months on the island before being rescued. During Civil War, commanded a gunboat in the taking of Port Royal, SC. With Commo Charles Wilkes's [*q.v.*] "Flying Sqdn." in Caribbean, captured several Confederate prizes while in search of raider *Florida*. Was at Battle of Mobile Bay while commanding *Winnebago*. Served as senior officer off Texas Coast during the last months of the war.

References

Personal Papers: a) 35 items (1810–1952) in Stevens Family Papers in NHF,LC. b) letters from on board *Ottawa* to Edward Hallam Saltonstall in NYHS. c) 144 items (1823–1902) in WPL. d) 4 items (1861–64) in SCL. e) 3 items, letters from Edgar S. Maclay (1894–95) in Fondren Library, Rice Univ., Houston, TX. f) Private Collection in possession of granddaughter, Mrs. Frederick E. Hicks, Washington, DC.

Writings: *Narrative of the Wreck of the Chilean Ship* Maria Helena (1849).

CHARLES STEWART Born in Philadelphia on 28 Jul 1778, son of Charles and Sarah (Ford) Stewart. Entered merchant service at age thirteen, becoming a master before entering navy. Married Delia Tudor on 25 Nov 1813. Two children. A grandson was Charles Stewart Parnell, the Irish Nationalist. Died in Bordentown, NJ, on 6 Nov 1869. Buried in Philadelphia's Woodlawn Cemetery.

Ranks Lt (9 Mar 1798); Mstr.Comdt. (17 May 1804); Capt (22 Apr 1806); placed on Reserved List (14 Sep 1855); Senior Flag Off. (20 Apr 1859); retired (21 Dec 1861); RAdm on Ret.Lst. (16 Jul 1862).

Career Summary Received appointment from PA (9 Mar 1798); *United States* and *Enterprise*, W.Indies (1798–Jul 1800); cdr, *Experiment*, W.Indies (Jul 1800–Apr 1801); *Chesapeake*, Norfolk, VA (Apr–Aug 1801); *Experiment*, Baltimore (Aug–Sep 1801); on furlough (Sep 1801–Jan 1802); *Chesapeake*, Hampton Roads, VA (Jan 1802); exec.off., *Constellation*, Med.Sqdn. (Jan 1802–Mar 1803); on furlough (Mar–May 1803); construction supt., then cdr, *Syren*, Med.Sqdn. (May 1803–Sep 1805); cdr, *Essex*, Med.Sqdn. (Sep–Nov 1805); cdr, *Chesapeake*, in ordinary (Apr–May 1806); superintended building of gunboats, Philadelphia (May–Jul 1806); supt. of gunboat construction, Navy Yard, NY (Jul 1806–Dec 1807); member, court-martial bd., Norfolk, VA (Dec 1807); on furlough (Dec 1807–Feb 1809); cdr, *Essex*, spec.serv. (Feb–Mar 1809); on furlough (Apr 1809–May 1811); court of inquiry (Jul 1811–Apr 1812); cdr, *Constellation*, Norfolk, VA (Apr–

CHARLES STEWART
1778–1869

Jun 1812); cdr, *Argus*, N.Atl.Patrol (Jun–Jul 1812); cdr, *Congress*, N.Atl.Patrol (Jul–Sep 1812); cdr, *Constellation*, Navy Yard, Washington, DC, and Hampton Roads, VA (Sep 1812–May 1813); cdr, *Constitution*, spec.serv. (May 1813–Jun 1815); on furlough (Jun 1815–Jan 1816); cdr, Med.Sqdn., then Pac.Sqdn., *Franklin* (Jan 1816–1824); w.o. (1824–1830); pres., Naval Exam.Bd. (1830); commissioner of the navy, Washington, DC (1830–1833); w.o. (1833–Jun 1837); cdr, Navy Yard and Naval Sta., Philadelphia (Jun 1837–Nov 1841); cdr, Home Sqdn., *Independence* (Nov 1841–Nov 1843); w.o. (Nov 1843–Jan 1845); spec. temp. serv., Philadelphia (Jan–Dec 1845); comdt., Navy Yard and Naval Sta., Philadelphia (Jan 1846–Oct 1849); w.o. (Oct 1849–Sep 1850); pres., Bd. of Rank, Washington, DC (Sep 1850–Jun 1853); comdt., Navy Yard and Naval Sta., Philadelphia (Aug 1853–Dec 1860); placed on Reserved List (14 Sep 1855); retired (21 Dec 1861).

Career Highlights Commanded *Experiment* in W.Indies during Quasi-War with France, capturing two vessels and a privateer. Served in the beginning conflicts with Tripoli. Was senior officer in charge of party in ketch *Intrepid* which recaptured and burned the *Philadelphia* in Tripoli Harbor on 1 Oct 1803. In War of 1812, commanded *Constitution* in famous actions against HMS *Cyane* and *Levant* on 20 Feb 1814, subsequently receiving the thanks of Congress. In 1840 considered as possible presidential candidate but not nominated. By 1852, became navy's senior officer, and by a special act of Congress in Apr 1859 was officially designated senior flag officer. Pres. Lincoln consulted with him on relief of Ft. Sumter in early 1861. Was senior officer for about seventeen years and in service seventy-one years when he died.

References

Personal Papers: a) 15 items (1850–65) in NHF,LC. b) 1 vol. (1843–55) in NL. c) record book from *Constellation* (1812–13) in New Jersey Historical Society, Newark, NJ. d) material in Floyd T. Starr Collection in Historical Society of PA, Philadelphia, PA.

EDWIN STEWART Born in New York City on 5 May 1837, son of John and Mary (Aikman) Stewart. From Williams College, received A.B. degree in 1862, the A.M. degree in 1882, and the LL.D. in Jun 1898. Married Laura S. Tufts on 24 Aug 1865. One son. Married again on 17 May 1877 to Susan M. Estabrook. Made his home in South Orange, NJ, where he died on 28 Feb 1933. Buried in Arlington National Cemetery.

Ranks Asst. Paymstr. (9 Sep 1861); Paymstr. (14 Apr 1862); Pay Insp. (8 Mar 1879); Pay Dir. (12 Sep 1891); Paymstr. Gen. and Chief, Bur. of Provisions and Clothing (16 May 1890); RAdm (3 Mar 1899); placed on Ret.Lst. (5 May 1899).

Career Summary Received appointment from NY (9 Sep 1861); w.o. (Sep–Oct 1861); *Pembina*, S.Atl.Blk.Sqdn. (Oct

EDWIN STEWART
1837–1933

1861–Jul 1862); w.o. (Jul–Sep 1862); *Richmond*, W.Gulf Blk.Sqdn. (Sep 1862–Jul 1865); s.a. and w.o. (Jul–Oct 1865); *Michigan*, on Great Lakes (Oct 1865–Sep 1868); s.a. and w.o. (Sep 1868–Apr 1869); Navy Pay Office, Washington, DC (May 1869–Jul 1872); s.a. and w.o. (Jul–Sep 1872); flt.paymstr., Asia.Sta., *Hartford* (Oct 1872–Oct 1875); home and w.o. (Oct 1875–Feb 1876); Bur. of Provisions and Clothing, Washington, DC (Feb 1876–Jan 1877); insp. of provisions and clothing, Navy Yard, NY (Feb 1877–Aug 1879); insp. of provisions and clothing, Navy Yard, League Island, PA (Sep 1879–Mar 1880); insp. of provisions and clothing, Navy Yard, NY (Mar 1880–Feb 1883); flt.paymstr., Eur.Sta., *Lancaster* (Mar 1883–Aug 1885); s.a. and w.o. (Aug–Oct 1885); spec. duty, Morgan Iron Works, NY (Oct 1885–May 1886); l.o.a. (May–Jun 1886); Navy Pay Office, NY (Jun 1886–May 1890); paymstr. gen., and chief, Bur. of Provisions and Clothing [Supplies and Accounts], Washington, DC (May 1890–May 1899); placed on Ret.Lst. (5 May 1899).

GEORGE WASHINGTON STORER Born in Portsmouth, NH, in 1789. Died in Portsmouth, NH, on 8 Jan 1864.

Ranks Midn (16 Jan 1809); Lt (24 Jan 1813); Mstr.Comdt. (24 Apr 1828); Capt (9 Feb 1837); placed on Ret.Lst. with rank of RAdm (16 Jul 1862).

Career Summary Received appointment from ME (16 Jan 1809); Naval Sta., Portland, ME (Feb–Apr 1809); *President*, E. Cst. (Apr 1809–Jun 1810); flgs. *Constitution*, N.Atl.Sqdn. (Jun 1810–Jan 1811); on furlough (Jan–Jun 1811); Naval Rndv., Boston (Jun–Oct 1811); Naval Sta., NY (Oct 1811–Apr 1812); duty, Gunboat No. 108, NY (Apr–Nov 1812); *John Adams*, Navy Yard, Washington, DC (Dec 1812–Feb 1813); gunboat duty, Potomac Flot. (Feb–Sep 1813); cdr, *Black Snake*, Potomac Flot. (Sep 1813); *Frolic*, spec.serv. (Oct 1813–Apr 1814); prisoner of war, New Providence, Bahama Islands (Apr 1814–c. Feb 1815); *Independence*, Med.Sqdn. (Apr–Jun 1815); cdr, *Lynx*, Med.Sqdn. (Jun 1815–Oct 1817); *Congress*, Braz.Sqdn. (Oct 1817–Sep 1818); *Constitution*, Med.Sqdn. (Sep 1818–May 1824); l.o.a. (May–Aug 1824); Navy Yard, Portsmouth, NH (Aug 1824–Apr 1830); cdr, *Boston*, Med.Sqdn. (Apr 1830–Dec 1832); l.o.a. (Dec 1832–Feb 1833); Navy Yard, Portsmouth, NH (Feb 1833–Mar 1837); w.o. (Feb 1837–Jun 1839); cdr, rec. ship *Columbus*, Boston (Jun 1839–Oct 1840); cdr, *Constellation*, Braz.Sqdn. (Oct 1840–Feb 1841); cdr, flgs. *Potomac*, Braz.Sqdn. (Feb–Aug 1841); l.o.a. and w.o. (Aug 1841–Oct 1843); comdt., Navy Yard, Portsmouth, NH (Oct 1843–Nov 1846); w.o. (Nov 1846–Jul 1847); cdr, Braz.Sqdn., *Brandywine* (Aug 1847–Dec 1850); l.o.a. and w.o. (Dec 1850–Jul 1854); gov., Naval Asylum, Philadelphia (Jul 1854–Sep 1857); w.o. (Sep 1857–May 1858); pres., Bd. of Examiners (May 1857–Sep 1860); pres., Bd. of Inspection and Survey

GEORGE WASHINGTON STORER
1789–1864

(Sep–Oct 1860); w.o. (Oct 1860–Oct 1861); member, Bd. to Examine Military Establishment, NY (Oct 1861–May 1862); w.o. (May–Jun 1862); pres., Naval Ret.Bd. (Jun–Oct 1862, May 1863, Jun–Dec 1863); placed on Ret.Lst. (16 Jul 1862).

CORNELIUS KINCHILOE STRIBLING
1796–1880

CORNELIUS KINCHILOE STRIBLING Born in Pendleton, SC, on 22 Sep 1796. Died in Martinsburg, WV, on 17 Jan 1880. Buried in Oak Hill Cemetery, Washington, DC.

Ranks Midn (18 Jun 1812); Lt (1 Apr 1818); Cdr (28 Jan 1840); Capt (1 Aug 1853); transferred to Ret.Lst. (21 Dec 1861); Commo on Ret.Lst. (16 Jul 1862); RAdm on Ret.Lst. (25 Jul 1866).

Career Summary Received appointment from SC (18 Jun 1812); duty, Charleston, SC (Oct–Dec 1812); *Macedonian,* NY and New London, CT (Dec 1812–1814); *Mohawk,* Lake Ontario (1814–1815); *Macedonian,* Med.Sqdn. (1815–1816); *Constellation,* Med.Sqdn. (1816–1817); Braz.Sqdn. (1819–May 1820); Navy Yard, Norfolk, VA (May 1820–Mar 1822); *Hornet,* W.Ind.Sqdn. (Mar–Nov 1822); *Peacock, John Adams,* and *Constellation,* W.Ind.Sqdn. (Nov 1822–Jun 1825); *United States,* Pac.Sqdn. (Jun–Sep 1825); l.o.a. and w.o. (Sep 1825–Jul 1826); *Brandywine,* Pac.Sqdn. (Jul 1826–Jul 1830); l.o.a. (Jun–Oct 1830); Navy Yard, Boston (Oct–Nov 1830); l.o.a. and w.o. (Nov 1830–Mar 1831); cdr, rec. ship *Congress,* Norfolk, VA (Mar 1831–Mar 1833); l.o.a. (Mar–Apr 1833); asst.insp. of ord. (Apr 1833–Feb 1835); *Peacock,* E.Ind.Sqdn. (Mar 1835–Oct 1837); l.o.a. and w.o. (Oct 1837–May 1839); Naval Rndv., Norfolk, VA (May 1839–Mar 1840); cdr, Naval Rndv., Norfolk, VA (Jul–Oct 1840); Navy Yard, Washington, DC (Oct 1840–Sep 1841); cdr, *Cyane,* then *United States,* Pac.Sqdn. (Sep 1841–Oct 1844); l.o.a. and w.o. (Oct 1844–May 1845); spec. duty, Norfolk, VA (May–Oct 1845); cdr, rec. ship *Pennsylvania,* Norfolk, VA (Nov 1845–Oct 1847); flt.capt, Pac.Sqdn., *Ohio* (Oct 1847–Apr 1850); l.o.a. (Apr–Jun 1850); supt., USNA (Jul 1850–Nov 1853); w.o. (Nov 1853–May 1854); member, Bd. of Exam. (May 1854); cdr, *San Jacinto,* spec.serv., Home and W.Ind. Sqdns. (Jul 1854–Jun 1855); member, Efficiency Bd., Washington, DC (Jun–Sep 1855); w.o. (Sep 1855–Apr 1857); comdt., Navy Yard, Pensacola, FL (Jun 1857–Apr 1859); cdr, E.Ind.Sqdn., *Hartford* (May 1859–Jul 1861); member, spec. Senate Committee on officers' compensation, Washington, DC (Dec 1861–Apr 1862); transferred to Ret.Lst. (21 Dec 1861); member, L.h. Bd., Washington, DC (Apr–May 1862); pres., Bd. of Examiners (May–Nov 1862); comdt., Navy Yard, Philadelphia (Nov 1862–Sep 1864); cdr, E.Gulf.Blk.Sqdn., *San Jacinto* (Oct 1864–Jul 1865); w.o. (Jul 1865–Aug 1866); member, L.h. Bd., Washington, DC (Sep 1866–Oct 1871).

Career Highlights Served during War of 1812 and saw service under Stephen Decatur on board *Macedonian* in 1815 against Algiers. He served as flt.capt of Pac.Sqdn. during the war with Mexico, taking part in operations against Monterey. Was supt. of USNA during time of major curriculum changes.

SILAS HORTON STRINGHAM Born in Middletown, NY, on 7 Nov 1797, son of Daniel and Abigail (Horton) Stringham. Married Henrietta Hicks in 1819. Four children. Died at his residence in Brooklyn, NY, on 7 Feb 1876. Buried in Greenwood Cemetery, Brooklyn, NY.

Ranks Midn (15 Nov 1809); Lt (9 Dec 1814); Mstr. Comdt. (3 Mar 1831); Capt (8 Sep 1841); placed on Ret.Lst. (21 Dec 1861); RAdm on Ret.Lst. (16 Jul 1862).

Career Summary Received appointment from NY (15 Nov 1809); *President*, spec.serv. (Jun 1810–May 1814); *Guerriere*, Navy Yard, NY, and Med.Sqdn. (May 1814–Jun 1815); *Spark*, Med.Sqdn. (Apr 1815–Jul 1817); *Erie*, Med.Sqdn. (Jul 1817–Nov 1818); *Peacock*, Med.Sqdn. (Nov 1818–May 1819); *Ontario*, Baltimore (Jun–Sep 1819); *Cyane*, and temp. cdr, prize schooner, *Plattsburg*, Afr.Cst. (Oct 1819–Jan 1821); *Erie*, Navy Yard, NY (Feb–Aug 1821); exec.off., *Hornet*, W.Ind.Sqdn. (Sep 1821–Feb 1822); supernumerary, *Washington*, NY (Mar 1822–Sep 1823); *Cyane*, Med.Sqdn. (Oct 1823–Oct 1825); rec. ship *Fulton*, NY (Nov 1825–Aug 1826); l.o.a. (Aug–Oct 1826); Navy Yard, NY (Oct 1826–Apr 1827); l.o.a. (Apr–Jul 1827); court-martial duty, NY (Aug–Sep 1827); Navy Yard, NY (Nov 1827–Feb 1829); l.o.a. and w.o. (Feb–Aug 1829); *Peacock*, W.Ind.Sqdn. (Sep 1829–Apr 1830); *Falmouth*, W.Ind.Sqdn. (Apr–Aug 1830); l.o.a. (Aug 1830–Nov 1831); spec. court-martial duty (Nov 1831–Jan 1832); w.o. (Jan 1832–Dec 1834); court-martial duty (Dec. 1834–Jan 1835); w.o. (Feb–Jul 1835); cdr, *John Adams*, Med.Sqdn. (Oct 1835–May 1837); comdt., Navy Yard, NY (May 1837–Jul 1840); w.o. (Jul–Sep 1840); cdr, *Boston*, in ordinary, Navy Yard, NY (Sep–Oct 1840); w.o. and various bd. duties (Nov 1840–Sep 1842); cdr, flgs. *Independence*, Home Sqdn. (Sep 1842–Jun 1843); comdt., Navy Yard, NY (Jul 1843–Oct 1846); w.o. (Oct–Nov 1846); cdr, *Ohio*, Home Sqdn. (Nov 1846–Nov 1847); home and l.o.a. (Nov 1847–Feb 1848); bd. duties (Feb 1848–Jan 1851); comdt., Navy Yard, Norfolk, VA (Feb 1851–Mar 1852); cdr, Med.Sqdn., *Cumberland* (Apr 1852–Jul 1855); l.o.a. (Jul–Sep 1855); comdt., Navy Yard and Sta., Boston (Nov 1855–Apr 1859); pres., Bd. of Examiners, USNA (May–Oct 1859); w.o. (Oct 1859–Sep 1860); member, Sailing Boat Bd. (Sep–Oct 1860); w.o. (Oct 1860–Feb 1861); senior member, gen. court-martial, Navy Yard, NY (Feb–Mar 1861); spec. duty, Navy Dept., Washington, DC (Mar–Apr 1861); cdr, Atl.Blk.Sqdn., *Minnesota* (May–Sep 1861); l.o.a. (Sep–Dec 1861); placed on Ret.Lst. (21 Dec 1861); bd. duties, War Dept., Washington, DC (Jul 1862–Dec 1863); comdt., Navy Yard, Boston (Dec 1863–Dec 1866); w.o. (Dec 1866–Jan 1867); pres., Naval Ret.Bd., Washington, DC (Jan–Apr, Oct–Nov 1867);

SILAS HORTON STRINGHAM
1797–1876

w.o. (Nov 1867–Apr 1869); cdr and port adm, Naval Sta., NY (Apr 1869–Jun 1872).

Career Highlights With outbreak of Civil War, first assigned to command the relief force for Ft. Sumter which, however, never materialized. Commander of small first blockading force that extended from VA to southern part of FL. In command of naval forces which captured Fts. Hatteras and Clark in 1861, the North's first naval victories of the war.

EDWARD TRASK STRONG Born in Ipswich, MA, on 10 Feb 1840, son of Dr. Simeon E. Strong. Educated at Andover, MA. Married Annie G. Strong on 11 Jun 1867. Served throughout Civil War as volunteer officer, being commissioned in regular navy in 1868. Resided in Albany, NY. Died in Andover, MA, on 18 Mar 1909.

Ranks Act.Mstr's Mate (24 Nov 1862); Act.Ens (15 Oct 1863); resigned (15 Jun 1865); reappointed Act.Ens (5 Jul 1866); Ens (12 Mar 1868); Mstr (18 Dec 1868); Lt (21 Mar 1870); LCdr (2 Jul 1882); Cdr (9 Jan 1893); Capt (10 Oct 1899); retired with rank of RAdm (21 Nov 1900).

Career Summary Received appointment from MA (24 Nov 1862); *Macedonian*, Navy Yard, Boston (Nov 1862); flgs. *Ticonderoga*, W.Ind.Sqdn. (Nov 1862–Oct 1863); *Rachael Seaman*, W.Gulf Blk.Sqdn. (Nov 1863–Nov 1864); *Savannah*, Navy Yard, NY (Nov–Dec 1864); l.o.a. (Dec 1864–Jan 1865); Naval Rndv., NY (Jan–Apr 1865); training ship *Savannah* (Apr–May 1865); *Emma Henry* [renamed *Wasp*], Hampton Roads, VA (May–Jun 1865); resigned (15 Jun 1865); received appointment from MA as act.ens (5 Jul 1866); *Paul Jones*, Gulf Sqdn. (Jul 1866–Mar 1867); apprentice ship *Portsmouth* (Jun 1867–Oct 1868); rec. ship *New Hampshire*, Norfolk, VA (Oct 1868–Feb 1869); Navy Yard, Boston (Feb–Mar 1869); *Seminole*, N.Atl.Sta. (Apr 1869–Feb 1870); w.o. (Feb–May 1870); rec. ship *Vermont*, NY (May 1870); rec. ship *Ohio*, Boston (May–Jun 1870); flgs. *California*, Pac.Sqdn. (Dec 1870–Jul 1873); w.o. (Jul–Nov 1873); *Terror*, Philadelphia (Dec 1873); Navy Yard, Boston (Dec 1873–Jan 1874); *Shenandoah*, N.Atl.Sta. (Jan–Apr 1874); w.o. (Apr–Jul 1874); rec. ship *Ohio*, Boston (Jul 1874–Oct 1875); rec. ship *Wabash*, Boston (Oct–Dec 1875); *Vandalia*, Eur.Sta. (Jan 1876–Jan 1879); w.o. (Jan–Jul 1879); equip. duty, Navy Yard, Boston (Jul 1879–Apr 1882); Torp.Sta., Newport, RI (May–Jul 1882); w.o. (Jul–Aug 1882); exec.off., training ship *Minnesota* (Aug 1882–Jan 1883); *Swatara*, N.Atl.Sta. (Jan 1883–Nov 1885); w.o. (Nov 1885–Feb 1886); rec. ship *Wabash*, Boston (Feb–May 1886); equip. duty, Navy Yard, Boston (May 1886–Nov 1889); PA Nautical Schoolship *Saratoga* (Nov 1889–May 1892); l.o.a. abroad (Jun 1892–Feb 1893); cdr, PA Nautical Schoolship *Saratoga* (Feb 1893–Dec 1895); apprentice ship *Essex* (Jan 1896–Mar 1898); Navy Yard, League Island, PA (Mar–Apr 1898); cdr, *Mon-*

tauk, League Island, PA (Apr 1898); Navy Yard, Portsmouth, NH (May 1898–Nov 1899); ord. instruction, Navy Yard, Washington, DC (Nov 1899–Mar 1900); cdr, *Monadnock*, Asia.Flt. (May–Sep 1900); home and w.o. (Sep–Oct 1900); sick lv. (Oct–Nov 1900); retired (21 Nov 1900).

JAMES HOOKER STRONG Born in Canandaigua, NY, on 25 Apr 1814, son of Elisha Beebe and Dolly (Hooker) Strong. Attended the Polytechnic School in Chittenango, NY, graduating in 1829. Married Maria Louisa Von Cowenhoven in 1844. Two children. Died in Columbia, SC, on 28 Nov 1882. Buried in Newburgh, NY.

Ranks Midn (2 Feb 1829); PMidn (4 Jun 1836); Lt (8 Sep 1841); Cdr (24 Apr 1861); Capt (5 Aug 1865); Commo (2 Mar 1870); RAdm (25 Sep 1873); placed on Ret.Lst. (25 Apr 1876).

Career Summary Received appointment from NY (2 Feb 1829); w.o. (Mar 1829–Mar 1831); *Lexington* and *Enterprise*, Braz.Sqdn. (Apr 1831–Apr 1834); l.o.a. and w.o. (Apr 1834–Mar 1835); Naval School, NY (Mar–Jun 1835); l.o.a. (Jun–Aug 1835); *Constellation*, W.Ind.Sqdn. (Aug 1835–Apr 1836); l.o.a. and w.o. (May–Sep 1836); rec. ship *Hudson*, NY (Oct 1836–Jan 1837); *Independence*, Braz.Sqdn. (Jan 1837–Apr 1840); l.o.a. (Apr–Nov 1840); *Fulton*, spec.serv. (Nov 1840–Nov 1842); *Oregon*, Navy Yard, NY (Nov–Dec 1842); w.o. (Dec 1842–Jan 1843); *Truxtun*, Med.Sqdn. (Feb 1843–Jan 1844); l.o.a. and w.o. (Jan–Apr 1845); *Columbus*, E.Ind.Sqdn. (Apr 1845–Sep 1847); sick lv. and w.o. (Sep 1847–May 1848); rec. ship *Franklin*, Boston (May–Jul 1848); rec. ship *North Carolina*, NY (Jul 1848–May 1849); *John Adams*, Afr.Sqdn. (May–Nov 1849); sick lv. and w.o. (Nov 1849–Jan 1851); rec. ship *North Carolina*, NY (Jan 1851–Apr 1852); *Levant*, Med.Sqdn. (May 1852–May 1855); l.o.a. (May–Sep 1855); rec. ship *North Carolina*, NY (Sep 1855–Aug 1856); Naval Rndv., NY (Aug 1856–Feb 1858); cdr, *Relief*, Home Sqdn. (Feb 1858–Jan 1859); s.a. and w.o. (Jan 1859–Mar 1861); cdr, *Mohawk*, S.Atl.Blk.Sqdn. (Mar 1861–Apr 1862); cdr, *Flag*, S.Atl.Blk.Sqdn. (Apr 1862–Jun 1863); w.o. (Jun–Jul 1863); cdr, *Monongahela*, then cdr, *Pensacola*, W.Gulf Blk.Sqdn. (Aug 1863–Apr 1864); cdr, *Monongahela*, W.Gulf Blk.Sqdn. (Apr 1864–Apr 1865); spec. duty (Apr–May 1865); Navy Yard, NY (May 1865–Jan 1867); cdr, *Canandaigua*, Eur.Sqdn. (Feb 1867–Feb 1869); w.o. (Feb–Mar 1869); Navy Yard, NY (May 1869–Apr 1870); w.o. (Apr–Sep 1870); insp., 4th L.h. Dist., Philadelphia (Sep–Dec 1870); insp., 3rd L.h. Dist., Tompkinsville, NY (Dec 1870–Jul 1873); cdr, S.Atl.Sta., *Lancaster* (Sep 1873–Aug 1874); home and w.o. (Aug 1874–Apr 1876); placed on Ret.Lst. (25 Apr 1876).

Career Highlights During Civil War, commanded *Monongahela* at Battle of Mobile Bay on 5 Aug 1864, his being the first ship to ram Confederate *Tennessee*, helping to cripple the ship and force her surrender.

JAMES HOOKER STRONG
1814–1882

GEORGE WATSON SUMNER
1841–1924

GEORGE WATSON SUMNER Born in Constantine, MI, on 31 Dec 1841, son of Dr. Watson and Hester Ann (Welling) Sumner. Married Maudthilde Willis on 20 Feb 1886. Died at his home in Patchogue, Long Island, NY, on 20 Feb 1924. Survived by two sons and a daughter. Buried in Rock Creek Cemetery, Washington, DC.

Ranks Act.Midn (20 Sep 1858); title changed to Midn (16 Jul 1862); Lt (1 Aug 1862); LCdr (25 Jul 1866); Cdr (13 Jun 1876); Capt (2 Oct 1891); RAdm (3 Mar 1899); placed on Ret.Lst. (31 Dec 1903).

Career Summary Received appointment from KY (20 Sep 1858); USNA (Sep 1858–May 1861); *Colorado*, Gulf Blk.Sqdn. (May–Sep 1861); *Brooklyn*, Gulf Blk.Sqdn. (Nov–Dec 1861); spec. duty, *Harriet Lane* and Vicksburg batteries, Mortar Flot., MS River (Dec 1861–1862); exec.off., *Pinola*, then nav.off., *Pensacola*, W.Gulf Blk.Sqdn. (1862–Apr 1864); USNA (May–Aug 1864); *Massasoit*, N.Atl.Blk.Sqdn. (Aug 1864–Jan 1865); cdr, *Massasoit*, N.Atl.Blk.Sqdn. (Jan–Jun 1865); l.o.a. (Jun–Jul 1865); exec.off. and nav., *Desoto*, N.Atl.Sqdn. (Jul 1865–Sep 1868); w.o. (Sep–Nov 1868); watch off. and nav., flgs. *Franklin*, Eur.Sqdn. (Dec 1868–Nov 1871); w.o. (Nov–Dec 1871); Hydrographic Office, Washington, DC (Dec 1871–Aug 1877); cdr, *Monocacy*, Asia.Sta. (Sep 1877–Sep 1880); w.o. (Sep–Dec 1880); spec. duty, Washington, DC (Dec 1880–Sep 1881); Bur. of Ord., Washington, DC (Sep 1881–May 1886); l.o.a. (May–Oct 1886); torp. instruction, Newport, RI (Oct 1886–Sep 1887); NWC, Newport, RI (Sep–Dec 1887); home and w.o. (Dec 1887–Apr 1888); Torp.Sta., Newport, RI (May–Aug 1888); NWC, Newport, RI (Aug–Nov 1888); cdr, flgs. *Galena*, N.Atl.Sta. (Dec 1888–Jul 1890); l.o.a. (Jul–Oct 1890); asst., then equip.off., Navy Yard, NY (Oct 1890–Mar 1893); cdr, *Baltimore*, Hampton Roads, VA (Mar–May 1893); gen.insp., *Columbia*, Philadelphia (May 1893–Apr 1894); cdr, *Columbia*, N.Atl.Sqdn. (Apr 1894–Sep 1895); suspended from duty (Sep 1895–Jan 1896); cdr, *Monadnock*, Pac.Sta. (Feb 1896–Jun 1897); capt.yd., Navy Yard, NY (Jul 1897–Apr 1899); home and w.o. (Apr–May 1899); comdt., Naval Sta., Port Royal, SC (Jun 1899–Jan 1901); comdt., Navy Yard and Sta., Philadelphia (Jan 1901–Feb 1902); cdr, S.Atl.Sqdn., *Iowa*, *Chicago*, and then *Newark* (Mar 1902–Sep 1903); home and w.o. (Sep–Dec 1903); placed on Ret.Lst. (31 Dec 1903).

Career Highlights During Civil War, participated in actions against forts on lower Mississippi River and at Vicksburg in 1862. Fought against Confederate ironclads on James River in early 1865. Commanded triple screw cruiser *Columbia* at opening of Kiel Canal in Germany in 1895, racing her home from Southampton to NY, achieving fastest long distance run yet for a warship.

References
Personal Papers: 1 item (1862) in NHF,WNY.

ALFRED TAYLOR Born in Alexandria, VA, on 23 May 1811. Married twice: to Nancy Massey Bronaugh, then to Katherine Dimick. At least three children. Died in Washington, DC, on 19 Apr 1891. Buried in Portsmouth, NH.

Ranks Midn (1 Jan 1825); PMidn (4 Jun 1831); Lt (9 Feb 1837); Cdr (14 Sep 1855); Capt (16 Jul 1862); Commo (27 Sep 1866); RAdm (29 Jan 1872); placed on Ret.Lst. (23 May 1872).

Career Summary Received appointment from VA (1 Jan 1825); *Brandywine*, Med.Sqdn. (Jul–Oct 1826); *North Carolina*, Med.Sqdn. (Oct 1826–Jun 1830); l.o.a. (Jun–Dec 1830); Naval School, Norfolk, VA (Dec 1830–Mar 1831); w.o. (Mar–Jun 1831); l.o.a. (Jun–Sep 1831); Navy Yard, Portsmouth, NH (Sep 1831–Jul 1833); l.o.a. (Jul–Sep 1833); Navy Yard, Boston (Sep 1833–Jan 1834); rec. ship *Columbus*, Boston (Jan–May 1834); *Erie*, Braz.Sqdn. (Jun 1834–Sep 1837); l.o.a. (Sep 1837–Sep 1838); *Ohio*, then *Grampus*, Med. and Afr. Sqdns. (Sep 1838–Aug 1841); l.o.a. (Aug–Dec 1841); rec. ship at Alexandria, VA (Dec 1841–Feb 1842); Navy Yard, Washington, DC (Feb 1842–Sep 1843); *Boston*, Braz.Sqdn. (Sep 1843–Jan 1846); l.o.a. and w.o. (Jan 1846–Jan 1847); Naval Observatory, Washington, DC (Jan–Sep 1847); *Cumberland*, Home Sqdn. (Oct 1847–Aug 1848); w.o. (Aug 1848–Mar 1849); Navy Yard, Washington, DC (May 1849–Oct 1851); w.o. (Oct 1851–Mar 1852); *Mississippi*, E.Ind.Sqdn. (Mar 1852–Sep 1854); return and l.o.a. (Sep 1854–Apr 1855); temp. duty, insp. of provisions, Navy Yard, Washington, DC (Apr–May 1855); w.o. (May–Oct 1855); cdr, Naval Rndv., NY (Oct 1855–Oct 1858); w.o. (Oct 1858–Oct 1860); cdr, *Saratoga*, Afr.Sqdn. (Oct 1860–Aug 1861); return and w.o. (Aug 1861–Feb 1862); cdr, *Galena*, Mystic, CT (Feb–Apr 1862); Navy Yard, Boston (Apr 1862–Apr 1865); cdr, flgs. *Susquehanna*, Braz.Sqdn. (May 1865–Jun 1866); w.o. (Jun 1866–Oct 1868); court-martial duty (Oct–Nov 1868); w.o. (Nov 1868–Feb 1869); insp., 12th L.h. Dist., San Francisco (Feb 1869–Feb 1872); w.o. (Feb–May 1872); placed on Ret.Lst. (23 May 1872).

Career Highlights Served with Commo M. C. Perry and the expd. to the Far East and Japan in 1852–54.

ALFRED TAYLOR
1811–1891

WILLIAM ROGERS TAYLOR Born in Newport, RI, on 7 Nov 1811, son of William Vigneron and Abby (White) Taylor. Married Caroline Silliman on 30 Apr 1840. Two children. Died in Washington, DC, on 14 Apr 1889. Buried in the Congressional Cemetery in Washington, DC.

Ranks Midn (1 Apr 1828); PMidn (14 Jun 1834); Lt (10 Feb 1840); Cdr (14 Sep 1855); Capt (16 Jul 1862); Commo (25 Jul 1866); RAdm (19 Jan 1871); placed on Ret.Lst. (7 Nov 1873).

Career Summary Received appointment from RI (1 Apr 1828); w.o. (Apr–Jul 1828); *Hudson*, Braz.Sqdn. (Jul 1828–Aug 1831); l.o.a. (Aug 1831–Feb 1832); *Peacock*, Braz.Sqdn. (Feb–Aug 1832); l.o.a. (Aug 1832–Feb 1833); Naval School, NY

WILLIAM ROGERS TAYLOR
1811–1889

(Mar 1833–May 1834); l.o.a. and w.o. (May 1834–Mar 1835); *Peacock,* E.Ind.Sqdn. (Mar 1835–Feb 1839); l.o.a. and w.o. (Feb 1839–Oct 1841); Depot of Charts, Washington, DC (Nov 1841–May 1842); l.o.a. (May–Aug 1842); rec. ship *North Carolina,* NY (Aug–Oct 1842); *Oregon,* survey duty (Oct 1842–Jul 1843); *Perry,* spec.serv., and *Columbus,* Med.Sqdn. (Sep 1843–May 1844); l.o.a. and w.o. (May–Oct 1844); *St. Mary's,* Home Sqdn. (Oct 1844–May 1847); l.o.a. and w.o. (May 1847–Feb 1848); rec. ship *Franklin,* Boston (Feb–Jul 1848); *St. Lawrence,* spec.serv. (Jul 1848–Jan 1849); l.o.a. and w.o. (Jan–Aug 1849); Naval Asylum, Philadelphia (Aug 1849–Feb 1850); Naval Observatory, Washington, DC (Feb–Oct 1850); *Albany,* Home Sqdn. (Oct 1850–Jul 1852); ord. duty, Navy Yard, Boston (Jul 1852–Aug 1855); *Saratoga,* Navy Yard, Boston (Aug–Oct 1855); w.o. (Oct 1855–Apr 1856); ord. duty, Washington, DC (Apr 1856–Nov 1859); w.o. (Nov 1859–May 1860); member, Bd. of Examiners, USNA (May–Dec 1860); insp., 1st L.h. Dist., Portland, ME (Dec 1860–May 1861); Bur. of Ord., Washington, DC (May 1861–May 1862); flt.capt, S.Atl.Blk.Sqdn., and cdr, *Housatonic* (Jun 1862–Aug 1863); sick lv. (Aug–Oct 1863); spec. duty, Navy Dept., Washington, DC (Oct 1863–Apr 1864); w.o. (Apr–May 1864); cdr, *Juniata,* N.Atl.Blk.Sqdn. (May 1864–Jan 1865); sick lv. (Jan–Apr 1865); ord. duty, Navy Yard, Washington, DC (Apr–Jul 1865); pres., Bd. to Revise Navy Regulations, then ord. duty, Navy Yard, Washington, DC (Jul 1865–Aug 1866); l.o.a. and w.o. (Aug–Dec 1866); ord. duty, Fort Pitt Foundry, Pittsburgh, PA (Dec 1866–Apr 1867); w.o. (Apr–May 1867); l.o.a. and w.o. (May 1867–Mar 1868); member, Naval Exam.Bd., Boston (Mar–Oct 1868); various shore duties (Oct 1868–May 1869); cdr, N.Pac.Sta., *Ossipee* (May 1869–Feb 1871); w.o. (Feb–Sep 1871); pres., Bd. of Examiners (Oct 1871–Mar 1872); cdr, S.Atl.Sta., *Lancaster* (Oct 1872–Oct 1873); home and w.o. (Oct–Nov 1873); placed on Ret.Lst. (7 Nov 1873).

Career Highlights Saw action at Vera Cruz during war with Mexico. During Civil War, was a senior officer off Charleston during the first unsuccessful attacks by ironclads. Also served as flt.capt to RAdm John A. Dahlgren [*q.v.*] against forts in Charleston Harbor in Jul 1863.

WILLIAM GRENVILLE TEMPLE

Born in Rutland, VT, on 23 Mar 1824, son of Robert and Charlotte Eloise (Green) Temple. Married Catlyna Totten on 7 Oct 1851. Died in Washington, DC, on 28 Jun 1894. Buried in the Congressional Cemetery there.

Ranks Act.Midn (18 Apr 1840); PMidn (11 Jul 1846); Mstr (21 Jul 1854); Lt (18 Apr 1855); LCdr (16 Jul 1862); Cdr (3 Mar 1865); Capt (28 Aug 1870); Commo (5 Jun 1878); RAdm (22 Feb 1884); retired (29 Feb 1884).

Career Summary Received appointment from VT (18 Apr 1840); rec. ship *Columbus,* Boston (May–Sep 1840); *Con-*

WILLIAM GRENVILLE TEMPLE
1824–1894

stellation, spec. cruise (Sep 1840–May 1844); l.o.a. (May–Aug 1844); flgs. *Potomac*, Home Sqdn. (Aug 1844–Mar 1845); *St. Lawrence*, Navy Yard, Norfolk, VA (Mar–Oct 1845); *Potomac*, W.Ind.Sqdn. (Oct–Dec 1845); Naval School, Annapolis, MD (Dec 1845–Jul 1846); w.o. (Jul–Oct 1846); *Boston*, W.Ind.Sqdn. (Oct–Dec 1846); rec. ship *Pennsylvania*, Norfolk, VA (Jan–Feb 1847); court-martial duty, Norfolk, VA (Feb 1847); *Scourge*, Home Sqdn. (Feb–Nov 1847); *Scorpion*, Home Sqdn. (Nov–Dec 1847); *Mississippi*, Gulf of Mexico (Dec 1847–Apr 1848); l.o.a. (Apr–Jun 1848); Naval Observatory, Washington, DC (Jun 1848–May 1849); cst.surv. duty (May 1849–Aug 1850); Cst.Surv. Office, Washington, DC (Aug–Oct 1850); Naval Observatory, Washington, DC (Oct–Nov 1850); l.o.a., Isthmus of Tehuantepec hydrographic survey (Nov 1850–Apr 1852); *Levant*, Med.Sqdn. (Apr 1852–May 1855); l.o.a. (May–Jun 1855); cst.surv. duty (Jun–Dec 1855); Cst.Surv. Office, Washington, DC (Dec 1855–May 1856); cst.surv. duty (May 1856–Oct 1858); Cst.Surv. Office, Washington, DC (Oct 1858–Apr 1859); flgs. *Lancaster*, Pac.Sqdn. (Apr 1859–Oct 1861); l.o.a. (Oct–Nov 1861); cdr, *Flambeau*, S.Atl.Blk.Sqdn. (Nov 1861–Jan 1862); *Savannah*, S.Atl.Blk.Sqdn. (Jan–Feb 1862); w.o. (Feb 1862); ord. duty, NY (Feb–Apr 1862); insp. of ord., Navy Yard, NY (Apr–Sep 1862); cdr, *Pembina*, W.Gulf Blk.Sqdn. (Sep–Nov 1862); flt.capt, E.Gulf Blk.Sqdn., *San Jacinto* (Nov 1862–Sep 1864); temp. duty, cdr, *San Jacinto*, spec.serv., Key West, FL (Apr 1864); ord. duty, West Point Foundry, Cold Spring, NY (Sep–Nov 1864); cdr, *Pontoosuc*, N.Atl.Blk.Sqdn. (Nov 1864–May 1865); l.o.a. (May–Aug 1865); cdr, flgs. *Tacony*, N.Atl.Sqdn. (Aug 1865–Oct 1866); insp. of ord., Navy Yard, Portsmouth, NH (Nov 1866–Oct 1869); member, Permanent Ord. Bd., Navy Dept., Washington, DC (Oct 1869–Oct 1870); asst. judge advocate, U.S. Navy, Navy Dept., Washington, DC (Oct–Dec 1870); cdr, *Tennessee*, spec.serv. (Dec 1870–Apr 1871); w.o. (Apr–May 1871); Bur. of Ord., Washington, DC (May–Oct 1871); chief of staff, Eur.Sta., *Wabash* (Oct 1871–May 1873); cdr, *Wabash*, Eur.Sqdn. (Jul 1872–May 1873); l.o.a. (May 1873–Dec 1874); spec. duty, in charge of reception of Hawaiian King, Kalakaua, to Washington, DC (Dec 1874); capt.yd., Navy Yard, NY (Feb 1875–Oct 1877); w.o. (Oct 1877–Oct 1878); temp. duty, *Hartford*, Navy Yard, NY (Oct 1878–Feb 1879); w.o. (Feb–Oct 1879); member, Naval Exam. and Ret. Bd., Navy Dept., Washington, DC (Oct 1879–Sep 1882); member, Naval Advisory Bd., Navy Dept., Washington, DC (Jul 1881–Sep 1882); w.o. (Sep–Oct 1882); pres., *Jeanette* court of inquiry, Washington, DC (Oct 1882–Apr 1883); w.o. (Apr 1883–Feb 1884); retired (29 Feb 1884).

SILAS WRIGHT TERRY Born in Wallonia, Trigg County, KY, on 28 Dec 1842, son of Abner R. and Eleanor (Dyer) Terry. Married Louisa G. Mason on 14 Oct 1873. Two chil-

SILAS WRIGHT TERRY
1842–1911

dren. Died at his home in Washington, DC, on 9 Feb 1911. Buried in USNA Cemetery.

Ranks Act.Midn (28 Sep 1858); title changed to Midn (16 Jul 1862); Ens (16 Sep 1862); Lt (22 Feb 1864); LCdr (25 Jul 1866); Cdr (11 Jul 1877); Capt (9 Jan 1893); RAdm (29 Mar 1900); placed on Ret.Lst. (28 Dec 1904).

Career Summary Received appointment from KY (28 Sep 1858); USNA (Sep 1858–May 1861); found deficient and turned back (Jun 1859); Navy Yard, NY (May–Jun 1861); *Dale*, Atl.Blk.Sqdn. (Jun 1861–Sep 1862); flgs. *Wabash*, S.Atl.Blk.Sqdn. (Sep–Oct 1862); *Alabama*, S.Atl.Blk.Sqdn. (Oct 1862); l.o.a. and w.o. (Oct–Nov 1862); aide, N.Atl.Blk.Sqdn., *Minnesota* (Dec 1862–Mar 1863); *Dakotah*, N.Atl.Blk.Sqdn. (Mar–Jul 1863); *Black Hawk*, and cdr, *Benefit*, MS Sqdn. (Sep 1863–Oct 1864); detail off., N.Atl.Blk.Sqdn., *Malvern* (May 1864–May 1865); w.o. (May–Jul 1865); *Agawam*, N.Atl.Blk.Sqdn. (Jul–Aug 1865); *Ticonderoga*, Eur.Sta. (Aug 1865–Oct 1868); w.o. (Nov–Dec 1868); rec. ship *Vermont*, NY (Dec 1868–Apr 1869); USNA (Apr 1869–Mar 1871); exec.off., flgs. *Severn*, N.Atl.Sta. (Mar–Dec 1871); exec.off., flgs. *Worcester*, N.Atl.Sta. (Dec 1871–May 1873); w.o. (May–Jul 1873); Naval Observatory, Washington, DC (Jul–Oct 1873); l.o.a. (Oct 1873–Jul 1874); USNA (Jul 1874–Aug 1877); insp., 5th L.h. Dist., Baltimore (Aug 1877–Jun 1880); s.a. and w.o. (Jun 1880–Jun 1881); cdr, *Marion*, S.Atl.Sta. (Jul 1881–Dec 1882); w.o. (Dec 1882–Apr 1883); Navy Yard, League Island, PA (Apr 1883–Oct 1884); cdr, Training Sqdn., *Portsmouth* (Oct 1884–Apr 1886); cdr, training ship *Jamestown* (Apr–May 1886); w.o. (May 1886–Oct 1887); nav.off., Navy Yard, Washington, DC (Oct 1887–Aug 1889); bd. duties (Jul 1888–May 1893); cdr, *Newark*, Naval Review Flt. and S.Atl.Sqdn. (May 1893–May 1895); l.o.a. (May–Jul 1895); cdr, rec. ship *Franklin*, Norfolk, VA (Jul 1895–Sep 1898); cdr, *Iowa*, Pac.Sta. (Sep 1898–Sep 1899); home and w.o. (Sep–Nov 1899); member, Naval Exam.Bd. (Dec 1899–Mar 1900); comdt., Navy Yard, Washington, DC (Mar 1900–May 1903); w.o. and bd. duties (May–Jul 1903); comdt., Naval Sta., Honolulu, Hawaii (Aug 1903–Dec 1904); placed on Ret.Lst. (28 Dec 1904).

Career Highlights During Civil War, served on the Red River Expedition: commended by RAdm David D. Porter [*q.v.*] for his gallantry in delivering despatches through hostile action. Served on Porter's staff for much of the war's remainder. Saw action at Ft. Fisher. Accompanied Pres. Lincoln and RAdm Porter into Richmond.

HENRY KNOX THATCHER Born in Thomaston, ME, on 26 May 1806, son of Ebenezer and Lucy Flucker (Knox) Thatcher. Grandfather was MGen Henry Knox of Revolutionary War fame. Attended U.S. Military Academy for a few months in 1822. Married Susan C. Croswell on 26 Dec 1831. One adopted child. Died in Boston on 5 Apr 1880.

HENRY KNOX THATCHER
1806–1880

Ranks Act.Midn (4 Mar 1823); PMidn (23 Mar 1829); Lt (28 Feb 1833); Cdr (14 Sep 1855); Commo (16 Jul 1862); Act.RAdm (25 Jan 1865); RAdm (25 Jul 1866); placed on Ret.Lst. (26 May 1868).

Career Summary Received appointment from ME (4 Mar 1823); Navy Yard, Washington, DC (Sep–Nov 1823); flgs. *United States*, Pac.Sqdn. (Nov 1823–Apr 1827); l.o.a. (Apr 1827–May 1828); *Independence*, in ordinary, Navy Yard, Boston (May–Oct 1828); w.o. (Oct 1828–Sep 1829); l.o.a. and w.o. (Sep 1829–Aug 1830); act.mstr., *Porpoise*, then *Erie*, W.Ind.Sqdn. (Aug 1830–Oct 1831); l.o.a. and w.o. (Oct 1831–Nov 1833); Navy Yard, Boston (Nov 1833–Feb 1834); *Falmouth*, W.Ind.Sqdn. (Feb 1834–Aug 1835); l.o.a. and w.o. (Aug 1835–Jan 1838); *Erie*, spec.serv. (Jan–May 1838); l.o.a. and w.o. (May 1838–May 1839); *Brandywine*, Med.Sqdn. (May 1839–Jun 1841); l.o.a. (Jun–Nov 1841); Naval Rndv., Portland, ME (Nov 1841–Aug 1842); w.o. (Aug–Oct 1842); rec. ship *Ohio*, Boston (Oct 1842–Oct 1843); l.o.a. and w.o. (Oct 1843–Jul 1845); rec. ship *Ohio*, Boston (Jul 1845–Oct 1846); *Boston*, Navy Yard, NY (Oct 1846–Feb 1847); w.o. (Feb–Mar 1847); rec. ship *Ohio*, Boston (Mar–Jun 1847); *Jamestown*, Afr. and Med. Sqdns. (Jun 1847–May 1850); l.o.a. (May–Jun 1850); insp. duty, Navy Yard, Boston (Jun 1850–Mar 1851); cdr, *Relief*, Braz.Sqdn. (Mar 1851–Aug 1852); l.o.a. and w.o. (Aug 1852–May 1853); cdr, *Lexington*, Navy Yard, NY (May–Jun 1853); w.o. (Jun 1853–Sep 1854); exec.off., Naval Asylum, Philadelphia (Sep 1854–Mar 1857); cdr, *Decatur*, Pac.Sqdn. (Apr 1857–Aug 1859); w.o. (Aug–Sep 1859); exec.off., Navy Yard, Boston (Nov 1859–Nov 1861); cdr, *Constellation*, spec. duty, Med. (Nov 1861–Jul 1863); return and w.o. (Jul–Sep 1863); cdr, *Colorado*, and 1st Div., N.Atl.Blk.Sqdn. (Sep 1863–Feb 1864); w.o. (Feb–Apr 1864); temp. cdr, *New Hampshire* then *Vermont*, storeships, Port Royal, SC (Apr–Aug 1864); *Colorado*, N.Atl.Blk.Sqdn. (Aug 1864–Jan 1865); cdr, W.Gulf Blk.Sqdn., *Portsmouth* (Jan–Mar 1865); cdr, W.Gulf Blk.Sqdn., *Stockdale* (Mar–Jul 1865); cdr, Gulf Sqdn., *Estrella* (Jul 1865–May 1866); cdr, N.Pac.Sqdn., *Vanderbilt* then *Pensacola* (Jul 1866–Aug 1868); placed on Ret.Lst. (26 May 1868); port adm, Naval Sta., Portsmouth, NH (May 1869–Oct 1870).

Career Highlights During latter phase of Civil War, commanded a division in attacks and capture of Ft. Fisher. Commanding W.Gulf Blk.Sqdn, initiated operations against Mobile and along Texas Coast.

References
Personal Papers: a) 1 item (1866) in NHF,LC. b) 1 letter-book (1867–68) in GARL.

Additional Sources: George Henry Preble, *Henry Knox Thatcher, Rear Admiral, U.S. Navy* (1882).

HENRY DAVIS TODD Born in Cambridge, MA, on 25 Aug 1838, son of John N. Todd. Primary education in Nyack, NY. Married Flora Johnson on 28 Sep 1865. Two children.

Died at his home in Annapolis, MD, on 8 Mar 1907. Buried in USNA Cemetery.

Ranks Act.Midn (28 May 1853); Midn (10 Jun 1857); PMidn (25 Jun 1860); Mstr (24 Oct 1860); Lt (3 Apr 1861); LCdr (2 Jan 1863); resigned (19 Oct 1866); Prof. of Math. (16 Sep 1877); Prof. of Math. with rel. rank of Lt (15 Nov 1877); Prof. of Math. with rel. rank of Capt (29 Jul 1898); placed on Ret.Lst. as Prof. of Math. with rank of RAdm (25 Aug 1900).

Career Summary Received appointment from NY (28 May 1853); USNA (May 1853–Jun 1857); *Minnesota*, E.Ind.Sqdn. (Jun 1857–May 1859); l.o.a. and w.o. (May–Nov 1859); *Mohican*, Afr.Sqdn. (Nov 1859–Oct 1860); w.o. (Oct–Nov 1860); *Cumberland* and *Roanoke*, Home and N.Atl.Blk. Sqdns. (Nov 1860–Mar 1862); w.o. (Mar–Apr 1862); *Port Royal*, N.Atl.Blk.Sqdn. (Apr–Sep 1862); flag lt, Spec.W.Ind.Sqdn., *Wachusett* (Sep 1862–Mar 1863); w.o. (Mar–Apr 1863); USNA (Apr–Nov 1863); *Sangamon* (Nov 1863); *Sacramento*, spec.serv. (Nov 1863–Aug 1865); w.o. (Aug–Sep 1865); inst. of math., USNA (Oct 1865–May 1866); w.o. (May–Aug 1866); Naval Rndv., Boston (Sep–Oct 1866); *Ossipee*, Navy Yard, Philadelphia (Oct 1866); resigned (19 Oct 1866); received appointment from PA as prof. of math. (16 Sep 1877); w.o. (Sep–Oct 1877); Nautical Almanac Office, Washington, DC (Oct 1877–Oct 1878); head, Dept. of Physics and Chemistry, USNA (Nov 1878–Dec 1886); Nautical Almanac Office, Washington, DC (Dec 1886–Dec 1900); dir., Nautical Almanac Office, Washington, DC (Dec 1899–Aug 1900); placed on Ret.Lst. (25 Aug 1900).

References

Writings: (with J. J. Brown), *Total Eclipse of the Sun, May 28 1900* (Washington, DC: 1900).

JAMES EDWARD TOLFREE Born in Ithaca, NY, on 29 Aug 1837, son of John Edward and Caroline Rebecca (Cole) Tolfree. Educated at the Ithaca Academy and by private tutors in France and Italy. Married Caroline Overman on 9 Oct 1872. His brother-in-law was RAdm Charles Baldwin, USN [*q.v.*]. Resided in New York City. Died in Atlantic City, NJ, on 10 Jan 1920.

Ranks Act.Asst.Paymstr. (13 Sep 1862); Asst.Paymstr. (3 Mar 1865); Paymstr. (22 Jan 1866); Pay Insp. (10 Aug 1886); Pay Dir. (12 Feb 1898); placed on Ret.Lst. as Pay Dir. with rank of RAdm (29 Aug 1899).

Career Summary Received appointment from NY (13 Sep 1862); *Vanderbilt*, spec.serv. (Sep 1862–Feb 1867); s.a. and w.o. (Feb 1867–May 1868); training ship *Savannah* (May–Sep 1868); s.a. and w.o. (Sep–Oct 1868); *Richmond*, Eur.Sqdn. (Dec 1868–Nov 1871); s.a. and w.o. (Nov 1871–Apr 1872); rec. ship *Vermont*, NY (Jul 1872–Jun 1875); rec. ship *Colorado*, NY, and in charge of stores and accounts, *Intrepid* (Jun 1875–Feb 1877); purchasing pay off., Philadelphia (Mar–Apr 1877);

flt.paymstr., Eur.Sta., *Trenton* (Apr–Oct 1877); in charge, Naval Depot, Villefranche, France (Oct 1877–Jan 1879); s.a. and w.o. (Jan–May 1879); Pay Office, Navy Yard, Washington, DC (May–Aug 1879); flt.paymstr., S.Atl.Sta., *Shenandoah* (Sep 1879–May 1882); s.a. and w.o. (May–Sep 1882); rec. ship *Colorado*, NY (Oct 1882–Nov 1885); s.a. and w.o. (Nov–Dec 1885); flt.paymstr., Asia.Sta., *Trenton* (Feb–May 1886), *Omaha* (May 1886–May 1887), and *Brooklyn* (May 1887–May 1889); s.a. and w.o. (May–Jun 1889); gen. storekeeper, Navy Yard, NY (Jul 1889–Oct 1890); s.a. and w.o. (Oct–Dec 1890); training ship *Minnesota*, NY (Dec 1890–Dec 1893); additional duty, in charge, Navy Pay Office, NY (Dec 1892–Jan 1893); s.a. and w.o. (Dec 1893–Feb 1894); gen. storekeeper, Navy Yard, NY (Feb 1894–May 1896); in charge, Navy Pay Office, NY (May 1896–Jun 1899); s.a. and w.o. (Jun–Aug 1899); placed on Ret.Lst. (29 Aug 1899).

STEPHEN DECATUR TRENCHARD Born in Brooklyn, NY, on 10 Jul 1818, son of navy Capt Edward (1784–1824) and Eliza (Sands) Trenchard. Educated at Kenyon College in Gambier, OH, in 1829. Married Ann O'Conner Barclay on 1 Dec 1848. One son. Died at his home in New York City on 15 Nov 1883. Buried in the Cemetery of St. James the Less in Philadelphia.

    Ranks Midn (23 Oct 1834); PMidn (16 Jul 1840); Lt (27 Feb 1847); Cdr (16 Jul 1862); Capt (25 Jul 1866); Commo (7 May 1871); RAdm (10 Aug 1875); placed on Ret.Lst. (10 Jul 1880).

    Career Summary Received appointment from NY (23 Oct 1834); w.o. (Oct 1834–Feb 1835); *Constitution*, spec.serv. (Feb–Aug 1835); rec. ship *Hudson*, NY (Aug 1835–Jan 1836); *Concord*, W.Ind.Sqdn. (Jan 1836–Dec 1838); Naval School, NY (Dec 1838–Nov 1839); Naval School, Philadelphia (Nov 1839–Jun 1840); l.o.a. (Jun–Sep 1840); Navy Yard, NY (Sep–Dec 1840); *Preble* and *Fairfield*, Med.Sqdn. (Dec 1840–Jan 1845); l.o.a. and w.o. (Jan–Jun 1845); cst.surv. duty (Jun 1845–Mar 1848); *Saratoga*, Home Sqdn. (Mar 1848–Nov 1849); l.o.a. and w.o. (Nov 1849–Apr 1850); rec. ship *Union*, Philadelphia (Apr–Nov 1850); *Albany*, Home Sqdn. (Nov 1850–Sep 1852); rec. ship *Union*, Philadelphia (Sep 1852–Mar 1853); cst.surv. duty (Mar 1853–Oct 1857); *Powhatan*, E.Ind.Sqdn. (Nov 1857–Aug 1860); l.o.a. and w.o. (Aug 1860–Apr 1861); Naval Rndv., Philadelphia and cdr, *Keystone State* (Apr–Jun 1861); Navy Yard, Philadelphia (Jun–Jul 1861); cdr, supply ship *Rhode Island* (Jul 1861–Aug 1865); exec.off., Navy Yard, NY (Sep 1865–Aug 1866); insp., 4th L.h. Dist., Philadelphia (Sep 1866–Apr 1867); Navy Yard, NY (May 1867–May 1869); cdr, flgs. *Lancaster*, S.Atl.Sqdn. (May 1869–Jul 1871); w.o. (Jul–Oct 1871); member, Bd. of Examiners, Washington, DC (Oct 1871–May 1873); insp., 3rd L.h. Dist., Tompkinsville, NY (Aug 1873–Sep 1875); w.o. (Sep 1875–Aug 1876); cdr,

STEPHEN DECATUR TRENCHARD
1818–1883

N.Atl.Sta., *Hartford* (Aug 1876–Aug 1878); w.o. (Aug 1878–Apr 1879); bd. duties (May 1879–Jul 1880); placed on Ret.Lst. (10 Jul 1880).

Career Highlights Served in Commo Matthew C. Perry's sqdn. during Mexican War, participating in action off Vera Cruz and against Tabasco in 1847. While commanding the *Vixen*, rescued the HMS *Adieu* off Massachusetts's coast in 1856, receiving a sword from Queen Victoria in gratitude.

References

Additional Sources: Edgar S. Maclay, *Reminiscences of the Old Navy; from the Journals and Private Papers of Edward Trenchard and Stephen Decatur Trenchard* (NY: 1898).

JOSEPH TRILLEY Born in Ireland on 25 Sep 1837, son of Samuel and Ann Trilley. Emigrating early to United States, attended schools in Philadelphia and in Baltimore, then studied engineering at Maryland Institute School of Design. Married Blanche Haynes on 25 Apr 1868. Died in San Francisco on 6 Mar 1911. Buried in San Francisco.

Ranks 3rd Asst.Engr. (11 Aug 1860); 2nd Asst.Engr. (30 Jul 1862); 1st Asst.Engr. (20 Jul 1864); Chief Engr. (31 Jan 1873); Chief Engr. with rel. rank of Cdr (2 Mar 1892); Chief Engr. with rel. rank of Capt (27 Jun 1896); title changed to Capt (3 Mar 1899); placed on Ret.Lst. with rank of RAdm (25 Sep 1899).

Career Summary Received appointment from MD (11 Aug 1860): *Pawnee*, Gulf and N.Atl. Blk.Sqdns. (Sep 1860–Jun 1862); examination and w.o. (Jun–Sep 1862); *Monongahela*, W.Gulf Blk.Sqdn. (Sep 1862–Apr 1865); w.o. (Apr–Jul 1865); spec. duty, NY (Jul–Dec 1865); *Algonquin* [never commissioned], NY (Dec 1865–Mar 1866); *Idaho*, on trials (Mar–May 1866); temp. duty, Navy Yard, Boston (May 1866–Apr 1867); sick lv. (May–Nov 1867); spec. duty, Naval Rndv., Boston (Nov 1867–Jun 1868); w.o. (Jun 1868–Apr 1869); *Seminole*, N.Atl.Sta. (Apr 1869–Feb 1870); w.o. (Feb–Aug 1870); Navy Yard, Norfolk, VA (Aug 1870–Mar 1871); *Shawmut*, N.Atl.Sta. (Mar 1871–Nov 1872); home and w.o. (Nov 1872–Mar 1873); examination and w.o. (Mar–Oct 1873); member, Bd. of Examiners, USNA (Oct–Nov 1873); recruiting duty, Chicago (Nov–Dec 1873); w.o. (Dec 1873–Jan 1874); *Ossipee*, N.Atl.Sta. (Feb 1874–Mar 1875); home and w.o. (Mar 1875–Aug 1876); *Vandalia*, Eur. and N.Atl. Sqdns. (Aug 1876–Jul 1879); w.o. (Jul–Aug 1879); rec. ship *Wabash*, Boston (Sep 1879–Aug 1883); additional duty, Naval Rndv., Boston (Mar 1881–Aug 1883); *Trenton*, Asia.Sqdn. (Sep 1883–Jun 1884); flt.engr., Asia.Sqdn., *Trenton* (Jun 1884–Jun 1885); *Trenton*, Asia.Sqdn. (Jun 1885–Sep 1886); w.o. (Sep 1886–Jun 1887); member, Bd. of Inspection and Survey, NY (Jun–Dec 1887); rec. ship *Wabash*, Boston (Oct 1887–Jun 1888); chief engr., Navy Yard, Portsmouth, NH (Jun 1888–Nov 1891); insp., Union Iron Works, San Francisco (Dec 1891–Feb 1893); *Mon-*

terey, Pac.Sta. (Feb 1893–Jan 1895); flgs. *Olympia,* Asia.Sta. (Jan–Jul 1895); flgs. *Philadelphia,* Pac.Sta. (Jul 1895–Jan 1896); home and l.o.a. (Jan–Apr 1896); duty at, then chief engr., Navy Yard, Mare Island, CA (May 1896–Sep 1899); placed on Ret.Lst. (25 Sep 1899).

JAMES RUFUS TRYON Born in Coxsackie, NY, on 24 Sep 1837, son of Benjamin and Jane (Smith) Tryon. Received the A.B. degree in 1858, an honorary Ph.D. in 1891, and an honorary LL.D. in 1895 from Union College in Schenectady, NY. Received the M.D. from the Univ. of PA in 1861. Remained unmarried. Resided in Coxsackie, NY. Died on 20 Mar 1912 at the Naval Hospital in NY. Buried at Morristown, NJ.

Ranks Act.Asst.Surg. (19 Mar 1863); Asst.Surg. (22 Sep 1863); PAsst.Surg. (21 Dec 1866); Surg. (30 Jun 1873); Medl.Insp. (22 Sep 1891); Surg.Gen. with rank of Commo (7 Sep 1893); Medl.Dir. (21 Jan 1897); placed on Ret.Lst. as RAdm (24 Sep 1899).

Career Summary Received appointment from NY (19 Mar 1863); Naval Hosp., NY (Mar–May 1863); Naval Hosp., Pensacola, FL (Jun 1863–Jul 1864); W.Gulf Blk.Sqdn., Pensacola, FL (Jul 1864–Jul 1865); sick lv. (Jul–Sep 1865); Navy Yard, Boston (Sep–Nov 1865); Naval Hosp., Boston (Nov 1865–Feb 1866); spec. duty, Bur. of Medicine and Surgery, Washington, DC (Feb–Jun 1866); asst., Bur. of Medicine and Surgery, Washington, DC (Jun 1866–Feb 1870); *Colorado* then *Idaho,* Asia.Sta. (Mar 1870–Mar 1873); temp. duty, in charge, Smallpox Hosp., and supt., U.S. Naval Hosp., Yokohama, Japan (1871); return to U.S., w.o., and l.o.a. (Mar–Jun 1873); Marine Rndv., NY (Jun–Dec 1873); Naval Hospital, NY (Dec 1873–Sep 1874); Naval Rndv., NY (Sep–Oct 1874); spec. duty, Navy Yard, Pensacola, FL (Oct–Dec 1874); Naval Rndv., NY (Dec 1874–Jun 1876); w.o. (Jun 1876–Mar 1877); *Swatara,* N.Atl.Sta. (Mar 1877–Oct 1878); w.o. (Oct 1878–Jan 1879); *Vandalia,* N.Atl.Sta. (Mar–Dec 1879); w.o. (Dec 1879–Jan 1880); spec. duty, NY (Jan 1880–May 1882); *Alaska,* Pac.Sta. (Jun 1882–Jan 1883); w.o. (Jan–Feb 1883); member, Naval Medl. Exam.Bd., Philadelphia (Feb 1883–Jun 1884); delegate, International Medl. Congress, Copenhagen, Denmark (Jun–Sep 1884); *Quinnebaug,* Eur.Sta. and Afr.Cst. (Sep 1884–Jun 1887); home and w.o. (Jun–Sep 1887); Marine Rndv., NY (Oct 1887–Jun 1888); spec. duty, NY (Jun 1888–Jan 1889); member, Medl. Exam.Bd., NY (Jan 1889–Sep 1891); flgs. *Chicago,* N.Atl.Sta. (Oct 1891–May 1893); surg.gen., and chief, Bur. of Medicine and Surgery, Washington, DC (Sep 1893–Sep 1897); Bur. of Medicine and Surgery, Washington, DC (Sep–Oct 1897); gen.insp. of hospitals, Washington, DC (Oct 1897–Sep 1899); delegate, International Congress of Hygiene and Demography, Madrid, Spain (Apr–May 1898); placed on Ret.Lst. (24 Sep 1899).

JAMES RUFUS TRYON
1837–1912

THOMAS TURNER
1808–1883

THOMAS TURNER Born in VA near Washington, DC, on 23 Dec 1808. Died on 24 Mar 1883 at his home in Glen Mills, near Media, PA. Buried in Laurel Hill Cemetery in Philadelphia.

Ranks Midn (21 Apr 1825); PMidn (4 Jun 1831); Lt (22 Dec 1835); Cdr (14 Sep 1855); Capt (16 Jul 1862); Commo (13 Dec 1862); RAdm (27 May 1868); placed on Ret.Lst. (21 Apr 1870).

Career Summary Received appointment from VA (21 Apr 1825); *Constellation*, Med.Sqdn. (Jun 1825–Nov 1827); w.o. (Nov 1827–Feb 1828); Naval School, Norfolk, VA (Feb–Dec 1828); *Warren*, Med.Sqdn. (Dec 1828–Sep 1830); Navy Yard, Norfolk, VA (Sep 1830–Mar 1831); w.o. (Mar–Jun 1831); l.o.a. (Jun 1831–Feb 1832); *Constellation*, Med.Sqdn. (Feb 1832–Sep 1835); l.o.a. and w.o. (Oct 1835–Mar 1837); *Macedonian*, spec.serv. (Mar 1837–Feb 1838); *Columbia*, E.Ind.Sqdn. (Feb 1838–Jun 1840); l.o.a. (Jun 1840–Dec 1841); Naval Rndv., Kensington, PA (Dec 1841–Jan 1842); rec. ship *Experiment*, Philadelphia (Jan 1842–Jul 1843); *Falmouth*, Home Sqdn. (Jul 1843–Jan 1844); l.o.a. (Jan–Apr 1844); Naval Rndv., Philadelphia (Apr 1844–Apr 1846); w.o. (Apr–Oct 1846); *Albany*, and cdr, *Fredonia*, Home Sqdn. (Oct 1846–Dec 1847); w.o. (Dec 1847–May 1848); rec. ship *Union*, Philadelphia (May 1848–Apr 1850); exec.off., *Congress*, Braz.Sqdn. (Apr 1850–Jul 1853); l.o.a. and w.o. (Jul–Nov 1853); ord. duty, Philadelphia (Nov 1853–Aug 1857); w.o. (Aug 1857–Jun 1858); cdr, *Saratoga*, Home Sqdn. (Jun 1858–Jul 1860); l.o.a. and w.o. (Jul 1860–Feb 1861); cdr, Naval Rndv., Philadelphia (Feb–Sep 1861); Navy Yard, Philadelphia (Sep 1861–Jun 1862); cdr, *New Ironsides*, spec.serv. (Jun 1862–Jul 1863); Navy Dept., Washington, DC (Aug–Oct 1863); spec. duty, NY (Oct 1863–Jul 1865); spec. duty, Philadelphia (Jul 1865–Jan 1867); w.o. (Jan–Apr 1867); ord. duty, Navy Yard, Philadelphia (Apr 1867–Jun 1868); cdr, S.Pac.Sqdn., *Saranac* (Jul 1868–Sep 1870); placed on Ret.Lst. (21 Apr 1870).

JOHN HENRY UPSHUR
1823–1917

JOHN HENRY UPSHUR Born in Northampton County, VA on 5 Dec 1823, son of John Evans and Elizabeth Parker (Upshur) Nottingham. Legally changed his name to his mother's surname, Upshur. Uncle was Secretary of Navy Abel Upshur. Attended William and Mary College in Williamsburg, VA, before entering the service. Resided in Washington, DC, where he died on 30 May 1917. Buried in Arlington National Cemetery.

Ranks Midn (4 Nov 1841); PMidn (10 Aug 1847); Mstr (18 Apr 1855); Lt (14 Sep 1855); LCdr (16 Jul 1862); Cdr (25 Jul 1866); Capt (31 Jan 1872); Commo (11 Jul 1880); RAdm (1 Oct 1884); retired (1 Jun 1885).

Career Summary Received appointment from VA [under name of John Henry Nottingham] (4 Nov 1841); w.o. (Nov 1841–Jan 1842); rec. ship *Pennsylvania*, Norfolk, VA

(Jan–Apr 1842); *Congress* and *United States*, Med.Sqdn. (Apr 1842–Oct 1844); l.o.a. (Oct–Nov 1844); *St. Mary's*, Home Sqdn. (Oct 1844–Jun 1847); l.o.a. (Jun–Sep 1847); Naval School, Annapolis, MD (Oct 1847–Aug 1848); Naval Observatory, Washington, DC (Aug 1848–Jun 1849); *Cumberland* and *Constitution*, Med.Sqdn. (Jul 1849–Jan 1851); l.o.a. (Jan–Feb 1851); ord. duty, Norfolk, VA (Feb 1851–Mar 1852); storeship *Supply*, E.Ind.Sqdn. (Mar 1852–Feb 1855); l.o.a. (Feb–Apr 1855); ord. duty, Navy Yard, Washington, DC (Apr 1855–May 1857); flag lt, *Cumberland*, Afr.Sqdn. (Jun 1857–Jul 1859); home and l.o.a. (Jul–Oct 1859); instructor, USNA (Oct 1859–May 1861); *Wabash*, S.Atl.Blk.Sqdn. (May 1861–Jan 1862); cdr, *Flambeau*, S.Atl.Blk.Sqdn. (Jan 1862–Sep 1863); ord. duty, Navy Yard, Philadelphia (Oct–Nov 1863); cdr, flgs. *Minnesota*, N.Atl.Blk.Sqdn. (Nov 1863–Sep 1864); cdr, *Advance* [renamed *Frolic*], N.Atl.Blk.Sqdn. (Oct 1864–Apr 1865); cdr, *Frolic*, Eur.Sqdn. (Apr 1865–Jul 1867); home and w.o. (Jul–Sep 1867); cdr, *Saratoga*, coastal operations (Oct 1867–Apr 1869); spec. duty, New London, CT (May 1869–Jun 1872); cdr, *Pensacola*, and chief of staff, S.Atl.Sta. (Sep 1872–Sep 1873); l.o.a. (Oct 1873–Jul 1874); Naval Sta., New London, CT (Jul 1874–May 1875); cdr, flgs. *Brooklyn*, S.Atl.Sta. (Jun 1875–Jul 1876); w.o. (Jul–Oct 1876); member, Bd. of Examiners (Oct–Nov 1876); w.o. (Nov 1876–Mar 1877); member, Bd. of Inspection (Mar 1877–Mar 1880); l.o.a. (Apr 1880–Jun 1881); member, Bd. of Examiners (Jun 1881–Mar 1882); comdt., Navy Yard, NY (Apr 1882–Mar 1884); cdr, Pac.Sta., *Hartford* (Mar 1884–May 1885); w.o. (May–Jun 1885) retired (1 Jun 1885).

WILLIAM KNICKERBOCKER VAN REYPEN Born in Bergen, NJ, on 14 Dec 1840, son of Cornelius C. and Christina Cantine (Van Alen) Van Reypen. Received the A.B. degree in 1858, the A.M. in 1863, both from NY Univ., and the M.D. in 1862 from the Univ. Medl. College of NY Univ. Married Nellie C. Wells on 21 Sep 1876. Resided in Washington, DC, where he died on 22 Dec 1924. Buried in Arlington National Cemetery.

Ranks Volunteer Army (1 May 1861); discharged (31 Jul 1861); Asst.Surg. (26 Dec 1861); PAsst.Surg. (26 May 1865); Surg. (12 May 1868); Medl.Insp. (16 Aug 1887); Medl. Dir. (30 Mar 1895); Surg.Gen. with rel. rank of Commo (18 Dec 1897); Surg.Gen. with rel. rank of RAdm (3 Mar 1899); retired with rank of RAdm (25 Jan 1902).

Career Summary Volunteer Army (May–Jul 1861); discharged (31 Jul 1861); received appointment from NJ as asst.surg. (26 Dec 1861); w.o. (Dec 1861–Mar 1862); Naval Hosp., NY (Mar–Sep 1862); *St. Lawrence*, E.Gulf Blk.Sqdn., and Marine Hosp., Key West, FL (Sep 1862–Dec 1864); Naval Hosp., Chelsea, MA (Jan–Dec 1865); *Lenapee*, Atl.Sqdn. (Dec 1865–May 1867); w.o. (May–Jun 1867); *Ticonderoga* and *Frolic*,

WILLIAM KNICKERBOCKER VAN
REYPEN
1840–1924

Eur.Sqdn. (Jul 1867–May 1869); spec. duty, New Orleans (May–Jul 1869); w.o. (Jul–Aug 1869); Naval Hosp., Chelsea, MA (Aug 1869–Apr 1870); sick lv. (Apr–Oct 1870); Naval Hosp., Norfolk, VA (Oct 1870–Jun 1871); Naval Hosp., Annapolis, MD (Jun 1871–Feb 1872); *Iroquois*, Asia.Sta. (Feb 1872–Apr 1874); return and w.o. (Apr–Sep 1874); Naval Hosp., NY (Sep 1874–May 1877); l.o.a. (May–Sep 1877); w.o. (Sep 1877–May 1878); *Alaska*, Pac.Sta. (Jun 1878–Jun 1880); return and w.o. (Jun–Oct 1880); Navy Yard, Norfolk, VA (Oct–Dec 1880); w.o. (Dec 1880–Jan 1881); Naval Hosp., NY (Jan 1881–Oct 1883); *Powhatan*, spec. duty (Oct 1883–Feb 1884); asst. chief, Bur. of Medicine and Surgery, Washington, DC (Feb 1884–Apr 1892); flt.surg., Pac.Sqdn., *San Francisco* (May 1892–Jul 1894); member, Bd. of Inspection and Survey (Jul 1894–Oct 1897); delegate, 12th International Congress of Medicine, Moscow, Russia (Jul–Sep 1897); surg.gen., and chief, Bur. of Medicine and Surgery, Washington, DC (Oct 1897–Jan 1902); retired (25 Jan 1902).

Career Highlights As surg.gen. and chief, Bur. of Medicine and Surgery during war with Spain, outfitted *Solace* as ambulance ship, the first ever used in naval warfare. After retirement, was a delegate to the Red Cross Conference in St. Petersburg in 1902. Served as pres. of American Red Cross from 1904 to 1905.

HENRY WALKE
1808–1896

HENRY WALKE Born at "The Ferry," Princess Anne County, VA, on 24 Dec 1808, son of Anthony and Susan (Carmichael) Walke. Raised in Chillicothe, OH, where his family moved when he was two. Educated at the local Chillicothe academy. Married three times: Sara J. Aim, Jane Ellen Burgess, and Julia Reed. Four children. Died at his home in Brooklyn, NY, on 8 Mar 1896.

Ranks Midn (1 Feb 1827); PMidn (10 Jun 1833); Lt (9 Dec 1839); placed on Reserved List (13 Sep 1855); promoted to Cdr on Reserved List (14 Sep 1855); recalled to Active List (29 Jan 1858); Capt (16 Jul 1862); Commo (25 Jul 1866); RAdm (13 Jul 1870); placed on Ret.Lst. (26 Apr 1871).

Career Summary Received appointment from OH (1 Feb 1827); rec. ship *Alert*, Norfolk, VA (Mar–Jul 1827); *Natchez*, W.Ind.Sqdn. (Jul 1827–Feb 1829); l.o.a. (Feb–May 1829); Navy Yard, Portsmouth, NH (May–Jun 1829); *Ontario*, Med.Sqdn. (Jun 1829–Nov 1831); l.o.a. and w.o. (Nov 1831–Mar 1834); rec. ship *Sea Gull*, Philadelphia (Mar–Oct 1834); l.o.a. (Oct–Dec 1834); on furlough (Dec 1834–Jan 1836); Navy Yard, Philadelphia (Jan–Sep 1836); *North Carolina*, Pac.Sqdn. (Nov 1836–Jul 1839); l.o.a. (Jul–Oct 1839); rec. ship *North Carolina*, NY (Oct 1839–Oct 1840); *Boston*, E.Ind.Sqdn. and spec. cruise (Oct 1840–Aug 1843); l.o.a. and w.o. (Aug 1843–May 1844); *Bainbridge* and prize brig *Albert*, Braz.Sqdn. (May 1844–Sep 1845); l.o.a. (Sep 1845–Feb 1846); rec. ship *North Carolina*, NY (Feb 1846–Feb 1847); exec.off., *Vesuvius*,

W.Ind.Sqdn. (Feb–Oct 1847); rec. ship *North Carolina*, NY (Sep 1848–Jun 1849); *Cumberland*, Med.Sqdn. (Jun 1849–Jan 1851); return and l.o.a. (Jan–Apr 1851); Naval Observatory, Washington, DC (Apr–May 1851); w.o. (May–Jun 1851); rec. ship *North Carolina*, NY (Jul 1851–Sep 1853); *St. Mary's*, Navy Yard, Philadelphia (Sep 1853); rec. ship *North Carolina*, NY (Sep 1853–Jul 1854); w.o. (Jul 1854–Sep 1855); placed on Reserve List (13 Sep 1855); on furlough (Sep 1855–Jan 1858); recalled to Active List (29 Jan 1858); w.o. (Jan 1858–Aug 1859); cdr, *Supply*, Afr. and W.Ind. Sqdns. (Aug 1859–Feb 1861); under arrest and w.o. (Feb–May 1861); *Mount Vernon*, spec.serv. (May–Sep 1861); insp., 11th L.h. Dist., Detroit, MI (Sep 1861); cdr, gunboat *Tyler*, then cdr, *Carondelet*, MS Flot. (Sep 1861–Feb 1863); cdr, *Lafayette*, MS Flot. (Feb–Aug 1863); l.o.a. (Aug–Sep 1863); cdr, *Sacramento*, spec.serv. (Sep 1863–Aug 1865); w.o. (Aug 1865–Feb 1868); cdr, Naval Sta., Mound City, IL (May 1868–Apr 1870); w.o. (Apr–Oct 1870); bd. duties (Oct 1870–Apr 1871); placed on Ret.Lst. (26 Apr 1871); spec. duty, Navy Dept., Washington, DC (Apr–Oct 1871); member, L.h. Bd., Washington, DC (Oct 1871–Apr 1873).

Career Highlights During Mexican War, was present at taking of Vera Cruz, Tabasco, Tuspan, and Alvarado. Just before outset of Civil War and while commanding *Supply*, removed the garrison at the Pensacola Navy Yard and the small force from Ft. Barrancas to Ft. Pickens owing to the occupation of Pensacola by secessionist forces. His actions, which technically disobeyed previous orders, resulted in a court-martial, but he received a "complimentary reprimand" from secretary of the navy. Saw action on upper Mississippi at Fts. Henry and Donelson, and at Island Number 10. Walke was an accomplished artist as well as naval officer.

References

Writings: *Naval Scenes and Reminiscences of the Civil War . . . 1861, 1862 and 1863* (NY: 1877).

Art Work Collections in: a) The Dept. of the Navy, Washington, DC. b) Ross County Historical Society, Chillicothe, OH. c) The Library of Congress. d) The Franklin D. Roosevelt Library, Hyde Park, NY. e) The Mariners Museum, Newport News, VA. f) The Dillon Collection, Far Hills, NJ. g) Free Library of Philadelphia. h) The Peabody Museum, Salem, MA. i) The U.S. Naval Academy Museum.

JOHN GRIMES WALKER Born in Hillsborough, NH, on 20 Mar 1835, son of Alden and Susan (Grimes) Walker. Moved to Iowa after mother's death in 1846. Lived with uncle, John W. Grimes, who later served as gov. of IA. Married Rebecca W. Pickering on 12 Sep 1866. Two sons and four daughters. Died on 15 Sep 1907 at Ogunquit, ME. Buried in Arlington National Cemetery.

Ranks Act.Midn (5 Oct 1850); PMidn (20 Jun 1856),

JOHN GRIMES WALKER
1835–1907

Mstr (22 Jan 1858); Lt (23 Jan 1858); LCdr (16 Jul 1862); Cdr (25 Jul 1866); Capt (25 Jun 1877); Commo (12 Feb 1889); Act.RAdm (1 Oct 1889); RAdm (23 Jan 1894); placed on Ret.Lst. (20 Mar 1897).

Career Summary Received appointment from IA (5 Oct 1850); USNA (Oct 1850–Nov 1851); *Portsmouth*, Pac.Sqdn. (Nov 1851–Apr 1855); l.o.a. (Apr–Sep 1855); USNA (Oct 1855–Jun 1856); w.o. (Jun–Dec 1856); *Falmouth* and *St. Lawrence*, Braz.Sqdn. (Jan 1857–May 1859); l.o.a. (May–Sep 1859); instructor of math., USNA (Sep 1859–Jul 1860); *Susquehanna*, spec.serv. (Jul 1860–Jun 1861); w.o. (Jun 1861); ord. duty, Navy Yard, Boston (Jun–Jul 1861); *Connecticut*, Atl.Cst. (Jul–Oct 1861); 1st lt, *Winona*, W.Gulf Blk.Sqdn. (Nov 1861–Aug 1862); cdr, *Baron de Kalb*, MS Sqdn. (Oct 1862–Aug 1863); cdr, naval battery, 15th Army Corps, Vicksburg, MS (Jun–Jul 1863); w.o. (Aug–Sep 1863); temp. duty, Navy Yard, Boston (Sep–Dec 1863); cdr, *Saco*, N.Atl.Blk.Sqdn. (Jan 1864–Jan 1865); cdr, *Shawmut*, S.Atl.Sqdn. (Jan 1865–Jun 1866); asst.supt., USNA (Jul 1866–Apr 1869); cdr, training ship *Sabine* (Apr 1869–Jul 1870); w.o. (Jul–Sep 1870); insp., 2nd L.h. Dist., Boston (Oct 1870–Apr 1872); l.o.a. (Apr 1872–Jan 1873); Navy Yard, Boston (Jan–Apr 1873); secretary, then member, L.h. Bd., Washington, DC (May 1873–May 1878); w.o. (May 1878–May 1879); l.o.a. (May 1879–Mar 1881); cdr, *Powhatan*, N.Atl.Sta. (Mar–Aug 1881); w.o. (Aug–Oct 1881); chief, Bur. of Nav., Washington, DC (Oct 1881–Oct 1889); cdr, Sqdn. of Evol., *Chicago* (Oct 1889–Sep 1892); cdr, N.Atl.Sta., *Chicago* (Sep–Dec 1892); temp. duty, Washington, DC (Dec 1892–May 1893); member, Naval Exam.Bd. and Bd. of Inspection and Survey, and other bd. duties (Jun 1893–Nov 1896); cdr, Pac.Sta., *Philadelphia* (Mar–Dec 1894); chairman, L.h. Bd., Washington, DC (Dec 1894–Mar 1897); chairman, Deep Water Harbor Bd., southern CA (Nov 1896–Jul 1897); placed on Ret.Lst. (20 Mar 1897); member, then pres., Nicaraguan Canal Commission (Jul 1897–Jun 1899); pres., Isthmian Canal Commission (Jun 1899–Apr 1905).

Career Highlights Graduated first in class of 1856. During Civil War, saw action on lower Mississippi River, at capture of New Orleans, and at Vicksburg. Participated in capture of Wilmington, NC. Thereafter commanded all major squadrons, including the Sqdn. of Evolution. While commanding Pac.Sta. in 1894, was given special charge of maintaining peace and order in Hawaiian Islands.

References
Personal Papers: a) 1750 items (1873–1903) in NHF,LC. b) 5400 items (1865–1907) in Wichita State Univ. Lib. Wichita, KS. c) 3 vols. (1851–94) in USNAM.

Writings: a) *Report of the Nicaraguan Canal Commission, 1897–1899* (Baltimore: 1899). b) *Report of the Isthmian Canal Commission, 1899–1901* 2 vols. (Washington, DC: 1901–1902).

Additional Sources: Daniel Howard Wicks, "New Navy

and New Empire: The Life and Times of John Grimes Walker" (Ph.D. dissertation, Univ. of CA, Berkeley, 1979).

THOMAS CAMERON WALTON Born in Cumberland, England, on 31 May 1838, son of Thomas and Ann (Watson) Walton. Emigrated to N. America in 1847, educated at the Toronto Academy and at McGill University in Montreal, Canada, graduating from the latter in 1860. Received the M.D. from the Univ. of the City of New York in 1862. Married Kate Lane Lynch in Feb 1871. Three children. Died at his home in Annapolis, MD, on 2 Mar 1909. Buried in USNA Cemetery.

Ranks Asst.Surg. (5 Oct 1861); PAsst.Surg. (20 Jan 1866); Surg. (22 Oct 1868); Medl.Insp. (18 Sep 1887); Medl.Dir. (25 May 1895); placed on Ret.Lst. with rank of RAdm (31 May 1900).

Career Summary Received appointment from NY (5 Oct 1861); w.o. (Oct 1861–Jan 1862); *Jamestown*, N.Atl.Blk.Sqdn. and E.Indies (Jan 1862–Oct 1865); w.o. (Nov 1865–Mar 1866); recorder, Medl. Exam.Bd. (Mar–May 1866); rec. ship *Ohio*, Boston (May 1866–Jul 1867); *Suwanee*, N.Pac.Sqdn. (Aug 1867–Jul 1868); *Mohican* and *Resaca*, Pac.Sqdn. (Jul 1868–Dec 1870); return and w.o. (Dec 1870–Feb 1871); rec. ship *New Hampshire*, Norfolk, VA (Feb 1871–Feb 1873); *Juniata*, spec. duty and Eur.Sta. (Feb 1873–Feb 1876); rec. ship *Worcester*, Norfolk, VA (Feb 1876–Feb 1877); rec. ship *Franklin*, Norfolk, VA (Feb 1877–Feb 1881); *Powhatan*, spec.serv. (Feb 1881–Aug 1883); senior medl.off., USNA (Sep 1883–Jun 1889); *Chicago*, Sqdn. of Evol. (Jun 1889–Oct 1891); l.o.a (Oct 1891–Oct 1892); USNA (Oct 1892–Jan 1897); Naval Laboratory, NY (Jan 1892–May 1900); placed on Ret.Lst. (31 May 1900).

THOMAS CAMERON WALTON
1838–1909

JOHN CRITTENDEN WATSON Born in Frankfort, KY, on 24 Aug 1842, son of Dr. Edward Howe and Sarah Lee (Crittenden) Watson. She was daughter of KY Gov. John Jordan Crittenden who was also attorney gen. under Pres. William Henry Harrison. Married Elizabeth Anderson Thornton on 29 May 1873. Five sons and two daughters. Died at his home in Washington, DC, on 14 Dec 1923. Buried in Arlington National Cemetery.

Ranks Act.Midn (29 Sep 1856); Midn (15 Jun 1860); Mstr (31 Aug 1861); Lt (16 Jul 1862); LCdr (25 Jul 1866); Cdr (23 Jan 1874); Capt (6 Mar 1887); Commo (7 Nov 1897); RAdm (3 Mar 1899); placed on Ret.Lst. (24 Aug 1904).

Career Summary Received appointment from KY (29 Sep 1856); USNA (Sep 1856–Jun 1860); *Susquehanna*, spec.serv. (Aug 1860–Mar 1861); *Richmond*, Med.Sqdn. (Mar–Jul 1861); *Sabine*, Navy Yard, Portsmouth, NH, and Atl.Blk.Sqdn. (Jul 1861–Jan 1862); *Hartford*, W.Gulf Blk.Sqdn. (Jan 1862–Dec 1864); l.o.a. and w.o. (Dec 1864–

JOHN CRITTENDEN WATSON
1842–1923

Apr 1865); flgs. *Colorado*, Eur.Sqdn. (Apr 1865–Jul 1867); on staff, Eur.Sta., *Franklin* (Jul 1867–Jul 1868); exec.off., *Canandaigua*, Eur.Sta. (Jul 1868–Feb 1869); w.o. (Feb–Apr 1869); Navy Yard, NY (Apr–Jun 1869); spec. duty, Philadelphia (Jun–Sep 1869); *Albany*, N.Atl.Sta. (Sep–Oct 1869); w.o. (Oct 1869–Jan 1870); *Congress*, Navy Yard, Philadelphia (Jan–Feb 1870); l.o.a. (Feb–Mar 1870); exec.off., *Alaska*, Asia.Sta. (Apr 1870–May 1871); cdr, stationary storeship *Idaho*, Yokohama, Japan (May 1871–Apr 1873); home, l.o.a., and w.o. (Apr–Dec 1873); ord. duty, Navy Yard, NY (Dec 1873–Jan 1874); insp. of ord., Navy Yard, Mare Island, CA (Apr–Nov 1874); senior aide to comdt., Navy Yard, Mare Island, CA (Nov 1874–Apr 1877); w.o. (Apr 1877–Feb 1878); cdr, *Wyoming*, Eur.Sta. (Feb 1878–Feb 1880); w.o. (Mar–Apr 1880); torp. instruction, Newport, RI (Jun–Sep 1880); asst., then insp., 11th L.h. Dist., Detroit, MI (Sep 1880–Oct 1883); s.a. and w.o. (Oct–Nov 1883); equip.off., Navy Yard, NY (Nov 1883–Nov 1884); w.o. (Nov 1884–Apr 1885); equip.off., Navy Yard, NY (Apr 1885–Aug 1886); cdr, *Iroquois*, S.Pac.Sta. (Sep 1886–May 1887); w.o. (Jun 1887–Feb 1888); pres., Bd. of Inspection, Mare Island, CA (Feb 1888–Jul 1890); capt.yd., Navy Yard, Mare Island, CA (Jul 1890–Jun 1892); cdr, *San Francisco*, Pac.Sqdn., and flgs., N.Atl.Sqdn. (Jul 1892–Jul 1894); member, Naval Ret.Bd. (Aug 1894–May 1895); gov., Naval Home, Philadelphia (May 1895–Apr 1898); special duty, N.Atl.Sqdn. (May–Jun 1898); cdr, 1st Sqdn., N.Atl.Flt., *Newark* (Jun–Sep 1898); comdt., Navy Yard, Mare Island, CA (Oct 1898–May 1899); cdr-in-chief, Naval Forces, Asia.Sta., *Baltimore* (Jun 1899–Apr 1900); home, w.o., and l.o.a. (Sep–Dec 1900); pres., Naval Exam.Bd. (Dec 1900–Jul 1902); naval representative, Coronation of King Edward VII, London, England (Apr–Sep 1902); bd. duties (Sep 1902–Aug 1904); placed on Ret.Lst. (24 Aug 1904).

Career Highlights During the Civil War, participated in numerous actions, including Fts. Jackson and St. Philip, Chalmette Batteries, Vicksburg Batteries, Port Hudson, Grand Gulf, Mobile Bay, and Warrington, where he was wounded by a shell fragment. In the war with Spain, commanded a division of the Atl.Flt. and also the Eastern Sqdn., which in Jul 1898 was designed to threaten Spain's coast and to reinforce the Asia.Flt. in the P.I.

References
Personal Papers: a) 1500 items (1845–1960) in NHF,LC. b) See: Lib. of Congress, MSS Div., *John Lansing Callan, John Crittenden Watson: A Register of their Papers in the Library of Congress* (1968).

Writings: "Farragut and Mobile Bay—Personal Reminiscences," U.S. Naval Institute *Proceedings* 291 (May 1927): 551–57.

AARON WARD WEAVER
1832–1919

AARON WARD WEAVER Born in Washington, DC, on 1 Jul 1832, son of navy Lt William Augustus and Jane (Van

Wyck) Weaver. Married Ida Hyatt on 13 Feb 1864. Died on 2 Oct 1919 in Alexandria County, VA.

Ranks Act.Midn (10 May 1848); PMidn (15 Jun 1854); Mstr (15 Sep 1855); Lt (16 Sep 1855); LCdr (16 Jul 1862); Cdr (25 Jul 1866); Capt (8 Aug 1876); Commo (7 Oct 1886); RAdm (27 Jun 1893); retired (26 Sep 1893).

Career Summary Received appointment from OH (10 May 1848); *St. Louis* and *Congress*, Braz.Sqdn. (Jun 1848–Jul 1853); home and w.o. (Jul–Oct 1853); USNA (Oct 1853–Jun 1854); w.o. (Jun–Sep 1854); *Fulton*, Home Sqdn. (Sep 1854–Jul 1856); l.o.a. (Jul–Oct 1856); cst.surv. duty (Oct 1856–Nov 1857); *Marion* and prize brig *Ardennes*, Afr.Sqdn. (Dec 1857–Jun 1859); w.o. (Jun–Aug 1859); Navy Yard, Philadelphia (Aug 1859–Aug 1860); *Susquehanna*, Med. and S.Atl.Blk. Sqdns., then cdr, *Winona*, W.Gulf Blk.Sqdn. (Aug 1860–Jun 1864); w.o. (Jun–Aug 1864); cdr, *Chippewa*, and *Mahopac*, N.Atl.Blk.Sqdn. (Aug 1864–May 1865); Navy Yard, Boston (Jun 1865–Nov 1866); w.o. (Nov–Dec 1866); cdr, *Tallapoosa*, Gulf Sqdn. (Dec 1866–May 1867); cdr, Naval Rndv., Washington, DC (May 1867–Jun 1868); w.o. (Jun–Aug 1868); l.o.a. (Jun 1868–May 1869); insp. of supplies, Navy Yard, Washington, DC (May 1869–Sep 1870); equip. duty, Navy Yard, Norfolk, VA (Oct–Nov 1870); cdr, *Terror*, N.Atl.Sqdn. (Nov 1870–Jan 1872); Navy Yard, Washington, DC (Feb 1872–Aug 1873); in charge, munitions depot, Malden, MA (Sep 1873–Sep 1875); w.o. (Sep–Nov 1875); cdr, *Dictator*, N.Atl.Sta. (Dec 1875–May 1877); w.o. (May 1877–Jul 1879); in charge, Equip. Dept., Navy Yard, Norfolk, VA (Aug 1879–Oct 1880); capt.yd., Navy Yard, Norfolk, VA (Oct 1880–Oct 1881); cdr, *Brooklyn*, S.Atl.Sta. (Nov 1881–Oct 1884); w.o. (Oct 1884–Feb 1885); member, then pres., Naval Ret.Bd. (Feb 1885–Jan 1890); member, then pres., Naval Exam.Bd. (Apr 1885–Jan 1890); comdt., Navy Yard, Norfolk, VA (Jan 1890–Jan 1893); pres., Naval Exam. and Ret. Bds. (Jan–Sep 1893); retired (26 Sep 1893).

Career Highlights During the Civil War, participated in the action at the Hatteras Forts, NC, at Fts. Beauregard and Walker, and at Port Royal, SC. Present at the retaking by Union forces of the Navy Yard at Norfolk, VA. Saw considerable action on Mississippi through summer of 1863. Subsequently completed the war on the Atlantic coast at Ft. Fisher, the fall of Charleston, and at the fall of Richmond.

References
Personal Papers: 77 items (1851–87) in NYPL.

CLARK HENRY WELLS Born in Reading, PA, on 22 Sep 1822. Married, with a family. Died at his home in Washington, DC, on 28 Jan 1888. Buried in Laurel Hill Cemetery, Philadelphia.

Ranks Midn (25 Sep 1840); PMidn (11 Jul 1846); Mstr (1 Mar 1855); Lt (14 Sep 1855); LCdr (16 Jul 1862); Cdr (25 Jul

1866); Capt (19 Jun 1871); Commo (22 Jan 1880); RAdm (1 Apr 1884); placed on Ret.Lst. (30 Sep 1884).

Career Summary Received appointment from PA (25 Sep 1840); w.o. (Sep–Oct 1840); rec. ship *Hudson*, NY (Oct–Dec 1840); *Franklin*, in ordinary, and *Brandywine*, Med.Sqdn. (Jan 1841–Jul 1842); l.o.a. and w.o. (Jul–Nov 1842); *Independence*, Home Sqdn. (Nov 1842–Jun 1843); *Levant*, Pac.Sqdn. (Jun 1843–Aug 1845); l.o.a. (Aug–Oct 1845); Naval School, Annapolis, MD (Oct 1845–Jul 1846); w.o. (Jul–Aug 1846); *Somers* and *Petrel*, Home Sqdn. (Aug 1846–Aug 1847); l.o.a. and w.o. (Sep 1847–Jan 1848); *Plymouth* and *Dolphin*, E.Ind.Sqdn. (Feb 1848–Jun 1851); l.o.a. (Jun–Sep 1851); rec. ship *Princeton*, Philadelphia (Sep 1851–Mar 1852); Naval Observatory, Washington, DC (Mar–Sep 1852); storeship *Fredonia*, Valparaiso, Chile (Oct 1852–Jun 1855); return to U.S., l.o.a., and w.o. (Jun–Nov 1855); Naval Observatory, Washington, DC (Nov 1855–Oct 1856); exec.off., *Resolute*, spec.serv. (Oct–Nov 1856); l.o.a. (Nov 1856–Apr 1857); *Niagara*, Atl. Cable Expd. (Apr–Sep 1857); *Susquehanna*, Med.Sqdn. (Sep 1857–Apr 1858); l.o.a. (Apr–May 1858); *Water Witch*, Home Sqdn. (May–Jul 1858); w.o. (Jul–Nov 1858); exec.off., *Metacomet*, Paraguay Expd. (Nov 1858–Mar 1860); sick lv. (Mar–Oct 1860); exec.off., *Susquehanna*, Med. and Atl.Blk. Sqdns., then *Vandalia*, then cdr, *Dale*, S.Atl.Blk.Sqdn. (Oct 1860–Oct 1862); w.o. (Oct–Dec 1862); exec.off., Navy Yard, Philadelphia (Dec 1862–Sep 1863); cdr, *Galena*, W. and E. Gulf Blk.Sqdns., and James River (Oct 1863–Jun 1865); cdr, *Kansas*, S.Atl.Sqdn. (Jul 1865–Aug 1867); return and w.o. (Aug 1867–Jun 1868); Navy Yard, Portsmouth, NH (Jul 1868–Jul 1870); cdr, *Shenandoah*, Eur.Sta. (Aug 1870–Jan 1874); return to U.S. and w.o. (Jan–Feb 1874); exec.off., Navy Yard, Boston (Mar–Oct 1874); capt.yd., Navy Yard, Philadelphia (Oct 1874–Jan 1876); capt.yd., League Island, PA (Jan 1876–Nov 1877); w.o. (Nov 1877–Apr 1879); chief signal off., Washington, DC (May 1879–Nov 1881); comdt., Navy Yard, Portsmouth, NH (Nov 1881–Sep 1884); placed on Ret.Lst. (30 Sep 1884).

Career Highlights During the Mexican War, saw action in attacks against San Juan d'Ulloa and Vera Cruz and in the captures of Tuspan and Tampico. During the Civil War, participated in actions at Port Royal, SC; Fernandina, FL; and in the Battle of Mobile Bay.

REED WERDEN Born in Delaware County, PA, on 28 Feb 1818, son of Col William Werden, USA. Married with no children. Died in Newport, RI, on 11 Jul 1886. Buried in NY.

Ranks Midn (9 Jan 1834); PMidn (16 Jul 1840); Lt (27 Feb 1847); Cdr (16 Jul 1862); Capt (25 Jul 1866); Commo (27 Apr 1871); RAdm (4 Feb 1875); placed on Ret.Lst. (27 Mar 1877).

Career Summary Received appointment from OH (9 Jan 1834); w.o. (Jan–Apr 1834); *Enterprise, Ontario,* and *Erie,* Braz.Sqdn. (Apr 1834–Sep 1837); l.o.a. (Sep–Dec 1837); Naval School and Navy Yard, NY (Jan–May 1838); *Cyane,* Med.Sqdn. (May–Dec 1838); l.o.a. and w.o. (Dec 1838–Jan 1840); Naval School, Philadelphia (Jan–Jul 1840); l.o.a. (Jul–Oct 1840); *Boston* and *Constellation,* E.Ind.Sqdn. (Oct 1840–Aug 1843); l.o.a. and w.o. (Aug 1843–Apr 1844); rec. ship *Pennsylvania,* NY (Apr 1844–Jan 1845); l.o.a. and w.o. (Jan 1845–Mar 1847); *Germantown,* Home Sqdn. (Mar–Aug 1847); l.o.a. (Aug–Oct 1847); rec. ship *Vermont,* Boston (Oct 1847–May 1848); l.o.a. and w.o. (May 1848–Jul 1849); *Vandalia,* Pac.Sqdn. (Jul 1849–Jul 1852); return to U.S. and w.o. (Jul–Nov 1852); Naval Rndv., Baltimore (Nov 1852–Sep 1853); *Albany,* Home and W.Ind. Sqdns. (Sep 1853–Apr 1854); sick lv. and w.o. (Apr 1854–Nov 1855); spec. duty, W.Indies (Nov 1855–Mar 1856); Naval Observatory, Washington, DC (Nov 1856–Jul 1857); *Cumberland,* Afr.Sqdn. (Aug 1857–Sep 1859); l.o.a. and w.o. (Sep 1859–Apr 1861); *Minnesota,* Home Sqdn. (Apr–May 1861); cdr, Philadelphia ice boat, Delaware River (May–Jun 1861); cdr, *Yankee,* N.Atl.Blk.Sqdn. (Jun–Jul 1861); l.o.a. (Jul–Aug 1861); cdr, *Stars and Stripes,* N.Atl.Blk.Sqdn. (Aug 1861–Apr 1862); sick lv. (Apr–Jun 1862); cdr, *Connemaugh,* S.Atl.Blk.Sqdn. (Jun 1862–May 1863); return and w.o. (May–Sep 1863); Navy Yard, Philadelphia (Sep 1863–Nov 1864); flt.capt, E.Gulf Blk.Sqdn., *San Jacinto* (Nov 1864–Jul 1865); w.o. (Jul–Oct 1865); spec. duty, Navy Yard, NY (Oct–Dec 1865); cdr, *Bienville,* W.Ind.Sqdn. (Jan–Nov 1866); w.o. (Nov 1866–Apr 1867); l.o.a. and w.o. (Apr 1867–Jul 1868); Navy Yard, Mare Island, CA (Aug 1868–May 1871); w.o. (May–Dec 1871); cdr, Naval Sta., New London, CT (Dec 1871–Dec 1874); l.o.a. (Dec 1874–Aug 1875); cdr, S.Pac.Sta., *Richmond* (Sep 1875–Jul 1876); w.o. (Jul 1876–Mar 1877); placed on Ret.Lst. (27 Mar 1877).

Career Highlights During war with Mexico, commanded a party of bluejackets at capture of Tuspan. During the Civil War, present at capture of Roanoke Island.

CHARLES HENRY WHITE Born in Centre Sandwich, NH, on 19 Nov 1838, son of Dr. Charles and Sarah (French) White. Educated in academies there and at Northfield, NH. Received the M.D. from Harvard Univ. in 1862. Home was Centre Sandwich, where he died on 25 Jul 1914 and where he was buried.

Ranks Asst.Surg. (26 Dec 1861); PAsst.Surg. (30 Oct 1865); Surg. (18 Nov 1869); Medl.Insp. (10 Jul 1888); Medl.Dir. (8 Jun 1895); placed on Ret.Lst. as Medl.Dir. with rank of RAdm (19 Nov 1900).

Career Summary Received appointment from MA (26 Dec 1861); w.o. (Dec 1861–Apr 1862); Naval Hosp., Chelsea, MA (May–Oct 1862); *Huron,* S.Atl.Blk.Sqdn. (Oct 1862–Apr

CHARLES HENRY WHITE
1838–1914

1864); return home and w.o. (Apr–Jun 1864); Navy Yard, Portsmouth, NH (Jun–Aug 1864); USNA (Aug–Oct 1864); *Roanoke*, N.Atl.Blk.Sqdn. (Oct 1864–Jun 1865); w.o. (Jun–Nov 1865); Navy Yard, NY (Nov 1865–Mar 1866); *Ashuelot*, Asia.Sta. (Mar 1866–Jul 1869); return to U.S. and w.o. (Jul–Sep 1869); sick lv. (Sep–Nov 1869); Navy Yard, Boston (Nov–Dec 1869); Naval Laboratory, NY (Dec 1869–Jul 1872); *Benicia, Idaho,* and *Monocacy,* Asia.Sta. (Mar 1872–Feb 1875); return to U.S. and w.o. (Feb–Apr 1875); Naval Laboratory, NY (Apr 1875–Dec 1878); w.o. (Dec 1878–Oct 1879); Naval Hosp., Mare Island, CA (Oct 1879–May 1880); *Lackawanna,* Pac.Sqdn. (May 1880–Jun 1883); return and w.o. (Jun–Aug 1883); Museum of Hygiene, Washington, DC (Aug 1883–Jun 1888); w.o. (Jun–Jul 1888); flt.surg., Pac.Sta., *Trenton* (Aug 1888–Jul 1889); w.o. (Jul–Aug 1889); *Pensacola,* N.Atl.Sta. (Sep 1889–Jul 1890); w.o. (Jul–Oct 1890); *San Francisco,* Pac.Sta. (Nov 1890–Mar 1891); flt.surg., Pac.Sqdn., *Baltimore* (Mar–Jul 1891), then *Pensacola* (Jul 1891–Jan 1892); l.o.a. and w.o. (Jan 1892–Jan 1893); spec. duty, Smithsonian Institution, Washington, DC (Jan–Jul 1893); member, then pres., Naval Medl. Exam. and Ret. Bds., NY (Jul 1893–Oct 1897); in charge, Museum of Hygiene, Washington, DC (Oct 1897–Nov 1900); placed on Ret.Lst. (19 Nov 1900).

EDWIN WHITE Born in Ohio on 20 Dec 1843, son of Lyman White. Married Antonia Thornton Emmons, daughter of RAdm George F. Emmons, USN [*q.v.*]. Resided in Princeton, NJ. Died on 23 Dec 1903 at the Navy Yard in NY. Buried in USNA Cemetery.

Ranks Act.Midn (29 Nov 1861); title changed to Midn (16 Jul 1862); Ens (1 Nov 1866); Mstr (1 Dec 1866); Lt (12 Mar 1868); LCdr (15 Sep 1869); Cdr (4 Mar 1886); Capt (25 Dec 1898); retired with rank of RAdm (28 Dec 1899).

Career Summary Received appointment from OH (29 Nov 1861); USNA (Nov 1861–Nov 1864); l.o.a. (Nov 1864–Feb 1865); rec. ship *Vermont,* NY (Feb–Apr 1865); flgs. *Colorado,* Eur.Sqdn. (Apr 1865–Mar 1867); *Shamrock,* Eur.Sta. (Mar 1867–Jul 1868); w.o. (Jul–Sep 1868); nav., *Yantic,* W.Ind.Sqdn. (Oct 1868–Nov 1869); w.o. (Nov–Dec 1868); Hydrographic Office, Washington, DC (Jan–Sep 1870); USNA (Sep 1870–Jan 1871); rec. ship *Potomac,* Philadelphia (Jan–May 1871); ord. duty, Navy Yard, Philadelphia (May–Sep 1871); exec.off., and temp. cdr, *Kansas,* W.Indies (Sep 1871–Aug 1872); cdr, *Onward,* S.Pac.Sta. (Aug 1872–Mar 1875); aide to cdr, Asia.Sta., *Tennessee* (Mar 1875–Aug 1877); l.o.a. and w.o. (Sep 1877–May 1878); Torp.Sta., Newport, RI (Jun–Sep 1878); l.o.a. and w.o. (Oct 1878–Jun 1879); instructor in seamanship, USNA (Jun 1879–Jun 1882); exec.off., flgs. *Hartford,* Pac.Sta. (Jun 1882–Apr 1884); sick lv. (Apr–Dec 1884); spec. duty, Navy Dept., Washington, DC (Dec 1884–Apr 1885); exec.off., training ship *New Hampshire,* Newport, RI

EDWIN WHITE
1843–1903

(Apr 1885–May 1886); torp. instruction, Newport, RI (Jun–Sep 1886); w.o. (Sep–Nov 1886); cdr, training ship *Portsmouth* (Dec 1886–Oct 1888); equip.off., Navy Yard, Portsmouth, NH (Nov 1888–Nov 1892); w.o. (Nov 1891–Apr 1892); cdr, *Concord*, spec. duty, Mississippi River, then N.Atl.Sqdn. (Apr 1892–Jun 1893); Naval Review, Hampton Roads, VA, and NY (Mar–Jun 1893); home and w.o. (Jun–Jul 1893); equip.off., Navy Yard, NY (Jul 1893–Feb 1895); l.o.a. (Feb–May 1895); NWC, Newport, RI (Jun–Oct 1895); comdt. of cadets, USNA (Nov 1895–Sep 1898); cdr, *Terror*, Hampton Roads, VA (Sep–Oct 1898); cdr, flgs. *Philadelphia*, Pac.Flt. (Oct–Nov 1898); sick lv. (Nov–Dec 1899); retired (28 Dec 1899).

CHARLES WILKES Born in New York City on 3 Apr 1798, son of John De Ponthieu and Mary (Seton) Wilkes. Was the great nephew of celebrated late-18th-century British politician John Wilkes. Educated at various schools and by various tutors before entering merchant service in 1815. Married Jane Jeffrey Renwick on 16 Apr 1826. Married again on 3 Oct 1854 to Mary H. (Lynch) Bolton. Four children. Died on 8 Feb 1877 in Washington, DC. Buried in Rock Creek Cemetery, Washington, DC; reinterred in Arlington National Cemetery in 1920.

Ranks Midn (1 Jan 1818); Lt (28 Apr 1826); Cdr (13 Jul 1843); Capt (14 Sep 1855); Commo (16 Jul 1862); Act.RAdm (15 Sep 1862); promotion to Commo rescinded and placed on Ret.Lst. with rank of Capt (12 Nov 1862); RAdm on Ret.Lst. (25 Jul 1866).

Career Summary Received appointment from NY (1 Jan 1818); *Independence*, Boston (Jan–Jul 1818); *Guerriere*, Med. and Eur. Sqdns. (Jul 1818–Mar 1821); *Washington*, NY (Mar–Jun 1821); *Franklin*, Pac.Sqdn. (Jun 1821–Nov 1823); on furlough (Nov 1823–Apr 1825); court-martial duty, Washington, DC, and Philadelphia, then l.o.a. and w.o. (Apr 1825–Jun 1830); *Boston*, Med.Sqdn. (Jun 1830–Feb 1831); *Fairfield*, Med.Sqdn. (Feb–May 1831); l.o.a. (May–Dec 1831); sick lv. (Dec 1831–May 1832); survey expd., Narragansett Bay (May 1832–Feb 1833); supt., Depot of Charts and Instruments, Washington, DC (Feb 1833–Jun 1837); cdr, *Porpoise*, survey duty of St. George's Bank and Savannah River (Jun 1837–Mar 1838); cdr, U.S. Surveying and Expl.Expd., flgs. *Vincennes* (Mar 1838–Jul 1842); spec. duty, preparing report of expd. (Jul 1842–Apr 1861); cdr, *Pawnee*, Navy Yard, Norfolk, VA (Apr–May 1861); cdr, *San Jacinto*, spec.serv., W.Indies (Aug–Nov 1861); bd. duties (Dec 1861–Jul 1862); cdr, James River Flot., *Wachusett* (Jul–Aug 1862); cdr, Potomac Flot., *Wachusett* (Sep 1862); cdr, W.Ind. ["Flying"] Sqdn., *Wachusett* (Sep 1862–Jun 1863); placed on Ret.Lst. (12 Nov 1862); w.o. (Jun 1863–Apr 1864); suspended from service (26 Apr 1864); spec. duty, Washington, DC (Jun–Sep 1870, May 1872–Mar 1873).

CHARLES WILKES
1798–1877

Career Highlights Interested in exploration, studied under founder of U.S. coast survey, Ferdinand Hassler. In charge of the new Depot of Charts and Instruments, began to build a rudimentary astronomical observatory which became forerunner to U.S. Naval Observatory. Commanded the very successful U.S. Surveying and Expl.Expd. of 1838–42. In 1847, awarded Founder's Medal by Royal Geographical Society. In 1861, commanded *San Jacinto* which stopped British mail steamer *Trent* in West Indies, taking off the Confederate agents James Mason and John Slidell. Seen by many as a hero, but the *"Trent* Affair" caused much international tension between the U.S. and Great Britain. Holding several more commands during the Civil War, was subsequently court-martialled for disobedience, disrespect, insubordination, and conduct unbecoming an officer owing to his comments against Secretary of the Navy Gideon Welles. Found guilty and sentenced to public reprimand and suspended three years, a sentence reduced to one year.

References

Personal Papers: a) 6500 items (1607–1959) in LC. b) papers of U.S. Exploring Expedition (1838–42) in Smithsonian Institution, Washington, DC. c) 5 vols. (1837–42) in KS State Historical Society, Topeka, KS. d) 50 items (1848–73) in Gray Herbarium Library, Harvard Univ., Cambridge, MA. e) 33 items (1838–1952) in NYPL. f) 15 items (c.1838–50) in American Philosophical Society Lib., Philadelphia, PA. g) 1 box (1801–80) with William Compton Bolton Papers in State Historical Society, Madison, WI.

Writings: a) *Narrative of the United States Exploring Expedition during the Years 1838, 1839, 1840, 1841, 1842* (5 vols., 1844). b) *Voyage Around the World* (Phil.: 1849). c) *Western America, Including California and Oregon* (Phil.: 1849). c) *Meteorology* (1851). d) *The Theory of the Wind* (Phil.: 1855). e) *Theory of the Zodiacal Light* (1857). f) *On the Circulation of Oceans* (1859). g) *Hydrography* (1861). h) *Autobiography of Rear Admiral Charles Wilkes, U.S. Navy, 1798–1877,* ed. William James Morgan, et al. (Washington, DC: 1978).

Selected Additional Sources: a) Angelo Michele Costi, *Memoir of the* Trent *Affair* (Washington, DC: 1865). b) James D. Hill, "Charles Wilkes—Turbulent Scholar of the Old Navy," U.S. Naval Institute *Proceedings* 341 (Jul 1931): 867–87. c) William W. Jeffries, "The Civil War Career of Charles Wilkes," (Ph.D. dissertation, Vanderbilt University, 1941). d) Daniel MacIntyre Henderson, *The Hidden Coasts: A Biography of Admiral Charles Wilkes* (NY: 1953; Westport, CT: 1971). e) Daniel C. Haskell, *The United States Exploring Expedition, 1838–1842, and its Publications, 1844–1874* (NY: 1968). f) David B. Tyler, *The Wilkes Expedition. The First United States Exploring Expedition (1838–1842)* (Philadelphia: 1968). g) Vincent Ponko, Jr., *Ships, Seas, and Scientists: U.S. Naval Exploration and Discovery in the Nineteenth Century* (Annapolis: 1974). h)

William Stanton, *The Great United States Exploring Expedition of 1838–1842* (Berkeley: 1975). i) Norman B. Ferris, *The Trent Affair: A Diplomatic Crisis* (Knoxville: 1977).

JOHN ANCRUM WINSLOW Born in Wilmington, NC, on 19 Nov 1811, son of Edward and Sara (Ancrum) Winslow. Raised in MA. Married cousin Catherine Amelia Winslow on 18 Oct 1837. At least three children, one of whom was RAdm Herbert Winslow, USN (1848–1914). Died in Boston Highlands, MA, on 29 Sep 1873. Buried in Forest Hill Cemetery in Boston.

JOHN ANCRUM WINSLOW
1811–1873

Ranks Midn (1 Feb 1827); PMidn (10 Jun 1833); Lt (9 Dec 1839); Cdr (14 Sep 1855); Capt (16 Jul 1862); Commo (19 Jun 1864); RAdm (2 Mar 1870); died (29 Sep 1873).

Career Summary Received appointment from NC (1 Feb 1827); *Fulton*, Navy Yard, NY (Aug–Nov 1827); *Falmouth*, W.Ind.Sqdn. (Nov 1827–Aug 1830); l.o.a. (Aug–Dec 1830); Naval School, NY (Dec 1830–Mar 1831); *Falmouth*, Pac.Sqdn. (Mar 1831–Feb 1832); Naval School, NY (Feb–Aug 1832); on furlough (Aug–Sep 1832); l.o.a. (Sep 1832–Jan 1833); Naval School, Norfolk, VA (Jan–Apr 1833); l.o.a. (Apr–Sep 1833); Navy Yard, Boston (Sep 1833–Jan 1834); on furlough (Jan 1834–Jun 1835); *Ontario*, Braz.Sqdn. (Jun 1835–Jan 1836); *Erie*, Braz.Sqdn. (Jan 1836–Sep 1837); Naval Rndv., Boston (Jan 1838–Jan 1840); w.o. (Jan–Feb 1840); *Enterprise*, Braz.Sqdn. (Feb–Oct 1840); sick lv. (Oct 1840–Feb 1841); rec. ship *Columbus*, Boston (Feb 1841–Jun 1842); *Missouri*, Home Sqdn. (Jul 1842–Aug 1843); *Cumberland*, Home Sqdn. (Dec 1845–Dec 1846); cdr, *Morris*, Home Sqdn. (Dec 1846); l.o.a. (Dec 1846–Jan 1847); *Mississippi*, Home Sqdn. (Jan 1847); l.o.a. (Jan–Mar 1847); Navy Yard, Boston (Mar 1847–Mar 1848); *Saratoga*, Gulf Sqdn. (Apr 1848–Sep 1849); w.o. (Sep 1849–Oct 1851); *St. Lawrence*, Pac.Sqdn. (Oct 1851–Apr 1855); l.o.a. (Apr–May 1855); cdr, Naval Rndv., Boston (May 1855–Jul 1858); w.o. (Jul 1858–Dec 1860); insp., 2nd L.h. Dist., Boston (Dec 1860–Sep 1861); cdr, *Benton*, MS Sqdn., St. Louis, MO (Sep–Dec 1861); sick lv. (Dec 1861–Feb 1862); cdr, *St. Louis*, MS Sqdn. (Feb–Jun 1862); cdr, *Baron de Kalb*, MS Sqdn. (Jun–Oct 1862); on furlough (Oct–Nov 1862); w.o. (Oct–Dec 1862); cdr, *Kearsarge*, spec.serv. (Apr 1863–Nov 1864); home and w.o. (Nov 1864–Feb 1865); spec. duty with RAdm Francis H. Gregory [*q.v.*] and ironclad steamers, Philadelphia and NY (Feb–Dec 1865); cdr, Gulf Sqdn., *Estrella* (Jan 1866–Jun 1867); l.o.a. and w.o. (Jun 1867–Jan 1868); member, Bd. of Examiners, Navy Yard, Boston (Mar–Oct 1868); w.o. (Oct 1868–Jun 1869); comdt., Navy Yard, Portsmouth, NH (Jun 1869–Jul 1870); cdr, Pac.Flt., *Saranac*, *Pensacola*, then *California* (Aug 1870–Jul 1872); l.o.a. and w.o. (Jul 1872–Sep 1873); died (29 Sep 1873).

Career Highlights In 1841, helped fight a fire in the hold of a British Cunard liner vessel in Boston Harbor;

subsequently decorated with sword knot and a pair of epaulets by Queen Victoria. During war with Mexico, distinguished himself by leading landing party at Tabasco and at Frontera. Commanded *Kearsarge* in 1864 on special assignment in search of Confederate raiders, finding and eventually defeating CSS *Alabama* commanded by Raphael Semmes on 10 Jun.

References

Personal Papers: a) 10 items (1864–88) in NHF,LC. b) papers in NYHS. c) 2 items (1843, 1873) in WPL.

Additional Sources: John Morris Ellicott, *The Life of John Ancrum Winslow, U.S. Navy* (NY: 1902).

JOHN LORIMER WORDEN
1818–1897

JOHN LORIMER WORDEN Born in Sing Sing, Westchester County, NY on 12 Mar 1818, son of Ananias and Harriet (Graham) Worden. Married Olivia Taffey. Four children. Died in Washington, DC, on 18 Oct 1897. Buried in Pawling, NY.

Ranks Midn (10 Jan 1834); PMidn (16 Jul 1840); Mstr (13 Aug 1846); Lt (30 Nov 1846); Cdr (16 Jul 1866); Capt (3 Feb 1863); Commo (27 May 1868); RAdm (20 Nov 1872); retired (23 Dec 1886).

Career Summary Received appointment from NY (10 Jan 1834); *Erie*, Braz.Sqdn. (Jun 1834–Sep 1837); Navy Yard, Boston (Apr–May 1838); *Cyane*, Med.Sqdn. (May 1838–Dec 1839); Naval School, Philadelphia (Dec 1839–Jul 1840); w.o. (Jul–Oct 1840); *Relief*, Pac.Sqdn. (Oct 1840–Sep 1842); *Dale*, Pac.Sqdn. (Sep 1842–Oct 1843); l.o.a. and w.o. (Oct 1843–Apr 1844); Naval Observatory, Washington, DC (Apr 1844–May 1846); l.o.a. and w.o. (May 1846–Feb 1847); *Southampton*, Pac.Sqdn. (Feb 1847–May 1848); *Independence*, Pac.Sqdn. (May–Jul 1848); *Warren*, Pac.Sqdn. (Jul 1848–Sep 1849); *Ohio*, Pac.Sqdn. (Sep 1849–Apr 1850); l.o.a. and w.o. (Apr–Oct 1850); Naval Observatory, Washington, DC (Oct 1850–Mar 1852); *Cumberland*, Med.Sqdn. (Apr 1852–Feb 1855); *Levant*, Med.Sqdn. (Feb–May 1855); Naval Observatory, Washington, DC (Oct 1855–Mar 1856); Navy Yard, NY (Mar 1856–Jul 1858); *Savannah*, Home Sqdn. (Jul 1858–Nov 1860); l.o.a. and w.o. (Nov 1860–Apr 1861); spec. duty, Washington, DC (Apr 1861); spec. duty to Pensacola, FL (Apr 1861); prisoner of war (13 Apr–18 Nov 1861); Naval Rndv., NY (Nov 1861–Jan 1862); cdr, *Monitor*, spec.serv. (Jan–Mar 1862); sick lv. (Mar–Aug 1862); asst. in ironclad construction, NY (Aug–Oct 1862); cdr, *Montauk*, S.Atl.Blk.Sqdn. (Oct 1862–Apr 1863); supt. of ironclad construction, NY (Apr 1863–Feb 1866); cdr, *Idaho*, trial and experimental duty (Feb–May 1866); ironclad duty (Jun–Aug 1866); cdr, *Pensacola*, Pac.Sqdn. (Aug 1866–May 1867); l.o.a. (May 1868–Dec 1869); supt., USNA (Dec 1869–Sep 1874); cdr, Eur.Sqdn., *Franklin* and *Marion* (Dec 1874–Oct 1877); member, then pres., Naval Exam. and Ret. Bds. (Dec 1877–Dec 1886); retired (23 Dec 1886).

Career Highlights Just prior to outset of the Civil War, sent with secret and memorized despatches to the sqdn. reinforcing Ft. Pickens near Pensacola, FL. Was captured while returning, remaining a prisoner of war until Nov 1861. Given command of new *Monitor*, he remained with her until forced to leave owing to injuries sustained during famous engagement with Confederate *Virginia* (formerly *Merrimack*). Given a vote of thanks and promoted for his conduct in the fight. Participated in Jul 1863 ironclad attack on Charleston, for which he and his crew were thanked by Congress. Remainder of war spent overseeing construction of ironclad vessels in NY. Served as supt. of USNA. Helped to found and served as first pres. of U.S. Naval Institute.

References

Personal Papers: a) 65 items (1861–98) in NHF,LC. b) 75 items (1835–91) in Lincoln Memorial Lib. Harrogate, TN. c) 1 in., 20 items (1862–99) in Long Island Historical Society.

Writings: *The* Monitor *and the* Merrimac; *Both Sides of the Story* (NY: 1902).

ROBERT HARRIS WYMAN Born in Portsmouth, NH, on 12 Jul 1822, son of navy Capt Thomas White and Sarah (Harris) Wyman. Married Emily Madeline Dallas on 27 Sep 1847. Three children. Died in Washington, DC, on 2 Dec 1882. Buried in Oak Hill Cemetery, Washington, DC.

Ranks Midn (11 Mar 1837); PMidn (29 Jun 1843); Lt (16 Jul 1850); Cdr (16 Jul 1862); Capt (25 Jul 1866); Commo (19 Jul 1872); RAdm (26 Apr 1878); died (2 Dec 1882).

Career Summary Received appointment from NH (11 Mar 1837); *Independence, Fairfield, John Adams,* and *Concord,* Braz. and W.Ind. Sqdns. (Mar 1837–Jun 1840); l.o.a. (Jun–Sep 1840); *Levant,* W.Ind.Sqdn. (Sep–Nov 1840); *Concord, Delaware,* and *Potomac,* Braz.Sqdn. (Nov 1840–Aug 1842); Naval School, Philadelphia (Aug 1842–Jul 1843); *Onkahage,* E.Ind.Sqdn. (Jul–Aug 1843); *Perry* and *Brandywine,* E.Ind.Sqdn. (Aug 1843–Oct 1845); l.o.a. (Oct 1845); Navy Yard, Boston (Nov 1845–Mar 1846); *Princeton* and *Porpoise,* Home Sqdn. (Mar 1846–Jun 1847); l.o.a. (Jun–Jul 1847); Naval Rndv., Boston (Jul–Sep 1847); *Albany,* Home Sqdn. (Sep 1847–Jan 1848); sick lv. and w.o. (Jan–Feb 1848); Naval Observatory, Washington, DC (Feb–Jun 1848); rec. ship *Franklin,* Boston (Jun 1848–Jun 1850); w.o. (Jun–Sep 1850); *St. Mary's,* Pac. and E.Ind. Sqdns. (Sep 1850–Dec 1852); l.o.a. (Dec 1852–Feb 1853); Naval Observatory, Washington, DC (Feb 1853–Oct 1854); training ship *Preble* (Oct 1854–Oct 1856); w.o. (Oct–Nov 1856); *St. Mary's* and *Independence,* Pac.Sqdn. (Nov 1856–Aug 1857); *St. Mary's,* Pac.Sqdn (Aug 1857–Jan 1859); Navy Yard, NY (Jan–Apr 1859); training ships *Preble* and *Plymouth* (Apr 1859–Aug 1860); *Richmond,* Med.Sqdn. (Sep 1860–Jul 1861); cdr, *Yankee,* Potomac Flot. (Jul–Oct 1861); temp. cdr, *Pawnee,* S.Atl.Blk.Sqdn. (Oct–Nov

ROBERT HARRIS WYMAN
1822–1882

1861); sick lv. and w.o. (Nov–Dec 1861); cdr, Potomac Flot., (Dec 1861–Jun 1862); cdr, *Sonoma*, James River Flot. (Jul–Sep 1862); cdr, *Wachusett*, Potomac Flot. (Sep–Nov 1862); spec. duty, Washington, DC (Nov 1862–Mar 1863); cdr, *Santiago de Cuba*, spec.serv., W.Indies (Apr–Aug 1863); spec. duty, Navy Dept., Washington, DC (Aug 1863–May 1865); cdr, flgs. *Colorado*, then cdr, *Ticonderoga*, Eur.Sqdn. (May 1865–Apr 1869); w.o. (Apr–Oct 1869); Hydrographic Office, Washington, DC (Oct 1869–Sep 1870); in charge, Hydrographic Office, Washington, DC (Oct 1870–May 1878); spec. temp. duty, Bur. of Nav., Washington, DC (May 1878–Jan 1879); cdr, N.Atl.Sta., *Tennessee* (Jan 1879–May 1882); spec. duty, Washington, DC (May 1882); chairman, L.h. Bd., Washington, DC (Jun–Dec 1882); died (2 Dec 1882).

References

Writings: a) *Navigation of Coasts and Islands in the Mediterranean Sea* (1872). b) *Coasts of Chile, Bolivia and Peru* (1876).

NOTE ON SOURCES

One of the most frustrating aspects of seeking biographical information is the diverse, varied, and frequently unreliable or conflicting nature of the material. In some cases, there might exist an extremely accurate and complete career record, although only in manuscript form. The careers and personal information for many others, unfortunately, have never been compiled. Discovering one man's entire military career or, for example, pinpointing just if and when he was stationed on a particular vessel or at some navy yard requires many tedious and often disappointing hours of research at various inconveniently located repositories. The following is intended both as an explanation of this volume's sources and as a guide for those pursuing further research into the biographies of those in the navy.

MANUSCRIPT SOURCES AND REPOSITORIES

There are, naturally, many collections of manuscripts on naval history scattered all over the country. Many of these provide very valuable information of a biographical nature. By far the best catalogue of these collections is *U.S. Naval History Sources in the United States*, compiled and edited by Dean C. Allard, Martha L. Crawley, and Mary W. Edmison (Washington, D.C.: Department of the Navy, Naval History Division, 1979). This very convenient, thorough, and essential guide lists and in many cases describes collections on a state-by-state basis. It is well indexed and should be one of the first sources consulted to find records and manuscripts, biographical in nature or not, on naval history.

The National Archives of the United States in Washington, D.C., is the central depository for official records and documents of a historical nature or value. While there are numerous guides for the manuscripts in the National Archives, the *Guide to the National Archives of the United States* (Washington, D.C.: Government Printing Office, 1974) is the best. The *Catalogue of National Archives Microfilm Publications* (Washington, D.C.: Government Printing Office, 1974) is also very useful. The Archives groups information into various categories. Some of the more valuable records groups for naval biographical material are: Record Group 19 (records of the Bureau of Ships); Record Group 24 (records of the Bureau of Personnel); Record Group 45 (naval records collection of the Office of Naval Records and Library); Record Group 80 (general records of the Department of the Navy); and Record Group 405 (records of the U.S. Naval Academy). Besides these and other valuable collections in the central repository, the National Archives also operates the National Personnel Records Center in St. Louis, MO. While containing much, the National Archives normally takes considerable time to respond to requests for information.

The Manuscript Division of the Library of Congress in Washington, D.C., has many collections on naval subjects and personnel. For information on what the library holds, see *The National Union Catalogue of Manuscript Collections* (Washington, D.C.: Library of Congress, 1959–) as well as Philip M. Hamer, ed., *A Guide to Archives and Manuscripts in the United States* (New Haven: Yale University Press, 1961). The library's annual accessions are reported in the *Quarterly Journal of the Library of Congress*. In addition, Richard B. Bickel compiled *Manuscripts on Microfilm: A Checklist of the Holdings in the Manuscript Division* (Washington, D.C.: Library of Congress, 1975).

Besides its own collections, the Library of Congress also houses part of the very rich and extremely valuable collections owned by the Naval Historical Foundation, a nonprofit, private organization that preserves material on naval and maritime subjects. Those collections held by the Library of Congress are described in *Naval Historical Foundation Manuscript Collection: A Catalogue* (Washington, D.C.: Library of Congress, 1974). Those sources not deposited in the Library of Congress are located in the same building as the Naval Historical Center at the Washington Navy Yard.

The Naval Historical Center is a very convenient central repository of many sources and manuscript collections, both official and private. There are several different departments within the Naval Historical Center. Of great importance is the Operational Archives branch. This branch contains the Early Records Collections, which house the historical reference (Z) files, including biographical material (ZB). Other important branches of the Naval Historical Center are the Ships' History Branch and the Still Photo Library. Located in the same building is the Navy Department Library, which owns many publications difficult to find elsewhere. The center and library are extremely pleasant places to work, and the staffs are most professional, cordial, and helpful.

Another extremely important storehouse of manuscripts and information on naval history and naval personnel is the U.S. Naval Academy in Annapolis, MD. The Academy's Nimitz Library, like the Navy Department Library, contains many rare and difficult-to-find monographs and journals. The Nimitz Library also has Special Collections and Archives departments. Private collections of papers as well as some of the more essential printed primary sources are housed here and overseen by extremely helpful and professional staff members. Similarly, the Naval Academy Museum possesses manuscripts, photographs, and memorabilia that are most useful to the researcher.

Also in Annapolis is the U.S. Naval Institute. While located on the grounds of the Naval Academy, the Institute is separate and owns both a naval library and an extremely valuable photographic collection.

The United States Naval War College in Newport, RI, also owns much valuable information, including manuscript collections, information and documents on the college itself, as well as naval documents of a more general nature from the nineteenth and twentieth centuries.

While the above material is intended to describe most of the sources used for the information found in this volume, it does not cover all. Manuscript collections as well as secondary sources from which specific biographical information was extracted are found under the bibliographical sections for those particular admirals.

PRINTED PRIMARY AND SECONDARY SOURCES

One of the most useful sources of career information is the *Abstract of Service Records, 1798–1893*. These are microfilmed manuscripts from the Record Group 24 (records of the Bureau of Personnel) in the National Archives. While not particularly easy to use and containing numerous discrepancies, especially up to the Civil War, they provide good career summaries. The *Register of Commissioned and Warrant Officers of the United States Navy, Including Officers of the Marine Corps* (Washington, D.C.: Department of the Navy, 1814–) gives the names, dates of commission, ranks, and present stations for all officers of the sea services and has appeared annually since 1814, with some variations. Sadly, some volumes are more complete than others, and normally the month when an officer saw a change of duty is not given. Beginning in July 1908, the *Register* became the *Navy and Marine Corps List and Directory*. The information within each volume since 1908 becomes far more detailed and reliable. A source of obituaries and social news is the *United States Army-Navy Journal*, which began its weekly publications on 29 August 1863.

Another source is Lewis Randolph Hamersly's *The Records of Living Officers of the U.S. Navy and Marine Corps*, 7 editions (Philadelphia: L. R. Hamersly and Co., 1870–1902), which is considered the standard work for career information on naval officers to the early twentieth century. Hamersly acquired his information from the official records of the Bureau of Personnel, but the editions are far from complete, leaving large gaps within the careers and normally not including the squadron or fleet with which a man served while on board a particular ship. Other works produced by Hamersly are: *A Naval Encyclopedia, Comprising a Dictionary of Nautical Words and Phrases; Biographical Notices, and Records of Naval Officers. . . .* (Philadelphia: L. R. Hamersly and Co., 1884; Rpr. 1971); *Biographical Sketches of Distinguished Officers of the Army and Navy* (New York: L. R. Hamersly and Co., 1905); and *List of Officers of the Navy of the United States and of the Marine Corps from 1775 to 1900*, edited by Edward W. Callahan (New York: L. R. Hamersly and Co., 1901, Rpr. 1969).

Along the same lines are Thomas Holdup Stevens Hamersly's *General Register of the United States Navy and Marine Corps for One Hundred Years, 1782–1882* (Washington, D.C.: 1882), and his *Complete General Navy Register of the United States, from 1776 to 1887, Containing the Names of all the Officers of the Navy, Volunteer and Regular* (New York: L. R. Hamersly, 1888).

There are more recent works dealing with the careers of those in the military. A work that deals only with select individuals is Roger J. Spiller, ed., with Joseph G. Dawson and T. Harry Williams, *Dictionary of American Military Biography*, 3 vols. (Westport, CT: Greenwood Press, 1984). See also *Webster's American Military Biographies* (Springfield, IL: G. & C. Merriam Co., 1978). The most recent work that includes almost every major military figure is *Who Was Who in American History—The Military* (Chicago: Marquis Who's Who, Inc., 1975). While including many individuals, this work contains only short and abbreviated, albeit reliable, information. Finally, there is Karl Schuon's *U.S. Navy Biographical Dictionary* (New York: Franklin Watts, 1964), which is very selective in choosing officers for inclusion.

For personal information on officers, there are standard biographical dictionaries. Among these are: *Dictionary of American Biography*, eds. Allen Johnson and Dumas Malone, 20 vols. (New York: Charles Scribner's Sons, 1928–1936); *Appleton's Cyclopaedia of American Biography*, eds. James Grant Weston and John Fiske, 10 vols. (New York: Appleton, 1887–1924); and *The National Cyclopaedia of American Biography*, multivolume (New York: James T. White & Company, 1898–). Lastly, an extremely useful, indeed essential, work that associates officers and the location of ships on which they served is James L. Mooney, ed., *Dictionary of American Naval Fighting Ships*, 8 vols. (Washington, D.C.: Government Printing Office, 1959–81).